The British Journal of Nursing

(Volume LXI)

Editor: Mrs. Bedford Fenwick

Alpha Editions

This edition published in 2020

ISBN : 9789354036040

Design and Setting By
Alpha Editions
www.alphaedis.com
email - alphaedis@gmail.com

THE
BRITISH JOURNAL OF NURSING
WITH WHICH IS INCORPORATED
THE NURSING RECORD
EDITED BY MRS BEDFORD FENWICK

No. 1,579.   SATURDAY, JULY 6, 1918.   Vol. LXI

EDITORIAL.

A CALL TO ARMS.

The great Procession of Homage of Women War Workers received by the King and Queen in the quadrangle of Buckingham Palace on Saturday last, when an address of congratulation upon their Silver Wedding was presented, was a magnificent success. Princess Mary was present in her uniform of Commandant-in-Chief of the V.A.D., and V.A.D. workers took precedence of all other branches of women's work, including the Trained Nurses of the Metropolitan Asylums Board led by Miss Ambler-Jones. The King's Reply to the Address, delivered in a resonant voice, was distinctly heard by some thousands of people present, and His Majesty spoke most sympathetically and appreciatively of the part played by women in the great war.

"The Queen and I," said the King, "are touched by the thought that the first expression of loyalty and devotion on the occasion of our silver wedding should come from this representative body of women who, by their services, have assisted the State in the full mobilization of its man power. In our visits to various centres we have had opportunities of seeing and appreciating the great part which the women of our land are taking in all branches of war service, and everywhere we have been filled with admiration at their achievements, an admiration which I believe to be shared by the whole nation.

"When the history of our country's share in the War is written no chapter will be more remarkable than that relating to the range and extent of women's participation. This service has been rendered only at the cost of much self-sacrifice and endurance."

Referring to nurses and V.A.D. workers His Majesty said, "They have often faced cheerfully and courageously great risks, both at home and overseas, in carrying on their work, and the Women's Army has its own Roll of Honour of those who have lost their lives in the service of their country. Of all these we think to-day with reverent pride."

There should not be to-day an idle woman in the three kingdoms. All able-bodied women between the ages of eighteen and forty, not otherwise employed, should enrol themselves as full-time workers in one of the great organizations of those who are prepared to make every sacrifice in order to assist their country at this supreme crisis in its history.

AN IMPORTANT DEPARTURE.

At the request of the Council of the Royal British Nurses' Association we shall henceforth publish fortnightly a Special Supplement, which will take the place of its official organ, the *Nurses' Journal*.

As one of the founders of the Association we are in full sympathy with the policy of the Hon. Officers for professional consolidation and for the protection of the interests of the thoroughly trained nurse, with which are interwoven those of the public.

Owing largely to the glorification of the semi-trained war worker by the Nurses' Department in the Red Cross Office, competition with the certificated nurse has already become a serious menace to our professional ideals.

By a new Army Order Queen Alexandra's Imperial Military Nursing Service will be reserved for V.A.D.s who conform to a term of general training, and private nurses must recognize the coming competition with semi-trained women of social influence which may deprive them of their livelihood after the war.

The nurses' organizations which are affiliated to the Royal British Nurses'

Association are prepared to support its work for the profession whole heartedly, but every individual nurse should do so individually. We invite nurses to fill in and send to the Secretary of the Association the application form which appears on the back cover of this issue.

OUR PRIZE COMPETITION.

WHAT IS A PARASITE? WHAT EXTERNAL PARASITES ATTACK MAN. DESCRIBE IN DETAIL THE TREATMENT AND MANAGEMENT OF A CASE OF SCABIES. WITH SPECIAL REFERENCE TO THE PREVENTION OF THE DISEASE.

We have pleasure in awarding the prize this week to Miss Catherine Wright, Dryden Road, Bush Hill Park, Enfield.

PRIZE PAPER.

A parasite is a living organism; it may be of animal or vegetable origin; it derives its existence from feeding on another living organism. Choosing for its environment preferably "man," it breeds prolifically; the power of movement is constant and sustained. Parasites move together in large numbers; surviving best in crowded and unwholesome atmospheres, they create a serious condition, which learned bacteriologists have proved by unquestionable scientific research to cause epidemic diseases, resulting in a very high mortality amongst human beings.

The parasites which most commonly attack man are the "louse" family, either as "pediculi capitas," those attacking the scalp, or "pediculi corporis," those attacking the body, and the "pediculi pubis"; the latter form is rare.

The former pediculi hatch their nits, or eggs, which adhere to the hair, cause great irritation; the skin becomes abrased by scratching, crusts form, the glands of the neck become infected; the victim thus becomes a source of infection, and this condition is found, in England, principally amongst school children.

The procedure of the "pediculi corporis" is the same, the body lice causing indescribable discomfort, and causing the same degree of danger by infection. The pediculi pubis are found in the eyebrows, axilla, or pubis, and necessitate medical treatment. The larvæ of these parasites are a source of great danger, and food for human consumption must receive special protection and scrupulous hygienic precautions to avoid contamination.

There are two vegetable parasites which attack human beings. Children of foreign origin principally have the affection of "favus." It is found in the form of a fungus in the head, yellow incrustations of a cup-like shape form; it is treated medically, often in the X-ray department of the London hospitals, and is highly infectious unless isolated.

The second vegetable parasite is the fungus of ringworm, attacking the scalp and the body. Both should receive medical attention, which will lessen their infectivity.

"Scabies," or "itch," is due to a parasitic insect, "acarus scabies," a minute object, invisible to the naked eye; the female acarus forms a burrow in the skin. Here it lays its eggs, and this is a source of incessant irritation; the hands, between the fingers, are affected, spreading to the inside of the wrist; other parts of the body become infected. The irritation is intense, especially at night, resulting in a very short time in a highly nervous condition through restlessness and sleeplessness. School children are very open to the infection, which may spread through the whole family.

The hands of school children should be frequently examined, because an early diagnosis and exclusion from school may be of practical use in preventing the spread of the disease.

A daily bath of soap and water, and an application of sulphur ointment, repeated for two or three days, relieves this condition. The clothes worn should be steeped in boiling water, and the child should have its own toilet requisites and sleep by itself. Exclusion from school is an important point.

This disease of scabies is prolific in the East End of London, and is intensified in crowded areas. The London County Council have arrangements for municipal baths, where a routine treatment of medicated baths is supervised by the trained nurses on the school staff. The children are kept under careful supervision until all infection is over and every symptom of the disease has disappeared. All clothing is specially sterilized. Mercurial ointment is a valuable asset in curing the condition of impetigo, which may follow the scabies condition, and good food and hygienic conditions will act as remedial and preventive measures for further or future infection.

HONOURABLE MENTION.

The following competitors receive honourable mention :—Miss M. M. Bielby, Miss A. M. Burns, Mrs. E. E. Farthing, Miss J. Robinson.

QUESTION FOR NEXT WEEK.

What points would you endeavour to impress upon a mother as of primary importance for the rearing of a healthy baby?

THE ROYAL RED CROSS.

On Saturday, June 29th, the following ladies were awarded the R.R.C. by the King at Buckingham Palace. Miss Elizabeth Humphries, who received the Military Medal, received also a great ovation from the public :—

The Royal Red Cross.

FIRST CLASS.

Sister Ellen BALDREY, Queen Alexandra's Imperial Military Nursing Service, Matron Helen PALIN, Territorial Force Nursing Service, and Matron Jessie SMALES, Territorial Force Nursing Service.

SECOND CLASS.

Territorial Force Nursing Service.—Sister Elsie BENNETT.

British Red Cross Society.—Matron Annie PEEL.

Voluntary Aid Detachment.—Miss Emma COLEMAN, Miss Margaret CRANAGE, and Miss Gertrude MILLER.

The Military Medal.

Matron Elizabeth HUMPHRIES, Territorial Force Nursing Service.

The Royal Red Cross.

The King invested the following ladies with the Royal Red Cross at Buckingham Palace on Wednesday, June 26th :—

FIRST CLASS.

Matron Kathleen PRENDERGAST, Queen Alexandra's Imperial Military Nursing Service Reserve.

SECOND CLASS.

Queen Alexandra's Imperial Military Nursing Service.—Sister Sadie TYLER.

Queen Alexandra's Imperial Military Nursing Service Reserve.—Sister Stella BURRELL, and Sister Dora SHANKLIE-SMITH.

Territorial Force Nursing Service.—Sister Martha MORRISON.

British Red Cross Society.—Matron Kate MOORE.

Voluntary Aid Detachment.—Miss Clare DAGLISH.

Queen Alexandra received at Marlborough House the Members of the Military and Civil Nursing Services who have been awarded the Royal Red Cross, subsequent to the Investitures at Buckingham Palace this morning.

The Royal Red Cross.

The King has been pleased to award the Royal Red Cross, 2nd class, to the undermentioned ladies, in recognition of their valuable nursing services in connection with the war :—

SECOND CLASS.

ABELL, Miss F. M., Matron, Henley Park, and Sister-in-Charge, Daneshill Mil. Hospl., Surrey ; ADAMS, Miss D. P., Sister (Lady Supt.), V.A.D. Hospl., Cranbrook, Kent ; ALLHUSEN, Miss E., Nurse, V.A. Hospl., Rhode Hill, Uplyme ; ALLWOOD, Miss M. J., Nursing Sister, Can. Nursing Service, No. 12 Can. Gen. Hospl., Bramshott, Hants ; ANDERSON, Miss E., Sister, V.A. Hospital, Torquay ; ANDERSON, Miss E. R., Charge Nurse, Waverley Abbey, Farnham ; ANDERSON, Miss I., Sister, Q.A.I.M.N.S.R., Barnet War Hospl., Herts ; ASPINALL, Miss E., Sister, Liverpool Stanley Hospl., Stanley Road, Liverpool.

BAGNALL-OAKELEY, Miss B., Lady Supt., Priory Hosp., Cheltenham ; BAGULEY, Miss F., Matron, St. John Aux.

V.A.D., Southport ; BAINES, Miss M. L., Asst. Matron, Horton War Hosp., Epsom ; BANKHEAD, Miss A., A. Asst. Matron, Richmond, Whitworth and Hardwicke Hospl., Dublin ; BARBER, Miss E. M., Sister, Horton War Hospl., Epsom ; BARROWCLIFF, Miss S. E., Sister, Q.A.I.M.N.S.R., Mil. Hospl., Bagthorpe, frmly. Hursley Camp Mil. Hospl., nr. Winchester ; BAYFIELD, Mrs. A., Sister, Hanover Park V.A.D. Hospl., Rye Lane, Peckham, S.E. 15 ; BAYNE, Miss A. E., Matron, Isolation Hospl., Southampton ; BELL, Miss A. B. H., Sister, T.F.N.S., 2nd Northern Gen. Hospl., Leeds ; BELL, Miss M. H., Asst. Nurse, King George's Hospl., Stamford Street, London, S.E. 1 ; BELLVILLE, Mrs. G., Matron, Darell Hospl., Queen Anne Street, W. ; BEVAN, Miss A. G., Sister, T.F.N.S., 5th Lond. Gen. Hosp., St. Thomas's, Lambeth, S.E. 1 ; BEVAN, Miss S. S., Asst. Matron, Fulham Mily. Hospl., Hammersmith, W. ; BEWSEY, Miss E. E., Sister, Q.A.I.M.N.S.R., Mily. Hospl., Fargo, Salisbury Plain ; BINGLEY, Miss F., Sister, War Hospl., Bradford ; BINNS, Miss L., Lady Supt., Matron, Royal Infirmary, Hull ; BIRKIN, the Hon. M. D. H., Matron (unpaid), Arnot Hill V.A. Hospl., Daybrook, Notts ; BIRT, Miss M. C., Matron, Red Cross Hospl., Huntingdon ; BLATCH, Mrs. K. M., Matron, Red Cross Hospl., Kenilworth, Warwickshire ; BLAYNEY, Miss E. K., Matron, R. Infirmary, Chester ; BLENKARN, Miss M., Lady Supt., Cooden V.A.D. Hospl., Bexhill ; BLOTT, Miss M. E., Nursing Sister. Can. Nursing Service, Granville Can. Spec. Hospl., Buxton ; BOATH, Miss E. M., Matron, Dundee War Hospl., Dundee ; BORTON, Miss F., Matron, Victoria Hospl., Blackpool ; BOSS, Miss A., Matron, Masonic Hall V.A.D. Hospl., Bromley, Kent ; BOTTOMLEY, Mrs. A. C., Matron (unpaid), St. John's Ambulance, 2, Bodorgan Road, Bournemouth ; BOUGHEY, Miss L. M., Matron, Lady Cooper's Hospl. for Officers, Hursley Park, Winchester ; BOWRING, Miss F., Nurse, Hart House Hospl., Burnham, Somerset ; BOWYER, Miss R., Sister, T.F.N.S., 2nd Southern Gen. Hospl., Bristol R. Infirmary, Bristol ; BRACE, Miss C A. M., Sister, Q.A.I.M.N.S.R., R. Victoria Hospl. Netley ; BRAMLEY, Mrs. M., Commdt., Dunraven Castle Red Cross Hospl., Glam. ; BRODRICK, Miss K. E., Nursing Sister, Can. Nursing Service, Queen's Can. Mily. Hospl., Beechborough Park, Shorncliffe ; BROTHER-TON, Miss H., Asst. Matron, T.F.N.S., 1st Northern Gen. Hospl., Newcastle-on-Tyne ; BROWN, Miss E., Nurse, Aux. Mil. Hospl., 9, Cedars Road, Clapham, S.W. ; BROWN, Miss F. E., Matron, Jaw Hospl., 78, Brook Street, London ; BRUCE, Miss A. L., Nursing Sister, Can. Nursing Service, Granville Can. Spec. Hospl., Buxton ; BUFFORD, Miss D. F., Matron, Ridley Hospl., 10, Carlton House Terrace, S.W. ; BURBIDGE, Miss C., Lady Supt., Standish Hospl., Glos. ; BUTLER, Miss G., Sister, Huddersfield War Hospl. ; BUXTON, Miss M., Matron, Princess' Royal Hospl. for Officers, 4, Percival Terrace, Brighton

(To be continued.)

UNIVERSITY COLLEGE HOSPITAL.
TRAINING OF V.A.D.s

We are informed that, as a special mark of their valuable work during the present war, the course of training at University College Hospital usually extending over four years will be reduced to three years in favour of V.A.D.s who have served for two years in a military hospital, and who are well recommended by their Matron.

This appears a fair arrangement as a fourth year is one of service and not training.

NURSING AND THE WAR.

On Saturday in last week the Royal Red Cross awarded to Miss L. V. Haughton, late Matron of Guy's Hospital, was presented to her by Dame Ethel Becher, G.B.E., with the King's approval, in the little Surrey village where she is slowly recovering from her very serious illness. His Majesty also, through Dame Becher, expressed great regret that Miss Haughton was unable to attend a public Investiture owing to her continued ill-health. Everyone will unite in congratulating Miss Haughton on this distinction, and will wish that before long she may be restored to health and be able to fulfil her wish of paying a visit to her many friends in Ireland, as she is still interested in their nursing activities.

Miss L. Jolley, R.R.C., until recently Matron of the Royal Southern Hospital, Liverpool, and who has done good service in France in Q.A.I.M.N.S.R., since the beginning of the war, has been appointed Matron-in-Chief of the Air Service. Miss Jolley is highly qualified, and her colleagues will wish her well in this new and interesting post.

Sister N. M'Kenzie was recommended for the R.R.C. by General Allenby. She has been a member of Queen Alexandra's Imperial Nursing Service (Reserve) since October 1914. Sister M'Kenzie has been on service since August, 1915, and was mentioned in General Murray's dispatches in June last. We are indebted to the courtesy of the Editor of *The Scots Pictorial*, Glasgow, for permission to reproduce Sister M'Kenzie's portrait and for the loan of the block. We have many Scottish readers at home and abroad who are interested in the recognition of the fine national work of their compatriots.

SISTER N. M'KENZIE, R.R.C., Q.A.I.M.N.S.R.

they often are of men of all types—should be more carefully supervised.

At Marylebone Police Court recently Peggy Robertson, aged twenty-one, was charged with permitting a maisonette at Connaught Street, Hyde Park, to be used for improper purposes.

The prisoner, in evidence, said that the officers who had called at the maisonette were friends whose acquaintance she had made during the two years she was acting as a V.A.D. nurse in Egypt and elsewhere.

This young girl was fined £20, with the alternative of six weeks' imprisonment; and she was ordered to pay five guineas costs.

We have always condemned the practice of the authorities sending young untrained girls to work in military hospitals abroad. We hope that both the War Office and the Joint War Committee will make it impossible for girls of twenty-one and under to be subjected to the temptations to which Peggy Robertson evidently succumbed.

In the *Times* recently Dr. Wigram extolled the value of short-time service in hospital work, and said 200 members of the Marylebone V.A.D. were able to run a hospital for soldiers with only one trained nurse in charge! We wonder when this unfortunate professional was supposed to be off duty, if she ever went to bed, and who "ran" the hospital in her absence. Let us hope there were no "cot" cases admitted. Anyway medical practitioners do a vast amount of harm in depreciating the value of skilled nursing where our sick and wounded men are concerned. We could wish that Dr. Wigram was on duty night and day in charge of 200 unskilled women nursing in and out of a hospital—perhaps he might then appreciate the worry and disorganisation of such a system.

A DAY OF PRAYER.

The King desires that August 4, the fourth anniversary of the war, shall be observed with special solemnity as a national day of prayer.

ASPECTS OF THE V.A.D. QUESTION.

We have come into intimate touch with several tragedies of late—affecting young inexperienced V.A.D.'s—which lead us to think that their free and easy and uncontrolled work—in charge as

CARE OF THE WOUNDED.

" France's Day," in aid of the British Committee of the French Red Cross, will be celebrated in the City, West End, and Greater London on Friday, July 12th. Ladies willing to help should write to the Honorary Secretary, " France's Day," 34, Wilton Place, S.W. 1. The souvenirs will include models of the famous 75mm. French gun. The Lord Mayor is again acting as Honorary Treasurer of the fund, for which last year over £200,000 was raised in the British Empire.

In connection with " France's Day," La Musique du Premier Zouave, the leading Zouave band of the French Army will visit London, being met by Lieut.-General Sir Francis Lloyd, and played through the streets by British bands. The eighty Zouaves, fresh from the battle front, will, on July 12th, play in the City and West-End.

The Order of St. John of Jerusalem in England has sent out a touching appeal for financial support to re-establish the fine Brigade Hospital splendidly equipped and maintained by the Order at Etaples since 1915, and which was barbarously bombed and much of it smashed to atoms by the Germans, when the casualties were sixty-four, including sixteen killed—a colossal crime, for which these murderers are quite impenitent. The circular, approved by H.R.H. the Grand Prior, the Duke of Connaught, gives illustrations of this beautiful hut hospital before and after the bombardment—the former showing its excellent formation in such perfect surroundings—where the best of care and comfort was at the disposal of our sick and wounded men ; the latter showing the cruel devastation wrought by outrage and fire—a sorry sight indeed !

The Military Authorities have ordered the evacuation of the hospital, and expressed their desire, that it should be re-erected on another site in France, and the Council of the Order have decided that this shall be done, and with the least possible delay. It will, however, entail heavy expenditure to re-equip the hospital and maintain the high standard of efficiency for which the St. John Ambulance Brigade Hospital when at Etaples was so widely known. Cheques should be sent to Lord Ranfurly, Director of the Ambulance Department, St. John's Gate, Clerkenwell, London, E.C. 1.

THE MILITARY MEDAL.

The Military Medal has been awarded to the following members of the nursing staff of the St. John Ambulance Brigade Hospital at Etaples.— Miss C. E. Todd (Matron), Miss M. A. Chittock (Assistant Matron), Miss M. McGinnes, Miss M. H. Ballance, Miss J. Benrose, and Miss C. Warner (Sisters). When the Hospital was deliberately bombed by the Germans, and a number of patients and members of the staff killed and injured, we may be sure that the nursing staff behaved with heroism, and congratulate Miss Todd, Miss Chittock, and the Sisters on the honour conferred upon them.

WAR POSTERS DEFACED.

A number of placards issued by the Ladies' Emergency Committee of the Navy League, showing a German Red Cross Nurse wilfully spilling the water for which British prisoners of war, herded in an open truck, are waiting, were found one morning last week to have been defaced. An examination of several of the principal hoardings in London revealed the fact that all the posters were mutilated in the same way. The nurse's face was in each case obliterated—in some cases torn out and in others covered with stamp edging.

The Huns in our midst evidently give short shrift to posters to which they object.

The King of the Belgians has conferred the Médaille de la Reine Elisabeth on a long list of ladies in recognition of " the kind help and valuable assistance personally given to the Belgian refugees and the Belgian soldiers during the war."

OUR ROLL OF HONOUR.

Again we have to mourn with our Canadian colleagues at the determined murder on the high seas of fourteen Sisters who, together with 80 Canadian Army Medical Officers, were on board the Canadian hospital ship *Llandovery Castle*, deliberately sunk by a German submarine commander about 120 miles from the Irish coast. Of the 258 souls on board only 24 in one boat have been saved alive. The belief is strong among the survivors that of seven boats launched, all, saving their own, were deliberately wrecked by the fiendish way in which the submarine charged up and down among the wreckage, sinking everything in sight.

One more most horrible crime to add to the score that must be paid by these dastardly murderers before they are classed as human beings by a civilised world.

All our sympathy goes out to those who loved these brave Canadian nurses.

TRUE TALE WITH A MORAL.

Lady Superintendent of Nurses to a friend. —" I think it simply disastrous to the future economic independence of the Nursing Profession to have all this begging upon their behalf. Much better help them to get just remuneration for their work."

Clear-sighted Friend : " My dear, I think the reason the Nation's Fund for Nurses was started by the hospital officials who control the College was that Nurses should *not* put up their fees. Much better give them a dole and control the charity."

FRENCH FLAG NURSING CORPS.

Mrs. Fenwick entertained the Sisters of Ambulance 12/2 and some of their fellow-Sisters to dinner at the Holborn Restaurant last Thursday, before their return to duty, as the ambulance is being re-established. Miss Roberts, R.R.C. (Chief Matron, British Committee, French Red Cross), Miss Hutchinson, F.F.N.C., Miss M. Breay, and Miss Isabel Macdonald, R.B.N.A., were also present, and it was a very cheery party. The unit returned to France the following day, and were all most eager to be at work again in the war zone.

which you were able to give us for a few days. The few days we had them we were very busy, and I really don't know what we should have done without them. They were such a nice well-trained capable set of women, and simply set to to help as if they had been here for weeks. The Med. Chef, I think, is writing to you also to thank you."

That is as it should be, but in these days of uncertain standards of nursing in military hospitals the help given is often far from efficient. In her reply, Miss Haswell asked Miss du Sautoy to thank her staff on behalf of the F.F.N.C. Sisters, for they all agreed that they had never worked in such a happy atmosphere, where

FRENCH FLAG NURSING CORPS SISTERS, AMBULANCE 12/2.

Miss Owens, of the Registered Nurses' Society, has joined the F.F.N.C., and has been posted to Lisieux, where the hospital has been largely extended.

During the recent great stress of work, the beautiful Hôpital Bénéval No. 4, located in the Astoria at Paris, was full to overflowing, and some of the F.F.N.C. Sisters had the privilege of giving a helping hand. Miss Haswell has since received the the following letter from Miss C. C. du Sautoy, the Matron of the hospital :—

" Dear Miss Haswell,—Would you convey to Mrs. Bedford Fenwick my thanks, and that of the Sisters, for the services of the F.F.N.C. Sisters

everyone, without exception, did everything in their power to make them welcome, and feel at home.

British nurses working in Paris are showing splendid nerve, bombed as they are nearly every night.

MORE SISTERS REQUIRED.

Several more Sisters have been requisitioned by the Service de Santé—for work in France. Candidates, aged from 26 to 40, must hold a three years' certificate of general training, must have good health, and know some French. Mrs. Fenwick will see candidates by appointment. Address, 431, Oxford St., London, W. 1.

THE COLOURED WOMEN OF MID-WEST AND THE RED CROSS.

HELPING THE REST OF THE WORLD'S PEOPLE TO THEIR OWN DEARLY WON LIBERTY.

Many and varied were the phases of the gigantic parades held all over America in commemoration of Uncle Sam's first anniversary of entrance upon the world-war, as well as in celebration of the opening of the big "drive" for the third Liberty Loan; none were more affecting, to those realising its import, than the march of the coloured women workers of Cincinnati with the Red Cross.

Cincinnati lies on the Ohio, just across from the Kentucky shore. Placed thus, the city was the

FREE COLOURED WOMEN HELPING TO FREE THE WORLD.

creature comforts for the coloured soldiers, but now given over to all the regular Red Cross activities.

On Liberty Day, the first anniversary of America's taking definite share in the stupendous conflict, Cincinnati marked the opening of the big drive for the Third American Liberty Loan with one of the largest parades in her history.

Among others, the Red Cross workers turned out, marching in their attractive white habits and veils, the endless cohorts having their snowy whiteness punctuated by the red caps of supervisors here and there.

Boundless applause greeted all these workers along the line of march; but no one unit received more acclaim than the one hundred and fifty negro women of the Soldiers' Comfort Club—the dusky faces of these faithful knitters and sewers and the makers of dressings and comforts for the sick all the more picturesque in contrast with their white attire.

As black troops are available from America to take part in the war in Europe, the woman President of the National Association of Coloured Graduate Nurses offers 2,000 black nurses, ready trained for service at military hospitals in Europe and America.

There are already 34 black chaplains in the American army.

logical gateway between American North and South before the Civil War, and, therefore, the Mecca of no end of fugitive slaves. Here lived the abolitionists Coffin and Beecher, and here Harriet Beecher Stowe penned her "Uncle Tom's Cabin." In fact, here, if anywhere, the big fight for the liberty of the black man may be said to have concentrated.

In and about Cincinnati still you may find any number of men, or women, who received freedom from the Emancipator President. Their children, the children of others, who fled from slavery, and, again, the children of those, more fortunate, who saw the results of slavery just across the Dixie line here.

Now free themselves, at the call to help other lands—in fact, to save all the world from autocracy—these coloured women are not to be behindhand in the good work.

Affiliated with the Red Cross—in fact, now one of its definite units—they have formed a Soldiers' Comfort Club, originally for providing various

THE BRITISH LION GROWLS.

The swishing of the British Lion's tail on the enemy alien question has produced some effect. The Prime Minister has asked five members of Parliament to make a thorough investigation of the enemy alien problem, and to advise him what action should be taken to allay public anxiety.

The remedy is simple. There is to be a great public demonstration in Trafalgar Square on Saturday, July 13th, at 2.30 p.m., at which a resolution calling for immediate internment of all aliens of enemy blood will be submitted.

Let us all be there to see it is passed by acclamation, and later make sure that the demands of the people are carried into effect by the Government. The feeling concerning these dangerous and crafty spies will soon be out of hand unless firm action is enforced.

Royal British Nurses' Association.

(Incorporated by  Royal Charter.)

THIS SUPPLEMENT BEING THE OFFICIAL ORGAN OF THE CORPORATION.

Cumberland Lodge,
Windsor,
June 28th, 1918.

TO THE MEMBERS OF THE AFFILIATED SOCIETIES,

I desire in this Supplement, the first issue of the new official organ of the Royal British Nurses' Association, to express the sincere gratification the affiliation of your Societies with my Association affords me.

I am confident that my own Nurses would like me to say that they, too, welcome most cordially closer union between you and them. I have appreciated warmly the support given by your Societies to the Chartered Association, and I earnestly hope that the powers conferred by the Royal Charter may be used in every way possible to aid your Societies, in all they undertake, to further the interests of all fully trained Nurses.

I trust that this union between your Societies will not be a matter of organisation alone, but that it will inspire a spirit of comradeship between you and the Members of the Royal British Nurses' Association—individually and collectively.

The welfare and happiness of our Nurses is a matter very near to my heart, and I have watched with great pride and admiration the magnificent and self-sacrificing work they have done.

It is therefore a source of much gratification to me to feel that your Societies have all united under the Royal Charter granted to my Association by my beloved Mother, Queen Victoria.

Helena

President of the Royal British Nurses' Association.

THE OFFICIAL ORGAN OF THE ROYAL BRITISH NURSES' ASSOCIATION.

A NEW DEPARTURE.

For several years the conviction has been growing in the minds of Members of the Council of the Royal British Nurses' Association that a monthly organ, which circulates only to its own Members, is no longer adequate to the requirements of the Corporation. The events of the past twelve months have brought this point of view more prominently than ever before those to whom the management of the Corporation has been entrusted by its Members, particularly as the action of the Association and its Council has been repeatedly misrepresented in sections of the nursing press. The opinion of some Members of the General Council has been that the object of such misrepresentation was not merely to obscure the powers which the nurses possess in their Charter and the use which they could make of it to improve their economic position, but also to spread dissension in the Association, and to undermine the confidence of the Members in those whom they have elected to the governing body of the Association. If such has been the intention it has failed utterly, for at no time have the Members been more strongly united; nevertheless the Council feel that the time has now arrived for adopting an organ, wherein to publish fortnightly a report of what is taking place in connection with the Association and its work. Too often it happens that matter, inserted in a monthly journal, has already appeared in the weekly press, and not as official information from the Association. These considerations led the Council to the decision that some change was now called for to enable the Members to keep in close touch with their Corporation. At a quarterly meeting, at which Her Royal Highness the President of the Corporation presided, it was decided that steps should be taken in order to arrange that official information should be inserted in a weekly organ. It was the unanimous opinion of the Meeting that THE BRITISH JOURNAL OF NURSING was the Journal best suited in which to insert the official Supplement of the Chartered Corporation of fully qualified nurses. Instructions were given to the Executive Committee to proceed with whatever negotiations and arrangements they might deem advisable, in order to give effect to the proposals of the General Council. At the next Meeting of that Committee the Honorary Officers were asked to approach Mrs. Bedford

Fenwick, Editor of THE BRITISH JOURNAL OF NURSING, and to request that some arrangement should be made whereby that Journal should become the organ of communication with Members of the Association. The proposals of the Executive Committee were met in the most generous spirit by Mrs. Fenwick, and ultimately the Committee laid before the General Council a formal recommendation that a Supplement be inserted fortnightly in THE BRITISH JOURNAL OF NURSING as the Official Organ of the Corporation. This recommendation was unanimously adopted at a Special Meeting of the General Council.

The decision of the Council in this matter is a very important one, apart from those aspects in which it nearly concerns the Association itself, for such a decision embodies the vital principle that control of the professional press should be in the hands of the profession. THE BRITISH JOURNAL OF NURSING, is the only weekly nursing paper in England edited by nurses. It is, therefore, the Journal best calculated to promote the interests of the nurses, to voice their opinions, and to keep them informed on questions relating to their professional affairs; moreover, directly and indirectly, it is undoubtedly the publication which has educated the public and the nurses of all countries on the necessity for the organization of nursing education and the need for Registration by the State of those who have qualified themselves to be entrusted with the care of the sick.

Some regret was expressed at the Council Meeting that the *Nurses' Journal* should be discontinued, but just as "new times demand new manners and new men," so also a time has come when the Journal, which has served its purpose so usefully in the past twelve months of controversy, by conveying to the Members full verbatim reports of the proceedings at Meetings of the Corporation and its Council, must now be laid aside in favour of another which is in a position to be of greater value to the Members and to the profession at large. We hope that the Members will look upon their new organ as an important and tangible part of their Association. As Members of the only Corporation of Nurses recognised by the State they have great powers, and consequently great responsibilities. In order to discharge those faithfully they must see to it that they use the means provided for them in order to keep themselves informed on all questions relating to the policy of their Corporation, for the present time is one of grave crisis for themselves and all members of their profession, and questions call for consideration which are of vital importance to them and to the nurses of the future.

One word to those who are not Members of the Association : the Royal Charter gives to the Royal British Nurses' Association prestige and powers which no other body of nurses in the Empire possesses or is ever likely to possess, powers granted to the *nurses* under the sign manual of a sovereign of the realm.   The extent to which such powers shall be used to protect them and to promote their welfare is entirely dependent upon the nurses themselves, their comradeship, their willingness to unite with one another, and to line up under the banner of the Royal Charter, each stepping into her place in the Royal Corporation prepared to take her part as an architect in the building of a mighty fabric composed of individuals, each individual strengthening and being strengthened by the other.   By the Royal Charter nurses are given the powers to form such an organization, and one so powerful that, if all the nurses in England would come forward to help, there is nothing within reason which it could not demand for them and *get*.

ROYAL RED CROSS.

The Royal Red Cross (second class) has been awarded to Miss Caroline Cattell, Matron of the Uffculme Military Hospital, Birmingham. Miss Cattell held appointments as Sister and, later, as Matron in Military Hospitals in France, between 1914 and 1916.   Later, she acted as Sister in a Military Hospital in London, and left this for the appointment which she now holds.   We notice that in the same list of awards, a similar honour has been conferred upon Miss Bertha Cattell (Sister Mary Peter of the Little Company of Mary), and the information will give pleasure to many of our members to whom these ladies are well known. Both are sisters of Miss Alice Cattell, a popular member of the Council of the R.B.N.A.

AFFILIATED SOCIETIES.

Since the General Meeting of the Corporation, information has reached us that the Scottish Nurses' Association has accepted the invitation of H.R.H. the President and the Council to become affiliated to the Corporation, and Miss Isabel E. Henderson has been nominated as its representative on the Council. Miss Henderson has been a member of the R.B.N.A. since 1909.   The following Societies are also now affiliated :—The Matrons' Council of Great Britain and Ireland, the Society for the State Registration of Trained Nurses, the National Union of Trained Nurses, the Irish Nurses' Association, and the Fever Nurses' Association.

(Signed)   ISABEL MACDONALD,

Secretary to the Corporation.

THE LEAGUE OF ST. BARTHOLOMEW'S HOSPITAL NURSES.

The summer general meeting of the League of St. Bartholomew's Hospital Nurses was held in the clinical theatre of the hospital on Saturday, June 29th.   In the unavoidable absence of the President, Miss Helen Todd, the chair was taken by the senior Vice-President, Miss Juliet Curtis. Miss Todd wrote expressing her extreme regret at her absence, and saying that it was the first summer meeting of the League she had missed since its foundation ;   only urgent duty would have kept her away.

SATISFACTORY REPORTS.

Very satisfactory reports were presented.   The Treasurer, Mrs. Turnbull, showed a balance in hand of over £67, after paying for three issues of *League News* in one year. Miss Cutler, the General Secretary, reported that forty-seven new members had joined during the year and one resigned, and that the League now numbered 973 members.

The decorations conferred on members of the League included a Military Medal bestowed upon Miss Dorothy Foster, two bars to the Royal Red Cross, and seven first-class and seventeen second class R.R.C.s, and two Serving Sisters of the Order of St. John of Jerusalem.

The Chairman said that many members of the League working on land and sea had gained decorations.   The members of the League would like them to know how they valued their courage and work, and that we should welcome them on their return with pleasure, love and gratitude.

We felt their good work was needed, for we saw the results of other work which was not so skilled, and we felt that our broken men needed the very best we had to give and the most skilled nursing care ;   therefore, when honours came to the skilled workers we rejoiced at this recognition.

Mrs. Matthews, Treasurer of the Benevolent Fund reported a balance in hand of over £90. One grant of £10 had been made during the year.

THE EXECUTIVE COMMITTEE.

Miss M. Appleyard, R.R.C., and Miss Lister were elected members of the Executive Committee in place of the retiring members.

THE ISLA STEWART MEMORIAL.

Mrs. Shuter presented the Report of the Isla Stewart Memorial Standing Committee, which showed the total amount received to be £600, and an income from investments (including the £5 annual subscription of the League) of £30 per annum.

REPORT ON STATE REGISTRATION.

Miss Le Geyt, delegate of the League on the Executive Committee of the Society for the State Registration of Trained Nurses, then presented her report, in which she said, in part :—

" In taking a general survey of the work of the Society during the past year, it would seem as if the President and the Executive Committee had, like the nation at large, experienced the need to exercise great vigilance in this instance in guarding the ideals and interests of the nursing profession.

"With truth it might be said that 'Vigilance' could be called the watchword of the Society for the State Registration of Trained Nurses from its foundation in 1902."

Mrs. Bedford Fenwick briefly outlined the present position up to date, commenting, in this connection, on the seventh draft of the Nurses' Registration Bill of the College of Nursing, Ltd. Three important points had now been conceded, but the Bill still incorporated the College Company; it also made provision for establishing registers of specialists. The claim for such registers was a claim on the part of institutions. To take women and half train them was to put them outside the pale. The first duty of any Council considering the State Registration of Trained Nurses was to do justice to the members of the nursing profession.

This view was strongly supported by Miss Helen Pearse.

The Chairman said that the nursing profession appeared at the present time to be in great jeopardy. It was used, put aside, and other people put forward; training did not count We must see that the profession was not overlooked. She hoped if amalgamation of the two Bills took place we should keep the profession at the top, and hold firmly to standards, ideals, and principles.

The meeting then terminated, and adjourned for tea, which was served in the Nurses' Home and the cloisters.

THE NURSES' MISSIONARY LEAGUE CAMP.

This is the first, but I trust not the last, time that I have attended the "Camp" of the Nurses' Missionary League. It was held from June 20th to 27th, at Old Jordans Hostel, Beaconsfield, an ideal spot with such a beautiful old-world garden and lovely woods and country all round, most restful and peaceful. We started with twelve members, but were soon fourteen, and several were prevented at the last from joining us. We met each morning after breakfast for prayers, and then most of the mornings and afternoons were spent in walks or rambles in the woods, in gathering strawberries or in cycle rides. One afternoon two of the nurses made an excursion to Burnham Beeches, most beautiful woods, some six miles away. On three mornings there were Bible Circles, which we found most helpful; but best of all perhaps were the evenings, when we had inspiring addresses on such subjects as "God's Plan for the World" and "The Great Adventure," always ending with prayer and intercession. We remembered all our members, very especially those in the foreign mission field. We were very fortunate in having with us Miss Herbert, from

China; Miss Mathew, from Uganda; Miss Jones from North India; and Miss Edwards, who has done mission work in France. Other members represented health welfare, civil and military hospitals and private and district work. We had wonderful examples of God's answers to prayer in Miss Herbert's most interesting talks about China and Miss Mathew and Miss Jones interested us keenly in their work by their conversation and photographs. They showed us how very urgent is the call for more workers; while the letters read to us from members abroad showed how more than usually under-staffed many hospitals are at present, making always difficult work well-nigh impossible. They showed us too, however, that the difficulties are as nothing in comparison with the privilege of carrying the message of Christ all over the world. Many of these letters told how deeply the members abroad appreciate the prayers of their friends, and one of the lasting memories of Camp will be the emphasis upon prayer.

It was the most enjoyable and most restful holiday I have ever had, and we all hope that the second Camp, which is to be held at Mottram St. Andrew, Cheshire, from July 17th to 24th, will be as great a success. Any nurses who are free at that time should write at once for particulars to Miss Macfee, 21, Frognal Lane, Hampstead, London, N.W. 3.

A VISITOR TO THE CAMP.

NURSES AND INSURANCE.

The National Insurance Commissioners have issued a summary of the Provisions of the National Insurance (Health) Acts, 1911–18, for the information of the members of Approved Societies. These helpful leaflets can be obtained, cost 1d. through any bookseller, or directly from H.M. Stationery Office, at the following addresses:—Imperial House, Kingsway, London, W.C. 2; or 28, Abingdon Street, London, S.W. 1; 37, Peter Street, Manchester; 1 St. Andrew's Crescent, Cardiff; 23, Forth Street, Edinburgh; and E. Ponsonby, Ltd., 116, Grafton Street, Dublin. Nurses who are insured would do well to procure and study these leaflets, as they will find them very useful to refer to in dealing with the Secretary of the Approved Society in which they are insured.

A NEW RULE.

The amended Act (1918), Clause 27, instructs a member who becomes incapable of work through illness to give notice to her Society *at once*, together with a medical certificate of incapacity. If she does not give notice *within three days* from the commencement of her incapacity, benefit will not commence until the day following that on which the notice is given. This is a new rule, to which insured nurses must give heed, as under the old provisions of the Act, they were often most casual in notifying illness, sometimes not doing so for weeks and then expecting benefit in full, although all rules had been broken. For the future they will do well to obey the law.

GAMBOLS *v.* NATIONAL SERVICE.

It is deeply to be deplored that His Majesty the King has, with the kindest intentions no doubt, given permission for a Garden Party, to be held at St. James' Palace, for the War Charity, the Nation's Fund for Nurses, as it is in no sense national, and its methods are detested by self-respecting professional nurses.

We have as a result a new outburst of costly advertisements in the daily Press in support of the Fund, which continues to boycott the opinions of those opposed to the subsidising of the lay consti-tuted College of Nursing Company, in its attempt to control the Nursing profession.

Once again our sense of propriety is out-raged by the reappearance on the hoardings of the poster of a semi-nude female, purporting to be a nurse, tenaciously clutching a wounded (and evidently abashed) young man !

Throughout, the tone of the advertisements in support of this War Charity have been tactless and offensive in the extreme, and we note amongst other advertised attractions there are to be "Gambols" at the Garden Party ! Who is going to "Gambol" ? Surely not the heads of our Nurse-training Schools who are thrusting this Society Charity on the profession they should be the first to protect. But that the supposed indi-gence of our profession is to be the excuse for this unseemly rout, is nothing short of an outrage, when we know that brave men, many of them our nearest and dearest, are dying or risking death for us in every hour.

We have in our midst an army of rich, vain and idle women, underdressed and overfed, whose life has, and presumably always will consist of self-indulgence, excitement and vapidity, women who never have done an hour's real useful work since the war began, and who clutch at any excuse to amuse themselves. If this heartless clique must "gambol" whilst the nation is in danger, we strongly object to our profession being used as an excuse for their antics, and the sooner Parliament conscripts the lot, and compels them to do some really useful work for the benefit of the country the better. Young, strong, able-bodied women should be on the land, in the shipyards, or in the factory in this hour of the nation's needs. Any-way we nurses protest against their "gambols" in our name, under a cloak of Charity.

MISS ELIZABETH ASQUITH LETS ANOTHER CAT OUT OF THE COLLEGE BAG.

As widely advertised, Miss Elizabeth Asquith and others have been selling tickets for the "Gambols" at St James' Palace at the big drapers' shops during the week, which has given nurses who object to being placed at the mercy of the College Constitution an opportunity of expressing their views concerning lay patronage.

The Daily Mirror man also availed himself of the opportunity to seek information, to judge by the following " par " which appeared on Tuesday last :—

FUTURE OF THE V.A.D.
COLLEGE AND FULL EDUCATION SCHEME FOR NURSES AFTER THE WAR.

What is to become of the V.A.D.'s after the War ? Miss Elizabeth Asquith told *The Daily Mirror* yesterday : "A College of Nursing has been founded by the Nation's Fund for Nurses as a thankoffering for what the nurses have done.

" Undoubtedly," Miss Asquith added, " vast numbers of V.A.D.'s will want to continue nursing, but they must be adequately trained, and the college has a full education scheme, with scholar-ships, so that they can finish their course.

" In peace days, when wounds and shell shocks are no more, they must know the women's side of nursing as well as the men's."

Trained nurses will do well to consider their future if they hope to make a living in com-petition with " vast numbers " of V.A.D.'s, who are being projected into the profession through the Nation's Fund for Nurses

---

A PROTEST.

Under the heading of " A Protest," a communi-cation from Miss Alicia Lloyd Still, Matron of St. Thomas' Hospital, London, and Miss Amy Hughes late General Superintendent of Queen Victoria's Jubilee Institute for Nurses appeared in the June number of the *American Journal of Nursing.* These ladies write : " Our attention has been drawn to an article, headed ' English Nursing Politics,' published in the *American Journal of Nursing* for February. As this article is evidently written under a misapprehension of the situation, and as it is based upon a biassed account given in THE BRITISH JOURNAL OF NURSING of the present condition of the Nursing World in England, may we be allowed to give a short account of the exist-ing state of affairs in the nursing world ?

" The article in question (written by Miss Dock) says that an ' odious element which has been the affliction of British nurses for thirty years, is still busy trying to enslave them in a web wherein the College of Nursing, State registration, and public alms are woven with the intent to keep them professionally helpless."

" The Protest " of the two signatories is full, no doubt unintentionally, of inaccuracies which can be quite easily refuted from the printed matter so lavishly issued by the College of Nursing, Ltd., which it is designed to support.

The confusion of mind of the College Matron advocates concerning their own Constitution is amazing. Apparently they have never studied it, or are incapable of discriminating concerning the " odious " provisions of its Memorandum and

Articles of Association (which we know were drafted before they were consulted) but which they have made no attempt to alter.

Next week, in justice to THE BRITISH JOURNAL OF NURSING, we propose to prove that it is neither biassed nor inaccurate in its surmises concerning the fundamental policy of the promoters of the College of Nursing, Ltd.

Anyway, those members of the nursing profession in England, Scotland and Ireland, who are economically independent do not intend to submit to its Constitution, as so many ignorant young nurses have been persuaded by their employers to do.

A CONVENIENT SHOPPING CENTRE.

Proprietors of Nursing Homes and private nurses in the Marylebone District will find in the establishment of Messrs. Gayler & Pope, 112-117, High Street, Marylebone, W., a convenient shopping centre, whether for materials for nursing uniforms, or for general shopping purposes. Those requiring furniture, whether for the equipment of nursing homes or its renewal, should inspect the varied stock of this firm.

A POPULAR PUBLISHER.

Messrs. H. & K. Lewis, Ltd., of 136, Gower Street, and 24, Gower Place, W.C. 1, publish a variety of literature popular with and useful to nurses, masseuses and midwives in connection with their work. In this connection we may mention " The Theory and Practice of Massage," with numerous illustrations by Miss Beatrice M. G. Copestake, Member of and Examiner to the Incorporated Society of Trained Masseuses.

SOME VALUABLE FOODS.

Just now when the anxieties of the war are apt to bring many people somewhat below par, and rationing and considerations of economy restrict the diet, it is well to recall some of the valuable foods which we can utilise with advantage, for adults, children and infants. THE ALLENBURYS' FOODS (37, Lombard Street, London) (Milk Food No. 1 and No. 2 and Malted Food No. 3) will be found most satisfactory in the feeding of infants, while their Diet is largely used and of proved value for invalid and aged persons.

ROBINSON'S " PATENT " BARLEY (Keen, Robinson & Co., Ltd., London), for making barley water for diluting cow's or goat's milk for infant feeding is a preparation which midwives and nurses find invaluable, and nothing could be better than their " Patent " Groats, for preparing milk gruel and porridge for nursing mothers.

BENGER'S FOOD (Otter Works, Manchester) is an invaluable preparation in the dietary of invalids, a unique feature of which is that it is self-digestive and that the extent of the digestive process can be regulated to suit individual patients.

FALIÈRES' PHOSPHATINE (F. H. Mertens, 84, Holborn Viaduct, E.C. 1) is also a valuable food, which, associated with milk, is much liked by patients, while its food value is undoubted.

APPOINTMENTS.

MATRON.

Welsh Hospital, Netley. — Miss Kathleen S. Stewart has been appointed Matron. She received her general training at the Royal Infirmary, Sunderland, and maternity training at the Royal Maternity Hospital, Edinburgh. She was subsequently district and ward Sister at the Deaconess Hospital, Edinburgh, and Night Superintendent and Housekeeping Sister at the Royal Infirmary, Sunderland. She has also been Housekeeping Sister at Charing Cross Hospital, Assistant Matron at the Royal Hospital for Sick Children, Edinburgh, and Matron of the York County Hospital. She was awarded the Royal Red Cross (2nd Class) in January, 1917.

Isolation Hospital and Sanatorium, Belvedere Road, Burton-on-Trent. — Mrs. A. Ellis has been appointed Matron. She was trained at the Royal Infirmary, Derby, and the Fountain Fever Hospital, Tooting, where she also held the positions of Ward Sister, Night Superintendent and Housekeeper. She has also been Matron of the District Hospital, Settle, and for the last five years of the Joint Hospital and Sanatorium, Smethwick.

Royal Surrey County Hospital, Guildford. — Miss R. A. Longland has been appointed Matron. She was trained at the Great Northern Hospital, London, where she has been Sister and Night Superintendent, and has also held the positions of Assistant Matron and Acting-Matron at the Royal Surrey County Hospital.

Tuberculosis Sanatorium, Pelsall Hall, near Walsall. — Miss P. Partington has been appointed Matron. She has previously been Matron of the Observation Hospital for Tuberculosis at Bury, Lancs.

ACTING MATRON.

National Hospital for Diseases of the Heart, London. — Miss Cecilia Beaton has been appointed Acting Matron. She was trained at the Taunton and Somerset Hospital, and has been Sister at the General Infirmary, Worcester, and the County Hospital, Bedford, and Home Sister at Bolingbroke Hospital, Wandsworth Common.

ASSISTANT MATRON.

Hendon Grove Asylum, Hendon, N.W. — Miss Elizabeth J. Thompson has been appointed Assistant-Matron. She has been on the Staff of the Prestwich Asylum for fifteen years, and for the past two years has been Assistant-Matron of Palmerston House, Palmerston, co. Dublin.

WARD SISTER.

Dudley Union Infirmary. — Miss H. Hollies has been appointed Ward Sister. She was trained at the Wolstanton and Burslem Union Infirmary, and is at present pupil midwife at Queen Victoria's Nursing Institute, Northampton.

NURSING ECHOES.

Miss Mollett's many friends will be sorry to hear that on Thursday, June 27th, she met with a serious accident when cycling from Bournemouth to her home at Three Cross, near Ringwood. Apparently no immediate help was at hand, and she lay in the road for a considerable time, until a gentleman came by and rendered aid, taking her in a taxi cab to Miss Forrest's Nursing Home, 4, Cambridge Road, Bournemouth. On examination it was found that the injuries sustained were an impacted fracture of femur, a bruised head, and cut arm. Throughout all this Miss Mollett was full of the courage and cheerful endurance which never fails her. She may be sure now, as ever, of affectionate regard and sympathy, and also of good wishes for a steady convalescence and recovery.

Long before the war we claimed just educational and economic conditions for nurses, but until recent events has caused the supply of nurses in all directions to fall short of the demand, those who employed them appeared well content to continue at sweated rates of remuneration. Especially has this been apparent in various branches of district nursing. We note with pleasure the recent awakening of conscience (necessity has a way of driving her lessons home) on this question.

There has been far too much patronage and too little pelf in the conduct of County Nursing Associations in the past, and our Lady Bountifuls are seldom lavish where working women are concerned.

We observe that Mrs. Cooke-Hurle, speaking at the annual meeting of the Somerset Nursing Association at Taunton, said : " She would like to see the time when the salaries of nurses would be raised to such an extent that they would be able to have their full training and adequate payment for their services."

It is the fault of the women organizers and managers of the County Nursing Associations that these just terms have not prevailed in the past. A network of social influence and self-appointed control by the laity has defined the standards of knowledge and the remuneration of district and village nurses all over the country. The standards are woefully insufficient, and the remuneration a sweated wage. The sooner the nursing of the poor is directed by a State Department controlled by a Ministry of Health the better—better for patient and nurse. Class government has had its day.

The Local Government Board has sanctioned a joint scheme entered into between the Nottingham Guardians and the Guardians of the Basford Union for the training of probationary nurses, under which the probationers will receive their first year's training at Basford, and then proceed to Bagthorpe for a further three years' training, including midwifery and massage. By this arrangement the services of candidates who desire to qualify as fully certificated nurses will be secured for the Basford Union.

The King Edward Nurses were organized as a South African Memorial to commemorate the life and aims of King Edward VII, and comprises two divisions (*a*) European ; (*b*) Coloured and Native, and its immediate object is to make good deficiencies now existing in nursing circles in South Africa.

From the Report of 1917, just to hand, we learn from Miss J. E. Pritchard, Superintendent of the Order, that 1917, like the two previous years, has been one of many difficulties owing to the war. The year was begun with a staff of 15—and ended with 11. The centres have been understaffed, and it is impossible to estimate the work lost, but we gather that much good work has been done, and on visiting the various centres the Superintendent found the nurses much appreciated in the districts.

A new centre was opened during the year at Empangeni, a malarial district, and during the floods, when it was cut off for some time, it was most fortunate that, as there was no doctor, a qualified nurse-midwife was in the place, more particularly as some cases who had arranged to go to a Maternity Home in Durban were unable to get through.

Several applications for resident nurses have not been able to be met owing to the shortage of nurses, but considerig the serious understaffing in some of the large civil hospitals, the Superintendent considers the Order fortunate to begin the year with 11 nurses, and she hopes when times are normal to expand the work in many directions.

The Committee report with great satisfaction that upon the completion of her term of contract, Miss Pritchard has consented to continue in her post. The Committee also records its appreciation of the services of Miss Brailsford (Senior Nursing Sister at Ladysmith), and other members of the Order.

The South Australian Branch of the R.B.N.A. was welcomed by the South Australian Branch of the A.T.N.A. at its annual meeting, when joint consideration was given to raising the fees of private nurses in the State from £2 2s. to £3 3s. a week. Dr. Cecil Corbin, R.B.N.A., addressed the meeting, and it was agreed that other States having adopted the higher scale of fees was undoubtedly attracting many nurses from South Australia. The Council recommend raising the fee, and the members will have an opportunity of voting on it.

The future organization of the nursing profession was the subject for discussion at the Women's Institute on June 21st, when Mrs. Alderton, of Colchester, presided. It is a hopeful sign that women are beginning to show concern in this question, as, so far, they have taken deplorably little interest in trained nursing. Beyond the address of Miss Georgina K. Sanders, who described the methods of nurse training in America, and emphasised the importance of dietetics in the curriculum, there was nothing of great value in the discussion. We were sorry to hear the Secretary of the College of Nursing, Ltd., defending the indefensible provision in its Memorandum whereby power is given to the Council to remove a member from its Register without giving her a power of appeal. Miss Rundle also, in advocating autocratic control, confused the Constitution of the College of Nursing Company with the Constitution of the Council. It is high time both the officials and nurses realised the difference between the two. Miss Cowlin, also speaking of Registration in the United States of America, said that during a visit there it had not taken her long to realize that the value of registration in some of the States was practically *nil*, and said, " We put education first." Miss Cowlin did not appear to realize that the primary purpose of a Registration Bill is to standardize and test nursing education, and that it is this great reform which the State Registrationists have been fighting for, for a quarter of a century, and which the nursing schools have opposed. She also divulged a unique plan for roping in the small cottage hospitals. They could not be used for training purposes, she said, because they did not provide sufficient clinical material. The proposal was, therefore, to send round a Sister-Tutor to instruct the nurses. How the advent of the Sister-Tutor would miraculously provide the clinical material she did not explain, nor what would be the position of the Matrons of the smaller hospitals in relation to Sister-Tutors.

BOOK OF THE WEEK.

SIR ISUMBRAS AT THE FORD.*

" And weel ye ken, Maister Anne, ye should have been asleep lang syne," said Elspeth severely.

Master Anne, le Comte Anne-Hilarion de Flavigny, gave a little sigh from the bed. " I have tried . . . if you would say ' Noroway ' perhaps ? Say ' Noroway—over the—foam ' Elspeth, *je vous en prie.*"

" Dinna be using ony of yer French havers to me wean," exclaimed the elderly woman thus addressed. However, she sat down, took up her knitting, and began

" The king sat in Dumferline toun
 Drinking the blude-red wine."

Anne-Hilarion had not chosen well the date of his entry into this world.

On the very July day when René and Janet de Flavigny and all their tenants were celebrating the admirable prowess displayed by M. le Comte in attaining without accident or illness, without flying back to heaven, as his nurse had it, the age of one year, the people of Paris also were keeping a festival, the first anniversary of the day when the bloody head of the governor of the Bastille had swung along the streets at the end of a pike.

Before that summer was out the Marquis de Flavigny, urged by his father-in-law, had decided to place his wife and child in safety, and so, bidding the most reluctant of good-byes to the tourelles and the swans which had witnessed their two short years of happiness, they left France for England."

But on the journey home the little French boy's Scottish mother caught a chill from which she never recovered, and the openng of the story finds Anne in the London house of his maternal grandfather in the charge of his Scottish nurse, at the hour when his father, in concert with other notable *emigrés* were, in the room below, talking of the intrigues and counter intrigues which ate like a canker into the heart of the Royalist cause.

There are many charming pictures drawn of the little Franco-Scottish boy. Anne-Hilarion was quite aware in a general way of his father's occupations. In fact, as he lay in his bed, looking through the curtains at the wardrobe door, he was meditating upon the important meeting Papa was having with his friends in the dining-room.

His lively imagination, coupled with Elspeth's grim ballads, and something he had heard about papa going to France, made him decide that there was nothing for it but to go down to the conclave below and ascertain the truth.

" Messieurs, a new recruit ! Welcome small conspirator. Come in, but shut the door." And all the rest turned on the instant to look at the little figure clad only in a nightshirt which was visible in the doorway behind René de Flavigny's back.

He made a dash for his father.

---

* By D. K. Broster. John Murray. London

" Papa," he burst out, " Do not go to ' Noroway over the foam.' You know how it says the feather beds floated about in the waves and the sea came in and they were all drowned fifty fathoms deep."

Little Anne learned more at that conclave than it was prudent he should know in those troublous times.

Following almost immediately after this he is kidnapped and taken by a ruse to the house of two *charming* (?) old ladies, who posed as his father's old friends.

The conception of these two treacherous old pieces of Dresden china is one of the cleverest things in the book.

Mme. de Chaulnes first dealt effectively with old Elspeth, who had also been inveigled away with her charge.

" Elspeth having arranged about the baggage, they went upstairs into a spotless little bedroom smelling of lavender. She informs the old Scotch woman that she will have to sleep out of the house.

Elspeth looked mutinous, and her mouth took on a line that Anne well knew.

" A'm thinkin' Mem," she replied, " it wad be best for me tae hae a wee bit bed in here."

Mme. de Chaulnes shook her head. " I am afraid," she said, " that that arrangement would not suit us at all."

Elspeth was very glum as she put the little boy to bed.

" At ony rate" she said, " A'll no leave till A please."

" They are very kind ladies," said little Anne, who was excited. " I think Mme. de Chaulnes is a beautiful old lady like a fée Marraine."

Little Anne's tongue did a great deal of mischief to his father that night, and the adventure ended with his being smuggled out to France, from which country, so perilous at that time to the aristocrats, he was rescued after exciting adventures by M. de la Vireville.

But Anne's are not the only adventures in this exciting story. Far from it. The whole book teems with exciting episodes, and lovers of historical romance will find much to delight them in its pages.

H. H.

IN GOOD CHILDREN STREET.

There's a dear little home in Good Children Street,
Where my heart turneth fondly to-day ;
Where tinkle of tongues and patter of feet
Make sweetest of music at play ;
Where the sunshine of love illumines each face
And warms every heart in the old-fashioned place.

For dear little children go romping about,
With dollies and tin tops and drums.
And my ! how they frolic and scamper and shout,
Oh, the days they are golden and days they are fleet
With the dear little folks in Good Children Street.

EUGENE FIELD.

COMING EVENTS.

July 4th.—Royal British Nurses' Association. General Council Meeting. 10, Orchard Street, Portman Square, W. 2.45 p.m.

July 6th.—Central Committee for the State Registration of Nurses. Council Chamber, British Medical Association, 429, Strand, London, W.C. 2.30 p.m.

LETTERS TO THE EDITOR.

Whilst cordially inviting communications upon all subjects for these columns, we wish it to be distinctly understood that we do not IN ANY WAY hold ourselves responsible for the opinions expressed by our correspondents.

THE COST OF PROPAGANDA.

To the Editor of THE BRITISH JOURNAL OF NURSING.

DEAR MADAM,—Every member of the Society for State Registration of Nurses and also all trained nurses who have any sense of professional responsibility, owe THE BRITISH JOURNAL OF NURSING a great debt for the most comprehensive official Report of the work of the Society, and the manner in which our professional interests have been safeguarded, which filled fourteen columns of space in last week's issue. I wonder how many of your readers realized the cost of the production of such a Report—the year's voluntary labour, the compiling, reporting, transcribing, editing, printing, paper and publication. In these days of costly labour, such results could not have been attained by the expenditure of £20 —if at that. I know few of my colleagues are women of business, but many of them appreciate the labour and financial expenditure upon their behalf ; and I venture to suggest that those who are able to do so should send a subscription to the Hon. Secretary of the Society for State Registration, at 431, Oxford Street, towards the expense of producing this invaluable Report.

I am, Madam,
Yours gratefully,

HENRIETTA HAWKINS.

ONE AND INDIVISIBLE.

To the Editor of THE BRITISH JOURNAL OF NURSING.

DEAR MADAM,—THE BRITISH JOURNAL OF NURSING confirms my understanding on the subject of the affiliated societies for State Registration. I am so very glad that we have again joined up with the R.B.N.A., and enclose to you what I deem a thankoffering on " St. John's Day," towards our aims for State Registration, as you described it, " all one and indivisible making the perfect circle."

Sincerely trusting our " sweet reasonableness " will continue.

Believe me, yours as ever, also

A LIFE MEMBER OF R.B.N.A.

1st South African General Hospital,
B.E.F., France.

RECIPROCAL TRAINING FOR MENTAL NURSES.

To the Editor of THE BRITISH JOURNAL OF NURSING.

DEAR MADAM,—A recent issue of THE BRITISH JOURNAL OF NURSING contains an account of the annual meeting of the Asylum Workers' Association held at the Mansion House under the presidency of the Lord Mayor; and one of the speakers, Captain Kirkland-Whittaker, M.D. called attention to some advertisements appearing in a contemporary nursing paper, emanating from one or two asylums, inviting candidates for the posts of Matron and Assistant Matron, and specifying that such candidates should have received both training in a general hospital and hold the Medico-Psychological certificate—that is to say, they should have been trained in both general and mental hospitals.

A nurse in a mental hospital has, ordinarily, no opportunity of satisfying these requirements of general hospital training, and if she has already thought of devoting her life to mental work, the fact that the higher posts in asylums are barred against her, must give her seriously to consider whether it is worth her while to remain in mental work.

To obtain the Medico-Psychological certificate, three years' training in a mental hospital are required; while to obtain a certificate of general training, the same period is demanded. The nurse who is trained in both institutions would certainly be fully-equipped and eligible for the higher positions, and this either in a general or mental hospital. This would be an ideal training and one I should personally recommend, but it must not be forgotten that a nurse who left asylum work to spend three years in general hospital training would lose the benefits of the Asylum Officers' Superannuation Act, as far as her previous years of service were concerned, unless by some arrangement with the asylum authorities she could still be regarded as being " on the strength."

It would certainly be of the greatest advantage to a nurse to be trained in both general and mental hospitals, for each of these institutions would contribute towards the development of the qualities of tact, organisation, discipline, &c., so essential for making the nurse thoroughly efficient in her work and fit her for responsibility in either institution.

At the same time, seeing that the training in both general and mental hospitals covers, to some extent, the same ground, one is tempted to ask, whether a full three years of training in each institution should be made a *sine quâ non*. For instance, if a nurse has received a certificate of three years' training at a general hospital, she is allowed to sit for the Medico-Psychological certificate after two years of training in a mental hospital, yet, on the other hand, the nurse who has received the Medico-Psychological certificate is not allowed to proceed to the certificate in general nursing, after a similar experience in the general hospital.

Believe me, yours truly,
MARY LORD,
Matron, Banstead Mental Hospital.

[We regret that lack of space compels us to hold over a most interesting letter on this question from Dr. George M. Robertson, of the Royal Edinburgh Asylum.—ED.]

KERNELS FROM CORRESPONDENCE.

E. G. Fosbroke.—" I have had to attend many cases of scabies lately amongst quite clean people, who, owing to expense, have given up wearing gloves. As it was usually on the left hand, I wonder if the infection comes from touching the brass handle in mounting busses—or can your readers suggest another source ? "

———

A Red Cross Nurse writes :—" How about the dangers of inexperienced Commandants and Quarter Masters (girls often just out of their teens) and fires in Red Cross Hospitals ? I have known the kitchen chimney left unswept for six months at a time, and been told ' to mind my own business ' when I suggested the danger of fire with blocked flues. I see another fine War Hospital has been burnt down. ' Sparks from the kitchen chimney ignited the roof,' to be observed by a gardener. When was the kitchen chimney at Oakwood Hall swept last ? "

———

Another Dublin Sister writes :—" I also want to protest against English Nurses subsidising the College of Nursing Irish Board. Unless it is self-supporting it should be closed down. We Irish nurses object to it on every count. It has been thrust upon Ireland by the trainees of St. Thomas' Hospital. It will always be an apple of discord here. We mean to have Home Rule professionally, as Irish doctors do, and we told Sir Arthur Stanley so when he was recently over here."

OUR PRIZE COMPETITION.

July 13th.—What points would you endeavour to impress upon a mother as of primary importance for the rearing of a healthy baby ?

July 20th.—State fully how you would disinfect a bedroom and its furnishings.

TERMS FOR " BRITISH JOURNAL OF NURSING."

Do not fail to order THE BRITISH JOURNAL OF NURSING through your newsagent, price 2d. per week. If you prefer to subscribe the JOURNAL costs 10s. 10d. annually, 5s. 6d. for six months, or 2s. 9d. for three months. Abroad, 13s. 4d.

Trained Nurses who are members of organised Nurses' Societies are given preferential terms of 6s. 6d. annually.

Apply to the Manager, BRITISH JOURNAL OF NURSING, 431, Oxford Street, London, W. 1.

The Midwife.

NATIONAL BABY WEEK.

CONFERENCE AND EXHIBITION.

On Monday, July 1st, the National Conference on Maternal and Infant Welfare and the Educational Mothercraft Exhibition were opened at the Central Hall, Westminster, by the Dowager Marchioness of Londonderry, who said it afforded her the greatest possible pleasure to open an exhibition of every possible appliance for bringing up children in the best manner. So many children were born and so few came to maturity that she welcomed any knowledge which would teach mothers and potential mothers—as well as fathers—to bring up their children healthy and well.

On behalf of the National Union of Women Workers of Great Britain and Ireland, whose Child Welfare Committee organized the Exhibition, the President (Mrs. Ogilvie Gordon) expressed its thanks to Lady Londonderry.

At three o'clock, the Conference was inaugurated by a Mass Meeting, at which Major Waldorf Astor presided. After paying a tribute to Lord Rhondda, who, when at the Local Government Board, with the true instincts of a statesman, had grasped the fundamental principle that the horrible waste of child life must be reduced and that the immediate creation of a Ministry of Health was a necessity, to co-ordinate the Health efforts of all Departments, he spoke of the Departmental jealousy which delayed such co-ordination, and said that the first essential was the amalgamation of existing officials in a department engaged in fighting against disease, instead of their being engaged in fighting one another.

The first speaker was the Bishop of Birmingham who moved the following resolution :—

MOTHERHOOD.

" This meeting being confidently assured that the existing rate of infant mortality is unnecessary and uneconomic and the cause of much misery, calls upon the electors to demand complete and effective action from all candidates for and Members of Parliament or Municipal Councils for the better protection of the mothers and children of the Nation "

Referring to environment as it affects the mother and child, he said there were two main influences on the character of a child— one heredity the other environment. There might be some difference of opinion as to the effect of heredity, but there was none as to environment. He instanced the boys brought up in Poor Law schools, 98 per cent. of whom did well because their characters developed in good conditions. No true community, said the Bishop, could shirk its duty to the up-growing citizen, and had no right to expect to endure if it neglected infant life. We asked of the State that it should safeguard the mother and child, that girls should understand the sacred duty of their office, and receive due instruction in their future duties. He hoped no girl would grow up without three months' experience in these matters ; he would prefer to substitute years for months.

Then there was the wage problem. No married man should receive pay which did not enable him to support his wife who was bearing children. There was also the problem of the unmarried mother. Whatever the moral offence of the father or mother, the child should not suffer.

Mrs. Pember Reeves had said that motherhood was the most sweated and the worst paid of all the professions. He refused to ask people to have numbers of children under wretched conditions and unsuitable environment. A Department of Government was required to deal with these matters. At present the child was struggled for by many Departments and was in danger of being dismembered. The country was expectant to-day but it would not always be patient, even with Parliament. He had pleasure in moving the resolution.

Sir Owen Seaman, in supporting the resolution, claimed that every child at birth should have an equal chance of life.

Mrs. H. B. Irving sympathetically and eloquently pleaded for pensions for widows. The right of every baby was a mother to feed it, a father to work for and protect it. Many of Britain's babies were fatherless. The mothers should be assisted by the State.

Mr. Ben Tillett spoke on the relationship of the State towards the expectant mother ; and Dr. Truby King insisted that unpreparedness for motherhood was a main handicap of modern civilization.

The resolution was carried unanimously.

On both Wednesday and Thursday interesting and instructive addresses and lectures were given.

THE EXHIBITION.

An extremely interesting exhibition, open from 10.30 a.m. to 8 p.m. throughout the week, aims at the education of the infant welfare worker and presents to the public the general scope and varied aspects of the movement for the care of mothers and children.

MOTHERCRAFT.

In the section devoted to Mothercraft, as taught in the elementary schools, Mrs. Truelove, L.C.C. School, Tollington Park, exhibits articles used by girls attending mother-craft classes. Simple but effective is the baby's basket, costing only 8½d., *i.e.*, a strawbery basket 1d., pink sateen 3d., muslin 4½d. An oval glass, originally a potted meat dish, serves as a soap dish, and other fittings are quite inexpensive.

The Battersea Polytechnic, where a thorough training is given extending over a year, and recognised by the Local Government Board, show sets of infants' clothes made by students. A feature is a collection of soaps suitable and unsuitable for infants (mostly the latter). The test of phenolphthalein is applied, and if it is unsuited for a baby's use, the soap turns a deep pink.

CLEAN MILK.

The model of a modern cowbarn made to scale at the Lord Roberts' Memorial Workshops, and a second of a dirty and unventilated barn actually in existence, is an object lesson in the necessity for clean dairy farms.

WOMEN'S LEAGUE OF SERVICE.

By the kindness of Mrs. O'Rourke, of the Women's League of Service for Motherhood, 128, Pentonville Road, London, N. 1, we are able to reproduce their striking poster of a working-class mother and her infant. Their exhibit is a reproduction of their dining-room for mothers and children, showing equipment and menus. There was the dining-table for toddlers, whose meal is

served first, and then they are cared for in another room while the mothers sit down, free from distraction, to a well-cooked and well-served meal at a cost to themselves of 2d.

MIDWIVES' INSTITUTE.

The Midwives' Institute have arranged a midwife's room containing the necessary equipment for the efficient booking of patients, including various charts for ante-natal records exhibited by practising midwives ; also apparatus used by teachers of midwifery when preparing pupils for the examination of the Central Midwives' Board.

MATERNITY HOSTEL.

The Maternity Hostel arranged by the Croydon Mothers' and Infant Welfare Association is very complete, including a well-equipped labour ward and a lying-in ward. The new jointless flooring supplied by the British Doloment Co., Ltd., is utilized with good result.

SYDENHAM INFANT WELFARE CENTRE.

The Sydenham Infant Welfare Centre of Adamsrill Road, S.E., has arranged (1) a ward for ailing babies, (2) other equipment. Particularly noteworthy is the fitted shelf for the soap, towels, &c., used for different babies. The soap is in its own numbered dish, and each towel and washer is numbered and kept apart.

ST. PANCRAS SCHOOL FOR MOTHERS.

The St. Pancras School for Mothers—the *doyenne* of such schools—has arranged an Infant Welfare Centre, showing the methods followed and the equipment required for weighing the babies, &c. On the walls are educative posters, case papers and card indexes form part of the well-ordered equipment.

Even more interesting is the second section of this exhibit, a room, eleven feet by twelve in a hostel for working mothers. The room is intended for a mother and one or two children whose husband is at the war ; or for a munition worker. The floor is covered with black and white linoleum. The convenient wooden furniture made by the boys of the Technical Institute, Shoreditch, can all be easily scrubbed, spotless curtains hang at the open window, the mother's bed is covered with a bright quilt. By her side is the baby's cot, a cheerful rug is laid down in front of the fire, a clothes-horse is converted into a screen. There is a small chart for the baby, as well as the other necessary equipment including a dresser with bright coloured crockery. The baby's larder, in which the milk for his use is kept, was designed by a father. There is a hay-box for cooking, such as is now used by many frugal mothers, and a charming diminutive gas cooker supplied by the London Light & Coke Co. It is a most attractive little home.

EUGENICS.

An interesting exhibit is that lent by the Eugenics Education Society, 11, Lincoln's Inn Fields. A selection of striking posters are illustrative of the various aspects of syphilis.

NORTH ISLINGTON MATERNITY CENTRE AND SCHOOL FOR MOTHERS.

There are 1,200 Infant Welfare Centres, or Schools for Mothers, or Babies' Welcomes (whichever you like to call them, they are practically interchangeable terms) in the kingdom. No doubt all are doing excellent work.

Having a little time and much inclination, and having consulted the Superintendent on the telephone as to her convenience in the matter, I paid a visit to the North Islington School on June 28th. During the five years of its existence it has grown rapidly. The premises consist of two adjoining semi-detached houses in Manor Gardens, which stand in a fair-sized garden. The exquisite cleanliness and order of the whole place is the first thing that strikes the visitor. The next is the extreme cordiality and courtesy of the Superintendent, Miss Le Geyt, who, although obviously very busy, takes her visitors round—there were several on this occasion—explaining everything with pardonable pride. There are rooms of a good size for every purpose : Weighing-rooms, consultation-rooms, lecture-rooms, a room for social gatherings.

There are three main factors in every school for mothers, namely : — 1. Infant consultations. 2. Classes. 3. Home visiting. This forms the basis of all the rest of the work. Here, as elsewhere, great attention is paid to these essentials. But the activities of the North Islington School do not end here. Dinners for expectant and nursing mothers are provided by the Invalid Kitchens of London, which rent four rooms at the school. The L.C.C. also use it as a dental clinic for elementary school children two or three times a week. One of the nurses is employed to attend the dentist and keep the records. Another room is fitted up as a surgery for the treatment of minor ailments and for the instruction of the mothers in such treatment.

The records of the Centre are kept by means of a card index system. Case papers take the form of cards—pink for girls, blue for boys, grey for the expectant mothers, and white for the visitors. A chart of the child's weight is attached to the case paper.

The staff includes the Superintendent and several other nurses, some of them resident. About thirty-seven voluntary workers, most of whom are visitors, also two women medical officers. The most recent development of the work is an infants' ward with accommodation for about fifteen ailing babies. Children who are not ill enough to be taken into a hospital, and yet require to be under observation and have skilled care and attention. Dr. Truby King has visited the school and given an address there. His comment is that it is *first-rate*—the real thing. From such an authority this is praise indeed, and Miss Le Geyt values it as such. Certainly no Institution of the kind could be *better*.

B. K.

POST GRADUATE WEEK FOR MIDWIVES AT YORK ROAD LYING-IN HOSPITAL.

On June 26th, a party of post-graduates visited Queen Charlotte's Lying-in Hospital. Here they were received most courteously by the Matron, who deputed one of the Sisters to escort the numerous visitors round the wards of the hospital.

Many interesting cases were pointed out and described, the midwives eagerly reading the notes on the very comprehensive case papers. The babies, as usual, came in for a large amount of admiration, for midwives like mothers, seem to have an inexhaustible stock of love for infants, and one unusually fine or charming drew forth universal appreciation. The tiny " prem " was in a tent made of blankets and warmed by an electric lamp. At Queen Charlotte's they do not use incubators. Blankets are considered preferable to cotton covering on account of their being porous.

One small ward was a centre of interest, as it contained two Cæsarian section cases, and one bad case of mitral disease.

The labour wards are roomy and thoroughly equipped, and are used in turn. This arrangement enables each ward to be thoroughly " spring cleaned " each month.

Adjoining the hospital is the ante-natal and infant clinic department.

At the conclusion of the visit, tea was most kindly provided by the Matron in the pupils' lecture room, and so a very instructive and pleasant afternoon was brought to a close.

EXAMINATION.

As the result of the examination held at the conclusion of the week, the first prize was awarded to Mrs. Walters (trained at the General Lying-in Hospital) and the second prize to Mrs. McLaren.

———◆———

A nursery hospital for 15 babies suffering from marasmus, &c., has been opened under the auspices of the Birmingham Public Health Committee. It affords an opportunity for gaining or increasing experience in the treatment and physiological feeding advocated by Dr. Holt and Dr. Eric Pritchard. Volunteers interested in this form of war work may write for particulars to Miss Margesson, Nursery Hospital, Barnt Green, near Birmingham.

———◆———

The Midwives Bill, to amend the Midwives Act, 1902, was considered by the House of Lords in Committee on July 2nd. On the motion of the Marquess of Salisbury the contentious and objectionable Clause (Clause 12) was struck out of the Bill. Lord Salisbury then moved the insertion of a new Clause, *i.e.*, " Section nine of the principal Act (which enables county councils to delegate their powers and duties to district councils) shall be repealed." So far so good. Friends of midwives must now watch the Bill in the House of Commons.

THE
BRITISH JOURNAL OF NURSING

WITH WHICH IS INCORPORATED
THE NURSING RECORD

EDITED BY MRS BEDFORD FENWICK

No. 1,580.   SATURDAY, JULY 13, 1918.   Vol. LXI

EDITORIAL.

OUTSIDE THE PALE—LONDON HOSPITAL NURSES.

The following instructive discussion took place in the House of Commons on July 4th :—

Major Chapple asked the Chancellor of the Exchequer whether his attention had been called to the existence of a system of farming out of nurses in the London Hospital under which nurses were taken from their training in the wards at the end of their second year, were paid 13s. per week, and sent out to nurse as trained nurses in private cases at £2 2s. per week, the hospital profiting by this means to the extent of over £6,000 per year before the war ; and whether he intended to introduce legislation to protect nurses and patients from this system.

Mr. Walsh, Parliamentary Secretary to the Local Government Board, who replied, said :—The arrangements made by the London Hospital with their nurses are not a matter over which the Government have any control. There is no intention of introducing legislation on the subject.

Sir C. Henry : Has the hon. member satisfied himself of the accuracy of the statements in the question ?

Captain Carr-Gomm : Are not the statements in the question of a controversial character, and is not the expression "farming out," though perhaps picturesque, very unfair to an institution which has done much good work for a great number of years ?

Major Chapple : Is my hon. friend not aware that the London Hospital is the only great hospital which takes its nurses from their training in the wards at the end of the second year, and admittedly pays them only 13s. a week while it draws two guineas a week ?

The Speaker : This question should not have appeared on the paper. No Government Department has any control over the affairs of the London Hospital. If my attention had been called to the preamble of the question I should have struck it out.

We are all conversant with the commercialism of the Nursing Department of the London Hospital. No doubt it will pass with the present Prussianised incarnation, but what is of vast importance to the nursing profession, as a whole, is the unblushing confession of the Parliamentary Secretary to the Local Government Board that arrangements made by employers of voluntary charitable institutions, in connection with workers under their control, no matter how injurious they may be, are beyond the power of Parliament. Again, the Speaker, in supporting this view, boldly said had his attention been called to the preamble of the question he would have struck it out !

In our opinion this is a most indefensible attitude for Parliament to assume in relation to any class of worker. Here we have a class of women whose work in civilian and military hospitals, and in the homes of rich and poor is of the utmost value to the well-being of the State, and we find members of Parliament—to whose emoluments many of these workers are compelled to subscribe, calmly repudiating all responsibility for their conditions of labour. By what right, human or divine, are hospital governors empowered to treat their nursing staffs as helots, to work them and exploit them as they please ? We are not living in pre-Reformation days when the religious houses were barred and bolted, and their conduct above the control of the State, and that is the position claimed by Mr. Speaker for the London Hospital in this year of grace. It is amazing!

Do not let us forget, however, that there is no Act on the Statute Book for the protection of trained nurses, and until we get a modern Parliament we fear no just Act will be enforced. We trained nurses must not fail to realise the significance of Mr. Speaker's attitude towards us. It is indeed high time some Government Department was given control over every institution where persons assume arrogant authority over the lives of their fellows.

The subtle provisions for the perpetuation of this unrestricted control by Nurse Training Schools is what we have been fighting in the draft Bill, seven times revised, by hospital governors and officials who control the College of Nursing, Limited.

OUR PRIZE COMPETITION.

WHAT POINTS WOULD YOU ENDEAVOUR TO IMPRESS UPON A MOTHER AS OF PRIMARY IMPORTANCE FOR THE REARING OF A HEALTHY BABY?

We have pleasure in awarding the prize this week to Miss Theodora Harris, Slack Lane, Derby.

PRIZE PAPER.

I should endeavour to impress on the mother the following points as essential to the successful rearing of a healthy baby :—

1. That Nature's way is always the best, and that to keep to the plans of Nature will ensure the best results. Nature intended breast-feeding, therefore breast-feeding is the right method. But to ensure her infant getting the full value from its natural food the mother must bear in mind the following points :—

(*a*) That her own physical health must be safeguarded by abundance (if possible) of plain, nourishing food and milk; by sufficient sleep and rest; by sufficient work, exercise, and fresh air; and by the avoidance of constipation, hot rooms, and any other unhealthy condition.

(*b*) That her mental condition must be kept as healthful and peaceful as possible, and agitations, excitements, fits of passion, &c., strictly avoided as far as is possible. An anxious, worried, or angry mother will find her milk suffer.

If from any unusual cause it is absolutely necessary to feed the baby artificially (and a baby should not be weaned except under medical advice, as a condition serious enough to necessitate weaning would be serious enough to necessitate a doctor's attendance), the artificial feeding must adhere as closely as possible to Nature's plan, and, in that case, I should advise the mother to procure a pamphlet (price 2d.) by Dr. Eric Pritchard on " Artificial Feeding," and follow the directions closely. No other food must, of course, be given—no " bits."

2. Regularity in *all* things : regular three-hourly feeding; regularity in holding out, so that the infant is soon habituated to connect certain times with certain things; regular hours for putting to bed, for getting up, for bathing, &c. An infant's life should go by clockwork, not only for the sake of present comfort and health, but also for the sake of educating the child. An infant's education begins on the first day of its life : in the first few hours he is being taught habits, either good or bad.

3. Fresh air is an essential whatever the season, and the windows should never be shut, except just at bath-time. Baby should spend a large portion of his time in the open air, not with the sun beating on him, and not inside the leather hood of a perambulator, and not with his face covered with muslin. If a garden is available, it is a good plan to place a cot under a tree, and allow him to sleep there. A perambulator is too cramped to sleep in.

4. Which brings us to another point—rational clothing. Away with stiff binder, linen shirt, &c., and supplant them with loose, knitted wool vest and binder, high neck and long sleeves, *no* head flannel, and gowns that do not pin up over the feet, but allow for exercise.

5. Absolute cleanliness for the baby and all appertaining to him is a point the importance of which cannot be over-estimated, and too much stress cannot be laid on the dangers arising from lack of it.

6. Sleep and rest are things many babies are deprived of. A baby should sleep most of his life that is not occupied by feeding and bathing. He should be allowed to be peaceful when awake, and not be " on show " to friends and relatives, who endeavour to attract his attention; that way lies a nervous child. Give baby every needful attention, and then judiciously *let him alone.* It is as bad to deprive a baby of sleep as to deprive it of food.

7. Baby must have a separate bed, be it but a clothes-basket or orange-crate, and with no curtains to keep out the air. An orange-crate and a mattress of chopped straw, that can be easily replaced, are within the means of even very poor mothers.

8. *No dummy!* Adenoids, misshapen mouths, and deformed teeth may result from this evil practice; and the danger of infection when one is used is almost impossible to guard against.

9. Flies are some of baby's worst enemies, and must be fought and exterminated. All food must be covered; damp refuse, tea-leaves, green stuffs, &c., burnt, and the dustbin be always covered, and no accumulations allowed anywhere.

To sum up, all baby's surroundings must be clean, sunny, sanitary, and airy, and not over-crowded, either by persons or things. And as a child is trained to good habits in infancy, so will he be in adult life.

HONOURABLE MENTION.

The following competitors receive honourable mention :—Mrs. Farthing, Miss M. M. G. Bielby, Miss Alice M. Burns, Mrs. S. A. Box, Miss Olive M. Balderstone, Miss P. Thompson, Miss J. James.

QUESTION FOR NEXT WEEK.

State fully how you would disinfect a bed-room and its furnishings.

THE ROYAL RED CROSS.

The King conferred the decoration of the Royal Red Cross upon the following ladies at Buckingham Palace, on July 3rd, as follows:—

Bar to the Royal Red Cross.
FIRST CLASS.

Matron Ada YORKE, late Queen Alexandra's Imperial Military Nursing Service.

The Royal Red Cross.
FIRST CLASS.

Queen Alexandra's Imperial Military Nursing Service. —Matron Alexina GUTHRIE, and Lady Superintendent Edith BEESBY.

Queen Alexandra's Imperial Military Nursing Service Reserve.—Assistant Matron Grace ROWLATT, and Sister Gwendoline WILLIAMS.

Territorial Force Nursing Service.—Matron Ethel BUCHANAN.

Civil Nursing Service.—Matron Emmeline BANN, Matron Clare FIRTH, Matron Agnes HUNT, Assistant Matron Eleanor RODGERS, and Assistant Matron Martha ROGERS.

British Red Cross Society.—Matron Mary GUY.

Voluntary Aid Detachment.—Miss Maud GOODHUE, and Miss Kate HOWARD.

Canadian Army Nursing Service.—Matron Bessie MITCHELL, Matron Elizabeth ROSS, Acting Matron Irene CAINS, Acting Matron Jessie SCOTT, Acting Matron Jean STRONACH, Sister Hilda CORELLI, Sister Alison DICKISON, and Sister Minnie McAFFEE.

SECOND CLASS.

Queen Alexandra's Imperial Military Nursing Service Reserve.—Sister Elsie BEWSEY, Sister Annie FLOREY, and Sister Sarah HUGHES.

Territorial Force Nursing Service.—Sister Lillian LOVELL.

Civil Nursing Service.—Matron Lilian BOUGHEY, Assistant Matron Lilian BAINES, Assistant Matron Agnes BANKHEAD, Sister Elizabeth ANDERSON, Sister Edith ASPINALL, and Sister Edith BARBER.

British Red Cross Society.—Matron Pauline PETER.

Voluntary Aid Detachment.—Miss Pollex ADAMS, Miss Edith ALLHUSEN, Miss Betty ANDERSON, Miss Frances BAGULEY, Mrs. Elsie HUGHES, Miss Beatrice BAGNALL-OAKLEY, Miss Katherine TOMPSON, and Miss Mary WILKINSON.

Canadian Army Nursing Service.—Acting Matron Gertrude RADCLIFFE, Sister Gertrude RAMSDEN, Sister Gertrude SPANNER, Sister Letitia STEVENSON, Sister Jean SWORD, and Sister Mary WHITE.

Queen Alexandra received at Marlborough House the Members of the Military and Civil Nursing Services who have been awarded the Royal Red Cross, subsequent to the Investiture.

The King has been pleased to award the Royal Red Cross to the undermentioned ladies, in recognition of their valuable nursing services in connection with the war.

SECOND CLASS.

CABLE, Miss A. E., Matron, Gen. Infirmary, Salisbury; CALLAN, Miss H., Sister, T.F.N.S., 2nd Lond. Gen. Hospl., Chelsea; CAMERON, Miss J. W., Sister, Q.A.I.M.N.S.R., Mily. Hospl., Tidworth; CAMERON, Miss M., Sister, T.F.N.S., 4th Sco. Gen. Hospl., Stobhill, Glasgow; CAMERON, Miss M. C., Sister, Tooting Mily. Hospl., Tooting, S.W. 17; CAMPBELL, Miss A. G., Matron, The Red Cross Hospl., Sussex Lodge, Newmarket; CAMPBELL, Miss E. N., Nursing Sister, Can. Nursing Service, No. 4 Can. Gen. Hospl., Basingstoke, Hants; CAMPBELL, Miss M. S., Sister, Q.A.I.M.N.S.R., Wharncliffe War Hospl., Sheffield; CARPENTER-TURNER, Miss E. M., Matron, R. Hamp. County Hospl., Winchester; CARR-HARRIS, Miss S. M., Nursing Sister, Can. Nursing Service, No. 16, Can. Gen. Hospl., Orpington, Kent; CARRIER, Miss E., Charge Sister, V.A. Hospl., Lydney, Glos.; CARTER, Miss A. M., Matron, Broomlands Aux. Hospl., Kirkcudbright; CATTELL, Miss C. L., Matron, Uffculme Aux. Hosp., Birmingham; CHANDLER, Miss G., Sister, T.F.N.S., East Leeds War Hospl., 2nd Northern Gen. Hospl.; CHRISTMAS, Miss M. L., Sister i c Ward, N.Z.A.N.S., No. 2 New Zealand Hospl., Walton-on-Thames; CLERK, Miss E. M., Sister, T.F.N.S., 3rd Northern Gen. Hospl., Sheffield; CLAYTON, Mrs. C., Lady Supt., Dollis Hill House, Gladstone Park, Willesden; CLERY, Miss M., Sister, Q.A.I.M.N.S.R., Mily. Hospl., Curragh, Ireland; CLOWES, Miss C., Hilder's Mily. Hospl., Haslemere, Surrey; COATH, Miss E., Sister, American Women's War Hospl., Paignton, Devon; COCKBURN, Mrs. S., Matron, Royston, Herts; COCKERAM, Miss E., Asst. Matron, Gen. Hospl., Birmingham; COMYN, Miss K., Asst. Matron, Dublin Castle Red Cross Hospl., Dublin City; CONLEY, Miss B., Sister, Q.A.I.M.N.S.R., R. Herbert Hospl., Woolwich; CONNON, Miss A. H. J., Matron, Murtle House Aux. Hospl., Aberdeenshire; COOK, Miss M., Masseuse, Bath War Hospl., Bath; COOMBY, Miss A., Sister, Q.A.I.M.N.S.R., King George's Hospl., Stamford Street, London, S.E. 1; CORRIGAN, Miss F., Night Sister, Nell Lane Mily. Hospl., West Didsbury, Manchester; CORT, Miss F. M., Matron, R. Bath Hospl., Harrogate; COTTRELL, Miss A., Asst. Matron, Gen. Mily. Hospl., Edmonton; CRAMP,

Miss F. G., Sister, Q.A.I.M.N.S.R., Reading War Hospl.; CRAWFORD, Miss J., Matron, Stapleton Park, Pontefract, W. Yorks; CRAWSHAW, Mrs. F., Matron, Stubbins Vale Red Cross Hospl., Ramsbottom; CROCK-WELL, Miss H., Matron, Basford House Red Cross Hospl., Old Trafford, near Manchester; CROSFIELD, Lady D., Commdt., Highgate V.A.D. Hospl., " By-culla "; CRUMP, Miss E. M., Matron, Red Cross Hospl., Belper, Derbyshire; CULLIMAN, Miss A. M., Sister, Weston Favell, Northampton, Aux. Mil. Hospl.

DARLEY, Mrs. L., Matron, St. John's Ambulance Bde. Hospl., 6, Kensington Terrace, Newcastle-on-Tyne; DAVIES, Miss C., Matron, V.A.D. Hospl., High Wycombe; DAVIES, Miss E. A., Sister, Q.A.I.M.N.S.R., Council School Mil. Hospl., Aylesbury; DAVIES, Miss E., Matron, Countess of Pembroke's Hospl. for Officers, Wilton House, Salisbury; DAVIS, Miss M., Sister, Q.A.I.M.N.S., The Co. of Midd'x War Hospl., Naps-bury, St. Albans; DAWE, Miss A. M., Sister, Q.A.I.M.N.S.R., Mily. Hospl., Ripon, Yorks; DEAN, Miss N., Senior Sister, Oakdene Hospl., Rainhill; DE BELLEFEUILLE, Miss K., Nursing Sister, No. 14 Can. Gen. Hospl., Eastbourne; DENNIS, Miss L., Sister, T.F.N.S., 1st Northern Gen. Hospl., Newcastle-on-Tyne; DENTON, Miss L., Matron, Normanby Park Aux. Hospl., near Doncaster; DODDS, Miss J. C., Sub-Matron, N.Z.A.N.S., No. 3 N.Z. Mil. Hospl., Codford; DODGSON, Miss G. E., Matron, Dane John V.A.D. Hospl., Canterbury; DOUGLAS, Mrs. M., Nurse, Princess Christian Hospl., South Norwood Hill, London; DOW-SON, Mrs. A., Senior Nurse, St. John's Hospl., Chelten-ham; DRAPER, Miss E. A., A./Asst. Matron, Highfield Mil. Hospl., Knotty Ash, Liverpool; DUGDALE, Mrs. E. I., Matron, Eggington Hall Hospl., Derby, DUMBLE, Miss J., Asst. Matron, Welsh Metropolitan War Hospl., Whitchurch, near Cardiff; DUNBAR, Miss M. A., Sister, Q.A.I.M.N.S.R., Mil. Hospl., Sheerness; DUNN, Miss V., Matron, St. John's V.A.D. Hospl., Sevenoaks; DURWARD, Miss A. J. D., Sister, Q.A.I.M.N.S.R., Queen Mary's Mil. Hospl., Whalley, Lancs.

(To be continued.)

Matron Ada Yorke, Q.A.I.M.N.S. (Winchester Divisional Red Cross Hospital), received a Bar to the Royal Red Cross on the same day as her son, Captain H. Yorke, R.A.M.C., received the M.C. Proud mother and proud son! We congratulate them both.

NURSING AND THE WAR.

It is reported that the Queen is particularly anxious that wounded women should be permitted to wear a little gold-braid stripe on their sleeves after the manner of the men. She is of opinion that it is the least recognition they can have. For some time now there has been a rumour that women should receive orders for distinguished service, and we hear that this is under consideration and is likely to bear fruit.

We hope to hear that trained nurses under the authority of the *Service du Santé*, in France, may be granted the right to wear the *galons* for length of service, as soldiers are. The Sisters of the F.F.N.C. rank as officers in the French Army, and have many of their privileges.

We hear that some of the American masseuses in France are doing remarkably clever work in manipulating bad facial wounds. These masseuses were originally beauty doctors, and—like all the American specialists of this order—are very clever at their work.

In France, where the " religious " have been for so long the nurses of the sick, the modern civil and military nurse is a new species, not yet quite understood or approved. For instance, when the Americans first came to Talence, the fact that they were provided with recreation and gaily tripped the light fantastic toe with their fellow workers the doctors rather shocked the French. But recreation is a most necessary provision in the maintenance of a sound mental and physical balance, especially in war—and dancing may be harmless enough.

Miss Jane A. Delano, R.N. (Chairman of the National Committee on Nursing Service of the American Red Cross), writes of " Recreation Houses for Nurses " in the *American Journal of Nursing*. The A.R.C., at the request of the Surgeon-General, is erecting forty of such recrea-tion houses, which are in reality club houses for nurses working in the cantonment hospitals. Most exacting care is being given to the comforts within. The main room (30 by 75 ft.), to be used ordinarily as a living room, will also be adapted for an assembly hall, and can be used for dances and receptions. There will be a small balcony, which may be utilised, among other ways, for operating moving pictures. From the great room will open a library, a sewing room equipped with machines and all conveniences, a small laundry, and a fully equipped kitchen. A piano and victrola and dainty lounges, and everything else necessary to express a sense of home, and to supply the needs and add to the comfort of cantonment life, have been provided. These clubs will be connected with the nurses' quarters.

Major Chapple recently asked the Under Secretary of State for War, in the House of Commons, whether any advance in the mess allowance to nurses had recently been made to meet the increased cost of food ; and whether he had satisfied himself that the increased and increasing strain being put upon nurses in the execution of their duties was being fully met by an adequate supply of nourishing food ?

Mr. Forster replied, as follows : " An advance of 4s. 2d. was authorised in February, 1917. I have no information to suggest that the nurses are suffering in consequence of an inadequate supply of nourishing food."

A Sister we know, now supervising W.A.A.C.s, appears to have put on lbs. of weight. " No wonder," she remarked, cheerfully, " we are magnificently fed; meat twice a day, and as much of everything as we can stuff." Moral : To avoid the vacuum nature abhors, become a woman soldier.

FRENCH FLAG NURSING CORPS.

So many of the Sisters were working behind the French lines between the last German push and the Marne that their ambulances, in many instances, have had to be set up anew. This the Service du Santé has accomplished in the most admirable manner—and we have received numbers of letters expressing the gratitude of the Sisters for the great consideration, kindness and appreciation they have received from the medical officers under whom they work.

One Sister writes : " I cannot express to you *how* good the doctors have been to us . . . they have looked after us and spared us in every way possible, and treat us as *camarades*—the greatest compliment. This ambulance has been very well *noteé* at Headquarters in the retreat. We left C——— at mid-day and at mid-night were working at M———. Never shall we forget that night, with bombs falling all round us, knowing that the Boches were advancing so fast."

This brave woman once expressed the opinion that she would consider it a glorious death to die on duty at the Front. So it may be, but we cannot spare these heroines—the wounded have too great need of them.

Another Sister says :—

" All the six weeks I was there (somewhere in France) I only had two quiet nights—the Germans bombarded alternately by cannons and avions. We got nearly all the Boches from R———and we were kept very busy. The wounds were very terrible—many deaths ; we had some who had lain out three, four and five days on the ground, and it was awful to see enormous quantities of worms come out when the dressings were taken off."

In French hospitals, German wounded share all the good care that is going equally with the heroic Frenchmen. This is the law of chivalry—entirely superseded by the law of " frightfulness " so far as our brutalised enemies are concerned.

The Ambulance 12/2 Unit have arrived at their destination and had a very warm welcome upon their return.

Sisters Gill, Hanning and Jones have rejoined Ambulance 16/21, and have also enjoyed the " fatted calf." It is indeed a matter for congratulation that the medical officers of the Service de Santé value their services so much. Both units have been told their care means the saving of life. This is *the* great reward to the true nurse.

Miss Mildred Aldrich, the author of that most fascinating little book, " A Hill-top on the Marne," has published a second volume, " On the Edge of the War Zone," in which she gives a palpitating picture of the emotion with which an American resident near Meaux has lived through the exciting events down to the advance on Soissons. This is a book many F.F.N.C. Sisters will want to possess.

CARE OF THE WOUNDED.

July 4th, American Independence Day, has been celebrated in great form by the Allied nations, and we were all with President Wilson in spirit, when, on that date, he stood by the tombs of Washington and his wife, Martha, within the grounds of Mount Vernon, their lovely home on the banks of the Potomac, now consecrated by the Daughters of the Revolution to their imperishable memory.

July 14th, which typifies to all Frenchmen the victory of Liberty over Absolutism, when, in 1789, they stormed and captured the Bastille—a victory which swept away the *ancien regime*—is in this year of grace to be celebrated in London as " France's Day," on the 12th inst. A solemn mass of requiem for the French soldiers and sailors who have fallen in the war will be held at Westminster Cathedral at 11.30 a.m. in connection with the British Committee of the French Red Cross, when the splendid premier Zouave band of the French Army will play before lunching with the Lord Mayor. A whole day collection will be made in London for the benefit of French sick and wounded—the refugees from the devastated districts, and other sufferers from the invasion of France by the ruthless Hun. Thousands of sympathisers will sell souvenirs and a splendid response is expected. We shall all be wearing favours in support of the good cause on the 12th, to show our admiration for the unquenchable spirit which is France.

Why Poilu ? Many nurses want to know the reason for the name, which now stands for all the most splendid attributes of the fighting man. According to the French dictionary, the word means hairy, shaggy, bristling, and it is said that the name was given to French soldiers who have served in the trenches because the first French soldiers on leave thronged into Paris wearing whiskers. Such a sight had never been seen before and the people cried : " Oh ! les poilus, which may be freely translated : " Oh ! the whiskers," and the name stuck. Has anyone another explanation ?

TRUE TALE WITH A MORAL.

An experienced sister, who is blest with a sense of humour, was asked the other day by her wounded soldiers : " How long does it take to be a nurse ? "

" How long does it take to learn to nurse soldiers, do you mean ? "

" Well, yes ! "

" Oh," she returned, with a twinkle, " you require six months in a children's hospital and six months in the police force."

Her patients were hugely delighted.

OUR ROLL OF HONOUR.

With grief and pride we publish the names of our Canadian sisters murdered on the high seas by the sinking of the *Llandovery Castle.*

CAMPBELL, Christine, N.S., Victoria, B.C. ; DOUGLAS, Carola Josephine, N.S. Manitoba ; DUSSAULT, Alaxina, N.S., Montreal ; FOLLETTE, Minnie, N.S., Cumberland Co., N.S. ; FORTESCUE, Margaret Jane, N.S., Montreal ; FRASER, Matron Margaret Marjory, Moosejaw, Sask. ; GALLAHER, Minnie Katherine, N.S., Ottawa ; MCDIARMID, Jessie Mabel, N.S., Ashton, Ontario; MCKENZIE, Mary Agnes, N.S., Toronto ; MCLEAN, Rena, N.S., Prince Edward Island ; SAMPSON, Mac Belle, N.S., Duntroon, Ont. ; SARE, Gladys Irene, N.S., Montreal ; STAMERS, Anna Irene, N.S. New Brunswick ; TEMPLEMAN, Jean, N.S., Ottawa.

To hundreds of officers and men of the Canadian Overseas Forces, the name of Nursing Sister Miss Margaret Marjorie (Pearl) Fraser, will recall a record of unselfish effort, a fitting tribute to this nation's womanhood. Volunteering for active service in the C.A.M.C. on September 29th, 1914, Miss Fraser went to France with the 1st Canadian Division, and for almost three years had been on duty in casualty clearing stations. Her faithfulness was only typical, however, of that service for humanity exhibited by every one of these precious 14 lives.

The Minister of Overseas Military Forces of Canada (Sir Edward Kemp, K.C.M.G.), having made careful inquiries into the sinking of the hospital ship *Llandovery Castle,* on June 27th has authorised publication of a report, which affords convincing evidence of the deliberate intent and dastardly character by the latest German outrage on non-combatants.

THE SPLENDID COURAGE OF THE SISTERS.

In an extract from Sergeant A. Knight's stirring record of the supreme devotion and valiant sacrifice of the medical personnel, nothing stand out more heroically than the coolness and courage of the fourteen Canadian Sisters, every one of whom was lost. We learn :—" Unflinchingly and calmly, as steady and collected as if on parade, without a complaint or a single outward sign of emotion, our fourteen devoted nursing sisters faced the terrible ordeal of certain death, only a matter of minutes, as our lifeboat neared that mad whirlpool of waters where all human power was helpless."

The majority of the fourteen Sisters volunteered for service at the very outbreak of hostilities in 1914, came to England and France with the first Canadian Division, had seen active service, chiefly in casualty clearing stations in France, throughout the intervening period, and recently had been transferred to transport duty. For many months, and in some cases, two years these Sisters had endured the hazards of the shelled areas in France, splendidly contributing to the efficiency of our medical service. How magnificently they faced the final ordeal on that awful evening of June 27th is simply yet graphically related in the story of Sergeant A. Knight, the non-commissioned officer of the C.A.M.C. who took charge of lifeboat No. 5, into which the fourteen nurses were placed.

It is a story calculated to make every heart throb with admiration and gratitude to have been born British, and to be a member of the Nursing Sisterhood.

There is much feeling throughout the nursing community over the sinking of the *Llandovery Castle.* The International Council of Nurses in London is compiling a full list of members deliberately assassinated by the Germans. Canada's loss is most grievous.

Elliott & Fry.

SISTER FOX HARVEY, TRIPLE CHEVRONS.

THE ROYAL NAVAL NURSING SERVICE.

Sister Fox Harvey, whose portrait appears on this page, wears three chevrons for service afloat as a naval nurse. She is now on duty at the Royal Naval Hospital, Chatham. We hear very little of the work done by the members of Queen Alexandra's Royal Naval Nursing Service, but our sick and wounded sailors realize its value.

THE CENTRAL COMMITTEE FOR THE STATE REGISTRATION OF NURSES.

A Meeting of the Central Committee for the State Registration of Nurses was held in the Council Chamber of the British Medical Association, 429, Strand, London, W.C., on Saturday, July 6th, at 2.30 p.m.

Mr. T. W. H. Garstang, M.R.C.S., was in the Chair.

Reports were received from the Hon. Secretaries and the Executive Committee.

NEW DELEGATES.

Upon the nomination of the Royal British Nurses' Association, Mrs. Shuter and Miss Isabel Macdonald were elected in the place of Mr. Comyns Berkeley and Miss Grace Gordon.

Upon the nomination of the National Union of Trained Nurses, Miss Farrant was elected in the place of Miss Carruthers.

REPRESENTATION OF THE IRISH NURSING BOARD.

Upon the recommendation of the Executive Committee, the request for representation of the Irish Nursing Board, approved by the Royal College of Surgeons in Ireland, was agreed to.

AMENDMENTS TO THE NURSES' REGISTRATION BILL.

The following Amendments to the Bill were agreed to :—

1. To insert the word " Nursing," to read " General Nursing Council " throughout the Bill.

2. To substitute two for one representatives for Male Nurses and Mental Nurses on the General Nursing Council.

DUTIES AND POWERS OF COUNCIL
TO PROVIDE FOR RECIPROCAL CURRICULA.

The following new Clause was agreed to :— " Prescribing the conditions necessary to be fulfilled by any hospital desirous of having any portion of its training recognised *pro tanto* towards the three years' training required under the Act."

NOMINATION FOR ELECTION OF DIRECT REPRESENTATIVES ON THE GENERAL NURSING COUNCIL.

The following new Clause was agreed to :— " The registered nurses entitled to be elected on the General Nursing Council must be duly nominated on a Form prescribed for the purpose. Each nomination paper must be signed by at least twelve registered nurses. Form of Nomination Paper :—We, the undersigned, being registered nurses resident in (England and Wales or Scotland or Ireland), hereby nominate (name in full), of (address and qualification), a registered nurse, as a proper person to be elected to the General Nursing Council by the registered nurses resident in (England and Wales or Scotland or Ireland)."

RESOLUTIONS.

The following Resolutions were approved :—

AN INDEPENDENT COUNCIL.

1. " That in the opinion of this Committee the Registration of Trained Nurses should be carried out by an independent Nursing Council, constituted by Act of Parliament, entirely dissociated from any one Organization of Nurses, such as the College of Nursing, Ltd."

THE REGISTRATION OF SPECIALISTS.

2. " That this Committee desires to protest against the Clause recently inserted in the Nurses' Registration Bill drafted by the College of Nursing, Ltd., which provides for the Registration of Specialists, other than male and mental nurses.

" In the opinion of this Committee the compiling of such Supplementary Registers is injurious to the best interests of the nursing profession, and the public, and is calculated to undermine the value of a Three Years' General Training, a One Portal Examination for the Nursing Profession, and the efficient standard of a General Register of Trained Nurses."

LETTER FROM MAJOR CHAPPLE, M.P.

A letter from Major Chapple, M.P., concerning the re-drafted Bill of the College of Nursing, Ltd., was read, and it was agreed to refer it to the Executive Committee for consideration and report.

ETHEL G. FENWICK, *Hon. Nurse Sec.*
E. W. GOODALL, *Hon. Medical Sec.*

THE CONSECRATION OF THE NURSING PROFESSION.

The Address of the President, Miss Annie W. Goodrich, R.N., to the American Nurses' Association, delivered recently at Cleveland, Ohio, might well be reprinted in leaflet form and scattered broadcast throughout the nursing world. The theme is the consecration of the nursing profession, in the most momentous period in the history of the world, to the service of humanity. It is an inspiring trumpet call.

" Never," says Miss Goodrich, " in our history have we been so under fire, never perhaps again will there be such a period of testing. With all the strength we have, with all the undreamed-of strength we can summon, through every avenue of service we can find, we should seek to raise the standard of nursing immeasurably above the service rendered in all previous wars, that, after this ghastly struggle is over, freed, through a record of high service, our profession may contribute in fullest measure to the restoration of this crippled, scarred humanity."

Royal British Nurses' Association.

(Incorporated by   Royal Charter.)

THIS SUPPLEMENT BEING THE OFFICIAL ORGAN OF THE CORPORATION.

LOYAL CONGRATULATIONS TO THEIR MAJESTIES.

On behalf of the Royal British Nurses' Association, Her Royal Highness the Princess Christian, President of the Corporation, has been graciously pleased to convey to their Majesties the King and Queen the loyal and dutiful greetings and respectful congratulations of the Hon. Officers, of the General Council, and of the Members of the Corporation on the occasion of their Majesties' Silver Wedding.

MEETING OF THE GENERAL COUNCIL.

A Meeting of the General Council was held at 10, Orchard Street on July 4th, at 2.45 p.m.

Before the Minutes were read, Mr. Paterson, who occupied the Chair, extended a very warm welcome to the new Members of the General Council. He hoped that the precedent made by the harmonious co-operation of the Representatives of the Affiliated Societies and other Members of the R.B.N.A. on the Council of the Chartered Corporation of Nurses would be followed by the nurses themselves, and if this happened he had very little doubt but that there would soon be a great improvement in the conditions under which the nurses worked.

REPORTS OF THE EXECUTIVE COMMITTEE AND THE HON. TREASURER.

The report of the Executive Committee for April and May was read, the Medical Honorary Secretary remarking that already most of the information contained therein had already been conveyed to Members of the Council through other channels, as the summer Meeting of the Council had been somewhat delayed owing to the fact that one of the Byelaws stipulated that it should not be held within a fortnight of the Annual Meeting. The Report of the Hon. Treasurer for the same two months showed a balance of £269 in the General Fund, and £1,489 and £2,406 in the Helena Benevolent and Settlement Funds respectively. Expenses for print-

ing formed an extremely heavy item in the expenditure account of the General Fund.

LOYAL CONGRATULATIONS TO THE KING AND QUEEN.

Mrs. Bedford Fenwick moved, and Miss Easton seconded, a Resolution that an expression of loyalty and the congratulations of the Royal Corporation of Nurses be sent to their Majesties on the celebration of their Silver Wedding. This was carried unanimously.

ELECTIONS OF HON. OFFICERS AND EXECUTIVE COMMITTEE.

It was moved by Miss Cattell, seconded by Miss Sendall, and carried, that the following be elected Hon. Officers for the ensuing year :—Vice-Chairmen, Miss Heather-Bigg, R.R.C., Sir James Crichton Browne, Dr. Percival White; Medical Hon. Secretary, Mr. Herbert Paterson; Nurse Hon. Secretary, Mrs. Campbell Thomson; Hon. Treasurer, Dr. Kenneth Stewart. It was moved by Mrs. Campbell Thomson, seconded by Mrs. Sherliker, and carried, that the following be elected to fill vacancies on the Executive Committee :—Dr. A. P. Beddard, Dr. A. S. Currie, Dr. J. T. C. Laing, Dr. Eric Pritchard, Dr. Leonard Williams, Mrs. Bedford Fenwick, Miss Easton, A.R.R.C., Miss Roberts, R.R.C., Miss Sinzininex, A.R.R.C., Miss Bedwell, A.R.R.C., Miss Alice Cattell, Miss Beatrice Kent, and Miss Liddiatt. Miss Henderson, the nominee of the Scottish Nurses' Association, was elected to a vacant seat on the General Council.

The Medical Hon. Secretary read a report of a Meeting of the Consultative Committee, and instructions were given to the Executive Committee with regard thereto.

THE MIDWIVES ACT AMENDMENT BILL.

Miss Breay then moved the following Resolution :—

The Council of the Royal British Nurses' Association desire to place on record their satisfaction that Clause 12 has been deleted from the Midwives Act Amendment Bill, a Clause which the Council consider to be against the interest of the Public and of the Midwives.

This was seconded by Mrs. Scott and carried unanimously. The Secretary was instructed to forward a copy of the Resolution to the Lord President of the Council, the Right Hon. the Marquis of Salisbury, the President of the Local Government Board, and the Chairman of the Central Midwives' Board.

The Meeting then terminated.

APPOINTMENTS.

Miss Margaret Tait has been re-appointed Matron of the Government Hospital, Sarawak. Four years ago the late Rajah of Sarawak asked the Royal British Nurses' Association to recommend to him a nurse to undertake the duties of Matron in this hospital, where the patients are all Europeans. Miss Tait was appointed for the term of three years. At the end of that time, much to the disappointment of all connected with the hospital, she decided to return to England. The Government of Sarawak again asked the Corporation to recommend one of its Members, and Miss Ina Macdonald secured the appointment, which is a very desirable one in many respects. Some six months after she sailed the news of her engagement to the Chief Medical Officer of Sarawak reached us, and considerable pressure was brought to bear upon Miss Tait by the Sarawak Government in order to persuade her to return and take charge of the hospital again. Much appreciation has been expressed regarding her work in Sarawak, and many friends will extend to her a warm welcome upon her return. Miss Tait was trained at the Royal Infirmary, Edinburgh, and became a Member of the Corporation in 1914.

Miss Louisa Kate Clarke has been appointed Night Superintendent at Gateshead Hospital. Miss Clarke gained the Diploma of the Royal British Nurses' Association, and became a Member in 1908.

Miss Alice M. Brittain has been appointed District Nurse in Bournemouth. She joined the Association in 1902.

ENGAGEMENT.

As we go to press we learn that Miss Jean MacLauchlin is shortly to be married to Mr. Deltman, of Belmont Park, Blackheath. Miss Maclauchlin joined the Association in 1915. Until recently she was Matron in a Government Colony for Munition workers, an appointment which she obtained through the Association.

MARRIAGE.

On March 11th, at St. Andrew's Church, Singapore, by the Venerable Archdeacon Swindell, Dr. Downes Latimer Greene, Principal Medical Officer to the Government of Sarawak, was married to Miss Ina Macdonald, second daughter of Roderick Macdonald, Esq., of Ashford. The ceremony was a very quiet one, the only witnesses being Lieut. Gibson-Fleming, who gave the bride away, and Captain and Mrs. J. C. Moulton. The honeymoon was spent in Penang and Singapore, and a month later Dr. and Mrs. Greene returned to Sarawak. Mrs. Greene joined the Association in 1914.

The marriage took place recently, at the Brompton Oratory, of the Hon. M. P. E. R. Antelme to Miss Mary C. Lewis. Miss Lewis became a Member of the Association in 1917, and took private cases from it for some time.

DONATIONS RECEIVED.

GENERAL FUND.

Mrs. Rogers, £3; Miss Coward, £2; Miss Eden, £2; Mrs. Broadfoot, £1 1s.; Miss Habgood, £1 1s.; Miss Boldero, £1; Miss Cattell, £1; Miss Glover, £1; Mrs. Raikes, £1; Miss Jordan, 15s.; Miss Conway, 10s. 6d.; Miss Liddiatt, 10s.; Miss Sumner, 10s.; Miss Hawkes, 5s.; Mrs. Roberts, 5s.; Miss Oldham, 3s. 6d.; Miss Randall, 3s. 2d.; Miss Shorter, 2s. 6d.; Miss Young, 2s. 6d.; Miss Coates, 2s.; Miss Stewart, 1s. 6d.; Miss Consterdine, 1s; Miss Munson, 1s.

STATE REGISTRATION FUND.

Miss Easton, £2; Miss Budd, £1 6s. 6d.; Miss Cureton, £1; Miss Farquharson, £1; Miss Clifford, 10s.; Miss Copeland, 10s. 6d.; Miss Davis, 10s.; Miss Glover, 10s.; Miss Holmes, 10s.; Miss Robinson, 10s.; Miss Ault, 5s.; Miss Bedwell, 5s.; Miss Gurnett, 5s.; Miss Byard, 2s. 6d.; Miss Coull, 2s. 6d.; Miss Jones, 2s. 6d.; Miss Leigh, 2s 6d.; Miss Standing, 2s. 6d.; Miss Tarry, 2s. 6d.

HELENA BENEVOLENT FUND.

Maintained by the Members for the benefit of their fellow-Members in times of sickness or distress.

Miss Habgood, £1; Miss Cutler, 10s.; Miss Glover, 10s.; Miss Cattell, 8s. 6d.; Mrs. Hewer, 5s.; Miss Chippendale, 5s.; Miss Oldham, 4s.; Miss Garland, 2s. 6d.; Miss Hooper, 2s. 6d.; Miss Smith, 2s. 6d.; Miss Young, 2s. 6d.; Miss Bayley, 2s.; Mrs. Dalton Holmes, 2s.; Miss Humphry, 2s.; Miss Newcombe, 2s.; Miss Dyke, 1s. 6d.; Miss Ansett, 1s.; Miss Blizard, 1s.; Mrs. Douglas, 1s.; Miss Fewkes, 1s.; Miss Haynes, 1s.; Miss Henry, 1s.; Miss Henson, 1s.; Miss Hore, 1s.; Miss Kenten, 1s.; Miss Millar, 1s.; Miss Morris, 1s.; Miss Ommaney, 1s.; Miss Pardy, 1s.; Miss Pike, 1s.; Miss Relph, 1s.; Miss Robertson, 1s.; Miss Slater, 1s.; Miss Steuart, 1s.; Miss Tabuteau, 1s.; Miss Wilson, 1s.; Miss Groom, 6d.

SETTLEMENT FUND.

Subscribed to by the Members for the maintenance of the Princess Christian Settlement Home for aged nurses.

Miss Henry, £1; Miss Baskerville Smith, 2s. 6d.

(Signed) ISABEL MACDONALD,
Secretary to the Corporation.

A PROTEST.

We referred last week to a letter of protest addressed by Miss Lloyd Still, Matron of St. Thomas' Hospital, and Miss Amy Hughes, in the June issue of the *American Journal of Nursing*, against an article by Miss L. L. Dock entitled " English Nursing Politics," which they state was based on a biassed account in THE BRITISH JOURNAL OF NURSING of the present condition of the Nursing World in England.

The two ladies think it right American nurses should hear both sides ; so do we.

They claim that the College of Nursing, Ltd. came into existence as a result of the great lack of uniformity, and (in many instances) the lack of efficiency in the training of nurses, and state that its avowed objects are to obtain (1) State Registration for the trained nurses, (2) the protection of the interests of trained nurses, (3) the raising of the standard of training, (4) the establishment of a uniform curriculum of training and the one-portal examination, (5) the establishment of lectureships and scholarships.

Whose the fault for this deplorable condition of affairs, that all these reforms have not long ago been instituted ? Certainly not that of the State Registration Party, who have called urgently for one and all through their organ, THE BRITISH JOURNAL OF NURSING, for thirty years but of the lay governors of hospitals, and Matrons like Miss Lloyd Still, who have opposed by every means in their power the organisation of trained nursing education, and registration through an Act of Parliament, and who have signed manifestoes without end to Members of Parliament and the public, stating that :—

" We believe that any system of State Registration would be detrimental to the public, and harmful to the nurses themselves," and further

" A State Register of Nurses, far from being a security, to the public, would be an actual source of danger."

No, the College did not come into existence to effect the State Registration of Nurses. It came into existence to attempt to circumvent State Registration by a voluntary system of Registration controlled by the employers of nurses, and only recanted when its promoters found we State Registrationists had, by thirty years' work and the expenditure of upwards of £20,000, convinced the country and the legislators of the justice of our cause. Then they adopted the letter of registration law without its spirit.

We claim a just Bill, incorporating self-determination and self-government. The College Company and its nominees have denied this fundamental basis of good government and have attempted to thrust a Bill upon us incorporating a lay company and its tyrannical Constitution as the General Nursing Council of our profession. The College has the support of the laity who control the large Nursing Schools and Nursing

Institutions, the Anti-Registration Party ; their Bill is inspired by some of the most subtle anti-feminists in our midst, and their claim that the government of the College is democratic is, presumably, a huge joke.

Take a few of its provisions :—

2. This Council has power :—

(a) To appoint any persons (whether already members or not) to be members of the Council. (Article 37.)

(b) To exclude from office Matrons of Hospitals or Superintendents of Nursing, Sisters or Nurses who are not engaged in the active practice of their profession. (Article 35.)

(c) To adopt, if thought fit, the results of examinations held by approved Nursing Schools as sufficient evidence of proficiency. (Memo. 3 (D).)

(d) To grant certificates . . . Provided that the College shall not grant or profess to grant titles or diplomas. (Memo. 3 (E).)

(e) To remove from the Register the name or names of any person or persons as the Council may in its discretion think proper. (Memo. 3 (J).)

We claim professional independence.

We take exception to the appeal made by the British Women's Hospital Committee because (1) as professional women we object to be made the objects of a War Charity by a self-appointed committee of Society women and actresses who know nothing of our professional needs, (2) because to endow a lay Company of employers, the College of Nursing, Ltd., with unlimited funds means the subjugation of the class of working women they are attempting to control, and we object to our independence being bought up.

Enough. Our American readers will not have far to seek to realise our claim that if these anti-registrationists are converted and truly penitent for their unreasoning obstruction to nursing reform in past years, and its consequent injury to the sick, and are prepared to refund to working women the £20,000 they have spent in conscientious agitation, they could prove their *bona fides* by evincing sympathy with our professional aspirations, without adopting our programme, and claiming it as their own.

The truth is the attitude of the Governors and officials of our Nurse-Training Schools is British to the backbone. We are in the aggregate creatures of habit, a dull, worthy, unimaginative people, but we are credited with being honest.

The founders of the College must repent them of their stupidity before they can hope to inspire confidence in those whose ideas they have exploited with such avidity.

Miss Lloyd Still and Miss Amy Hughes are much respected ladies, but their environment is circumscribed. They look down on mere mortals from the heights of Olympus.

We claim a fair field and no favour.

We will not be cooped up in the College compound.

A LITTLE BIT OF SUGAR.

We hope we shall not be accused of undue vanity if we reprint the following paragraph from the "Foreign Department" of the *American Journal of Nursing*, in charge of Lavinia L. Dock, R.N.; but to have struggled for the past thirty years for professional ideals in an antagonistic and reactionary atmosphere at home, makes the appreciation we have always received abroad doubly sweet. It has been the "spirit" which has sustained the "Dynamos" and made the wheels go round.

OUR DEAR DYNAMOS.

For many years we have been in the habit of calling Mrs. Bedford Fenwick and Miss Margaret Breay affectionately, the "Dynamos," because of their unceasing and untiring energy in all the manifold crises met with in the process of conducting a weekly nursing journal, which is also an organ of the most vital propaganda—really a watch tower quite as much as a brilliantly-edited magazine. The chief lady dynamo, Mrs. Fenwick, has completed, on the first of April past, her fortieth year of professional work, sixteen of which she spent in varied pieces of active nursing, including the matronship in one of England's most famous hospitals, St. Bartholomew's, where she laid the foundation of the modern democratic, educational, enlightened discipline of training-schools as against the older autocratic, repressive methods; while her last twenty-four years of the most intense and unremitting labours for the advanced education and organisation of nurses in self-governing professional bodies, with the attainment of State regulation of nurses' training as the goal, have been given their special fire and fervour by the necessity of combating the most solid, determined and obstinate hostility to the economic progress of women that has been encountered by any nurses in any otherwise progressive country. We do not, of course, here consider those countries which are distinctly unprogressive as regards women. In these forty years, Mrs. Fenwick has seen her ideals supported and developed in many countries, and these proofs of their merit have given her courage and joy even though "State registration still hangs in the balance" in Great Britain.

A marvellous, self-renewing spring of energy has been hers. She writes: "It has been splendid to have been given health and strength, energy and spirit, to keep the cause alive for all these years, and to realise that victory is at hand." Not only on these well-known lines, but in myriad ways of civic and war work is she now busy.

Twenty-five teaching Sisters from Roman Catholic convents in Ontario are taking a special course in agriculture at Guelph College. This is a fine example to thousands of idle young Society women in England.

THE IRISH NURSING BOARD.

The first of the three yearly elections of the Irish Nursing Board was held in the Royal College of Surgeons in Ireland, Dublin, on July 4th. The voting was by postal ballot, and 38 nurses had been nominated to fill 22 vacancies.

The following 22 names received the largest number of votes, and were duly declared elected :—

Miss E. T. Bacon, St. Vincent's Hospital.
  ,,   L. Bradburne, The Meath Hospital.
Hon. A. L. Brodrick, Caher Daniel, co. Kerry.
Miss T. Doorly, 9, Blackhall Place.
  ,,   E. Hezlett, Richmond Hospital.
  ,,   J. Hughes, Temple Hill Hosp., Blackrock.
  ,,   M. Huxley, Elpis, Lower Mount Street.
  ,,   J. Jordan, Mercer's Hospital.
  ,,   K. Kearns, 29, Gardiner's Place.
  ,,   M. A. Keating, National Maternity Hosp.
  ,,   N. McArdle, Castle Red Cross Hospital.
Mrs. F. Manning, Elpis, Lower Mount Street.
Miss G. O'Donel, 24, Eccles Street.
  ,,   M. O'Flynn, Children's Hosp., Temple St.
  ,,   A. M. Phillips, Dr. Steevens Hospital.
  ,,   C. Pike, 38, Ranelagh Road.
  ,,   A. Carson Rae, 34, St. Stephen's Green.
  ,,   L. Ramsden, Rotunda Hospital.
  ,,   A. Reeves, Royal Victoria Hospital.
  ,,   A. S. Rhind, Cork Street Fever Hospital.
  ,,   E. Sutton, St. Vincent's Hospital.
  ,,   M. Thornton, Sir Patrick Dun's Hospital.

A Meeting of the Irish Nursing Board was held in the Royal College of Surgeons on July 12th, to elect the Committee.

We learn that certificated Irish Nurses are supporting this movement for the improvement of their professional education and status in a very satisfactory manner, and many intend to register as soon as they have completed their three years' training and have obtained their Certificates.

APPOINTMENTS.

MATRON.

Ilford Maternity Home.—Miss Edith Waring has been appointed Matron. She held the position of Ward Sister at the Chelsea Hospital for Women.

ASSISTANT MATRON.

St. Mary, Islington, Infirmary, Highgate Hill, N. 19.—Miss Jean McKenzie has been appointed Assistant Matron. She was trained at the Toxteth Infirmary, Liverpool, where she was afterward ward and theatre Sister. She has also been Night Sister at the Mile End Military Hospital, and Assistant Matron at the Westminster Infirmary, Hendon. She has also had experience of District Nursing as a Queen's nurse.

SISTER.

General Hospital, Northampton.—Miss Annie Askew has been appointed Sister. She was trained at the Workhouse Infirmary, Portsmouth, and has been Staff Nurse at the Royal London Ophthalmic Hospital, and Sister at the Birmingham Midland and Eye Hospital.

A DESIRABLE APPOINTMENT.

A desirable appointment in the nursing world is now vacant in the Cheltenham General Hospital. For particulars in regard to it we refer our readers to our advertisement supplement.

QUEEN ALEXANDRA'S MILITARY NURSING SERVICE FOR INDIA.

Miss Helen Dorothea Campbell and Miss Margaret Deans Scott have been appointed Nursing Sisters in Queen Alexandra's Military Nursing Service for India.

QUEEN VICTORIA'S JUBILEE INSTITUTE.

TRANSFERS AND APPOINTMENTS.

Miss Miriam Booth is appointed to Charlton; Miss Celia R. Clapson to South Wimbledon; Miss Agnes C. Cottrill to Brixton; Miss Mary Crosse to Leeds (Armley); Miss Ivy A. Fawkes to Manchester (Harpurhey); Miss Eva Markby to Portsmouth; Miss Adelaide J. Pringle to Prestwich; Miss Mary F. Ronchetti to Leeds (Armley); Miss Janet Wilcock to Radcliffe; Miss Edith J. Woodhouse to Charlton.

COLONIAL NURSING ASSOCIATION.
Imperial Institute, S.W. 7.

The Committee of the Colonial Nursing Association desire to notify that at a meeting of the Executive Committee, held at the Imperial Institute on Wednesday, June 5th, 1918, the following Resolution was unanimously carried :—

" That from and after the date of the next General Meeting (July 3rd, 1918), the name of the Association shall be the Overseas Nursing Association."

By Order of the Committee.

EDITH CAVELL HOMES.

A large number of applications are being received from nurses by the committee of the Edith Cavell Homes of Rest for Nurses, of which Queen Alexandra is the patron, and new homes are in the course of being opened. Funds are urgently required. Subscriptions should be sent to the Hon. Secretary, 25, Victoria Street, S.W.

PRACTICAL POINTS.
Vaseline in Ether Anesthesia.

" M.P.A." writes in the *American Journal of Nursing* : " Carbolised vaseline applied to the nasal mucosa has been found to overcome post-operative vomiting and to do away with the unpleasant taste of ether while taking it and afterwards. It is not infallible, but in a number of cases it has been most successful and is worth trying."

AN INTERESTING ANNOUNCEMENT.

Mr. J. S. Wood, the Chairman, has purchased the entire interest in *The Gentlewoman* and the Press Printers, Ltd., held by Mr. Alex. J. Warden, who has now no connection with either company.

NURSING ECHOES.

The Report of the Treasurer of St. Bartholomew's Hospital for 1917 remarks :—

" The inadequate and unsatisfactory housing of the Nurses in the Hospital is a subject to which I have referred on numerous occasions, and in my Report for 1916 I expressed the opinion that the provision of a suitable Home must be dealt with immediately upon the termination of the war.

" I fully realise that the task of raising a large sum which will be required for this purpose will be an extremely difficult one, but I would urge that, as a preliminary, a Special Committee should be appointed forthwith to consider the question of a site, arrange for the preparation of plans, and advise as to the means to be adopted to obtain the necessary funds for the erection of the building.

" The urgency of this matter is naturally more apparent to those actively engaged in the administration of the Hospital, and I venture to think the views I have expressed will be fully endorsed by my colleagues, the Almoners, and by those members of the Visiting Governors' Committee whose duty it is to periodically inspect the existing accommodation."

The fact is that the housing of the Nursing Staff at St. Bartholomew's Hospital is quite inadequate and the sanitary arrangements obsolete. Upwards of thirty years ago the question of providing a Nurses' Home was under the consideration of the then Treasurer and Almoners, and that a catastrophe from fire has not happened is more from good luck than good looking for; there has been more than one narrow escape. Again, the Nursing School attached to the hospital has been most seriously handicapped for need of proper classrooms and teaching facilities for many years past. The neglect of the Nurses' interests in these particulars at the premier royal hospital in the Empire is a lesson to the community that no class of worker should be entirely left to the mercy of irresponsible employers, however benevolent in intention. The sooner we have a Ministry of Health, responsible for the expert inspection of every institution where sick people are attended, the better. Generations of professional women will then be protected from the control of philanthropists where education is concerned, and conditions of housing dangerous to life. His Majesty the King, who is President of St. Bartholomew's Hospital, expressed his solicitude for the health and comfort of Nursing Staffs of Hospitals in Lord Stamfordham's letter to the Council of King Edward's Hospital Fund for London in December last : it is doing His Majesty a very poor service to permit him to run the risk of blame for neglect and injury to the devoted nursing staff at Bart's. We hope the Governors will respond whole-heartedly, as suggested by Lord Sandhurst, as to providing a new Nurses' Home.

We are glad to note the Nursing Staff are congratulated on the honours they have received for war work, and that the emolu-ments of the probationers have been consider-ably increased. The Sisters and senior officers are generously remunerated, and their off-duty time at St. Bartholomew's Hospital is most liberal.

The Establishment Committee of the London County Council reported to the Council last Tuesday that they have not deemed it desirable to revise the scale of salaries of the school nurses in the Public Health Department during the war, though they have granted war wages of 9s. a week, but the nursing staff—141 in number—have submitted a petition asking that the matter may be reconsidered. The Com-mittee still think the time inopportune for a revision of the scale, but consider there is justification for increasing the amount of war wages, especially as there has been a consider-able number of resignations among the staff in order to take up more remunerative work. They now recommend that, as from the 1st July, 1918, until the expiration of six months after the declaration of peace, the war wages of 9s. a week granted to the assistant super-intendents of school nurses and the nurses serving on the permanent staff in the public health department, be increased by £50 a year. This recommendation is approved by the Finance Committee, and provision is made in its estimates for the necessary increase as a matter of urgency.

We hear from several Matrons of country hospitals that it is almost impossible to get suitable trained women to fill the positions of sister and night sister. We wonder if an increase of salary to £50 annually would not meet with some response. Hospital com-mittees should realise that the supply of really well-trained and first-class women is not at present equal to the demand. The law of economics demands an uprising scale of re-muneration. The new-laid summer penny egg is now 5d. ; for a spring chicken anything from 10s. to 15s. Either you must pay for them or go without. It appears a simple proposition.

OUTSIDE THE GATES.

THE NEW REGISTER.

The new Parliament Bill brings the next general election a little nearer, for it is understood that this Bill will be the last of the series. If an election is to take place before the end of the year a great speeding up of the new register will be necessary. Women are all longing for a new Parliament which they have helped to elect. We want young fresh men (and women, if we may have them) full of patriotism and energy. We want to set to and get things done for the benefit of the people.

MAKE SURE.

The new voters' lists are being posted at post offices, churches, chapels, and public buildings. All qualified, including women over 30, should see their names are included. If not, information must be given to the local registration officer before July 17.

WE OFFER SYMPATHY.

We offer sincere sympathy to our American Sisters, that after all their strenuous work, into which many of them, like Lavinia Dock, have put their whole heart, the requisite two-thirds majority in the Senate of the United States was not obtained for the Woman Suffrage amendment to the Federal Constitution, in spite of the President having openly advocated woman suffrage for the United States, as part of the creed of democracy for which the war is being fought. A few reactionary Senators have turned it down, men, we learn, described as " crusted Tories and Junkers, old slave holders." The result is that, after a battle of nearly thirty years to get the Federal Amendment through Congress, it will be necessary for the women to begin all over again at the next session to put the measure through the lower House. Anyway, these " old slave holders " who defeated the amendment have given abroad in enemy countries the impression that America is not as far advanced as her slogans of democracy would indicate. She must wipe out this impression at the first possible opportunity.

SANITAS.

A most satisfactory report was presented at the twentieth ordinary general meeting of the " Sanitas " Company, Ltd., on July 3rd, at Winchester House, Old Broad Street, E.C. The Chairman, Mr. C. T. Kingzett, F.I.C., F.C.S., in moving the adoption of the report and accounts said that the business of the company had been well maintained. In some directions there had been great extensions, notwithstanding the diffi-culties attendant upon trading in these days—the scarcity of materials, difficulties of securing licences to obtain them, scarcity of freight, deple-tion of staff, and so forth. The volume of trade had nevertheless increased proportionately. Both sales and profit constituted a record in the history of the company. The reserve fund has been increased by over £7,000, and the total dividend for the year has been 8 per cent.

LETTERS TO THE EDITOR.

Whilst cordially inviting communications upon all subjects for these columns, we wish it to be distinctly understood that we do not IN ANY WAY hold ourselves responsible for the opinions expressed by our correspondents.

WHY NOT STOP THE SALE OF THIS MISLEADING BADGE?

To the Editor of THE BRITISH JOURNAL OF NURSING.

DEAR MADAM,—The attention of the Council of the Nightingale Fund has been drawn to the fact that a trading association has been selling a badge which they call the "Nightingale Badge," and the Council feel, therefore, that they ought to explain that the selling of this badge is not authorised by them, and that its possession does not imply that the owner has received a training at the Nightingale School.

It would appear that the badge can be purchased by any nurse, or indeed anyone, if she wishes.

My Council, therefore, feel it right to make this explanation and disclaimer in response to requests that have come to them from influential quarters in the nursing world, and they will be much obliged if you will give it as wide publicity as possible.

I am, dear Madam,
Yours faithfully,
W. H. BONHAM-CARTER,
Secretary of the Nightingale Training School.

[It will be remembered that a correspondent drew public notice to this matter in this Journal a few weeks ago. At the request of the Matron of St. Thomas' Hospital we placed further information at her disposal, and congratulate the Committee of the Nightingale School for Nurses on disclaiming responsibility for this "Nightingale Badge." For the protection of "Nightingales" we suggest the Committee should take steps to prevent the sale of this "badge," which any person trained or not can buy, and wear. It is calculated to mislead the public.—ED.]

HUMILIATING HUMBUG.

To the Editor of THE BRITISH JOURNAL OF NURSING.

DEAR MADAM,—I wonder how much deeper of the cup of humiliation the nursing profession will have to drink—to the very dregs? I happened to walk into Waring & Gillow's shop the other day, where I saw a most extraordinary entertainment in progress. Miss Elizabeth Asquith was exhibiting a wax doll, which she informed me represented Queen Alexandra in her wedding dress. Upon further questioning, I learned that this toy was to be raffled for "The Nation's Fund for Nurses," so called. I gave her to understand very clearly that self-respecting nurses resented being held up as objects of charity. I further informed her that the only thing we did want was what her father—when Prime Minister—had had the power to give us, and had refused, namely,

State Registration; and that what we did *not* want was that she should patronize the nurses in such an insulting way as to invite raffling (gambling is the most honest term) over a wax doll to obtain charity money for trained nurses. What has Miss Asquith to do with the Nursing Profession I should much like to know. Instead of this unjustifiable interference, she would be better employed doing some work of national importance, and this I told her as a parting word of advice. Where is the *esprit de corps* among nurses if they can tolerate this ignoble treatment of what is often called by those who delight to humiliate it—"a noble profession"?

Yours indignantly,
BEATRICE KENT.

P.S.—I am in perfect sympathy and agreement with Henrietta Hawkins in the views she expresses about the work which the splendid official report of the work of the Society for State Registration represents, and I enclose a donation towards the expenses with the greatest pleasure and gratitude.

[Appreciation, as well as financial support for a just Bill, is most welcome.—ED.]

A QUESTION OF IMPORTANCE TO MENTAL NURSES.

To the Editor of THE BRITISH JOURNAL OF NURSING.

DEAR MADAM,—I was much interested in Captain Kirkland-Whittaker's remarks at the Annual Meeting of the Asylum Workers' Association (*The Asylum News*, p. 18) on the promotion of mental nurses to the posts of Assistant Matron and Matron, and from the applause they received it would appear that the sentiments were approved of by the whole meeting. It is interesting to record that he repeats in England the views which were expressed in Scotland by Dr. Yellowlees, of Gartnavel (the Father of the Medico-Psychological Association), so long ago as 1898. While agreeing with Captain Kirkland-Whittaker that the matron of an Asylum ought to be fully qualified in her profession, and hold both the Certificates of Hospital Nursing and of Proficiency in Mental Nursing, he thought the best matrons were those who had first been mental nurses and had subsequently completed their training in the wards of a General Hospital. The Asylum, he eloquently said, was their "first love," and their interest in work of this kind of institution would be greater.

Dr. Yellowlees' remarks were made during a discussion on the training of hospital nurses in mental work for the purpose of fitting them to become matrons of Asylums. A considerable number since 1880 had been appointed matrons of Asylums in Scotland, and, owing to their want of training, with indifferent success in many cases. I thought this defect should be rectified, and I induced the first hospital nurses to enter the wards of an Asylum in the year 1896. The prestige of the Asylum service was then so low that it took nearly a year before I could get a single candidate. Two others came shortly afterwards. All three became matrons of Asylums within three years, and after

that candidates became numerous. The full double training is, of course, a tremendous advantage to any applicant for a matron's post. No person should, however, be appointed matron of an Asylum, if it can be avoided, who does not hold the Certificate of Proficiency in Mental Nursing, and the training which was instituted in 1896 for hospital nurses, and adopted in many other Asylums since then, obviates the necessity of doing this.

In answer to Dr. Yellowlees I replied that enterprising and intelligent mental nurses, meeting hospital nurses in the wards of Asylums, would be induced to complete their training in Hospitals, and would in their turn be available for matrons' posts. Also that the status of Asylum nurses would be improved by Hospital nurses working in the wards of Asylums. My surmises both proved correct. Scores of my nurses have taken their hospital training. I fancy this practice is more prevalent in Scotland than in England, as our Asylums have become more hospitalised and we employ more hospital nurses in them. The result of this is that many mental nurses who have completed their double training in hospitals are afterwards appointed assistant matrons, and some do ultimately become matrons of Asylums. Lately, I think four out of five assistant matrons at the West House of the Morningside Royal Asylum had begun their career as mental nurses. During the last three years three at least, if not more, of my former assistant matrons, who started as mental nurses, have been appointed matrons of English Asylums. More mental nurses may be appointed matrons than Captain Kirkland-Whittaker suspects, but they usually have the double training, which we all think so desirable. In any case, good mental nurses are now coming into their own in this respect, as I predicted twenty years ago they would, and the status of mental nurses is much higher now than then.

Hard lines still occur, as when a faithful experienced mental nurse is passed over for a younger woman who holds both certificates. Some weight must, of course, be attached to the possession of the second certificate, and the interests of the patients and the institution must come first. One cannot fail to sympathise with these older officials; not so much, however, with the younger generation of mental nurses. Those of them who are enterprising and ambitious should know by this time that if they aspire to the higher posts they must complete their training in a general hospital. If they do this, there are many I know of, like Dr. Yellowlees, who will give them a preference when opposed by candidates who are equally qualified, but whose " first love " has not been the Asylum.

I do not think there is any difficulty such as Captain Kirkland-Whittaker suggests in a mental nurse completing her training in a general hospital. My experience, which is not exceeded by anyone, is opposed to this. She must, of course, resign her asylum post after obtaining her certificate, which she can do by giving a month's notice. She will find she will have less difficulty than the untrained woman in entering a Hospital, as the certificate of the Association which she possesses, I am proud to say, is held in high esteem. The matron of the Hospital knows that she is not a raw, untrained, ordinary probationer. If she has done good service in the Asylum, the Superintendent and the Matron will help her to enter a Hospital.

I think it distinctly hard that one year should not be deducted from the three required for Hospital training, in virtue of her mental certificate, as is done when a hospital nurse enters for the mental certificate. This point has already been brought by the Medico-Psychological Association to the notice of the College of Nursing, and the favour will no doubt be obtained in time. It was several years before the Medico-Psychological Association itself granted the favour to hospital nurses. As I was the first to train hospital nurses in Asylums, I naturally proposed at the meeting that this favour should be accorded them, but I underwent the trying experience of not finding anyone to second my proposal. Several years afterwards, at a large meeting in London at which I was present, Dr. Mercier made a similar proposal, and he not only found a seconder, but his motion was enthusiastically carried without a dissentient voice. His argument may have been as lucid, interesting, and convincing on that occasion as his speech was at the Annual Meeting, and the times may have been ripe.

I am, Madam, &c.,

GEORGE M. ROBERTSON, M.D., F.R.C.P.Ed.,
*Physician-Superintendent of the
Royal Edinburgh Asylum.*

KERNELS FROM CORRESPONDENCE.

Self-supporting Nurse :—" I ventured into Selfridges the day last week that actresses and others were selling tickets for the Nation's Fund for Nurses. I told one lady how strongly many nurses objected to its being done as a war Charity. She kept repeating, " Nonsense, Miss Davies must know ! " I resented this. Who is Miss Davies, and what has she to do with my freedom of opinion ? She is neither the keeper of my conscience nor my purse. I claim the right to form and express my own opinions. To the little actress in question, this appeared entirely superfluous."

[It would.—ED.]

- - - • - - -

OUR PRIZE COMPETITIONS.

July 20th.—State fully how you would disinfect a bedroom and its furnishings.

July 27th.—What are the chief racial poisons ? What steps should be taken to prevent and counteract their effects ?

- - - • - - -

OUR ADVERTISERS.

Do not omit to buy, as far as possible, everything you need from " Our Advertisers," and to recommend them to your friends. They are all first-class firms.

The Midwife.

THE MIDWIVES' ACT AMENDMENT BILL

On Tuesday, July 2nd, as we briefly notified last week, the House of Lords resolved itself into Committee to consider the Midwives Bill, the Earl of Donoughmore being in the chair.

FUTURE REVISION OF CONSTITUTION OF CENTRAL MIDWIVES' BOARD.

Clause I of the Midwives' Act Amendment Bill is important, because, if passed into law, it confers on the Central Midwives' Board of England powers which, so far, it has not possessed. It provides that :—

1. (1) The Central Midwives' Board may at any time represent to the Privy Council that it is expedient to modify the constitution of the Board, either by

(*a*) increasing or diminishing the number of persons appointed by any body or person ; or

(*b*) abolishing the power of appointment by any body or person ; or

(*c*) conferring on any body or person a power of appointment of one or more persons ; or

(*d*) altering the term of office or qualifications of any members.

The Privy Council is then to cause such representation to be laid before both Houses of Parliament ; and, if within forty days, either House presents an address to His Majesty, declaring that the representation, or any part thereof, ought not to be given effect to, no further proceedings shall be taken in respect of the representation in regard to which the address has been presented ; otherwise, it shall be lawful for His Majesty, by Order in Council, to give effect to the same.

This provision is made both in the Midwives (Scotland) Act, 1915, and the Midwives (Ireland) Act, 1918 ; but the Amending Bill makes no provision for " bringing the English Act into line with those in the other parts of the United Kingdom," by the inclusion of certified midwives upon their governing body.

A VITAL OMISSION.

This omission has always been a very grave blot upon the English Act.

In the Amending Bills introduced into the House of Lords in 1910 by Lord Presidents of the Council, first Viscount Wolverhampton and then Earl Beauchamp, steps were taken to rectify it. Both Bills proposed that two certified midwives should be appointed on to the Central Midwives' Board—one by the Incorporated Midwives' Institute, and one by the Royal British Nurses' Association. During the passage of Earl Beauchamp's Bill through the House of Lords, the representation of the Midwives' Institute was increased by the addition of a medical representative, and that of the R.B.N.A. was (by a majority of six) altered to give it the option of appointing a representative

other than a certified midwife—though Lord Beauchamp opposed the amendment on the ground that out of a Board of fourteen appointed to deal with midwives, it was not unreasonable that two of the members should be midwives. Before the Bill passed into law, the House of Commons of 1910 was dissolved.

The Central Midwives' Board for Scotland consists of eleven persons. Three of these are appointed by the Lord President of the Council and two of the three must be certified midwives.

The Central Midwives Board for Ireland consists of eleven persons, four of whom are midwives.

The Central Midwives' Board for England consists of nine persons, none of whom need be midwives.

Why should not the Amending Bill provide for the addition of two certified midwives to the Board ? The grievance of English midwives will be accentuated if a Bill of which the declared purpose is to bring it into line with those in other parts of the United Kngdom fails to do so in this vital particular. It is a point which midwives should not allow to be lost sight of in the House of Commons, and should urge upon their local Members of Parliament—and especially upon Labour Members.

An Amendment was adopted on July 2nd to section five of the principal Act. This section provides that the Central Midwives Board shall, as soon as practicable after December 31st in each year, publish a financial statement, and submit a copy to the Privy Council. If there is any balance against the Board, and the balance is approved by the Privy Council, the Board may apportion such balance between the councils of the several counties and county boroughs *in proportion to the number of midwives who have given notice during the year of their intention to practise in those areas* respectively, and may recover from the councils the sum so apportioned.

The amendment provides that the apportionment of such balance shall be *in proportion to the population of those counties and county boroughs,* according to the returns of the last published census for the time being. This is obviously an improvement, and a more just arrangement. If the basis of apportionment is the number of practising midwives, then the more active a county or county borough is in inducing midwives to practise, the larger the amount of the subsidy which can be recovered by the Central Midwives' Board, while a slack authority gets off lightly.

Section 3 makes the following necessary addition to section 7 of the principal Act :—

" A certificate purporting to be signed by the Secretary of the Board that the name of a woman whose name appears in the roll of midwives has been removed from the roll and of the date of such removal shall be evidence that such woman is not certified under this Act, and of the date as from which she ceased to be so certified."

Section 4 makes provision for the payment of reasonable expenses to members of the Board in respect of their attendance at meetings on a scale approved by the Privy Council.

Section 5 deals with the annual report of the Board to the Privy Council. Such a report is, in fact, already made by the Board. The section provides that it shall contain " such particulars as the Privy Council may direct."

Section 6 (1) authorises the Central Midwives Board to frame rules deciding the conditions under which midwives may be suspended from practice and includes a power of framing rules—

(*a*) Authorising the Board to suspend a midwife from practice in lieu of striking her name off the roll and to suspend from practice any midwife accused before the Board of disobeying rules or regulations, or of other misconduct, until the case has been decided and, in the case of an appeal, until the appeal has been decided.

(*b*) Authorising the local supervising authority which takes proceedings against a midwife before a Court of Justice, or reports a case for consideration by the Central Midwives Board, to suspend her from practice until the case has been decided.

At present, neither the Central Midwives Board nor a local supervising authority has power of suspension in a punitive or disciplinary sense, though, under its rules, local supervising authorities may suspend a midwife from practice to prevent the spread of infection.

Section 6 (2) provides that when a case has been decided in favour of a midwife who has been suspended from practice pending its decision, the Board, or local supervising authority concerned, " may, if they think fit, pay her such reasonable compensation for loss of practice as under the circumstances may seem just."

"Breaking a Lance for the Midwife."

On this Clause, the Earl of Meath moved to delete the words we have quoted, and to insert " shall pay her reasonable compensation for loss of practice," because, as he explained, it appeared to him there is a want of elementary justice in this second sub-section.

" I wish," he continued, " to break a lance for the midwife. It appears to me she is hardly properly treated. You give power to the Central Midwives' Board and to the local supervising authority to suspend her, but if it is proved that she is innocent it would be only justice that some reasonable compensation should be given to her for loss of practice. . . . Once upon a time, Mr. Gladstone said that we, in this House, lived up in a balloon ; but I think we know enough of affairs terrestrial to be aware of the fact that a prosecutor is not likely to do justice to a defendant if it is proved that the defendant is innocent, and that the prosecutor is the very last person to give compensation and thus be likely to stultify himself."

Viscount Peel said he did not think the noble Earl need display any anxiety that there would not be plenty of noble Lords in that House who would break lances on behalf of midwives, because in his experience they had many strong friends, not only there, but in the other House. He was advised that the particular proposal of the noble Lord would make little, if any difference in practice. Further, he believed it would be far better to leave the whole matter to the fair discretion of the Board. He hoped the noble Earl would not press his amendment.

The Earl of Meath said the noble Viscount had alluded to the Central Midwives' Board, but not to the local supervising authority, which was the body least likely to give the compensation needed.

On question, the Amendment was negatived and Clause 6 agreed to.

(*To be concluded.*)

NATIONAL BABY WEEK.

Presiding at a meeting at the Central Hall, Westminster, during Baby Week, Sir Francis Champneys, Chairman of the Central Midwives' Board, advocated a closer co-operation between medical practitioners and midwives and a longer training for the latter. Their status, he said must be increased and the calling made more attractive. He also spoke of the great future before ante-natal clinics and the necessity for the provision of decent houses—housing conditions affected the health of mother and child enormously.

Pathological Section of the Exhibition.

Admission to this section was restricted to doctors, nurses, midwives, sanitary inspectors, health visitors and infant welfare workers. Very terrible, but very informing, were some of the exhibits, showing various diseases and abnormalities, including the ravages of syphilis.

"ORDER OF THE BRITISH CRADLE."

At the opening of a day nursery at Stuart Crescent, Wood Green, last Saturday, Mr. Pett Ridge said that while a great many Orders had been given to more people than wanted them, no one had thought of creating the Order of the British Cradle, to be given to mothers who brought up their children well under difficulties. A small boy of three, on being brought one day to a Hoxton nursery, cried bitterly when his mother left him. The next morning the mother stayed chatting with the sister for a few moments to break the anguish of the parting, but the boy glanced up from his playthings on the floor and said, " 'Op it, mother."

We don't like that little boy.

THE
BRITISH JOURNAL OF NURSING
WITH WHICH IS INCORPORATED
THE NURSING RECORD
EDITED BY MRS BEDFORD FENWICK

No. 1,581.   SATURDAY, JULY 20, 1918.   Vol. LXI

EDITORIAL.

FRANCE'S DAY.
REQUIEM FOR THE FALLEN.

" Pray for my soul. More things are wrought by
prayer than this world dreams of."

It is the common instinct of humanity to
honour the dead who have fallen gloriously
in battle, or have died in the defence of their
country of wounds and sickness, and it is
the practice of all branches of the Catholic
Church, from primitive times, to associate
that honour with prayers for the departed.

It was fitting and natural, therefore, that
on France's Day a Solemn Mass of Requiem
for the Fallen should be sung at the Cathedral at Westminster for the French soldiers
and sailors who have fallen in the war, and
the great congregation which filled the
Cathedral to overflowing was proof that
this remembrance of their dead was appreciated by a large number of the relatives
and friends of these fallen heroes.

The King, Queen Alexandra, and the
Government were represented, and the
Lord Mayor and Sheriffs attended in state,
and there were present the French Ambas-
sador and the full staff of the Embassy, as
well as many of the Diplomatic Corps, the
French Commission, the French Red Cross,
Members of Parliament and the Consular
Service, Ministers of the Allied Countries,
representatives of British Overseas
Dominions, the wives of French soldiers,
and many others.

At the foot of the Sanctuary steps was
the Catafalque adorned with the Tricolour.
Around it burned six tall candles, and by
each, erect and motionless, stood a Zouave,
in his striking red and blue uniform, with
fixed bayonet, and facing the Catafalque
was an officer in khaki, with red, blue, and
gold laced cap. Bishop Butt, the celebrant,
was vested in black, but on the High Altar
burned many candles, and colour was the

prevailing note, for the Cardinal Archbishop wore his red robes and cappa magna,
the Metropolitan Chapter wore exquisite
rose-coloured cappas, and the Cathedral
clergy grey silk.

The Zouave band played before the
service, and then was silent for the music
of the Mass, when the plain-song melodies
in the Mass of Anerio, a 16th century
composer, were sung by the choir under
the direction of Dr. Terry with beautiful
effect, the men's and boys' voices alternat-
ing in the *Dies Iræ*.

In the Offertorium the Zouave Band
played a fragment from Gounod's Jeanne
d'Arc Mass, and at the Elevation of the
Host, signalized by fanfares of trumpets,
the Zouaves at the Catafalque presented
arms, and the officer's sword came to the
salute.

After the departure of the Celebrant, the
Cardinal, vested in cope and mitre, and the
choir, sang the *Libera Me*, and then with
his procession, carrying lighted torches, he
came down to the Catafalque, sprinkling
and censing it and giving the Absolutions.

Then came the heart-stirring roll of the
drums, which re-echoed through the Cathedral, the Last Post sounded by the buglers
of the Grenadier Guards, and the " Marche
Heroique," rendered with consummate
skill and inspiring beauty by the Zouave
Band. After these the " Marseillaise "
thrilled the great congregation, and a profoundly impressive service concluded with
the National Anthem.

In many a quiet side chapel in our
churches to-day an increasing number of the
faithful avail themselves of the opportunity,
and consolation, afforded them of praying
for their dear ones, quick and dead, in the
presence of the Blessed Sacrament.

" To souls departed in the fear of the
Lord, grant refreshment in the land of
peace, Jesus, God of life and death."

A MINISTRY OF HEALTH.

The most pressing of all reconstructive problems is the foundation of a Ministry of Health; and Major-General Sir Bertrand Dawson, G.C.V.O., in an address on "The Future of the Medical Profession," in his Cavendish Lecture delivered recently before the West London Medico-Chirugical Society, emphasised this point.

There is, he said, "a growing appreciation of the fact by the medical profession and the public that much disease is preventible; a growing sense that health is of supreme importance alike to the State and the individual; that the best means for preserving health and curing disease should be available for (not necessarily given to) every citizen, irrespective of his position, and by right and not by favour.

"There is an interesting parallel between provision for education and health, both as regards historical development and present needs. Education was at one time patchy, unorganized, and dependent on voluntary effort. In 1870 Parliament stepped in, with the result that State and voluntary education proceeded side by side. Since then the State Service has gradually overgrown the voluntary one, because it has been recognized that education should be available for all, that the State is responsible for the education of its citizens, and that the cost is too great to be supported by fees, or by voluntary effort alone. This cost is in part defrayed by an education rate chargeable on householders, and Dr. Gordon Dill's suggestion that a similar rate should be charged for health has a great deal to recommend it; it would be a local contribution to the cost, and would not be altogether an additional burden, for its application would soon be followed by a diminution in the poor rate.

"Health organization is following a similar development, though tardily and at a distance. Yet in reality health is a more fundamental need than education, and without doubt the two together form the foundation stone of the State. Notwithstanding there exists no Ministry of Health, and even now, when it is proposed to form one, such a Ministry is to be tied politically to the Local Government Board."

Sir Bertrand Dawson considers that medical services must have some kind of State aid and central control; that for their efficiency they need co-ordinated effort installed in specially equipped institutions, and reaches, by what he regards as the irresistible logic of facts, the following conclusions :—

1. State aid : central control.
2. Co-ordinated effort—team work.
3. Development of institutions specially designed for diagnosis and treatment, styled for brevity institutional treatment.

To the foregoing he adds a fourth—that curative and preventive medicine are no longer separated in accordance with any sound principle, and should be brought together in thought, teaching, and organization.

The Administration of the Medical Services.

Conditions he regards as essential to any plan are that "all the buildings and equipments, such as hospitals, clinics, laboratories, necessary for the medical services, will be constructed and maintained by the new health authority. They would be available for all citizens, though in practice they would be only partially used by the well-to-do. . . .

"All professional and technical questions must be determined alone by the doctors, and administrative questions by a health board composed of both lay and professional members. Neither the professional nor lay members should be chosen from any area smaller than a county or large borough... . . Though granted adequate powers, the health boards should be controlled as regards larger questions of policy, by the Ministry of Health.

"By this plan of choosing big areas for the Health Board electorate, one would hope to avoid the evils of local politics and to secure a better type of representative. By retaining the determination of policy, and the confirmation of the more important administrative acts at the Health Ministry, one would secure control without over-centralization. . . .

"But whatever the actual plan, the principle that technical matters must be decided by medical men must be adhered to, and thus one of the errors of the Insurance Act put right.

"The practice of putting the skilled under the control of the unskilled must cease. . . .

"With so much of the flower of our manhood sacrificed for the great cause, the rearing of a healthy race has become a supreme necessity.

"The Ministry will need to draw to its counsels representatives from all departments of medicine, both preventive and curative, and these counsellors must have real power, with direct access to the Minister, in contrast to the baneful tradition at the Local Government Board, whereby the medical officer can only advise the Minister through the intermediary of a lay official."

FOR DAUNTLESS FRANCE.*

France, dear to men that honour human things,
To have helped or heartened any of these your maimed
And homeless, is itself felicity.
—From the Dedication.

" For Dauntless France " ! The heart of many an English nurse who has worked in French hospitals throbs responsive to the words ; for her admiration and liking for the French poilu, so brave, so gentle, so courteous, so grateful, is unbounded, and she desires no greater privilege

a singularly happy one. Let us say at once the book is one to possess, not, like so many war books, one to be read with enjoyment and then laid aside. Enjoyment certainly, may be promised, but as a history of the work of Englishmen and Englishwomen for the dauntless people of France, carefully and sympathetically compiled, it merits an abiding place on our bookshelves.

His Excellency the French Ambassador, M. Paul Cambon, who contributes the preface, writes :—

" Le budget des œuvres auxquelles Mr. Laurence Binyon a si bien rendu justice, en dit long sur la générosité britannique. Mais il ne l'exprime

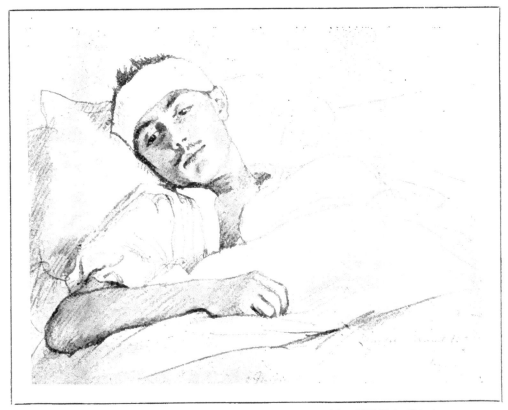

"THE WOUNDED POILU." By JANE DE GLEHN (Mrs. Wilfrid de Glehn.)
Reproduced from Laurence Binyon's New Book, FOR DAUNTLESS
FRANCE, by kind permission of Messrs. Hodder & Stoughton.

than to serve him till peace once more reigns and happily he no longer needs her skilled services.

" For Dauntless France " is the title chosen by Mr. Laurence Binyon for his book compiled for the British Red Cross Societies, and the British Committee of the French Red Cross, which contains an account of Britain's aid to the French wounded and victims of the war, and the title is

* By Laurence Binyon. Hodder & Stoughton, St. Paul's House, Warwick Square, London, E.C. 4. 10s. 6d. net.

qu'en termes d'argent et de matériel. Les pages qui suivent nous montrent l'œuvre admirable des hommes et des femmes venus de Grande Bretagne comme à une sainte croisade, au secours de leurs frères de France. Les nurses anglaises qui ont, dès le premier jour, offert le secours précieux de leur expérience au service médical français, les ambulances automobiles qui, équipées en Angleterre, montées et conduites par des volontaires anglais, ont suivi nos armées jusque sur la ligne de feu, par les chemins que balayait l'artillerie, où il fallait passer de nuit et sans lumière ; les groupes de Quakers qui, sans renoncer à leur attitude traditionelle à l'égard de la guerre sont venu réconstruire nos villages détruits, et soigner les femmes et les enfants chassés de leur foyer par l'invasion ; les cantines créees sur les routes ou s'écoule le flot incessant des combattants et des blessés ; la quantité des hôpitaux fondés, recrutés, entre-tenus par nos amis de l'Empire britannique, tout cela forme un tableau auquel l'auteur a su donner la grandeur qui lui appartient. Nous ne souhaitons qu'une chose, et elle est facile à réaliser : c'est que son livre puisse être lu en France comme en Angleterre."

THE CALL AND THE ANSWER.

Part I deals with the Call and the Answer, and includes three chapters " The Scene Surveyed," " A Day's Work at the Office of the Comité Britannique," and " British Nurses in France : The French Flag Nursing Corps."

The Scene Surveyed enables us to look down as from an aerial vantage-point upon the regions of Western Europe—upon a world at war.

" That scarred line from Yser to Jura attracts like a magnet ; it sucks up like a sponge. All Europe and much more than Europe is conscious of it. Not a hamlet by the Atlantic or the remote Pyrenees—not a village in the British Isles but has a vision of it ; and far away in the South Seas and beyond the North Atlantic it is the same. To it men and women are sending, sending, sending. They have sent sons and brothers, lovers and husbands. They have sent arms and ammunitions. They are sending letters and little gifts. Those that have nothing send their thoughts and their fears. Could we use that other vision of the mind, we might see those thoughts, prayers, curses, apprehensions, hopes and passionate desires flying in that one direction like the birds that fill the sky at the time of their migration. But we should see also, pressing thither, streams of embodied human energy—passion and calculation alike translated into active force and absorbed into the momentum of a single will."

Writing of the British workers for the French soldier Mr. Binyon says that when they have returned to their homes in Britain " they will testify to what they have seen and known.

" They will have learnt that Paris is not France, and that the tourist of other days but rarely came into touch with the true French nature, with France herself. They will grow to understand how fine is the texture of human qualities and human resources which underlie French history, French art and civilisation, and which have made the French so great and renowned a people."

Of the British nurses in French hospitals Mr. Binyon writes :—

" Who, that has seen them at work, has not admired their skill, their resource, their patient deftness ? They have behind them a hard and splendid training, which ensures that only enthusiasts for the vocation become fully-qualified nurses. Very few had experience of war and the wounds a modern war produces ; therefore their

interests were all the more engaged. But it is not only their own work that has been invaluable, it is the training they have given to others less skilled. For under the nurses or sisters work the V.A.D. probationers.

" The V.A.D.s," says a surgeon, " are undoubtedly the surprise. They are splendid, and as probationers under trained nurses in a ward, nothing that I can say is good enough for them."

(We wish the V.A.D.'s were always, or commonly, content with the position of probationers.)

AT THE OFFICE OF THE COMITÉ BRITANNIQUE.

The day's work at the Office of the Comité Britannique, at No. 9, Knightsbridge, S.W., begins " when, at a punctual nine o'clock in the morning, the purple-scarfed Boy Scout, who with so polite a firmness guards the door, lets in the arriving Director-General." From that time onwards its manifold activities are ceaseless.

" Seating ourselves beside the Director-General, and looking unabashed over his shoulder, we get a glimpse of his morning's correspondence. It is comprehensive and formidable."

But first there are some fifty " Ordres de Mission " to be signed, those valuable vouchers which, by a special concession to the Comité, enable its workers to travel free in France.

One touch will amuse trained nurses.

" Two drivers write to ask about their passports, their *fiches* and their *carnets*. The *fiche* is a paper of identification ; but I dare not try to explain what the *carnet* is ; it is just a little book that gives a great deal of trouble."

We cannot even peep into the many rooms, all hives of industry, in this busy building, but mention must be made of the room on the ground where the President, the Vicomtesse de la Panouse, reigns, who, Mr. Binyon explains, " holds all the threads of the Comité s activities. No one is so intimate with the condition of things in France ; no one knows better the real needs of the sick and wounded ; and with her large sympathy with the English people, her knowledge of the right persons to do the right things on both sides of the Channel, she has done, and continues to do, inestimable service to the cause of the friendship between the two nations."

THE FRENCH FLAG NURSING CORPS.

We congratulate the Sisters of the French Flag Nursing Corps on being accorded the position of honour in the book, the first chapter after that on the office in London being devoted to their work ; for although the need of skilled nursing to mitigate the sufferings of the French wounded was obvious in the early days of the war, the assistance offered by this Corps was discountenanced and discouraged by the War Office and the British Red Cross Society, and it was not until the Director-General and the President of the Comité de Londres, now the Comité Britannique of the French Croix Rouge, recognising the value of the fine work of the Corps in the French Military Hospitals, affiliated it as a department of its own work, that the Corps received the appreciation and sympathy which was its due, and its services were offered as a gift to our French Allies.

Mr. Binyon writes :—

"There was unlimited devotion, immense eagerness to serve, but of trained and expert help there was an inevitable deficiency. The ladies of Paris staffed the Red Cross Hospitals, and did all they could. It was the same in other towns. Some of the most devoted nursing work in those days was done, let it be recorded, by women of the streets. But the crying need was for skill, training, experience. And it is told that a-Frenchwoman who knew what nursing requirements really were, and who had seen a well-appointed English ambulance train, sat and wept because so many of her dear countrymen lacked the comforts and the help they so sorely needed."

It was then that an Englishwoman went to t he head of the French Army Medical Corps, and proposed to raise the Corps of fully-trained British nurses, known as the French Flag Nursing Corps, an offer which was eagerly accepted.

"It was an opportunity for testing the value of skilled nursing in war time ; and the testimony of the French doctors and surgeons under whom they have worked, shows what precious metal the test revealed."

A high official wrote ; "The nurses of the French Flag Nursing Corps are considered by the doctors of our armies as assistants of the first class, and their presence in France, in a number the insufficiency of which we regret, is one of the most touching evidences of the sympathy of the English nation towards our country."

(To be concluded.)

THE ROYAL RED CROSS.

The King conferred the Decorations recorded below on the following ladies on July 10th, at Buckingham Palace :—

Bar to the Royal Red Cross.

Queen Alexandra's Imperial Military Nursing Service.—Matron-in-Chief Caroline KEER (retired), and Matron Edith NIXON.

The Royal Red Cross.
FIRST CLASS.

Queen Alexandra's Imperial Military Nursing Service.—Acting Matron Bertha PERKINS.

SECOND CLASS.

Queen Alexandra's Royal Naval Nursing Service.—Sister Isabella LONG.

Queen Alexandra's Imperial Military Nursing Service Reserve.—Assistant Matron Nellie MERRIOTT, Sister Sara BARROWCLIFF, Sister Harriett PERFREMENT, Sister Elizabeth RUSSELL, Sister Lizzie VARLEY, Sister Lillie WRIGHT, Sister Lilian WYNN, and Staff Nurse Grace MANNELL.

Civil Nursing Service.—Matron Alice BAYNE, Matron Edith BLAYNEY, Matron Elizabeth BOATH, Matron Florence BORTON, Matron Adeline CARLE, Matron Caroline CATTELL, Matron Emily CARPENTER-TURNER, Lady Superintendent Lucy BINNS, Assistant Matron Sophia SMITH-BEVAN, Assistant Matron Kathleen COMYN, Sister Florence BINGLEY, Sister Margaret BIRT, Sister Gertrude BUTLER, Sister Cargill CAMERON, Sister Elizabeth COATH, and Sister Sophie FRY.

British Red Cross Society.—Matron Alice BOTTOMLEY, Matron Frances BROWN, Matron Maria BUXTON, Assistant Matron Clara HENDERSON, Assistant Matron Lois MARSDEN, and Sister Eliza WORKMAN.

Voluntary Aid Detachment.—Mrs. Agnes BAYFIELD, Miss Mary BELL, Mrs. Gladys BELLVILLE, the Hon. Mrs. Margaret BIRKIN, Mrs. Katherine BLATCH, Miss Maud BLENKARN, Miss Ada BOSS, Miss Freda BOWRING, Mrs. Margaret BRAMLEY, Miss Edie BROWN, Miss Cicely BURBIDGE, Miss Ellen CARRIER, Miss Anna CARTER, Mrs. Caroline CLAYTON, and Miss Claudia CLOWES.

Queen Alexandra received at Marlborough House the members of the military and civil Nursing Services after the investiture.

The King has been pleased to award the Royal Red Cross to the undermentioned ladies, in recognition of their valuable Nursing Services in connection with the war :—

SECOND CLASS.

EAGER, Miss F. E., Sister, Queen Mary's Hospl. for the East End, Stratford ; EDGAR, Miss A., Sister, T.F.N.S., 4th Sco. Gen. Hospl. ; EDWARDS, Miss E. A., Supt. of Nurses, Toxteth Park Mil. Hospl., Liverpool ; EDWARDS, Mrs. H., Matron, Boothroyde and Longroyde Hospls., Brighouse, Yorks ; ELLIOTT, Miss A., Sister, T.F.N.S., 3rd Northern Gen. Hospl., Sheffield ; ELLWOOD, Miss P. H., Sister, Red Cross Hospl., Horncastle, Lincs ; ELMS, Miss J., Matron, Sussex Eye Hospl., Brighton ; EPPS, Miss E. M. T., Lady Supt., Rauceby Hall, near Grantham, S. Lincs ; EVANS, Miss B., Supt. Nurse, Jericho Mil. Hospl., Bury, Lancs ; EVANS, Miss C., Sister, Aux. Mil. Hospl., Tranmere, Birkenhead.

FANNING, Miss R. G., Sister, Matron's Asst., N.Z.A.N.S., No. 1 N.Z. Gen. Hospl., Brockenhurst, Hants ; FARMER, Miss A., Sister, Cyngfeld, Shrewsbury ; FARMER, Miss M., Sister, Q.A.I.M.N.S.R., R. Victoria Hospl., Netley ; FEARON, Miss M. I., Nursing Sister, Can. Nursing Service, No. 11 Can. Gen. Hospl., Moore Barracks, Shorncliffe ; FITZGERALD, Miss N. A. L., Staff Nurse, War Hospl., Bradford ; FRICKER, Miss M., Sister, N.Z.A.N.S., No. 2 N.Z. Gen. Hospl., Walton-on-Thames ; FRY, Miss S. C., Sister, R Sussex County Hospl., Brighton ; FERGUSON, Mrs. C. F., Commdt., Bredbury V.A.D. Hospl., Tunbridge Wells.

GALBRAITH, Miss L. E., Nursing Sister. Can. Nursing Service, No. 4 Can. Gen. Hospl., Basingstoke, Hants ; GALE, Miss E. G., Matron, Hospl. for Sick and Wounded, Boscombe, Hants ; GALLOWAY, Miss J., Sister, Q.A.I.M.N.S.R., Queen Alexandra Mil. Hospl., Grosvenor Road, S.W. 1 ; GALT, Miss C., Nursing Sister, Can. Nursing Service, No. 15 Can. Gen. Hospl., Taplow, Bucks ; GARDINER, Miss M , Senior Sister i/c., St. John Ambulance, Radcliffe ; GAY, Miss F. E., Sister, T.F.N.S., 4th Lond. Gen. Hospl., Denmark Hill ; GIBBON, Miss L. C., Matron, R. Infirmary, Blackburn ; GIBSON, Mrs. L. M., Matron, Gatcombe House, Isle of Wight ; GOOSEMAN, Miss F., Asst. Matron, T.F.N.S., 2nd Western Gen. Hospl., Ducie Avenue, Manchester ; GORDON, Miss J. W., Sister, R. Infirmary, Manchester ; GOULD, Miss I. M. H., Sister, Pembroke Aux. Mil. Hospl., Lytham ; GOWAN, Miss F. W., Sister, Mil. Orthopædic Hospl., Shepherd's Bush, W. ; GRAHAM, Mrs. E S. (Mrs. W. V. Graham), Matron, Hdqrs., B.R.C.S. ; GRAHAM-SMITH, Miss M. M., Staff Nurse, Regent's Park Hospl., Southampton ; GREEN, Miss L. M., Sister, Union Infirmary, Darlington ; GREEN, Miss L. E., Matron, Ilford Emergency Hospl., Ilford ; GRIFFITHS, Mrs. L., Staff Sister, Aux. Mil. Hospl., Quarry Place, Shrewsbury. *(To be continued.)*

OUR ROLL OF HONOUR.

MISS ISOBEL M. MACKINTOSH, A.R.R.C., SISTER, BERMONDSEY MILITARY HOSPITAL.

We regret to have to record the death, at the early age of 31, of Sister Isobel Mackintosh, who died at her post on July 10th.

Miss Mackintosh, who was a daughter of Mr. A. R. Mackintosh, of Glenlyon Lodge, Nairn and Kincorth, Forres, received her four years' training at the Prince of Wales's General Hospital, London, and almost immediately after war broke out she volunteered for active service at the Front. From 1914 to 1916 she served in British hospitals at Wimereux, Calais, and Le Touquet, and was recently awarded the Mons Ribbon.

In 1917 she was appointed Sister-in-Charge of one of the medical blocks at Bermondsey Military Hospital, Ladywell, where her death from acute influenzal pneumonia took place. She had had a number of soldiers with influenza under her charge, whom she had nursed with great devotion.

Sister Mackintosh (Sister "Mac" as she was affectionately called) was a great favourite with staff and patients alike, and acted as Night Superintendent at Ladywell before being appointed Sister-in-Charge. She was recently awarded the Royal Red Cross (2nd Class) for her valuable services during the war.

The large attendance at her funeral indicated how deeply she was mourned. The medical and nursing staff with the invalid soldiers filled the hospital chapel, while men from her own wards carried the coffin, which was draped with the Union Jack and covered with flowers. One beautiful wreath was labelled "from the 'Boys' of D Section, in grateful and loving memory."

MISS ISOBEL M. MACKINTOSH, A.R.R.C.

I take my heart in my hand, I shall not die
   but live.
  Before Thy face I stand, I for Thou callest
   such.
  All that I have I bring, all that I am I give;
   Smile Thou, and I shall sing but shall
    not question much.

                C. ROSSETTI.

NURSING AND THE WAR.

THE TRAINING OF V.A.D. MEMBERS AS NURSES.

Mr. W. H. Bonham-Carter, Secretary, Nightingale Training School, informs us in the following letter of the terms on which V.A.D. members will be received for training at St. Thomas' Hospital :—

Dear Madam,—The conditions under which V.A.D. Nursing Members and Special Military Probationers, who have served in military hospitals for a consecutive period of not less than two years, who are considered suitable, and who desire to become trained nurses with a view to subsequently entering Queen Alexandra's Imperial Military Nursing Service, have now been defined. Three years' training in a civil hospital training school being a necessary condition, it has been decided by the Committee of the Nightingale Training School at St. Thomas' Hospital to admit such candidates under the conditions now applying to special probationers but without payment of the usual fees, and they will therefore, after passing the short preliminary training in the Preliminary School, and subject to their qualifying in the usual examinations, receive their certificate on the completion of three years' work in the wards.

I, therefore, crave the courtesy of your columns to make this decision public.

    I am, dear Madam,

      Yours faithfully,

      W. H. BONHAM CARTER,

      Secretary, Nightingale

          Training School.

It is an open secret that it was the influence brought to bear through the British Red Cross Society, supported by the Matrons on the Army Nursing Boards, and the College of Nursing Council, which has induced the Army Council to issue Instruction 678, styling V.A.D. nursing members and special military probationers, when they enter a general hospital for training, "Probationers for Queen Alexandra's Imperial Military Nursing Service" and giving them priority of promotion to the Service when trained.

This Instruction will, *in practice*, make it impossible for civil probationers, even with four years' certificates, to enter this Imperial Nursing Service for years to come, as a rota of V.A.D.s after three years' general training will be kept, and if no vacancy exists for them they are promised future vacancies as they occur; so that practically Queen Alexandra's Imperial Military Nursing Service is no longer open to the whole nursing profession, as all Government Nursing Services should be.

Imagine the Army Council enforcing an Instruction that no medical practitioner should be permitted to enter the Royal Army Medical Corps unless he had worked under the Red Cross Society or the Order of St. John during the war ! Such a suggestion for men would not be tolerated for an hour.

We presume trained nurses on the Reserves who have joined the College of Nursing, Ltd., realise that its promoters have helped to deprive them of military promotion in three years' time and used their influence to have them superseded by V.A.D.s.

The Royal Victorian Trained Nurses' Association of Australia has refused to consider service in a military hospital as supplementary to training schools under any circumstances.

BRISQUES.

It is well to let it be known that nurses have no right to wear the French Military Service Brisque (gold braid) worn by soldiers.

In the case of Nurses working in the French Military or Benevole Hospitals there is the "Ensigne de Service" for which their Med. Chef cites them. This consists of two small palm leaves with a tiny red cross in the centre. The leaves are Bronze for one year's service, Silver for two years' service, and Gold for three years. With the "Ensigne " is given a short citation indicating the length of service.

In the case of Canteen Workers, whose service is as a rule rather disconnected, long vacations being taken between each period of service, there does not appear to be any distinguishing Service Badge.

It is interesting to note that H.M. the King of the Belgians has conferred upon Miss Edith Mawe, of Lee Hurst, Weston-super-Mare, the Medaille de la Reine Elisabeth. It will be recalled that during the dark days of 1914 and the early part of 1915 a great many wounded Belgian soldiers were sent to this country to be cared for. At this time Miss Mawe was Honorary Lady Superintendent of the Royal West of England Sanatorium, Weston-super-Mare, and 800 of the Belgians came under her care. It is in recognition of the care bestowed upon these men that the medal has been conferred.

The same honour has been conferred upon Mrs. Bernard Allen, hon. organizer of the Belgian Hospital Fund, in recognition of the work which she has done since January, 1915, in aiding the military and civil hospitals and institutions in France and Belgium; and on Mrs. Rowland Fisher in recognition of her work in establishing and conducting the Belgian Children's Home at Aldeburgh, Suffolk.

CARE OF THE WOUNDED.

A ROYAL GIFT.

Since our last issue, the King and Queen of the Belgians have flown over from France and back again, just to be with our King and Queen on their Silver Wedding Day. King Albert has about him so much of the glorious tradition of a fairy King that he should come and go on wings is all in the picture !

The Queen of the Belgians, before leaving London handed to Queen Mary £500, with the request that she would distribute it among any charities in which she was specially interested.

The Queen has decided to allot the money thus :—£100 each to the War Refugees Committee for the Relief of Belgians in England, Queen Mary's Convalescent Auxiliary Hospital for Widows of Soldiers and Sailors at Roehampton, Queen Mary's Hospital at Frognal, Queen Mary's Royal Naval Hospital at Southend, and Queen Mary's Hostels for Nurses.

Dr. Mary M'Neill, of the Scottish Women's Hospital at Salonica, has had conferred upon her the Order of St. Sava by the King and the Crown Prince of Serbia for services rendered to sick and wounded soldiers.

The following British women motor ambulance drivers working under the Red Cross in France have been mentioned in French Army Orders, and awarded the Croix de Guerre for bravery during an air attack :

Miss M. Thompson, First Aid Nursing Yeomanry, O.C., M.A.C.

Miss M. Lowson, First Aid Nursing Yeomanry, Sergt., M.A.C.

Miss M. Mordaunt, First Aid Nursing Yeomanry, Sergt., M.A.C.

The brigade order citing them states that on May 18th, during a bombardment by aeroplanes which lasted over five hours, they went at once to the point of danger, and picked up the dead and wounded to transport them to hospitals. " They showed absolute disregard of danger, and at the same time gave to all the finest example of courage and *sang froid.*"

The largest American military hospital in Great Britain, to be established near Southampton, will accommodate nearly 3,000 wounded. The site is a country estate of 186 acres, formerly known as Sarisbury Court. The central building of the hospital will be the old Manor House, round which the American Red Cross is building nearly 10 acres of frame hutments. There will be separate buildings for the medical and nursing staffs, the other employees, the kitchens, and the operating rooms, and a large isolation hospital.

Everything is planned in the most wonderful way.

The 10 acres of vegetable gardens will be intensively cultivated. The hospital will produce a considerable part of its dairy requirements, its bacon, and its eggs and poultry.

Ambulances will bring the American wounded from the piers at Southampton. The convalescent soldier will find several miles of sunny or shaded walks without going outside the hospital grounds.

Captain F. Harper Sibley, of the Red Cross, formerly President of the Chamber of Commerce of Rochester, N.Y., who has been in charge of the American Red Cross work at Southampton since April, is supervising the construction of the hospital.

Part of the beds will at first be placed in tents of the Bossoneau type, with windows set in the walls to make them light and airy and a double roof with air-chamber between to insulate them from the heat of the sun. Some of the tents may be retained for convalescents or reserved for emergencies.

JOINT WAR COMMITTEE.

The following Sisters have been deputed for duty in Home Hospitals :—

Red Cross Hosp., Chippenham.—Miss C. L. Still.
Barham Lodge, Weybridge.—Miss E. Redmile.
Dunraven Castle Red Cross Hosp., Bridgend.—Miss P. Palmer.
Hanover Park V.A. Hosp., Peckham.—Miss A. H. Murray.
Weir Hosp., Balham.—Miss C. A. H. Rhodes.
Kingwood Park Hosp., Tunbridge Wells.—Miss C. C. Krelle.
V.A. Hosp., Burnham-on-Crouch.—Miss M. Johnston.
Hosp. for Officers, 16, Bruton Street, W.—Miss E. A. Nurse.
Park House Aux. Hosp., Newbury.—Miss E. Gribben.
Brackenhurst Hall Aux. Mil. Hosp., Southwell.—Miss L. Poole.
Hosp. for Facial Injuries, 24, Norfolk Street.—Miss M. C. Thompson.
6, Kensington Terrace, Newcastle-on-Tyne.—Miss E. G. Elliott.
Beach Red Cross Hosp., Holyhead.—Miss H. A. G. Hawley.
Victoria Aux. Hosp., Stretfold, Lancs.—Miss E. Rycroft.
V.A. Hosp., Northwood, Middlesex.—Miss M. B. May.
Kempston Red Cross Hosp., Bedford.—Miss K. Aitken.
Officers' Red Cross Hosp., Worsley, Lancs.—Mrs. E. L. Lamb.
De Walden Court, Eastbourne.—Miss M. P. Peter.
Newnham Paddox Hosp., Lutterworth.—Mrs. M. E. C. Swann.
Kempston Red Cross Hosp., Eastbourne.—Miss V. Kendal.
Auxiliary Hosp., Bitterne, Southampton.—Miss M. G. Welch.

THE COLLEGE OF NURSING, LTD., AND AMERICAN NURSES.

A REPLY TO MISS LLOYD STILL AND MISS AMY HUGHES.

The following article appears in the July number of the *American Journal of Nursing* in the Foreign Department, which is in charge of Miss L. L. Dock, the Hon. Secretary of the International Council of Nurses.

A PERIL TO INDEPENDENCE AND SELF-GOVERNMENT.

The peril to the independence and professional self-government of English nurses through the College of Nursing, Ltd., of which we have often spoken in these columns, is growing daily more imminent, and it now concerns American nurses more closely to understand this peril, since a very definite attempt is now being made to enlist them in support of the College. The letter in its behalf, which appeared last month in the *Journal*, and the suggestions of re-enforcement of its structure in the invitation to individual Americans to accept associate membership in the College, are indications of this approach, and we think it is highly important that American nurses who may be asked to align themselves in any way with the College should understand that if they do so they will, in effect, no matter how well-meaning and friendly their intentions, be helping to strangle their British Sisters' long, hard efforts to obtain that professional freedom which we Americans have been fortunate enough to obtain for ourselves. No American nurse would knowingly do a thing of this kind. Let us urge them, earnestly, not to do it unknowingly. Let it be remembered that, in the first place, the alumnæ association is by no means the accepted starting point of English nursing organization, as in this country. This grouping of graduates by their schools, which we consider so necessary as the first step in self-government, has never been liked by the conservative hospital managers of England and their matrons, and only those nursing schools that came under the influence of Mrs. Fenwick, the late Miss Isla Stewart, and their group of progressives in the Matrons' Council, developed the alumnæ association under the name of " Nurses' League."

The historic school at St. Thomas', of which Miss Still is matron (Miss Still is one of the signers of the letter to the Editor in June), has no alumnæ association, and would regard the idea with the utmost disapproval. Still less do such conservative matrons tolerate the idea of their nurses (they do not willingly admit that they are ever " graduates " or free from school control, but like to keep this control over them for life) joining *general* societies, such as the county, city, or State groups, which Americans, in their precious freedom, have been able to build up, and which we know to be so all-important in breaking down lines of narrow separation and bringing all together in one circle, in enabling nurses to compare their views and to unite their strength for true standards and principles.

How far should we have progressed in State Registration had we not had our self-governed county and State societies?

When such matrons, then, talk of demo-cratic management and control, it simply means that they do not understand the essence of such control, since their own nurses have never been permitted to learn it. They have taken up the popular catchwords of the day, no doubt in good faith, but do not know their actual implications.

The structure of the College of Nursing, Ltd., is essentially autocratic. The letter itself, signed by Miss Still and Miss Amy Hughes, shows this, as it is perfectly clear therein that this College Company is a close corporation.

The Leaflet issued by the Trained Nurses' Protection Committee, exposing the autocratic Constitution of the College of Nursing, Ltd., is republished in the *American Journal of Nursing* in support of Miss Dock's criticism.

We have once again to thank Miss Dock for her clear-sighted and courageous advocacy. Many years ago Miss Dock took the trouble to tour Europe, and to enquire into Nursing con-ditions in nearly every country. Her opinions are not formed on accounts, " biassed " or otherwise, which appear in the press. She has studied " English Nursing Politics " on the spot, and is fully conversant with the antagonism with which hospital authorities and their discreditable " press " have treated the State Registration question as advanced by what she terms the " intelligentsia,"—that is, by the women who years ago had the brains to evolve a well-defined policy of reform.

AN HISTORICAL SURVEY.

Mrs. Bedford Fenwick has consented to repeat her address to the National Party, " An Historical Survey of the Registration Move-ment," as the younger generation of nurses have had little opportunity of instruction on the question.

"THE LANCET" AND THE SOCIETY FOR THE STATE REGISTRATION OF TRAINED NURSES.

In its issue of July 6th, *The Lancet* published, in an article on " Registration of Nurses," comments on the conduct of business at the Annual Business Meeting of the Society for the State Registration of Trained Nurses, based on misapprehension, which reflected adversely on the policy of the Society.

Having pointed out that Major Chapple, who is in charge of the Central Committee's Bill, was prepared " to assist in an agreed Bill " with the College of Nursing, Ltd., *The Lancet* remarked :

" We welcome an assurance made by Mrs. Bedford Fenwick from the Chair, speaking on behalf of the Society for the State Registration of Trained Nurses, that the Society has never been obstructionist ; and now is evidently the time to give practical proof of this. A resolution was passed at the Annual Meeting of the Society for the State Registration of Nurses, and sent to the Central Committee for State Registration, which contained a clause dissociating the Society from the College of Nursing. The affirmative vote was by no means a large one, but an amendment to secure freedom from ' the domination ' of the College of Nursing, ' without dissociation from it ' was not accepted by the chair. We find this attitude hard to distinguish from obstruction ; we have every confidence in the ability of nurses to settle their own polity without help from outside . . . nothing is more certain than that the profession of nursing is likely to undergo profound changes within the next few years ; and, provided that it is placed in a position to manage its own affairs, plasticity is altogether desirable."

As quite inadvertently, no doubt, *The Lancet's* statement was calculated to give a wrong im-pression, Mrs. Bedford Fenwick, whose conduct of business was criticised, sent an explanation to *The Lancet*, too late, she was informed, for insertion in its issue of July 13th : and upon asking that it might appear this week, she has been informed that—

" We shall, of course, be glad to insert a state-ment that the amendment was proposed by a person not a member of your Society and therefore not accepted by you as Chairman. I fear con-siderations of space will hardly permit of dealing with the other matters at length, especially as they would give rise to correspondence for which we could not possibly find room."

To which Mrs. Fenwick replied :—

" I much regret that you are unable to find space for my letter on the article which appeared in *The Lancet* on July 6th, on the ' Registration of Nurses,' as it is calculated to give a wrong impression, so far as the policy of the Society is concerned, and also of my *personal* attitude and conduct of business. Frankly, this is unfair. If by inadvertence, reports are published which are not correct, the person named should have the right of reply. I had hoped *The Lancet* would have agreed with this ethical journalistic standpoint. From the lay press, generously subsidised by our opponents, we have ceased to expect fair play.

"I shall do myself the justice of publishing my reply to *The Lancet* in THE BRITISH JOURNAL OF NURSING."

Letter sent to the Editor of "The Lancet" by MRS. BEDFORD FENWICK, *President of the Society for the State Registration of Trained Nurses.*

REGISTRATION OF NURSES.

SIR,—I observe that in your last issue, July 6th, you refer to the character of the proceedings at recent meetings of the College of Nursing, Ltd., and the Society for the State Registration of Trained Nurses. The single object of the latter Society since its inception in 1902 has been " To obtain an Act of Parliament providing for the Legal Registration of Trained Nurses," and it naturally restricted itself to the question of Nurses' Registration at its annual business meeting.

The College of Nursing, Ltd., which purports to control Nursing Education, together with Registration and Discipline, and also to associate the members of the Nursing Profession under its direction, at its recent Conference chose a wider field for discussion.

As you refer to my statement made at the former meeting, that the Society for the State Registration of Nurses had never been obstructionist, adding, " now is evidently the time to give practical proof of this," I feel sure you will grant me the opportunity of disabusing your readers of a wrong impression.

The Society for the State Registration of Nurses, which first drafted a Nurses' Registration Bill, passed in 1908 by the House of Lords, and read a first time under the ten minutes' rule in the House of Commons in 1914 with a majority of 229, has stood, and will continue to stand, for fundamental principles of good government in any Nurses' Registration Bill to which it gives its support. In opposing five successive drafts of the Bill promoted by the College of Nursing, Ltd., we have so far acted in protection of the interests of the Nursing Profession as a whole, the four vital principles for which we contend having been omitted from the drafts. Fighting for principles is not obstruction.

You state further that " A resolution was passed . . . and sent up to the Central Committee for State Registration, which contained a clause dissociating the Society from the College of Nursing . . . but an amendment to secure freedom from " the domination " of the College of Nursing without dissociation from it " was not accepted by the Chair."

May I explain that my Society is not, and never has been, associated with the College of Nursing, and that the amendment to which you allude was not accepted by me as Chairman, as it was proposed by a person who was not a member of the Society, and was therefore not in order.

May I express my appreciation of your statements " we have every confidence in the ability of nurses to settle their own polity without help from outside . . . and " Nothing is more certain than that the profession of nursing is likely to undergo profound changes within the next few years, and, provided that it is placed in a position to manage its own affairs plasticity is altogether desirable."

It is this power of self-determination and plasticity for which the organised Societies of Nurses grouped in the Central Committee are contending, and which will be rendered impossible if the College of Nursing, Ltd., and its present restrictive and inelastic Memorandum and Articles of Association are incorporated in an Act of Parliament, bestowing upon it powers exercised in the Medical Profession by three separate bodies, which maintain the balance of power in that profession, *i.e.*, the Royal Colleges of Physicians and Surgeons (Education) the General Medical Council (Registration and Discipline) and the British Medical Association (free action in the body politic).

The Constitution of the College of Nursing, Ltd., (a company of laymen) is calculated to establish a Nursing monopoly, which in our opinion would undermine the professional and economic independence of the Nursing Profession.

We claim in our Bill a democratic and independent Governing Body authorised by Act of Parliament, entirely free from the restrictive Constitution of the College of Nursing, Ltd., and this principle of democratic organisation we must continue to support. Hoping for the sympathy of *The Lancet* for our professional claims.

I remain,
Yours faithfully,
ETHEL G. FENWICK,
President.

As this explanation has not been inserted, the readers of *The Lancet* are left to assume that the members of the Society for the State Registration of Trained Nurses, who have largely inspired, and paid for, the campaign for nursing reform for the protection of the public, and the nursing profession, are contumacious obstructionists, and its President incapable of conducting its business without prejudice.

A most unmerited aspersion upon the public-spirited character of the Society, and one we cannot permit to pass without protest.

WEDDING BELLS.

At the reception held after the wedding of Mr. Cyril Thatcher to Miss Ethel Benjamin, Assistant Commandant of the Women's Legion, the bride was presented by the wife of the Serbian Minister with the Order of the Royal Red Cross of Serbia, in recognition of her services to that country.

PROGRESS OF REGISTRATION IN CANADA.

The Canadian Nurse publishes the good news that after nearly six years of preparation and attempts to get it, " the Nurses' Registration Act has been passed in British Columbia, and she now joins the rest of the Western Provinces in such recognition." One interesting feature about the support given to the Bill was the very general feeling among members that, by having established affiliation, the evident attempts of the Graduate Nurses' Association to help the smaller hospitals formed a good reason for passing the Bill. The Bill was introduced as a Public Measure, and was generally recognised as a protection to the public as well as the graduate nurse.

The Act seems a thoroughly sound one, and follows closely the principles laid down in the Central Committee's Bill in this country—Independent Governing Body, three years' term of training, protected title, affiliation of special hospitals, and a ten-dollar (£2) registration fee. Good. Hearty congratulations to our Canadian colleagues.

COLLEGE OF NURSING, LTD.

Centres of the College have been formed at Derby and Bristol. At the latter centre Sir Arthur Stanley stated that the local centre would include the adjoining counties, and everything would be done to encourage its power of initiative. At the moment they were not bothering about big buildings in London, but they did need an annual income of about £5,000, which they hoped to secure by means of an endowment fund of £100,000. Sir Arthur then announced that six prominent laymen had consented to serve on the finance committee, so the system of placing the laity in charge of the money means placing the practical control of these local centres in their hands. Nothing can be more stultifying to "initiative" on the part of the nurses than to deprive them of the financial control of their own affairs. But this is the College policy throughout. There is no truer proverb in our language than "those who hold the purse-strings call the tune." All the College nurses need do is to toe the line.

THE IRISH NURSING BOARD.

At the meeting of the Irish Nursing Board, held on July 12th, the following seven members were elected by ballot as the Executive Committee, to hold office for three years :—Miss Huxley, Miss Carson Rae, Dr. Kirkpatrick, Miss O'Flynn, Miss Ramsden, Miss Reeves, Miss Kearns. Colonel Sir Arthur Chance, F.R.C.S.I., was elected Chairman of the Board for the ensuing year.

The Board have every reason to be satisfied with the first year's work. Nurses have joined in numbers, fully realising the value of a strong Register to support them, and of the Irish Nursing Board to look after their interests when Parliament grants State Registration of Nurses.

PRESENTATION.

Miss Ellen Chippindale, on leaving the Clapham Maternity Hospital, of which she has been Matron for six years and Sister for five years, was presented, on July 12th, by past and present nurses with a silver tea-tray and tea kettle and stand.

Her departure is very deeply regretted by all who have worked with her or had the privilege of training under her. She also received other gifts.

APPOINTMENTS.

MATRON.

District Hospital, Newbury. — Miss Phœbe Jones has been appointed Matron. She was trained at the Royal Infirmary, Liverpool, and has been Sister at No. 2 Red Cross Hospital, Rouen ; Night Superintendent at the British Red Cross Hospital, Netley ; and Matron at Groesynyd Hospital, Conway.

NIGHT SUPERINTENDENT.

Welsh National Hospital, Netley.—Miss Emily Godfrey has been appointed Night Superintendent. She was trained at the York County Hospital, and subsequently held the position of Sister in the same institution, and that of Night Superintendent at the Royal Infirmary, Perth.

THEATRE SISTER.

North Lonsdale Hospital, Barrow-in-Furness.— Miss Alys M. Hatton has been appointed Theatre Sister. She was trained at the Royal Salop Infirmary, Shrewsbury, has been Night Sister and Sister at the General Hospital, Walsall, and Sister at the Miller General Hospital, Greenwich, and at the Red Cross Hospital, Sandivery, Cheshire.

SISTER.

Ormskirk Military Hospital.—Miss Nellie Walton has been appointed Sister. She was trained in general nursing at St. Luke's Hospital, Halifax, and in Fever Nursing at Morton Banks, Keighley.

SECOND MASSAGE SISTER.

Leicester Royal Infirmary.—Miss Ella H. Cozens has been appointed Second Massage Sister. She was trained at Bristol Royal Infirmary, and holds the certificate of the Incorporated Society of Trained Masseuses.

WELCOME HELP.

The President of the Society for the State Registration of Trained Nurses acknowledges with thanks the following donations to the funds of the Society :—Miss A. E. Hulme, £5 ; Anon., £2 ; Miss F. Sleigh, £1 1s. ; Mrs. Turnbull, £1 1s. ; Miss M. N. Cureton, £1 ; Miss E. J. Hurlston, £1 ; Miss J. C. Child, £1 ; Miss Beatrice Kent, 10s. ; Mrs. G. F. Wates, 10s. ; Miss C. A. Little, 6s. ; Miss L. Huggins, 8s. 6d. ; Miss C. MacCarthy, 6s. ; Miss E. Ross, 5s. ; Miss Macvitie, 5s. ; Miss Lucy Woodrow, 5s. ; Miss Muriel Withers, 5s. ; Miss E. Martin, 5s. ; Miss L. M. Havers, 3s. 6d. ; Miss C. Wright, 2s. 6d. ; Miss F. E. Batt, 2s. ; Miss M. G. Allbut, 1s. 6d. ; Miss McGimpsey, 1s.

NURSING ECHOES.

The beautiful verses which appear in this JOURNAL from time to time, signed " C. B. M.," are written by the sister of the Editor. We note that " Rachel Weeping " has been inserted in a nursing exchange without acknowledgment to THE BRITISH JOURNAL OF NURSING. We are glad to give permission for our exclusive contributions to be re-published by professional journals, but courtesy and the law of copyright demand that their source should be acknowledged.

Mrs. Baines and Miss Imandt, of the Society of Women Journalists, are to be At Home to meet the Colonial Matrons-in-Chief, at 2–4, Tudor Street, E.C., on Thursday, July 18th, from 3.30–6. We surmise this will be a very interesting occasion. We have quite a number of nurse journalists in these days, and many of our matrons have quite the literary touch. The pre-war teas of the Society of Women Journalists were renowned. Alas ! we fear that delectable raisin cake our souls loved no longer graces the menu. Let us hope good-fellowship continues to make up for luxuries of a more material nature.

The Committee of the County Hospital, York, has decided to raise the salaries of the probationers in training from £6, £12, and £16 per annum to £18 and £20 respectively. If they remain on for special experience they will be paid at the rate of £24 for the first six months, and of £40 for the time they act as Sister. The Sisters' salaries start at £40, with £5 war bonus, with a yearly rise up to £50.

Dr. H. C. Cameron, the examiner of probationers at the Portsmouth Infirmary, has reported very favourably on their standard of knowledge.

" As a whole," said Dr. Cameron's report, " and especially in the second and third years, the standard attained by the nurses was uniformly high—higher than I have met with elsewhere."

The Infirmary Committee has decided to admit probationers at the age of 19 instead of 21, owing to the difficulty in obtaining probationers.

The Scottish Nurses' Club in Glasgow, promoted by the Scottish Nurses' Association, is having a wonderful success. £5,000 has been raised, and a capital fund of £10,000 is aimed at. Premises have been obtained at 206, Bath Street, Glasgow, and are being suitably equipped.

Mrs. Strong, formerly Matron of the Royal Infirmary, is giving much personal help with the organization, and Dr. McGregor Robertson is encouraging the nurses to help themselves. This is the right policy where professional women are concerned if success of the right kind is to be attained.

A correspondent sends the following advertisement from the *Glasgow Herald* :—

PROBATIONERS wanted for general training, hospital, 60 beds (North of England), recognised as a training school by the College of Nursing; applicants must be strong, well educated, age 20 to 28 ; salary, first year, £15 ; second, £17 ; third, £20, with a yearly bonus of £5 ; indoor uniform provided after two months.

She thinks it is misleading to young candidates for training, as the College of Nursing, Ltd., cannot possibly know anything of the result of the teaching and training at this hospital.

THE TRAINED WOMEN NURSES' FRIENDLY SOCIETY.

We have pleasure in informing the members of the Trained Women Nurses' Friendly Society that their Committee (owing to careful management) has just invested £1,200 on behalf of their Sick Benefit Fund, so that now their invested savings are nearing £5,000—a splendid result. This proves how thrifty women are in managing public money, and should encourage trained nurses to join their own professional society, and help to pile up an invested fund, so that in the future they can expend the income in extra benefits. Each member should get her friends to join, and prove women's capacity for financial responsibility.

Now that the Insurance Act has been amended, the bad habit of omitting to give notice to the Secretary of illness, sometimes for weeks after the event, must be discontinued by Nurses, as they are only to receive benefit from the day following that on which notice of incapacity is given. Thus a serious loss may be sustained. On the other hand, nurses who continue to break the law must expect to suffer for it. They must learn to be business-like, and not treat an Act of Parliament like a scrap of paper.

THE OVERSEAS NURSING ASSOCIATION.

The twenty-second annual report of the Colonial Nursing Association (now the Overseas Nursing Association) states that in the face of the present difficulties it was hardly to be expected that any new developments in the work would take place. The Committee are, therefore, pleased to record that in three instances requests for nurses in new fields of labour have been met. A Matron and two nurses have been supplied to the British Hospital, Lisbon; a female Head Attendant to the St. Anne's Lunatic Asylum, Trinidad; and two nurses for Government service in what before the war was German East Africa.

The Committee continue to receive encouraging reports of nurses serving abroad. In Nyasaland Miss R. Paterson, Matron of the Government Hospitals, and Nursing Sister A. Pallot have been decorated with the Royal Red Cross, and were mentioned in a Dispatch from Brigadier-General Northey " for their splendid work during the past year." Nineteen additional badges for meritorious service for five years and upwards have been awarded. The Committee record with deep regret the death of two of their nurses on their voyage home to this country on leave. Miss M. Graham, from Southern Nigeria, was a passenger on the ss. "Abasso," torpedoed on May 17th. and Miss M. Poulter on the ss. "Appapa," torpedoed in December last.

Nothing definite appears to have been done towards supplying midwives to the outlying districts of Canada, concerning which proposal there was some strong criticism expressed from Canada last year. The report states :—" It is felt that this matter can only be taken in hand in compliance with the wishes of the Canadian Authorities, but active steps are being taken to make it known that the Association is anxious to lend its aid in the selection and provision of nurse midwives from the Mother Country."

The Dowager Countess Grey, Miss Amy Hughes, and Major D. K. McDowell, C.M.G., R.A.M.C., have been elected to fill vacancies on the committee.

HOSPITAL WORLD.

In consequence of the increasing number of Child Welfare Centres in North London, the Committee of the Great Northern Central Hospital, Holloway, have established a Consultative Centre for Children. Consultations will be on Wednesday and Thursday each week, when children referred from any Welfare Centre in North London will be seen by appointment. At a later date a Clinic for Children will be inaugurated.

LONDON HOSPITAL NURSES.

A lively correspondence has been kept up in the *Times* on the "farming out" of two years' trained nurses at the London Hospital, subsequent to Major Chapple's question on the subject in the House of Commons.

Lord Knutsford, the Chairman, and a keen supporter of the lucrative intensive system of training at the London Hospital, repeats his convictions, and accuses Major Chapple of trickery in the House.

Colonel Maurice, A.M.S., supports in a well-reasoned speech the sound economic claims of Major Chapple.

Then, of course, in butts Sir Henry Burdett, and presumes to " voice the wish of the nursing profession," and " ventures " incidentally " to appeal to the Chairman of the London Hospital " to do justice to the probationary nurses under his control, and abandon the ambiguous system of giving a two years' certificate of training, and supplementing it with a second at the end of two years' private work—a system Sir Henry has supported with vehemence in his nurses' papers, especially when " Bart's " nurses protested against the depreciation of their three years' certificate, when a " Londoner " was thrust upon them as Matron with the lower qualification !

Lord Knutsford returns to the attack on July 11th and 16th, and points out that neither Sir Henry Burdett nor " his son-in-law," Colonel Maurice, " have given any reason why the London Hospital should change its methods." He trots out the well-known fact that both the Matrons-in-Chief—in England and France—of Q.A.I.M.N.S. are " Londoners," but fails to inform the public that he and other officials of the London Hospital have seats on the Nursing Board which made these appointments ! As the dispute is one of the exploitation of the Nursing Profession, Lord Knutsford might very pertinently have invited Sir H. B. to disclose the profits on his nurses' papers, and prove how entirely disinterested has been his connection with our profession for the past thirty years !

Up to date Major Chapple sits on velvet ; he repeats his statements categorically, and no one can disprove them.

Nurses with only two years' experience are certified as " trained " and " farmed out " for the profit of the charity, under a contract for a further two years' service.

It is significant that the emoluments paid to the Matron who originated, and controls, this profitable business are considerably in advance of those of any other Matron in the kingdom.

OUTSIDE THE GATES.

DIED FOR THEIR COUNTRY.

The King and Queen went to St. Paul's to pray on July 13th, with over 4,000 Woolwich munition workers.

The special prayer said by the Bishop of Southwark was : " Almighty God, we commend into Thy hands of mercy the souls of our brothers and sisters who have laid down their lives whilst devoting their skill and industry to the service of their country. Grant that they may be accounted worthy of a place amongst Thy faithful servants in the Kingdom of Heaven; and give both to them and to us forgiveness for all our sins and increasing understanding of Thy will; for His sake Who loved us and gave Himself for us, Thy Son, our Saviour, Jesus Christ. Amen."

There was a moment of great emotion when the King and his people stood and listened to the " Last Post " and Reveille, sounded by the trumpeters of the Royal Regiment of Artillery, " as a tribute to those who in Woolwich munition factories have laid down their lives for their country."

The House of Commons accepted without a division the second reading of the Government Bill for prolonging the life of Parliament for another six months to January 30th, 1919. Then it is to be hoped this tired Parliament will cease to exist, and women have a chance of recording their votes for men of a very different type.

ENEMY ALIENS.
A CLEAN SWEEP.

Mrs. Dacre-Fox, the organizer of the enthusiastic mass meeting held in Trafalgar Square last Saturday in support of a " clean sweep " of Germans at large and in office, had reason to be well satisfied with the spirited determination it evinced. The speakers used good old Saxon English, and the following resolution was passed with loud and prolonged acclamations :—

That this mass meeting regards the proposals made by the Home Secretary on Thursday in the House of Commons as futile and useless to deal with the alien enemy, and refuses to accept any such compromise on the part of the authorities.

It demands the immediate internment of all aliens of enemy blood, whether naturalised or unnaturalised, the removal of all such aliens from every Government and public office, and calls upon the Government to take whatever steps are necessary to put this resolution into effect.

When the resolution was carried, Mrs. Dacre-Fox said she would ask the Prime Minister to receive a deputation in order to convey to him the determination of the meeting to see that no half-measures were adopted by the Government in the treatment of the enemy alien peril.

BOOK OF THE WEEK.

THE SINGER.*

There is enough good material in this book to make two stories and so many interesting personalities that it is impossible to do them justice in a short notice.

Pauline, the singer, is the central figure and her career is full of interesting details.

It was when singing at a country house that she first met Doctor Carnovious, who opened the door for her to all that her ambition had dreamed of. He fell in love with her voice, with her beauty, with everything that belonged to her at that first meeting, and from the first was determined to marry her. But it must be well understood that he was a German, that the time was that prior to the war and that he was in England studying *coast erosion.* It was he who procured for her an introduction to the great Ottenscheiner, who in his turn introduced her at the German Embassy. Although Pauline was as yet unaware of any deep feeling for Carnovious, the thought of another woman in the field of his favour was vaguely distasteful to her. The face of the beautiful Baroness whom her friend Florrie Keppel had designated ' a cat, but a beautiful cat," persisted in Pauline's remembrance when that of others to whom she had spoken was blurred. " What was she to Carnovious or he to her ? And did the answer to either question matter to her who devoted her immediate future to art ? " But of course she married him, because he had determined that she should do so, and she apparently was quite happy with him until she regained from him by a trick the secret code of the disposal of the British Navy, which the beautiful Baroness had obtained for the German Secret Service, of which she and Carnovious were illustrious members. Pauline loved her German husband (strange as may seem to us), but she unhesitatingly tricked him when the honour of her country was at stake.

He condemned her to die by her own hand in consequence, but the same night he was electrocuted, in his study, by a naked wire on his electric lamp. Not by any means an accident, we are led to believe.

The excitement and colour of beautiful Pauline's career is balanced by that of the super-mother, Mrs. Barbacre, to whom we are introduced at the moment that she has selected the golf course as a suitable place for a picnic for her infant son.

Her husband was a novelist, but Mrs. Barbacre's interests were somewhat circumscribed. At irregular intervals she had taken an interest in his later books, but it had more reference to their sales than their composition. It will be possible, therefore, to believe that when Mr. Barbacre announced that he was taking lessons in golf, she did not enquire what golf was, in what manner it was played, or where, but simply said, " How nice. You might pass the mustard."

---

* By W. J. Escott. Blackwood & Sons, London.

So it came to pass that she and her infant settled to their picnic upon the golf course.

"A tall gentleman came rapidly up to her and lifting his cap, said most urbanely :

"You'll excuse me, madam, but might I remove your chair and things to a better place ? "

"Not at all. Oh, don't trouble, please. We are quite comfortable here."

"But the danger, madam, to your little boy !

"Cows ? " said Mrs. Barbacre, looking round in various directions.

"No, no, madam ; golf balls."

"Oh, yes," said she, still bewildered.

"This, madam, is what we call a 'green,' a little over here would be quite safe."

Pretty little slangy Patricia, her young daughter, is the very antithesis of her matter-of-fact mother, but she is a charming little person, and we are glad that she is happy with Jules at last.

"Pat, Cherie, I love you a thousand times more than anyone else in the world."

Jules sealed the betrothal, and so did she.

"How could I ? " said she, blushing furiously. "Now go downstairs and face the music. I am going to change my face."

"Then I shan't marry you," said Jules.

H. H.

MISSING.

Tell me he's dead or dying ; say he stands
Seeking for guidance the warm touch of hands,
Doomed in an instant to eternal night,
With only mind and memory for sight—
For I could cheer him.—But, Lord, quench this drought,
The unfathomable immensity of doubt,
Tell me he's maimed or crippled, torn or blind,
Staring through eyes that show his wandering mind,—
Tell me he's rotting in a place abhorred,—
Not this, not this, O Lord !

—From Poems by Geoffry Dearmer.

WHAT TO READ.

In these days of difficulty in getting books it is well to know of the best, so as not to waste time in reading rubbish. Read, if you can get them, " General von Sneak," by Robert Blatchford ; " Towards Morning," by Miss I. A. R. Wylie ; " That Which Hath Wings," by Richard Dehan ; " On the Edge of the War Zone," by Mildred Aldrich ; " Yellow English," by Dorothy Flatau ; and " First the Blade," by Clemence Dane.

COMING EVENTS.

July 25th.—Central Midwives' Board. Monthly Meeting. 1, Queen Anne's Gate Buildings, Dartmouth Street, S.W.

August 1st.—Central Midwives' Board. Examination in London, Birmingham, Bristol, Leeds, Liverpool. Oral Examination a few days later

LETTERS TO THE EDITOR.

Whilst cordially inviting communications upon all subjects for these columns, we wish it to be distinctly understood that we do not IN ANY WAY hold ourselves responsible for the opinions expressed by our correspondents.

NATIONAL BABY WEEK.

To the Editor of THE BRITISH JOURNAL OF NURSING.

DEAR MADAM,—On behalf of National Baby Week Council I wish to thank you most warmly for the generous help you have given to our work.

Free publicity at a time like this, when space has to be so severely curtailed, can only be given at the cost of real individual sacrifice, and I should like you to realise how deeply my Committee appreciate all you have done.

Yours faithfully,
ERIC PRITCHARD,
Chairman of the Executive Committee.

THE HEALTH OF THE RACE.

To the Editor of THE BRITISH JOURNAL OF NURSING.

DEAR MADAM,—If Dr. Truby King could have brought with him New Zealand skies, open spaces, healthy homes and conditions generally prevailing there, he might have added greatly to his reputation as a " baby saver "—a title which is being claimed for him by the lay press.

But the world is as it is. When he compares figures and conditions in his own country and in this, he will, one hopes, admit that *our* medical men must be given the palm for the reduction of infantile death rate.

They have improved the health of the race in spite of tremendous obstacles ; Dr. Truby King is improving it by harnessing his knowledge to the chariot of a beneficent nature ; aided by social conditions which are the outcome of experience for which we are still paying the price.

L. E. SHERLIKER,
Member, Royal British Nurses' Assoc.

A "NURSE'S BADGE" MISLEADING.

To the Editor of THE BRITISH JOURNAL OF NURSING.

DEAR MADAM,—Since writing to you my letter with reference to the badge which was being sold as the " Nightingale Badge," I have been in communication with the Nurses' Outfitting Association, Ltd., which was selling it, and, as the result of my protest, they have agreed in future to drop the word " Nightingale " from the title of the badge and to call it in future the " Nurses' Badge," and they have added that the badge has always been sold simply as a distinguishing mark for nurses in general.

Whilst it is doubtful whether any nurse can be advised to wear such a badge, which implies no certificate of efficiency but might be interpreted as carrying that certificate, I think it is fair to the Nurses' Outfitting Association to mention that they have met the objection to their using the title " Nightingale." Yours faithfully,

W. H. BONHAM CARTER,
Secretary Nightingale Training School.

WAS IT FAIR TO THE SICK NURSE?

To the Editor of THE BRITISH JOURNAL OF NURSING.

MADAM,—On a recent date, the Matron of a Nurses' Home in London called at a Hospital seeking advice regarding a member of her staff, who is very ill. She was received by the secretary of the hospital, to whom the details of the case were explained. The secretary said there was no bed available for some days, and in any case, the only suggestion she could make was that the sick nurse should attend at the out-patient department on Thursday at one o'clock (presumably with other casuals !) and see the medical officer then.

Does a trained nurse, who has gone under in the zealous performance of her duty in these strenuous times, not merit a little more privacy and delicacy in seeking professional advice ? This is the hospital for which your excellent Journal asks subscriptions from all classes of women workers to perpetuate the undying memory of one whom all professional women love, and who would never have meted out such casual courtesy to one of her sisters.

I enclose my card, and remain,

ANOTHER HARD-WORKING SISTER.

[We regret to hear of this treatment of a sick nurse at a Woman's Hospital. Our experience at the General Hospitals has been quite otherwise. Sick nurses are often given preference before the general public, and receive the very best of care and kindness. Sometimes we have asked ourselves the question : " Are medical women and women hospital officials as sympathetic towards nurses as men ? " We should be pleased to hear expert opinion on this point.—ED.]

HUMILIATING HUMBUG.

To the Editor of THE BRITISH JOURNAL OF NURSING.

DEAR MADAM,—I quite agree with the views expressed *re* " Humiliating Humbug," by Beatrice Kent, in your last issue. I am just back from France, a land of horror and sadness, and during my absence many nursing affairs may have changed. I do not know, but one thing I feel sure about is, that we women who have had the honour of nursing the greatest men in the world, both at home and abroad, do not want patronage from Miss Asquith, or charities such as the " Nation's Fund for Nurses."

It is to be hoped that trained nurses will wake up soon and let the nation know who and what we are in this great country of ours. Then, perhaps, Miss Asquith will —— understand and —— leave us alone.

Yours faithfully,

F. M. B.,
B.E.F.

Queen Mary's Hostel for Nurses.

[The whole War Charity scheme to finance the College has been manœuvred during the absence of the flower of the nursing profession on active service. No Bill should be hurriedly passed in their absence.—ED.]

KERNELS FROM CORRESPONDENCE.

" A Sister of Sixty " writes : " Gambols, indeed. I want no idle Society women gambolling on my behalf. Has not the Premier made a most touching appeal to every woman who has the great gifts of youth and strength to go on the land and save the harvest. He says, ' the harvest is in danger,' owing to lack of labour, and ' there is not a moment to lose.' Let young women gambol amongst the hay-cocks and the corn stooks, and later on let them plough and sow and spread manure. Forty years ago I could have given them a lead. If the Queen would express her displeasure with the waste of time by Society girls, and the Royalties refuse to give their patronage to ' gambols,' they would set a popular example and discourage these merry mummers. Anyway I protest with you that the nursing profession should be used as their excuse for frivolity and self-indulgence."

"Australian Sister " writes :—"As you advised, I attended the mass meeting in Trafalgar Square on Saturday, in support of interning Huns high and low. The speeches were hot and strong, but it is a pity the men and women who governed this country for ten years before the war were not in the crowd to hear what the man and woman in the street think of them. ' Hang the lot,' was the import of their suggestions—and in very ugly language with plenty of groans. I was surprised and pleased to hear calls for ' Hughes.' ' Give us Hughes ! ' ' Hughes is the man ! ' ' Hughes would soon settle their hash ! " I gathered some high-placed alien had to do with court-martials. This seemed infuriating to the boys in blue. ' Just you wait till the boys come home ; they'll soon hoof out the Hun and the men who have kept him in office ! ' One and all of the crowd spoke of bribery and corruption, and to hear them swear that oath proposed by the Mayor of Bury-St. Edmunds did one's heart good, and the women were as deep-throated as the men."

REPLIES TO CORRESPONDENTS.

Correspondent, Wimbledon.—The names of lady chemists who take pupils in dispensing can be obtained from the Secretary of the Pharmaceutical Society, 17, Bloomsbury Square, W.C. At the close of a three years' apprenticeship the student can enter for the " Minor " examination of the Pharmaceutical Society, the passing of which gives the legal right to dispense and sell poisons, and to use the title of " Chemist and Druggist " or " Pharmacist."

OUR PRIZE COMPETITIONS.

July 27th.—What are the chief racial poisons ? What steps should be taken to prevent and counteract their effects ?

August 3rd.—How may the play of children be directed so as to be a means of education ?

The Midwife.

THE MIDWIVES ACT AMENDMENT BILL.

On July 9th, in the House of Lords, the Report of Amendments to the Midwives Bill was received. The district councils are evidently still struggling to retain the right to act as Local Supervising Authorities. It will be remembered that in Committee the following Amendment was inserted at the instance of the Marquess of Salisbury as " Clause 12 " :—

" Section nine of the principal Act (which enables county councils to delegate their powers and duties to district councils) shall be repealed." An amendment to this Clause, moved by Lord Salisbury, has now been adopted which materially weakens it :—
" Provided that where, at the commencement of this Act, any powers or duties have been delegated, such delegation shall not be affected." To this amendment, on the third reading of the Bill on July 16th, Viscount Peel moved a further one :—
" Unless, on the representation of the County Council concerned, the Local Government Board otherwise direct."

The existing cases of delegation affected by this amendment are four.

The Bill was read a third time and passed.

THE MATERNITY AND CHILD WELFARE BILL.

The Maternity and Child Welfare Bill was debated at length in Committee in the House of Commons on July 9th, and read a third time and passed in that House on July 12th. The long discussion in Committee centred mainly round the question whether the powers given under the Act should be conferred on both large and small authorities, or whether it was desired to limit the use of these powers to boroughs of more than 50,000 population. Eventually it was decided that the County Councils in England and Wales exercising powers under this Act or under Section two of the Notification of Births (Extension) Act, 1915, should establish maternity and child welfare committees, and may delegate to such committees, with or without restrictions or conditions, as they think fit, any of the powers under either Act, except the power of raising a rate, or borrowing money.

EUGENICS.

A selection of striking posters shown at the recent Baby Week Exhibition at Westminster were illustrative of inheritance of ability, inheritance of defect, causes of infant deaths, insanity in the relation to heredity ; also of the various aspects of syphilis—as the result of heredity, of infection, &c. —and a study of worthy parentage.

BABIES OF THE EMPIRE.

On Tuesday in last week the Right Honble. W. F. Massey, P.C. (Prime Minister of New Zealand), presided at the opening of the Babies of the Empire Mothercraft Training Centre, 29 and 31, Trebovir Road, Earl's Court, S.W. The Babies of the Empire Society, of which Lord Plunket is Chairman, and Dr. F. Truby King, C.M.G., Medical Director, has its headquarters in the General Buildings, Aldwych, W.C. 2. Its objects are (1) To uphold the Sacredness of the Body and the Duty of Health ; (2) To acquire accurate information and knowledge on matters affecting the health of Women and Children , and to disseminate such knowledge ; and (3) To train specially, and to employ qualified nurses, whose duty it will be to give sound, reliable instruction. advice and assistance on matters affecting the health and well-being of women, especially during pregnancy and while nursing infants . . . with a view to conserving the health and strength of the rising generation, and rendering both mother and offspring hardy, healthy, and resistive to disease ; (4) To co-operate with any present or future organisations which are working for any of the foregoing or cognate objects.

At the Mothercraft Training Centre the main idea is to give a sound, simple, thorough grounding in the every-day needs of home and nursing. The desire is to make the course practical, helpful, and domestic, to encourage and stimulate commonsense and resourcefulness, and to render the knowledge conveyed as interesting and as widely applicable and adaptable as possible. The Matron is Miss A. Pattrick, and the Staff Sister Mrs. Cowey.

THE CARE OF MOTHER AND CHILD.

Under the auspices of the London County Council, which is the Local Supervising Authority for midwives in the county, Dr. Truby King is giving two courses of lectures on the Care of Mother and Child with special reference to the work of midwives, one at Birkbeck College, Bream's Buildings, Fetter Lane, E.C., the next lecture being given on July 22nd at 4 o'clock, and the other at Morley College, Waterloo Road, S.E. 1, where lectures will be given on July 18th and 24th at 4 o'clock. They will be illustrated by Lantern Slides and Practical Demonstrations.

A report compiled by the Local Government Board on information derived from German sources shows that the fall in the birth-rate in Germany during the three years, 1915-17, was equivalent to the loss of 2,000,000 babies.

THE
BRITISH JOURNAL OF NURSING
WITH WHICH IS INCORPORATED
THE NURSING RECORD
EDITED BY MRS BEDFORD FENWICK

No. 1,582.   SATURDAY, JULY 27, 1918.   Vol. LXI

EDITORIAL.

THE ARMY SCHOOL OF NURSING IN THE UNITED STATES.

Immediately America came into the War the leading nursing experts were on the *qui vive* to evolve a plan which would meet the needs of the stricken troops and provide them with trained skilled nursing. These ladies had watched with intelligent interest the progress of military nursing in Europe, and in its disorganised methods found little to emulate outside the Imperial and Territorial Nursing Services. Beyond these well-disciplined Services—our amateur Red Cross nursing system—placing the skilled work of the professional worker under the direction of the untrained commandant—was condemned *in toto*. The Nursing Department of the American Red Cross is superintended at Washington by an experienced Matron, Miss Jane A. Delano, R.N., who has had the very best medical and nursing support in the further organization of her department, and after the appointment of Miss Annie Goodrich, R.N., as Chief Inspecting Nurse of the Army Hospitals in the Surgeon-General's Office, Washington, D.C , Miss Delano and Miss D. E. Thompson, R.N., of the Army Nurse Corps, U.S.A., have worked to evolve a complete system of nursing for the Army in the field.

At the recent Convention at Cleveland, two important Papers were presented— one by Colonel W. H. Smith, which represents Miss Goodrich's plan, the other, entitled "A Nursing Crisis," by Dr. Goldwater, which advocated the employment of nurses' aides as they have been trained for the past three or four years through the educational committees of the Red Cross. Great satisfaction has been given throughout the American nursing world by the authorization, by the Secretary of War upon the recommendation by the Surgeon-General of the Army, of the establishment of the Army School of Nursing, evolved by the leading Nursing Superintendents and supported by Colonel W. H. Smith.

This School will put into operation a plan whereby the sick and wounded men in military hospitals will receive care through the method that has been found most effective in the civil hospitals. The course is to extend over a period of three years.

The military hospitals will provide experience in surgical nursing, including orthopedic, eye, ear, nose, and throat ; medical, including communicable, nervous, and mental disease. Experience in the diseases of children, gynecology, obstetrics, and public health nursing will be provided through affiliations in the second or third year course.

Lectures, recitations, and laboratory work, will be given in the required subjects, each hospital assigned as a training camp having its staff of lecturers, instructors, and supervisors, and teaching equipment. To be eligible for the Army School of Nursing candidates must be between 21 and 35 years of age, in good physical condition, and of good moral character. They must be graduates of recognised high schools or present evidence of an educational equipment. Credit of nine months, or approximately an academic year, will be given to graduates of accredited colleges. No tuition fee is required.

In many of the military hospitals are to be found men and women prominent in the medical and nursing world through whom the School is assured of a strong faculty, and the following advisory council appointed to advise concerning the general policy assures its success :—

Colonel W. H. Smith, chairman ; Colonel C. L. Furbush ; Colonel W. T. Longcope ; Miss M. Adelaide Nutting ; Miss Lilian D. Wald ; Miss Anna C. Maxwell ; Miss Dora

E. Thompson, the Superintendent of the Army Nurse Corps; Miss Lenah S. Higbee, the Superintendent of the Navy Nurse Corps; Miss Jane A. Delano, the Director of the Department of Nursing, American Red Cross; the President of the American Nurses' Association; the President of the National League of Nursing Education; the President of the National Organization of Public Health Nursing; and the Dean of the Army School of Nursing.

We congratulate the Surgeon-General on calling to his aid the representatives of all the leading Nurses' Organizations in the United States. Brains and Patriotism count some in America!

FOR DAUNTLESS FRANCE.*

(Concluded from page 43.)

THE RECORD.

"The Record" (Part II of Mr Laurence Binyon's book) deals with the Convoys, the Hospitals, the Canteens, and Relief Work in the Devastated Zones.

THE CONVOYS.

It became known in England in the early months of the war that more ambulances for the wounded were urgently required for the French Army's unprecedented needs. The Automobile Association at once appealed to their members to provide touring cars which might be converted into ambulance cars. As a result 250 cars were offered and about 200 were found suitable for conversion and shipped to France, and a large number who could not provide cars subscribed over £6,000. Of one mobile unit we read: "The devoted work of the unit was warmly appreciated, not only for the 'swiftness and comfort,' with which the wounded were carried, but for the 'spontaneity and warmth' of the English offers of aid. A French Army doctor wrote to thank the unit's commander for the 'precious help' it had given. The British ambulances had transported more than one hundred and fifty wounded to Amiens and to Doullens in three days. 'By this action,' the doctor wrote, 'you have greatly relieved our own convoys and secured a very swift and continuous evacuation for the severely wounded, some of whom, I do not scruple to say, will owe their recovery to you.'"

Amongst the ambulances which have done excellent work are those sent out by members of the Society of Friends, who were determined to serve their fellowmen in the struggle though resolved also not to be combatants. The pioneers

* By Laurence Binyon. Hodder & Stoughton, St. Paul's House, Warwick Square, London, E.C.4. 10s. 6d. net.

of the unit chose for their motto "Search for the work that no one is doing; take it, and regularise it later if you can."

Section 3 of the British Ambulance Committee has always been attached to a division in the Vosges. "The Germans were continually trying to block the mountain road by which supplies came up, and by which Section 3 carried down the wounded, by bursting huge shells upon it. . . . At one of the corners on the zigzag bends, directly under the fire of the German snipers, one man of Section 3 was killed and several more were wounded. To prevent repair the Germans constantly burst shrapnel over the road. But in spite of everything the wounded were all brought down safely. And when one remembers how they were formerly carried in springless carts, taking thirty hours to do what a motor ambulance accomplished in two or less, it is easy to imagine the incalculable value of an efficient service of automobiles. The protracted anguish of the long ride, with the constant result of septic poisoning, ended frequently in the loss of lives which are now saved by speed."

A service of motor-cycle side cars used for transporting the wounded over tracks where the ambulances could not run have, we are told, perhaps saved more lives than even the motor ambulances. They are able to go over the steepest and roughest roads, and the Alpine posts or field hospitals on the Vosges front are now all served by them.

In transporting wounded from Verdun, Section 17 found that for men in a state of exhaustion, as they often were when they came down from the trenches, to travel some thirty miles in the lorries over rough roads without any food was to run the risk of an utter collapse. It therefore started a soup kitchen which, until it was no longer required, was kept going night and day. Seventeen thousand bowls of soup were given out, and the timely refreshment made a great difference to the wounded and worn-out soldiers—in some cases, perhaps, the difference between life and death.

In the battle before the Côte de Poivre, Section 1 won the Croix de Guerre for the convoy, and Section 2 (which had had four of its men wounded at Verdun) received eight Croix de Guerre for individual members, and one Médaille Militaire.

We can only mention the convoy work of two groups of Englishwomen—the First Aid Nursing Yeomanry Corps (members of which have recently won distinction for courage and *sang froid* under fire), and the Hackett-Lowther Unit who draw soldiers' rations, and form a military unit like the sections which have been described.

THE HOSPITALS.

A Section is devoted to the hospitals and the supply depôts, for the Comité Britannique—besides sending supplies on its own account—forwards every day consignments of supplies of all kinds needed by the hospitals—the purely French as well as the Anglo-French. These supplies come to the Comité, not only from all parts of the United Kingdom, but from Canada, Australia, New Zealand, South Africa, India, Ceylon, Singapore, Trinidad, Mauritius, Newfoundland, Malta, Gibraltar, and elsewhere.

The French War Emergency Fund, the headquarters of which are at 44, Lowndes Square, London, has an admirable system of ascertaining the needs of the hospitals. A group of ladies in the provinces of France, with a supply of motor cars at their disposal and chosen for their knowledge of the French language and French ways, have a headquarters at some central point of the region they serve. Each of these delegates visits all the hospitals in her region, interviews the Médecin-chef, the heads of the *Pharmacie* and the *Lingerie*, and talks to the nurses; she is thus able not only to bring away a precise list of what each hospital requires, but to form an independent opinion of its merits as well as its needs. The lists of requirements are submitted to a special committee at Lowndes Square; and if the committee is satisfied that the need is real and urgent, precisely those things are packed and despatched forthwith.

For " The Story of the Hospitals " in detail we must refer our readers to the book itself. We would fain quote from it, but pressure on our space forbids, and many of the details have from time to time been already related in this Journal

THE DAY OF AN ORDERLY.

A most interesting chapter is that on " The Day of an Orderly." We commend it to Matrons and Sisters. They may, perhaps, see the vocation of orderly from a different view point henceforth.

One of the duties of the orderlies is to take stretchers to the wards and carry the patients to the operating theatre. The orderly writes :

" Forty-eight hours ago, perhaps, or less, this man was lying out on the churned and shattered slopes of the Mort Homme or Côte 304. . . . I marvel at their fortitude and elasticity. . . . The men we are getting now are mostly Territorials, between thirty and forty in age, who have been flung into the furnace of Verdun. And splendidly have they quitted themselves. These solid, sunburnt, quiet men—no light weight on a stretcher—seem to belong to the very core of the nation which so indomitably and tenaciously is holding the gate of France against the colossal blows of the German armies. They are taciturn, with gentle voices; but they will stand to the last for ' all they have and are '; they will flinch from no suffering or calamity to save their beloved country. It is for them mere matter of course; yet they hate the war. . . .

" Almost all, as soon as they are under the anæsthetic, go back to the battlefield; and you will hear sometimes the yell of the charge— ' Courage, les gars ! En avant, la baionette ! '— and the soldiers, hearing the cry ring out through the window, will listen with a kind of fascination. ' That's just how it is when we attack,' they will say.' "

The orderly thus concludes a modest and most interesting record : " Having set down these common tasks which make up the orderly's day, I feel half ashamed at proffering so trivial a record, when the real work of the hospital, the work of the doctors and nurses, who have not only hard labours to perform with their trained skill, but endless anxious responsibilities, is the story that ought to be told. Alas ! I have not the knowledge for the telling of it; I have only boundless honour and admiration for them and their wonderful work. We orderlies have glimpses only of what that work means, what lives it saves, what suffering it alleviates. We see rather the human side; yet that is my excuse for these pages, since I hope they may reflect something of the qualities of the Poilu whom we love, as we have learnt to know him in his hour of trial and suffering ; gentle in speech, courteous in bearing, constant in fortitude, fervent in the faith of his country's cause."

THE CANTEENS.

A very important and valuable branch of the Red Cross work done by the British for the trench wounded is that of the canteens. Quite early in the war, we are told, an organization for providing canteens for the refreshment of the sick and tired soldiers was set on foot in Paris by a patriotic Frenchman, called ' L'Œuvre de la Goutte de Café.' It was on a small scale on account of the limited funds available ; but the first canteens which it started were so greatly appreciated and so obviously needed that the founder of the Œuvre and his wife, whose hearts were very much in the work—looked about for means to extend it." The Présidente of the Comité Britannique was appealed to. She had a great desire to further the work and it occurred to her that here was at once an outlet for the enterprise and enthusiasm of Englishwomen who wanted to serve France in some way and yet had no specific training or qualification, and a golden occasion for furthering the friendship of the two countries. So it came to be arranged, by mutual consent, that the Comité Britannique should undertake the setting up of additional canteens, and should provide their *personnel*. The work they have done has been invaluable.

The Algerian Arabs, we are told, especially appreciate the coffee, as most of them keep strictly to their religion and never drink the wine which is served out in the barrack rations. The most pathetic men are the Senegalese, as they understand very little French, and seem to be like little children, drawn into a vortex which they do not understand. Like children, though, they are made very happy by very small things.

Elsewhere in the book the story is recalled of a Senegalese found wandering stark naked by a corporal, who proceeded to arrest him. " But it is all right, said the Senegalese, " we have had leave to go out in *mufti*."

RELIEF WORK.

The chapter on " Relief Work in the Devastated Zones " is concerned chiefly with the labours of the Society of Friends. As part of the schemes for providing employment, sewing and embroidery classes have been started and materials provided. One mother told how she heard her daughters, as they sat over their new found occupation, singing for the first time since the war began. And a child of seven confided gravely : " Pour les émigrés, vous savez, c'est désolant ; mais, avec la broderie, on s'ennuiera moins."

IMPRESSIONS.

Part III gives us a series of impressions from a variety of points of view, all interesting. In " A Thought for the Future " we read : " France, like other nations, has experienced what the sinister phrase-makers of Prussia call ' peaceful penetration.' She has experienced a foreign infiltration, professedly friendly, the extent and volume of which she never suspected till suddenly, in a night, she woke to find those myriad dwellers in her cities and country towns, industrious and ingratiating, useful and well-behaved, were smiling thieves of her secrets, priers into her resources and her weaknesses—returning in helmet and uniform as swaggering conquerors to the homes where they had been trusted and subservient, the implements of a patient and laborious perfidy."

Part IV contains a statistical index, a list of war hospital supply depots, and a list of over 7,000 British subjects who have gone abroad on Red Cross and kindred war work for the French up to December 31st, 1917. An admirable arrangement is that names are not mentioned in the text, but in the statistical index at the end of the book full credit is given to the workers.

The literary skill, the painstaking research, and the sympathy with dauntless France, which go to the making of this book, command our whole-hearted admiration ; and we offer our sincere congratulations to Mr. Laurence Binyon on his work. The charming illustrations add to its interest. It is a book to buy and treasure.

E. G. F.

THE ROYAL RED CROSS.

The following ladies were decorated by the King at Buckingham Palace, on July 17th :—

THE ROYAL RED CROSS.
FIRST CLASS.

Queen Alexandra's Imperial Military Nursing Service.—Acting Matron Helena HARTIGAN.
Queen Alexandra's Military Nursing Service for India.—Lady Superintendent Clara CUSINS.

SECOND CLASS.

Q.A.I.M.N.S.R.—Sister Hilda CONNELL, Sister Anne DAWE, Sister Rosina HOOK, Sister Helen PATERSON, and Staff Nurse Christina GUNN.

T.F.N.S.—Matron Alexandra CONNON, Sister Elsie BLACKBURN, and Sister Anne MUSSON.
Civil Nursing Service.—Matron Mary CORT, Matron Helen CROCKWELL, Matron Catherine DAVIES, Matron Elizabeth DAVIES, Matron Edith WILLIAMS, Assistant Matron Annie COTTRELL, and Sister Ellen DEAN.
British Red Cross Society.—Matron Anne CAMPBELL, Matron Lottie DARLEY, Matron Kate JONES, and Sister Alicia CULLINAN.
V.A.D.—Miss Gwendolyn CRAWFORD, Lady CROS-FIELD, Miss Ethel CRUMP, Miss Maud HEATHCOTE, Miss AGNES McDERMOTT, and Mrs. Edith MARSDEN.
Almeric Paget Military Massage Corps.—Sister Margery COOK.
Canadian Army Nursing Service.—Sister Mary ALL-WOOD, Sister Anna BRUCE, Sister Elizabeth CAMPBELL, Sister Katherine DE VELLEFEUILLE, Sister Margaret FEARON, Sister Lillie GALBRAITH, Sister Cicely GALT, Sister Alice GRINDLAY, Sister Phylis GUILBRIDE, Sister Alice HOGARTH, Sister Isabel Holden, Sister Mary HUBBS, Sister Edith LUMSDEN, Sister Jean LYALL, Sister Helena MacCALLUM, Sister Mary MacLEOD, Sister Theodora McKIEL, Sister Annie McNICOL, Sister Martha MORTON, Sister Mina MOWAT, Sister Cecil OATMAN, Sister Mae PRICHARD, and Sister Mary QUIGLEY.

Queen Alexandra received the Matrons and Sisters at Marlborough House after the Investiture.

The King has been pleased to award the Royal Red Cross to the undermentioned ladies, in recognition of their valuable nursing services in connection with the war.

SECOND CLASS.

GRIMBLY, Miss K. A., Staff Sister, Coulsdon and Purley Mil. Hospl., Purley ; GRINDLAY, Miss A. M., Nursing Sister, Can. Nursing Service, West Cliff Can. Eye and Ear Hospl., Folkestone ; GUILBRIDE, Mrs. P., Nursing Sister, Can. Nursing Service, No. 11 Can. Gen. Hospl., Moore Barracks, Shorncliffe ; GUNN, Miss J., Sister i/c., Handsworth Aux. Hospl., Birmingham.

HAGGAR, Miss L., Nurse, Broadwater Hospl., Belstead Road, Ipswich ; HALL-HOUGHTON, Miss M., Sister, T.F.N.S., Bishop's Knoll Sec., 2nd Southern Gen. Hospl., Stoke Bishop, Bristol ; HARROWER, Miss M. I., Asst. Matron, Q.A.I.M.N.S.R., University War Hospl., Southampton ; HATTON, Miss K., Sister, Weir Red Cross Hospl., Balham, London ; HAYHURST, Miss A., Nursing Sister, Can. Nursing Service, No. 10 Canadian Gen. Hospl., Brighton ; HEBERDEN, Miss I. M., Asst. Matron, Great Northern Central Hospl., Holloway Road, N. ; HEMMENS, Miss A. A., Sister, T.F.N.S., 3rd Western Gen. Hospl., Cardiff ; HENDERSON, Miss F. E., Sister, T.F.N.S., 5th Lond. Gen. Hospl. (St. Thomas's), Lambeth, S.E. 1 ; HENRICI, Miss M. L., Matron, The Cottage, Fleetwood Road, Southport ; HENSTOCK, Miss H., Sister, T.F.N.S., 3rd Northern Gen. Hospl., Sheffield ; HEPHERD, Miss M. I., Nurse, White Cross Mil. Hospl., Warrington ; HEYDE, Mrs. E., Matron, Bal-gowan V.A.D. Hospl., Beckenham ; HICKLING, Miss C. J., Matron, Red Cross Hospl., Long Eaton ; HILL, Miss L., Asst. Matron, Q.A.I.M.N.S.R., Belmont Prisoners of War Hospl., Sutton ; HOCKNELL, Miss E., Sister, Q.A.I.M.N.S.R., Military Isolation Hospl., Aldershot ; HODGE, Mrs. E. C., Matron, Passmore Edwards Hospl., Middlesex ; HODGES, Miss F. M., Lady Supt., Baptist School Red Cross Hospl., Yeovil ; HOGARTH, Miss A. G., Nursing Sister, Can. Nursing Service, No. 16 Can. Gen. Hospl., Orpington, Kent ; HOLDEN, Miss I., Nursing Sister, Can. Nursing Service, No. 13 Can. Gen. Hospl., Hastings ; HOWARD, Miss S.,

Sister, Northern War Hospl., Duston, Northampton; HUBBS, Miss M. B., Nursing Sister, Can. Nursing Service, Granville Can. Spec. Hospl., Buxton; HUGHES, Mrs. E., Sister, Red Cross Hospl., Winchester; HUGHES, Miss F. G., Staff Nurse (A./Sister), Mil. Hospl., Endell Street, Long Acre, W.C. 2; HUNT, Miss M., Matron, Welbeck Abbey Aux. Hospl., Worksop, Notts; HUSON, Miss A. R., Sister i/c., St. John's Relief Hospl., Harrow; HUSTON, Miss A., Nursing Sister, Can. Nursing Service, No. 4 Can. Gen. Hospital, Basingstoke, Hants.

IFFLAND, Mrs. M., Matron, City and County Infirmary, Londonderry; IND, Miss H. P., Matron, Gen. Hospl., Stratford-on-Avon; INGLES, Miss A. C., Sister i/c., N.Z.A.N.S., No. 1 N.Z. Gen. Hospl. (Forest Park Section), Brockenhurst, Hants; INMAN, Miss G., Sister, Huddersfield War Hospl.; IRWIN, Miss K. F., Matron, Red Cross Hospl. for Officers, 4, Percival Terrace, Brighton.

JACK, Miss C., Sister, Q.A.I.M.N.S.R., 1st Birmingham War Hospl., Rednall; JACKSON, Miss K. P., Sister, Naunton Park, Cheltenham; JAMES, Mrs. A., Joint Commdt., Aberdare and Merthyr Red Cross Hospl., Merthyr; JOHNSON, Miss M., Matron, Standswood Aux. Hospl., Fawley, Hants; JOHNSTON (*née* Walker), Mrs. L., Sister, T.F.N.S., E. Leeds War Hospl., 2nd Northern Gen. Hospl.; JONES, Miss E. C., Matron, Kingston, Surbiton, and District Red Cross Hospl., London; JONES, Mrs. E. R. G., Commdt., Y.M.C.A. Hospl., Swansea; JONES, Miss M. A., Sister, Bethnal Green Mil. Hospl.

KAYE, Miss A., Matron, Loughborough Gen. Hospl., Leic; KENNEDY, Miss M. C., Nursing Sister, Can. Nursing Service, No. 15 Can. Gen. Hospl., Taplow, Bucks; KIDSON, Miss S. E. A., Matron, St. Luke's War Hospl., Halifax; KNAPTON, Miss E. B., Matron, School Hill Aux. Hospl., Lewes.

(To be continued.)

FRENCH FLAG NURSING CORPS.

We congratulate the Corps on the honourable recognition of the Sisters attached to Ambulance 12/2.

MENTIONED IN DESPATCHES.

The following Sisters have been mentioned in Despatches "for courage and devotion" during the retreat :—Sister Ellen Bennett, Sister Annie Mackinnon, Sister Dora T. Simpson, Sister Mary Richard, Sister Lucy B. Giles, Sister Annie B. Banks, and Sister Gladys Hawthorne.

CROIX DE GUERRE.

Sister Annie Mackinnon has been decorated with the Croix de Guerre—which makes the third Croix awarded to members of the Corps—Sister Hilda Gill and Sister Madeleine Jaffray having been decorated in 1917.

A member of 12/2 Ambulance writes :—" I know you will be pleased to hear that one of our Unit, Sister Mackinnon, has this afternoon been decorated with the Croix de Guerre. We are all delighted that one of our number has received so great an honour.

" It was a great surprise to all of us, as we had heard nothing about it till this afternoon, when we were called to the hospital where the Med.

Principal is, and learned on arrival what was to take place. First our Med. Chef was decorated with the Croix de Guerre, then Sister Mackinnon, for our Unit, and two infirmières, a Dame de France and an American, and all our names were mentioned to the General."

THE CITATIONS.

Mrs. Bedford Fenwick, as Hon. Superintendent of the Corps, has received the following official notification from Le Médecin Inspecteur Lasnet, Médecin de l'Armée, approved by le Général Commandant en Chef, notifying the award of the Croix de Guerre to Sister Mackinnon, together with a copy of the Citation.

Secteur 178.   Q. G. le 14 Juillet, 1918.

MADAME LA PRÉSIDENTE,—

Je me permets de vous adresser ci-joint le relevé des citations à l'ordre du Service de Santé qui viennent d'êtres accordées aux Dames Infirmières de votre Société à l'occasion de leur dévouement et de leur énergie pendant les pénibles opérations du repli de l'Aisne du 27 Mai au 5 Juin.

Leur attitude a été très belle et je vous suis reconnaissant de vouloir bien me donner des collaboratrices, de pareille valeur.

Avec les félicitations que je vous présente en cette occasion, je vous prie de vouloir bien agréer, Madame la Présidente, l'assurance de mes sentiments respectueux et tout dévoués.

LASNET.

CITATIONS

A l'ordre du Service de Santé de l'Armee accordées au personnel des Dames Infirmières de la Société " French Flag Nursing Corps."

Miss Mackinnon Annie (Ambulance 12/2).— " Infirmière qui, dans les circonstances difficiles du repli de l'ambulance, sous la fusillade ennemie, a continué à soigner malades et blessés jusqu'à la dernière minute, avec un courage et un sangfroid remarquables, confirmant ainsi les qualités que tous ses chefs lui ont reconnues depuis trois années qu'elle se dévoue aux soldats français (27–28 Mai)."

Le Médecin Inspecteur Lasnet also sends a copy of the Citation of Miss Marion Pill, who has also been decorated with the Croix de Guerre :

Miss Pill Marion (Equipe Chirurgicale 299/A). —" L'équipe chirurgicale 299/A composée de . . .

. . . .

" Miss Pill Marion—

" A eu le 27 Mai, au poste chirurgical avancé de X . . . . où elle était détachée, une attitude digne des plus grands éloges prodiguant ses soins aux blessés sous un tir de barrage extrêmement violent, se refusant à chercher un abri et contribuant pas sa belle tenue à maintenir le calme parmi le personnel et les blessés."

THE BRITISH JOURNAL OF NURSING offers warm congratulations to both ladies.

CARE OF THE WOUNDED.

THE MACKINNON HOSPITAL.

When Captain Mackinnon, of the London Scottish, went on active service in the early days of the war his wife opened their house at 46, Queen's Gate Terrace, S.W., for the reception of wounded officers. In a few weeks' time Captain Mackinnon was amongst those who fell in defence of King and Empire, and of the freedom of the world, and, ever since, Mrs. Mackinnon has maintained their house as an officers' hospital of twenty beds.

The Sister-in-Charge is Sister Jones-Evans, trained at the Salop Royal Infirmary, Shrewsbury, who shares the day duty with Sister Holland, trained in the same institution. Sister Dixon is on night duty, and seven V.A.D.'s, including two of Mrs Mackinnon's sisters, complete the staff.

Most comfortable and restful the hospital seems to be. On the ground floor is a ward which opens into a lounge. The walls, grey in colour, tone admirably with the pretty flowered curtains, and each white bed has an eider-down covered with bright pink silk, the effect of which is charming, and this colour scheme is carried out throughout the house. On the floor above the French windows of the ward open on to a wide balcony, where are comfortable chairs in which the more convalescent patients can rest while enjoying the fresh air. On this floor, also, is the officers' dining-room, with service room, which has been arranged beyond. A gas stove has been installed, and a sink for washing up, and other conveniences added to make the service of food as easy and perfect as possible.

On the floor above is the operating theatre, which is fitted very completely with up-to-date fixtures, appliances, and instruments.

There are also two single wards used for cases requiring special attention and quiet, or for such potentates as colonels, who like a room to themselves.

On the ground floor, at the back of the house, is a room used by the nursing staff; all the rest are given up to the patients. It has French windows opening on to a small garden, a fact fully appreciated by the three months' old puppy—a Clumber spaniel—whose handsome ears dip, to their detriment, into the saucer of tea which he so appreciates.

That the hospital serves the purpose for which it is designed is amply evinced by the way in which departing convalescents express the hope that if they are again returned to "Blighty" for treatment they may find themselves once more within its hospitable doors. It must be a satisfaction to their hostess that its work is so appreciated.

SISTER JONES-EVANS.

Food for the mind as well as care of the body is a great need of our wounded and convalescent soldiers, and the excellent example set by the Great Northern Central Hospital, in organizing a series of lectures for soldiers warded there, might well be followed by many other hospitals.

"LIBERTY."

The lecture of this series for Friday, July 12th, was given by Mr. Shadrach Hicks, Principal of the Shoreditch Technical Institute. Mr. Hicks said that liberty was one of the spiritual forces which had moved men to noble and useful deeds through all ages. He said that it was a very strong quality in the character of the very earliest inhabitants of these islands, and traced its influence upon the history and development of the British people from the early days of the Witan to the present. He rightly drew attention to the great Charter of 1215, and said that on that rock had been built not only British liberty, but also that of the Great American Republic, as well as of our Dominions beyond the Seas.

The future of the country was in the balance, and liberty in its widest and best sense would enable the people to produce a better standard of living and to develop personal character and the material resources of the Empire to their fullest extent. The men expressed their grateful thanks to Mr. Hicks, who promised to deal on a subsequent date with a similar subject.

Mr. F. Hammond, F.R.I.B.A., delivered the usual weekly lecture in the Military Annexe, on Friday, July 19th. His subject, which was illustrated by slides kindly lent by the Ministry of Pensions, was " The After-Care of Discharged Disabled Soldiers and Sailors "—a national question of first importance.

IN A RUSSIAN DISPENSARY.

The time is 8 a.m., the day Friday, the market day of the large Russian village where the English doctor and nurse are in sole charge of a district of 60,000 people ; in area about the size of Wales. The season is winter, consequently the outside temperature is well below zero, and inside, thanks to the splendid Russian stoves, of a warmth and comfort utterly unknown in England, where we still live under the delusion that our climate is a mild one.

The nurse looks out through the living-room window and notices that already a long string of sledges drawn by small, shaggy horses, whose coats are white with hoar-frost, are waiting outside the dispensary. Market day is our busiest time. Everyone, sick or well, who comes in to buy and sell makes it a point of etiquette to go and see the English doctor and try and wheedle from him some much-coveted " măs " (ointment) or " kaple " (drops), while we shrewdly suspect that our waiting room is made the dumping ground for the old grannies and grandpas whose relatives want to get rid of them while they do their business elsewhere. We live in a wooden house, surrounded by blocks of buildings, one of which is our hospital, another the Aptek or dispensary. They are all about 100 yards from the house, and it is necessary to put on high felt boots, a sheepskin coat, and a thick shawl over one's cap to run even that short distance in the icy cold.

In the dispensary there is already a crowd of moujiks similarly clad. The Austrian dispenser has been giving out tickets in rotation, with a sharp eye on the bright boys of the village, who are shrewd enough to arrive very early for tickets and then sell their places to late-comers at a handsome profit !

The doctor and nurse by now have picked up sufficient Russian to cope with the patients without an interpreter, and enough experience to tell, as they survey the crowd, that, as usual, they fall into three classes—the chronics, the certificate hunters and the really ill. The last-named are the smallest, and, in the eyes of the other patients, the most negligible class. The Russian peasants firmly believe that a headache of 30 years' standing (and they will tell you quite seriously that they have had one continuously for that period) is far more worthy of attention than a high fever of only three days' duration.

But let us begin work, and see some typical instances of the three classes for ourselves. A little Polish refugee girl named Dunia is our doorkeeper, a by no means easy post. Directly she unbolts the portal that separates the doctor's little room from the waiting-room a noise rather like a menagerie assails our ears, and the call of " Number One " is a signal for Nos. 8, 19 and 40 to try and push their way in. Dunia valiantly forces them back, and repeats the call for " No. 1." This time No. 10 comes forward triumphantly, certain that he will be entirely acceptable. " Where is No. 1 ? " repeats our handmaid firmly. " She has gone out to the market, but I am her uncle, I will do as well ; I can tell you all about her," remarks a peasant hopefully. Much surprised is he when his helpful offer is refused and No. 2 is called. Enter No. 2 supporting an aged grandma on one arm and in the other carrying a stout infant, two children clinging to the skirts of her sheepskin coat. With a quick sleight-of-hand movement she drops one ticket into the bowl placed for the purpose and faces us with a guileless smile. " Four more tickets, please," says the doctor, well versed by now in the wiles by which many a woman has endeavoured, under only one ticket, to obtain advice and medicine for an entire family, some of whom were not even present ! " I don't understand," replies the culprit innocently. But this excuse will not wash. " Well thou understandest, thou," retorts the stern Dunia, and the protesting family retires to obtain the needful tickets from the Austrian dispenser.   G. T. W.

OUR ROLL OF HONOUR.

DIED.

Ross, Sister A. J., Can. Nursing Service.

STAR OF MONS.

Some of those entitled to the Star of Mons have now received it, as well as the ribbon which has already been widely distributed, so we may hope, shortly, to see nurses wearing this much-coveted emblem.

A TRUE TALE WITH A MORAL.

" I COULD ILL SPARE IT."

District Nurse visiting house of very poor patient.
Patient (cheerfully) : " Oh ! nurse, I've given a shilling to your Fund."
Nurse (puzzled) : " My Fund ! What do you mean, Mrs. Smith ?"
Patient : " Why the Fund that they are collecting for the nurses, wot you will have some of."
Nurse : " Oh ! you mean the Nation's Fund for Nurses, I expect. No ; I don't approve of the way that it is raised at all. I shall have none of it, and I am quite sure you have many other things to do with your money."
Patient (crestfallen) : " Oh ! nurse, I would never have given to it if I'd 'ave known. I could do very well with that shilling. But you've been rare and good to me, and you would never have anything off of me, and I thought it was a chanst to give you somethin'. But I'd never have given it if I hadn't have thought you'd get some of it, for I could ill spare it."

Royal British Nurses' Association.

(Incorporated by   Royal Charter.)

THIS SUPPLEMENT BEING THE OFFICIAL ORGAN OF THE CORPORATION.

LETTER ACKNOWLEDGING THE CON-GRATULATIONS OF THE MEMBERS OF THE ROYAL BRITISH NURSES' ASSOCIATION ON THE OCCASION OF THEIR MAJESTIES' SILVER WEDDING.

BUCKINGHAM PALACE,
July 6th, 1918.

MADAM,—I am commanded to beg Your Royal Highness to be so good as to convey to the Members of the Royal British Nurses' Association, of which Your Royal Highness is President, the expression of the sincere thanks of the King and Queen for the kind message of congratulation and good wishes on Their Majesties' Silver Wedding, communicated through Your Royal Highness on behalf of the Members and also in the name of the Honorary Officers of the Council.

     I have the honour to be, Madam,
         Your Royal Highness' humble and
            obedient servant,
                 STAMFORDHAM.
H.R.H. the Princess Christian.

A PROPOSED CONFERENCE ON PRESENT-DAY NURSING PROBLEMS.

The Council of the Corporation have under consideration arrangements for holding a Conference in the autumn, which will deal chiefly with the problems of the day in so far as they affect fully qualified nurses.

ROYAL BRITISH NURSES' ASSOCIATION.

It has been suggested that, in one of the early issues of the new official organ of the Association, a very brief account should be given of the ordinary work of the Corporation, apart from the other business—lectures, meetings, &c.

which it undertakes from time to time. Repeatedly it has been stated by the promoters of the College of Nursing, Ltd., that, until this company was founded, there was no organisation of nurses and we hear references frequently to the " inspiration " which led to its foundation. A short scrutiny of its activities up to the present will serve to show that, apart from its form of incorporation and the methods adopted to finance it, its founders ought to have offered their " grateful acknowledgments " to those of the R.B.N.A. so far as any " inspiration " or imagination is concerned. As a matter of fact, however, the College cannot claim to be one of the nurses' organisations, for its Council is representative only of the employers of the nurses, so that the independent working nurses have no voice in the management of the company. Under the by-laws of the R.B.N.A. equal representation is given, on the governing body, to medical men, to matrons and to the working nurses, and therefore it is the fault of the nurses themselves if they do not take their share in the management of their own affairs and make good use of the powers placed in their hands by Royal Charter. In the Council and Executive Committee no expression of opinion is given more courteous consideration or receives more ready sympathy than when it comes from one of the elected nurses.

THE REGISTER.

The Association has kept a Register of Nurses since 1890, and on this are entered full particulars of the training and qualifications of those whose names are, for the time being, inscribed thereon. The fee for registration has been temporarily reduced to five shillings in order to make it easily possible for all fully-qualified nurses to belong to the Association and to use the Royal Charter for their own benefit, and that of their fellow workers.

MEMBERSHIP.

Duly qualified medical men, matrons and superintendents of nurses and those nurses whose names have been placed on the Register of the Corporation are eligible for election as members of the Corporation. In accordance with By-law VIII, the annual subscription is five shillings. For life membership a single payment of two guineas is necessary.

BADGE.

We give, in the present issue, a reproduction of the pretty badge worn by the members of the Royal British Nurses' Association. That of H.R.H. the President is of gold, while past and present members of the General Council wear a silver badge; the ordinary member's badge is of bronze. In each case the design is the same.

DIPLOMA IN NURSING.

The Corporation grants a Diploma in Nursing to such fully qualified nurses as pass a higher examination in nursing. The Royal British Nurses' Association is the only organisation which grants this honour, and, therefore, it takes precedence, in the nursing world, as an educational and academic body at the present time.

STATE REGISTRATION.

The Association is a constituent part of the Central Committee for the State Registration of Nurses and is therefore one of those societies which for years have been promoting the Bill for State Registration. Through its representation on that Committee the powers

THE BADGE.

and prestige, given by the Royal Charter, are used in support of a Bill in every way just both to the public and the nurses.

CO-OPERATION BETWEEN THE MEMBERS.

There are two Private Nurses' Co-operations in London which are maintained solely for Registered Members of the Royal British Nurses' Association; the Members of those societies receive the full fees charged for their services less a small commission for working expenses. The Association also finds a considerable number of permanent appointments for its members throughout the year, and in regard to this it often has the co-operation of the members themselves, as nurses who are giving up their posts frequently put those responsible for appointing their successors into communication with the Secretary. The Australian Branch of the Association also has a flourishing private staff, and Members going out from the parent Association frequently find employment through this.

BENEVOLENCE.

The Helena Benevolent Fund is maintained by the nurses for their fellow-members in times of sickness and distress, as also is the Princess Christian Settlement Home for Aged Members of the Corporation. Each nurse there has a pretty room of her own for the nominal rent of 4s. 4d. annually.

ROYAL RED CROSS.

We learn with pleasure that the Royal Red Cross has been awarded to Sister Sarah Ellen Howard and that she has been commanded to attend at Buckingham Palace on the 31st inst. in order to receive this. Miss Howard, in addition to her certificate in General Training, holds one in Midwifery, and has been a Member since 1910. She has always been enthusiastic in her efforts to attain to the highest possible standard in her professional work and we congratulate her warmly upon this well-earned award.

AN APPRECIATION.

We note with pleasure that, in its report for 1917, the Middlesex Hospital pays a well-earned tribute to Miss Langridge, an early Member of the Royal British Nurses' Association. The report, in placing on record an appreciation of her twenty years' work, states that this was "marked by intense devotion to the patients under her care and all her actions were influenced by a sincerity of purpose and a true spirit of helpfulness which brought bodily comfort and ease of mind to many who turned to her in their hour of trial. She was," adds the report, "an ideal Sister in every sense of the word."

NOTICES TO THE MEMBERS.

Members are requested to return all books borrowed from the Library not later than 31st inst., and, as is customary, the Library will be closed during the month of August.

The Club Room at 10, Orchard Street is open to Members from 10 a.m. until 4 p.m. Various nursing, medical and lay periodicals are available for the use of Members there, but they cannot be circulated from the office by post.

Members are requested to send at once to the Office of the Corporation notices of new appointments, changes of address, &c., in order that those may be inserted on the Register and Membership Roll.

Members may arrange to have their letters addressed to the office and forwarded to them, and those residing abroad may, by special arrangement with the Secretary, use the telegraphic address for communicating with their friends.

Application forms for Registration and Membership can be obtained from the Secretary, 10, Orchard Street, Portman Square, W. 1.

DONATIONS RECEIVED.

The Honorary Treasurer acknowledges with thanks donations from the following:—S. W. Harrison, Esq. (per Mrs. Raikes), £5 5s.; Mrs. Charles Hughes, £5; Mrs. Martin, £1 1s.; Mrs. Raikes, £1 1s.; Miss Hutton (per Miss Cattell), £1.

(Signed) ISABEL MACDONALD,
Secretary to the Corporation.

THE SOCIETY FOR THE STATE REGIS-TRATION OF TRAINED NURSES.

A Meeting of the Executive Committee of the Society took place on July 2nd at 431, Oxford Street, W. Mrs. Bedford Fenwick presided.

The Sixth and Seventh Drafts of the Nurses' Registration Bill drafted by the College of Nursing, Ltd., were considered clause by clause.

The Committee recognised that the firm attitude of the Central Committee in maintaining the vital principles of just legislation in the Nurses' Registration Bill drafted by it in 1910, has apparently convinced the College of Nursing, Ltd., that no agreement between the two Bills was possible until it recognised the determination of the State Registrationists to oppose any attempt to govern the Nursing Profession without adequate representation.

Thus, the College Council (the Nurses have never been consulted in meeting assembled) has inserted provisions in the recent drafts of its Bill :

(1) For the direct representation of the organised Nurses' Societies on the Provisional Council to frame the rules.

(2) For the *security* of representation of the Registered Nurses on the Permanent Council.

(3) For a term of three years' training and examination under a definite curriculum prescribed by the Council after the three years' term of grace.

(1.) The Committee objected to the College of Nursing, Ltd., being incorporated in the Bill under its existing Memorandum and Articles of Association and empowered to govern the whole Nursing Profession in the United Kingdom, as it is a lay Corporation, and gives undue power of control to the Nurse-Training Schools over registered Nurses, for whom they are not financially responsible. The Committee claims for the Profession of Nursing an independent governing Body in the General Nursing Council, with no ultimate power and control behind it, such as the Bill secures for the College of Nursing, Ltd.

(2) The Committee also strongly deprecates the undermining of the status of the General Register of three-years' trained general nurses by the Clause in the College Bill, providing for the institution of Supplementary Registers of Specialists—such as Children's Nurses, Fever Nurses, Tuberculosis Nurses, Maternity Nurses, &c.—as such registers would be compiled for the benefit of institutions and employers, and not of nurses themselves, who, semi-trained, would be ineligible for promotion to the best work and pay.

(3.) The Committee also took exception to preferential treatment for nurses on the register of the College of Nursing when a Bill becomes law. It agreed that all trained Nurses should have equal rights to registration during the term of grace.

The Committee intends to uphold these vital principles.

The Committee received with deep regret the resignation of Miss Elinor Pell-Smith, who had been the delegate of the Royal Infirmary Leicester Nurses' League for a number of years.

It was proposed from the Chair that a sincere vote of thanks be sent to Miss Pell-Smith, thanking her for her very valuable services during the long time she had been on the Committee, and expressing the regret of the Committee in losing her most kind help. This was unanimously agreed to.

Miss Irene Sumner, who had been appointed to represent the Royal Infirmary Leicester Nurses' League, was present, and received a cordial welcome.

New members were elected.

MARGARET BREAY,
Hon. Secretary.

LONDON HOSPITAL NURSES.

Major Chapple, M.P., has given notice in the House of Commons of the following motion :—

" That the system carried on at the London Hospital, under which nurses are taken from their training in the wards at the end of their second year, sent out to attend private cases, paid at the rate of 13s. per week while they receive £2 2s., the hospital appropriating the difference of 29s. per week earned by them, is adopted by no other great hospital in Britain, gravely interferes with the professional training in the wards of such nurses during their third and most important year, and is a cruel exploitation of women for the sake of pecuniary gain, and this House calls upon the Government to introduce legislation to remedy the abuse."

Lord Knutsford has again written to the *Times* denying the truth of Major Chapple's statements, and Sir Henry Burdett has cast his sucking dove attitude, and now states that Lord Knutsford's reply to his letter " is mere camouflage."

But whilst these well-known exploiters of the nursing profession fly at one another's throats, the nurses themselves either remain dumb, or their opinions are excluded from the discussion as usual.

The nursing profession at large are somewhat out of patience with London Hospital nurses. They are not children, and it is time they realised that, by accepting unjust conditions, they injure their colleagues as a whole : (1) by undermining the recognised nursing standard of three years' training ; and (2) by themselves, insufficiently trained, competing with their efficiently trained colleagues in private nursing for the same fees, and thus sapping their economic status. To be plain, this conduct, in trade-union parlance, constitutes the "blackleg," and it is high time conscientious and courageous members of the nursing staff at the London Hospital made it plain to the Matron and Committee that they can no longer tolerate being placed in such an invidious position. It is now upwards of a quarter of a century since the redoubtable Miss Yatman exposed this commercial system of exploiting the nurses' training and earnings at the London Hospital before a Select Committee of the House of Lords, and although the late Lord Kimberley described it as "almost fraudulent," social influence has been permitted by Parliament to continue it till this day. London Hospital Sisters and Nurses, we your colleagues call upon you to come out and purge the profession of the abuses to which you have so long submitted—to *our* injury as well as your own.

The medical staff also might give a helping hand.

THE COLLEGE OF NURSING LTD., AND LONDON HOSPITAL STANDARDS.

It should be of interest to nurse members of the College to realise that in defining standards for the College "Register," a special clause was inserted to include London Hospital nurses, "with two years' training and two years' service." Thus the College Council protects the commercial interest of the Hospital, as against that of its exploited probationers. As the whole Council is composed of hospital officials (including employers), the danger of their policy in this instance is apparent.

This is why the independent Nurses' Organizations demand an independent and representative Governing Body, and mean to work for it.

Many of their members feel that the Matrons on the Council have failed to protect their professional interests.

THE SHEFFIELD CENTRE.

A Centre of the College of Nursing is being formed in Sheffield, and Miss Hancox, of the Queen Victoria Nursing Association, Glossop Road, Sheffield, and Miss Bolton, of the Jessop Hospital, have consented to act as Hon. Secretaries.

We hope these ladies have read the Memorandum and Articles of Association of the College, and are prepared to have them eliminated from the Bill. We make this remark because we have never yet met a nurse member who has seen the constitution to which she has subscribed.

APPOINTMENTS.

NIGHT SISTER.

Bridge of Weir Consumption Sanatoria, Scotland. —Miss Eleanor Harvey has been appointed Night Sister. She was trained at the Leeds Township Infirmary, and has held the position of Staff Nurse in that institution, and at the Leeds Sanatorium, Gateforth.

SISTER.

The Sanatorium, Middlesborough. — Miss A. Lilley has been appointed Sister. She was trained at the South Shields Borough Hospital, and has been Staff Nurse at Deans Hospital in the same place, and Night Charge Nurse at the West Lane Hospital, Middlesborough.

General Hospital, Nottingham.—Miss J. Morgan has been appointed Outpatient Sister. She was trained at the General Hospital, Wolverhampton, and has been Night Sister at the General Hospital, Weston-super-Mare, and Ward Sister and Sister in the X-Ray Department at the Hospital, Rugby.

HOUSEKEEPING SISTER.

General Hospital, Nottingham. — Miss Edith Gething has been appointed Housekeeping Sister. She was trained at the East Suffolk Hospital, Ipswich, where she has held the position of Outpatient Sister. She has also been Night Sister at the Royal Gwent Hospital, Newport; and had housekeeping training at the Norfolk and Norwich Hospital.

QUEEN VICTORIA'S JUBILEE INSTITUTE.

TRANSFERS AND APPOINTMENTS.

Miss Helena Mathieson is appointed to Norfolk N.F. as Assist. Co. Superintendent; Miss Ethel Daniells to High Wycombe; Miss Constance M. Deering to Hampstead Garden Suburb; Miss Margaret Heritage to Chatham; Miss Edith Matthews to Hampstead; Miss Edith A. Richardson to Brixton.

"THE MECCA OF THE THRIFTY."

The establishment of Thomas Wallis & Co., Ltd., Holborn Circus, London, E.C., is a well-known landmark to Londoners, for there are few busses plying on the main route from the City to the West End which do not draw up in front of it. The firm have for many years been contractors for hospital furnishing, and recently they were selected to furnish the Edith Cavell Home for Nurses at the London Hospital. It has also an extensive *clientele* in connection with its department for Nurses' Uniforms and Outfits; and the reasonable prices which prevail have earned for it the sobriquet, "The Mecca of the Thrifty."

Among the gifts at Queen Mary's Royal Naval Hospital, Southend, was a cheque for £100 from Queen Mary.

NURSING ECHOES.

The Council of Queen Victoria's Jubilee Institute for Nurses, in their Report for the year 1917 to the Patron, Her Majesty Queen Alexandra, report " satisfactory progress, notwithstanding the extremely difficult conditions caused by the war. The chief developments have again been in connection with the work in country districts and with the County Nursing Associations in particular; but a considerable increase has been shown in the number of Associations affiliating with the desire to employ Queen's Nurses; and no doubt the number would have been larger had it not been for the shortage of nurses. At the end of the year, 592 Queen's Nurses were on leave for service in connection with the war, and the supply of candidates for training shows no improvement. Every effort is being made to secure the services of nurses who are not required for war nursing, but the number of these available is small, and it is not anticipated that there will be any great increase until the war ceases. Steps are under consideration to organize the training of more Queen's Nurses, so that the machinery may be in order when nurses are set free from War Service.

" The Local Government Board has again co-operated with the Nursing Associations, by means of the grants given for midwifery work, with the object of securing the provision of a satisfactory service of midwives for country districts. It is essential that there should be an adequate supply of well-trained and efficient midwives to check the wastage of infant life. . . . These nurses can also act as school nurses and health visitors."

The supply of efficient midwives is most essential, but unless they are trained as nurses, and conform to the standard for Queen's Nurses, *i.e.*, three years' general and six months' district training, they should not, in our opinion, be enrolled in Nursing Associations with the prestige of the Queen Victoria's Jubilee Institute for Nurses. Their work is sufficiently extensive and important to be organized in County Midwifery Associations, whether under the authority of the " Queen's " or otherwise. " Village nurse-midwives " have their status under the Midwives' Act, but their nursing is an amateur and unknown quantity, and the suggestion that these midwives can act as school nurses is not one which can be supported.

It is disquieting to find that the number of " Village Nurses " employed by County Nursing Associations affiliated to the Institute is 1,327, while the total number of Queen's Nurses in England on December 31st, 1917, was 1,357, including Queen's Nurses who are undertaking duty in connection with the war, of whom there were 592 in the United Kingdom. The total number of Queen's Nurses in the United Kingdom on December 31st, 1917, was 2,056.

There have been two new features in the constitution of the Council appointed by Queen Alexandra during the year. For the first time the Superintendents of the Training Homes, and the Superintendents of the County Nursing Associations have each been allowed to appoint a representative.

Her Royal Highness Princess Louise visited the Kensington Infirmary on Friday last, and expressed her warm admiration at all she saw. The Princess was received by the Chairman, the Chaplain, and the Matron. After visiting the beautiful Church of St. Elizabeth, Her Royal Highness passed through the wards, and chatted with the patients.

The " At Home " to meet the Colonial Matrons-in-Chief, held by the Society of Women Journalists at 2–4, Tudor Street, E.C., on July 18th, was a great success. Mrs. Baines and Miss Imandt were the hostesses, and together with the President, Miss Billington, welcomed the guests. Australia, Canada, New Zealand, South Africa, and the United States of America were represented, and we noticed all sorts of interesting people present, including leading women journalists, all apparently warmly interested in cementing friendship with our overseas nurses, whilst the Matrons-in-Chief expressed the opinion that " it does us a lot of good to come into touch with all these bright women—whose sphere of work is different to our own. We are apt to get a bit narrow in the nursing world." We are bound to admit we found nothing narrow in the views of our overseas Matrons, who one and all appear inspired not only with professional zeal, but with a liberal outlook on life.

The Asylums and Mental Deficiency Committee of the London County Council reported at its meeting on Tuesday that as a war measure it has been necessary to employ women on agricultural and farm work at the mental hospitals. Some nurses have been so employed, and have received a special rate of pay while doing farm work. As there is such difficulty in obtaining nurses, and as it now seems possible to obtain from other sources the services of women for work on the land, the committee think it undesirable to second nurses wholly for farm work, and have directed that they shall no longer be so employed.

The Committee have granted extra duty pay to a large number of members of the nursing staff at the Banstead mental hospital.

The Hon. Albinia Brodrick's pamphlet, "Professional Development and Organization," is on sale, price 2d., at the office of the National Union of Trained Nurses, 46, Marsham Street, London, S.W. 1, the keynotes of which are Democracy, Comradeship, Organization. Every nurse should own it, study it, and live up to it.

Miss Grace Ross Cadell, L.R.C.P., L.R.C.S., late of Edinburgh, left £1,000 to the Queen's Nurses in Scotland, and £300 to the Leith Branch of the Queen's Nurses—a legacy which will bring comfort to many a sick body.

LEGAL MATTERS.

A case involving important principles was recently brought by the Norfolk Nursing Federation, in regard to a broken agreement, the defendant being Miss Rose Snelling, of 20, Junction Road, Norwich.

Mr. F. A. Bainbridge said the Federation was a charitable institution, to obtain suitable candidates and train them as village nurses. The vice-presidents were ladies and gentlemen of leading position and standing in Norfolk. There were two agreements, one for training at Plaistow, under which £24 0s. 11d. was claimed for non-fulfilment. Under the second the defendant was " to become a trained nurse at the Norwich Isolation Hospital," but left before completing her training.

The judge held that the first agreement could not stand. It was superseded by the second. In this he gave judgment for 30s.

The necessity for the statutory definition of a standard of what constitutes a trained nurse is manifest in this case. Certainly training at Plaistow—for the most part in district midwifery—and in a fever hospital, does not do so. " Ladies and gentlemen of leading position " would do well to refrain from interfering with the economic and professional standards of candidates for a skilled profession, unless they are prepared to enforce a just standard of training, which qualifies the nurses for their responsible duties, and enables them to compete with others in the open market.

THE PAPAL SCHOOL OF NURSING.

We quote the following interesting article on the Papal Nursing School from *The Universe* of a recent issue. The training of nuns in the science, in conjunction with the practice, of nursing, is one of the most progressive and necessary reforms amongst Religious Orders. We know how in the past the good Sisters in hospitals have excelled in the care of the cuisine and the linen; for the future every facility should be provided for them to care intelligently for the body in health and disease.

" The autumn and winter course of training for outside pupils at the Papal School of Nursing, our Rome correspondent writes, has come to its conclusion with the examinations at the end of Lent, and after Holy Week the Spring course opens. The existence of this school is still unknown to the majority of Catholics, yet its institution ranks easily among the greatest works of Pius X's Pontificate. As the founder and organiser of the school said to me on the morning when she was kind enough to take me over it : ' How many people are aware of the fact that His Holiness Pius X collected the Statutes and Constitutions of every religious nursing Order in the Church, in order to study the best means of providing facilities for their members to follow a modern training and pass up-to-date examinations while yet living in accordance with their rule, and that the record of this research is filed in the secret archives of the Congregation of Religious?'

This is briefly the history of the school. In 1904 (during the first year of Pius X Pontificate) a certain French lady, who had devoted her life to hospital organisation in her own country and had just completed the foundation and equipment of the Hôpital St. Joseph in Paris, was paying her annual visit to Rome. In a private audience she asked a blessing on her work, of which she gave an account to His Holiness. The Holy Father, after enquiring into every detail, asked her to stay in Rome and take charge of a training school he wished to organise, in which members of religious Orders could obtain an up-to-date training in the right spiritual conditions. This she was unable to do, but she promised to return the following year, when she would have finished the work she was engaged on in France. She was true to her word, and in 1906 the school was opened on a very modest scale in temporary quarters in the *Prati*. It grew and prospered, and in 1912, funds being assured, its own building was begun under the shadow of St. Peter's next to but independent of the Hospital of Sta. Marta. The outbreak of the war has temporarily suspended the progress of fitting up the building, as the quarters which were destined to the ' in patients ' have been handed over to the 'Cross of Malta' for wounded soldiers, but the work of the dispensary is in full swing. There is a resident staff of trained nurses in charge, working under some of the best doctors here, and already representatives of twenty-seven different nursing Orders have gone through their training there. The dispensary is always crowded with ' out patients ' of every age and sex, and suffering from every variety of human complaint. The operating-rooms, sterilisation plant, bandage department, sanitation, &c., are irreproachable, and the names of the doctors in attendance warrant the excellence of the surgery. After the war there will be accommodation for in-patients under medical and surgical treatment, with a larger operating theatre and more extensive accommodation for the subjects under training. It will then be possible to receive at least two members of any given Order to ensure the maintenance of their religious life. The chapel is already in use, and on its wall hangs the autograph blessing and approval of the present Holy Father. There is also a course of training in dispensing and first aid for ladies and girls. The course, theoretical and practical, is conducted by excellent doctors and lasts four months; it is concluded by an examination, on passing which a certificate is granted.

The attention of His Holiness Pope Pius X was first drawn to the need of a reform in the practical training of the older nursing Orders by the fact that while he was still Patriarch of Venice, a surgeon in one of the hospitals there protested against the removal of one of the nuns assisting in the operating theatre, for the reason that no one of the other sisters was capable of replacing her in the theatre.''

OUTSIDE THE GATES.
THE ENEMY ALIEN DANGER.

' Now that the people are beginning to realise the fine mesh of the financial net in which Hun bankers and millionaires in this country are strangling our national life and liberties—and what the " Hidden Hand " really means—they are becoming inspired with a deep and smouldering fury against the political system which has placed the Empire in such danger, and are slowly but surely rousing themselves to action. The Prime Minister has refused to receive a deputation on the enemy alien question, proposed by Mrs. Dacre Fox ; and on Sunday, this valiant lady, speaking to a great meeting in Hyde Park, said, " for the first time since the war broke out there was an open fight between the British public and German influence at work in this country. We had to make a clean sweep of all persons of German blood, without distinction of sex, birth-place or nationality. Any person in this country, who was suspected of protecting German influence, should be tried as a traitor and, if necessary, shot. The Home Office was impregnated with German influence and the Foreign Office used men protected by the Home Office.'' Mrs. Dacre Fox announced she had booked the Royal Albert Hall for a national demonstration on the subject on Tuesday, July 30th, at 7.30 p.m., and a sympathiser present offered £100 towards the expenses. Mr. R. Wilson, Secretary of the British Empire Union, said that Sir George Cave (the Home Secretary), must be made to understand that unless he applied drastic legislation he would be impeached.

We learn that there is a type of enemy blood against whom strong precautions are needed. This is the British-born son of German parents. It may have been only by accident that his birth took place in this country. He has not to be registered with the police or submit to any of the restrictions imposed on his parents; and there are men of this sort doing confidential Government work and manning the Labour battalions—safe from the bombs and bullets of their blood compatriots. Recently we heard of one of these insolent Huns wearing the King's uniform, during leave, boasting of what " they intended to do after the war. *We* are not going to have Germany isolated,'' he boasted—" we hissed the King's portrait on the cinema screen ''—and '' you English ran at Cambrai and now have to be stiffened up with Frenchmen at the front ''— and more of such blasphemy. A lady present wrote down the sayings of this young traitor in khaki, and has handed them to the right quarter. But is there a right quarter, that is the question ?

The proposed legislation in the Naturalisation of Aliens Bill is weak and wobbling. Not to our taste. We want a few women in Parliament to tone it up.

WOMEN IN PARLIAMENT.

It is stated that the Labour Party are determined to force a decision on the eligibility of women for membership of the House of Commons before the General Election. The Executive, by endorsing the candidatures of several Labour women for industrial constituencies, have staked out their claim. They have decided to have a qualifying Bill ready, in case the Law Officers should advise the Government that, under the present law, women are not eligible for membership of the House of Commons.

The National Labour Party have officially endorsed the prospective candidature of Miss Macarthur for the Stourbridge Division at the next election.

BOOK OF THE WEEK.

"TOWARDS MORNING."*

This book may be compared to a film—a terrible, realistic series of moving pictures, which is marshalled before our fascinated eyes with relentless force.

It may awaken, perchance, for the first time, our pity for the unfortunate victims of the German military system, as page after page depicts for us the remorseless crushing of the individual into the powder that is destined to cement the nation, or, to use the simile of the author, " the cog mattered only so long as it served its purpose—it was the machine, the machine that mattered always."

To illustrate this system, this amazingly strong book has been produced, which follows from the cradle to the grave, nay even while the child was yet in its mother's womb, one unit of that vast army which, after long years of like preparation, have been ruthlessly sacrificed to satisfy the insolent claims of the War God.

The Herr Amtshreiber is awaiting with nervous expectation the advent of his first born. He himself had never been a success. How this is he doesn't know. " My Bureau Chief doesn't like me. I don't know why. I have always done my best."

On the other hand his brother-in-law was a great man. He had no sympathy with the expectant parents at the supreme crisis.

" Women have to go through with it. It's their duty. They were made for it. Mustn't make a fuss. We fight—they bear children. Na gut, it must be a boy, then. You know the good old custom, the first child to the Kaiser. A fine boy. See to it, my dear fellow."

The young Helmut was ten when he first went to the Gymnasium, and the sufferings of the unhappy, nervous child on the first day there and the cynical callousness which was meted out to him could not fail to raise the compassion of the hardest heart. His return home to his mother in the evening is told with a brevity and force that is a good example of the fine work of the writer.

" Well, Helmut."

He did not answer, and she took off the bright yellow cap of the Lower Fifth and ran her hand with a caress over the close-cropped head. " Why, you're going to be a real man, Helmut." She helped him to unstrap his books. There were ten of them. He had got to take everything that was in those dull covers and squeeze them into his head. And his head ached now, as if it were full to overflowing.

Suddenly he turned, and there was a note of quivering hysteria in the boy's voice.

" And shall I never play again, mother ? "

For a moment they stared at each other. There was an aghast look on the woman's dull, pale face. She turned away, as though there were something in his eyes she could not meet.

" You must be a man, Helmut," she said quietly. " Life isn't a game."

He was ten years old when he found out that life wasn't a game.

And the end of it all was that he failed to pass the necessary examination and was compelled to enlist as an ordinary soldier. We suppose one must be a German lad of the better class to appreciate what the humiliation of that would mean.

We cannot give, for want of space, the description of the cruel twenty-four hours' march, to satisfy the ambition of rival divisions whose officers had laid a bet on the endurance of their respective men.

It was Viet Thomas who told them—

" If we don't play up it will cost our little officers fifty bottles of fizz. You'll see how they'll hound us along. Of course you know it's all unofficial ; but you know what *that* means. If we win, the Herr Oberst can begin thinking about himself as brigadier. If we don't, he'll wake up one morning with a top-hat on."

It was the little Herr Leutnant Müller that first spoke words of kindness and encouragement to Helmut, which for one brief evening lifted him out of his sullen despair. The little Leutnant was killed in a duel next morning at dawn. Helmut recalled a voice he had heard say, " We'll get our little Müller out soon—freeze him out, or kick him out ; somehow. You'll see ! "

So they drove the body of the little Leutnant home.

Johan cried. The tears splashed on to his tunic, and made big stains on the blue cloth.

But Helmut did not cry. His eyes were empty —stupid-looking.

That night he succumbed for the first time to the bestial pleasures of his companions, because his loneliness and isolation were more than he could bear. After his rapid descent into brutality it is said of him, " There were stains on the field grey uniform, grotesque stains on the peaceful face half hidden on the curve of his arm. It was as though while he slept, an enemy had wilfully besmeared him."

And the end of it *all* was—

" Helmut Felde, at dawn, for disobedience in the face of the enemy."

But Helmut by this very disobedience made good, and the incidents connected with it are stirring and pathetic beyond description.

The relating of the grinding to powder of this human soul is no mere figment of the imagination, it is rather the play of the imagination around facts ; but it is an embodiment of the system which no fiction can over-estimate—the relentless Juggernaut which, please God, we, in our turn, are out to crush.

This book should be read with sympathy and understanding.

H. H.

* By I. A. R. Wylie. (Cassell & Co., London.)

LETTERS TO THE EDITOR.

Whilst cordially inviting communications upon all subjects for these columns, we wish it to be distinctly understood that we do not IN ANY WAY hold ourselves responsible for the opinions expressed by our correspondents.

RENDER TO CÆSAR, &c.

To the Editor of THE BRITISH JOURNAL OF NURSING.

DEAR MADAM,—I have to thank one of your correspondents for a most gratifying reference to the work done at the North Islington Maternity Centre, in your issue of July 6th.

In justice to the founder and other pioneer workers to whom the credit of the success is really due, I feel compelled to rectify the mis-statement in connection with the Infant Welfare Ward, which is not under my charge. The whole department, which is re-opening on the 24th on an enlarged scale, will have a complete residential staff, and the late Superintendent of the North Islington Maternity Centre has been appointed Matron of the American Infant Welfare Wards, by which title it will be known in future.

The work of the wards will be of immense benefit to the residents of this district who attend our Centre, and we workers hope to co-operate most cordially for the general good of Welfare Work.

Yours sincerely,

G. LE GEYT,

Superintendent.

6, Manor Gardens,
Holloway Road, N. 1.

WANT OF CONSIDERATION.

To the Editor of THE BRITISH JOURNAL OF NURSING.

DEAR MADAM,—A couple of weeks ago THE BRITISH JOURNAL OF NURSING reported that Major Chapple recently asked in the House of Commons whether any advance had been made in the mess allowance to nurses to meet the increased cost of food. To this it was possible to answer truthfully in the affirmative, but is it not time that the Government increased their nurses' uniform allowance, which remains still at the pre-war figure of £8 per annum, in spite of the fact that all materials and also dressmaking cost almost twice as much as at the beginning of the war? And does there exist anywhere in this country a class of employment where salaries have not been largely advanced to meet the enormous increase in the cost of living? Yet the Government has not raised by one penny the salaries of its nurses, except to those who sign a contract for the duration of war, and the many women who, on account of home and other responsibilities, are unable to agree to such a contract must continue to struggle along with an income which in pre-war days was hardly sufficient.

I shall be grateful if you will give publicity to this letter, as I know there are many members of the Army Nursing Service who feel strongly the want of consideration shown to them in these matters. I enclose my card and remain,

AN ARMY SISTER.

A VEXATIOUS ARRANGEMENT.

To the Editor of THE BRITISH JOURNAL OF NURSING.

DEAR MADAM,—I should be very glad if any of your readers could enlighten me as to the following point. All nurses who have joined the Royal National Pension Fund for Nurses, and getting an annuity, have, as you know, every month to send a doctor's certificate and a clergyman's certificate. This, surely, especially for nurses living in a country district, is a little humiliating as it means that their business is more or less known. Is there any obscure reason for the multiplication of these signatures, for it surely is a waste of time for the clergyman and doctor—though that is not my point. My point is, that surely every nurse getting a pension naturally feels she would like to keep her affairs private, and the getting signatures every month seems to me an unnecessary bringing to light of her own business.

If you could find space in your valuable paper for my letter I should be very grateful.

Yours truly,

M. SHEPHERD,

Trained Nurse, C.M.B. Cert.

[This system is surely annoying, especially as nurses insured in the N.P.F.N. have paid in full for their annuities, which are *not* pensions.—ED.]

KERNELS FROM CORRESPONDENCE.

From a Sister in France :—" For the first time I have seen ' A History of Nursing ' (Nutting & Dock). What a mine of wealth to explore ! Why did I never hear of this greatest of educational works in my training school (Guys) ? "

[Because our training-schools have hitherto been too narrow in their outlook to teach nursing history, and, incidentally, because you have not read a professional Journal—THE B.J.N. !—which keeps you in touch with professional affairs.—ED.]

From a Sister in Savoy.—" We follow with interest the professional struggle in the *B.J.N.* . . . It seems incredible that outsiders should consider themselves capable of directing our profession. What would some of our interfering friends think if we offered to stage manage some of their productions. Our profession is indeed fortunate in having you at its head to fight its battles, otherwise without your leadership I do not know where we should be landed."

OUR PRIZE COMPETITION.

We regret that no prize competition has this week been received which comes up to the standard which justifies us in awarding a prize. No doubt all nurses are just now very busy, and those who are not working at full pressure are taking a well-earned rest.

QUESTIONS.

August 10th.—What have you learnt of new nursing methods in a Military Hospital ?

August 17th.—What is pernicious anæmia ? How have you seen it treated ?

The Midwife.

THE MIDWIVES' ACT AMENDMENT BILL.

(Concluded from page 38)

When the Midwives' Act Amendment Bill comes on in the House of Commons, two points in particular will need careful watching. (1) As we have already pointed out that " to bring the English Act into line with those in other parts of the United Kingdom," which is the intention of the Bill as declared in its memorandum, provision must be made for adding midwives to the Central Midwives Board. (2) The final form of Clause 12. It will be remembered that the Marquess of Salisbury, when the Bill was before the House of Lords, secured an Amendment providing that " Section nine of the principal Act (which enables county councils to delegate their powers and duties to district councils) shall be repealed." This was qualified later by the addition of the words " Provided that where at the commencement of this Act any powers or duties have been delegated, such delegation shall not be affected, unless, on the representation of the County Council concerned, the Local Government Board otherwise direct." This provision affects four district councils. Any further attempt at weakening Lord Salisbury's amendment in the House of Commons must be strenuously resisted.

THE MATERNITY AND CHILD WELFARE BILL.

The committee stage of the Maternity and Child Welfare Bill in the House of Lords is down for Thursday, July 25th.

NATIONAL BABY WEEK.

A meeting of the Council was held at the Armitage Hall, 224, Great Portland Street, on Tuesday, July 23rd. The chair was occupied by Dr. Eric Pritchard, Chairman of the Executive Committee, in the regretable absence of Major the Hon. Waldorf Astor, whose duties as Parliamentary Secretary to the Ministry of Food, to which office he has just been appointed, were too pressing to admit of his being present. It was quite obvious that those present in the body of the hall were animated by a spirit of enthusiasm and hope, which augurs well for the future welfare of mothers and babies in particular and for the health of the nation in general. They were not merely lookers-on, but social workers taking a deep interest in this work of great national importance, which was shown by the lively discussion which followed upon speeches recommending a Ministry of Public Health. The following reports were submitted :—That of the Executive Committee by Mrs. H. B. Irving (Hon. Sec.) That of the Hon. Treasurer, by Dr. Eric Pritchard, in the absence of Sir Edward Penton. That of the Jewel Fund Administrative Committee, by Miss Halford.

The National Baby Week Council is doing good service in publishing a series of pamphlets bearing upon its work. Included in these are four lectures to which reference has already been made in this journal. " National Baby Week, from the Working-class Mother's Point of View," by Mrs. H. B. Irving ; " The Factors of Infant Mortality," by Dr. C. W. Saleeby, F.R.S.E., F.Z.S. ; " Civic Responsibility with regard to Child Welfare," by Dr. Harold Scurfield, D.P.H., and " Baby Week : its Objects and its Future," by Miss Alice Elliott. " The Nation's Wealth " is a Composite Message from the Well Wishers of the Campaign, including General F. Foch. The most vital message is from a working woman in St. Pancras, and most nurses and midwives will agree with her when she says, " People that do not know much about children should not be allowed to give advice." The message sent two months ago by the late Lord Rhondda has a special interest. He wrote : " The care of the children is a sacred duty we owe to those who are giving their lives for us at the Front, and we can best help our country in these critical times by helping the children. . . .

" The establishment of a Ministry of Health, which would do much for the nation's children and coming generations is an object for which all well-wishers of the Empire should work, and one for which I hope we shall not have long to wait."

Alas, Lord Rhondda did not live to see the reform he so earnestly desired. We agree with the National Baby Week Council that the best memorial to his memory would be the immediate establishment of a Ministry of Health.

WORD FOR THE WEEK.

" To those who say that an abundant supply of cheap juvenile labour is necessary to industry we answer ' Hands off the children ! ' They are the nation of the future. They ought to be regarded as potential parents and potential citizens, not to be sacrificed—as they have been in the past—to the temporary convenience of industry and to considerations of private profit. Industry exists for human beings, not human beings for industry and if the exigencies of employers and the welfare of the children conflict, then the former must give way to the latter, not the latter to the former."—*Mr. Arthur Henderson, M.P.*

THE
BRITISH JOURNAL OF NURSING
WITH WHICH IS INCORPORATED
THE NURSING RECORD
EDITED BY MRS BEDFORD FENWICK

No. 1,583. SATURDAY, AUGUST 3, 1918. Vol. LXI

EDITORIAL.

REMEMBRANCE DAY.

The Lord Mayor of London rightly interpreted the national feeling when he proposed " that Great Britain should pause for a moment in the midst of the great struggle to turn to the past four years, and reconsecrate itself in the memory of those high traditions, to the demands of the future."

So it comes to pass that, throughout the Empire, Sunday, August 4th, will be kept as " Remembrance Day." We shall have in remembrance our fighting men, our sick and wounded, our prisoners of war, and surely our nurses, and our women's army.

The Roll of Honour of members of our profession who bravely and simply have laid down their lives in the cause of the world's freedom, is a long and growing one. We will have them in remembrance proudly and gracefully on Sunday next, and year by year as " Remembrance Day " comes round.

At the instance of the Prime Minister a solemn service of intercession will be held on Sunday morning at St. Margaret's, Westminster, the parish church of the Royal Palace of Westminster. Apart from its special intention, it will be of historical interest, as the King, accompanied by the Queen, will attend, and it will be the first occasion in English history on which the Sovereign has officially attended Divine Service at the head of His Lords and Commons.

In the afternoon there will be a service in Hyde Park, where a Floral Shrine will be erected, which it is hoped may be visited by Their Majesties. These War Shrines will be a feature of the day, and will be erected in the market places, or at the town halls in provincial towns, so that floral offerings may be made in honour of the dead. These will afterwards be collected by volunteers, and boy scouts, and taken to the local military hospitals. A short service, at which the Bishop of London will be the preacher, and a mass meeting will be held, when the following resolution will be proposed, and subsequently despatched to the Prime Minister :—

" That the citizens of London here assembled on Remembrance Day, August 4th, 1918, silently paying tribute to the Empire's sons who have fallen in the fight for freedom on the scattered battlefields of the world-war, whether on sea or shore, and mindful also of the loyalty and courage of our sailors, soldiers, airmen, and men of the Mercantile Marine every day and everywhere, and those who are working on the munitions of war and helping in other ways for the preservation of civilisation, unanimously resolve to do all that in their power lies to achieve the ideals on behalf of which so great a sacrifice has already been made."

Of those who most need our thoughts, our sympathy, and our practical help, the prisoners of war surely come first, and the suggestion of the Duke of Connaught that the collections made in the churches on Sunday next should be given in whole, or in part, to our prisoners of war in enemy hands will be widely approved.

PANSIES FOR THOUGHTS.

The simple heartsease is by common consent the flower of remembrance. Why should we not adopt it as the flower of Remembrance Day, and wear " Pansies for Thoughts " on Sunday next, and every year when the Day comes round in honour of our heroes and heroines, living and departed ?

There is no flower more appealing than the heartsease, and in its manifold variety it presents a diversity of colour and form to suit all tastes. Far and wide let us wear the emblem, and, more important still, let us cultivate and cherish the attribute of the heartsease. The world never needed those who possess it, and the power of communicating its secret to others more than at the present time.

OUR PRIZE COMPETITION.

HOW MAY THE PLAY OF CHILDREN BE DIRECTED SO AS TO BE A MEANS OF EDUCATION?

We have pleasure in awarding the prize this week to Miss Emilie Mona Clay, Colwyn Crescent, Rhos-on-Sea, North Wales.

PRIZE PAPER.

In the year 1837, Friedrich Froebel opened his first Kindergarten at Blankenburgh. The idea of using play for educational ends was carried out by him in that early infants' school.

It was Friedrich Froebel who first thought of educational play, that is, of so using the natural characteristic of the child in loving play, to teach the child what it is good for him to know.

Froebel's explanation of why he thought it important to use play educationally would be something like this :—

It is the child's nature to play; it will be easiest to teach a child through play because the child loves to play.

By using nature and natural means, the child will learn unconsciously.

Play is a means of expression. This is important, because at an early age the child expresses himself more through actions than words.

Play is the child's world.

For these and other reasons, having regard to child psychology, it is important to use nature and what is natural to meet our ends educationally.

Thus, if we want a child to realise some of life's activities—the work of the baker, the shoemaker, the blacksmith, and so forth—we do not take a book and read to the child a discourse on the work of the baker, the shoemaker, the blacksmith, we follow nature, and we picture out through play the activities of these tradesmen. Or, again, we may be wishing to draw a child to close realisation of the beauties of nature, as in the life of the butterfly, the squirrel, the bee, the daffodil. To do this we may dramatise simply through play the simple facts of nature : the butterfly's beautiful transformation, the life of the squirrel in saving food, the wonders of bee life, the daffodil with other bulbs, and the future of that brown-looking object.

Through nature play the child sees his own life reflected in some life outside his own, and the plays or simple dramatisations make sure his knowledge about the animal life so near him. This kind of acquisition is the " learn by doing " which does not merely apply to children's play, but is the great fundamental principle in all teaching.

The child who has pictured out the activities of the baker, the shoemaker, the blacksmith—or represented through play some of Nature's wondrous lore—will not forget the knowledge gained in this way. Such knowledge will be the child's very own in a more far-reaching sense than it could possibly be were the child only *told* about the baker, the shoemaker, the blacksmith, or about the butterfly, the bee, or the daffodil, the squirrel, and so on.

Educational play is learning by doing ; it is using something so natural to the child, the love of play and activity and dramatisation, to impart that knowledge which in after years will be added to and glorified.

Froebel says in connection with hand plays :

If your child's to understand
   Things which other people do,
You must let his tiny hand
   Carry out the same thing too.

The hand plays were instituted as the earliest form of educational play. In these the child imitated the actions of the " other people " and of Nature's phenomena, as the turning round of a weather vane through the action of the wind, an unseen force which the child cannot see, but an early indication of the law of cause and effect, though not clear to the child at the moment.

Some have been heard to say that " educational play " is over-directed. It should not be this in the hands of a skilful teacher. She should tell the children in simple words the facts that need representing, and leave the representation to them. She should simply change the centre of interest for the children if the play is degenerating into uselessness, but she should *not* be the director of the play.

As cannot be too often said, " educational play " is only really successful when the teacher simply remains the inspirer, but not the manager of a game.

Educational play is a great factor in education of an all-round character, more than merely the imparting of facts and giving knowledge, it may be a means of moral training untold. It may well help to make citizens as well as professors !

HONOURABLE MENTION.

The following competitors receive honourable mention :—Miss M. M. G. Bielby, Miss R. E. S. Cox, Miss O. M. Balderton, Miss C. Wright, Mrs. Farthing.

QUESTION FOR NEXT WEEK.

What have you learnt of new nursing methods in a military hospital?

MEDICAL MATTERS.

FEBRIS WOLHYNICA.

A perfect maze of publications, long and short, with this heading has appeared in the German and Austrian medical press, says the *British Medical Journal,* which has been drenched with a sort of printer's drum fire on this subject. Out of this tangle, Dr. Oluf Thomsen, of the Serum Institute of Copenhagen, has picked out the most salient features of a disease which was practically unknown before the war, except to Polish physicians, who seem to have regarded it as a form of malaria. Early in 1916 the disease was observed in soldiers on the German Eastern front. Its geographical name, *Febris wolhynica,* was as misleading as its symptomatic name, *Febris quintana,* which suggested a variety of malaria, for it was observed also on the Western front, and no bodies resembling the malarial parasite have been found in the blood, and laborious searches for them have been made. It presents many of the characteristics of trench fever. They may, indeed, prove to be identical, though Wolhynian fever, as referred to by certain German writers, would appear to be a very definite fever, with a far more uniform clinical picture than that of trench fever. According to Dr. Thomsen, the first symptom is lassitude, followed in a day or two by a sudden rise of temperature to about 40° C. The early symptoms, which may be preceded by rigors, are a sense of great heat and profuse sweating. The patient is giddy, and his muscles feel bruised. A very characteristic and most unpleasant symptom is pain in the legs, especially the shins. This pain— gaiter pain—is often worst in the evening or at night, and is stabbing, boring, or burning. After lasting about forty-eight hours the temperature falls almost to normal, and this may be the end of the attack. It may, however, recur as often as ten or twelve times, at intervals of five to six days. These intervals may last only two to three days, or may be as long as seven to eight. The prognosis is good, and the disease is seldom if ever fatal. Slight jaundice, great pallor, herpes, a scarlatiniform or small papular rash, and slight enlargement of liver and spleen have all been observed. There is an absolute and a relative increase in the number of the polymorphonuclear neutrophil leucocytes, and, after two or three attacks of fever, the red cells may show slight polychromasia. The disease can be experimentally transmitted to man by lice, which, it is thought, are probably always responsible for the development of the disease in man. Various bodies have been found in the digestive system of the louse and in the blood of man, but the evidence on these points is still conflicting. No satisfactory treatment has yet been found.

LICE AND DISEASE.

In connection with a correspondence on the above subject appearing recently in the *Times,* the Local Government Board has contributed an interesting note :—

The relation between trench fever—and, it may be added, typhus fever—and body-louse infection has been recognized from an early period in the war, and active and extensive precautions have been adopted to combat pediculosis (lousiness) in camps in this country and abroad. The difficulties of " delousing " have been extremely great, especially in the earlier days of rapid mobilization, when arrangements for personal cleansing and disinfection had to be rapidly improvised. At present such arrangements are fairly complete and adequate for military needs. It is noteworthy in this connection that few if any cases of trench fever have originated amongst soldiers in home camps or billets. The same holds good for civilians. In view of the medical publicity given to this disease, there is little doubt that cases would have been reported had they occurred.

In *Parasitology* for April and May of this year, Professor Nuttall, F.R.S., the Quick Professor of Biology at the University of Cambridge, has published the results of investigations in which he has been engaged, partially on behalf of the Local Government Board, during the last three years, on the whole question of pediculosis. In this publication he has added considerably to our previous knowledge of the subject, and has incorporated a full account of the mass of work which has been done by various expert workers for the Army Medical Department. The practical methods for destroying lice and their eggs, which have been adopted on a large scale, with excellent results, in military camps are also described. . .

A question somewhat similar to that of trench fever has been under consideration by the Local Government Board in connection with complaints from different parts of the country as to the unusual prevalence of scabies (itch). In some areas in which scabies has been particularly prevalent, the Board have consented to its being made temporarily notifiable as part of the systematic measures proposed to be undertaken to control its spread. In the same connection the Board have in preparation a circular letter to all local authorities, embodying practical suggestions for the control of the parasites of scabies and pediculosis.

THE ROYAL RED CROSS,

The King conferred decorations as follows at Buckingham Palace, on July 26th :—

THE ROYAL RED CROSS.

FIRST CLASS.

Queen Alexandra's Imperial Military Nursing Service. —Sister Margaret PERCIVAL.

Queen Alexandra's Imperial Military Nursing Service Reserve.—Assistant Matron Mary CHAPMAN, and Sister Annie MacLEOD.

SECOND CLASS.

Queen Alexandra's Imperial Military Nursing Service. Sister Jane GALLOWAY and Sister Frederica ROCHE.

Queen Alexandra's Imperial Military Nursing Service Reserve.—Matron Margaret MULLALLY, Sister Aggie DURWARD, and Sister Elizabeth WELLER.

Civil Nursing Service.—Matron Louisa DENTON, Matron Jessie ELMS, Matron Elsie GALE, Matron Lilian GIBBON, Assistant Matron Edith DRAPER, Sister Frances EAGER, Sister Phœbe ELLWOOD, Sister Clara EVANS, Sister Anne FARMER, Sister Jean GORDON, Sister Ida GOULD, Sister Lavinia GREEN, Staff Nurse Norah FITZGERALD, Miss Esther EDWARDS, and Miss Beatrice EVANS.

British Red Cross Society.—Matron Ethel GRAHAM, and Sister Ruby COCKBURN.

Voluntary Aid Detachment.—Mrs. Marguerite CARRABINE, Miss Grace DODGSON, Mrs. Margaret DOUGLAS, Mrs. Annie DOWSON, Mrs. Ethel DUGDALE, Mrs. Henrietta EDWARDS, Mrs. Cecilia FERGUSON, Mrs. Lilian GIBSON, Miss Theodora MARSH, Miss Elsie RIGBY-MURRAY, and Miss Millicent GRAHAM-SMITH.

Queen Alexandra received at Marlborough House the Members of the Civil and Military Nursing Services who have been awarded the Royal Red Cross, subsequent to the Investiture at Buckingham Palace.

NURSING SERVICES IN EAST AFRICA.

The King has been pleased to award the Royal Red Cross to the following ladies of the Nursing Services in recognition of their valuable services with the British Forces in East Africa :—

FIRST CLASS.

Miss R. PAUL, A.R.R.C., Sen. Nursing Sister, E.A.N.S.

SECOND CLASS.

Miss M. ARNOLD, Sister, S.A.M.N.S.; Miss J. E. BRODIE, Sister, North'n Rhod'n Med. Serv.; Miss E. M. CAMPBELL, Staff Nurse, Q.A.I.M.N.S.R.; Miss T. A. CLAVIN, Sister, S.A.N.S.; Miss R. DAVY, Staff Nurse, Q.A.I.M.N.S.R.; Miss V. DONKIN, Sen. Nursing Sister, E.A.N.S.; Miss K. F. DUFF, Sister, Q.A.I.M.N.S.R.; Miss A. M. FLETCHER, Staff Nurse, Q.A.I.M.N.S.R.; Miss H. FRANKLIN, Staff Nurse, Q.A.I.M.N.S.R.; Miss D. M. GRAVES, Staff Nurse, S.A.M.N.S.; Miss B. HOOPER, Sister, S.A.M.N.S.; Miss A. N. MARTIN, Sister, S.A.N.S.; Miss A. M. SARGENT, Actg. Matron, Q.A.I.M.N.S.R.

The King has been pleased to award the Royal Red Cross to the undermentioned ladies, in recognition of their valuable nursing services in connection with the war :—

SECOND CLASS.

LAING, Miss H., Matron, Princess Patricia's Hospl., Bray, co. Wicklow; LAWSON, Miss C. A., Matron, "Sutherlands," Aux. Hospl., Reading, Berks; LAWTON, Miss E., Sister, Mil. Hospl., Endell Street, Long Acre, W.C. 2; LEARMOUTH, Miss E. F., Nurse, Ryecroft Hall, Audenshaw; LEAVESLEY, Miss S., Staff Nurse, T.F.N.S., 4th North. Gen. Hospl., Lincoln; LINDSAY, Miss M. O., Nursing Sister, Can. Nursing Service, No. 16, Can. Gen. Hospl., Orpington, Kent; LINDSAY, Miss R., Sister i/c St. John's V.A. Hospl., Kingswood School, Bath; LINTALL, Miss M., Anstie Grange, Dorking; LLEWELLYN, Mrs. H., Commndt., Coytrahen Park Red Cross Hospl., Tondu, Glam.; LLOYD, Miss S., Nurse, 3rd Lond. Gen. Hospl., Wandsworth, S.W.; LOVELL, Mrs. A. L. S., Matron, and Officer i/c., Aux. Mil. Red Cross Hospl., Llanelly; LOVELL, Miss L. A., Sister, T.F.N.S., 2nd Eastern Gen. Hospl., Division 1, Brighton; LOWE, Miss A. M., Sister, T.F.N.S., 1st Eastern Gen. Hospl., Cambridge; LUMSDEN, Miss E. E., Nursing Sister, Can. Nursing Service, No. 5 Can. Gen. Hospl., Kirkdale, Liverpool; LYALL, Mrs. J. D., Sister, Can. Nursing Service, Can. Red Cross Spec. Hospl., Buxton, Derbyshire.

MACCALLUM, Miss H. B., Nursing Sister, Can. Nursing Service, West Cliff Can. Eye and Ear Hospl., Folkestone; MacDERMOTT, Miss A., Sister, Beech House Aux. Hospl., 16 and 18, The Avenue, N.W. 6; MACGREGOR, Miss J. K., Matron, Dalmeny House Hospl., Edinburgh; MacINTYRE, Miss M. F., Sister, T.F.N.S., 3rd Lond. Gen. Hospl., Wandsworth, S.W.; MACLEOD, Miss M. E., Nursing Sister, Can. Nursing Service, No. 9 Can. Gen. Hospl., Shorncliffe; MARR, Miss E., Sister, R. Infirmary, Sunderland; MARSDEN, Mrs. E., Matron, Beech House Aux. Hospl., 16 and 18, The Avenue; MATTHEWS, Miss O., Staff Nurse, Q.A.I.M.N.S.R., S. African Mil. Hospl., Richmond; MAYNE, Mrs. C., Matron and Theatre Sister, Flanders and Brooklands; McDOWELL, Miss A., Sister, Q.A.I.M.N.S.R., Mil. Hospl., York; McGLASHAN, Mrs. M. H., Sister-in-Charge, Mil. Hospl., Newhaven, Sussex; McKIEL, Miss T., Nursing Sister, Can. Nursing Service, No. 13 Can. Gen. Hospl., Hastings; McNICOL, Miss A. H., Nursing Sister, Can. Nursing Service, No. 11 Can. Gen. Hospl., Moore Bks., Shorncliffe; MERRIOTT, Miss N., Asst. Matron, Q.A.I.M.N.S.R., Mil. Hospl., Prees Heath, Salop; MESSUM, Miss A. M., Matron, Kent and Canterbury Hospl. (Civil); MICHELMORE, Mrs. E., Masseuse, Alton Red Cross Hospl., Hants; MILLER, Miss E. A., Asst. Matron, T.F.N.S., 1st Lond. Gen. Hospl., Camberwell; MILNES, Miss M., Nurse, V.A. Hospl., Torquay; MOFFAT, Miss A., Hermitage Aux. Hospl., Lucan, Dublin; MONEY, Miss G., Matron, Field House, Daisy Hill, Bradford; MOONEY, Miss L. (Sister Alphonsus), Head Sister and Theatre Sister, Mapperley Hall V.A.D. Hospl., Nottingham; MOORE, Miss E. M., Sister, T.F.N.S., 5th Northern Gen. Hospl., Leicester; MORRIS, Miss J. G., Asst. Matron, Mil. Orthopædic Hospl., Shepherd's Bush, W.; MORTON, Mrs. F. A., Matron and Lady Supt., Mil. Hospl., Scarborough; MORTON, Miss H., Sister, Edinburgh War Hospl., Bangor, W. Lothian; MORTON, Miss M. Y. E., Nursing Sister, Can. Nursing Service. No. 16 Can. Gen. Hospl., Orpington, Kent; MOSELEY, Miss E., Matron, T.F.N.S., Oakbank War Hospl., 3rd Sco. Gen. Hospl., Glasgow; MOWAT, Miss M., Nursing Sister, Can. Nursing Service, No. 11 Can. Gen. Hospl., Moore Bks., Shorncliffe; MULLALLY, Miss M., Matron, Q.A.I.M.N.S.R., Mil. Hospl., Buttevant, Co. Cork; MURRAY, Miss C., Sister-in-Charge, Cuerden Hall Hospl., Bamber Bridge.

NURSING AND THE WAR.

The Governors of St. Bartholomew's Hospital have decided, with many other general hospitals, to admit for training a limited number of nursing members of voluntary aid detachments and special military probationers who have satisfactorily completed not less than two consecutive years' work in a military or an auxiliary hospital. The hospital certificate of training will be granted after the passing of the final examination on the completion of three years' training, the fourth year of the usual course being excused. Regular probationers are now received at St. Bartholomew's Hospital at the age of 21.

An Injustice to Regular Probationers.

As the fourth year's work exacted by the training schools is one of service and not of training, this is a fair arrangement ; but where regular probationers will suffer is that those who train in hope of making military nursing their career, will, in the future, be excluded from the Imperial Nursing Service, as the new Instruction 678, recently adopted by the Army Council, promoted by the British Red Cross Society and the Nursing Board, provides for priority of promotion to the Service for members of voluntary aid detachments and special military probationers, who are to be admitted to our large training schools on the privileged three years' term. This is specially unjust to those regular probationers who have entered for four years' training and service this year.

But throughout this war, members of the Nursing Profession have, by the unfortunate influence of the Matron-in-Chief of the Joint War Committee, been treated with a lack of recognition, to which it is surprising that they should have submitted.

Instruction 678 is the latest evidence of the danger of the control of our professional standards by lay persons of social influence, the leisured wealthy, and their subservient officials.

What next ? First the " serf clause " ; now the most honourable service under the State closed to open competition. As we trained nurses are compelled to pay the taxes to support the War Office, we must place our opinion on record concerning this class job.

The Ulster Nurses' Unit, since their hospital at Lyons was closed, have been working with an American ambulance on the Western front, but they are anxious not to lose their identity, and an appeal for funds is being made. This Unit has had a strenuous time. They were close to the battle for an important point, and their hospital drew the usual attention from the Germans. Finally, they got orders to evacuate in the night, packed all, and arrived safely at the next point, where they are now in charge, after almost miraculous escapes. Every window broken and roofs moved by injuries to the walls, yet the only building completely destroyed was their goods store and the only lives lost by bombardment were seven horses close outside the nurses' quarters. The Germans fired on them while removing the stretcher cases, and on the doctors, and again on the orderlies finally clearing off. Ulster nurses who would like to join the unit should apply to the Matron, Samaritan Hospital, Belfast. They must speak French fluently, and not object to hard work and some discomforts.

Miss Dora E. Thompson, Chief of the American Army Nurse Caravan Corps, whose hospitals are mounted on motor trucks and trailers, is organising staffs of fifty nurses for each unit, who will go up within five miles of the fighting lines when their caravans respond to emergency calls. Each unit is planned to be equivalent to an evacuation hospital, and the nurses are each given the field kit of an officer, prepared to camp where night finds them.

Real Good Work.

Sister Mary Walker, holder of the Serbian Croix de Charité, a former student of the Keighley Girls' Grammar School, gave an address at the Keighley Temperance Institute recently on the work of the Scottish Women's Hospital in Serbia and Corsica. Sir John Clough (chairman of the Governors) presided over a large audience, and Serbian national songs were sung by girls of the Grammar School. Sister Walker, who expressed her pleasure at being able to come back to Keighley again, outlined the work of the Scottish Women's Hospitals with the Belgian and French armies, and subsequently with the Serbians. After the retreat from Serbia she and another nurse attached themselves to the women's hospital which went out with the Salonika Expeditionary Force. White aprons and caps were synonymous with nursing in England, but not so in Serbia, where they had no water to wash in, snow up to the hips, and blocks of ice over the only well in the village. In the hospital itself they had no means of obtaining heat, and the hot-water bottles put in bed at 5 o'clock at night were frozen at 10. Around the compound wolves gathered at night.

Sister Walker spoke of the removal of the hospital to Salonika, and subsequently to Corsica, where they had 10,000 refugees under their care. In Corsica 100 babies were born, and only three died. Here mothers were getting the ideas of Western and particularly British civilisation on the rearing of children, sanitation, and personal hygiene, so that when the Serbian nation was rebuilt its sanitary systems would be founded upon British and French examples. The Serbian people generally were greatly interested in Britain, and when they got back to their own land there would be an opening for British trade provided our manufacturers offered to Serbia the goods she wanted.

FRENCH FLAG NURSING CORPS.

CORDIAL CONGRATULATIONS FROM HIS EXCELLENCY THE FRENCH AMBASSADOR.

Madame la Vicomtesse de la Panouse, the Présidente of the Comité Britannique de la Croix Rouge Française, has, on behalf of His Excellency M. Paul Cambon, French Ambassador to the Court of St. James', and the whole Comité conveyed to the Sisters of the French Flag Nursing Corps attached to Ambulance 12/2, very hearty congratulations both upon the honour which the French Government has conferred upon them, and upon their

former, when Matron of Ambulance Mobile No. 1, earned the affection of every member of the Corps with whom she came in contact, and is a shining example of what a military nurse should be. She is back in her old place and everyone delighted to have her there. A Sister writes :— " When our nice General, whom we have known for so many years, recently asked us to a theatrical performance, and particularly asked as many of us as possible to come, it was a wonderful sight to see all our ' Poilus ' in their azure blues and various uniforms in this pretty theatre ; the *coup d'œil* would have made a wonderful painting. The General had Miss Warner in his box, and he told her he was glad to see us all back with them, and hoped we should never leave them again. It

MISS MITCHELL AND MISS WARNER, SISTERS HANNING, JONES AND GILL, F.F.N.C., AMBULANCE, 16/21.

admirable devotion to duty which has earned distinction for them, for the Corps, for the Comité, and for their country, and has wished them Godspeed in their beneficent service.

The seven Sisters will, we feel sure, value deeply this expression of appreciation upon the part of the French Ambassador and the Comité Britannique.

Miss Martha Oakley-Williams, R.N.S., has joined the Corps and has been posted to Lisieux, which is now in the war zone.

Miss Warner and Miss McMurrich have rejoined Ambulance 16/21, and with the three F.F.N.C. Sisters are happily reunited in their work. The

is so nice to be amongst old friends and to be appreciated.

" On July 4th Miss Warner gave a party to the patients, which was a great success, a very nice déjeuner, and surprise bags for all, which they greatly enjoyed. Our surprise came later when one of the patients came forward and presented the American and English nurses each with wonderful bouquets of crimson ramblers, lupins and Easter lilies tied with " Entente " ribbon. He made a most charming speech. He said he wished to present the flowers to each of us in the name of the patients, on this great day of Independence, and said how much they all appreciated their English and American brothers having come to fight by their side for the great cause of Humanity, and for Liberty, and Justice and Right, and that he also wished to thank ' les bonnes Dames Infirmières Anglaises et Americaines pour tout leurs grands dévouements et soins minuteuses qu'elles donnent à nous tous,' a most beautiful and touching speech. They gave a sounding ' Vive l'Angleterre ' and ' Vive l'Amerique ' to end up with. They really are wonderful, our Poilus. I don't think anyone knows how truly wonderful they are apart from their splendid gallantry on the battlefield."

"As you have shown, since the very beginning of the war, so much understanding and real sympathy with France, I only wish you could see the joy of these dear people since the push back began," writes a Sister in the war zone. " Young men and old go rollicking by, laughing and singing, with garlands of flowers round their necks, their camions decorated, and the horses—flower-decked too—prance along as proud as can be, entirely in the know.

With what marvellous courage the French have borne their burden in these black years ! Is it any wonder, now that they know that the tide has turned—for indeed the beginning of the end is here and now—that their spirits rise, and after super-human restraint they let themselves go ?

To see these flower-decked warriors on the war-path fills one with exultation. We know victory will be their reward.

We have heard much of supermen. The real supermen in this war are not the brutes who have wallowed in carnage, but the wonderful patriots who, in resisting them, have all these years kept their courage, and their faith, and their spirits, and their souls—all alive, red hot, in spite of hell let loose, the murder of their dear ones, the devasta-tion of their homes, and the ruin of their glorious monuments.

We British Nurses rejoice to serve men of such mettle."

CARE OF THE WOUNDED.

Mr. Laurence Philipps, brother of Lord St. Davids, has given £15,000 towards homes for paralysed Welsh Service men.

Sir William Osler, Regius Professor of Medicine at Oxford University, unfurled the American flag at the new hospital for United States soldiers at Portsmouth.

In an inspiring speech at the annual meeting of the Order of St. John, the Viceroy referred to the magnificent result of " Our Day " appeal— 122 lakhs (£813,333). The attacks by the Germans on hospitals provided an additional reason for ungrudging help to the Red Cross. If the need arose, he would not hesitate to make another appeal to India, confident that she would again rise to the height of her opportunities.

The Vicomtesse de la Panouse writes to the press to express to the generous people of Great and Greater Britain her heartfelt thanks for their splendid response to the appeal for help on France's Day. We are pleased to learn that the gifts are likely to exceed those of last year.

The largest purely American hospital near London will be located in the grounds of Richmond Park, on land given for this purpose by the King. The hospital itself is to be a gift from the British Red Cross. It will stand in one of the finest sylvan sites in this country, situated on high ground and commanding an unequalled view of the Thames Valley and the historic countryside. It is intended that the institution shall be the finest example of a hut hospital which can be built in the light of the experience gained since the war broke out. Wounded Americans in hospital in Great Britain are visited weekly by American women, more than 600 of whom in all parts of England are now enrolled in the " Care Com-mittee " of the American Red Cross. For con-valescent soldiers, the " Care Committee " co-operates with the British Hospitality Committee in organizing excursions, teas, theatre parties, and similar entertainments.

M. Clemenceau has awarded the Legion of Honour and the Croix de Guerre to Miss Fraser, a British motor-driver, who was wounded while in the exercise of her duties. The award was accompanied by the following glowing tribute to the act of gallantry which earned her these decorations : " Ordered to transport wounded, she accomplished her mission under a violent bombardment, and though sustaining two very serious wounds during the journey she had the superb courage to run 200 yards. On collapsing from weakness, she was transported to hospital to undergo an operation, but insisted upon not being attended to before the wounded for whom she was responsible."

Steel traps, equipped with springs of bone-crushing strength and jagged teeth two inches long, are being used by the Germans to catch patrols in " no man's land." Corporal Leonard Manser, U.S. Army, relates how he discovered one at night in an unnamed American-held sector and brought the trap to their trenches. The con-trivance is three feet long, and has jaws eighteen inches wide, with teeth two inches long. It is designed to give the victim great pain and make him call for help. This attracts his comrades, who become targets for a German machine-gun fusillade, which results in the annihilation of the entire party.

When we were young we were greatly interested in the pictures of Chinese tortures which used to line the walls in descending to the dark and gruesome Chamber of Horrors at Madame Tous-sand's. But why go so far afield as China to seek for hideous cruelty ? Germany is comparatively close and could evidently give points to the heathen Chinee.

NIGHTINGALE NURSING IN FRANCE.

PROGRESS AT THE MAISON DE SANTÉ PROTESTANTE, BORDEAUX.

Of all the world's nursing pioneers since the days of Florence Nightingale, none has perhaps had a harder fight than Dr. Anna Hamilton of Bordeaux. Of her truly it can be said, "a prophet is not without honour," &c., and the reputation of the work she has been doing for 18 years is now returning to France via the U.S.A. As the U.S. delegates land in Bordeaux and visit the one school of nursing run on Nightingale lines, they are all astonished that such a splendid work has not had better recognition, and the French are astonished that a work which has been quietly (and almost unnoticed in their midst) establishing itself should be so well known in the States.

example. After visiting the School Major Cabot asked Dr. Hamilton how much it cost to train a nurse. He was told £110, and he has sent her that amount and the following charming expression of appreciation :—

" ' I believe your training school is not only the best in France, but one of the best in the world. With more money and a better hospital it could become, under your management, the best. I congratulate you.   RICHARD C. CABOT.' "

The scholarship so graciously bestowed by Major Cabot has been won by Mdlle. Guelfucci of Gard.

Miss Emily Kemp, who has been such an indefatigable worker for the French wounded since the beginning of the war, has sent Miss Grace Ellison £100 to train a nurse for three years at Dr. Hamilton's hospital at Bordeaux. Miss Kemp

NEW DIPLOMÉES OF THE MAISON DE SANTÉ PROTESTANTE.

We have received an interesting account of the recent examinations for the Nursing Diploma at this school, when all the senior pupils were eminently successful.

NEW DIPLOMÉES OF THE MAISON DE SANTÉ PROTESTANTE, BORDEAUX.

Mdlle. Long (Nice), Mdlle. Casalis (Paris), Mdlle. Harrioo (Port Menois, Finisterre), Mdlle. Sélzer (Jonina, Algeria), Mdlle. Midas (Royan), Mdlle. Coste (St. Étienne), Mdlle. Laverniez (Clermont Ferrand), Mdlle. Charcusol (St. Croix Voltee Français), Mdlle. Bravois (Bonfritz, Algeria), Mdlle. Mentello (Nice).

The examinations in which Major Richard Cabot (Massachusetts Hospital, Boston), Med. Chef of the great American Hospital at Talence, took part, were held in public, and the day ended with a delightful dinner and concert. Miss Grace Ellison, who was present, writes :—

" I have so often, in the 'B.J.N.' spoken of the Americans as a practical people. Here is an

is much in sympathy with this plan for training nurses, especially when the candidates are what we in Great Britain call "the right sort." So many daughters of French Protestant pastors wish to take up nursing as a profession, but their parents have not been able to pay the fees ; it is for women like these that Miss Kemp's money will be used in memory of Miss Lydia Kemp, her sister, who has just died and who worked indefatigably for the sick and poor and blind.

By and bye it is hoped to build and endow a beautiful hospital and Nursing School at Bagatelle, the property left by Mdlle. Bosc to the Maison de Santé Protestante at Bordeaux. Under the direction of Dr. Anna Hamilton this school has always been organised on the Nightingale principles of nursing, and we hear that it is probable that the new school will be known as the Florence Nightingale College of Nursing. £100,000 could accomplish magnificent results if only it was to hand. We have great hopes for the future.

LONDON HOSPITAL SYSTEM.

How It Injures the Profession.

In the House of Commons, on Thursday, July 18th, Major Chapple asked the Under-Secretary of State for War (1) whether, in appointing nurses to the nursing staff of the Army, any discrimination is made against nurses trained in hospitals that farm out their nurses after the end of their second year's training, taking them away from their training in the wards and paying them 13s. per week while they are earning £2 2s. for the hospital. (2) whether the certificate given to nurses at the end of their second year's training in the London Hospital is accepted by the Army nursing authorities as qualifying for appointment to the Army nursing staff?

Mr. Macpherson, in replying, said : The regulations regarding the qualifications for appointment to the Queen Alexandra's Imperial Military Nursing Service provide that a candidate must possess a certificate of not less than three years' training and service in medical and surgical nursing in a civil hospital having not less than 100 beds. Time spent in private nursing is not allowed to count towards the qualifying period of three years' training. The answer to the second question is in the negative.

Major Chapple, on July 25th, asked the Under-Secretary of State for War whether the certificate of training given by the London Hospital is accepted as qualifying for appointment to the Army Nursing Service ; whether the certificate states that the nurse has had not less than three years' training in the hospital ; whether he is aware that nurses in the hospital are taken from their training in the wards and are sent out at the end of their second year to nurse private cases for the purpose of appropriation by the hospital of not less than 29s. per week of their earnings and not for professional training ; and whether if time spent in private nursing is not allowed to count towards the qualifying period of three years' training, any steps are taken to discover what period of the years of training in the case of a London Hospital nurse applying for a post in the Army Nursing Service have been spent in private nursing ?

Mr. Macpherson said : In reply to questions by my hon. and gallant friend, on Thursday last, I stated what certificate of training must be possessed by candidates for appointment to Queen Alexandra's Imperial Military Nursing Service. Steps are always taken to ascertain that a nurse has completed the necessary training.

And so the principle at issue—of justice to the worker—is befogged every time.

The fact is that Miss Lückes, the Matron of the London Hospital, is permtited to use the nurses as she chooses—as one does the lint and the bandages ! If she elects to send them out private nursing to make money for the hospital, she may do so, and thus disqualify them for all the higher positions in the profession for which a three years' certificate of training is obligatory.

But as the London Hospital has always had so much influential representation on the Nursing Board of Queen Alexandra's Imperial Military Nursing Service the rules continue to provide a loophole for the admission of London Hospital nurses with a two years' certificate and service.

It is high time all these irregularities and privileges for the London Hospital were abolished.

The London should train and certificate its nurses after a three years' systematic training in the wards ; it should shut down its " nurse farm " or work it on the co-operative plan for the benefit of members of the nursing staff who have gained a three years' certificate. Thousands of pounds would be thus paid to the workers instead of in support of the charity, and to provide huge salaries for senior officials.

The Nursing Board of Q.A.I.M.N.S. should cease to pander to the commercial régime of the London Hospital, establish the standard of the three years' certificate, and cease to recognise " service," whatever that may mean. Incidentally, the senior and best paid posts in the service should not, in the future, be reserved for London Hospital trainees, who carry on the obsolete traditions of their Alma Mater.

GIVING DIRECTIONS TO PARLIAMENT.

In discussing the Maternity and Child Welfare Bill recently in Committee in the House of Commons, the Chairman ruled out of order, on the ground that it would be giving directions to Parliament in regard to future legislation, a new clause, which Sir W. Cheyne and Major Hills had given notice of their intention to propose, providing that on the appointment of a Minister of Public Health, the powers and duties conferred and imposed by the Bill on the Local Government Board or on the President thereof should be transferred forthwith to the Minister of Public Health.

We have pointed out the unparliamentary proceeding of the Council of the College of Nursing in pledging Parliament in their prospectus to nurses as an inducement to register with the College—

(1) " If, therefore " (the prospectus states), " you are on the College Register you will, automatically, and without further fee, be placed upon the State Register, when the ' Nurses Registration Bill ' is passed."

Thousands of nurses have been induced to join the College on this printed promise, which is " giving directions to Parliament in regard to future legislation " concerning which it has never been consulted, and which it may very naturally repudiate.

Miss Matheson, the Secretary of the Irish College Board, in her pamphlet, is even more unconstitutional in her pie-crust pledges.

Parliament is *very jealous* of its prerogatives, as people presuming to deal with legislation should be well aware.

THE BANNER OF QUEEN ALEXANDRA'S IMPERIAL MILITARY NURSING SERVICE

Queen Alexandra, accompanied by the Princess Victoria, was present on Monday at a service for the dedication of the banner of Queen Alexandra's Imperial Military Nursing Service, which was hung in the Royal Albert Hall on the occasion of the commemoration of the First Seven Divisions, which was held in the Chapel of the Queen Alexandra Military Hospital, Millbank.

The banner was handed over to the custody of Queen Alexandra's Imperial Military Nursing Service.

The service was conducted by the Archdeacon of London (the Venerable E. E. Holmes), the Rev. R. Bartlett (Chaplain to Queen Alexandra Hospital for the Nursing Service), and the Rev. J. C. Knapp (Chaplain to the Queen Alexandra Military Hospital).

Queen Alexandra afterwards visited the sick and invalid nurses who are patients in the hospital.

OUR ROLL OF HONOUR.
NURSING SERVICE.
WOUNDED.
WRIGHT, Sister M., B.R.C.S.

THE MILITARY MEDAL.

The *London Gazette* of July 30th publishes the names of 38 ladies (mostly trained nurses) who have been awarded the Military Medal for distinguished services in the field, in connection with the bombing of hospitals in France.

APPOINTMENTS.

MATRON.

General Hospital, Cheltenham.—Miss L. C. Fox-Davies has been appointed Matron. She was trained at the General Hospital, Birmingham, and has held the positions of Ward Sister, Theatre Sister, Night Sister, and Home Sister at the General Hospital, Cheltenham.

Home of Recovery, Allerton Tower, Liverpool.—Miss Grace C. Maywood has been appointed Matron. She was trained at the Manchester Royal Infirmary, and has been Assistant Matron, British Red Cross Hospital, Netley; Matron, Ilfracombe Private Nursing Home; and was for three years previous to taking up war work, on the Staff of the London Association of Nurses.

THEATRE SISTER.

Royal Albert Edward Infirmary, Wigan.—Miss Henrietta Follevaag has been appointed Theatre Sister. She was trained at the Royal Albert Edward Infirmary, and has done private nursing.

SISTER.

Royal Albert Edward Infirmary, Wigan.—Miss S. A. Eddy has been appointed Sister. She was trained at the Royal Infirmary, Sheffield.

"BRITISH NURSES AND THEIR FIGHT FOR FREEDOM."

Under the above heading the *American Journal of Nursing* just to hand publishes an admirable letter by Miss Beatrice Kent, placing clearly before our American colleagues the situation in this country in regard to the College of Nursing, Ltd., and British nurses. Trained nurses in this country owe a debt of gratiude to the editor of our contemporary for the space she has devoted to making the position plain to our American colleagues, and to Miss L. L. Dock and Miss Beatrice Kent, most forceful of advocates, for their articles.

NOCTURNE.

(In a Nursing Home.)

Grey scudding clouds and a sodden sky,
  The distant sound of the rolling sea,
And on my back in my bed I lie,
  Counting the hours to early tea.

The trees outside fling back and fro,
  Whipt by the early morning wind;
And Time is moving remarkably slow,
  And night is long and far from kind.

And all the ghosts of long ago,
  They gather around with much to say;
They gather around and bother me so,
  And the bed feels hard—I wish it were day.

The stars grow faint and the sky grows light,
  The first tram rumbles along its way;
Past and gone is the weary night,
  And—surely that is nurse with the tray.
         —M. MOLLETT.

NO FLOWERS BUT A CROWN.

(Lines beneath a picture of our Lord; quoted in a recent sermon by the Rt. Rev. the Bishop of Edinburgh.)

I said, "let me walk in the fields";
He said, "nay, walk in the town";
I said, "there are no flowers there";
He said, "no flowers but a crown";
I said, "but the skies are black,
There is nothing but noise and din";
But He wept as He sent me back,
"There is more," He said, "there is *sin.*"

I said, "but the air is thick,
And fogs are veiling the sun";
He answered, "yet hearts are sick,
And souls in the dark undone."
I said, "I shall miss the light,
And friends will miss me, they say";
He answered me, "choose to-night,
If I am to miss you, or they."
I pleaded for time to be given;
He said, "is it hard to decide?
It will not seem hard in Heaven
To have followed the steps of your Guide."

Then into His hand slipped mine
And into my heart came He.
And I walked in the light Divine
The path I had feared to see.
      (From "Nurses Near and Far.")

NURSING ECHOES.

The Report of Lady Minto's Indian Nursing Association for 1917 records the retirement in May of Mrs. Davies, Chief Lady Superintendent of the Association since its earliest days, and the appointment of Miss R. E. Darbyshire, R.R.C., as her successor. It places on record that Mrs. Davies' zeal and devotion have proved of the greatest service, and the perfect order in which she left the affairs of the head office is an eloquent testimony to her business capacity and years of hard work.

A scheme has been inaugurated for maintaining small nursing homes, principally for maternity cases, in Simla and Delhi. It is anticipated that these Homes will meet a real need.

The Chief Lady Superintendent states in her report that the greatest difficulty encountered during the year has been the serious depletion of the nursing staff, and the impossibility of supplying the needs of the Association from England. Though short-handed the branches have done a great deal of good work, and seven members of the staff loyally remained on after the expiration of their contract, in spite of the attractions of other branches of their profession.

The fees charged to patients have been raised by 1 rupee per diem, and the salaries of the nursing staff raised. The Lady Superintendents of the Provincial branches receive an additional 30 rupees per month, Sisters an increase of 10 rupees per month in the third and fourth year, and a further increase of 10 rupees a month in the fifth year of service.

The commencing salaries of Nursing Sisters have also been increased to 90 rupees a month, increasing annually till 135 rupees a month is reached in the tenth year.

The rules relating to the engagement and employment of Nursing Sisters have been revised, and those relating to agreement, discipline, and refunds made somewhat more stringent.

The value of the skilled help of trained Sisters cannot be too highly estimated, and there is evidence that they are appreciated. Thus in connection with the Rajputana Branch the reports of medical officers and patients are said to be invariably commendatory and frequently laudatory. " Anxiety disappears when your well-trained Sisters take charge of a case " is a typical instance.

As usual, the report is admirably produced and illustrated.

We are glad to learn that, owing to a Petition organized by Miss Charlotte M. Markwick, and sent to the Governors of the Victoria Infirmary, Glasgow, the scale of the salaries of the nursing staff has been substantially raised :—

In the 1st year from	...	£12—£16.
In the 2nd year from	...	£16—£20.
In the 3rd year from	...	£20—£25.
In the 4th year from	...	£30—£40.
For the Sisters from	...	£45—£60.

There are other points which the nurses would like to bring before the Governors, but are hampered in their action for lack of legal advice. This is one of the things which they hope may be made available when their new Club is opened in Bath Street.

We are always seeing nonsensical paragraphs in the quack nursing press and elsewhere, making statements about our views and opinions, which we have never expressed— penny-a-line trash which presumably is good enough for the type of person who reads these unprofessional publications.

If anyone cares what we think, and wishes to know what we say, we advise them to subscribe to this JOURNAL. They would then not be fobbed off with twaddle.

LEAGUE NEWS.

The second number of the *League News* of the Royal Infirmary, Bradford, just issued, contains many interesting items, including a Foreword by Major Phillips, Hon. Surgeon to the Infirmary, who, talking on Reconstruction, says that one feels quite sure that after the war, as before it, and during it, there will be reason to be proud of the work of nurses, and that any woman who takes up that work will be employing herself in a profession in which she can find occupation for all that is in her. The fortunate people in the world are surely those whose work is also their hobby. The first essential of a hobby is that its possibilities can never be exhausted; it must be an El Dorado which is unattainable. . . . The zest of the business lies in the fact that, however splendid the collection may be, it is always, will always continue always to be possible to improve it. And so with nursing. There are many nurses who know a tremendous lot about nursing. It has been my privilege to know not a few nurses whose work has been just splendid; but there has never been a nurse who was a perfect nurse in the sense that she knew all there was to know about nursing.

Amongst the letters from nurses that by Miss M. Wroe on A Visit to Seville is specially interesting.

A MODERN INDUSTRY.

THE PREPARATION OF CONDENSED MILK.

Most people are familiar with the appearance of a tin of Nestlé's milk, for this far-famed brand is used all over the world ; but probably comparatively few people know precisely of what this milk consists or how it is prepared.

It was my good fortune to see the process under ideal conditions at the Aylesbury Condensery, one of the most important of the English factories of the Nestlé and Anglo-Swiss Condensed Milk Company, St. George's House, 6 & 8, Eastcheap, London, E.C.

An hour's run from London with only a stop at Harrow, with its far-famed hill and steeple-crowned church, brought us to Aylesbury, the county town of Buckinghamshire, with its interesting market-place where stands conspicuous the virile statue, in bronze, of John Hampden, known to fame as the Buckinghamshire patriot who refused to pay the 'ship money' levied by Charles 1, and whose honourable public and private life was ended at Chalgrove Field where he fell mortally wounded in a skirmish

AYLESBURY CONDENSERY, FROM THE OFFICE GARDEN.

with the King's troops under Prince Rupert. The verdure of the surrounding country and the luxuriance and beauty of the creepers on many of the houses of Aylesbury made one realize that the valley in which it is situated must be ideal for dairy purposes, and one was not surprised at its widespread reputation as a centre of dairy farming.

Manifestly, the Anglo-Swiss Milk Company did wisely to plant a Condensery just here.

Its object is, of course, to procure fresh, rich milk, and to preserve it under hygienic conditions in portable form, so that it can easily be transported far and wide.

Milk, as originally drawn from the cow, contains approximately 87.55 per cent. of water ; therefore, if you can eliminate a considerable proportion of that water, which can be replaced by the consumer before use, you have solved the problem of portability and easy distribution, and this is what is done so successfully at Aylesbury. The

full-cream condensed milk sent out from the factory contains only 24 per cent. water, the odd 63 per cent. being extracted in the process of condensation.

Many things, however, must contribute to the perfection of the finished product ; and essentially the quality and purity of the milk condensed. Therefore, supervision by the management begins before the milk—drawn as by a magnet from the surrounding farms—enters the factory gates, and inspectors frequently visit the farms under contract to supply the factory with milk, so as to ensure that only milk of fine quality, dealt with under sanitary and hygienic conditions, is used.

It is interesting to see the milk arriving at the Condensery in great cans, and, contrary to one's pre-conceived ideas, not measured, but weighed, in huge copper pans, so that the amount sent in by each farmer can be correctly estimated ; from these it passes on to a reservoir, from which it is pumped up into great tanks.

One next saw the care with which the empty cans are treated before being returned to the farmers. First they are thoroughly cleansed in hot water by brushes, one of which rotates inside, and the other scrubs the outside of the can, which is then turned upside down and a jet of steam sprayed into it.

To return to the milk. On leaving the receiving tanks it is raised to a temperature sufficiently hot to dissolve the sugar which is added to it as a preservative, although the " Ideal Milk," the brand supplied to the Navy and Army has no sugar or other preservative added. It is found in practice, however, that when used for infant feeding, the sweetened milk ordinarily gives the best results. In these days of the strict rationing of sugar, to pass through a room containing sack upon sack of glistening white sugar, is calculated to arouse feelings of envy, but the whole of the supplies to the Nestlé's Factories are " controlled." After the addition of the sugar the milk is passed through a series of fine sieves, so that any fibre or other foreign body inadvertently introduced from the sugar bags is removed.

CONDENSING.

Then comes the all-important process of condensing. For this purpose the hot milk is drawn into copper condensing pans from which the air is exhausted, and which contain a series of copper coils heated by steam, by which means the milk is raised to boiling point. But, it must be realised, for it is very important, that in a vacuum the milk boils at about half the temperature at which it would do so if treated in the ordinary way, and, therefore, is not heated sufficiently to destroy the vitamines which are so essential if it is to be relied upon as the sole food of the growing infant. In the condensing pans a considerable proportion of the water in the milk is converted into steam and removed in this form, to be later cooled and re-converted into water. It will be thus realised that Nestlé's Milk is simply pure milk, sweetened and condensed, and that its thickness is due solely to the extraction of water, and not to the addition of any thickening.

When the milk has been condensed it is transferred from the condensing pans to large cans, and cooled down in large tanks of cold water, by a method which ensures that the cooling shall be uniform. The process is now complete, and it is put up in tins by deft-handed girls.

The tins are made on the premises, and the process is an interesting one. First the sheets of tin are cut the required length by machinery, and each strip soldered to form the body of the can. The top and the bottom—with a small hole for filling the tin later—are also stamped out. These are then soldered together and the can is ready for filling, but first it is tested to see if it is airtight, and any defect in the soldering is remedied by hand. The tins are then filled and soldered, labelled, wrapped in paper, and packed in wooden boxes, also made on the premises.

Nurses travelling with patients by sea would be well advised to take with them a supply of Nestlé's Milk, as it is often a very great difficulty to obtain fresh milk for invalids.

In addition to Nestlé's Milk, their Milkmaid Brand Café au Lait is made at the Aylesbury Factory, and we see the green coffee berries roasted to a deep brown over the glowing embers in a great furnace by girls who carefully watch and turn them. They are then ground, and the strong coffee, when made, added in proper proportions to the milk, which is then condensed. Cocoa and milk is another "Milkmaid Brand."

Is it now clear to our readers that Nestlé's Milk is pure, rich milk from which nothing has been eliminated but water—so that it may be the more easily transported—under the most hygienic conditions, and to which nothing has been added except pure sugar? It follows that it must be a boon indeed to those mothers who are unable to nurse their own children, and whose milk supply is of uncertain purity.

If we consider the average milk supply of London, for instance, the method of its transportation for long distances in cans of uncertain cleanliness, in hot trains, and its subsequent exposure on the counters of shops and elsewhere, we must realise that Nestlé's milk, prepared under such conditions as I have described, is an infinitely safer and more reliable preparation to use than a large proportion of the milk supply of the metropolis.*

The firm, in "Nestlé's Baby Book," issues annually some very valuable information on the subject, with the testimony of thousands of mothers who have used Nestlé's Milk for their children. In eight years 3,572 children were thus reported on. Investigation showed that of this number 73 had died from disease, 7 from accidents, 25 were unwell at the time the report was made, and 3,467 children were in perfect health. To accurately appraise this most remarkable record is must be remembered that in a considerable proportion of these cases the children were given Nestlé's Milk practically as a last resort, when no other food could be tolerated, and that the average mortality of town-born children, between the ages of one and five years, is one in six. The pictures of the children with which the book is abundantly illustrated, also show how bonnie are many of the children brought up on Nestlé's Milk.

A particularly interesting book at the present time published by the firm is "Heroes All." It must be remembered that Nestlé's Milk has now been on the market for over fifty years, therefore many babies brought up upon it have long since grown to man's estate. "Heroes All" is a selection of voluntary testimony from mothers of men fighting for their country in the Great War. In addition to its valuable testimony to the virtue of Nestlé's Milk, the collection of so many portraits of our gallant soldiers and sailors must, in years to come, form a valuable historical record.

A word of caution is necessary. When I speak of Nestlé's Milk as a valuable and reliable substitute for breast feeding when this is impossible, I mean Nestlé's, and not any other brand of condensed milk. Nestlé's, as I have shown, is a full-cream milk scientifically condensed. But from some brands of condensed milk placed on the market the cream, or a large proportion of it, has been extracted before it has been condensed. A baby brought up on such milk would not thrive, any more than it would if fed with uncondensed skim milk.

Of course, Nestlé's Milk has a much wider sphere of usefulness than the feeding of infants, witness the fact that the "Ideal Milk" is supplied to the Services in large quantities, besides being greatly in demand by the general public. Lastly, I must mention that the Nestlé's Anglo-Swiss Condensed Milk Company were eight or nine years ago granted the Royal Warrant of Appointment, an honourable recognition which its services to the community have certainly merited. M. B.

Mrs. Hayes Fisher opened Parkside Orthopædic Hospital for Wounded Officers, Ravenscourt Park, Hammersmith, on July 25th.

---

* According to *The Times* of July 31st, the Hammersmith Public Health Committee states that "there is evidence to prove that milk is deliberately and scientifically reduced to the lowest possible standard so far as fatty substances are concerned."

OUTSIDE THE GATES.

THE ENEMY ALIEN DANGER.

There is no doubt in the minds of those who attended the Internment of Enemy Aliens Meeting in Hyde Park last Sunday that the Government is playing with fire, in not carrying into effect the will of the people in the most drastic manner. The people has now made up its mind that for the safety of the Realm all enemy aliens of every class, rich and poor, should be placed behind barbed wire, and the uncontrolled rage of a mob of some hundreds of persons in the Park, from whom the police had to rescue a dissenting German, proves that its patience is used up, and that the devilish devices of barbarians are no longer to be tolerated. What with the torture of our defenceless prisoners, the wholesale violation of women and children, the murder of our seamen nurses, and doctors, mantraps and other villainy, the British public is now thoroughly roused, and all feeble fumblers—otherwise professional politicians—will rue the day if they continue their effete treatment of these insolent traitors.

The House of Lords in its debate echoed public opinion. "Denaturalise them all, remove them from high places, from the Privy Council, Parliament, and Government Departments"—that is the sound advice of Lord St. Davids, and many noble Lords supported him.

AN INSULT TO EVERY SOLDIER AND OFFICER IN HIS MAJESTY'S SERVICE.

In the Commons Mr. Swift MacNeill asked the Prime Minister whether Mr. Felix Cassel, K.C., had resigned or intimated his intention of resigning the position of Judge Advocate-General, to which he was appointed in 1916; and, if so, whether, regard being had to the fact that the Judge Advocate-General was the president of the judicial department of the Army and the sole representative of the Government in all military proceedings before general Courts-martial, maintaining the interests of the Crown and prosecuting, either in person or by deputy, in the Sovereign's name, and that all matters arising out of the administration of martial law, including the examination of the sentences of Courts-martial and the reporting thereon to the Crown, come under his supervision, the new occupant of the position of Judge-Advocate-General would not, whatever might be his qualifications, be a person of enemy alien birth or origin.

The Chancellor of the Exchequer replied that Mr. Felix Cassel had not resigned.

After which Mr. MacNeill very pertinently asked : Is the right hon. gentleman aware that having a gentleman of alien origin and birth in full command of Courts-martial is an insult to every soldier and officer in His Majesty's Service?

It is more than that—it is an insult to every patriotic person of British blood in the Empire.

As the Aliens Advisory Committee set up by the Government is to sit *in camera*, and the public prevented from knowing the whole truth, it is proposed to form a new Parliamentary Watch Committee, and also to establish local watch committees. This is very significant. If we remember aright, it was the Committees of Public Safety which took the law into their own hands during the Terror. Well, we have had enough of the Terror, and we mean to protect ourselves from the crafty treachery of the thousands of Huns in our midst, especially from the result of their system of "peaceful penetration," which spells bribery and corruption.

BOOK OF THE WEEK.

"ON THE EDGE OF THE WAR ZONE."*

Those of us who read with pleasure and gratification "A Hill-top on the Marne," will welcome the new volume by Miss Mildred Aldrich, in which she relates the continuance of her most interesting experiences within the war zone, in her little, hitherto, peaceful retreat, "The Crest" on the hill-top.

This very talented lady has not only had almost a unique position, but is able to give her impressions of three years in a most attractive and yet quite natural way. This is, perhaps, explained because the book consists of letters written by her to a friend in America. It will be remembered that Miss Aldrich is herself of American birth. This volume has the advantage of a charming little drawing of "La Creste" on the title-page, and also a map of the surrounding neighbourhood, so that, with the aid of them, added to her graphic description, we are able in some measure to picture to ourselves the incidents so charmingly recorded. The period covered is from that immediately following the battle of the Marne to the entering in of the Stars and Stripes.

Her little French friend, Mdlle. Henriette, proposes "that I should harness Ninette and go with her to the battle-field, where, she said, they were sadly in need of help. At first it seemed to me that there was nothing to do but go, and go quickly. But before she was out of the gate, I rushed after to tell her I knew they did not want an old lady like me, very unsteady on her feet, absolutely ignorant of the simplest rules of 'first aid,' that they needed tried and efficient people, and that we could not lend efficient aid, but should be a nuisance.

"She argued that we could hunt for the dead and 'carry consolation to the dying.' I was afraid I was going to laugh at the wrong moment. The truth was I had a sudden vision of my chubby self—me, who cannot walk half-a-mile or bend over without getting palpitation—stumbling in my high-heeled shoes over fields ploughed by cavalry and shells, breathlessly bent on carrying

---

* By Mildred Aldrich. London : Constable & Co.

consolation to the dying." This decision of hers was eminently right and she found much more suitable and efficacious means of ministering to the army in her own little house on the hill-crest.

Here is a moving picture of a burying-ground at Chambry :—" First the graves are scattered, for the boys lie buried just where they fell, cradled in the bosom of the mother country that had nourished them and for whose safety they had laid down their lives. As we advanced they became more numerous, until we reached a point where as far as we could see in every direction floated little *tricolour* flags, like fine flowers in the landscape. . . . Here and there was a haystack with one grave beside it and again there would be one almost encircled with tiny flags which said : ' Here sleep the heroes.' It was a disturbing and a thrilling sight. I give you my word, as I stood there I envied them. It seemed to me a fine thing to lie out there in the open in the soil of the field their death has made holy, the duty well done, the dread over. You may know a finer way to go. I do not. Surely, since Death is, it is better than dying of age between clean sheets."

Further on in the book she says : " The only other thing I have done this month which could interest you was to have a little tea-party on the lawn for the convalescent boys of our ambulance, who were ' personally conducted ' by one of their nurses.

" When I got them grouped round the table in the shade of the big clump of lilac bushes, I was impressed, as I always am when I see numbers of common soldiers together, with the fact that no other race has such intelligent, such really well-modelled faces as the French. It is so rare to see a fat face among them. When the nurse looked at her watch and said it was time to return to the hospital, as they must not be late for dinner, they all rose. The law student came, cap in hand, and thanked me for a pleasant afternoon, and every man imitated his manners with varying degrees of success and made his little bow, turning back to wave their caps as they went round the corner."

She has some charming young officers billeted on her from time to time, and she describes the manner in which she is requested to offer her hospitality.

" It was just after lunch on Sunday—a grey, cold day, which had dawned on a world covered with frost—that there came a knock at the salon door. I opened it and there stood a soldier with his hand at salute, who said : ' Bon jour, madame, avez vous un lit pour un soldat ? '

" When you are to lodge a soldier in a house so intimately arranged as this one is, I defy anyone not to be curious as to what the lodger is to be like.

" There stood a tall, straight lad, booted and spurred, with a crop in one gloved hand, and the other raised to his fatigue cap in salute, and a smile on his bonny face. Of course, in twenty-four hours he became the child of the house. I feel like a grandmother to him. As for Amelie,

she falls over herself trying to spoil him and before the second day he became ' Monsieur André ' to her. Catch her giving a boy like that his military title, though he takes his duties most seriously."

This is really a charming volume and we hope that Miss Aldrich will be inspired to give her experiences of the fourth year of the war and that there may never be a fifth for her to experience.

H. H.

LETTERS TO THE EDITOR.

Whilst cordially inviting communications upon all subjects for these columns, we wish it to be distinctly understood that we do not IN ANY WAY hold ourselves responsible for the opinions expressed by our correspondents.

WE NIGHTINGALES KNOW BETTER.

To the Editor of THE BRITISH JOURNAL OF NURSING.

DEAR EDITOR,—We nurses desire to thank you for your speedy publicity concerning the Nightingale badge, and on reaching the proper authorities, viz., Mr. Bonham Carter.

Personally, I was roused to jealousy and indignation (having been trained as a Nightingale probationer) when first I noticed it worn by a midwife with a few months' training and passing as a qualified nurse here. We Nightingales know better, nothing of the kind having ever been issued from the training school to its probationers.

I can give a further instance of a village nurse half a mile from my district boundary, who was discharged by her committee for misconduct. The same always paraded the badge. All qualified nurses here, and, universally, I venture to add, will be indebted to you for your exposure of the degrading use to which our Lady of the Lamp's symbol has been subjected.

Again, I thank you in the name of all the profession around this district for sending that shaft home.

I am, yours faithfully,
ISABEL NICOLL,
Queen's Nurse, Member Society for State Registration of Nurses, National Union of Nurses, &c.
Hensingham,
Nr. Whitehaven.

WANT OF CONSIDERATION.

To the Editor of THE BRITISH JOURNAL OF NURSING.

DEAR MADAM,—I was much interested in the letter which appeared in your last number on the subject of the pay of Army Nurses and signed " An Army Sister," and I can endorse every word she says.

I should like particularly to draw attention to the salaries which the War Office pays the Matrons employed in the larger Territorial Hospitals at home, and which constitute a genuine hardship. Many of these ladies gave up good civil posts in order to fulfil their engagements to the War Office when war broke out, and have been working at high pressure for the last four years. The majority of them are in charge of hospitals of anything between 1,000 and 2,000 beds, and few, if any, even now receive as much as £150 per annum. When it is remembered that these posts are only temporary, that there is no pension attached to them, and no certainty of post-war employment, it will be seen how unfavourably they compare with civil matronships, even in small hospitals, where the work and responsibility are infinitely less and where the position is an assured and permanent one.

I should like to add that *so far* the yearly bonus to which all members of the Territorial Force Nursing Service are entitled by the terms of their enrolment, has been paid *only* to those members who have been invalided from the service, and it now transpires that if from any cause, except ill-health, a member resigns before the end of the war she will forfeit every penny of it.

If you can find room for this letter in your widely-read journal I shall feel grateful.

Yours faithfully,

A CIVILIAN MATRON.

THE V.A.D. QUESTION.

To the Editor of THE BRITISH JOURNAL OF NURSING.

DEAR MADAM,— May I give a concrete instance in support of the view that semi-trained nurses might be held to resemble, and possibly be treated like, Territorial officers. In the second year of the war I had much to do with the practical training and the supervision of a band of enthusiastic V.A.D.s. One of the best was the sister of the local draper, who himself enlisted in the Territorial battalion, and in less than six months earned a commission. He was a very gallant and efficient young officer and did valuable service before he gave his life for his country. Had he lived, he would, after the war, have returned to his business in the same simple spirit in which he left it (and practised it when on leave!). The sister yearned to serve her country in the same way. She could, by an effort, have been spared from home for a year or so, or as we then hoped for, the " duration of the war," and consulted me many times as to how she might at once get some real nursing to do. As far as she went she was very good, and had worked hard, but the three years' compulsory training was quite impossible for her ; and if she eventually went as a special military probationer (for I have now lost sight of her), I suppose after one-and-a-half or two years she is still one ! If all the nursing energies of the country were managed, as you suggest, by *one* central authority, no doubt these problems would be solved and waste of human material avoided ; but it would (shall we say it *will ?*) be a colossal task. I was much amused to find that one of my English-speaking friends, who has been

diligently reading the back numbers of the B.J.N., now talks glibly about *Vads* (as one syllable) !

I am, yours faithfully,

" RED CROSS WORKER."

Lyceum, Florence.

KERNELS FROM CORRESPONDENCE.

" Soldiers' Friend " writes : " Can nothing be done to supply sick soldiers with more food ? In the hospital I visit men have a light tea at 4.30 and nothing more till breakfast at 7.30 next morning. Also convalescent soldiers I entertain are all hungry. How would our political mandarins get on without their substantial luncheon and good dinner at 8 p.m. ? "

A Sister of Thirty :—" A Sister of Sixty," is the right sort. Since reading her letter, as I am to have my holiday in August, I have offered to work on the land. I feel sure I could help with the harvest, and as I love all animals should like to keep them clean and feed them. I have nothing but contempt for all these young society women who pose as patriots, but take care never to do a bit of real hard work for our country at this crisis. ' Merry Mummers ' is a very good description of them, and our once self-respecting profession is the sentimental peg and excuse for their silly ' gambols.' We owe ' Beatrice Kent ' a vote of thanks for her out-spoken courage. Let us hope Miss Asquith and her companions will take it to heart. Anyway we nurses have no respect for waste of time on social functions by young women able to *work*. Conscription of young unmarried women is what we approve."

OUR PRIZE COMPETITION.
QUESTIONS.

August 10th.—What have you learnt of new nursing methods in a Military Hospital ?

August 17th.—What is pernicious anæmia? How have you seen it treated ?

HOW TO HELP THE B.J.N.

1. Get new subscribers.
2. Send news and marked newspapers.
3. Secure new advertisers.
4. Read the advertisements.
5. Patronise the advertisers.
6. Tell the advertisers where you saw the advertisement.

OUR ADVERTISERS.

Do not omit to buy, as far as possible, everything you need from " Our Advertisers," and to recommend them to your friends. They are all first-class firms.

The Midwife.

CENTRAL MIDWIVES' BOARD (ENGLAND)

MONTHLY MEETING.

The Monthly Meeting of the Central Midwives' Board was held at 1, Queen Anne's Gate Buildings, Westminster, on Thursday, July 27th, Sir Francis Champneys presiding.

A letter was received from the Secretary of the Association for Promoting the Training and Supply of Midwives, enclosing for the information of the Board a copy of a revised edition of the Association's proposals for a State Midwifery Service, a summary of which we give in this issue.

In reference to the application of a candidate for the Board's Examination, it was resolved that she be required to satisfy the Board that she is not an enemy alien before admission to the examination.

A letter was read from the Medical Officer of Health for the County of Durham, raising various points in connection with the relation of medical practitioners to both certified midwives and uncertified women in their practice.

The letter concluded :—

" I am afraid that there is no doubt it is a common practice in many parts of the county for the doctors, especially in these times of stress, not to trouble to attend normal confinements if they know that an uncertified woman is present, though they attend later and sign the maternity benefit certificate. They thus tacitly encourage practice by uncertified women, and enable them to carry on a practice to the detriment and discouragement of any trained midwives in the district."

PENAL CASES.

A Special Meeting of the Central Midwives Board was held at 1, Queen Anne's Gate Buildings, Westminster, on Wednesday, July 24th, at 10.30 a.m., when the charges against a number of midwives were considered, with the following results :—

Struck Off the Roll and Certificate Cancelled.—Ellen Beesley (No. 12400), Alice Jemima Burnett, L.O.S. Cert. (No. 17397), Sarah Ann Dean (No. 18278), Hannah Hammond, C.M.B. Examination (No. 41117), Mary Jane Hartley (No. 20537), Clarissa Lister (No. 15068), Sarah Moxon (No. 2219), Rebecca Taylor (No. 7240), Gertrude Davies (No. 29355), Ada Rawlings (No. 9709).

Severely Censured.—Henrietta Haycock, C.M.B. Exam. (No. 30190).

Adjourned for Report in Three and Six Months.—Lucy Lake (No. 2519), Charlotte Major, C.M.B. Exam. (No. 41223).

There were several defended cases. The charges against one midwife included her carrying in the bag containing her appliances a " pig's black pudding."

PROPOSALS FOR A STATE-AIDED MIDWIFERY SERVICE.

In September last we discussed at some length the Proposals for a State-aided Midwifery Service in England and Wales embodied in a Memorandum by the Association for Promoting the Training and Supply of Midwives as a basis for necessary legislation. This Memorandum has now been revised, and we publish below the Summary of the proposals. We hope later to discuss them.

Summary.

(i) The greatest need in maternity and infant welfare is to secure an efficient midwifery service in *all* parts of the country, so that the most congested areas, where the rate burden is most severely felt, shall not be left with a defective service.

(ii) At present, though there are enough midwives competent to give efficient midwifery services, the fees obtainable are too small to enable them to earn an adequate livelihood. It is, therefore, necessary that every midwife attending a confinement must be secured an adequate fee; this is put at 25s.

(iii) In order that the areas most difficult to serve shall not be left without these services, it is necessary that the requisite sum for paying this fee shall be provided from the Exchequer, and not be met from local rates.

(iv) The fee of the midwife must be guaranteed, and must not depend upon the ability or willingness of the patient to pay.

(v) The Exchequer money should be disbursed through an efficient Local Body, which must supervise the systematic provision of midwives for the area; this body must be the same as that which is responsible for the inspection of midwives under the Act.

(vi) The scheme must include, and be conditional upon, the provision of greatly improved arrangements for the inspection of midwives everywhere.

(vii) The scheme must be accompanied by sufficient Exchequer money for the payment of requisite fees for doctors called in to abnormal cases by midwives under the C.M.B. rules.

(viii) These various items point to a sum of about £1,000,000 per annum being sufficient in England and Wales; its provision is intended to secure efficient midwifery services for every confinement in England and Wales where the income is too small to meet the charges involved.

(ix) The provision of Exchequer money for giving an increased maternity benefit *in cash*, or for giving *cash* allowances to the mother, would not meet the needs of the situation, since this does not secure that any *efficient services* are provided; but the present proposals, by securing efficient midwifery services in every case, guarantee that the whole of the money provided from the Exchequer is expended directly upon provision of services that immediately affect the welfare of mother and infant.

VERDICT OF WILFUL MURDER.

The adjourned inquiry as to the cause of the death of Kenneth Cedric Goodman at the Sydenham Infant Welfare Centre, on July 19th, was resumed by Mr. H. R. Oswald on Tuesday at Lewisham.

Miss Payne, the Superintendent of the Centre, explained that the worst kind of wasting and prematurely-born infants were taken, and those suffering from digestive disorders; no other diseases were admitted. Had she received Nurse Thompson's references before engaging her she would not have done so.

The medical officer at the Centre, Dr. Gladstone, said after his attention was called to Goodman's case he discovered the double fracture of the skull spoken of by Colonel Toogood in his evidence last week.

Nurse Eva Grace Thompson, who was cautioned by the Coroner, stated that she had charge of Goodman and four other children during the night of June 4th. She denied striking the child on the head. When she handed him over to the day staff on the morning of June 5th he was quite normal, and she could not account for the fractures of the skull and the three bruises. She denied that she took drugs or intoxicants.

The Coroner informed the jury that in the early days of June six children were found injured at the Centre, and four had died—one from double pneumonia. Another, still alive, had a fractured skull, and the sixth, also alive, had a fracture of the arm and a dislocation of the collar-bone.

The jury returned a verdict of wilful murder against Nurse Thompson, who was arrested in court and committed for trial.

£300 DAMAGES FOR MIDWIFE.

Damages were assessed by a Sheriff's jury at £300 at Green Street Courthouse, Dublin, as reported in the *General Advertiser*, in a case in which Mary Anne Herbert a midwifery nurse of Rush, claimed £1,000 damages from M. Sigman, 40, Lower Clanbrassil Street, dairy proprietor, for injury to herself and her bicycle by the negligent driving of a horse and trap on January 20th. Mr. Gavan Duffy (instructed by Messrs. Corrigan & Corrigan), for the plaintiff, said the plaintiff's right arm was broken, and the defendant made no defence or offered no apology. Dr. M'Elhinney, Meath Hospital, said the plaintiff would not be able to do her duties for two years.

LECTURES TO NURSES ON VENEREAL DISEASES.

The course of free lectures to nurses on Venereal Diseases at St. Paul's Hospital, Red Lion Square, by Mr. Leonard Myer, F.R.C.S., met a great need, judging by the large and increasing numbers of nurses who attended each week.

NATIONAL BABY WEEK COUNCIL.

In our last issue we drew attention to the fact that an interesting meeting of the National Baby Week Council took place at the Armitage Hall last week. The point of greatest interest—to which, for lack of space, we were unable to refer at the time—was the following resolution :—

" That the National Baby Week Council, whilst approving the objects of the Maternity and Child Welfare Bill, deplores the continued sacrifice of the nation's present health and future life, to *Departmental Vested Interests*, calls upon the Government to establish a Ministry of Health without further delay, and at no distant date ; and that the Council approach its affiliated organisations with a view to a free discussion of this important subject, and to carry on a co-ordinated propaganda and campaign in favour of a Ministry of Health during the coming autumn."

The italics are ours. The important and significant point about it is, that although one member suggested as an amendment, that the words " Departmental Vested Interests " should be deleted, as being too strong, and another seconded it, when the Chairman put it to the vote the meeting was solidly in favour of having the words retained. We see in this the first fruits of the movement for social and political purity, and are encouraged thereby. Those who are awakened have begun to " *march breast forward.*"

AMERICAN HELP FOR MOTHERS.

The American Red Cross has allocated the sum of £5,000 to the National League for Health, Maternity, and Child Welfare, to promote the establishment of maternity centres and day nurseries in areas where much war work is being done.

Mrs. Whitelaw Reid, chairman of the London Chapter of the American Red Cross, on July 24th, opened the new buildings for the crèche at the North Islington Maternity Centre, arranged by the Committee of the American Infant Welfare Centre. The buildings are at 9, Manor Gardens, Holloway Road, Islington.

THE BEST.

" We all have held in fee one woman's heart :
Have all been pillowed on one woman's breast,
Have knelt and worshipped at one woman's knee—
A mother's. If this be the only part
We have learned of woman's love, it is the best."

A. G. SHERRIFF.

From "A Sonnet to Mother-love."

THE
BRITISH JOURNAL OF NURSING
WITH WHICH IS INCORPORATED
THE NURSING RECORD
EDITED BY MRS BEDFORD FENWICK

No. 1,584. SATURDAY, AUGUST 10, 1918. Vol. LXI.

EDITORIAL.

THE UNCHANGING RESOLVE OF THE BRITISH EMPIRE.

Three messages stand out amongst those delivered on the fourth anniversary of the entrance of the British Empire into the War ; that of his Majesty the King to the Heads of Allied countries, that of the Bishop of London, representative of the Church, delivered at the morning service, on Sunday, at St. Paul's to the great congregation which filled the Cathedral to the doors, and that of the Prime Minister, representative of the State, delivered in sealed packets and read on Saturday evening to audiences in the theatres and elsewhere.

THE KING'S MESSAGE TO THE HEADS OF ALLIED COUNTRIES.

On this the fourth anniversary of the day on which my country joined in the great conflict which still distracts the world it is my privilege to convey to you my greetings, and to emphasize once again the unchanging resolve of the British Empire to concentrate its entire energy upon a victorious conclusion of the struggle. Thanks to the determination of our peoples and the splendid achievements of our brave sailors and soldiers, I feel confident that the dawn of a victorious peace is not far distant.

" Go FORWARD."

The Bishop took for his text the words " Wherefore criest thou unto me ? Speak unto the children of Israel that they go forward." He spoke of the necessity and the power of prayer, and said :—

" Prayer which is to move the world must be accompanied by the resolute action which attests its sincerity—back to the desk to-morrow or after the needed holiday ; out into the battlefield again after the precious days of leave ; on to the land to gather in the harvest. Away with all doubts and all fears, all croakers, and all those who weaken the knees of the valiant. Be strong and of good courage ; be not afraid and be not dismayed ; the Lord shall fight for you."

" HOLD FAST."

The Prime Minister's Message to the Nation was " Hold Fast." He wrote in part :—

" The message which I send to the people of the British Empire on the fourth anniversary of their entry into the war is ' Hold Fast.'

" We are in this war for no selfish ends. We are in it to recover freedom for the nations which have been brutally attacked and despoiled, and to prove that no people, however powerful, can surrender itself to the lawless ambitions of militarism without meeting retribution, swift, certain, and disastrous, at the hands of the free nations of the world. To stop short of Victory for this cause would be to compromise the future of mankind."

THE WAR SHRINE.

Thousands of people who worshipped in the churches and chapels in the morning were present at the blessing by the Bishop of London of the War Shrine in Hyde Park in the afternoon, and placed there their floral offerings in remembrance of the valiant men and women with the Expeditionary Force, the sick and wounded, the prisoners and captives and the heroic dead. The shrine still remains, close to the Marble Arch and to Park Lane, that great highway of traffic where all may see, testifying to the affectionate remembrance of the Nation for those who in concert with our Allies are keeping the flag of freedom aloft on land, on sea, and in the air.

LABORATORY WORK FOR WOMEN.

By A. KNYVETT GORDON, M.B., B.C., B.A. Cantab.

Some years ago, when in charge of a large hospital, it was my duty to examine candidates for the post of probationer nurse. The standard was high, because I did not accept anyone whom I thought would be likely to break down anywhere on training : consequently many, otherwise of excellent physique, were rejected on account of slightly deformed feet or varicose veins.

I have often wondered what became of these girls, many of whom must have had a natural aptitude for medical work of one kind or another, and it is a pity that they should be lost altogether to the profession. Nowadays, however, they need not be, and I think that the opening that awaits them in the laboratory is perhaps insufficiently realised. Let me, then, briefly describe the position, and then put in a plea for the pathologist who requires their services.

Until recently, pathology was a science of its own, and it got its facts mainly from the examination of tissues removed in the theatre and from the performance of post-mortem examinations; the pathologist himself was often a man without very much clinical inclination, and was, anyhow, concerned more with the advancement of science than with the treatment of the particular patient.

Small blame to him ! The science he loved, however, gave him scarcely a living wage, and certainly led to no pecuniary or social advancement, and very seldom was he permitted to see the practical result of his work. So, many brilliant men were lost to science by being pitchforked into general practice by the force of circumstances.

Gradually, however, the barrier between the clinician and the pathologist was broken down, and a new department of clinical pathology came into being. By this I mean that the pathologist was called in during the life of the patient to find out what he could from examination of any material he could collect, instead of having simply to find out after death how the horse had been stolen ! Of the value of this co-operation, the diagnosis of diphtheria and of phthisis by the detection of the characteristic microbes in the throat and sputum are good examples.

This child of the alliance grew apace, until the facilities for diagnosis afforded by the laboratory were demanded not only by the practising clinician, but even by his patient.

This necessitated a considerable increase both in the number of laboratories and in the staff which each employed.

Then came the war, and everybody knows how incalculable has been the value of laboratory work, not only in the treatment of the wounded, but also in the prevention of sickness which in former campaigns was more deadly than the weapons of the foe. On their return to civil practice many medical men now serving will demand the laboratory facilities which they have enjoyed in the field for all classes of their patients, and it is evident also that in any schemes for improvement of the national health research must find a place.

In the past, pathology has almost entirely been confined to men, though I have often thought—and taught—that this was unnecessary. Women are eminently fitted for pathological work, and nowadays they are taking to it in increasing numbers.

In a laboratory there are two classes of worker : the qualified pathologist, who has passed through the whole medical curriculum, and the technical assistant; it is the latter which we will now consider. What sort of life will the woman aspirant lead, and what advantages does the career hold out?

Well, in the first place she need not be physically robust; the hours of duty are not excessive, and she can sit or stand at her work at will. Consequently her night's rest is not broken by the cry of the aching back or the incipient flat foot.

Then she earns a living wage from the start, and at once begins to take a hand in the fascinating work of finding out what is wrong with the patient.

If she can afford it, there is distinct advantage in taking a preliminary course of instruction in Bacteriology and Chemistry at one of the teaching centres in London or elsewhere, but this is not essential, and she can start, if she prefers it, on the lowest rung of the ladder in the laboratory itself.

Probably she begins by spreading films of pus, sputa, and so on, and later on perhaps staining them for the pathologist to examine. At this stage she also learns something about microscopy itself.

Pathologists are often chatty souls, and in the intervals between one specimen, or batch, and the next, are usually keen on teaching. Generally they are also enthusiasts, and their reminiscences and day dreams are often fascinating.

Then she learns the gentle art of glass-blowing, and it is extraordinary how skilful many girls become at this in a very short time. It is important, for well-made apparatus tends to careful work.

Then there is the department of chemical pathology, where she learns not only how to make up solutions, but also the elements of chemistry, beginning with simple urine-testing, and going on to the chemical part of the analysis of drinking-water and foods. Then she learns how to cut and stain sections of tumours and of organs removed post-mortem, and also the details of bacteriology, such as the sowing of culture media with discharges from wounds, &c., and observing what comes up. Incidentally, this is a type of gardening quite as fascinating as the tending of the fashionable allotment. And so she goes on in a daily task that is never dull because it is always lit up by flashes of light from the pathological elysium where the answers to the eternal problems are kept.

All this makes for an atmosphere of comradeship. I never knew anyone give themselves airs in a laboratory for very long. In fact, swagger is impossible, if only because in research everyone is always making mistakes, or perhaps I should say following temporarily the wrong byroad.

The only essential preliminary qualifications are keenness—and this is the most important of all —and a certain degree of natural dexterity. For the hopelessly awkward and heavy fingered the laboratory has no place.

Then the candidate must not be absolutely hopeless at " Figures." Later on she will have to work out chemical reactions and statistics, and if this has to be done by counting her fingers she will be left behind in the race. But the majority of girls nowadays have these qualifications—and especially for those who prefer mental to physical work, a laboratory career offers many and interesting possibilities.

Messrs. Debenham & Freebody have given up two of their large workrooms in Welbeck Street to the West End Hospital. They will be known as the Debenham wards.

MISS MARY COURTENAY, R.R.C.,
Matron, Montgreenan Auxiliary Hospital, Kilwinning.

NURSING AND THE WAR.

We are indebted to the courtesy of the editor of the *Scots Pictorial* for our portrait of Miss Mary Courtnay, Matron of Montgreenan Auxiliary Hospital, Kilwinning, who was recently decorated with the Royal Red Cross.

At an Investiture held in the Quadrangle of Buckingham Palace on July 31st, the King conferred the following decorations :—

ROYAL RED CROSS.

FIRST CLASS.

Territorial Force Nursing Service.—Assistant Matron Ada TAYLOR.

Civil Nursing Service.—Assistant Matron Isabel KEMP, Sister Elizabeth MACAULAY.

Canadian Army Nursing Service.—Matron Myra GOODEVE.

SECOND CLASS.

Queen Alexandra's Imperial Military Nursing Service Reserve. — Sister Georgina HESTER, Sister Florence HUGHES, Sister Clara ROBINSON, Sister Amy McDOWELL, Staff Nurse Mercy HUFFER, Staff Nurse Euphemia LORAINE, and Miss Margaret PIERSON.

Territorial Force Nursing Service. — Sister Charlotte FITZMAYER.

Civil Nursing Service.— Matron Ethel CAREW-HODGE, Matron Marianne IFFLAND, Matron Phillimore IND, Matron Kathleen IRWIN, Matron Mabel JOHNSON, Matron Amy KAYE, Matron Ellen KIDSON, Matron Blanche KNAPTON, Matron Edith WAKE, Matron Marie WHEELER, Assistant Matron Isabel HEBERDEN, Sister Ellen HOWARD, Sister Gertie INMAN, Sister Minnie JONES, and Mrs. Marian McGLASHAN.

British Red Cross Society. —Matron Mabel HUNT, Sister Jessie GUNN, Sister Kate HATTON, and Sister Kathleen NIXON.

Voluntary Aid Detachment.—Miss Kate BISHOP, Mrs. Sibyl COCKBURN, Miss Lily HAGGAR, Mrs. Evelyn HEYDE, Miss Catherine HICKLING, Miss Mabel HODGES, Miss Amy HUSON, Miss Kate JACKSON, Mrs. Agnes JAMES, Mrs. Eva JONES, and Miss Gertrude MIRRINGTON.

Canadian Army Nursing Service.—Sister Alba ANDREW, Sister Irene BRADY, and Sister Sophie HOERNER.

THE MILITARY MEDAL.

Queen Alexandra's Imperial Military Nursing Service Reserve.—Sister Mary BROWN.

At the opening of Australia House by the King on Saturday last, Head Sister Ida O'Dwyer, Australian Army Nursing Service, R.R.C., was presented to the King and Queen.

THE MILITARY MEDAL.
FOR DISTINGUISHED SERVICES IN THE FIELD.

A special supplement to the *London Gazette* issued on July 30th states that the King has approved the award of the Military Medal to the under-mentioned ladies for distinguished services in the field. In each case the act of bravery recorded was performed during enemy air raids on hospitals :—

Sister C. L. A. ROBINSON, A.R.R.C., Q.A.I.M.N.S.—A stationary hospital was struck by four bombs from an enemy aeroplane and one wing was practically cut in two, many patients being buried in the debris. Sister Robinson, at very great personal risk, went in amongst the ruins to assist in recovering the patients, quite regardless of danger, her one thought being the rescue of the patients. She displayed magnificent coolness and resource.

A.-Sister N. GALVIN, Q.A.I.M.N.S.R.—Four enemy bombs were dropped on the building occupied by the hospital, causing much damage to the ward in which Sister Galvin was on night duty. She remained in the ward attending to the sick, several of whom were wounded, and carried on her work as if nothing had happened. She displayed the greatest coolness and devotion to duty.

A.-Sister M. M. DE GUERIN, Q.A.I.M.N.S.R.—The building occupied by the hospital was hit by four bombs, which cut in two the ward in which Sister Guerin was on night duty. Several patients were wounded and buried in the debris of the destroyed building, but she remained on duty in her ward, displaying the greatest coolness and courage in attending to the wounded and helping to rescue the buried.

Sister L. A. WILKINSON, Q.A.I.M.N.S.R.—Although her ward was demolished, she continued to attend to the wounded whilst the raid was still in progress.

Staff Nurse B. DASCOMBE, Q.A.I.M.N.S.R.—Her ward being destroyed by a bomb and herself wounded, she insisted on remaining at her post and attending to the wounded.

Sister (A.-Matron) L. M. M. TOLLER, R.R.C., Q.A.I.M.N.S.—When the sisters' quarters were wrecked and nurses wounded, Sister Toller collected the staff and placed them in comparative safety. By her fine example she undoubtedly saved life.

Staff Nurse A. M. McGRATH, Q.A.I.M.N.S.R.—In charge of a ward of serious cases. She showed throughout a quiet confidence and set a fine example during a most critical period.

Sister M. E. DAVIS, Q.A.I.M.N.S.—When the sisters' quarters were wrecked and bombs were falling, she showed a fine example, and assisted materially in controlling the situation and attending to the sisters who were wounded.

Staff Nurse S. D. MUNRO, Q.A.I.M.N.S.R.—An enemy air raid wrecked three of her wards. She showed coolness and contempt of danger and a solicitude for her patients which was invaluable.

Staff Nurse K. R. LOWE, T.F.N.S.—Bombs destroyed a large portion of the ward in which she was on night duty, wounding and burying many of the patients. She continued to carry out her duties with great composure, and showed much resourcefulness in looking after the injured.

Miss M. THOMPSON, F.A.N.Y., Miss W. M. ELWES, F.A.N.Y., Miss E. A. CORRIS, F.A.N.Y., Miss M. RICHARDSON, F.A.N.Y., Miss M. O'CONNELL-BIANCONI, F.A.N.Y., Miss H. M. DICKINSON, F.A.N.Y., Miss E. B. CALLANDER, F.A.N.Y.—All these lady drivers were out with their cars during the raid, picking up and in every way assisting the wounded and injured. They showed great bravery and coolness, and were an example to all ranks.

Miss K. M. FRESHFIELD, V.A.D.—The ward in which she was working was destroyed by a bomb, but she continued to attend to her patients, and was herself very severely wounded.

Miss L. A. GREGORY, V.A.D.—Her ward was destroyed by bombs, but she insisted on remaining at her post, and attended the wounded during the progress of the raid.

Miss K. FABLING, Miss S. DICKSON, Miss J. PENNELL, Miss M. DAVIDSON, B.R.C.S. (V.A.D.).—All these lady drivers were out with their cars during the raid, picking up and in every way assisting the wounded and injured, and showed great bravery and coolness, and were an example to all ranks. They also carried to safety and helped in every way many French civilians.

Miss W. A. BRAMPTON, B.R.C.S.—This lady continued at duty throughout the raid, although the ward in her charge was almost completely wrecked, several patients killed, and she herself was wounded.

Miss D. M. L. CREWDSON, B.R.C.S. (V.A.D.).—Although herself wounded, this lady remained at duty and assisted in dressing the wounds of patients.

Commandant W. E. S. MOUNT BATTEN, B.R.C.S.—She superintended the work of the convoy, drove an ambulance car herself during the raid, and by her coolness and disregard for her own safety ensured the prompt removal of the wounded to hospital.

Sub-Section Leader G. M. CUTHBERT, B.R.C.S.—She showed exceptional coolness and courage in directing her section.

Section Leader G. F. JOHNSTON, B.R.C.S.—She directed her section with coolness and courage under very trying circumstances.

Senior Section Leader J. V. MELLOR, B.R.C.S.—She showed exceptional courage and efficiency as senior section leader.

Nurse M. G. CAMPBELL, B.R.C.S.—During a raid buildings were set on fire. She moved about in full glare, regardless of imminent danger, taking patients to safety, and inspiring confidence in all.

V.A.D. M. CAVANAGH, St. John's Ambulance Brigade. —Miss Cavanagh was in charge of four wards, two of which were entirely wrecked. She continued to perform her duty; in addition was very active in removing the wounded to a place of comparative safety.

Nurse E. HOUNSLOW, A.R.R.C., St. John's Ambulance Brigade.—A bomb fell between two of her wards and injured many patients. She behaved with the utmost coolness, and set a fine example, attending wounded under most trying circumstances.

Asst. Matron M. CHITTOCK, St. John's Ambulance Brigade Hospital.—She displayed great presence of mind, and instilled courage and confidence throughout a very trying time.

Matron C. E. TODD, St. John's Ambulance Brigade Hospital.—She moved freely about the wards during the bombing, encouraging the sisters and patients, and displayed great bravery and presence of mind throughout.

Sister G. WARNER, St. John's Ambulance Brigade Hospital.—She displayed the utmost coolness and maintained a cheery spirit throughout, showing great bravery.

Sister J. BEMROSE, St. John's Ambulance Brigade Hospital.—She showed disregard of danger, and continued to attend the wounded in her charge during the heavy bombardment.

Sister M. McGINNIS, St. John's Ambulance Brigade Hospital.—She showed great courage, took charge of a ward, and sustained her patients.

Sister M. H. BALLANCE, St. John's Ambulance Brigade Hospital.—Her fortitude and courage were most conspicuous. She devoted herself entirely to her patients.

CARE OF THE WOUNDED.

PARKSIDE ORTHOPÆDIC HOSPITAL, RAVENSCOURT PARK, HAMMERSMITH.

In any kind of weather this, the newest of auxiliary war hospitals, would have been attractive, but on a warm summer day, with the breath of the flowers sweetening the air, and the bright sunlight making everything look cheerful, the impression left on the mind of the visitor was particularly pleasant. It stands in two acres of ground and is approached by a shady avenue of beautiful old sycamore trees. It is a handsome, well-built, commodious house, admirably adapted to its present purpose. The need of a hospital of this sort for officers has long been felt ; the Infirmary in Ducane Road is used for the accommodation of men only, requiring orthopædic treatment. It seems that it was only necessary to mention the fact to the Mayor of the Borough (Alderman H. Foreman, O.B.E., J.P.) for the idea to materialise. It is owing to his great generosity and that of Mrs. Foreman that Parkside has been acquired, redecorated and furnished to accommodate thirty officers besides the staff. No expense has been spared in making it as cheerful, cosy and comfortable as money plus a kind heart could make it. There may be hospitals as nice, but it is certain there could not be any *nicer.*

There is uniformity without monotony. Polished floors everywhere ; a mat of artistic colouring beside each bed, white embroidered coverlet, with an eiderdown quilt on each bed, and each of a different coloured silk. Shot silk appeared to be the favourite. White-painted lockers with glass tops, upon each of which stands an electric lamp with a shade of the same colour and material as the quilt. Harmony and proportion spell art, and this is evident everywhere, and is, we were told, the taste of the Mayoress. The walls are distempered in a soft shade of grey. The architect is to be congratulated upon the liberal provision of window space ; had he designed the house for the purpose he could not have done better.

The lavatory and bathroom accommodation is abundant, also sluices for bedpans, &c.

A winter garden or conservatory is used as a lounge and smoke room. There is a large and handsomely furnished dining room for the officers on the ground floor, and the same in the basement for the V.A.D. staff. The resident staff consists of the Matron, Miss Dible, and one Sister ; also the cook. Thirty-six V.A.D.s come in in three shifts of twelve. These as well as the Commandant are, of course, non-resident.

The sitting room for the officers is as comfortable as the rest of the house. The *pièce de resistance* there is a splendid new Grafonola, the gift of Messrs. Watsons, Sons & Room. There is a good-sized vegetable garden, which is not the least of the many attractions of the hospital.

We are greatly indebted to Miss Dible for her courtesy in showing us this admirable hospital.

Many generous people have given handsome subscriptions, but many more would be gratefully accepted.

The hospital was opened on Thursday, July 25th, by Mrs. Hayes Fisher, accompanied by the Right Hon. W. Hayes Fisher, President of the Local Government Board.

                                 B. K.

FRENCH FLAG NURSING CORPS.

WHAT THE " TIMES " THINKS OF OUR WORK AND POLICY.

" The French Flag Nursing Corps, which has supplied from 100 to 200 of the best trained British nurses for French Army hospitals, since 1914, came into prominence in the recent retreat from the Chemin des Dames, where they gave an example of their mettle by sticking to their posts till all the wounded were evacuated, and only escaped as the Germans entered the hospitals. These British women, scattered in twos and threes in great military hospitals throughout France, have raised the whole standard of nursing and made thousands of friends for us—friends who will not forget."

The good, kind " Henriette," femme de ménage at Verneuil, is now a refugee in Savoy. She was in attendance on the Sisters at the old Chateau to the last day when the retreat began. A Sister writes :—" Poor girl, she was very good to us, and has lost everything. Would it be possible to send her a gift of clothing or any help ; they are glad of such gifts. I send you her address." Poor Henriette ! Well we remember her and the lovely déjeuner she prepared for us the happy day we visited the Sisters in their romantic surroundings. Very happy we should be to forward her a gift of clothing, if any kind friend will help to make up a parcel. We could do with a tidy coat and skirt, two pairs of warm stockings, a good pair of boots, a warm petticoat, underlinen, and some tidy aprons, and any useful additions. " Henriette " is tall and stout and requires garments of ample proportions. It would be nice to send her a parcel from " Friends in England " now she is far from her home. Let us hope it may not be for long ; but, alas ! we know the devastation of the fair land of France, where the hoof of the Hun has passed. Please address gifts to the Editor, 431, Oxford Street, London W., marked " For Henriette."

A Sister in the war zone writes :—" We are having very bad nights, as we have nightly visits from the Boches. We get big rushes of wounded when the brutes have gone. . . . Nearly all our windows have gone, and some of our wounded have been cut with the falling glass. My flat has its disadvantages, so I lie down on any spare bed in the hospital, dressed of course. . . . The hospital where we are working was a mill before the war."

Royal British Nurses' Association.

(Incorporated by Royal Charter.)

THIS SUPPLEMENT BEING THE OFFICIAL ORGAN OF THE CORPORATION.

THE TRAINING OF CHILDREN OF FROM TWO TO FIVE YEARS OF AGE.

Synopsis of a Lecture given at Woolwich under the auspices of the City Parochial Charities by MISS KATE C. ATHERTON, *M.R.B.N.A., Medallist of the Royal Sanitary Institute.*

In commencing a very interesting lecture on "The Training of Children," Miss Atherton drew attention to the fact that, although one cannot change the nature of a child, much can be done by careful training and by environment so to direct his tendencies that his character will be such as to help, and not to hinder him, in the battle of life, and to make him in every sense a useful member of the community. Undue repression in the training of children is just as harmful as over-indulgence; to this, as well as to a shock or perhaps some nervous condition in childhood, mental trouble in after life is not infrequently traceable. Children have the same emotions as older people—love, jealousy, hope, and fear—and it is to be remembered that a child who has a great capacity for love has often a similar capacity for jealousy, so that his very love for others may indirectly be made the cause for stimulating a tendency to jealousy, and may give rise to a great deal of unhappiness, and even to ill-health. A child, being immature, is very crude and simple, and one of the first lessons to teach him is that of obedience. This can often be practised as a game, and, where there are two children, they can compete as to who will perform the command most quickly. In this exercise care must be taken not to carry it to the point of fatigue. Drill answers much the same purpose for older children. Organised exercises, as soon as the child is able to perform these, are very beneficial; they improve physical development, lead to unfolding of the mind, cause the child to realise that there is a right way and a wrong

way of doing the simplest thing, and unconsciously they develop in the child the habit of doing promptly what he is told.

Observation is of the greatest importance in those to whom there is entrusted the care of child life; in fact, to deal successfully with children one must, so to speak, become a child, must observe and understand to the utmost possible extent the psychology of the child mind. By observations and comparisons we arrive at conclusions which help us to understand each individual child. Take for instance, the immoral child. Very often he will be found to be in some respect, perhaps only in a very minor degree, physically defective. It is wrong to train such a child, or one whose health is not good, on the same lines as a normal child. In such cases suggestion often plays a very important part in the training. Then there is the rheumatic child, constantly quarrelling and "grizzling"; in all probability he is nervous, delicate, timid, and difficult to please, but rarely actually ill. Such children should be treated with the greatest consideration, but should be encouraged to mix much with other children, or they are apt to develop into the "mother's darling" type, and to become an affliction alike to themselves and their elders. In studying children always observe the signs of nutrition, expression, movement, and posture. Fatigue, for instance, is often indicated by posture. Ask a tired child to extend the arms on a level with the shoulders, and it will invariably happen that the arms will droop and the thumbs hang down.

Self-control and independence should be cultivated in children. A well-managed child in this respect is usually a well-balanced adult in later life. Regularity is really the keynote to successful training, and indeed applies to a period previous to the actual birth of the child; we, who have much to do with welfare work, are constantly impressing upon the mother the importance of regular habits during pregnancy.

Out of regular habits self-control is evolved, and, in order to develop independence, never do for a child what he is quite capable of doing for himself; rather, indeed, he should be encouraged to do things for those around him. He will enjoy performing little duties, and even the boys should be taught to help in the home; this will teach them to use their hands, and will sharpen their faculties. It is impossible to overrate the pleasure a child has in using his hands, and it is never too early to teach him to handle, to grasp, and later to pile up and throw about his toys. Complaints are sometimes made about the " destructiveness " of children, but it must be remembered that sometimes this arises from the mere desire to be creative, and then it should be encouraged rather than otherwise. Those of us who have worked among children in the hospitals and elsewhere often hear the demand, " more pictures, more scissors, and some paste, please."

Some children have a great difficulty in being accurate, and this must not be confused with lying, for they are often delighted to relate an experience which is really all imagination. In such cases the child should be taught to explain that he is " only pretending."

AN ATTRACTIVE CLUB FOR NURSES.

Members coming up to town for the holidays frequently write to enquire where they can find a comfortable and central club at which they may stay. They will find nowhere more pleasant quarters than the Kensington Gardens Nurses' Club, 57, Kensington Gardens Square, W. It is within easy reach of all the important parts of the city, and the Principal of the Club, Miss B. Cave, had a very intimate knowledge of club life and the requirements of private nurses before ever she established her own very popular club. Its rooms are large, airy, and very tastefully furnished, while the numerous contrivances for adding to the convenience and comfort of the nurses, and the exactitude with which their telephone messages are attended to, add very much to the value of the club as a residential one for private nurses. One much-travelled nurse expressed the view that she had never sojourned in any club where the atmosphere seemed more homelike or offered a greater sense of freedom.

Miss Cave is a Member of the Royal British Nurses' Association and of the Incorporated Society of Trained Masseuses, and her club is one of the very few large clubs for nurses in London which has a trained nurse at its head.

CORRESPONDENCE.
THE BADGE OF MEMBERSHIP OF THE ROYAL CHARTERED CORPORATION OF NURSES.
To the Secretary, R.B.N.A.

DEAR MADAM,—I have seen a picture of the badge of our Association in the official organ, and I should like to draw attention to the fact that all the members should make a point of wearing it who can. I often meet nurses from our Association, and we always recognise one another as fellow members through our badge. I have heard of two of our members who met out on the Rockies, and one was able to give the greatest help to the other, when, but for the R.B.N.A. badge, they would never have known that they were members of the same body, or even fellow nurses. I am, &c..

H. MACWILLIAM,
M.R.B.N.A.

A KIND THOUGHT.
To the Secretary, R.B.N.A.

DEAR MADAM,—A few days ago I heard of a member, suffering from an incurable disease, who felt the keenest disappointment because she could not afford, owing to the expenses of her illness, to take THE BRITISH JOURNAL OF NURSING, as she had been in the habit of doing our monthly paper. Her subscription was promptly paid for her by another member, but I hear that there are quite a number of the old nurses who find the cost of a weekly paper too much for their slender incomes.

We have had to discontinue the Recluse Club since the war began. Might I suggest that it now be revived for a slightly different purpose than its original one—that of supplying our old members with an illustrated paper each week? We used to subscribe a shilling annually, and I think it would be nice if we young members could link up and subscribe the same amount again, just to prevent the old members who helped to found the Association, and who have belonged to it for so long, from feeling shut out or left behind. Seven of us could keep one old nurse in touch with it right to the end in this way, and I know that it is a real grief to some to feel that they will no longer have their NURSES' JOURNAL each month.

The President's letter has given us all pleasure, and I for one warmly endorse what she says about welcoming other nurses to a share in our Charter. I am glad, too, that you have made this new arrangement about the official organ, for many of us have been very indignant about the one-sided propaganda for the College in the other papers. I hope that other nurses will follow the example of the R.B.N.A. members and " wake up."

I am, &c.,
V. M. CORBETT,
M.R.B.N.A.

Application forms for registration and membership can be obtained on application to the Secretary, R.B.N.A., 10, Orchard Street, Portman Square, W. 1.

(Signed) ISABEL MACDONALD,
Secretary to the Corporation.

LONDON HOSPITAL SYSTEM.

In the House of Commons on July 31st Major Chapple asked the Under Secretary for War whether the certificate of training presented in evidence of qualification by London Hospital nurses applying for posts in the Army Service states that the nurse has had three years' training in the hospital or only two years' training ?

Mr. Macpherson replied that steps are always taken to ascertain that a nurse has completed the necessary period of training and service in the wards. In reply to Sir C. Henry he said that there was no differentiation in the nurses that come from the London Hospital and from others.

Major Chapple then said : " Is the Right Hon. gentleman aware that he told us that a three years' certificate of training is necessary for appointment to the Army Nursing Service, and I ask him in the present question, does the London Hospital certificate of training say two years or three years ? "

Mr. Macpherson replied : " I cannot add anything to the answer I have given, but I would like to point out that the three years includes two years' training and one year's service in the wards."

Pressed further by Major Chapple, Mr. Macpherson said : " We are satisfied in every case with the nurse who comes from the London Hospital, or any other hospital, if she has completed the necessary period of training and service in the ward."

Thus, though the London Hospital certifies its nurses at the end of two years, the War Office requires that they shall serve another year in the wards before they are eligible for Queen Alexandra's Imperial Military Nursing Service, which, presumably, indicates that it does not consider a nurse certified at the end of two years adequately qualified.

Major Chapple also asked the President of the Board of Education whether nurses trained at the London Hospital have been appointed to any posts under the jurisdiction of the Board. Before putting the question he also asked, as a point of Order, why the following words were deleted from the question : " Whether he is aware that nurses at the London Hospital are taken from their training in the wards and sent out to do private nursing at the end of their second year, receiving 13s. per week, while the hospital draws not less than 29s. per week profit from their earnings ; and whether he will see that no nurses are appointed from hospitals that exploit their nurses in this way "—with those words deleted the question is meaningless ? "

The Speaker replied that the words were in the nature of giving, and not asking, information to a Department which was not responsible for it, and further that the Board of Education had no control over the training of nurses at the London or any other hospital.

THE GRAVE OF FLORENCE NIGHTINGALE.

" A Londoner," who appealed recently in the *Telegraph* for support for the Gold and Silver Fund of the British Red Cross Society, should know his London and his nursing history better before he conjures up the soul of Florence Nightingale in support of the appeal. He (or is it she?) writes :—

" Among your tarnished treasures you will find gold bracelets that even for your husband's sake you could never wear again, and that hitherto you have never dared to get rid of. To day the soul of Florence Nightingale cries to you insistently that the Red Cross can best be helped by those very discarded trinkets that meant so much to the women of her own generation. There were life and labour in the trenches of that day too. From her grave in the Abbey she will thank you—if it is thanks you ask for."

" A Londoner " will search in vain amongst the graves of the great ones of the earth in the Abbey at Westminster for that of Florence Nightingale. The nation would willingly have paid that last tribute to her genius, but Miss Nightingale expressly directed in her will that her funeral should be of the quietest possible character, and those who wish to stand beside her grave must make a pilgrimage to the quiet little Hampshire town of Romsey, and thence drive deep into the heart of the country across the lovely river Test, and, if they can get permission from the present owner, through Embley Park, close under the windows of Embley House, which Miss Nightingale in her ardent girlhood would like to have converted into a hospital, and so, through deep hedgerows, till they come to the tiny village of East Wellow, and, arrived at its typically English church, with its high-pitched, red-tiled roof, and black wooden tower, pass through the turnstile, at the side of the lych gate, to the Nightingale tomb. On three of the sides of this are inscribed the names of Miss Nightingale's father, mother, and sister respectively. The fourth panel bears the simple inscription :

F. N.

Born 12 May, 1820.
Died 13 August, 1910.

It faces the church where Miss Nightingale so often worshipped. She is still remembered by old inhabitants, and on the day of her funeral a former porter at Romsey, then blind, who knew her at Embley, begged to be led on the platform to hear the footsteps of the bearers " bringing her home "; the coffin was preceded by six old tenants and workmen on the Embley estate who knew her, and, in the porch of the church, as the procession passed in, stood John Kneller, a Crimean veteran who served in the trenches at Sevastopol, and was for three months in the hospital at Scutari, and familiar with the sight of " The Lady of the Lamp " on her night rounds. M. B.

OUR ROLL OF HONOUR.
NURSING SERVICE.
DIED.
HILLS, Sister M. E., T.F.N.S.

Miss Hills, who was trained at St. Bartholomew's Hospital, London, had a charming personality and was much loved by the staff and patients of the 53rd General Hospital, B.E.F., France, to which she was attached, and where she was very happy in her work.

The following announcement appeared in the Daily Orders of the 53rd General Hospital on July 24th :—

" The Commanding Officer much regrets to announce the death of Miss M. E. Hills, Sister T.F.N.S., which took place in Queen Alexandra's Military Hospital, London, on July 22nd, 1918.

" Sister Hills was called up for duty at the 1st London General Hospital on March 31st, 1916, and served there until she came out for duty with No. 53 General Hospital on April 24th, 1917. She was at once posted to Calais and rejoined this Unit on October 13th, 1917.

" As Sister-in-Charge of Wards 7 and 8, as Night Sister, and again as Sister-in-Charge of Hut No. 7, she endeared herself to all who had the privilege of working with her or under her, and the patients under her charge had something more than respect and regard for her.

" Skilful, kind, capable and devoted to her work, her death is a great loss to No. 53 General Hospital, and the sympathies of all ranks will go out to Miss Hills' relatives and friends in their bereavement."

Amongst the floral tributes sent was one from the nursing staff of the 53rd General Hospital, a copy of the Badge of the Territorial Force Nursing Service in scarlet and white flowers.

A memorial service was held in the Church Tent at the 53rd General Hospital on July 5th.

The sinking of the Australian Ambulance Transport, *Warilda*, carrying some 600 seriously wounded men, adds to the heavy score to be settled with an inhuman foe when the day of reckoning comes. It is feared that over 100 of those on board lost their lives, the majority being wounded helpless soldiers. Amongst the drowned is Mrs. Long, Chief Controller, Q.M.A.A.C.

MASQUERADED AS A V.A.D. NURSE.

The suspicious conduct of a woman wearing the uniform of a V.A.D. nurse on the occasion of the arrival of a trainload of wounded at the Victoria Station recently attracted attention, and the sequel was that at the Nottingham Guildhall she admitted that she had no right to appear in such a dress.

She was Emma Elizabeth Hunt, of Kirkstead Terrace, Kirkstead Street, and Captain J. A. H. Green, prosecuting, explained that the woman was noticed by Dr. T. Lindley, who was in charge of the special constables. Asked to produce her certificate, she was unable to do so. On her uniform were brass shoulder titles indicating that she was a member of the Notts. 20th Detachment, which had no existence. She gave a false address, but was tracked to her real one by a detective, to whom she stated that she had been admitted as a member of a detachment by Mrs. Coulby. A week or ten days previously she had been seen at the Midland Station dancing about with soldiers in uniform, and kissing them " Good-bye." Emphasising the necessity that tailors and drapers should take care not to supply the uniform to unauthorised people, Captain Green pointed out that otherwise no end of mischief might arise.

Defendant was sent to prison for 14 days.

If this masquerader had worn the uniform of the trained staff of the General Hospital, Nottingham, she might have kicked capers from now till Doomsday, as the civil professional nurse's uniform is not protected by law.

APPOINTMENTS.
MATRON.
County Hospital, Ayr.—Miss I. M. Crichton has been appointed Matron. She was trained at Chalmers Hospital, Edinburgh, and has held the position of Sister at the West Kent Hospital, Maidstone, and of Staff Nurse at the Edmonton General Hospital.

NURSE MATRON.
Infectious Diseases Hospital, Montrose. — Miss A. R. Hay has been appointed Nurse Matron. She was trained at the Alloa Infectious Diseases Hospital, and at the Royal Infirmary, Halifax.

CHARGE NURSE.
The Infirmary, Lichfield.—Miss G. M. Foster has been appointed Charge Nurse. She was trained in the same institution.

QUEEN ALEXANDRA'S IMPERIAL MILITARY NURSING SERVICE.
Miss D. M. Priestley to be Staff Nurse.

PRESENTATION.

On leaving Kensington Infirmary to take up work as a Chaplain to the Forces the Rev. A. Lombardini was the recipient of many gifts, including a dressing case from the Nurses' League, and a fountain pen, and field water bottle from the patients.

NURSING ECHOES.

The Lord Mayor of Norwich has announced that Queen Alexandra has consented to open the new Edith Cavell Memorial Home at Norwich, a decision which will give great pleasure to many nurses.

The Royal Sanitary Institute, 90, Buckingham Palace Road, London, S.W. 1, has now issued its prospectus for its autumn courses of lectures for the examinations for Women Health Visitors, School Nurses, and Maternity and Child Welfare Workers, beginning on Wednesday, September 18th, and Monday, September 23rd, at 6 p.m. Candidates must possess a nursing qualification before entering for these examinations. Not only is the knowledge obtained by attendance at these lectures and demonstrations valuable to its possessor, including instruction on many subjects not dealt with in the ordinary curriculum of a nurse's training, but the certificates awarded to successful candidates after the examination held at the end of the courses, are definite assets, as the Women Health Visitors and School Nurses' certificate of the Royal Sanitary Institute is recognized by the Local Government Board as qualifying for the appointment of Health Visitor, and that in school hygiene is accepted by the Education Committee of the London County Council and other large towns as a qualification for certain appointments.

A Convalescent Home for American nurses, of whom there are some 500 now working in this country, exclusive of the thousands in France, has been opened by the American Red Cross Society at Colebrook Lodge, West Hill, Putney Heath. The house, which belongs to Colonel Ryan, will accommodate twenty-five nurses, stands in three acres of lovely grounds, and is ideal for the purpose. By and by, when the nurses, now for the most part full of energy, are feeling the strain of war work and the need of rest and recuperation, the hospitality of Colebrook House will be welcome indeed. At present it is under the direct charge of Miss Carrie M. Hall, R.N., Chief Nurse for the American Red Cross in Great Britain, but she hopes to delegate this duty as the demands on the Home become more strenuous.

By permission of Mr. Frank M. America, Director on Information of the American Red Cross in London (the headquarters of which are at 40, Grosvenor Gardens, S.W.), and by the courtesy of the Editor of the *Gentlewoman*, we are able to publish the accompanying portrait of Miss Carrie Hall, taken in her office at Headquarters. It will be remembered that about a year ago Miss Hall came over in charge of the Harvard Unit, which has seen active service in France, and her experience in this connection, as well as her administrative work as Superintendent of Nurses at the Peter Bent Brigham Hospital, Boston, U.S.A., are excellent qualifications for her present position, which demands a woman of tact, professional skill, and experience. On the wall behind her desk hangs a large map of Northern France, of the details of which Miss Hall has an intimate knowledge.

MISS CARRIE M. HALL, R.N.,
Chief Nurse for the American Red Cross in Great Britain.

Sir William Treloar, who has done so much for tuberculous children, by founding the hospital at Alton, announces further developments in prospect at Hayling Island.

NURSES' MISSIONARY LEAGUE.

[*Contributed.*]

Another Nurses' Missionary League Camp—this time arranged to suit dwellers in the North. It was with feelings of great equanimity I embarked from Ireland and wended my way to Mottram-St. Andrew, Cheshire. I was rejoicing in the thought that I was an outsider going to have a good time as such, looking on, and finding pleasure in the observance of others from a nice, quiet corner—so I told myself. But—and such a big but—little by little my idea fell to pieces, as I realised I was not to be an island out on my own, but a member of a very happy, gladsome community. My disillusionment commenced at the station, where I was met by the sister of our hostess who handed my belongings to the official for delivery and we set off together for the Camp. The country was charming, and every few moments one felt it impossible to be silent and had to exclaim about the beauty of it all. As we neared Green Dale we were met by our indefatigable hostess and secretary, who extended me a very warm welcome. How at home I felt ; the "corner" was quietly disappearing.

Arrivals continued at frequent intervals What a joyful whirl of excitement meeting everyone ; parties on the road coming up, crossing others on the way down to meet still further comers from hospitals, &c., there being but one small regret—you could not be going both ways at once.

We quickly shook into our places, and our daily course took shape. Early tea and the energetic hurried off to try to raise an appetite (none too difficult to woo) for breakfast. We laughed and chatted over this meal, plans were discussed, arrangements made for meeting those who could only pay short visits, objects of interest to be seen &c. After singing, reading and prayers, we all hastened out of doors, returning at noon. We then assembled for a Bible study. On three occasions we were led by Mrs. Kirk (*née* Stubbs). These studies were most helpful as each was asked to take part if inclined. No hesitation was felt in the asking of questions or testifying to any passage that had been in any wise illumined.

After dinner at 1 p.m., we followed our own devices, whether resting, walking, reading, writing or sewing. We were such a jolly, happy lot. Tea at four o'clock was served out of doors if weather permitted. Conversation then frequently ensued on missionary subjects, Mrs. Kirk telling of her hospital experiences in China, from whence she had recently returned. She was brimming over with interest, and we all felt how very delightful it was to listen.

One also who came from Ceylon and India could find an audience at any moment to talk over the methods of work, &c., among the many varied nationalities there found, each of which is of intense interest from the missionary point of view.

Our camp (as the outsider in the corner now

calls it) has been a great help all round. One feels freshened and restored in every way—mind, body, soul and spirit. We felt it was good to be here, even for a short time.

I would like to refer to the kindness of the curate of the parish church, who welcomed us to all the services and arranged for a special early celebration, where we could all unite and renew our vows to Christ our Head, pledging ourselves to be His faithful servants and followers to our life's end. Then again we would thank the Rev. H. E. Stevens, who, though greatly pressed for time, came over to the camp and held a short service.

Our farm friends were most kind in seeing to our bodily wants. In these days of permits, ration-cards, &c., one cannot enlarge upon it, but sit down, marvel, and be thankful. Our happy week came to an end all too soon, but one and all echo the words of the old toast : " To our next merrie meeting."

DORMIGENE.

We have received several inquiries from our readers concerning this drug, and a London physician to whom we referred the question has been good enough to answer as follows :—Dormigene used to be known and was widely used under the trade name of " Bromural." It is, in simple language, a bromide valerian combination and I have found it valuable in nerve cases as a very efficient sedative. Especially in the extremely troublesome series of nervous and organic congestions associated with the menopause in women, and due of course to the presence in the body of the blood previously lost each month and the consequent stress on the circulation. I have found that Dormigene is more useful than the ordinary bromides of potash or ammonium, which have for so many years been our great resource in medicinal treatment of these cases. Moreover Dormigene does not seem to me to exert either the depressing effects which bromides so often cause, nor do patients while taking it seem to suffer from the acne eruptions which are so frequent and troublesome a consequence of a continued bromide course. I have not used this drug as a hypnotic and cannot therefore give you any opinion on that point ; but as a matter of fact I have found the bromides in nerve cases only act as sleep producers when given in large doses, and I have, therefore, come to rely on such drugs as trional for that purpose.

Gen. Sir Arthur Sloggett, K.C.B., K.C.M.G., K.C.V.O., has joined the Board of Bovril, Ltd. Sir Arthur was Director-General of the Army Medical Service from June 1st, 1914, to June 1st 1918, and from October, 1914, to June 1st, 1918, was Director-General of the British Armies in France and Chief Commissioner of the Order of St. John of Jerusalem and the British Red Cross Societies.

WELL EARNED DISTINCTION.

The King has conferred on Dr. Alfred Cox the Order of the British Empire and the rank of Member of the same Order on Miss Laurence.

At the Annual Representative Meeting of the British Medical Association Dr. Garstang, chairman of the Medico-Political Committee, referred to the fact that as a result of Dr. Cox's work for the Central Medical War Committee he had been honoured by the King, and proposed a vote of very hearty congratulations to Dr. Cox, and also of congratulations to Miss Laurence, whose work had been of great value to the office. This was warmly seconded by Dr. Jenner Verrall, and acknowledged by Dr. Cox.

BOOK OF THE WEEK.

KAREN.*

" I am going to Germany," I said looking up from my letters,

" What for ? " said Dad. He never wasted words.

" Eugénie Gutheim is going to be married, and wants me to come to her wedding. I promised her I would if she won her bet."

" What do you mean by saying she has won her bet ? "

" We had a bet together when she left school. I said she would marry a business man, and she said she would marry an officer, however difficult it was."

" Why should it be difficult ? "

" Because the Gutheims are Jews. Eugénie told me that no officers visited at their house. Yet she has pulled it off."

This conversation gives the key to the eventful visit of Karen to Germany prior to the war. It was in the train between Cologne and Reichenstadt that she met the German officer that she afterwards married. There was a great gulf fixed between the vulgar Gutheims and the noble family of Karen's fiancé, and, of course, this made complications from the outset. Added to this, Oscar Strauss, upon whom Emma Gutheim had set her somewhat heavy affections, had chosen to regard Karen attentively whilst he sang, " Du bist wie eine Blume." The result was a violent outburst from Emma and the return of Karen to England. This was before her engagement to Graf Wolfram.

Karen, however, got a great deal of amusement out of the affair.

" To watch Frau Gutheim and Eugénie conduct Emma's love affairs was like watching an old-fashioned play, or reading an old-fashioned novel in which characters play their part with a simplicity we cannot achieve. I began to wonder why Herr Strauss hesitated over the word that was to make him the happiest man till Eugénie told me

*By Mrs. Alfred Sidgwick. Collins, Sons & Co. London.

he was waiting for the betrothal ring. It would arrive shortly from Reichenstadt, and at the same time there would be a moon.

" You see," she said, " one morning he will receive a sealed packet, and after supper he will suggest to Emma that it is a glorious night."

" Supposing it rains," I suggested.

" Then he will find some other plan, Oscar is highly ingenious and original."

" Did he sing " Du bist wie eine Blume " to Emma ?

" He did at our house, about six weeks ago, it was highly exciting."

Karen's own wedding took place in England, and she returned with her husband to life in a German noble family, where we are glad to say she held her own.

The Grafin was large, fair and dignified. The Graf stared at my maid and said in a tone of surprise :

" Who is this, then ? "

" Its only Wilkins, my maid."

Wilkins was devoted to me and an excellent maid, but she had her tiresome side, and when I told her to say " Ja," as if she meant " Yes," had bridled in an irritating way and pointed out that she had been taught to consider " Yah " a vulgar expression only used by the lower classes.

" Of course, you mustn't put your tongue out and say it in a defiant tone," I explained. " You must say ' Ja,' gently and firmly when you want a thing. When you don't want it you say ' Nein.' "

" Nein," echoed Wilkins, " what a peculiar language. Why not ten ? "

I told her she must expect that everything would be a little different, but she had only replied that she supposed German gentry were like gentry everywhere else and knew what was expected.'

Wilkins was whole-hearted in her dislike of everything German, in which matter she showed her power of perception, even in those pre-war days.

" I had to speak to the Grafin and explain to her that Wilkins was used to tea and bread and butter at half-past seven, porridge, tea, bacon and marmalade at nine, and a solid early dinner at one, and that she would feel faint if she were supplied with less than this.

" Then let her feel faint," said the Grafin " such demands I will not satisfy."

So I had to wrap up this ultimatum in different language and deliver it to Wilkins as best I might.'

Once more, we have brought into prominence the cruelty of the educational methods applied to German boys as exemplified in little Max. The book ends with the death of Wolfram and the escape of Karen and Wilkins from the German frontier at the outbreak of the war. Wolfram it must be admitted, had some good points ; but we are glad that the concluding pages leave Karen happily married to a True Blue.

H. H.

LETTERS TO THE EDITOR.

Whilst cordially inviting communications upon all subjects for these columns, we wish it to be distinctly understood that we do not IN ANY WAY hold ourselves responsible for the opinions expressed by our correspondents.

RECONSTRUCTION IN THE NURSING PROFESSION.

To the Editor of THE BRITISH JOURNAL OF NURSING.

MADAM,—So much interest is being shown in the problems connected with the re-building of the nation that I feel this is not an inappropriate moment to draw the attention of your readers to an important movement in the organisation of the nursing profession, which has been developing for a number of years. The essence of the movement makes it unostentatious and un-clamorous for assistance, but that very fact will enlist the sympathy of those who believe in sound organisation and self-respecting effort.

I need say nothing in these days about the immense importance to the community of the nursing profession, and I merely allude to it in order to show that this being so, it is also a matter of real interest to the public that nurses should be organised on right lines. As stated in a recent publication : " All the proposals which are connected with the re-organisation of public health must, for their efficient treatment, depend greatly upon the work of nurses."

An upward turning point comes in the history of a profession when its members realize that the responsibility for its development rests on their shoulders. Those who have studied the history of the medical profession know what a great influence for good was brought to bear when the rank and file of medical men banded themselves together into the British Medical Association. The keynote of such an organisation is that the responsibility for a profession shall be shouldered by the profession itself. Self-respect, self-government, self-development, self-support. The National Union of Trained Nurses has had for a number of years a system of Branch organisation, providing for post-graduate lectures, opportunities for discussion and practical demonstration. It assists its members with free legal and professional advice. It upholds the interests of nurses in Parliament and on public bodies. It runs an employment bureau for nurses which has proved to be of great value. Many nurses—members and non-members—have expressed their appreciation of the friendly welcome and expert advice they receive at the Central Office, 46, Marsham Street, Westminster.

The Society has a very carefully thought out democratic constitution and is managed entirely by members of the profession on the system of local representation on a central body. It is run on practical business lines for the benefit of nurses, but it has from the beginning always borne the good of the country in mind, thus avoiding one of the great pitfalls of similar organisations—a narrow professionalism.

The National Union of Trained Nurses is affiliated to the Royal British Nurses' Association, which is the only society of women possessing a Royal Charter, with the powers that result therefrom.

The members of the public who understand the importance of professional development will be glad to realize the existence of so soundly organised a society for nurses and will doubtless give it their support, and nurses should join in large numbers to give it the strength necessary to carry out its reason for existence. The body which will administer the affairs connected with State Registration must be one representing all nursing interests, and a bill safeguarding this has for years been before Parliament, but it is of the utmost importance that there should be a strong society such as the National Union of Trained Nurses—representing trained professional opinion —in existence, both whilst the bill is being considered and after the Act comes into force, in order that the beneficent effect of a wide range of free opinion may be brought to bear on all matters affecting the profession.

All information can be procured from the Secretary, 46, Marsham Street, Westminster, S.W. 1. Yours faithfully,
E. L. C. EDEN.

A VEXATIOUS ARRANGEMENT.

To the Editor of THE BRITISH JOURNAL OF NURSING.

DEAR MADAM,—In answer to your correspondent *re* R.N.P.F. annuitants, I should like to state the annuitant has no need to send either doctor's or clergyman's certificate in acknowledgement of her quarterly allowance. It is sufficient for her receipt paper to be signed by someone who knows her personally, and who will also witness her signature, which implies that she is alive. Therefore there is no need for publicity in respect to her private affairs. Neither is Income Tax deducted from her annuity. The amount of her annuity must be recorded in the ordinary way if she is liable to Income Tax duty. A *special certificate* was sent out last March to be signed by others than friends, but that is the only occasion I know of.

ONE OF THE SECOND THOUSAND.

OUR PRIZE COMPETITION.
QUESTIONS.

August 17th.—What is pernicious anæmia ? How have you seen it treated ?

August 24th.—What points would you observe in paying an ante-natal visit to an expectant mother ? What would you impress upon the patient ?

OUR ADVERTISERS.

Do not omit to buy, as far as possible, everything you need from " Our Advertisers," and to recommend them to your friends. They are all first-class firms.

The Midwife.

CENTRAL MIDWIVES' BOARD (ENGLAND)
EXAMINATION PAPER.

The following are the questions set at the examination of the Central Midwives Board (England) at the London and Provincial Centres on August 1st :—

1. Describe the relative positions of the contents of the female pelvis, illustrating your answer with a diagram.

2. What investigation would you make of a patient at the seventh month who engages you to attend her in her confinement ? Under what circumstances would you advise the patient to see a doctor ?

3. What is meant by presentation and prolapse of the cord ? How would you treat these conditions ?

4. What are the causes of subinvolution of the uterus, and what symptoms accompany it ?

6. What is the best method of feeding an infant, and why ? Describe the care of the breasts of the nursing mother.

5. What is the importance of irregular bleeding from the vagina in a woman aged fifty ?

CENTRAL MIDWIVES' BOARD (SCOTLAND)

The Examination of the Central Midwives' Board for Scotland, held on July 29th last, simultaneously in Edinburgh, Glasgow and Dundee, has concluded with the following results :—

LIST OF SUCCESSFUL CANDIDATES.
EDINBURGH.

Miss Elizabeth Baxter, Mrs. Henrietta G. Deller, Miss Helen O. Driver, Miss Margaret J. Elliot, Mrs. Jemima M. Ferguson, Miss Barbara Galloway, Miss Helen Grant, Miss Esther J. Hewes, Miss Margaret C. McCluskie, Miss Mary Missett, Miss Jeanie M. Motson, Mrs. Annie F. Tait, Miss Isabella N. Wanless, Mrs. Ellen G. Watson, Miss Jemima Young.

GLASGOW.

Mrs. Mary A. Ablett, Miss Alexandrina Anderson, Mrs. Elizabeth Foster, Miss Annie Fraser, Miss Bridget Gavin, Miss Mary L. W. Hall, Miss Annie Hardie, Miss Elizabeth F. Horn, Miss Helen L. Hosie, Miss Elizabeth Kay, Miss Jessie Kelso, Miss Mary King, Miss Isabel W. McClymont, Miss Catherine McGillivray, Miss Catherine M. McInnes, Mrs. Jeanie McLellan, Miss Catherine McMillan, Miss Mary Munn, Miss Lizzie G. Polwart, Mrs. Beatrice A. Reid, Miss Margaret B. Summers, Miss Susan Turner, Mrs. Jessie Williamson.

DUNDEE.

Miss Davina B. Anderson, Miss Magdalena M. Baxter, Miss Barbara W. Craigen, Miss Janet M. Drummond, Miss Margaret M. Dunn, Miss Emily I. Gilbert, Miss Isabella Gordon, Miss Charlotte McGregor, Miss Annabella Mackay, Miss Isabella McKenzie.

EXAMINATION PAPER.

The following are the questions set at the examination of the Central Midwives Board for Scotland on July 29th :—

1. Define the third stage of labour. Give its management when normal and mention the complications which may occur.

2. What medical conditions must the midwife inquire into on the occasion of her first visit after labour (*a*) as regards the mother, and (*b*) as regards the new-born infant ?

3. If a patient has bleeding from the uterus about the seventh month of pregnancy, what may it be due to, and what are the risks to her and to the fœtus ?

4. What do you understand by prolapse of the umbilical cord ? How would you manage such a case until the doctor arrived ?

5. In a private house what methods would you use and how would you proceed to sterilise and disinfect the following :—Your hands, surgical instruments, and the patient ?

6. State the cases in which a midwife must send notification as soon as possible to the Local Supervising Authority according to the Rules of the Central Midwives Board.

FIRST VACANCY IN THE SCOTTISH BOARD.

We regret to announce that Sir Robert Kirk Inches, who had been present and taken an active interest in the meetings of the Board on the Thursday afternoon, died suddenly on Friday morning. Sir Robert Inches was elected by the Convention of Royal Burghs of Scotland as its representative on the Board, when it was constituted on February 18th, 1916. He was appointed Convener of the Finance Committee, an office which he discharged with much acceptance. His shrewdness and business ability were highly appreciated by the Board, and his relations with his colleagues were at all times of the kindliest and most genial character.

THE PSYCHOLOGY OF MOTHERHOOD.

An exceedingly interesting meeting of the Workers Section of the A.J.W.M.C. was recently held at the National Institute of Public Health (by kind permission of the secretary).

The speaker was Dr. Jessie Murray, and she came to talk about the " Psychology of Motherhood," a subject that is of great interest to those who are working amongst mothers. Dr. Murray gave an interesting account of the development of the human organism, and then went on to an absorbing analysis of the present-day mother. The discussion afterwards was keen, and in answer to questions that followed, some further points were elucidated. The thanks of the meeting to the lecturer were proposed by Miss Atherton and seconded by Miss Eliot.

THE
BRITISH JOURNAL OF NURSING
WITH WHICH IS INCORPORATED
THE NURSING RECORD
EDITED BY MRS BEDFORD FENWICK

No. 1,585.　　　　　SATURDAY, AUGUST 17, 1918.　　　　　Vol. LXI.

EDITORIAL.

THE SOUL OF NURSING.

We can hardly touch upon any question of social reform which does not affect the work and the interests of intelligent, educated nurses, for the term " trained nursing " has an ever-widening meaning and scope, and its aims are preventive as well as curative.

Nurses of the present day have a much greater knowledge of the evil in the world than those of the past. That bare fact shows very significant and important progress; because, with wider knowledge of existing evil, comes the stronger, more passionate aspiration to abolish it, and to make our beloved country cleaner, and therefore healthier and happier. We are well aware, for instance, of the widespread evil caused by the preventable infection of venereal disease. We are up against that accusing fact, also that in spite of the numerous public health agencies, that are doing such excellent work, these preventable things are not prevented. Nevertheless, there is another side to the melancholy picture, which fills us with encouragement and hope. Endued with power that comes of knowledge and adequate training, nurses are beginning to realize themselves. When all stultifying limits and barriers to progress are removed, and the full powers of nurses (more especially social service nurses) are liberated, the opportunities of our profession will be boundless.

There is a beautiful expression in a well-known hymn ;—" fire of love." It is just this fire of love—love for our fellow-creatures which is the highest form of love, which impels enlightened men and women, whose consciences are aroused to a sense of their corporate responsibilities as their weaker brothers' and sisters' " keepers," to desire more power to do more and more

good in the world, which is " white already to harvest." The one supreme hindrance to progress which has for so many years strangled endeavour, and stultified effort, has now been removed. Women are now enfranchised citizens. All conscientious nurses endued with the " fire of love " and having the necessary qualifications will realize that they dare not repudiate their responsibilities in this matter. They are fully aware also of the high privilege of having a voice—through their representatives—in the Councils of the Nation.

Questions of public health are now being recognized as vitally important to the future welfare of our great Empire, and the next Parliament—the first that will be elected by *the people* (women as well as men) will have to deal with them, and none will be more competent than well-trained, educated nurses.

Hitherto the emphasis upon the work and usefulness of nurses has been placed too much upon the heart, and too little upon the head. We do not mean for a moment to minimize the importance of the former, the highest qualities of the heart are needed, but an *understanding* heart is what is most required. A woman who is all heart and has no head will make as bad a nurse as the one who is unbalanced in the other direction. The soul of nursing consists of wisdom, understanding, counsel, strength and knowledge, combined in a well-balanced whole.

Thus equipped, and with the opportunities and powers referred to above, we believe that trained nurses will, in the near future, take a large share in the reforms and destinies of their country. The way will not be easy, the path will not be smooth. There will be vested interests and other antagonisms to combat, but—

" I hold that it becomes no man to nurse despair,
　But in the teeth of clench'd antagonisms
　To follow up the worthiest till he die."

OUR PRIZE COMPETITION.

WHAT IS PERNICIOUS ANÆMIA? HOW HAVE YOU SEEN IT TREATED?

We have pleasure in awarding the prize this week to Miss Alice M. Burns, East Suffolk and Ipswich Hospital, Ipswich.

PRIZE PAPER.

Pernicious anæmia is a somewhat obscure disease of the blood. It resembles simple anæmia in that it produces the symptoms of unhealthy pallor, breathlessness, languor, debility, and constipation, and differs from it in that it is associated with a diminution and also enucleation of the red blood corpuscles which would seem to destroy their capacity for holding iron and attracting oxygen, for iron, so valuable in the treatment of simple anæmia, is of no avail in these cases.

The disease is a very insidious one, and said to be invariably fatal, though periods of improvement may be looked for.

How I have seen it treated:—(1) Drugs, (2) bone marrow, (3) rest, (4) good food, (5) fresh air.

(1) We give first place to drugs, and one drug—arsenic—because they would seem to arrest the destruction of the blood elements. It may be given as a simple mixture, but is now usually given by either intravenous or intramuscular injection in the form of Salvarsan or its English substitute Galyl (20 to 40 c.c.gs.).

(2) Bone marrow is looked upon as a source of supply of new red blood corpuscles, and is often given in sandwiches.

(3) Rest is esssential, in the later stages in bed. The heart is always overtaxed in these cases, and may give out under strain.

(4) Good food of an easily digested character should be abundant, and the patient's appetite fostered, although unfortunately in the nature of the disease he cannot take advantage of all he eats.

One investigator has discovered that the blood destruction is greatly diminished by the use of a farinaceous diet and increased by nitrogenous foods.

(5) I have placed fresh air last because, since the blood is deficient in hæmoglobin and iron, the patient can only derive a minimum of benefit from oxygen, yet it goes witout saying that he should be placed in a position to obtain that minimum without loss of time.

These patients come to suffer great exhaustion and emaciation, and require unwearying care in the keeping of the bed clean and the skin whole, and the relieving of painful symptoms which are the outcome of their enfeebled conditions.

HONOURABLE MENTION.

The following competitors receive honourable mention :—Miss Ethel E. Hall, Miss E. F. Thompson, Miss M. Robinson, Miss B. James, Miss A. M. M. Cullen. Miss Ethel Hall writes :

It is probable that a group of diseases are collected together and called pernicious anæmia because the blood changes are similar in all of them. The usual type is generally fatal, and may occur both in men and women after the age at which chlorosis is common ; and its chief characteristic is failure to improve under iron, which often proves of benefit in ordinary anæmia. The cause of it is not yet known, but it follows many conditions in which the system is depressed either physically or mentally.

The disease is a very insidious one, the patient gradually becoming weak and bloodless, and the colour of the skin is yellowish, the mucous membranes are also pale, there is marked shortness of breath on exertion, due to the fact that there is but little hæmoglobin to carry oxygen to the tissues, the blood thus requiring much more aeration in the lungs than usual. There is often severe and distressing palpitation of the heart, and the sufferer is feeble, languid, and incapable of physical or mental exertion of any kind. Constipation is often a marked feature, also pain after food, with constant attacks of diarrhœa and vomiting, or both, but there is no marked wasting. There is often fever, the urine is dark in colour, and there may be tenderness of the bones. Changes also occur in the retina, and death usually ensues from exhaustion. Another special feature is the iiability to hæmorrhages.

QUESTION FOR NEXT WEEK.

What point would you observe in paying an ante-natal visit to an expectant mother? What would you impress upon the patient?

RECTAL FEEDING.

An article on this subject in the *Journal of the American Medical Association* says that as there is no proof that the colon possesses adequate digestive capacity, all food introduced by way of the rectum should be completely predigested. Flesh and eggs are undesirable because of their tendency to putrefy. Milk is comparatively free from this disadvantage, and appears to be the ideal source of protein for a nutritive enema. It should be fresh and unboiled, thoroughly peptonized and pancreatized. It should be skimmed, as fat introduced into the colon is useless and may be harmful. Glucose in solution supplies carbohydrate in an available form. Strained fruit juice may supply desirable salts to a limited extent.

NURSING AND THE WAR.

RECOGNITION OF HOME HOSPITAL WORK.

The names of a very large number of ladies have been brought to the notice of the Secretary of State for War for valuable nursing services rendered in connection with the war. The lists are issued from the War Office under dates August 10th and 12th.

AFRICAN CAMPAIGN.

GEN. DEVENTER'S LIST OF MENTIONS.
EAST AFRICA.

The names of the following have been brought to the notice of the Secretary of State for War by Lieutenant-General Sir J. L. van Deventer, K.C.B., Commanding-in-Chief, British Forces, East Africa, for distinguished services during the operations from May 30th to December, 1917, described in his dispatch of January 21st, 1918 :—

NURSING SERVICES.
IMPERIAL SECTION.

CORMACK, Miss J., Sister, N.Z.A.N.S. ; ROBERTS, Miss F. N., Sister (A./Matron), R.R.C., Q.A.I.M.N.S. ; THORNBORROW, Miss M. A., Staff Nurse, T.F.N.S. ; TOWNLEY, Miss E. J., Staff Nurse, Q.A.I.M.N.S.R. ; WATSON, Miss E. N., Staff Nurse, Q.A.I.M.N.S.R. ; WREFORD, Miss K. E., Staff Nurse, T.F.N.S.

SOUTH AFRICAN SECTION.

FITZHENRY, Miss D., Sister, S.A.M.N.S. ; LAMBERT, Miss J., Sister, S.A.M.N.S.

EAST AFRICAN SECTION.

BROWN, Mrs. N. M., Hon. Nurse, E.A.N.S. ; DRAYTON, Miss L. A., Nursing Sister, E.A.N.S. ; SHELDON, Miss A., Nursing Sister, E.A.N.S.

NORFORCE.

SPENDLER, Miss F., Sister, Nyasaland Fd. Force Med. Serv. ; WILSON, Miss R. L., Sister, Northern Rhodesia Med. Serv.

ITALIAN MISSION.

GUNDENE, Nursing Sister.

THE V.A.D.

The Surrey Branch, British Red Cross Society, have passed the following resolution :—

" That in view of the large number of other services now open to women, it is essential for maintaining the *personnel* of Voluntary Aid Detachments that service in such detachments should be placed on a more satisfactory basis. That, as a step in this direction, the opinion of this branch is that approved whole-time service in auxiliary hospitals, for a specified period, should be reckoned to excuse some portion of the training of such members as professional nurses in general civil hospitals."

Lord Ashcombe, Chairman of the Surrey County Committee, writing from Denbies, Dorking, says in the *Times* that concessions of this kind have already been made by at least four of the great hospitals of this category in London, but, the Committee feel that the principle should be universally adopted by civil hospitals in Great Britain and Ireland. They know that views of a like nature are largely shared by other county branches and persons connected therewith, but that there are difficulties in the way of their expression. They are prepared to take the lead in a movement to forward this purpose if sufficient support is forthcoming, and ask, therefore that those in sympathy with them in this respect will communicate with the Secretary, Surrey Branch, British Red Cross Society, 13, Charterhouse Street, E.C. 1.

We have always foreseen that the claim would be made that war service should rank as systematic training in nursing, but it has not been organised as such, and cannot, therefore, be rightly so regarded.

THE EDINBURGH BRANCH OF THE BRITISH RED CROSS SOCIETY.

The following appointments have been made by the *Personnel* Committee of the Edinburgh Branch of the British Red Cross Society during the past half-year :—Miss Mary Gordon Smith, Kippenross Hosp., Dunblane ; Miss McBain, Edenfield Hosp., Fife ; Mrs. Allan, Edinburgh War Hosp., Bangour ; Mrs. Green, Battery Hosp., Dunbar ; Miss Macleod, Edinburgh War Hosp., Bangour ; Miss Gordon, St. Leonard's Aux. Hosp., Edinburgh ; Miss Stobo, Bowhill Officers' Hosp., Selkirk ; Miss Gray, St. Leonard's Hosp., Edinburgh ; Miss Farquhar, Dingallon Hosp., Oban ; Miss Mitchell, Edinburgh War Hosp., Bangour ; Mrs. King, Mayfield Aux. Hosp., Edinburgh ; Miss Jennings, Hopeton House Hosp., South Queensferry ; Miss E. Forsyth, Marchhall Hosp., Edinburgh ; Miss McBain, Leven Hosp., Fife ; Miss F. Cameron, Tillyric Hosp., Milnathort ; Miss Methven, Coldingham, Berwickshire ; Mrs. Macdonald, Ceres Aux. Hosp., Fife ; Miss Doig, Castle Milk Hosp., Dumfries ; Miss A. B. Watson, Ranfurly Hosp., Bridge of Weir ; Miss Thomson, Ranfurly Hosp., Bridge of Weir ; Miss Lorimer, Bowhill Hosp., Selkirk ; Miss E. Chowler, Polkemmet Hosp., Whitburn ; Miss Cowan, Tayside Aux. Hosp. ; Miss Hastie, Mayfield Aux. Hosp., Edinburgh ; Miss Torrens, Wemyss Castle Hosp., Fife ; Miss Terriss, Edenfield Hosp., Fife ; Miss Field, Dunblane War Hosp. ; Miss Janet Dickson, Dalmeny House Hosp. ; Miss Belcher, The Gables, Gullane ; Miss Campbell, Whitehill Aux. Hos., Rosewell ; Miss C. M. Grant, Dunblane War Hosp. ; Miss Campbell, Morelands, Peebles ; Miss Gillon, Wemyss Castle Hosp., Fife ; Miss F. Urquhart, Royal Naval Hosp., Peebles ; Miss Binnie, Whitehill Red Cross Hosp., Rosewell ; Miss Locke, Lochiel Hosp., Banavie, Fort William ; Miss Belcher, Kippenross Hosp., Dunblane ; Miss M. Thomas, Coldingham, Berwickshire ; Miss Wray, Miss Grant, Miss Field and Miss Pearce, Dunblane War Hosp. ; Miss Maude Martin Craiglockhart War Hosp., Slateford, Edinburgh ; Miss Macdonald, Dunblane War Hosp. ; Miss Ruddock, Marchhall Aux. Hosp., Edinburgh.

THE ROYAL RED CROSS.

The King has been pleased to award the Royal Red Cross to the undermentioned ladies in recognition of their valuable nursing services in connection with the war.

SECOND CLASS.

NIPPARD, Mrs. E., Matron, Alderney Isolation Hospl., Newtown, Dorset; NUTSEY, Miss E. M., Sister, N.Z.A.M.S., No. 2 N.Z. Hospl., Walton-on-Thames.

OATMAN, Miss C. M., Nursing Sister, Can. Nursing Service, No. 4 Can. Gen. Hospl., Basingstoke, Hants; O'DONOGHUE, Miss A., Matron, Kitebrook, Moreton-in-Marsh; O'NEILL, Miss M., Matron, Southgate Aux. War Hospl., Grovelands, Southgate; O'NEILL, Miss M. E., Matron, Q.A.I.M.N.S.R., Mil. Hospl., Woking, Surrey; O'SULLIVAN, Miss J., Matron, Quarry Hill V.A.D. Hospl., Tonbridge.

PALMER, Miss H. S., Sister, Thorncombe Mil. Hospl., Bramley; PARKER, Mrs. C. E., Sister, Gifford House Aux. Hospl., Roehampton, London; PARKINS, Miss M. F., Nursing Sister, Can. Nursing Service, I.O.D.E., Can. Red Cross Hospl. for Officers, 1, Hyde Park Place, W. 1; PATEN, Miss E. M., A. Matron, Aust. A.N.S., 2nd Aust. Aux. Hospl., Southall, Middlesex; PATERSON, Miss H. C., Sister, Q.A.I.M.N.S.R., Central Mil. Hospl., Herne Bay; WILLIAMS, Mrs. J. P., Commdt., Sandy Hospl., Beds; PEEBLES, Miss J. M., Matron, R. Infirmary, Stirling; PEEL, Miss A. M., Matron, Gerstley-Hoare Hospl. for Officers, 53, Cadogan Square, London; PERCY, Lady V. A., Matron, Mil. Hospl., Alnwick; PERRIN, Miss H., Sister, Aust. A.N.S., No. 3 Aust. Aux. Hospl., Dartford, Kent; PERRY, Miss M., Sister, T.F.N.S., 5th Northern Gen. Hospl., Leicester; PETER, Miss M., Sister, Brompton Mil. Hospl., East Yorks; PETER, Miss P., Matron, Hdqrs., B.R.C.S.; PETTIGREW, Miss E., Asst. Matron, Catterick Mil. Hospl., Yorks; PHILIP, Miss A. T., Matron, Forres Aux. Hospl., Morayshire; PHILP, Miss E. K., Matron, St. Leonards Stonehaven Red Cross Aux. Hospl., Kincardineshire; PICKERING, Mrs. A. M., Commandant, Arnold Hospl., Doncaster, Yorks; PINNOCK, Mrs. R. H., Commandant, Warden House Hospl., Deal; PITTS, Miss R., Nurse, Hart House Hospl., Burnham, Somerset; PORTER, Miss E. A., Matron. Banbury Red Cross Hospl., Banbury, Oxfordshire; PRICE, Miss E., A. Matron, Highfield Mil. Hospl., Liverpool; PRICHARD, Miss M. A., Nursing Sister, Can. Nursing Service, No. 10 Can. Gen. Hospl., Brighton; PROWSE, Miss M. T., Sister-in-Charge, Bramhall and Cheadle Hulme Aux. Mil. Hospl., near Stockport; PUGH, Mrs. E. M., Sister, Woolton Aux. Hospl., W. Lancs; PUMPHREY, Miss L., Matron, Queen's Hospl., Birmingham; PURCELL, Miss L. E., Nurse, V.A.D. Hospl., Exmouth; PURDIE, Miss N. M., Matron, Brabyns Hall, Marples Bridge, Cheshire.

QUIGLEY, Miss M. E., Nursing Sister, Can. Nursing Service, Granville Can. Spec. Hospl., Buxton; QUINN, Miss A., Sister-in-Charge, Spencer Street Aux. Hospl., Keighley, Yorks.

RADCLIFFE, Miss G. S., Nursing Sister, Can. Nursing Service, No. 16 Can. Gen. Hospl., Orpington, Kent; RAINBOW, Miss H. K., Night Sister, Brook War Hospl., Woolwich; RAMSBOTHAM, Mrs. E. M., Sister-in-Charge, Redburn War Hospl., Eastbourne; RAMSDEN, Miss G., Nursing Sister, Can. Nursing Service, No. 12 Can. Gen. Hospl., Bramshott, Hants; RIGBY-MURRAY, Miss E., Matron, V.A.D. Hospl., Hatton Grange, Shifnal, Shropshire; RIDGEWELL, Miss L. M., Staff Nurse,

Q.A.I.M.N.S.R., King George's Hospl., Stamford Street, London; ROBERTS, Mrs. F., Matron, Holmfirth Aux. Hospl., nr. Huddersfield; ROBERTSON, Miss C. C. B., Sister, Aux. Mil. Hospl., Moor Park, Preston; ROCHE, Miss F., Sister, Q.A.I.M.N.S.R., Queen Alexandra's Mil. Hospl., Grosvenor, S.W. 1; ROGERS, Miss A., Sister, Q.A.I.M.N.S.R., Pavilion Gen. Hospl., Brighton; ROMER, Miss H. E., Asst. Matron, T.F.N.S., 3rd Sco. Gen. Hospl., Glasgow; ROOKE, Miss R. M., Asst. Matron, Q.A.I.M.N.S., Mil. Hospl., Park Hall Camp, Oswestry; ROSE, Miss E., Matron, Wych Red Cross Hospl., Forest Row, Sussex; ROSE, Mrs. M., Asst. Matron, T.F.N.S., 1st Scot. Gen. Hospl., Oldmill Section, Aberdeen; ROWLANDS, Miss B., Commdt., St. Pierre's Red Cross Hospl., Cardiff; RUSSELL, Miss A., Sister, Q.A.I.M.N.S.R., Mil. Hospl., Dover; RUSSELL, Miss E., Sister, Q.A.I.M.N.S.R., Mil. Hospl., Prees Heath, Salop.

SADLER, Miss M. T., Sister, Mil. Hospl., Alnwick; SAUNDERS, Miss M. A. G., Matron, Plas Tudno, and St. Tudno Aux. Hospl., Llandudno, Carnarvon; SCOTT, Mrs. M., Sister, Red Cross Hospital, Christchurch, Hants; SHIELD, Mrs. M., Matron, 20th Durham V.A. Hosp., St. Gabriel's, Sunderland; SHORT, Miss B., Nursing Sister, Exeter War Hospl., No. 1 Section; SIDDELLS, Miss F., Sister, N.Z.A.N.S., No. 1 New Zealand Gen. Hospl., Brockenhurst, Hants; SINCLAIR, Mrs. J., Commdt., Red Cross Hospl., Maesteg; SLAYDEN, Mrs. E., Sister, County Hospl., Lincoln; SLOCOCK, Miss R., Sister, Harnham Red Cross Hospl., Salisbury; SLOCOMBE, Miss J., Masseuse, V.A. Hospl., Totnes; SMITH, Mrs. E. M., Theatre Sister, Myrtle Aux. Hospl., Liverpool; SMITH, Miss G. E. S., Sister, T.F.N.S., 2nd Sco. Gen. Hospl., Craigleith; SMITH, Miss L. G., Sister, Q.A.I.M.N.S.R., Mil. Hospl., Fort Pitt, Chatham; SMITH, Miss M. E., Matron, Lady Forester Hospl., Much Wenlock, Shrops.; SMITH, Miss M. L., Matron, Burntwood Red Cross Hospl., Surrey; SMITH, Miss M. E., Matron, Red Cross Hospl., Leek, Staffs; SMITH, Miss S. E., Sister, V.A.D. Hospl., Coalville, Leics; SMYTHE, Miss I., Sister, Q.A.I.M.N.S.R., Stoke-on-Trent War Hospl., Newcastle, Staffs; SPANNER, Miss G. L., Nursing Sister, Can. Nursing Service, No. 12 Can. Gen. Hospl., Bramshott, Hants; STEIN, Mrs. M. McK., Asst. Commdt. and Sister-in-Charge, Park House V.A. Hospl., Shipston-on-Stour; STEVENS, Miss G. A. B., Matron, Aux. Mil. Hospl., Frodsham, Ches.; STEVENSON, Miss L. C., Nursing Sister, Can. Nursing Service, No. 10 Can. Gen. Hospl., Brighton; STRIKE, Miss M., Sister, Q.A.I.M.N.S.R., Mil. Hospl., Belton Park, Grantham; SWORD, Miss J. E., Nursing Sister, Can. Nursing Service, No. 12 Can. Gen. Hospl., Bramshott, Hants.

Miss Kate Maxey, who gained the Military Medal, the Red Cross Medal, and the Mons Ribbon, has been presented with a silver set of salts and spoons, in recognition of her heroic work in France, by the Spennymoor Ambulance Brigade and Nursing Division. She was wounded by hostile aircraft when in charge of a hospital in France.

The Military Medal won by Sister McGinnis was awarded her for conspicuous bravery and devotion to duty during attacks by Germans on a St. John Ambulance Brigade Hospital from May 19th to June 1st. Miss McGinnis was on the staff of the City of Dublin Nursing Institution before joining the Red Cross at the outbreak of war, and has served over three years in France.

AMERICAN RED CROSS NAVAL HOSPITAL,
ALDFORD HOUSE, PARK LANE, W.

One of the latest American Red Cross Hospitals in this country, and the first devoted to the needs of the sick and wounded of its Navy, is Aldford House, erected on a unique site in Park Lane, where it occupies an entire block. It has been placed at the disposal of the American Red Cross by Mrs. Frederick Guest, wife of Captain Guest, M.P., and accommodates 50 patients—men on the ground floor, officers above.

The nursing staff, who are members of the

its purpose; damask panels on the walls have been covered up by calico stretched over them, and the ceiling in the operating theatre has been subjected to the same treatment.

One ward on the ground floor opens on to a verandah, where chairs can be placed, overlooking Park Lane. Its pretty pink quilts and screens give it a very attractive appearance. In the opposite ward the quilts are white, and the screen-covers a rosy pink. The hospital has a garden of quite considerable size for London—an invaluable asset, especially for sailors, not used to living within four walls. It even boasts of a rabbit-hutch and rabbits.

There is also a winter garden, where the

Miss Powell, R.N.   Miss Akroyd, R.N.   Mrs. Buckingham, R.N.
          Miss Lamb, R.N.   Dr. McGrath.   Miss Taylor, R.N.   Miss Fifield, R.N.
[Photo. Bassano.]   (Matron.)

NURSING STAFF OF THE AMERICAN RED CROSS NAVAL HOSPITAL.

American Red Cross, are all Registered Nurses, and proud of the fact. Most of them have been war nursing for two or three years, and have served in Mesopotamia, Gallipoli, East Africa, and France, as well as in hospitals in this country. The Matron, Miss Catherine Taylor, was trained at St. Luke's Hospital, New York, by Miss Anna W. Goodrich, for whose personality and work she has unbounded admiration. The V.A.D.s undertake pantry work and kindred duties, but do no nursing.

The medical officers are Dr. L. W. McGrath and Dr. Agnew, both of the United States Naval Corps.

The house, with its central airy hall, and wide shallow staircase, is very well adapted for

patients can sit when the weather is unsuitable for life in the open air.

On a level with the floor above is a wide roof garden, where long chairs can be set, and from which an extensive and charming view is obtained.

The hospital, which for the first years of the war was used for British patients, has only been open as an American hospital for seven or eight weeks. The cases admitted are at present chiefly medical, accident, and operation ones.

Miss Taylor wears the dainty white uniform of the Chief Nurses of the American Red Cross, with the distinguishing black band and tiny red cross on the cap. The other members of the staff wear grey.

CARE OF THE WOUNDED.

The Queen, accompanied by Princess Mary, visited the Brook War Hospital on Wednesday in last week and spent a long time in the wards. Her Majesty was received by the President of the Local Government Board, the Chairman and the Vice-Chairman and Clerk of the Metropolitan Asylums Board. Major Swainston, Acting Senior Medical Officer, and Miss E. M. Baum, the Matron.

Her Majesty has also visited Queen Mary's Hospital at Stratford, the Pavilion General Military Hospital at Brighton, and the Hospital for Sick Children, Great Ormond Street, where she saw Princess Mary at work in the wards.

In a Summary of Work of the Joint War Committee of the British Red Cross Society and the Order of St. John of Jerusalem in England, the Commissioner of the Committee in France and Belgium—Colonel the Hon. Sir Arthur Lawley, K.C.M.G.—writes of Ambulance Train, No. 16 :—

No. 16.—The following extracts referring to this train will be of interest :—

" It is not long since that I recommended to your notice the excellent behaviour of this unit on the night of the 26th-27th March, 1918. I then particularly drew attention to the gallantry and courage shown and efficient work done by the Sister-in-Charge and Q.M.-Sergt

" This time . . . No. 16 Ambulance Train arrived at . . . in the midst of an air raid. ' A ' Coach got a direct hit from a large bomb, wrecking it and setting the stores on fire—the details of the damage done will have been made known to you.

" The Sisters were taken out of the cutting and placed under a hedge. I then returned to the train, where Q.M.-Sergt. had already engaged the men in trying to extinguish the fire ; in this he was ably assisted by one volunteer. . . . The burning coach was disconnected by this officer and Q.M.-Sergt. . . . while I directed the engine-driver what to do. The engine-driver and fireman had remained at their post—the brakesman had disappeared.

" It must be remembered that this was carried out while the raid was still in progress and 'planes humming overhead, three out of the four injured men assisting at the salvage.

" The personnel to a man did their very best."

Colonel Sir E. W. D. Ward, Director-General of Voluntary Organisations, asks for strong walking sticks for the use of wounded soldiers, for which he continues to receive large and increasing demands. It is necessary, if these requests are to be fully and punctually met, that he should receive a far larger number. If householders will made a point of sending one good strong walking-stick to the Comforts Depôt, 45, Horseferry Road, Westminster, S.W. 1, the required number will be secured.

SOCIAL SERVICE.

The American Red Cross has not only allocated £5,000 to the National League for Health, Maternity, and Child Welfare, 4, Tavistock Square, London, W.C. 1, to establish and maintain infant welfare institutions for a year, but has also given it £10,000 for maternity hostels. It is hoped to establish one in each of the three kingdoms and one in London, in addition to ante-natal clinics and factory crêches in various parts of the country. An emergency home for babies and two day nurseries for children of the professional classes, whose mothers are obliged to work to supplement their Army and Navy allowances, are also to be set up in London. Offers of empty houses are invited.

The report on the working of the Tuberculosis Department started at the Great Northern Central Hospital—by arrangement with the Islington Borough Council in May, 1917—shows that, during the year ended April 30th last 841 cases from the northern half of the borough were treated, and that there were 3,472 attendances. In addition, 1,510 visits were made to patients' homes, and a considerable number of contacts examined. This appears to be a very satisfactory report of the first year's working of the new dispensary.

THE PASSING BELL.

We regret to record the death on August 1st, at the Bradford Royal Infirmary, of Miss Janet McGill, of 93, Horton Lane, since 1894 the much valued matron of the Bradford District Nursing Association, a branch of the Nursing Institution in Manningham. The Home became a separate institution in 1904. The funeral took place on the 5th inst. at the Scholemoor Cemetery, a short service having previously been held at the Home. Both services were conducted by the Rev. C. Stewart Douglas, Vicar of Thornbury. Amongst many who sent wreaths were the members of the committee, the staff, the house surgeon, the matron and nursing staff of the Royal Infirmary.

Miss McGill was widely known, respected, and loved by the sick poor, and her death is a great loss not only to the Association but to the whole city. She was a good organiser, kind and sympathetic. Her whole life was centred in her work, and her activities were not confined to nursing. She was especially interested in getting patients away for a change of air, and took endless trouble to accomplish this.

OUR ROLL OF HONOUR.

NURSING SERVICE.

WOUNDED.

Watkins, Sister E. F., Q.A.I.M.N.S.R.

DIED.

Young, Miss M. C., V.A.D.

QUEEN VICTORIA'S JUBILEE INSTITUTE.

Her Majesty Queen Alexandra has been graciously pleased to approve the appointment of the following to be Queen's Nurses, to date July 1st

ENGLAND.—James, Gladys L. H. ; Rider, Grace: J. E. ; Fitzpatrick, A. T. ; Kemp, Rose E. ; Burgon, Jane ; Gough, Hilda S. ; Robson, Gladys S. ; Shotter, H. A.

WALES.—Jones, Janet ; Owen, Gwladys..

SCOTLAND.—Coghlan, Annie ; Dewar, Jessie ; Macfarlane, Sarah ; McLellan, Ellen ; McPhee, Mary ; Swanson, Margaret S. ; Walsh, Marian ; Graham, Margaret G. ;

IRELAND.—Collery, Nora ; O'Doherty, Sarah T. ; Phelan, Clare.

TRANSFERS AND APPOINTMENTS.

Miss Selina Collier is appointed to Worcester C.N.A. as Assistant Superintendent and Training Sister ; Miss Minnie A. E. Banks, to Margate ; Mrs. Ada Bulkeley-Jones, to Garston ; Miss Kate Clarkson, to Irlam ; Miss Gertrude M. Fraser, to Southall-Norwood ; Miss Evelyn I. Gallacher, to Dorking ; Miss Louie C. Lakin, to Horsham ; Miss Grace McCulloch, to South Wimbledon ; Miss Lucy McKinlay, to Horsham ; Miss Alice J. Maclachlan, to Crook ; Miss Emily M. Scott, to Wolverton ; Miss Ethel Thompson, to Brownhills.

APPOINTMENTS.

MATRON.

Mowsley Sanatorium (Leicestershire County Council).—Miss Jennie Cardwell Alcock has been appointed Matron. She was trained at the Crumpsall Infirmary, Manchester, and has been Sister-in-Charge of the New Hospital for Consumption, Kimberworth, Yorkshire, and Matron of the Hinckley Tuberculosis (Roadenhoe) Dispensary.

NATIONAL UNION OF TRAINED NURSES

SOME RECENT APPOINTMENTS MADE THROUGH THE N.U.T.N. EMPLOYMENT CENTRE.

Norfolk War Hospital, Thorpe, Norwich.—Ward Sister, Miss E. P. Darlington.

Women's After Care Hostels.—Miss Percival.

Addington Park War Hosp., Croydon.—Ward Sister, Miss A. M. Mann.

Exeter, No. II Military Hosp.—Ward Sister, Miss Ethel A. A. Moon.

St. Mary's Nursery Training College.—Nurse, Mrs. Eliz. Johnson.

Exeter No. 1 Hosp.—Night Superintendent, Miss A. Mackinnon.

Queen Mary's Aux. Mil. Hosp., Roehampton House.—Night Charge Sister, Miss S. E. McCracken.

St. Mark's Hosp., City Road.—Night Sister, Miss Sellers.

The London Temperance Hospital.—Night Staff Nurse, Mrs. M. M. Clarke.

NURSING ECHOES.

The interest aroused by the paper on "Laboratory Work for Women" by Dr. Knyvett Gordon, which we published last week, proves that the scientific side of their work is attractive to a proportion of members of the nursing profession. For such nurses the British Scientific Products Exhibition, organized by the British Science Guild, 199, Piccadilly, W., and opened on Monday, last at King's College, in the Strand, will hold attractions, and is undoubtedly instructive, and as it remains open until September 7th there are opportunities of a visit for all.

The aim of the Exhibition is to stimulate public interest and confidence in the capacity of British Science, combined with industrial enterprise, to secure and maintain a leading place amongst progressive nations, and the object is the full development of our mental and material resources. As Professor Gregory pointed out in an address given at the Exhibition, in purely scientific research of initiative quality we have been the pioneers ; where we have been deficient is in the practical use of the results obtained. In short, we need close association between the creative investigator, the industrial researcher who seeks to apply knowledge to useful ends, and the artisan, whose work is constructive and technical.

Amongst the exhibitors are firms of such world-wide repute as Messrs. Burroughs Wellcome & Co., Messrs. Allen & Hanburys, and Boots Pure Drug Company, Ltd., all of whom have exhibits of exceptional interest.

The dominant note of Messrs. Burroughs Wellcome & Co.'s exhibit is struck by the series of specimens showing the synthesis of "Kharsivan" and "Neokharsivan," which were the first British products to take the place of German salvarsan and neosalvarsan.

An exhibit which opens up to nurses a vista of an interesting hobby, which may also be a work of national utility, is that arranged by Mrs. Grieve, F.R.H.S., who has a School of British Medicinal and Commercial Herb Growing at the Whins, Chalfont St. Peter, Bucks, which represents an organized determination to recapture from Germany and Austria the Herb Growing Industry, which those countries have won from Great Britain. Before the war we spent annually £200,000 on importations of drug-yielding Herbs which we could have grown. What more interesting for a nurse living in the country than the cultivation of medicinal herbs? It is further of interest to know that the demand for properly trained herb growers far exceeds the supply, and good posts are obtainable for students when proficient.

The Council Meeting of the Metropolitan Hospital Sunday Fund have unanimously approved the report of the Committee of Distribution, and have directed the awards recommended to be paid. The sum available this year (£85,652) is a record one, exceeding the largest previous total by £15,000. It includes a gift of £5,000 from the American Red Cross Society, and £2,453 from St. Mark's, North Audley Street, the largest sum ever received from one London church, and £76 collected in pence from St. Andrew's, Lambeth, a very poor parish.

Seven and a half per cent. of the total sum available for distribution is appropriated to the purchase of surgical appliances during the ensuing year, and 2½ per cent. for district nursing associations.

The following are the awards to Nursing Associations : — Belvedere, Abbey Wood, £9; Brixton, £36; Central St. Pancras, £45; Charlton and Blackheath, £9; Chelsea and Pimlico, £18; Hackney, £63; Hammersmith, £81; Hampstead, £27; Isleworth, £18; Kensington, £81; Kilburn, £9; Kingston, £45; Lambeth Road (Catholic), £18; Metropolitan (Bloomsbury), £63; St. Olave's (Bermondsey), £36; Paddington and Marylebone, £63; Plaistow, £72; Plaistow (Maternity), £72; Ponders End, Enfield, &c., £18; Rotherhithe, £27; Shoreditch, £72; Sick Room Helps Society, £9; Sidcup, £9; Silvertown, £18; South London (Battersea), £54; Southwark, £36; South Wimbledon, £27; Tottenham, £27; Westminster, £36; Woolwich, £63; East London,

£135; North London, £81; Ranyard Nurses, £513.

Our illustration on this page shows a group of Sisters at the Jamsetji Jijibhai Hospital, Bombay, a hospital which owes its foundation to the munificence of Sir Jamsetji Jijibhai, a Parsi gentleman in Bombay.

How many English nurses know anything of the Parsis, a community of Persian origin, their customs, their faith, their family life based on the patriarchal system, the astuteness of their men, the beauty of their women?

It was on a journey to the East that the writer first got to know a Parsi family. Were it not for their Oriental dress, their olive-tinted complexions might be taken for those of Spaniards or Italians, but the quaint, stiff, shiny black hats of the men, not unlike a bishop's mitre without the point, and the rich graceful saris of the women, indicate unmistakably their Oriental extraction. A Parsi girl, lovely, graceful, modest, is a thing of beauty, though early middle age probably finds her

Sisters Gregory, Steinhoff, Green and Burke,
Sisters Burton, Klein and King.
Sister Beck
AT THE JAMSETJI JIJIBHAI HOSPITAL, BOMBAY.

slimness a memory of the past.

The group of hospitals in Bombay, including St. George's (the European Hospital), the Jamsetji, and the Cama, a women's hospital with a school of midwifery recognized by the Central Midwives Board in this country, in which the Sisters of the All Saints Community did such valuable pioneer work, have turned out many well-trained nurses, European, Eurasian, and native. For those who intend to work subsequently in India, the training given in these hospitals is specially valuable, as they not only receive a good professional education, but become acquainted with the conditions of life of those amongst whom they will subsequently work, and how to deal with the problems which will confront them.

THE HOSPITAL LAUNDRY.

Most of the provincial general hospitals have their own steam laundry attached in the grounds, the working and welfare coming under the Nursing department. The ideal laundry building is still to be planned, by the woman who knows its resources best, but until Utopia arrives what is at present in working order must be utilized to the best and fullest advantage.

The Staff.—The Board of Trade considers that to each 500 articles one worker must be allowed. This, taken all round, is a fair division, and, with care, should work easily and well.

All laundry workers come under the control of the same Board, they must work for the prescribed hours with stated times for meals, their Sundays must be free and Bank Holidays counted as holidays.

As a rule the hospital laundry workers prefer to be free from noon on Saturday until Monday morning, with hours off two evenings during the week, which enables them to get away from the heat and noise of the laundry.

A well-trained and experienced head laundress who though not required to run the machinery thoroughly understands it, is absolutely necessary, She arranges and controls the work of the laundry, keeping to the special time table which is as a rule drawn up by the Matron or her Assistant as best capable of taking in all the work of the week. Her work consists of sorting, packing, checking, superintending the calender and collar machines, and personally attending to the work of the patients, officers, nurses and maids.

It is better for the laundry staff, if possible to have their own sleeping apartments apart from the ordinary staff, and to have separate meals The hospital provides them with uniform and clogs for the wash-house, and with mackintosh aprons to protect them whilst actually washing the clothes,

For a hospital of 120 beds and the necessary staff, one head laundress and four maids, engineer and stoker should be ample—the weekly average of articles washed making a total of 3,800.

The Building.—This ought to be well apart from the main building so that the smoke from the stoke house and the noise of the plant will not disturb the patients. A prepared footpath should lead to it so that the staff in all weathers can go and come easily. The machinery should be well arranged so that each stage of the process may be got through in the best possible manner— washers, hydros, drying-room, calender, mangle, ironers, all following in their various degrees of use.

The ironing stove should not be in the same department as that where the actual ironing is done, as even with the aid of asbestos screens, ventilation, and electric fans, the heat in the summer months rises in a surprising way.

There should be pigeon-holes specially marked for each department and numerous laundry baskets and trollies to hold the clothes

Superintendent.—Under this heading comes the work of checking and entering all articles sent by the wards, nursing department, home, house, maids, &c

The special books are returned to the Matron's office weekly to be gone through and all missing articles reported. When possible, it is best for the Assistant Matron to obtain daily a list from the Ward Sisters and check this with that of the head laundress.

Where a venereal clinique is attached to the Out-Patients' Department, specially marked linen, which is treated in the same manner as that of infectious cases is the best and safest method.

Each day has its special work, the Nurses' and house linen being done on days which are not set apart for the ward linen.

The theatre washing, which in most busy general hospitals is a very heavy item, should be done daily and returned at a stated time for sterilization, this also applies to ward draw sheets and children's sundries.

Stores.—These are called weekly, preferably on Saturday, so that the soap may be melted, starch prepared, and soda portioned out, ready for the new week's work.

In a hospital where all garments are plainly and clearly marked and stocktaking is undertaken frequently there is very little trouble from lost articles. M. K. S.

The Law Officers of the Crown have expressed the opinion that a woman is not entitled to be a candidate for Parliament, but Mr. Bonar Law, replying to questions in the House of Commons, stated that the introduction of legislation to make this legal would be considered by the Government, and admitted that when the question of extending the Parliamentary Franchise to women was under discussion it was repeatedly said that when they gave the franchise to women they could not refuse their admission to the House.

Mr. Bonar Law, replying in the House of Commons to Colonel Sir J. Craig (Down, E., U.), also said, if there was a general desire he would be glad to arrange an opportunity after the recess for a discussion on the question of opening the available galleries of the House to women and men impartially.

The Home Secretary has expressed himself in entire sympathy with the proposal for the formation of a body of women police, and also of the establishment of women special constables during the war, and promised a deputation, introduced by Lord Sydenham, to consider the whole project with a view to its development.

BOOK OF THE WEEK.

THE GIRL FROM KURDISTAN.*

Miss Kerruish will be remembered as the author of " Miss Haroun Al-Raschid," which book won the thousand guinea competition offered by Messrs. Hodder & Stoughton ; so her present novel, dealing with Persian customs and intrigue must command our attention. Those who are acquainted with the position of European government officials in the east will be aware that their position is often one that requires very careful handling, and it is from this point that the book under consideration is written.

The opening chapter describes the position of a young Armenian lad, from, " forgetting he had a knife in his hand when he struck a man and God decreed that his neck vein should be cut. The blood ran all over my hand—see, all. And his brother said he would kill me." He was rescued from the infuriated relative by Europeans in a barouche driven by a Cossack coachman. Escorting it was a yelling and threatening mob of street roughs, slipshod policemen and a few respectable but enraged men of the better class and the inevitable rabble of urchins. Two figures emerged and stepped out for the Toup. The larger was a big man of five-and-thirty, undeniably British, his ruddy curls prematurely grizzled at the temples, his eyes choleric by habit. He led his companion by one gloved finger hooked in a greasy collar.

" The very shadow of the Pearly Gun is *Basr* (refuge)," said the European. He swung a foot back and shot his charge sprawling into the sanctuary.

He then made his stately way back to the carriage. The ladies were comparing torn flounces.

" No garden party after all, and a nasty, dirty criminal sitting on my feet all the way from Shimlah Gate."

It was unconventional Janet Macroy, who got herself into a nasty hole, by her friendship with Hajji Jaffier, the chief of a tribe, who was kept in Teheran by the Shah as a hostage for its good behaviour.

" The Hajji Khan was hawking and interrupted his sport to put me on the road," Janet explained to Perdita, as she made the introductions.

The Khan stroked down the diminutive falcon that was perched on his wrist and broke in deprecatingly. What was a lifetime's sport compared to the least service to the Shehzadeh Khanoum ? So he demanded, and vowed furthermore that the joy of meeting her had cured him of several specified diseases."

Self-willed Janet, although long resident in the East, chose to ignore the gulf that separates East from West, but in justice to her she was unaware of the havoc her friendship with the Eastern caused in the breast of his little wife. By strategy Janet's

friends contrive a meeting between her and the little heart-broken woman.

" You are a Hakim Khanoum, yea, and a white sorceress. I can see it in your eyes. You will give me a philtre, a love potion ? "

She fell full length and kissed Janet's shoes, not knowing her identity.

" The smallest Ferenghi philtre would bring him back. It is a Ferenghi woman who hath led him away, and may Allah send her swiftly to his kindled fire. And may he furthermore make every Ferenghi golden hair of her a serpent to gnaw the black Ferenghi heart of her to the last sounding of Serafil's Wakening Trump.

Janet Macroy, one of the best of women at heart, once having grasped the situation dealt with it thoroughly.

" Thou hast something better than spells," she said. " Thy little one doth but reckon her age in days. Take her and cherish her, O my sister, that when he returns she may be a sweet comfort to him, and a rosy link between ye twain."

She further assures Hajji Khan : " A Christian gentlewoman does not wed a Muslim. I never dreamed thou wouldst entertain such a thought. Hear thee that for it, I will have nothing more to do with thee, and leave thee to do to me as thou wilt."

" Do you deem I may, as I can, cast dirt on your name in the ears of Teheran ? "

But though, for political reasons, he did not dare to take this step, Janet came near to being ostracised for her foolishness, and it required all the finesse of her friends to prevent ugly consequences.

But as her friend, Madame Ecroy said : " Janet is always rather fine when she really knows what she is doing."

We feel sure that this story, that brings so vividly the atmosphere of the East around us, will be welcomed by many readers who are wearied by the commonplace.   H. H.

THE LAY OF THE LAZY NURSE.

Breathes there a nurse with soul so dead
Who never to herself hath said :
" To-morrow morning I will rise
Before the sun lights up the skies.
Soon as the calling maid shall ring,
Before the birds begin to sing,
Fresh as a lark I shall awake ;
An early morning walk I'll take."
And, when at an unearthly hour
Next morn, the maid with awful power
Makes noise enough to stir the dead,
And wake the nurse upon her bed,
Breathes there a nurse, I now repeat,
Who wouldn't send her twenty feet,
Then back beneath the counterpane
With restful sigh doze off again?

(With apologies to Scott.)

E. E. THIRKELL.

In the JOURNAL OF THE LEEDS TOWNSHIP
INFIRMARY NURSES LEAGUE.

* By Jessie Douglas Kerruish. (Hodder & Stoughton, London.)

LETTERS TO THE EDITOR.

Whilst cordially inviting communications upon all subjects for these columns, we wish it to be distinctly understood that we do not IN ANY WAY hold ourselves responsible for the opinions expressed by our correspondents.

A CERTIFICATE OF EXISTENCE.

To the Editor of THE BRITISH JOURNAL OF NURSING.

DEAR MADAM,—In your issue of THE BRITISH JOURNAL OF NURSING (July 27th), I saw a letter, complaining of hardship imposed on the annuitants of R.N.P.F.N. It sounded so unlike that valuable fund that I cut it out and asked what it meant. I enclose Mr. Dick's reply and should be so glad if you would make it public in your valuable paper. What a pity nurse did not find out facts before rushing into print.

I wish some of the letters about the "Merry Mummers" could be copied into the daily papers, so that the public could see what nurses think of those who are dragging down an honourable profession as an excuse to show off and gambol, and this while the greater number of the profession are living and sometimes dying for the men who are bleeding for their country. Is there no way in which we can stop this "War Charity"?

Believe me, Yours sincerely,
S. SULIVAN,
Harrow.   Member R.B.N.A.

LETTER TO MISS SULIVAN FROM THE SECRETARY R.N.P.F.N.

DEAR MADAM,—The cutting which you enclose contains a misrepresentation of the facts. It is quite untrue that we require our annuitants each month to send a doctor's certificate and a clergyman's certificate. The facts are these :—

About six months ago we requested our annuitants, for the first time in the history of the Fund, to obtain a Certificate of Existence, signed by a professional or other responsible man to the effect that she was alive at the date of signing the certificate. This formality was for the satisfaction of our actuaries, and was a measure framed in the interests of the policy-holders of the Fund. It may not be necessary to trouble the annuitants again, at any rate not for some considerable time.

In the ordinary course, all we require the Nurse to do is to sign a receipt for the quarterly instalment of her pension in the presence of a witness.

Yours faithfully,
LOUIS H. M. DICK,
Secretary.

To the Editor of THE BRITISH JOURNAL OF NURSING.

DEAR MADAM,—I have been much interested in the two letters published in your Journal as to the new condition to be complied with before annuitants of the R.N.P.F. for Nurses receive their annuity.

I was requested last March to get a signature from magistrate or doctor, &c., to say that I was alive. I did nothing that time. In June no cheque was sent, but another request for a certificate of existence. I wrote and declined, and gave as one reason for my refusal that I did not wish to add to the conditions under which I joined, especially as this would be so burdensome. I received another letter, arguing the point and saying the condition was covered by Article 5, which, however, simply says that in the first instance the applicant must satisfy the Council that she has given correct dates, and so on, at first, before any payment can be made, *and* (here your second correspondent has not taken in what will be asked of her) that they will not ask again for another certificate till September—just three months later.

I wrote again, saying it was not worth my while for £10 a year to undergo the worry and inconvenience entailed, but that if they were doubtful as to my existence they could pay the amount due into my bank, and it was paid.

The absurdity of it is that the annuity had never been paid without the signature of a witness, and either my partner or our secretary witnessed my signature. One can only suppose that, though women really have a vote now, that the Pension Fund Council still do not consider a woman's signature to be a trustworthy voucher, and the hardship of it is that nurses living in places where everyone's business is known will be obliged to ask outside people for signatures, thereby admitting them to a knowledge of their private affairs.

Yours faithfully,
CHRISTINA FORREST,
Matron Victoria and Bournemouth
Nurses' Institute.

A CHANGE NEEDED.

To the Editor of THE BRITISH JOURNAL OF NURSING.

DEAR MADAM,—In the early days of the war a large number of Nurses were sent to the Mediterranean, Egypt, and later to India.

Last week I was speaking to a medical man home from there, and he informed me that their lot is a very hard one.

Three years in a climate to which they were unaccustomed coupled with constant strain of hard and anxious work, unhealthy surroundings, has reduced them to a pitiable state, which calls for immediate attention.

They beg for a change to Europe, or even to Egypt, but no notice is taken of their request.

I am sure it is only necessary to call the attention of the higher authorities at home to this in order to bring about amelioration of the condition of those devoted women. Perhaps some Member would raise the matter by question in the House of Commons? Faithfully yours,
London, W. 1.   M. C. W.

OUR PRIZE COMPETITION.
QUESTIONS.

August 31st.—Mention some of the principal disorders of the nervous system, and the duties of the nurse in regard to them.

The Midwife.

IS A SPECIAL TRAINING FOR TEACHERS DESIRABLE ? *

By Miss M. Olive Haydon.

The certificated teacher is a feature of modern times, we have the certificated teacher of massage, cookery, laundry, and other arts and crafts ; the teaching of practical midwifery is on the same lines as these, but on a higher plane—a higher plane because indifferent bad, or careless teaching may endanger the lives of mothers and babies. At present practical teachers of midwifery have to satisfy the Central Midwives Board as to their experience, their management of their practice, their character, and their willingness to give adequate instruction to the pupils. All these are admirbale in themselves, and necessary, but it does not follow that such an approved teacher has the gift or ability for imparting her knowledge. It is as much a fallacy that any skilful midwife can teach as it is that every mother has an instinctive knowledge of how to manage a baby.

There are a few gifted persons who, without any special training for teaching do it inspiringly, originally, and brilliantly ; they are not always the most learned in theory, but they are usually people with love and enthusiasm for their work, progressive, and intensely interested in " leading out " the mental and physical capacities of their fellows. The born teacher loves the pupil to excel in his or her work, and even to excel him or her. There are exceptional pupils who have previously been educated in other branches of work who learn without teaching. But such teachers and pupils are rare.

In the educational world it is coming about more and more that a high degree is not sufficient to secure a good post as teacher, unless its possessor has also taken a course of practical training as a teacher.

There are, it must be confessed, men and women who would never make good teachers whatever courses they followed ; there are the " born " teachers who might profit little by them ; midway is the mass of average ability who greatly profit by such courses. The majority of practical teachers of midwifery would, I think, welcome a special training for their difficult and delicate task, and would do their work better if they were more conversant with the principles that underlie successful teaching, had some knowledge of psychology, were conversant with the methods of men and women who stand out as great teachers.

The teaching of practical midwifery is, in many respects, similar to the teaching of little children—

the training of the senses to observe accurately, manual training, the training in expression of sense impressions, in making discoveries, and in applying common sense and such knowledge as they possess, practically. Every teacher of midwifery would do well to study the work of such people as Froebel, Rousseau, James, Montessori. There are latent capacities in everyone that only need suitable environment and opportunities to develop, and our problem as practical teachers is how best to deal with each individual. Personally I found Madame Montessori's book a great inspiration and encouragement ; she thought out good methods for educating feeble-minded and backward children, and met with wonderful success. Most of us are backward, and many of us are comparatively feeble-minded (I mean in contrast to what we might be), and certainly many of our pupils, owing to the stupid way they have been taught in earlier years, are poor material. In desperation we are apt to perpetuate bad methods, learning by rote, unintelligent swallowing of information, slavery to printed matter, incapacity for retaining whatever is not written down, &c. A German girl once said to me, " in England it is always ' schreiber, schreiber ' (write, write) ; in Germany our professors say ' denken ' (think). They do not all do so. We teachers are faithful to Madam How. We are afraid of Madam Why ?

Practical teachers of midwifery have much the same job as the N.C.O.s of the Army. They may be weak on strategy, history, mathematics, but they have been through the mill ; they know " how " things should be done, if they do not know " why." So the teacher of practical midwifery usually knows how to manage normal pregnancies, labour, or puerperia ; although she may know little of embryology, bacteriology, and other sciences. The N.C.O. who was progressive enough to study theory, would probably get a commission ; why should not the practical teacher of midwifery, who studied theory more advanced than that required to be certified, be promoted ?

I understand that in Scotch universities it is the custom for aspiring graduates to take students for coaching outside the university ; if they gain a reputation as able men, they are likely to be offered a chair in the university with wider opportunities. I like to look forward to a time when the Midwives' Institute will be the College of Midwifery, with the ablest professors to pilot it, and midwives, who have distinguished themselves as teachers, will have opportunity to help practically juniors and midwives who are keen to train pupils.

This Conference, brief as it is, may be regarded as a course for practical teachers, for its aim is to inspire higher ideals. We hope that it may be held yearly in different centres. The demon-

* A Paper read at the Conference for Teachers of Pupil Midwives, Midwives' Institute, London, May 30th, 1918.

strations and clinics are not simply to give information, but to demonstrate good methods of conducting the same.

We are specially privileged to have lectures from the leading teachers of midwifery to pupil midwives; they cannot fail to inspire us to remodel our practical teaching in some cases, to realize how great a factor is the personality of the teacher, and to aspire to educate individually, more truly and thoroughly, each pupil that comes to us to be initiated into an art and science of which we ourselves feel that there is much yet to be perfected, to be discovered, to learn.

The question as to whether some test of the midwife's ability to teach practical midwifery is desirable is an open one. Personally, I think an oral and practical examination, which should include a demonstration, a clinic, and the taking of a coaching class, would be excellent. We are all apt to grow stale—to get " sick of perpetual pupil " (to modify Lamb's phrase), and we can only improve the education of our pupils by improving our own education. We ought to do that practically at every case we conduct, if we put our minds into it. New acquisition of knowledge will, in many cases, make us better midwives, and better teachers, and if there is anything to be said for a higher theoretical examination, demanding a wider knowledge of maternity and child-welfare than is required to become qualified as a midwife, it is that it will stimulate our lazy brains and keep us from numbness and rust, " the arch foe of women."

BILL TO AMEND THE MIDWIVES ACT, 1902.

On Thursday, August 8th, in the House of Commons (the day on which the House adjourned), the Bill to amend the Midwives Act, 1902, was presented by Mr. Hayes Fisher, President of the Local Government Board, on behalf of the Government, and read a first time.

Mr. Bonar Law, replying to Mr. Herbert Samuel, stated that when the House reassembled on Tuesday, October 15th, the Bill would be taken.

THE MATERNITY AND CHILD WELFARE BILL.

The Maternity and Child Welfare Bill, " An Act to make further provision for the Health of Mothers and Young Children," has now passed both Houses of Parliament. It provides that " any local authority within the meaning of the Notification of Births Act, 1907, may make such arrangements as may be sanctioned by the Local Government Board for attending to the health of expectant mothers and nursing mothers, and of children who have not attained the age of five years, and are not being educated in schools recognised by the Board of Education."

The Bill has received the Royal Assent.

CENTRAL MIDWIVES BOARD FOR SCOTLAND.

REPORT ON THE WORK OF THE BOARD.

The Report on the work of the Central Midwives Board for Scotland for the year ended March 31st, 1918, and presented to both Houses of Parliament by command of His Majesty, is now published, and may be purchased through any booksellers or directly from H.M. Stationery Office, Imperial House, Kingsway, London, W.C. 2, price 1d. net. The following items are of interest—

MIDWIVES' ROLL.

The total number of enrolments is made up of 1,351 by certificate, 1,695 in *bona fide* practice, and 264 after passing the Examination of the Board.

The returns made by the Local Supervising Authorities, under Section 16 (6) of the Act show that to date 1,408 midwives notified their intention of practising, and the names of these women have been prefixed by a star in the Roll.

FINANCIAL STATEMENT.

The work of the Board has been carried out in an efficient and economical manner. A credit balance has been carried forward to next year without requiring any levy on the Supervising Authorities.

VOLUNTARY RESIGNATIONS.

Certain enrolled midwives have resigned voluntarily on the ground of old age, ill-health, or inability to comply with the rules, and have applied to have their names removed from the Midwives' Roll.

The Board have instructed that their names should be retained in the Roll with a special mark in order that they may still be under the supervision of the Local Authority, with a view to discontinuance of any practice whatever under " cover " of a medical practitioner, so that the recommendation of the General Medical Council in this respect may be given full effect.

MATERNITY AND CHILD WELFARE SCHEMES.

The Board has been consulted in regard to the position of Health Visitors, who are not inspectors of midwives, attending and advising in the management of the mother or infant in a confinement case, where there is a certified midwife in attendance, and recommendations have been made to the Supervising Authorities whereby full co-operation of the existing organisations is secured for the benefit of the mother and the child.

THE MIDWIVES' (IRELAND) ACT.

At the recent election held pursuant to the provisions of the Midwives (Ireland) Act, 1918, the following four registered medical practitioners were elected to act on the Central Midwives Board for Ireland :—Sir Andrew J. Horne, Sir William J. Smyly, Sir John William Byers, and Professor Henry Corby.

THE
BRITISH JOURNAL OF NURSING
WITH WHICH IS INCORPORATED
THE NURSING RECORD
EDITED BY MRS BEDFORD FENWICK

No. 1,586.   SATURDAY, AUGUST 24, 1918.   Vol. LXI.

EDITORIAL.

THE KING'S VISIT TO FRANCE.

The King, after his recent visit to the Army in France, in the course of a letter addressed to Field-Marshal Sir Douglas Haig, warmly congratulating him and the troops that have fought so magnificently under his command on the triumphant issue of the recent operations, wrote :—

"I gratefully recognise that this high *moral* is in part the outcome of a hearty co-operation between the fighting Army and the great organisations behind the line ; the transport service by land and sea ; and those vast industries in which the men and women at home maintain the supplies of food and munitions of war.

"It was a pleasure to me to find from the admirable condition of the horses and mules of the various units I inspected that the new Armies fully uphold our national reputation as good horse-masters.

"Of the hospitals, their efficiency, skill, devotion, and untiring efforts of the staffs, I cannot speak in too high praise.

"I realise with thankfulness all that is done for the spiritual welfare of the troops by the chaplains of the different denominations.

"I return home with feelings of profound admiration for our Armies, convinced that in union with those of the Allied nations, we shall, with God's help, secure a victorious peace worthy of the noble sacrifices made ; a peace which must be a surety to coming generations against sufferings such as the present world has endured throughout these years of relentless war."

His Majesty visited several hospitals and casualty clearing stations near the fighting line and his visit was the source of much pleasure to both patients and staffs of these institutions.

A MINISTRY OF HEALTH.

At the instance of the Prime Minister, the National Memorial which urged the immediate establishment of a Ministry of Health as an urgent war measure has been laid before the Committee of Home Affairs. The Home Secretary, in a communication to Sir Kingsley Wood, states that the Committee have recently been considering the details of the scheme, and that the object of the Committee is to provide for the establishment of a Ministry with as complete powers as possible.

The President of the Local Government Board, who is a member of the Committee, has also announced that the Committee are about to conclude their deliberations, and that the scheme is practically completed.

It is expected that the Bill will be introduced at the beginning of the next Parliamentary Session.

No class of the community realise the necessity for a Ministry of Health more keenly than the trained nurses in the three kingdoms, whose work is largely concerned with the prevention as well as the cure of disease, and the maintenance of health. Sir Charles Booth in his " Notes on Social Influences " in the last volume of " Life and Labour of the People of London " wrote in reference to district nursing, " It is almost true to say that wherever a nurse enters, the standard of life is raised " and Dr. Thomas, at the last Conference of the National Union of Trained Nurses, said that the devoted, unflinching, steady, educational pressure of the L.C.C. School Nurses was revealed by the improving figures year by year, even in war time, when the chances of infection are multiplied a thousandfold by the close proximity of the hugger-mugger life of trench and camp to the homes of the people.

NURSING AS A FIELD OF NATIONAL SERVICE.

THE UNITED STATES STUDENT NURSE RESERVE.

The pamphlet by Miss Isabel M. Stewart, R.N., M.A., Assistant Professor in the Department of Nursing and Health at Teachers' College, Columbia University, U.S.A., on the above subject, is a personal message from the Committee on Nursing, General Medical Board, Council of National Defence, Washington, D.C., addressed to all young women of America who are well educated, physically capable, and otherwise able to put their full time and energy into some definite form of national service.

The pamphlet is in support of the Government call for 25,000 young women between the ages of 19 and 35 to join the United States Student Nurse Reserve, and hold themselves in readiness to train for service as nurses, and has been forwarded to us by the courtesy of Dr. Franklin Martin, member of the Advisory Commission of the Medical Section of the Council of National Defence.

In a recruiting leaflet, which is a reprint of matter included in Miss Stewart's pamphlet, it is pointed out that the war is creating an unprecedented demand for trained nurses. Only those who have taken the full training course are eligible for service with the American Forces overseas. Their places must be filled by student nurses enrolled for the full training course. Every young woman who enrols in the United States Student Nurse Reserve is releasing a nurse for service at the Front, and swelling the home army which must be relied on to act as the second line of hospital defence. Upon the health of the American people will depend the spirit of their fighting forces.

The need of the 1,579 nurses' training schools in the United States is as great and imperative as that of the Army School of Nursing. Those who enrol for these schools will be assigned as vacancies occur.

The enrolment card will indicate two classes of registrants—Preferred and Deferred. The Preferred class will be those ready to accept assignment to whatever hospital the Government directs them, although they may state what training school they prefer to be sent to. The Deferred class is composed of those who limit their pledge of service, *i.e.*, who will not engage to go except to certain hospitals. This class is intended largely for those who, for family reasons, cannot accept training at a distance from their homes. Those who register in the Deferred class will be assigned only after the Preferred class is exhausted.

The Government relies on the patriotism of those who enrol to fill out Preferred cards if they possibly can, thus volunteering to go where they are most needed.

Nobody will be assigned to any schools whose conditions of training are not approved by the State Board of Nurse Examiners.

After stating the terms of training, what the training course prepares for, and the earning capacity of the student after graduation, as well as referring to the honourable nature of the nursing profession, the recruiting leaflet concludes :—

"Enrol at the nearest recruiting station established by the Woman's Committee of the Council of National Defence."

The Committee on Nursing, whose message is voiced by Miss Stewart, assume at the outset that the person to whom it is addressed is not simply a dabbler, or a sentimental dreamer, but a serious, practical, patriotic girl or woman, sincerely anxious to throw her energies and her abilities into some form of work that is really going to count. Her brothers and friends have been called into the Army and Navy, and are now getting ready for a long period of hard and dangerous service for their country. That the girl is just as ready as they are to give up her own personal pleasures and pursuits and accept any of the sacrifices that may be called for, but that she does not want to squander her energy and waste her time in futile and unproductive forms of effort. That she wants to know how she can get into a *real* job.

Miss Stewart then proceeds to show what a nurse can do for her country, the need of recruits for the nursing army, the importance of thorough training, how the student recruit helps her country, what the training of the nurse offers, and the opportunities for service after graduation. She closes with the information already referred to in connection with the recruiting leaflet.

There is an Appendix of Information for College Graduates Desiring to enter Schools of Nursing. A special three months' nursing-preparatory course is offered this year to graduates of recognized colleges at Vassar College, University of Cincinnati, and elsewhere, the object of which is to provide an intensive preliminary training in subjects which are usually taken up in the early part of the hospital training course.

THE ROYAL AIR FORCE NURSING SERVICE.

It is fitting that the Royal Air Force, "the last creation of the fighting forces of the world," should have its own Nursing Service, which will build up its own traditions.

The appointment of Miss L. E. Jolley as Matron-in-Chief of the Service foreshadowed its development, and Miss Jolley is now prepared to receive applications from nurses who desire to join its ranks.

The rates of pay are as follows :—

Staff Nurses.—£40 per annum, rising by annual increments of £2 10s. to £45.

Sisters.—£50 per annum, rising by annual increments of £5 to £60.

Superintending Sisters.—£60 per annum, rising by annual increment of £5 to £75.

Matrons.—£75 per annum, rising by annual increments of £10.

There is no provision for Assistant Matrons, but the Superintending Sisters will have charge of units.

The Nursing Service will have a uniform of its own, and those members who sign on for the duration of the war will receive an extra bonus of £20 per annum.

Application for particulars should be made, in the first instance, to the Secretary, Air Ministry, Strand, W.C. 2.

The Service will assuredly be a popular one, for the splendid work of the gallant airmen who guard our coasts, and keep watch over the safety of the metropolis in the air, that lesser folk may sleep securely, commands both admiration and gratitude, and the privilege of serving those who are sick or wounded is one which should be very highly esteemed. So far the scope of the Service is restricted to the United Kingdom, as provision is made in the military hospitals abroad for the reception of airmen in need of medical and nursing care.

THE ROYAL RED CROSS.

The King has been pleased to award the Royal Red Cross to the following ladies in recognition of their valuable services in connection with the war :—

SECOND CLASS.

TALBOT, Mrs. K. H. E., Trained Matron and Commdt., 24th Durham V.A. Hospl., Middleton St. George, Durham ; TAYLOR, Mrs. B. D., Sister, Ridley House Hospl., Carlton House Terrace, S.W. ; TAYLOR, Miss D., Staff Nurse, Hooton Pagnell Hall Aux. Mil. Hospl. (V.A.D.), Doncaster ; TAYLOR, Mrs. M. A. J., Matron, Belmont Aux. Mil. Hospl., Anfield, Liverpool ; TAYLOR, Miss M. E., Sister, T.F.N.S., 1st Eastern Gen. Hospl., Cambridge ; TAYLOR, Miss N. H. R., Nurse, The Norlands Aux. Hospl., Erdington, Birmingham ; THOMAS, Mrs. A., Sister, Highbury Aux. Hospl., Birmingham ; THOMAS, Miss G. M., Sister-in-Charge, Temple Road Aux. Mil. Hospl., Birkenhead Section, 1st West Gen. Hospl. ; THOMPSON, Mrs. A. M., Sister, Northd. War Hospl., Gosforth, Newcastle-on-Tyne ; THOMPSON, Miss B. M., Sister, T.F.N.S., 1st West Gen. Hospl., Fazakerley, Liverpool ; THOMPSON, Mrs. L., Matron, The Woodlands, St. John's Aux., Southport ; TIMBRELL, Miss A. M., Matron, Lowestoft and N. Suffolk Hospl. ; TOLLEMACHE, Lady W., Commdt., Peckforton Castle and Bunbury Hospls., Ches. ; TOPHAM, Miss K., Sister, T.F.N.S., Becketts Park 2nd Northern Gen. Hospl. ; TOSH, Miss F. M., Matron, Q.A.I.M.N.S. (ret.), Mil. Hospl., Sheerness ; TOWNSEND-WHITLING, Mrs. J. G. M., Matron, Cottesbrook, Northants Aux. Mil. Hospl. ; TRACY, Miss M., Matron, Sedgeley Hall, Prestwich ; TURNBULL, Miss J. H., Matron, Carrick House Aux. Hospl., Ayr.

VERDIN, Miss E. G., Commdt., Winsford Lodge Aux. Hospl., Winsford, Cheshire.

WAKE, Miss E. E. P., Matron, Garswood Hall Hospl., W. Lancs ; WALKER, Miss A., Matron, Didsbury Lodge, Didsbury ; WALKER, Miss A., Sister, Red Cross Hospl., The Chalet, Hoylake ; WALKER, Miss C., Nurse, Parkfield, Crumpsall ; WALKER, Mrs. P., Sister i.c., Q.A.I.M.N.S. (ret.), Post Office Hospl., 20, Kensington Palace Gardens, W. 8 ; WALTERS, Miss H., Matron, Southport Infirmary ; WALTON, Miss B., Matron, Shenstone House, Higher Broughton ; WARRINGTON, Miss E. M., Asst. Nurse, King George's Hospl., Stamford Street, London, S.E. 1 ; WATT, Miss C., Matron, Woolton Conv. Institution, West Lancs ; WEBB, Miss F. A., Sister, Q.A.I.M.N.S.R., Wharncliffe War Hospl., Sheffield ; WELLER, Mrs. E. M., Sister, Q.A.I.M.N.S.R., Frensham Hill Mil. Hospl., Farnham, Surrey ; WELLICOME, Miss M. A. M., Matron, Malmesbury Red Cross Hospl., Wiltshire ; WELLSTED, Miss A. M., Matron, T.F.N.S., 5th South. Gen. Hospl., Fawcett Road Sec., Portsmouth ; WHITE, Miss A. E. N., Sister, T.F.N.S., 2nd South. Gen. Hospl., Bristol R. Infirmary, Bristol ; WHITE, Miss E., Matron, T.F.N.S., Cowley Sec. of 3rd South. Gen. Hospl., Oxford ; WHITE, Miss M., Nursing Sister, Can. Nursing Service, No. 11 Can. Gen. Hospl., Moore Barracks, Shorncliffe ; WHITEHEAD, Miss E. J., Sister, Woodlands, Wigan ; WHITING, Miss M. de G., Sister i.c., Colliton V.A. Hospl., Dorchester ; WILDING, Miss E. A., Matron, Rudyford, Nelson, E. Lancs ; WILKINSON, Miss M. E., Nursing Sister, Can. Nursing Service, No. 15 Can. Gen. Hospl., Taplow, Bucks ; WILLIAMS, Mrs. E., Joint Commdt., Aberdare and Merthyr Red Cross Hospl., Merthyr ; WILLIAMSON, Miss S. A., Sister, North'd War Hospl., Gosforth, Newcastle-on-Tyne ; WILLIS, Miss E., Matron, T.F.N.S., N. Evington Mil. Hospl. (5th North. Gen.), Leicester ; WILSON, Miss A. M., Commdt., the Red Cross Hospl., Melton, Suffolk ; WILSON, Mrs. B. M., Nursing Sister, Can. Nursing Service, No. 14 Can. Gen. Hospl., Eastbourne ; WINCH, Miss M. E., Sister, Salisbury and Dist. Joint Isolation Hospl., Salisbury ; WINDIMER, Miss M. E., Freemasons' War Hospl., 237, Fulham Road, Chelsea, S.W. ; WOOD, Miss A. E., Sister, T.F.N.S., 3rd West. Gen. Hospl., Cardiff ; WOODROW, Miss M., Sister, Aux. Mil. Hospl., Moor Park, Preston ; WOODWARD, Miss M., Matron, Aux. Mil. Hospl., Billinge Orrell, near Wigan ; WOOLLEY, Mrs. F. G., Hon. Matron, Mil. Hospl., Kingston-on-Thames ; WRIGHT, Miss L., Sister, Q.A.I.M.N.S.R., Reading War Hospl., Reading ; WYNNE, Miss E. A., Matron, R. Berks Hospl., Reading ; WRIGHT, Miss M. A., Sister, N.Z.A.N.S., No. 3 N.Z. Hospl., Codford ; WYLD, Miss K. M., Sister, Melksham Red Cross Hospl., Wilts ; WANN, Miss L., Sister, Q.A.I.M.N.S.R., Mil. Hospl., Bagthorpe, Notts.

YAPP, Miss C. S., Matron, Lake Hospl., Ashton-under-Lyne, Lancs ; YOUNG, Miss A. P., Sister, Q.A.I.M.N.S.R., No. 1 Mil. Hospl., Canterbury ; YOUNG, Mrs. M., Sister, Norfolk and Norwich Hospl., Norwich ; YOUNGE, Miss C., Sister, N.Z.A.N.S., N.Z. Convalescent Hospl., Hornchurch.

CARE OF THE WOUNDED.

The Hotel Petrograd, North Audley Street, W., has been procured by the Office of Works, on behalf of the War Office, for the purpose of converting it into a hospital for the Canadian Forces. The hotel is of modern construction, and very suitable for the purpose for which it has been acquired.

It is announced in the official organ of the British Red Cross Society that after careful consideration of the sites available in the royal parks for the hospital which is to be presented to the American Red Cross by the Joint War Committee of the British Red Cross Society and the Order of St. John, the one finally selected is in Richmond Park. The original intention was to place the hospital in Windsor Great Park, and His Majesty the King had graciously consented to give a site in that park for the purpose, but it was found impossible to carry out this intention, owing to difficulties of drainage, clay, soil, &c. The site which has now been selected in Richmond Park is pronounced by the War Office and other experts to be satisfactory in every way. It stands high ; it is on gravel soil ; water, gas, and electric light are easily procurable ; and it is within a mile of two stations on the main line from Southampton. The Office of Works has undertaken the construction, the necessary funds being provided by the Joint War Committee. Work will begin at once, and it is hoped that a hospital may be provided within the next few months which will be worthy of the acceptance of the American Red Cross and of the American sick and wounded for whom it is intended.

It is also announced that a new problem in hospital work was presented to the American Red Cross in Great Britain recently by the large number of small camps of American soldiers, particularly aviators, which have been opened in various parts of the British Isles. These camps are too small to require the installation of a large hospital, but there are frequent cases of illness or accident, and the camps are generally situated at points far distant from the regular military hospitals. The problem has been met by the establishment in each camp of a small "tent hospital," where American soldiers suffering from minor ailments can be cared for satisfactorily. More than fifty of these tent hospitals have been set up in various small American camps during the past few weeks, each accommodating from four to ten patients.

The Italian Red Cross Committee, 2, Albemarle Street, Piccadilly, W. 1, is extremely anxious to secure names of ladies who will be willing either to take charge of depôts or to act as sellers on the Flag Day on September 25th. Each seller will be subsequently notified as to the amount of her sales on the Flag Day, and will also receive an official letter of thanks from the Italian Red Cross.

General Humbert, in command of the Third French Army, has conferred upon Section 2 of the British Ambulance Committee the rare distinction of the Croix de Guerre with Palm. In a despatch of July 3rd the General wrote : "Attached to the division since January, 1917, the Section has, under the orders of its commandant, aroused universal admiration, especially during the operations from June 9th to 13th, 1918 (at Ribecourt). In spite of the fact that several of the ambulances were injured by the bombardment, the work of evacuating the wounded never ceased, the cars continuing to fetch the wounded from the most advanced and dangerous posts, close to the enemy." The distinction can only be awarded by a general in command of an army. The Section are entitled to paint it on their ambulances.

The public will learn with relief that our hospitals at the Front have been placed some distance from the fighting units. They are clearly marked, and, of course, when bombed were intentionally attacked. By-the-bye, we hear that the German aviation officer who was taken prisoner after the wholesale slaughter at Etaples and warded, demanded to be at once taken to a place of safety, and hysterically resented the chance of death at the hands of his cowardly compatriots !

IN GRATEFUL MEMORY.

A vase of red, pink, and mauve carnations, and spikes of red and white gladioli, with delicate green fern fronds, before the War Shrine in Hyde Park, on Saturday last, attracted considerable attention. Attached to the flowers, by a ribbon of the national colours, was a black-edged card bearing in Queen Alexandra's handwriting the words : "In grateful memory to our brave and splendid soldiers who gave their lives for King and country. God bless them all.—From Alexandra."

OUR ROLL OF HONOUR.
NURSING SERVICE.
DIED.

We regret to record the following death in the Nursing Service.

KEMP, Staff Nurse C. M. F., Q.A.I.M.N.S.R.

WEDDING BELLS.

A marriage has been arranged, and will very shortly take place, between the Rev. George Berens-Dowdeswell, Rector of Foot's Cray, Kent, and Miss Eveleen M. Hunter, Matron of the Cray Valley Hospital, St. Mary Cray. We wish them every happiness.

THE SCHOOL NURSE.

One of the most interesting and important developments of civic and social service in connection with nursing is that of the work of the School Nurse, and no one is better able to " survey the duties and responsibilities of the nurse in the maintenance of health and physical perfection, and in the prevention of disease among school children," than Mrs. Struthers, R.N., who, as Miss Lina Rogers, was Superintendent of School Nurses, first in New York City, and afterwards at Toronto.

In a book bearing the name of " The School Nurse," published by Messrs. G. P. Putnam's Sons, 24, Bedford Street, Strand, London, W.C., price 9s. net, Mrs. Struthers deals with many aspects of school nursing from the point of view of the expert. As she herself tells us in her preface, " school nursing is still in its infancy, and many changes in methods are to be expected, but the underlying essentials—child love and preservation of child health—will exist as long as child life."

" It is," says Mrs. Struthers, " very generally believed that so-called medical inspection of schools, or, more properly speaking, health supervision of school children, is of recent origin; that it is, in fact, one of the progressive measures of this century—an outcome of the newly aroused social conscience. Nevertheless, medical inspection of schools dates back to the palmy days of the ancient Greeks and Romans. Under these ancient and warlike people, the State trained, educated, and developed the child for his place in life. With them, however, the child was first the child of the State, and secondly the child of his parents, and to the State his physical training was more important than his mental training, because the chief duty of the State was to prepare the man for war."

The Policy of Exclusion.

Mrs. Struthers traces the successive steps in connection with the medical supervision of schools and school children of recent years. In the nineteenth century this only meant exclusion from school for communicable or loathsome diseases, and but little attention was paid to the child after exclusion. In most instances the parents failed, through ignorance, to obtain the necessary treatment, and he was even allowed to play on the street with other children after school hours, thereby making of no avail the first act of exclusion.

The Policy of Cure.

" The advent of the school nurse brought a radical change in the methods of dealing with diseased children. Instead of being excluded and neglected they were treated by the school nurse. Many cases were treated in the schools without danger of contagion to other children. The nurse visited the homes, pointed out to parents the dangers of such maladies, and specially interested the mother in getting the children well. The trained, and let us add the kindly and diplomatic, nurse became the guide, philosopher, and friend of the family. The school nurse who fails to get into intimate touch with the family must confess she has failed in her first mission. As a result of the nurse's work, school attendance increased fifty per cent. Interested and regular attendance took the place of exclusion and truancy."

The Policy of Prevention.

" During the last ten years the important outcome of the school health work has been the emphasis placed upon a policy of prevention. It is just the old story that prevention is better than cure; that education is better than reformation. . . . At the present time, therefore, health education is the fundamental basis of all school health work. To cure disease or remove physical defect is a necessary but incidental part of the work. The factors of greatest importance to the child's future welfare are wholesome food, proper clothing, personal cleanliness, physical drill and play, and plenty of fresh air in school and home. Unfortunately many have been slow to recognize that this last policy should be the primary function of the school in health work."

Mrs. Struthers gives the history of the development of school nursing both in America and in this country. She details the organization of a system of health supervision of school children, and gives suggestive rules.

A very interesting section is the description of the little mothers' classes and school, and of baby clinics, organized for the purpose of teaching little girls with younger brothers and sisters how to take care of their charges. Admirable illustrations show these little mothers as interested audiences at demonstrations of bedmaking, of the baby's bath, and of putting baby to bed. Considerable space is devoted to the Forest School at Toronto, and the uselessness of trying to cram a child's head full of knowledge when the body is enfeebled, poorly nourished, or sick, is emphasised.

A study of Mrs. Struthers' lucid and interesting exposition of the purpose of school nursing should do much to create a sympathetic understanding of the needs of school children and of the high value in the body politic of the work of school nurses.

Royal British Nurses' Association.

(Incorporated by Royal Charter.)

THIS SUPPLEMENT BEING THE OFFICIAL ORGAN OF THE CORPORATION.

COMPOUND FRACTURES OF THE HUMERUS.

PART I.—SPLINTS.

By Miss M. C. Sinzininex, A.R.R.C

*Diploma of the Royal British Nurses' Association ;
Matron of Queen Alexandra's Hospital for Officers.*

The aim in cases of compound fractures of the humerus is to get the arm into a comfortable position with the ends of the bone in apposition by means of a splint, the arrangment of which must give free acccess to the wound for purposes of dressing and drainage, and at the same time enable the patient to be nursed and to move about in bed in comfort.

At Queen Alexandra's Hospital, Highgate, a great number of very badly fractured humeri have been successfully treated. In many of these cases the bone has been so badly shattered that months (and in some cases a year) have elapsed before all the dead bone has come away, and until this has taken place the wounds will not heal satisfactorily nor will the fracture firmly set. The wounds are usually kept open by means of drainage tubes, as there is always sepsis where there is dead bone. Mr. Herbert Paterson (the surgeon-in-charge) has brought out a very good splint for use in fractures of the humerus or elbow joint, and it has been in use at Highgate for over three years. It is based on the Thomas's principle of extension, but the forearm is held at right angles to the upper arm, instead of being out straight, the former position being much more comfortable for the patient. A padded ring fits round the top of the humerus, and is pressed well up into the axilla, two bars are carried down from either side of this ring, parallel to the upper arm, and are joined by a cross piece below the elbow. About half-way down the inner bar is a space arranged for the forearm by dropping the bar for the distance of 4 in. to 5 in., thus ⌐⌐ From this dropped piece two bars extend at right angles

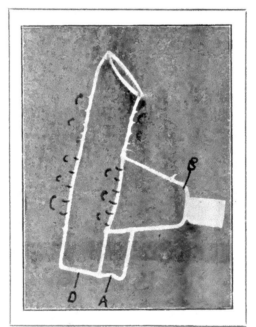

FIG. 1.—PATERSON'S SPLINT FOR FRACTURE OF HUMERUS OR ELBOW JOINT.

and between them the forearm rests, this also is joined under the wrist by a cross-bar to which a movable hand piece is attached. This is fastened on by means of a screw and can be raised or lowered at will. It is usually kept raised so as to prevent wrist-drop, but it can be lowered right down for purposes of movements and massage to hand and wrist.

In the case of a compound fracture, the method of extension is always a difficulty, as so often the wounds occur just where the pull is most needed. When it has been impossible to put an extension on the upper arm, a very good pull has been maintained by an extension round the forearm to the lower part of the splint below elbow but on the side nearer hand (see fig. 1, A.). When this method of extension is employed the wrist must be fixed by means of a firm bandage or buckle and strap to the upper bar of forearm piece at B., until such time as an extension can be put on the upper arm. Various armlets, to fit on part of the upper arm and part of the forearm have been devised, but nothing has been found to be so satisfactory as the old-fashioned stirrup made of strapping with block and cord. Armlets, however tightly laced, seem to have a way of slipping, and when tightly fastened they cut into the bend of the elbow and also impede the circulation of the forearm.

Even with a good pull from the axilla to the end of the splint, supports are necessary at intervals under the arm from the axilla to the elbow. The most suitable material for this purpose is rubber, as it can be easily cleansed and boiled when it comes in contact with discharges from the wounds. Old inner tubes of motor tyres, cut to the required size, are cheap, strong and serve the purpose well. These supports used to be held in place by very strong spring letter clips ; but as time progressed, these became unobtainable and safety-pins were used, the difficulty in pushing these through the tough rubber resulted in more than one pricked and septic finger. Then studs (fig. 1, C.) were made all down the bars on the new splints on which to fasten the rubbers. The rubber is nicked with a sharp knife in two or three places and pressed over the studs on the inner bar of the splint ; then it is brought under the arm and over the outer bar between the splint and the arm, drawn up to the requisite tightness, nicked again where the studs indicate by bulging through the rubber, and slipped over them, the elasticity of

FIG. 2.—FRACTURE BED, SHOWING DOUBLE BARS FOR SLINGING ARMS AND LEGS.

the tyre securing it. The studs are made thinner at the part nearer the splint to prevent the rubber slipping over and coming off. By this means the rubbers can be taken on and off with perfect ease when once the holes have been made. For dressing purposes only one side of the rubber need be detached from the studs. If several rubbers have to be used, it is wise to move only one at a time, as if too much support be taken away at once the fracture may sag and get out of position and also cause great pain to the patient.

The cords of the extension are passed through a screw pulley, which hooks over the cross bar at D. in fig. 1. This can be loosened or tightened by means of a key.

This splint can be worn by a patient who is able to walk about, the weight being supported by an ordinary arm sling. When the fracture

has set firmly, the arm is either put on a straight upper arm splint or put in plaster, the latter method being used where there has been great loss of bone.

This splint is slung by means of cords, pulleys and weights (sufficient to balance the arm) to a bar crossing the patient's bed (see fig. II). By this means the patient is able to move about in bed quite easily and can balance the arm himself at any height that is most comfortable. These fracture beds are fitted with two bars, so that either a left or right arm or leg, or both, may be slung, the bars also providing an attachment to which the flask of lotion may be hung.

DONATIONS RECEIVED.

The Honorary Treasurer acknowledges with thanks donations from the following :—

Misses A. E. and E. A. Boldero, 15s. ; Miss A. E. Billet, 5s. ; Miss Cruickshank, 2s. 6d. ; Mrs. Allan Robertson 2s. 6d. ; Miss A. Brentans 1s. ; Miss B. Carter, 1s. ; Miss E. Cowlan, 1s. ; Miss M. Ellis, 1s. ; Miss M. Lawford, 1s. ; Miss M. Littledale, 1s. ; Miss L. Pettigrew, 1s. ; Miss K. Rushton, 1s. ; Miss E. Starden, 1s.

THE THANKS OF THE MAYOR OF BIARRITZ TO AN ENGLISH NURSE.

Miss Constance Clarke, M.R.B.N.A., Matron of an American Hospital at Biarritz, has received a letter from Senator Forsan, Mayor of Biarritz, thanking her for the " enlightened zeal " with which she has accomplished the administrative work of the hospital, and conveying an expression of gratitude from the municipality of that town for the long months during which she has devotedly served the cause of humanity.

OBITUARY.

It is with regret that we have to report the death of Miss Mary Frost.

Miss Frost was trained at University College Hospital, and was for a considerable number of years on the staff of Great Ormond Street Hospital for Children. For many years she has been an inmate of the Princess Christian Settlement Home.

(Signed) ISABEL MACDONALD.

Secretary to the Corporation.

A SUPREME MOMENT.

Work was heavy and hands were few in a provincial hospital where I had gone to take temporary duty for three months ; in a word, we were understaffed. I was at once the Night Nurse and Night Sister on the male side of the hospital. Accidents I also had to admit, there being no night porter, and, if necessary, prepare the theatre for operations.

There was the usual, busy, rapid routine of hospital work, only rather more so than usually falls to the lot of one nurse. I had no time to sit still and think enviously of those who were spending the night in the conventional way, and deplore the anomaly of night nursing. I was, at any rate, spared the insidious temptation of sleepiness, which, in spite of the sustaining cup of tea, *will* assail the tired Night Nurse if she has not much to do. " Nurse, will you get the isolation ward ready at once, please for a bad case of diphtheria—a boy, seven years old—tracheotomy will be performed in the ward directly he arrives, in about an hour's time, and—will you take the case ? "

It was the house surgeon who spoke.

I replied in the affirmative, and then asked tentatively how my work was to be done. The best arrangement possible, under the circumstances, was made, and I was left free for my new and responsible duty. There is no such thing really as monotony in hospital life—that word should never find a place in a nurse's vocabulary, it savours of lack of imagination and sympathy on her part, who would do well to remember that what is an " interesting case " to her, spells something very different to the object of her interest.

Nevertheless, an emergency case is the trained nurse's opportunity and should not be discounted. But this in parenthesis.

To get the fire lit, bed made, tent erected, kettle half filled with boiling water and put in motion, and to make preparations necessary for the operation and for the nursing of such a case did not take very long.

One glance at the poor little sufferer convinced me that it was a very bad case ; the child was *in extremis*, semi-suffocated by the cruel disease so often characterised by the appearance of membrane of a more or less glutinous nature which attacks, and adheres to, the throat and nasal passages

The Surgeon arrived almost simultaneously, and the operation was performed at once. The immediate result of the incision into the trachea was a rush of confined air, and with it a splutter of mucus. The relief was instantaneous, and the look of strain and suffering on the little face was replaced by one of comparative comfort and ease. Johnny, however, was in a critical condition, and I watched him anxiously for eighteen hours, keeping the tube clear and giving constant nourishment, disinfecting and cleansing the throat, &c.

For that and the two following nights he did fairly well, and so I believed and hoped he would weather the storm. On the third night, or fourth —I cannot clearly remember—all went well for the first few hours, his breathing and his strength well maintained. Suddenly, without any warning at all, there appeared to be an interruption in the breathing of a very serious nature, and poor little Johnny was threatened with suffocation, due to the fact that a piece of membranous matter had become dislodged, and was blocking the trachea below the tube. As long as I live I shall never forget that poor child's face ; it was transfigured ; his eyes, big with terror, were turned to me in agonised mute appeal, while he clenched his fists and kicked out his legs with the force of impotent frenzy. It was obvious that removing the tube would be of no avail, the tube was clear.

For a moment my own helplessness was borne upon my mind with sickening dread. Must I watch the poor little fellow die ! There was only one thing to be done, and if that failed nothing could save him—artificial respiration. I took the arms and brought them above the head ; in bringing them down to the sides, I pressed against the ribs to force the obstruction upwards if possible. Hearing a nurse pass the door, I asked her to call up the house surgeon at once ; he appeared immediately.

" I can do nothing more than you are doing yourself," he said, and—unwilling, I suppose, to watch what seemed to be inevitable—he, half-reluctantly, left the ward. Time cannot be measured in such supreme moments of life ; it materialises to the overwrought brain and merges into tangible torture. Obviously, no length of time can elapse in a case like this. After the house surgeon had left the ward, the child became slightly easier soon he began to cough and I caught sight of something appearing at the mouth of the tube and was just about to seize it with the forceps, holding my own breath in the extremity of my suspense, when, with inspiration, it disappeared down the tube again. However the worst was over and the child could draw his breath. I waited anxiously with forceps in hand, watching the tube as a cat watches a mouse-hole, with a wildly-beating heart. Another cough and I had caught the thing, the cruel thing that had nearly cost my little patient his life. A large thick glutinous piece of deadly membrane. No sooner had the obstruction been removed than the child closed his eyes, breathed easily and slept with all the anguish that had distorted his face gone. I looked at the sleeping boy and then at the thing I held in the forceps, and my eyes filled with tears—tears of joy—as the tension of my brain was relaxed and I realized that my efforts to save the child's life had, under God, not been in vain. I put it into a bottle containing methylated spirit, I held it up to the light and looked at it again with—oh ! what different feelings. It was in the right place now, not in the wrong—that made all the difference. Now it was a bacteriological specimen ! I looked at it again, almost with affection, for had it not negatively saved my little patient's life ? The house surgeon returned just at the moment of my triumph ; he was surprised to find the child sleeping and breathing normally. I held the little bottle up to him with a triumphant smile ; he understood and gave an answering smile and went back to bed. Easy respiration was established after that, and there was no recurrence of the impediment. BEATRICE KENT.

NURSES' REGISTRATION ACT IN BRITISH COLUMBIA.

It is with pleasure we record that the Graduate Nurses' Association of British Columbia have secured the passage of their Nurses' Registration Bill. Hearty congratulations. In this connection Miss H. L. Randal, Editor of the *Canadian Nurse*, in a letter to Miss Beatrice Kent, writes : " I feel very strongly that we should give all the help we can to your efforts to secure Registration of Nurses, as we have it over here—a matter for the nurses alone and not of the laity. We have in British Columbia just got our Provincial Act passed after six years of work. Then, when all Provinces have their own Acts, we can formulate one Dominion Act with a very good chance of passing it, particularly as we have Dominion franchise."

APPOINTMENTS.
MATRON.
County Hospital, Ayr.—Miss I. M. Crichton, who has been appointed Matron of the County Hospital, Ayr, sends us the following details of her professional career. She was trained at Chalmers' Hospital, Edinburgh ; was Charge Nurse at the Victoria Infirmary, Glasgow ; and Theatre and X-Ray Sister, Housekeeper and Assistant Matron at Chalmers' Hospital. She has not held appointments at the West Kent Hospital, or the Edmonton General Hospital.

SISTER.
General Hospital, Nottingham. — Miss Alice Russell has been appointed Sister. She was trained at the Infirmary, East Dulwich Grove, and has been Sister in a Women's Surgical Ward at the Royal West Sussex Hospital, Chichester.

PRESENTATION.

At the Central Military Hospital, Fulford, York, on August 13th, Miss Kathleen Holmes, the retiring Matron, who is to resume nursing on the Western Front, was presented with a tea service on salver, a rose vase, a button-hook, and a shoe lifter, all in solid silver, the gifts of the nursing and medical staff of the hospital and the annexe at Haxby Road. Another gift from the annexe took the form of a piece of china beautifully designed to represent a wounded soldier. At the base was one word, " Blighty."

NURSING ECHOES.

An urgent appeal is made in the current issue of the *Queen's Nurses' Magazine* to all who are interested in its continuance. Owing to the war, and the large number of Queen's Nurses on active service, some hundreds of subscribers have ceased to take the Magazine, and of the rest no less than 208 have not yet paid for the current year, though they have given no notice of a wish to discontinue. Many others have not paid for 1917. The cost of paper and printing, as everyone knows, has increased to an alarming extent, and unless present readers discharge their obligations, and unless the number of subscribers is substantially enlarged quite quickly, the *Queen's Nurses' Magazine* must cease publication forthwith.

The dissertation on " Sister," by Corporal Ward Muir, R.A.M.C. (T.), of the 3rd London General Hospital, in that entertaining and interesting book, " The Happy Hospital," published by Messrs. Simpkin, Marshall, Kent & Co., Ltd., sums up the position with an insight so keen, and a humour so incisive, as to give both Sister and Staff Nurse pause for thought. Mr. Ward Muir writes :—

" There is a deal of difference, in hospital, between the word Sister and the word Nurse. Sister is, of course, a Nurse. But Nurse is not a Sister. However, there is nothing to prevent you calling Nurse ' Sister '—provided that Sister herself is not at your elbow. If she is, you had better be careful, both for your own sake and for Nurse's.

" Some wearily-wise orderlies, and many patients of experience, apostrophise all the female officials of a hospital as ' Sister.' The plan has its merits. . . . Apart from the fact that it can offend none, and will cajole not a few, some universal appellation of this sort is —the soldier finds—almost a necessity in his constant dealing with women who are strangers to him.

" He comes in contact with a host of women, especially after he is wounded ; not only nursing women, but women on the ambulances, women who serve refreshments at halting places, women clerks who take his particulars, women who trace casualties, women who transact postal errands, and so on. . . . To address them each indiscriminately as ' Miss ' is absurd . . . ' Madam ' is pedantic. ' Nurse ' is in many instances manifestly ridiculous ; you cannot call a clerical V.A.D. or a Y.M.C.A. waitress ' Nurse.' So, by a process of elimination, ' Sister ' is reached.

" Thus it comes to pass the Mlle. Peroxide of the Frivol Theatre who takes a turn at ladling out cups of coffee in a railway-station canteen (with a press photographer handy) finds that the mud-stained Tommies are saying, ' Another slice of cake, please, Sister,' or ' Any fags for sale here, Sister?' The Duchess, too, who is cutting bread-and-butter hears herself hailed by the same designation. And if both Miss Peroxide and the Duchess are not flattered (and maybe a little moved, too), I should be surprised.

" For really, you know, ' Sister ' is *the* happy word. It fits the situation—all such situations. Wouldn't it be possible to add one perfect touch : that our women comrades should drop into the habit of addressing us as ' Brother '? Officers and men alike— ' Brother '! It would be a symbol, this, of what the war ought to mean to us all : a fine collaboration of high and low, equals in endeavour. . . .

" When I was first put into a ward to serve as an orderly I was instructed beforehand that the only person to be entitled Sister was the goddess with the Stripes. Eager to be correct, I addressed the Staff Nurse as ' Nurse.' At once I divined there was something wrong. Her lips tightened. In a frigid voice she informed me of the significance of the Cape : all Cape-wearers held a status equivalent to that of a commissioned officer in the army, and must be treated as such by privates like myself. All Cape-wearers were to be accorded the proper courtesies and addressed as Sister. Furthermore, the speaker, realising that I was a new recruit, and therefore perhaps ignorant, would have me know that all Cape-wearers had undergone certain years of training. . . . The speaker concluded by a sketch of her past career—I was held up in the midst of an urgent job to hearken to it—and a rough estimate of the relative indispensability of the female as compared with the male staff. Finally I was dismissed with an injunction to hurry, and finish my incompleted task.

" ' Very good, Sister,' I replied.

" Half an hour later, in a pause in the morning's rush, I was beckoned aside into the ward kitchen by Sister herself. She gently apprised me that, as I was a new recruit, she thought perhaps I was not yet aware of the accurate modes of address and the etiquette customary in a military hospital. Etcetera, etcetera. She had overheard me call the Staff Nurse ' Sister.'

" Enough. One may smile at these exhibitions of feminine human nature (and I could match them, absolutely, on the male side), but when all is said and done ' Sister ' is a beautiful title, and most of the women who receive it— whether correctly or because, by war service, they have had it bestowed upon them—richly deserve it as a token of gratitude and honour."

The trustees of the Scottish Nurses' Club have purchased and are equipping premises at 205, Bath Street, Glasgow. The office-bearers appointed are the Marchioness of Ailsa, President; Mrs. J. W. Stewart, Vice-President; Convener, Mrs. David M'Cowan; Vice-Convener, Mrs. J. F. Pollock; Hon. Secretary and Treasurer, Sir John S. Samuel; Law Agent, Mr. Thomas Stark Brown. The Club has no official connection with any organization of nurses; the management will be in the hands of five representatives of the trustees, and individual nurses.

EARNEST WORKERS NEEDED.

Emphasising the need for recruits for Queen Mary's Army Auxiliary Corps (*alias* the " Waacs ") the *Times* says that " thousands of women are needed where hundreds only are coming forward. The appeals from the different commands are piteous. One commanding officer who had been promised a large contingent set to work and had the pleasantest portion of his camp fenced off and labelled, ' Q.M.A.A.C. only.' He had a garden laid out, had provided dining-rooms, recreation-rooms, sleeping huts, and everything of the best. As he looked sadly over the silent result, he said, ' These are my " Waackeries," but where are my " Waacs?" ' ' You can see them any afternoon from three to six on the river,' was the cynical reply of one who knew, ' they haven't joined up yet.'

" There are still thousands of idle women and girls in the country. Some of them, perhaps, do a little occasional voluntary work, but the average of their hours of industry is not great. The controllers of the Q.M.A.A.C., however, do not despair, and a big recruiting ' push ' has been begun, with a change of method.

" A valuable adjunct to recruiting will be an official film which is being prepared and will presently be shown throughout the country. It is called ' The Life of a Waac.' It will show her from the time she enlists, her life in Connaught Club, her work when training at a great military centre, and finally her embarcation for France. Later, it is hoped that oversea films will be prepared showing how the women live and work at the great bases and how they help to send more men up the line by doing work which in war time men ought not to do."

BOOK OF THE WEEK.

"THE NURSERY."*

Mr. Eden Phillpotts needs no recommendation, and no introduction. He is always worth reading. He most often deals with primitive and lawless men and women, but he would lose much of his power and charm if he attempted to lead his readers by conventional paths. "The Nursery" is an Essex story and the local colour is one of its chief attractions.

Aveline, the young widow, who turned out not to be a widow at all, appeared in the neighbourhood of Colchester to follow her profession of a painter. None knew from where she came, or aught of her, save that she was a beautiful woman. Her entry into the village life was marked by her rescuing a love-sick girl from suicide in the River Colne, and afterwards her consequent close friendship with the girl. The incident also provided an introduction to the village circle, for Margery came of decent people and was well known in the neighbourhood. Aveline's first coveted subjects for a picture were the tramps, who play a prominent part in the story.

"Both man and woman were somewhat extraordinary figures, and both smoked pipes. The woman bore the marks of beauty in ruins. She might have been forty-five, and was tanned brickred by exposure. Her eyes were bright and of the darkest brown; on her head she wore a bedraggled hat, with one great turkey feather set bolt upright upon it; her hair was cut short, and her thin bosom was buttoned up in an old Norfolk jacket. Her dress of withered brown ended in a fringe of rags.

The man accosting Aveline Brown says :—

"Me and Emma was wondering what you were up to."

"I'm going to paint a picture."

"Why?" asked the man.

"I live by it."

"Can't say as I've see you before, have you, Emma?"

"I'm a newcomer to Colchester."

"We're very well known—famous, in fact," explained Emma.

"But our liking for fresh air and objection to what they calls 'honest toil' makes us a people apart," drawled the man. "I'm William Ambrose and she's Emma Davey, better known as 'Marmalade Emma,' owing to a misunderstanding at the grocer's."

The brother of the male tramp was Aubrey Parkyn Ambrose, described by Emma as the "biggest nursery man in Colchester. Worth hundreds of thousands, I daresay—and the Mayor of Colchester this year into the bargain."

"I'm the thorn in his flesh," declared the tramp. He certainly was! If Mr. Phillpotts can draw the disreputable tramp true to life, he is no less successful when he paints nature in more

* By Eden Phillpotts. (London : Heinemann.)

attractive form, and his description of the summer glory in the nursery garden glows with colour.

It was while strolling in the gardens that Aveline met Peter Mistley, who was to play a great part in her life.

He was the designer of the water garden. Aveline asks if she may sketch there. "I'd love to try this lakelet, but I expect it would beat me," she confessed! "D'you know the underlying gold in it? But you made it, so no doubt you do. It's gold. You feel it more than you can see it, but it's there soaking everything. It actually flashes out on a dead water-lily leaf, or the edge of a reed, or in those warm, cloudy masses of plume poppy beyond."

Oyster-dredging at Brightlingsea is yet another aspect of industry from this versatile pen, and it is possible to learn a great deal on this subject from Mr. Rebow. Of the human interest, it is impossible to justify Aveline's treatment of Peter Mistley, for she married him well knowing that her husband was alive, but the war solved the problem of their relationship, as it has solved many other problems.

Even Marmalade Emma contrives to be pathetic, and she laments faithfully her disreputable partner, whose terrible death is depicted in characteristic fashion.

"Of course," she said, " we shan't tramp no more, nor nothing of that. But he believed we should meet again ; he often said he'd be terrible bored till I came to him. He'll be changed, but I hope not too much changed." Her simple faith is not shared by Aveline, who, speaking of Peter's death with the tramp—in the familiar fashion that Mr. Phillpotts makes natural—says, " He must have known that if he ever really came back that it would be ages before he could trust me or respect me any more. And no doubt he felt the game wasn't worth the candle.

" If you could only feel, same as I do that you're going back to him—if he's happy, then it's your place to be content."

But Aveline had the one adventure that Peter Mistley had declared that everyone needed, although it spelt disaster for herself and the man she professed to love.   H.H.

LIFE.

I play with life on different days
   In different moods,
Sometimes my wayward spirit strays
   In wonderful solitudes.
Sometimes I seek the crowded ways
   Of the world's gay multitudes.

Sometimes my soul is fierce and mad
   As a winter sea ;
Sometimes my soul is brave and glad,
   And the hours are good to me,
But often enough it is tired and sad,
   Poor waif of eternity !

—From *Rainbows*, by OLIVE CUSTANCE.

LETTERS TO THE EDITOR.

Whilst cordially inviting communications upon all subjects for these columns, we wish it to be distinctly understood that we do not IN ANY WAY hold ourselves responsible for the opinions expressed by our correspondents.

CERTIFICATE OF EXISTENCE.

To the Editor of THE BRITISH JOURNAL OF NURSING.

DEAR MADAM,—As one who has from time to time vouched for the existence of annuitants of the R.N.P.F.N., as well as witnessed the signature on receipt, I am at a loss to know why the receipt *had* to be returned to the office before the dispatch of cheque. Should not the endorsement of cheque to order satisfy the actuaries and protect the fund, besides being businesslike, even in transactions with women struggling to live for the remainder of their days on a small income? Postage counts, particularly in these days when a bonus is missed.

Yours truly,

CLARA LEE.

Letchworth.

NURSERY SCHOOLS.

To the Editor of THE BRITISH JOURNAL OF NURSING.

DEAR MADAM,—Mr. H. A. L. Fisher, at the opening of the Summer School for Teachers of Young Children at the Westfield College, Hampstead, in referring to the Nursery School, said this opens the way for " free voluntary experiment," and, it seems, he desires " suggestions and offers from people especially interested."

As a nurse who wishes her profession to take a definite form, and to command the same respect and similar remuneration from the Government and other employers as, for instance, the teaching profession, I object to the proposition that we should offer ideas founded upon our knowledge and training to authorities who did not heed our claims that this knowledge and training was essential to the success of the scheme. In my opinion the time has gone by for impressing the Ministry of Education with our views. The Nursery Schools are to be schools. Well, so be it.

Why should our services always be regarded as something to be had for mere asking?

Because *we have hitherto placed such little value on them ourselves.*

However, I am happy to say that there is to be plenty of scope for the ideas of nurses in their own *recognised* sphere, by the spurt given to the day nursery with the passing of the Child Welfare Bill.

Let our best nurses interest themselves more in the development of public health work, and take their proper place in it, and we will prove that our services are worth true recognition, and are no longer to be classed with voluntary efforts and benevolent societies. Then, indeed, will nursing rank with other professions and be able to claim its dues.

Yours faithfully,

Mosside, M/C.   THERESA MCGRATH.

THE HOSPITAL LAUNDRY.

To the Editor of THE BRITISH JOURNAL OF NURSING.

DEAR MADAM,—I was glad to see in THE BRITISH JOURNAL OF NURSING last week an article on " The Hospital Laundry," for in my experience the subject is one concerning which the knowledge of most nurses is sadly deficient. Yet, whether we consider it from the point of view of the nurse who is often recklessly lavish of clean linen, both in hospitals and private houses, of the Sister who is personally responsible for the correctness and good order of the supplies of her ward linen, or the Matron who should know approximately the average number of articles required to supply a given ward, the number which should be sent to the wash, and the amount of labour and materials needed to cope with them, the question of the laundry is all-important. Linen may be damaged or ruined, and expenditure in regard to the laundry be greatly in excess of what is necessary, if an expert and vigilant eye is not kept on all these departments. Added to this, most careful checking is needed when the clean linen is returned, or articles may disappear and not be forthcoming when stock-taking time draws on. Incidentally I may mention that this worry is minimised if the laundry is on the premises, as much closer supervision is possible.

Another advantage is that nurses in their fourth year can act as assistant to the Home Sister, or Assistant Matron, who arranges and controls the work of the laundry. This makes for smooth working in the hospital concerned, and the experience is invaluable to the nurse subsequently if she applies for an administrative post. For such a post high certificates in nursing, indispensable as they are, are only part of her equipment. Housekeeping experience, a knowledge of food values, and of the management of a laundry, also count for much, for she may have to supervise and control both these departments.

I am, Dear Madam,

Yours faithfully,

SUPERINTENDENT.

A CHANGE NEEDED.

To the Editor of THE BRITISH JOURNAL OF NURSING.

DEAR MADAM,—If nurses are run down through length of service in an enervating climate, they should have medical advice, and it should be followed. I may point out, however, that the climate of India differs widely, and that a visit to the hills would in most cases meet the needs of the situation. There are many places where the climate is as temperate and invigorating as that of the Homeland.

Yours truly,

ANGLO-INDIAN.

OUR PRIZE COMPETITION.
QUESTIONS.

August 31st.—Mention some of the principal disorders of the nervous system, and the duties of the nurse in regard to them.

September 7th.—What are the principal functions of a School Nurse? How may she assist in raising the standard of national health?

The Midwife.

MATERNITY AND CHILD WELFARE.

By direction of the President of the Local Government Board a circular has been addressed by the Secretary of the Board bringing to the notice of County Councils (other than the L.C.C.) and of Sanitary Authorities, the provisions of the Maternity and Child Welfare Act, 1918, which has recently been passed. The circular states :—

The Act widens the powers of Local Authorities in the matter of maternity and child welfare. It enables them to make such arrangements as may be sanctioned by the Board for attending to the health of expectant mothers and nursing mothers and of children who have not attained the age of five years, and are not being educated in schools recognised by the Board of Education.

A Council exercising powers under the Act must appoint a Maternity and Child Welfare Committee. This Committee may be specially appointed for this purpose or may be an existing Committee or a sub-Committee of an existing Committee, and it must include at least two women. Subject to two-thirds of the members of the Committee being members of the Council, persons specially qualified by training or experience in subjects relating to health and maternity who are not members of the Council may be appointed as members of the Committee. A Committee appointed under the section may also appoint sub-committees consisting wholly or partly of members of the Committee. Mr. Hayes Fisher considers it is important that working women should be represented on the Committee. In seeking such representatives the local branches of working women's organisations or the Standing Joint Committee of Industrial Women's Organisations, 33, Eccleston Square, London, S.W. 1, might usefully be consulted.

2. The Supreme importance of Maternity and Child Welfare work at the present time needs no emphasis. With a view to encouraging the provision of further services, which experience has shown would be of value for conserving infant lives and health, Mr. Hayes Fisher has obtained the sanction of the Treasury to a considerable extension of the scope of the Board's grant.

Regulations under which grants not exceeding one-half of approved net expenditure will be payable by the Local Government Board to Local Authorities and to Voluntary Agencies in respect of arrangements for attending to the health of expectant mothers and nursing mothers and of children under five years of age.

1. The Local Government Board will pay grants during each financial year, commencing on April 1st, in respect of the following services :—

(1) The salaries and expenses of Inspectors of Midwives.

(2) The salaries and expenses of Health Visitors and Nurses engaged in Maternity and Child Welfare work.

(3) The provision of a midwife for necessitous women in confinement and for areas which are insufficiently supplied with this service.

(4) The provision, for necessitous women, of a doctor for illness connected with pregnancy and for aid during the period of confinement for mother and child.

(5) The expenses of a Centre, *i.e.*, an institution providing any or all of the following activities : medical supervision and advice for expectant and nursing mothers, and for children under five years of age, and medical treatment at the Centre for cases needing it.

(6) Arrangements for instruction in the general hygiene of maternity and childhood.

(7) Hospital treatment provided or contracted for by Local Authorities for complicated cases of confinement or complications arising after parturition, or for cases in which a woman to be confined suffers from illness or deformity, or for cases of women who, in the opinion of the Medical Officer of Health, cannot with safety be confined in their homes or such other provision for securing proper conditions for the confinement of necessitous women as may be approved by the Medical Officer of Health.

(8) Hospital treatment provided or contracted for by Local Authorities for children under treatment.

(9) The cost of food provided for expectant mothers and nursing mothers and for children under five years of age, where such provision is certified by the Medical Officer of the Centre or by the Medical Officer of Health to be necessary and where the case is necessitous.

(10) Expenses of crèches and day nurseries and of other arrangements for attending to the health of children under five years of age whose mothers go out to work.

(11) The provision of accommodation in convalescent homes for nursing mothers and for children under five years of age.

(12) The provision of homes and other arrangements for attending to the health of children of widowed, deserted and unmarried mothers, under five years of age.

(13) Experimental work for the health of expectant and nursing mothers and of infants and children under five years of age carried out by Local Authorities or voluntary agencies with the approval of the Board.

(14) Contributions by the Local Authority to voluntary institutions and agencies approved under the scheme.

2. Grants will be paid to voluntary agencies aided by the Board on condition :—

(1) That the work of the agency is approved by the Board and co-ordinated as far as practicable with the public health work of the Local Authority and the school medical service of the local education authority.

(2) That the premises and work of the institution are subject to inspection by any of the Board's Officers or Inspectors.

(3) That records of the work done by the agency are kept to the satisfaction of the Board.

3. An application for a grant must be made on a form supplied by the Board.

4. The Board may exclude any items of expenditure, which, in their opinion, should be deducted for the purpose of assessing the grant, and if any question arises as to the interpretation of these Regulations, the decision of the Board shall be final.

5. The grant paid in each financial year will be assessed on the basis of the expenditure incurred on the service in the preceding financial year, and will be, as a rule, at the rate of one-half of that expenditure where the services have been provided with the Board's approval and are carried on to their satisfaction. The Board may, at their discretion, reduce or withhold the grant.

QUEEN CHARLOTTE'S HOSPITAL.

SISTER MEDCALF MEMORIAL.

We are asked by Mr. Arthur Watts, Secretary of Queen Charlotte's Hospital, Marylebone Road N.W., to notify that it is proposed to raise a permanent memorial to the late Sister Medcalf in recognition of her splendid record of work at Queen Charlotte's Hospital. She was a Sister at the Hospital for over twenty-four years, and from 1905 until the day of her death in January last also held the post of Assistant Matron.

Sister Medcalf was greatly esteemed by a large number of the midwives and monthly nurses trained at the hospital, and it is thought there are many who would wish to be identified with such a memorial. Any subscription, no matter how small, will be gladly received.

As Sister Medcalf was so closely identified with the chapel services and took such a care and interest in its upkeep, it has been thought fitting that the memorial should take the shape of something which will enrich and beautify the chapel which would thus be a permanent mark of her devotion to it.

Donations may be sent to the Matron, Miss A. Blomfield; the Chaplain, Rev. E. W. French; or the Secretary, Mr. Arthur Watts.

THE STORY OF THE TEETH.

" The Story of the Teeth and How to Save Them " is the title of an instructive and interesting booklet by Dr. Truby King, C.M.G., issued by the Babies of the Empire Society, under the auspices of the Overseas Club and Patriotic League, General Buildings, Aldwych, London, W.C. 2.

Writing of decay of the teeth Dr. Truby King says: " Decay of the teeth is not a mere chance unfortunate disability of the day; it is the most urgent and gravest of all diseases of our time—a more serious national scourge than cancer or consumption. Indeed, these and other diseases would be best attacked by establishing the strength and resistiveness of the whole human organism of which the mouth, jaws, teeth, and nose are the gateways—the gateways to health or disease according to our choice. Therefore, the mother's health and habits during pregnancy practically determine whether her baby's first set of teeth are to be strong and resistive or weak and subject to decay. In the next stage the main question (in addition to fresh air, exercise, &c.) is whether the baby is suckled or bottle-fed; and in the third stage whether he is brought up luxuriously, or with a Spartan simplicity and regularity—fed on food needing vigorous mastication—not coddled, spoiled, or pap-fed. Thus is the building and destiny of the permanent teeth also an intimate domestic and family question. Granted sensible upbringing, on the lines indicated, there would be no grounds for any anxiety as regards the future."

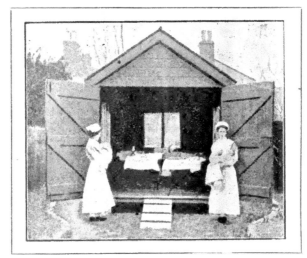

THE OPEN-AIR SHELTER IN CONNECTION WITH THE COUNTESS OF ATHLONE'S BABIES' HOME.

BABIES' OPEN-AIR SHELTER.

Our illustration, for which we are indebted to the courtesy of the editor of *The Gentlewoman*, shows the open-air shelter in connection with the Countess of Athlone's Babies' Home. It is an interesting and, we do not doubt, successful experiment.

THE
BritishJournal of Nursing
WITH WHICH IS INCORPORATED
THE NURSING RECORD
EDITED BY MRS BEDFORD FENWICK

No. 1,587.   SATURDAY, AUGUST 31, 1918.   Vol. LXI.

EDITORIAL.

THE RIGHTS OF TRAINED NURSES.

To all men and women of thoughtful and receptive minds, the war, notwithstanding all its horrors, has been a useful if stern instructor. Among the many valuable lessons learnt, and one of the most outstanding, is the value of intimate contact. We have watched with the deepest interest the ties which bind the Mother Country to the Colonies growing stronger and stronger. It has strengthened our patriotism as never before; it has given us a practical interpretation of solidarity—which we badly needed. Speaking broadly —in spite of strikes and rumour of strikes (perhaps because of them) — we are approaching nearer to the ideal of national solidarity. Nearer, but not very near even yet. We trained nurses might, with much profit, take the signs of the times as a parable applicable to ourselves. We have Imperial Conferences, and Inter-Allied Conferences. The deliberations and conclusions arising therefrom, constitute a force which has brought us within sight of victory. *L'union fait la force.* There is not the slightest doubt about that legend.

This intimate contact is needed in the nursing profession in order to make it " safe for democracy." We have an effective plant ready at hand. We have our own professional societies, well organised and properly constituted. We have self-governing societies of certificated nurses grouped in our National Council, and with other National Associations we are grouped in the International Council of Nurses, and few of us thus associated can express or perhaps even realize, what we owe to its inspiration. Again we have the Royal British Nurses' Association, the only body of nurses to possess a Royal Charter, of which every member is justly proud, for it confers both prestige and the power to promote good constructive work.

No progress can be made either in the government of a country, or the government of a profession, where the workers are denied representation—adequate representation—on the governing body. It is further necessary that nurses should realize the historical certainty that autocracy in their profession will die hard, and that their just rights can never be sufficiently secured, while it exists.

Nevertheless, with unity, determination and solidarity ultimate victory is assured. The true spirit of liberty is never defeated. Let us remember that we are fighting in our own beloved profession (as well as throughout the civilised world) to overthrow this wrongful power, in the best interests of the sick, and in the interests of posterity. A careful and critical study of the Bill for State Registration of Nurses promoted by the Central Committee, will abundantly repay those who are interested in nursing politics, so will the synopsis printed inside our front cover, which shows what nurses agree to who sign the application form for Registration and Membership of the College of Nursing, Ltd.

It is an interesting fact that the idea of self-government has found expression even in prisons: in some parts of America where prison reform is far advanced. The results have been all that could be desired. The spirit of self-determination pervades the whole world. It is no phantom spirit. It is quietly, though insistently palpable.

The lure of it is felt by all the most intelligent nurses in this country. But nothing worth having can come, or will come, by lazily wishing for it only, except in fairy tales. If workers want their rights, they must assert themselves in the only practical way—namely by working for them, and working for them in conjunction with others. *L'union fait la force.*

NURSES TAKE RANK AS OFFICERS.

It is with great pleasure that we draw attention to the announcement in the regulations for the members of the Royal Air Force Nursing Service published on pages 139 and 140, that honorary rank as officers is to be granted to the members of the Service, the Matron-in-Chief as major, Matrons and Superintending Sisters as captains, Sisters as lieutenants, and Staff Nurses as second-lieutenants.

Nothing could make the Service more popular, or conduce more to its efficiency by attracting a high type of nurse. The thanks of the nursing profession are due to the Air Ministry for conferring on the members of the newest Nursing Service the rank which has so far been withheld from the members of the sister Services.

A DEVICE FOR PREVENTION AND TREATMENT OF ADENOIDS.

Dr. Isabel Ormiston, Medical Inspector of Schools, Tasmania, gives in the *Lancet* the following interesting description of a device for prevention and treatment of adenoids :—

When in 1914 a non-operative method of treating adenoids, discovered by Mrs. E. Handcock, was brought under my notice I was not merely sceptical, but openly scoffed at the idea. I was bound to admit, however, that after two years' residence in a children's hospital and three years' medical inspection of school children I was not satisfied with the results of the usual operative treatment; as such a large percentage of cases remained mouth-breathers and continued to suffer from nasal catarrh. In many cases also the growth returned.

DESCRIPTION OF METHOD.

This new treatment consists in the production of a sneeze by lightly touching the nasal septum near the tip of the nose with a slightly irritant adhesive powder, made from powdered iris root and soap. The powder is not sniffed up into the nose.

The effect of the sneeze is to expel the catarrh or muco-pus from the nose and the adjacent sinuses. This stimulation should be repeated till a " dry " sneeze results. The free flow of lymph which accompanies the sneeze acts as a most efficient washout, and no doubt acts, too, as a natural protective fluid against the bacterial invasion present in adenoids.

The children who are old enough to blow their noses are then taught a handkerchief drill. They stand in line, and at the word of command they grasp the bridge of the nose and raise the elbow to the height of the shoulder, and then blow forcibly. The position of the elbow automatically expands the lungs and ensures a strong current of air being forced through the nose, which is held at the bridge to prevent pinching of the nostrils.

RESULTS.

Under the supervision of Dr. Octavia Lewin an experimental clinic of this nature has been in existence for six months at the Roll of Honour Hospital for Children, Harrow Road. The committee is so satisfied with the results that it is to be continued as part of the hospital routine.

I have been observing this simple method of treatment for the past four years, and have found the results most gratifying. The first marked improvement is, curiously enough, in the digestive system. The dyspepsia and constipation, which are so common an accompaniment of adenoids, are the first symptoms to disappear. Perhaps some student of reflex action could explain this. We know that the nose is an early indicator of indigestion, alcoholism, and gout; so perhaps it is not surprising if the digestive system can be reflexly affected by a nasal stimulus.

Deafness due to the blocking of the Eustachian tube also disappears quickly.

The time taken for the shrinkage of the growth varies. Generally speaking, the younger the child the quicker the results. A great deal depends on the intelligence of the mother, as the treatment must be carried out every day. In older children and adults with nasal obstruction a certain amount of manipulation of the head and neck is necessary to stimulate the lymphatic circulation.

One of the chief advantages of this form of treatment is that large numbers of school children should be treated simultaneously at little cost. School nurses could be quickly trained to carry out the treatment under the supervision of the medical inspectors of schools. At the present, when, owing to the shortage of staff, the out-patients' departments of the various hospitals find it impossible to cope with the number of cases from the board schools, it seems the ideal moment to introduce the system into our schools.

A clinic has lately been started at the Westminster Health Association, Greek Street, Soho, where the enthusiasm of the mothers over the improvement in their children is most encouraging.

OUR PRIZE COMPETITION.

MENTION SOME OF THE PRINCIPAL DISORDERS OF THE NERVOUS SYSTEM, AND THE DUTIES OF THE NURSE IN REGARD TO THEM.

We have pleasure in awarding the prize this week to Miss Mary D. Hunter, Section Hospital, Kineton, near Warwick.

PRIZE PAPER.

There are so many nervous disorders that perhaps the easiest method of mentioning some of the principal ones would be to classify them under three headings, *i.e.* :—

1. Disorders of the brain (organic), such as hemiplegia, meningitis, or tumours of the brain.

2. Disorders of the spinal cord, such as tabes dorsalis, anterior poliomyelitis, scoliosis.

3. Disorders of the nerves (functional), such as epilepsy, chorea, hysteria, and neurasthenia.

The duties of the nurse in regard to them varies considerably in the different diseases. But in any case the first thing for her to consider is the cause (and if any organic disease is present), and what steps the physician is taking to remove it or ameliorate. So much help can be given by careful and intelligent nursing in these cases. Suggestion plays a very important part in the nursing of all nervous disorders, and it is absolutely essential that the nurse inspires confidence in her patient.

To enumerate the nurse's duties more fully and draw attention to the various methods, I should like to briefly mention a few in connection with the disorders I have chosen as examples.

1—DISORDERS OF BRAIN.

Hemiplegia and Meningitis.—Guard against bedsores in both diseases, and give great attention to the bowels. Care must be taken that the diet is easily digested and nourishing. Pain is best relieved by cold applications to the head. In the former the nurse should try by careful treatment to prevent fixation of joints and faulty position of limbs.

Cerebral Tumour.—The intense headache being one of the symptoms, care is needed in choosing a suitable place for the bed : in the darkest corner, so that the light does not irritate the eyes. Absolute quiet is essential for all brain disorders, and the nurse would, of course, avoid any sudden noise, such as the banging of a door.

2—DISORDERS OF SPINAL CORD.

Tabes Dorsalis.—"Lightning pains," one of the many distressing symptoms, may be relieved by hot fomentations, massage, or counter-irritants of some kind. Suitable exercises to correct ataxia need to be practised daily. Constipation is frequently present, so that the question of aperients proves a troublesome detail. The nurse should impress upon the patient the importance of micturition at frequent and regular intervals, as disorders of the bladder generally arise to complicate matters. Between the attacks or crises, feeding up is required to make up for the loss of strength. In fact, to insist on a quiet, regular, abstemious life is the duty of the nurse in regard to this disease.

Anterior Poliomyelitis.—The most essential matter is *warmth,* which is best obtained by baths, suitable clothing, and gentle rubbings. See that the child has complete rest in a comfortable position, careful feeding, and that the bowels are kept regular.

Scoliosis.—Really more a deformity of growth than a disease, and to correct this deformity great attention must be paid to the clothing. Suitable exercise and correct breathing are also duties for the nurse to consider.

3—DISORDERS OF NERVES.

Epilepsy.—It is necessary to improve the general health by regular hours, suitable exercise and occupation, and most careful diet.

Chorea.—Absolute quiet and isolation should be insisted upon—rest being so important—combined with light food. The greatest care is needed in restraining the child, as too much restraint may do more harm than good. The sides of the bed will need padding. Proper nursing eliminates bed-sores. As arsenic is the drug usually given, the nurse must be well acquainted with the signs of an overdose.

Hysteria.—The duty of the nurse is to gain the patient's confidence and make use of judicious suggestion. Weir-Mitchell treatment is often most successful. Not too much fuss must be made, but the fact that it is a definite disease must not be lost sight of, and the nurse should refrain from showing any impatience.

Neurasthenia.—Due to some shock or worry and consequent mental strain, and therefore tact and sympathy are required in dealing with these cases. The nurse's chief duty is to ensure *rest.* There is usually loss of weight, so that diet must be considered to help improve the general health. A marked feature is insomnia, which requires great ingenuity on the part of the nurse to find out the best means of inducing sleep.

HONOURABLE MENTION.

The following competitors receive honourable mention :—Miss Catherine Wright, Miss Alice M. Burns, Miss P. Thomson, Miss J. Robinson.

NURSING AND THE WAR.

SOUTH-WEST AFRICAN CAMPAIGN.

LIST OF REWARDS.

The King has been pleased to give orders for a number of appointments for valuable services rendered in connection with military operations in German South-West Africa. Amongst them is the following :—

ORDER OF THE BRITISH EMPIRE.

CREAGH, Mrs. Elizabeth Rymer, R.R.C., Matron-in-Chief, South African Military Nursing Service.

ROYAL RED CROSS.

The King has been pleased to award the Royal Red Cross to the following ladies of the Nursing Services in recognition of their valuable services in the campaign in German South-West Africa, 1914-1915 :—

FIRST CLASS.

ALEXANDER, Miss I. G., Matron, S.A.M.N.S. ; BESTER, Miss H. L., A.R.R.C., Staff Nurse, S.A.M.N.S. ; FYNN, Miss M. A., A.R.R.C., Staff Nurse, S.A.M.N.S. ; WEISE, Miss H. H., A.R.R.C., Nursing Sister, S.A.M.N.S. ; WESSELS, Miss E. S., A.R.R.C., Nursing Sister, S.A.M.N.S.

SECOND CLASS.

BURGESS, Miss E., CHILD, Miss J. C., FERGUSON, Miss J. M., HAWKES, Miss C. J., NEWTH, Miss A. M., PEARSON, Miss E. M., WILDE, Miss B. J., WILSON, Miss E., Nursing Sisters, S.A.M.N.S. ; KROHN, Miss G., LANGMAN, Mrs. J. (*née* Patterson), VAN NIEKERK, Miss D. N. K., Staff Nurses, S.A.M.N.S.

A special supplement to the *London Gazette* contains the following list of honours and awards for valuable services with the British Forces in Mesopotamia :—

ROYAL RED CROSS.

FIRST CLASS.

COULSON, Miss M. G., Sister, T.F.N.S. ; EARLE, Miss A. L., Matron, T.F.N.S. ; GILMORE, Miss M. G., Matron, Q.A.M.N.S.I. ; McNAB, Miss M. M., A.R.R.C., Sister, Q.A.I.M.N.S.R. ; RAE, Miss M., Sister and Acting Matron, Q.A.I.M.N.S.R. ; WHEELER, Miss M. K., Sister, T.F.N.S. ; WILKINSON, Miss E. S., Sister, Q.A.I.M.N.S.R.

SECOND CLASS.

ARGO, Miss M. B., Staff Nurse, Q.A.I.M.N.S.R. ; BOTTOMLEY, Miss C. M., Sister, Q.A.I.M.N.S.R. ; CROSBIE, Miss M. F. D., Sister, T.F.N.S. ; CURTIES, Miss N., Sister, T.F.N.S. ; DAVIES, Miss A. M., Staff Nurse, Q.A.I.M.N.S.R. ; DAVIES, Miss E., Staff Nurse, Q.A.I.M.N.S.R. ; EMUSS, Miss E. A., Sister, T.F.N.S. ; HARTRICK, Miss A. L., Sister, Q.A.I.M.N.S.R. ; HUNSTONE, Miss M., Sister, T.F.N.S. ; KING, Miss E. S., Staff Nurse, T.F.N.S. ; MACLEAN, Miss M. E., Nursing Sister, Q.A.M.N.S.I. ; MARSHALL, Miss E. O., Nursing Sister, Q.A.M.N.S.I. ; REID, Miss A. E., Staff Nurse, Q.A.I.M.N.S.R. ; ROBERTSON, Miss M. A., Sister, Q.A.I.M.N.S.R. ; SEACOMBE, Miss B. E., Sister, T.F.N.S. ; WADSWORTH, Miss S. E., Sister, Q.A.I.M.N.S.R. ; WELLINGTON, Miss A., Staff Nurse, Q.A.I.M.N.S.R.

THE MILITARY MEDAL.

It is announced in the *London Gazette* of August 23rd that the King has approved of the following award of the Military Medal for distinguished service in the Field :—Staff Nurse Pearl Elizabeth Corkhill, Aust. A.N.S.—For courage and devotion on the occasion of an enemy air-raid. She continued to attend to the wounded without any regard to her own safety, though enemy aircraft were overhead. Her example was of the greatest value in allaying the alarm of the patients.

Miss M. Adelaide Nutting, Chairman of the Committee on Nursing of the Council of National Defence in the United States of America, in making a report to the twenty-first Annual Convention of the American Nursing Association, which is printed in full in the *American Journal of Nursing*, outlined the adoption of a very statesmanlike policy by that Committee. She said : " Women will ask themselves, ' What else is there that needs to be done that anybody could do, since the Red Cross and the Army and Navy are taking such care of the whole situation ? '

" Now this Committee on Nursing has found that while the Army and Navy controlled and the Red Cross mobilised, there was something else to be done, and that was to try to create something to take the place of that which was being called away. Let me say that last June the estimate was, if I remember right, that we would need something like 10,000 nurses for the Army Nursing Service. It did not seem to us that to find 10,000 nurses in this great country would be very difficult ; the Red Cross already had about that number mobilised. But before many months an order was made that said the United States Army Nursing Service is going to want 37,500 nurses, and a few weeks ago another body asked for an allowance of 40,000 nurses.

" Now it is perfectly clear that if we were going to put 10,000 into France or into active duty, we could not pick up 10,000 nurses without making 10,000 vacancies, because nurses do not belong to the idle classes, and we would have to have some way of replacing those nurses at their posts, wherever their posts might be. Therefore, one of the first things to be done was to try to find some good and satisfactory way of bringing into our schools more women and training more women, just as rapidly as was practicable, to go into the places left vacant by those nurses who were called to active duty. It was assumed that a good many of the posts in the hospitals would be filled by senior nurses."

After saying that with a very considerable amount of effort a very large number of students had been brought into the training schools, amounting to something over 7,000, Miss Nutting pointed out that the vacancies created pressed most hardly on the training schools.

CHEVRONS FOR AMERICAN NURSES ON HOME SERVICE.

" Some of you, I presume, are shortly going out of the training schools, some of you have come out of them, many of you will face what seems to be the great choice of a great opportunity. You will represent, over there in France, or wherever you go, the mothers, sisters, daughters and wives, and you take your places beside their loved ones that they would so gladly take if they could go, and all the world is looking. . . . Our work to-day presents to us a great crisis, and I know the American nurses will rise fully and thoroughly to meet it. Whether you will choose the thing you most want to do or whether you will choose the thing that most needs you, it will be an honourable thing for any young woman to choose to remain at her post as teacher, as supervisor, as public health nurse, if she is more valuable there, and if those who know most of her work feel that she can do better service there than she can do anywhere else. A very conspicuous insignia to show that, will be given to those nurses, and I think that is very necessary. For I can remember well as the war progressed, both in England and here, it was said a young man to-day does not like to be seen in the streets without a uniform. If you wear the chevron it explains why you are not at the front. All the country is looking to you with the greatest possible affection and with the greatest possible confidence."

———

Lieutenant-Colonel C. Yeatman, in command of the 1st Australian Auxiliary Hospital at Harefield Park, near Uxbridge, writes in the *Boomerang* :—
" After more than three years' service in the A.I.F., it is good to realise that in all this time there has been room only in one's mind for the deepest feelings of pride and affection for men of one's race and country. Appreciation of their soldierly qualities and magnificent achievement in battle does not exhaust by any means all that can be said or written of them, and I feel it a privilege to be able to record my unbounded admiration of the pluck and sticking power of my wounded or sick Australian comrades, and the triumphant will which gave exhausted and sick troops in Gallipoli the power to stand for months against superior forces, and I shall never lose the memory of the cheeriness and fortitude of my emaciated and worn-out typhoid and dysentery patients in Cairo, with " Gallipoli faces " and frames of a sort to make one weep, but with an unfailing spirit which made one happy to have been born and bred an Australian. Let me cite the case of a boy who in some manner became infected with small-pox. He was nursed by our own Sisters at the Fever Hospital at Abbasia, and when I went to visit him there, though he could not see me and was on the point of death, this poor, whispering boy, with the last flicker of life, had only words of gratefulness for the nurses who attended him. I have the same sense of pride in the qualities of the devoted women of the Australian Army Nursing Services on active service, and it is no unfounded or biassed statement to make that these are appreciated by soldiers of expeditionary forces other than Australians as they are by members of our own Imperial Forces. I count myself fortunate beyond measure to be serving in this great war with the Australian Imperial Forces."

THE ROYAL AIR FORCE NURSING SERVICE.

The following are the necessary qualifications and conditions of service for members of the temporary Air Force Nursing Service :—

A. CONSTITUTION.

(1) Matron-in-Chief, (2) Matrons, (3) Superintending Sisters, (4) Sisters, (5) Staff Nurses.

B. QUALIFICATIONS.

A candidate for appointment in the Royal Air Force Nursing Service must be duly qualified according to the following regulations :—

She must possess a certificate of not less than three years' training in a civil hospital, having not less than 100 beds.

She must be of British parentage and between 25 and 45 years of age, single or a widow.

The Matron-in-Chief will be required to satisfy the Advisory Board that, as regards education, character and social status, the candidate is a fit person to be admitted to the Royal Air Force Nursing Service.

The candidate will be required to fill in and return the form of application which will be forwarded to her, together with the following documents :

(*a*) Certificate of birth, or if this is not obtainable, a declaration made before a magistrate by one of her parents or former guardians, giving the date of her birth.

(*b*) Certificate of training (original to be produced when appearing before the Sub-Committee of the Advisory Board).

(*c*) Medical certificate.

(*d*) Dental certificate.

It is required that the candidate should have been vaccinated within the last two years and also inoculated against typhoid (A. and B.).

C. TERMS OF APPOINTMENT.

Forms of Agreement will be signed by candidates who are willing to serve :—

(*A*) So long as required during the present emergency, or (*B*) for a period of twelve calendar months.

D. PAY AND ALLOWANCES.

—	Initial Rate.	Annual Increment.	Maximum.	Washing.	Uniform.
Matrons ...	£75*	£10	£150		
Superintending Sisters ...	£60*	£5	£75	3 6 per week	£8 per annum
Sisters ...	£50	£5	£60		
Staff Nurses...	£40	£2 10s.	£45		

* And charge pay.

When quarters, board, fuel and light are not provided, a stated allowance is made.

A gratuity of £20 per annum is allowed to Sisters and Staff Nurses who sign Agreement

Form A., for serving as long as required during the present emergency.

E. LEAVE OF ABSENCE.

Twenty-eight days' leave of absence without deduction of pay will be allowed in each period of twelve months, *i.e.*, fourteen days on completion of each six months.

F. DRESS.

The members of the Royal Air Force Nursing Service are to provide themselves with the following uniform :—

The establishments selected to supply it will be intimated to them on application to the Matron-in-Chief.

MATRON-IN-CHIEF.

Dress : R.A.F. material, faced and braided ; cape : R.A.F. blue cloth ; bonnet : R.A.F. blue.

MATRONS.

One winter dress, serge R.A.F. blue ; 1 summer dress (alpaca), R.A.F. blue ; 6 muslin caps R.A.F. blue ; 6 collars (soft) 1⅛ in. turnover ; 6 pairs cuffs (soft) 1½ in. turnover ; 2 cloth capes R.A.F. cloth ; 1 bonnet R.A.F. blue ; 1 summer cloak (serge) and 1 winter cloak (serge), R.A.F. cloth collars.

In hospitals, where Matrons are required to nurse, 3 washing dresses and 5 aprons should be substituted for 1 alpaca dress.

SUPERINTENDING SISTERS AND SISTERS.

One winter dress and 1 summer dress, serge, R.A.F. colour ; 3 washing dresses, blue cotton ; 6 muslin caps ; 6 collars (soft), 1⅛-inch turnover ; 6 pairs cuffs (soft), 1½-inch turnover ; 8 aprons ; 2 cloth capes, R.A.F. cloth ; 1 summer hat, straw, three-cornered ; 1 winter hat, felt, three-cornered.

STAFF NURSES.

One winter dress ; 1 summer dress ; 3 washing dresses ; 6 muslin caps ; 6 collars (soft), 1⅛-inch turnover ; 6 pairs cuffs (soft), 1½-inch turnover ; 8 aprons ; 2 cloth capes.

In no detail whatsoever may the approved uniform be altered or added to.

In uniform, no furs, ornaments or jewellery are to be worn, neither coloured shoes nor coloured or fancy stockings.

Muslin caps are not to be worn outside the precincts of the hospital.

Waterproof caps of regulation material and design may be worn in bad weather in place of hats.

Waterproofs may be worn when necessary, but must be the same colour as the uniform, and of trench coat design.

G. HONORARY RANK.

Honorary rank in the Royal Air Force will be granted as follows :—

Matrons-in-Chief	.. Major.
Matrons ..	.. Captains.
Superintending Sisters ..	,,
Sisters ..	.. Lieutenants.
Staff Nurses ..	.. 2nd Lieutenants.

CARE OF THE WOUNDED.

The King has granted unrestricted permission to Miss Henrietta Fraser, Ambulance Driver attached to Section Sanitaire, S.S.Y. 2, to wear the Cross of Chevalier of the Legion of Honour with the Croix de Guerre, conferred upon her by the President of the French Republic in recognition of her courageous conduct when wounded recently while on duty ; to Miss Muriel Annie Thompson, First Aid Nursing Yeomanry, to wear the Cross of Chevalier of the Order of Leopold II, conferred upon her by the King of the Belgians in recognition of her services to the Belgian sick and wounded ; and to Miss Frances Elizabeth Latham to wear the Insignia of the Fifth Class of the Order of St. Sava, conferred upon her by the King of Serbia in recognition of her services to the Serbian sick and wounded.

The Lord Mayor has undertaken to make a special appeal to the City of London for funds for the British Red Cross and the Order of St. John in connection with Our Day, October 24th, and the collection of £1,000,000 in the City is the aim of his committee. The offices of the City appeal are at 3, Lombard Street, and the honorary organising secretary is Mr. J. H. Estill, of the Port of London Authority.

Miss Emma and Miss Kate Lansing, Sisters of the American Foreign Secretary, who are serving with the American Red Cross, have been mentioned in an Order of the Day of the 5th French Army for courageous conduct.

More than 6,000 women motor-drivers have now been enrolled in the United States in the Women's Motor Corps of the Red Cross. These women carry all official telegrams containing information regarding oversea casualties to the homes of the relatives of the killed.

President Wilson has approved the suggestion of the Women's Committee of the Council of National Defence that relatives of American soldiers and sailors lost in the Service wear a black sleeve-band with a gold star for each member of the family giving his life for the defence of the nation.

OUR ROLL OF HONOUR.

We regret to record the following announcements in the Casualty List.

NURSING SERVICE.

KILLED.

INGRAM, Miss E. A., V.A.D.

DIED.

CHAPMAN, Miss M. D., V.A.D.

WOUNDED.

THOMPSON, Sister M. C., St. John A.B.
HARRISON, Miss A., V.A.D.

THE COLLEGE OF NURSING, LTD., AND POOR LAW GUARDIANS.

A good deal of feeling has been aroused amongst Poor Law Guardians by the Council of the College of Nursing, Ltd., sending the following circular of inquiry over their heads to the Matrons of Poor Law Infirmaries—as in this breach of etiquette the College has failed to recognize that the Poor Law Infirmaries are public institutions administered under legal rules, and the Guardians are the authorized channel by which information is officially conveyed. The circular has also been addressed to Matrons of voluntary hospitals. No doubt in both cases the Matrons will obtain permission from their Boards before complying with the demands of the College.

THE COLLEGE AND HOSPITAL ETIQUETTE.

The College of Nursing, Limited,
6, Vere Street, Cavendish Square, London, W. 1.

The Matron,

Dear Madam,—The objects of the College of Nursing will be known to you as including the following :—To raise the standard of training, to promote a uniform curriculum and one portal examination, to establish lectureships and scholarships, and to make and maintain a Register of Trained Nurses.

Up to the present the Council of the College has largely centred its activities on the compilation of a Register which now numbers 8,800 nurses, and the Registration Committee acknowledges most gratefully the help and information you have given concerning applications for registration.

The Consultative Committee, appointed to consider the curricula of Training Schools, now appeals to you for further assistance in this important matter.

Before considering any plans for the future, the wisest course would appear to be to ascertain what is the present curriculum in the different Nurse Training Schools, and it would materially assist the work of this Committee if you would kindly supply the information requested on the following form, and any other particulars you may have that would be helpful in the matter.

With apologies for the trouble I am giving you,

I remain, yours faithfully,

M. S. RUNDLE, Secretary.

QUESTIONS.

1. For what period of training, or periods, do you grant your Certificate of General Nursing?
2. Is sick leave, or any time beyond recognised annual leave, made up after the period of training?
3. What Lectures are delivered to Probationers, and if you have a Syllabus, will you kindly send it?
4. Are your Nurses instructed in Sick Room Cookery?
5. Are the Examinations written and oral? How often are they held during the period of training, and by whom are they conducted?
6. What Beds have you besides those for General Medical and Surgical cases?
7. Are any facilities offered in the fourth year for preparation in special branches of work, e.g., Massage, Midwifery, &c.?

Space is provided for the answers, and for the signature thereto of the Matron or Superintendent of Nursing.

A COLONIAL OPINION.

The following letter appears in the issue of *Una*, the official organ of the Royal Victorian Trained Nurses' Association, just received in this country :

To the Editor of " Una."

Dear Sir,—I notice with surprise that up to the present time you have not in our nursing journal attempted to voice an opinion upon the College of Nursing which is now being launched in London by Sir Arthur Stanley. . . . It is of real live interest in the nursing circles of Great Britain, and as fellow-nurses I think it is about time we roused ourselves and became acquainted with the facts.

I have always been an advocate of direct representation upon any board or council of nurses. I fail to see how any lay control can ever be the right thing in the interests of the nurses themselves.

Sir Arthur Stanley holds the position of Treasurer of St. Thomas' Hospital as well as that of Chairman of the British Red Cross Society. His knowledge of the nursing profession would necessarily be that of an employer. There are several matrons of large hospitals also connected with the college. This I do not consider advisable, as after years of work with committees, &c., they more or less acquire the institutional mind. The general nurse wants someone in power who will be able to entertain her point of view in dealing with items of nursing.

Here in Victoria the personnel of the Council of the R.V.T.N.A. is regulated by the nurse voters, who elect members once a year. A few are nominated by the committees of the special training schools, and the appointment ratified by the Council. In most cases the hospitals suggest their matrons.

The readers of *Una* will well remember the firm stand this Council took when the then Minister of Health decided that there be no nursing member upon the proposed board to administer the State Registration Bill for nurses In the opinion of those best qualified to know, it was considered that it would be better to have no Bill at all unless the profession to be governed and regulated had a voice in the administration.

When I was in London, in 1912, Mrs. Bedford Fenwick and Dr. Chapple—who, by the way, was once in New Zealand—were working for their Bill, which, if I remember rightly, was introduced into the House of Commons by our present Governor-General, Sir R. Munro Ferguson, who passed it over to Dr. Chapple when leaving England. The aims and ideals of their proposed Bill seemed much the same as the objects we are striving for. As a keen registrationist I warmly support them in their efforts, as it appears to be the best course to uplift and safeguard the nursing profession. I hope now that so many nurses are eligible as women voters they will strive to place the important rôle they try to maintain, viz., the health of a nation, before their Parliamentary representatives, so that their services may become more efficient.—I am, &c.,

GRETTA LYONS.

REGISTRATION PROPOSALS IN VICTORIA.

Bills for the registration of nurses and of masseurs will be introduced into the State Parliament in Victoria, Australia, in the forthcoming session. It is proposed that the Governing Body under the Nurses' Bill shall be composed of representatives of the medical and nursing professions, the general public, and the Government.

LEGAL MATTERS.

Eva Grace Thompson, of Blackheath, was again brought up on remand at Greenwich last week, charged with the wilful murder of Kenneth Cedric Goodman, an infant aged eleven weeks, by striking him on the head, on or about June 4th, at the Sydenham Infant Welfare Centre. The prisoner was defended by Mr. G. W. Jones, and Sir Richard Muir appeared for the Director of Public Prosecutions. Miss Muriel Payne, the Superintendent of the Centre, said that the prisoner, a trained nurse, was alone in charge of the patients for several nights.

Medical evidence was given by Dr. Gladstone, Medical Officer of the Centre, and Lieut.-Colonel F. S. Toogood, R.A.M.C., in reference to post-mortem examinations on various children at the Centre whose skulls were found to be fractured.

The prisoner was again remanded.

APPOINTMENTS.

MATRON.

Isolation Hospital, Mortlake, S.W. 14. — Miss Mary Grace Lloyd has been appointed Matron. She was trained at Guy's Hospital, and held various positions of responsibility before being appointed Matron at the Accident Hospital, Rhymney.

SISTER.

St. Mary's Hospital, Plaistow, E. 13. — Miss E. E. Hibberd has been appointed Sister on the Children's Floor. She was trained at the Lewisham Infirmary, and has been staff nurse at the St. Mary's Hospital, Plaistow.

PRESENTATION.

Miss Gregory, who for twenty-one years has held the position of Matron at the Aldershot Hospital, has been presented by the management committee with a solid silver Georgian tea service and salver ; and a gold watch has been presented to Mr. W. Wren, its Hon. Secretary, who has also been associated with the work from the start.

LAVENDER BAGS FOR LINEN CUPBOARDS.

The Editor will be pleased to distribute lavender bags to military hospitals in London, if friends have any to spare. Address to 20, Upper Wimpole Street, London, W. 1.

NURSING ECHOES.

Members of the Royal British Nurses' Association will have a specially warm welcome for their Secretary, Miss Isabel Macdonald, who returns to town this week, and who has had during her holiday in Scotland an experience which might not have had a happy ending. Miss Macdonald writes :—" We had a very exciting evening yesterday ; we went out to fish without boatmen, and one of the worst squalls the boatmen remember on the loch came on unexpectedly. Oars were no more useful than teaspoons, and we had an exciting hour, twenty minutes of which was a *very* grim struggle. My brother said that had it been a nervous person with him we never would have survived, for every time the boat went down between the waves the least excited movement would have upset it. At last, after a terrific struggle on the part of the two men, we managed to get the boat up to a small island, climbed over the side and waded in. About nine it seemed a little better, so we made for the Castle (Loch Leven) Island, and just managed to reach it, which was consoling, as it meant the shelter of the ruin, and a possible fire if we had to spend the night out there. However, a club had been watching us with glasses from the shore, and later two boatmen came and took us off, but it took all the strength of them and the other two to make the shore. They told my brother very frankly that they would not have cared for him or his friend, but they were not going to let the 'leddy' spend the night out there if it was possible to get back, so don't say the age of chivalry is dead while there are boatmen on the Scottish lochs ! When the adventure was over it was entertaining, but at one stage we thought each wave would capsize the boat, and the water touched my fingers as I held on to the side."

Nurse Reid, of Dunleer, has just tendered her resignation to the Ardee Guardians, after thirty years' service. In asking a superannuation allowance, she stated, says the *General Advertiser,* she had not had an increase in her salary all that time.

Mr. James P. Chrystal, the Chairman of the St. George's Hospital Nursing Association, Bombay, in moving the adoption of the annual report at the Annual General Meeting of subscribers, held in Killick Buildings on June 10th, said, in part :—

" It will be observed from the report that considerable difficulty is being experienced in securing suitable probationers for training in the hospital, and also in maintaining the numbers on the Private Nursing Staff. The chief cause for the former difficulty is found to be the wide scope of better-paid employment for young women in work connected with the war and the attractions of the V.A.D. work in the war hospitals. The high nursing fees obtainable from the public by private nurses working on their own make it more profitable for nurses to commence nursing independently whenever they have completed their period of training and obtained their certificates of qualification. To in some measure counteract this effect the Committee have recently raised the grades of salaries of the Private Nursing Staff, and they hope under the new schedule that this staff may be strengthened. To meet this extra expenditure and the additional cost of maintenance due to a depleted staff it has been necessary to increase the charge for a nurse by Re. 1 per day.

" During the past year the work in the wards of the hospital has been particularly heavy and arduous. The small-pox epidemic and other infectious cases

MISS CHARLOTTE RICHMOND MILL.
Kaisar-i-Hind Medal, Matron St. George's Hospital, Bombay.

have called for a good deal of isolated nursing, which throws a great additional strain on the staff, and I desire to express the Committee's appreciation of the devoted manner in which the nurses have met the extra strain thus thrown upon them.

" I cannot conclude my remarks without referring with peculiar pleasure to the honour which has just been conferred by Government

on Miss Mill, the Lady Superintendent of St. George's Hospital. The award of the Kaisar-i-Hind medal is a high mark of Government's appreciation of her long and honourable nursing career in India. Miss Mill was brought out to India with one of the first drafts of Nursing Sisters in the early days of plague, and she remained in Government service till 1902, when she was permitted to join this Association as its Lady Superintendent when it took over the nursing of the hospital from the Sisters of All Saints. The St. George's Hospital Nursing Association was the first of all the Nursing Associations in India, and Miss Mill was consequently the first Lady Superintendent of such an Institution in this country. Her administration of the nursing staff during the last fifteen years has found great acceptance with the Committee and the surgical and medical officers at the hospital, and her sense of equity and justice, combined with her ability in training the nurses under her care, has always won for her the staff's respect and esteem. It therefore gives me great pleasure to take this opportunity of conveying to Miss Mill this Association's warmest congratulations on the public recognition which her services have so deservedly received."

The Bloemfontein Hospital Board has (says the *South African Nursing Record*) raised the question of nurses' hours, and considerable discussion took place on the subject. There seemed to be a general agreement that something on the lines of the recent Transvaal

Ordinance was required, though the possibility of three eight-hour shifts a day was also mentioned. Our contemporary continues :—" We are greatly averse to excessively long hours for nurses, and we think that they could in many cases be shortened with advantage. At the same time we should not like to see a matron's powers in 'this direction too rigidly limited. Off and on duty hours could well be adjusted to meet the needs of the institution at any particular time, and we do not think that either nurses themselves or the public will deny that it should be the privilege of the administrative head of a hospital to call upon the staff to work overtime if the welfare of sick people depends upon it, and provided that justice is always done. This call to self-sacrifice and the liability to uncertain and exhausting hours is one of the conditions both doctors and nurses accept when they take up the work, and is part of the discipline of our profession. We know that both these classes of workers recognise it themselves gladly."

"INTERN THEM ALL."

No one who watched the procession which streamed down Oxford Street on its way to Trafalgar Square last Saturday afternoon after the great meeting in Hyde Park, to demand the internment of all enemy aliens, naturalised or unnaturalised, could be in any doubt as to the temper of the People on this question, or of the wisdom of the National Party in organising the demonstration.

Brigadier-General Page Croft, who presided at the principal platform in the Park, emphasised his conviction that the right policy is to " intern them all." And the Government must begin with the dangerous wealthy Hun. Of what use is it to penalise the poor when the rich, who have bought themselves power, and who consequently count, are at large ? All must be interned in the interests of national safety.

Mrs. Dacre Fox was as emphatic as General Page Croft. She was " out for the internment of every alien of enemy blood, naturalized or unnaturalized." She moved the following resolution, which was carried by acclamation at all five platforms :—

" This meeting, representative of all sections of his Majesty's subjects in the United Kingdom and the British Dominions beyond the seas, calls upon his Majesty's Government to lose no further time in interning every enemy alien; in denaturalising those naturalised during the war or ten years prior thereto ; in immediately removing every enemy alien from Government employment, and generally in taking drastic steps to eradicate all enemy influence throughout the country."

Amongst the inscriptions on the banners borne in the procession were :

" Before you vote for a Party ask where their Funds came from."

" No German has ever subscribed to the National Party, can other Parties say the same ? "

" The National Party has No Secret Funds."

The Monster Petition to the Prime Minister, including over a million signatures, was presented at No. 10, Downing Street by General Page Croft, who subsequently reported the result to the waiting meeting in Trafalgar Square, on which the meeting passed a resolution, expressing its regret and dismay, that the message of the Prime Minister clearly indicated that his Majesty's Government does not appreciate the deep National feeling with regard to aliens at large. In forwarding the resolution General Page Croft, in an open letter, has requested the Prime Minister to state the earliest date on which he will personally receive a deputation, and adds :—

" On behalf of the demonstrators representing the National Party, the British Empire Union, the Discharged Soldiers' and Sailors' Association, and many other kindred bodies, may I take this opportunity of impressing upon you the intense feeling which exists throughout the country on this subject, and my fear that, unless immediate steps are taken to intern all enemy aliens, whether rich or poor, confidence in your Government may be impaired at this time when national unity is essential if complete victory is to be secured."

FORT=REVIVER.

Newman's Fort-Reviver is a beverage which has quickly won its way to public favour, and has many points to recommend it. As its name implies, it is a stimulant, and, moreover, a stimulant which is non-alcoholic, which will commend it to a large section of the public. If taken with this object it should be undiluted, but it is also a pleasant " long drink " when taken with aerated water. It is obtainable everywhere, the large-sized bottles being 5s. 6d., and the smaller 3s. 9d. If any difficulty is experienced in obtaining it application should be made to Messrs. H. & C. Newman, London Office, 41 and 42, Upper Rathbone Place, W. 1.

The Great Northern Central Hospital has received from the staff of the Argentine Estates of Bovril, Ltd., a remittance for £39, for the maintenance of the Santa Elena Bed in the Hospital's Military Annexe, Manor Gardens— as well as other overseas donations.

The *Entente Cordiale* has found recent expression in the arrangements made with Charing Cross Hospital for the reception for three months of French nurses endorsed by the French Red Cross, so that they may get an insight into English methods.

OUTSIDE THE GATES.

WOMEN.

The Deputy Registration Officer at Enfield, when asked, on August 30th, whether nurses in hospitals or institutions who had separate sleeping apartments or shared rooms in common with other nurses were entitled to the vote, said that unless it could be proved that, as part of her contract or engagement, a nurse was definitely entitled to the use of a specific room and could not be removed without due notice, she could not be accepted as occupying the room for the purposes of the Act.

In view of this decision it is extremely interesting to consider the usage at Charing Cross Hospital in regard to the nurses' quarters.

1. All the nurses have latchkeys to the Nurses' Home.

2. Every nurse has a bedroom allotted to her when she enters the hospital for training, and keeps it throughout the period of four years, whether on day or night duty, except in a very few instances when a nurse asks to be allowed to change her room.

3. The locks on the bedroom doors are similar to those on hotel doors. If a nurse takes her key out of her bedroom door it can only be opened by the matron with her pass key, and by the servant of the landing who has a pass key for cleaning purposes, so the nurse's room is really her own.

The Town Clerk and registration officer of Oxford City, Mr. Richard Bacon, had an important point to decide in the revision court on August 21st.

A number of the wives of Oxford Dons, according to the *Times*, claimed to be on the lists, but the Town Clerk pointed out that Section 257 of the Municipal Corporations Act provided that nothing in that Act should entitle any person to be enrolled as a citizen of the city of Oxford by reason of his occupation of any rooms, chambers, or premises in any college or hall of the University. Persons so occupying were, prior to the Act of 1918, placed on the Parliamentary but not on the municipal list. Unfortunately, in the new Act the lady's vote depended on her possessing the municipal vote, either in her own right or that of her husband. In the case under consideration, if the Warden of Wadham admitted, as he now did, that he was not entitled to what was called the Local Government vote, which was, of course, here the burgess vote, his wife lost in consequence not only her Local Government vote but also her Parliamentary vote. That, he thought, was regrettable. It could never have been intended by Parliament, and he thought the officers of the Crown in drawing the Act, or the Parliamentary draftsmen, must have overlooked this provision in the Municipal Corporations Act.

BOOK OF THE WEEK.

"THAT WHICH HATH WINGS." *

A book by Richard Dehan, author of "The Dop Doctor," is certain to be interesting and arresting, and "That which hath Wings" is true to type. It is a picture of Society just before and during the war, and the "Dop Doctor," now established in a fashionable practice in Harley Street, his wife Lynette, and their boy Bawne—the brave Boy Scout—play a prominent part in its pages, though the central figures are Francis Athelstan Sherbrand, Viscount Norwater, and his wife Margot, otherwise known as "Kittums."

"It was a genuine love-match, Franky being a comparatively poor Guardsman with only two thousand a year in addition to his pay as a Second Lieutenant in the Royal Bearskin's Plain, and Margot a mere Cinderella in comparison with heiresses of the American canned-provision and cereal kind."

It seemed to Franky that all his wooing had been done at Margot's Club, though he actually proposed to her at the Royal Naval and Military Tournament; "and Margot, hysterical with sheer ecstasy, as the horses gravely played at push-ball, had pinched his arm and gasped out ' *Yes*, but don't take my mind off the game just now—these dear beasts are so *heavenly*.' "

"The honeymoon might have been termed ideal—and four subsequent months of married life proved tolerably cloudless—until Fate sent a stinging hailstorm to strip the roses from the bridal bower, and an unexpected, appalling, inevitable discovery made in Paris, in the *Grande Semaine*, utterly ruined—for two people—the day of the Grand Prix"—for Margot made the discovery—which she deeply resented—that the crown of motherhood was to be hers.

"'I can't bear it! I won't bear it!' Margot reiterated. With her tumbled hair, swollen eyes, pink uptilted nose, and little mouth and chin that quivered with each sobbing breath intaken, she looked absurdly babyish for her twenty years, as she vowed wild horses shouldn't drag her to Longchamps, and railed against the injustice of Fate.

"'None of my married friends have had such rotten bad luck,' she asserted. She stamped upon the velvety carpet and flashed at Franky a glance of imperious appeal. ' Not Tota Stannus, or Cynthia Charterhouse, or Joan Delabrand, or anybody! Then why me! That's what I want to know! After all the mascots I've worn, or carried about with me . . . Gojo and Jollikins, and the jade tree-frog and the rest! . . . Every single one given me by a different woman who had been married for years and never had a baby! This very day I'll smash the whole lot!'

"' By the Great Brass Hat!'

"Franky exploded before he could stop himself, and laughed till the tears rolled down. So

---

* Wm. Heinemann, 21, Bedford St., W.C. 7/- net.

'Gojo' the black velvet kitten, and Jollikins, and all the army of gadgets and netsukis crowding Margot's toilette table and *secrétaire*, down to 'Pat-Pat,' the bog-oak pig, and 'Ti-ti,' the jade tree-frog, were so many insurances against the Menace of Maternity. By Jove! women were regular children . . . And Margot . . . Nothing but a baby this poor little Margot—going, in spite of Jollikins and Gojo, to have a baby of her own.

" 'What is one to believe ? Whom is one to trust in ?'

" 'Trust in . . . My best child, you don't mean that you believed those women when they told you that such two-penny gadgets could work charms of—that or any other kind ?'

" 'Indeed, indeed they do ! Tota Stannus was *perfectly serious* when she came to my boudoir one night at the club, about a week before our—the wedding. . . . She said—I can hear her now : *Well, old child, you're to be married on Wednesday, and of course you know the ropes well enough not to want any tips from me. . . . Still—*'

" 'That wasn't overwhelmingly flattering,' Franky commented, ' from a woman twice your age. What else did she say ?'

" 'She said I must be aware,' went on Margot, ' that a woman who wanted to keep her friends and her figure, simply couldn't afford to have kids !'

" 'And you—'

" Franky no longer battled with the grin that would have infuriated Margot. Something had wiped it from his face."

More revelations from Margot, till at length Franky said : " Look here, this is—strict Bridge. Do you loathe 'em—the kiddies—so horribly that the idea of having any is distasteful to you ? Or is it—not only the—the veto it puts on larking and kickabout and—the temporary disfigurement —you're afraid of—but the—the—the inevitable pain. . . . Tell me frankly." He waited an instant and then said in an urgent whisper : " Answer me ! . . . For God's sake, tell me the frozen truth, Margot !"

Poor Margot—thoughtless, irresponsible little humming bird—faced with the realities of life, confessed to her dread of the ugliness of the thing and her fear of the pain—the awful pain. " 'And besides—my mother died when I was born !' Margot's voice was a fluttering, appealing whisper ; her great eyes were dilated and wild with terror."

Franky, out of his love for his wife, able to understand something of her mental outlook, agreed that he was frightfully sorry for her. " All the more so because I can't help being thundering glad." Then he explained, " It's got to do with the Peerage . . . naturally enough— I want a boy to take the Viscounty when I succeed my father, and have the Earldom when I've absquatulated, just as the kiddy'll want one when his own time comes."

Later, at the sight of a mother and her babe in the public park, " a dimness came before his vision, and it was as though dimpled hands

plucked at his heart. He suffered a sudden revulsion strange in a young man, so modern, so up-to-date and beautifully tailored. He knew that he longed for a son most desperately. And the devil of it was—Margot did not."

Fate decreed that Franky and Margot should witness the trial ascent with a French pilot of a British monoplane (the Bird of War), fitted with an invention which the French experts were there to test with a view to purchase. The inventor was on the ground, for, as a French officer politely explained, " despite the Entente Cordiale, it would hardly be *convenable* or discreet to permit even an Englishman to fly over Paris or any other fortified City of France."

Franky, as he watched the Bird of War through his pocket field glass, was sensible of a thrill behind his immaculate waistcoat.

" If the English inventor had not solved the baffling Problem of Stability, he had come uncommonly near it, by the Great Brass Hat. And the dud heads at Whitehall had shown the door to him and his invention. 'Good Christmas ! how like 'em !' reflected Franky, lowering the glasses to chuckle and looking round for Margot."

We first make the acquaintance of Count von Herrnung, who is to play a prominent part in the story, at a dinner at the Hôtel Spitz in the Place Vendôme, where he had the insolence to propose that the guests—some of whom had been " rotting " him—should drink a toast " to show there is no ill will. . . . It would be amusing if you would all join me in drinking to The Day."

" Lord Norwater (Franky), lobster red and rather flurried, turned to von Herrnung, and said not loudly, yet clearly enough to be heard by every guest at the table—

" 'Stop ! Sorry to swipe in, Count, but you'd better not order that wine, I think !'

" 'You think not ? ' asked von Herrnung with coolest insolence.

" 'I—don't think so ? I'm dead sure !' said Franky, getting redder. ' We Britons laugh at brag and bluffing ; and the gassy patriotism shown by some foreigners we're apt to call bad form. We abuse our Institutions and rag our Governments ; we've done that since the year One—far as I can make out. And when other people do it we generally sit tight and smile. We've no use for heroics. But when the pinch comes—it ain't so much that we're loyal, we're Loyalty ; we're IT !— We're ready to make allowances—too rottenly ready sometimes. But I read off the iddy-umpties to Full Stop, a minute back. Count von Herrnung, when you ask English ladies and Englishmen—two of 'em in the Service—to drink that toast with you, you must know you're putting your foot in your hat ! ' "

That night the Assassinations at Sarajevo were announced in the papers. Berlin had had the story with its breakfast rolls and hot creamed coffee.

So the basis of the story ; and the principal *dramatis personæ*—Lord Norwater and Kittums, Sherbrand (the aviator who proves to be Franky's cousin), Dr. Saxham and his wife and boy, Count von Herrnung, Patrine Saxham (whose willing weakness was the cause of so much sorrow to herself and others) play for us the drama which keeps us absorbed to the last page.

According to the mental outlook of the reader, so will the verdict be. Some will disapprove, some will regard the book as a tract more powerful than many sermons. None can be indifferent, for the pen of Richard Dehan, which made " The Dop Doctor " one of the outstanding books of our time, has limned for us a living and glowing picture of current events, and of Society in the days preceding the war, which will be read by the children of those who fought the great fight, when Blue Books are buried in official departments, and lie unread on the shelves of the British Museum. So much greater the pity that the manner in which the Woman's Suffrage Movement is presented cannot be regarded as representing facts, rather they are so distorted as to be grotesque. P. G. Y.

WHAT TO READ.

We recommend to the attention of our readers Dr. Müehlon's Diary, published by Cassell & Co., Ltd. (5s. net), as a book to be read. Dr. Müehlon at the outbreak of the war was a director of Krupp's works at Essen. He severed his connection with the firm, left Germany, and settled in Switzerland. The Diary is of poignant interest.

They should also endeavour to procure a copy of a pamphlet entitled " Reality : the World's Searchlight on Germany," No. 135. It is printed by G. Binney Dibblee, and is obtainable in England and Wales through any branch of W. H. Smith & Son, and in Scotland through any branch of John Menzies & Co., Ltd.

"RED-ROBED FRANCE."

The Huns stripped off my own green gown
And left me stark and bare ;
My sons, they spread a red robe down
And wrapped me in it there.

The garb they brought was red as blood—
The robe was red as flame ;
They veiled me in it where I stood
And took away my shame.

Was ever web so costly wove,
Or warp so glorious spun ?
I'll wear no vestments prized above
That wide and scarlet one.

Though younger sons some happier day,
Weave me a fair green gown
Anew, or bid me don array
Of corn-ripe gold and brown,

The names (like beads, told one by one)
My heart will still repeat ;
Will call, with tears, each dear, dear son
Whose red robe wrapped my feet.

By Charles Buxton Going, in
"Everybody's Magazine."

LETTERS TO THE EDITOR.

Whilst cordially inviting communications upon all subjects for these columns, we wish it to be distinctly understood that we do not IN ANY WAY hold ourselves responsible for the opinions expressed by our correspondents.

NURSERY SCHOOL.

To the Editor of THE BRITISH JOURNAL OF NURSING.

DEAR MADAM,—I entirely agree with Miss Theresa McGrath as to the importance of nurses interesting themselves in the development of public health work, for it appears to me that such work is of more far-reaching importance than that of any other department of nursing. To help in maintaining a high standard of health is even more worth while than helping to cure disease. In the latter case we are trying to mend what is damaged : in the former, to maintain what is perfect in a state of perfection. The repair of a damaged article may be carried out so skilfully that few people can detect the flaw, but it is there all the same, and detracts from the value of the article in the eye of the expert.

In the same way, once health has been impaired it is never quite the same again; it may be most skilfully restored, but the flaw is there. For this reason it seems to me most desirable that trained nurses should have charge of the infants under five in nursery schools. These years are supremely important ones in the life and development of the child, and the daily supervision of these infants by a skilled nurse would have a far-reaching influence on their health in after life. What more worth while to a nurse, who sees things at their true value, than to fight, in the interest, not alone of the individual child, but of posterity, against the onset of a disease such as rickets, or the development of tuberculosis? Or, again, to build up the health of the child with a bad family history, so as to enable it to offer an effective resistance to the inroads of disease.

In work of this kind there is no picturesque background, no spectacular triumph, but nothing could be more solidly fruitful in good result. But if the importance of the trained nurse as a factor in preserving the health of young children is recognized, then the most skilled workers should be secured, and they should be paid salaries commensurate with their skilled services. It is unfortunately a lesson which, as a nation, we are very slow to learn, where women are concerned.

Yours faithfully,
PUBLIC HEALTH.

OUR PRIZE COMPETITION.
QUESTIONS.

September 7th.—What are the principal functions of a School Nurse? How may she assist in raising the standard of national health?

September 14th.— What do you know of Exophthalmic Goitre, its symptoms and nursing care?

The Midwife.

THE CENTRAL MIDWIVES BOARD.

At the Examination held by the Central Midwives Board (England) on August 1st, in London and the provinces, 494 candidates were examined and 400 passed the examination. The percentage of failures was 19.

HOSPITAL TREATMENT FOR INFANTS AND YOUNG CHILDREN.

The Mansion House Council on Health and Housing, of which the Lord Mayor is president, has recently instituted an inquiry as to the adequacy of hospital accommodation and treatment for infants and young children in London.

The general conclusion is that there is an insufficiency in most districts for the institutional treatment of infants and young children. Except in a few instances that deficiency cannot be made good by existing hospitals, save at the expense of the older children. In some cases additional accommodation could be provided in new buildings if funds were forthcoming.

To meet the need it has been suggested to the committee that wards should be set aside for infants and young children in existing hospitals, or small local wards set up for minor ailments; that each infant welfare centre should have attached to it a residential home or observation ward for delicate babies; that open-air schools should be provided for the prevention and cure of consumption; that minor operation cases ought not to be discharged so quickly as now; that delay in performing operations should be prevented and long waiting at the hospital curtailed; and that facilities should be available for daily attendance for simple treatment on the lines of school clinics.

In regard to Poor Law Infirmary facilities the Council consider the results unsatisfactory in the case of delicate babies. They think the Local Government Board and Boards of Guardians might consider whether the arrangements could not be improved.

OPHTHALMIA NEONATORUM.

By a new order of the Scottish Local Government Board cases of ophthalmia neonatorum become compulsorily notified in Scotland from November 1st, next. The Board advises local authorities to take counsel with their Medical Officer of Health so as to ensure skilled attendance for every case so notified.

VENEREAL DISEASES.

Much attention is just now being directed to the question of venereal diseases, owing to convictions under Clause 40D of the Defence of the Realm Act, and it is well that nurses and midwives should be well informed as to their chief symptoms. These were well described recently by Mr. Leonard Myer, F.R.C.S., in his course of lectures at St. Paul's Hospital, Red Lion Square.

Gonorrhœa, he said, ran a rapid and acute course, the incubation being three days, and it was a local disease.

Syphilis, on the other hand, was always chronic, its incubation was three weeks. The secondary stage began when the glands unconnected with the sexual organs became enlarged, e.g., those in the bend of the elbow.

In regard to the early complications in both sexes, syphilis had very few complications, though its existence predisposed the patient to other diseases, i.e., phthisis, malaria, diabetes and Bright's disease, the existence of the last-named also precluded the patient from treatment by mercury.

In gonorrhœa there were a whole host of complications, some affecting the male or the female only, and some common to both sexes.

Some of those common to both sexes were cystitis, ophthalmia, joint affection, meningitis peritonitis, flat-foot and blood poisoning.

In the male, orchitis, acute stricture, prostatic abscess.

In the female Bartolin's gland became enlarged and inflamed.

USE OF ABORTIFACIENTS.

The Local Government Board, in their Circular on Maternity and Child Welfare, addressed to County Councils and Sanitary Authorities, state that a report was published by the Privy Council Office in 1910 on the practice of medicine and surgery by unqualified persons. For the purpose of that Report the Board obtained some particulars from Medical Officers of Health, which showed that the sale of drugs intended to procure abortion and practice by abortion-mongers was prevalent in many parts of the country. From information obtained by Medical Inspectors of the Board in connection with their inquiries into Maternity and Child Welfare work and from other material, the Board have reason to fear that these practices continue. One of the drugs most commonly employed for this purpose is diachylon, and on April 27th, 1917, an Order in Council was made adding to the list of poisons for the purpose of Part I of the Schedule of Poisons "lead in combination with oleic acid, or other highly fatted acids, whether sold as diachylon or under any other designation (except machine spread plasters)." The Board would urge every Local Authority to bring this order to the notice of the druggists and of the practising midwives in their area, to explain to their Health Visitors and to the midwives the risks to life and health involved in the use of diachylon, and in every other way to do what they can to stop the traffic in abortifacients and the practice of abortion-mongers in their districts.

THE
BRITISH JOURNAL OF NURSING
WITH WHICH IS INCORPORATED
THE NURSING RECORD
EDITED BY MRS BEDFORD FENWICK

No. 1,588.　　　　　SATURDAY, SEPTEMBER 7, 1918.　　　　　Vol. LXI.

EDITORIAL.

A MONUMENT OF GRATITUDE.

We print in our correspondence columns a letter from the Right Hon. John Hodge, M.P., Minister of Pensions and Chairman of the Trustees for the King's Fund for the Disabled, which must go straight home to every one in these Realms, who lives securely, because others have barred the way to invasion by fire and sword with their flesh and blood, and have in consequence been disabled.

Surely the first instinct of gratitude is to see that the men who have thus suffered on our behalf shall have all the assistance possible to start business in civil life once again. So urgent is the need for this that the Minister of Pensions began last year to receive contributions to a Voluntary Fund which he administered himself, the primary object of which was to help discharged disabled men to start business in a small way—and roughly 2,000 men and a number of women have been so helped. It is however desirable to give more in certain specified cases than the £25 hitherto regarded as a maximum.

The £115,000, which Mr. Hodge collected without any special appeal, included £50,000 from Sir John Leigh. The Willis James' bequest for widows and dependants brought £15,000, the Chapman Fund £10,000 for men who had trained under the schemes of the Ministry, and donations from Mr. Bosanquet and others made up the balance. Alongside these separate Funds the donations were received by the Minister, until the whole of the Funds amounted to about £115,000 (a large part of this money has, of course, already been spent).

The King then took an active interest in the matter, and decided to hand over £53,000 (the City of London Silver Wedding Gift) and £25,000 from his own purse. The Duke of Connaught made this announcement at the Mansion House Meeting on the 31st July. It was decided that the Voluntary Funds, hitherto under the control of the Minister, should be known in future as The King's Fund for Disabled Officers and Men, to be administered by a Committee of Trustees appointed by the King, and with the patronage of His Majesty, through the Ministry of Pensions and its local War Pensions Committees.

The immediate object is to raise £3,000,000 to continue the work hitherto done by the Minister's Voluntary Funds, but on a more generous and wider scale. The existing funds are all but exhausted.

The weekly number of applications for grants is rapidly growing, and has already risen to close upon 600. Applications for grants must be made to the Local War Pensions Committees which are in every district throughout the country. (Officers apply direct to the Ministry.) The Local Committee sends a recommendation if the case is a suitable one, and the Trustees deal with it. A large staff at the Ministry is engaged on the work, and the applications are expeditiously dealt with without "officialism" or "red tape." Elasticity is the great feature of the Voluntary Scheme.

The need for the Fund is urgent, and already the most beneficent results have been obtained in resettling men. If the taxpayers' money were to be used there would require to be rigid regulations of universal application bound by hard and fast rules which would destroy the whole idea of this scheme.

We hope that every possible support will be given to this Fund, to help our disabled men to help themselves—a Fund which is not intended to be a substitute for a State Pension, but to supplement it.

OUR PRIZE COMPETITION.

WHAT ARE THE PRINCIPAL FUNCTIONS OF A SCHOOL NURSE? HOW MAY SHE ASSIST IN RAISING THE STANDARD OF NATIONAL HEALTH?

We have pleasure in awarding the prize this week to Miss Catharine Wright, Dryden Road, Bush Hill Park, Enfield.

PRIZE PAPER.

The principal functions of a school nurse cover a wide field of activities, all of which have for their object the raising of a higher standard of health among the school children, and in following up this ideal many other branches in connection with this school work have opened up, so that the school nurse of to-day has the opportunity of using her trained knowledge and experience, proving an invaluable help towards maintaining a national standard of health and fitness amongst the school children, many of whom live under the most adverse conditions of poverty, neglect, and ignorance.

It is in the elementary schools of the London County Council, principally, that her work begins, and usually the routine visit to the school is notified to the heads of the school previously, so that absentees may be present for the nurse's visit. Once in each term every child is examined for cleanliness, the hair and skin are inspected, and all conditions recorded. Verminous children are excluded : visits paid to the home, and the parents instructed as to the best method of cleansing. If this cannot be accomplished, the cleansing process may be compulsory under the Children's Act.

Any infectivity of skin is noticed, and the children referred to the school doctor, who will diagnose, and curative treatment then follows at a clinic or treatment centre.

Any eye disease, likely to be infectious, is also referred to the school doctor, and the same procedure followed, and aural disease is carefully supervised under curative treatment. This entails many visits to the homes of the children, and the school nurse is brought into touch with the family, and is almost invariably taken into confidence, and her sympathy and helpful advice readily accepted.

The medical inspections are of great importance. For these, the selected age-groups of children are prepared by weighing, measuring, and vision testing, an accurate record kept, which later on becomes useful for statistical purposes. The parents are urged to be present, and here again the school nurse is in touch with them, and has often to follow up the cases for curative treatment, getting vouchers for clinic and centre or hospital treatment, watching over the cases until they return to school.

In various districts, school clinics and treatment centres are in active progress, a very large number of defects being treated with the best result, supervised by the school doctors.

Dental centres are at work, the school nurse taking duty and helping the doctor and dentist in the recovery room. The X-ray department of a treatment centre utilizes the school nurse, she preparing the heads and keeping the children in suitable positions during the X-ray exposure. On certain days there are operations for tonsils and adenoids, the school nurses taking duty as in an ordinary operating theatre.

Mentally and physically defective children have their own school nurses, who well understand the supervision and care these children need.

The teachers of each school realise how beneficial the work of the school nurse has become, and the heads of the school nurses' department, realizing the many problems and difficulties that arise in this kind of work, are ever ready to receive and give suggestions bearing on these difficulties.

The work is intensely interesting, and may be more so, if, under the new Education Act, the services of the school nurses are as appreciated and used to the fullest extent, for the younger children will specially need trained knowledge, and the older children guided and taught a hygienic value of themselves.

With this wider knowledge the standard of national health will be on a good basis, which *must* result in future fitness and capacity for the girls and boys who are to be the parents of the future generation.

HONOURABLE MENTION.

The following competitors receive honourable mention :—Miss B. Courtenay, Miss M. James, Miss P. Thomson.

QUESTION FOR NEXT WEEK.

What do you know of ex-ophthalmic goitre, its symptoms, and nursing care?

We desire to draw the attention of nurses to the Form of Petition to the Prime Minister which appears inside the front cover. Although the principle of representation of the organized Nurses' Societies has been inserted in the 7th draft of the College of Nursing Bill, " there is many a slip between the cup and the lip," and the more representative the Petition the more influence it will have when our Bill is before Parliament.

NURSING AND THE WAR.

The many friends of Miss Violetta Thurstan will be glad to learn of her safe return to this country after her war service in Serbia. We learn it is probable that after a rest she will take up interesting work at home.

The Hon. Mrs. Waldorf Astor appeals for the loan or gift of river canoes for the use of the Nursing Sisters and staff of the 15th Canadian General Hospital, Cliveden, Taplow, Bucks.

Nurses of the American Army have now been given a definite status. They are not, however, to be commissioned, but to be warranted, as are sergeants and non-commissioned officers.

A Washington message says that orders have been issued by the United States War Department to the office of the Surgeon-General, which will enable coloured nurses who have been registered by the American Red Cross Society to render service to their own race in the Army. The nurses will be assigned to the hospitals at half-a-dozen camps, in which a total of about 38,000 coloured troops are stationed. General Pershing has been asked whether the services of coloured nurses can be utilised to advantage among the American Expeditionary Forces.

The *Nursing Journal of India* says: "Many names can be added to our list of heroine nurses by the splendid courage of those women who remained at the post of duty during the terrible

THE GARDEN AT COLEBROOK LODGE, PUTNEY HEATH, THE AMERICAN RED CROSS NURSES' REST HOUSE.

The Army regulations fixing the rank of officers in the Army has been amended by the insertion of the new grade of "nurse" below the grade of cadet, and above that of sergeant-major. The nurses are thus placed in authority over all men in the enlisted branch. Many of the nurses feel they should have commissioned rank, like their Canadian colleagues, thus giving them authority over all patients in military hospitals.

Our illustration, from an American Red Cross official photograph, gives a charming impression of the delights of Colebrook Lodge, West Hill, Putney Heath, the American Red Cross Rest House, for its convalescent nurses. It must surely be a joy to convalesce in surroundings so healthful and beautiful.

air raid which took place when the Germans bombed one of our military hospitals in France. The scene of the disaster was a big hospital camp composed of many huts and known to the enemy as being such, not only by its conspicuous marking with the Red Cross, but they had often seen it. The night was one flood of brilliant moonlight, when squadron after squadron flew over and dropped large bombs on the huts, which were nearly full of badly wounded men, who were mostly helpless to assist themselves and to whom movement was agony; some of the raiders flew very low and raked the huts and staff quarters with machine guns. There were several hundreds of casualties amongst the patients, orderlies and nurses. We read with pride and profound emotion the description of the behaviour of the nurses under the terrible ordeal."

GALLANT SERVICE IN MESOPOTAMIA.

GENERAL MARSHALL'S LIST OF MENTIONS.

WAR OFFICE, August 27th.

The Secretary of State for War has received the following dispatch addressed to the Chief of the General Staff, India, by Lieut.-General W. R. Marshall, K.C.B., K.C.S.I., Commanding-in-Chief, Mesopotamia Expeditionary Force :—

General Headquarters,
Mesopotamian Expeditionary Force,
April 15th, 1918.

SIR,—With reference to the concluding paragraph of my dispatch dated April 15th, 1918, I have the honour to submit herewith a list of names of those officers, ladies, non-commissioned officers, and men serving, or who have served, under my command, whose distinguished and gallant services and devotion to duty I consider deserving of special mention.

I have the honour to be, Sir,
Your obedient Servant,
W. R. MARSHALL,
Lieut.-General.
Commanding-in-Chief, Mesopotamian
Expeditionary Force.

QUEEN ALEXANDRA'S IMPERIAL MILITARY NURSING SERVICE.

WALKER, Miss M., Matron, R.R.C.

QUEEN ALEXANDRA'S IMPERIAL MILITARY NURSING SERVICE RESERVE.

ARGO, Miss M. B., Staff Nurse; BOTTOMLEY, Miss C. M., Sister; DAVIES, Miss A. M., Staff Nurse; DAVIES, Miss E., Staff Nurse; DE KOCK, Miss D., Sister; HARGRAVES, Miss D. O., Staff Nurse; HARTRICK, Miss A. L., Sister; LULHAM, Miss E. V. J., Staff Nurse; MARK, Miss M., Staff Nurse; McGAUGHEY, Miss M. A., Sister; McNAB, Miss M. M., Sister; MILLAR, Miss L., Staff Nurse; RAE, Miss M., Sister and A./Matron; REID, Miss A. E., Staff Nurse; ROBERTSON, Miss M. A. A., Sister; STUART, Miss A. L., Sister; WADSWORTH, Miss S. E., Sister; WELLINGTON, Miss A., Staff Nurse; WILKINSON, Miss E. S., Sister.

TERRITORIAL FORCE NURSING SERVICE.

COULSON, Miss M. G., Sister; CROSBIE, Miss M. F. D., Sister; CURTIES, Miss N., Sister; EARLE, Miss A. L., Matron; EMUSS, Miss E. A., Sister; HUNSTONE, Miss M., Sister; KING, Miss E. S., Staff Nurse; MANN, Miss T. J., Sister; POTTER, Miss M. M., Sister; SEACOME, Miss B. E., Sister; WHEELER, Miss M. K., Sister.

QUEEN ALEXANDRA'S MILITARY NURSING SERVICE, INDIA.

GILMORE, Miss M. G., Matron; MACLEAN, Miss M. E., Nursing Sister; MARSHALL, Miss E. O., Nursing Sister; WILSON, Miss J. S. R., R.R.C., Senior Nursing Sister.

TEMPORARY NURSING SERVICE, INDIA.

BURKE-ROCHE, Miss G., T./Matron; GASKIN, Miss J., T./Matron; MAY, Miss T., T./Nursing Sister; MINCHIN, Miss L. L. M., T./Nursing Sister.

VOLUNTARY AID DETACHMENT.

MARTIN, Miss C. A.

The Scottish Women's Hospitals have received from Major Endicott, American Red Cross Commissioner in this country, the first instalment of a most generous grant of 160,000 dollars.

FRENCH FLAG NURSING CORPS.

Miss Haswell, Matron in France, has taken part in the Allied Women War Workers' Congress in Paris, which we hear was most interesting, and a very valuable exchange of opinion of those deeply interested in women's part in organisation and the relief of suffering.

Noteworthy were the words of M. Pichon, Minister of Foreign Affairs, who represented M. Clemenceau at the great meeting at the Theatre Champs Elysées and who asserted that women's work is inseparable from the essential work of the war. He paid tribute to English women spending their lives in succouring those in the invaded districts, and the American women, who, he said, possessed in a supreme degree the idealism which is the gift of their race; and mentioned, as having earned for ever the admiration and gratitude of the nations—the Queen of the Belgians, Sister Julie, and Edith Cavell. "It is," he said to the members of the Congress, "a regular revolution which you have accomplished in placing yourselves by the side of the defenders of our soil and our right, and, indeed, everywhere where our deliverance and the constitution of a new society are being worked out. In the new society woman will no longer be what she was yesterday. She will no longer be content to leave to man affairs which concern her as much as him. She has acquired in the struggle a new rôle, and she will have had such a part in the liberation of the world that the world will not be able to keep her separated from the defence of great social causes. She will have penetrated further into the general organisation of society, which will have been saved partly by the action which she has exercised."

We hear of a Med. Chef remarking to an English lady who has worked with him for over a year :— "I like your British Nurses; they work all day, running about like mice; they don't talk, and they have been here a whole fortnight and I have not been called upon to adjust any quarrel!"

This same Med. Chef hopes that he will be able to have F.F.N.C. Sisters to work with him for the future.

Sister Dora Simpson has been awarded the Medaille des Epidemies, which she well deserves, after her excellent services in nursing contagious diseases in the war zone.

Members of the French Flag Nursing Corps will learn with pleasure that although General Vicomte de la Panouse is relinquishing his post as Military Attaché to the French Embassy in London, the Vicomtesse de la Panouse will continue her beneficent work as President of the Comité Britannique of the Croix Rouge Française.

An interesting report of Queen Mary's Hostels for Nurses, of which there are now three, has been published.

CARE OF THE WOUNDED.

THE INFLUENCE OF COLOUR.

As some people have greater perception of harmony and are more deeply moved by " concord of sweet sounds " than others, so some are more susceptible to the influence of colour and more consciously take pleasure in its effects. Yet subconsciously there are probably few people who are not influenced by it, and more especially the sick, who lie day after day in the same surroundings, which may depress them and retard their recovery, or inspire them to persevere on the road to recovery, and to regain the mental poise and concentration which for a time they have lost.

Nurses who have worked in a hospital where the walls are a drab colour, with perhaps a dado of brown paint chosen for its enduring quality, and who have escaped in their off duty time to the National Gallery, or one of the other great picture galleries, as a relief from their monotony, will realize their effect upon the mind, and the importance of the work for the sick and wounded of Mr. P. H. Kemp Prossor, who, having studied " colour-medicine " and the influence of colour on children and adults, is so convinced a believer in its benefits that he has closed down half his house, given up his motor car, and is devoting himself to arranging and supervising colour wards in military hospitals. Mr. Prossor's faith extends beyond the æsthetic effect of colour to its therapeutic influence.

We have already described the " Colour Ward " in the McCaul Hospital for Officers, and it was recently the good fortune of the writer to visit Section IV of the Maudsley Neurological Clearing Hospital at Denmark Hill, where shell-shock and kindred cases are received.

Imagine the change of being transported from the tortured battle-grounds of Europe, desolate, and reeking with the carnage of war, to these wards where " all the air is thrilling with the Spring," for that is the message of Mr. Kemp Prossor's colour wards, and the colours are nicely adjusted to the individual needs. The ceilings are in every case a soft firmament blue, and there are wards with apple-blossom pink walls— so many people need pink, says Mr. Prossor— with anemone mauve curtains, introducing the note of concentration and maybe Spring-green quilts, the bedsteads being painted the same colour, even the regulation army lockers are coloured to harmonize ; and the picture-frames are the same tone as the walls ; white sheets are not yet abolished, but that may come. Incidentally Mr. Prosser believes that much of the bad eyesight of to-day is due to the fact that so many people are constantly looking at white. No browns or mauves or reds are permitted ; " the men have seen far too much of those colours," says Mr. Kemp Prossor. Just at that moment the discordant note of red is introduced in the regulation red-bordered cape of the Territorial Sister, which sets one wondering why the War Office does not invite him to design a uniform for Sisters whose work lies amongst the mentally sick, which shall suggest peace and not war.

Why not ?

In a corridor on the officers' floor one gets a charming effect of sunlight and brightness. But the corridor really is dark, and it has been obtained by the sunlight yellow curtains to the window at the end, and will be further accentuated when the walls have been coloured a primrose yellow.

It should be known that Mr. Kemp Prossor is prepared to supervise a colour ward in any hospital, and under no circumstances will a fee be charged. All success to him in his important contribution to the work for the healing of the sick. He tells of a sleepless patient who fell asleep at once in a colour ward, and a letter received from a sergeant was eloquent in appreciation of the benefit he had received. The colours are all washable. Lastly, it is essential that they should be blended " with brains."

Lest it should be thought there is anything new under the sun, it may be mentioned that Aristotle was acquainted with the therapeutic influence of colour.

A BLACKGUARD NATION.

The German Army (says the *British Medical Journal*), which we are often told is one with the German people, is filling up the cup of its iniquities. When the Germans bombed hospitals the excuse was made for them that the buildings were not properly marked with the Red Cross, though the apologists forgot to add that the Germans used the Red Cross to protect their corps headquarters. A month or two ago an order was found to have been issued directing troops in the advanced line to shoot down stretcher parties collecting the wounded, not so much with the object of killing them, but, as was explained, to ensure that the wounded were left out so long that they would be beyond the reach of the surgeon's art. In this way it was sought to diminish allied effectives. The Ministry of Information has now sent through its wireless service particulars of certain gross outrages committed by the Germans upon British prisoners and wounded in March last. The stories have no doubt been seen by all readers, and it is only necessary to say that the sworn statements of soldiers belonging to a Scottish regiment are to the effect that, under the orders of a German officer, a a soldier who accompanied him turned a stream of liquid fire down the trench in which prisoners and wounded (16 men, of whom 10 were wounded) had been lined up. Some of the unwounded escaped, but all the wounded must have been either suffocated or burnt. The British Government has caused to be conveyed to the German Government a protest against the offences described, but, as they appear to be part of a deliberate policy, it is hardly to be expected to have any effect. The *Cologne Gazette* recently said that the Germans are a blackguard nation, and the epithet seems well chosen.

Royal British Nurses' Association.

(Incorporated by Royal Charter.)

THIS SUPPLEMENT BEING THE OFFICIAL ORGAN OF THE CORPORATION.

COMPOUND FRACTURES OF THE HUMERUS.

By Miss M. C. Sinzininex, A.R.R.C.

Diploma of the Royal British Nurses' Association ; Matron of Queen Alexandra's Hospital for Officers.

PART II.—DRESSINGS AND DRAINAGE.

In cases of compound fractures the wounds are usually kept open by means of drainage tubes. In war fractures the break is not an ordinary one, but in most cases the bone is badly shattered, and for months, possibly a year, pieces of bone that will not unite die and consequently come away or have to be removed, so there will, for a long time, be a septic wound, as where there is dead bone there is always sepsis. Experience has shown that if a wound be allowed to close too quickly it invariably has to be re-opened to admit of the removal of dead bone.

The Carrell-Dakin method of drainage and irrigation (not the solution) was used at Highgate long before it penetrated to the hospitals in France. At first normal saline was run through the wounds by means of a piece of bandage drawn through the arm and out at the counter opening, the solution draining into a pail below. Later on small bore tubes, tied at their lower ends, were inserted into the wounds, and an antiseptic solution, which was syphoned from an overhanging flask, was run into the wounds at intervals of about two hours, the flow being regulated by a screw tap on the connecting tube.

(It is important in inserting the tubes to see that all the small perforations are enclosed in the wound, or else, when the tap is turned on, the fluid will escape before it reaches the depth of the sinus.)

The Carrell-Dakin fluid was not used for several reasons. It requires very expert preparation, does not keep good for many days, and has an injurious effect on the skin around the wound, necessitating a protective form of dressing on the surrounding parts before the solution can be used. After trying various antiseptic solutions, Mr. H. J. Paterson, the Honorary Surgeon in Charge at Highgate, decided on using a preparation of sodium mono borate. This can be easily pre-

pared from the crystals, and will keep almost any length of time, so that a large quantity can be made at once. Ninety grammes of the crystals are dissolved in 3,000 c.c. of warm sterile water, the water being only sufficiently warm to melt the crystals. A little of any colouring matter added distinguishes the solution from saline or any other fluids in stock. Sodium mono borate is not nearly so expensive as the Carrell-Dakin solution, also it does not injure the skin unless used continuously for months, when, in some cases, the patient has developed a kind of wound eczema. A change of dressing and an application of Calamine lotion soon relieve matters. Sodium mono borate encourages a goodly flow of lymph to the wound and so "washes it out," carrying with it the pus. So quick and effectual is its action that sometimes within twenty-four hours of its application thick lymph will be seen mingling with the pus which is draining from the wound.

A solution of aluminium acetate was also tried, and is still used for the dressing of superficial wounds. It cleans up a large septic area in a marvellously short time, but it is not so good for irrigation purposes, as it seems to form a kind of crust in the wound which blocks up the smaller perforations of the tubes. The sodium monoborate and the aluminium acetate are both used mixed with the thick medicinal paraffin, and make an excellent dressing for wounds that do not need drainage, or are past the irrigation stage. This preparation has one very valuable asset—it prevents the gauze and wool from sticking to the wound, and so greatly lessens the pain and discomfort of a dressing.

In these days, interest is centred on anti-sepsis, so that asepsis, the most important factor of all in surgical cases, is a little apt to be pushed into the background. It should be borne in mind that the solutions used have quite enough work to do to kill the germs which are already in the wound, and it is the nurse's business to see that none are unnecessarily added. One is a little apt to think of war wounds as "dirty cases" and not to take the care one should with them. A nurse should always remember that she is dealing with open tissue, and her surgical cleanliness should be as punctilious as if she were dressing a clean abdominal case.

Another important point which should be remembered, especially with irrigation cases, is that germs travel up a moist track, and if, through a little over irrigation, the dressing becomes wet to the outside and has to be packed, the packing should be done with sterile pads and surgically clean hands. All the foregoing may be small points in themselves, but they are links in the chain that draws the patient to recovery.

In one's pre-war hospital days, simple fractures were the rule, compound ones the exception. Now the position is reversed, and not only are the majority of the fractures with which one meets compound, but comminuted as well.

APPOINTMENT.

Miss Florence Carver has been appointed Matron at the Military Hospital, Palavas, France, and writes that she finds the work there most interesting, and tells of the splendid surgery accomplished in this French Hospital, in which there are a hundred and fifty beds. Miss Carver was trained at St. George's Hospital and became a member of the Association in 1905.

MARRIAGE.

On Saturday, August 24th, Miss Emily Young was married quietly to Mr. Ernest Henry Collins, of 35, Bloomsbury Square. For a year, Miss Young has been working for the Association at a

HEADQUARTERS OF THE SOUTH AUSTRALIAN BRANCH OF THE R.B.N.A.

The treatment of compound fractures of the humerus and their attendant wounds is an especially interesting study. The arm is of such inestimable value to the patient that there is the greatest possible satisfaction in saving a badly smashed upper limb. Although the amputation of a leg may be a greater shock to the patient at the time than is the removal of an arm, the comparative loss in after life between the two limbs is enormous. A man with two arms and one leg will have a very much better prospect of a useful life than a man with one arm and two legs, even if fitted with the wonderfully efficient artificial limbs that are now in use. Therefore any extra trouble and patience expended in saving an arm is always repaid.

military hospital in Yorkshire, and has also done a considerable amount of private work for it. She became a member in 1915.

OBITUARY.

It is with regret that we have to report the death of Miss Mary Seamark.

Miss Seamark died in the Bush Township of Murat Bay, South Australia, in April last. She was trained at St. Thomas' Hospital, and, after holding several appointments in England, she went out to South Australia, where she did work for the Australian Branch of the Royal British Nurses' Association.

(Signed) ISABEL MACDONALD.

Secretary.

APPOINTMENTS.

MATRON.

St. John's Hospital Charity, Winchester. — Miss Annie Manning has been appointed Matron. She was trained at the Hackney Union Infirmary, London, and has been Superintendent Nurse at Oulton Infirmary, near Lowestoft, and at the Union Infirmary, Basingstoke, Hants.

OUT-PATIENT SISTER.

Great Northern Central Hospital, Holloway Road, N. — Miss Amy Martin has been appointed Outpatient Sister. She was trained at the Royal Free Hospital, and has been Sister at the Royal Albert Hospital, Devonport ; and at the National Hospital, Queen's Square, W.C.

QUEEN ALEXANDRA'S IMPERIAL MILITARY NURSING SERVICE.

Sister Mrs. E. Grazebrook resigns her appointment (August 26th).

THE NATION'S TRIBUTE TO IRISH NURSES.

The Fund for the Tribute to Irish Nurses is progressing slowly, not more than half the amount required being so far subscribed. The Fund, which will be administered by an Irish Committee, is intended to benefit civilian as well as war nurses.

LEGAL MATTERS.

The trial of Eva Grace Thompson, who claims to be a trained nurse, on a charge of wilful murder will take place at the Old Bailey, and may come on for hearing next week.

A serious charge was preferred against a woman named Tomkinson at the West Ham Police Court on Monday, namely of attempting to procure abortion in six cases. She is not a certified midwife, but was at one time assistant to a chemist.

LECTURES TO MASSAGE STUDENTS.

Masseuses, and nurses who are studying for their massage certificates will be glad to know that a series of classes in Anatomy for Massage Students, beginning on Monday, October 7th, have been arranged at the London (Royal Free Hospital) School of Medicine for Women, 6, Hunter Street) Brunswick Square, W.C. 1. Demonstrations on the cadaver will be given on Mondays, Tuesdays, Thursdays and Fridays at 5.30 throughout the Autumn term, under the direction of Dr. Mary Lucas-Keene, and Dr. Joyce Partridge. Further particulars may be obtained from Miss L. M. Brooks, Warden and Secretary.

RESIGNATION.

Many nurses and midwives who appreciate the excellence of the training they have received at the Rotunda Hospital, Dublin, under the able superintendence of Miss L. Ramsden, will learn with regret of her resignation of this important position, after over 20 years' service in the institution, for a short time as Assistant to Miss Hampson and then as Lady Superintendent.

NURSING ECHOES.

At the recent Annual Meeting of Princess Christian's District Nursing and Maternity Home at Windsor a letter received from the Town Clerk of Windsor proved how much the work of the Home is appreciated in the town.

The letter stated that it has been decided to give a donation of £10 10s. per annum to the funds of H.R.H. Princess Christian's Maternity Home as a recognition of the excellent work which the nurses of the Home are doing, and the great use that their services are to the poor of Windsor.

We continue to receive enquiries as to the prospects for those who undergo a course of training with the view of taking up laboratory work as described by Dr. Kynvett Gordon in this JOURNAL, and we are informed that Dr. Gordon has also been "inundated" with enquiries. After a course of training extending over three months, the prospects for a candidate who successfully passes the subsequent examination are good, as she would probably easily obtain the post of junior assistant at a commencing salary of £2 2s. a week.

The National Union of Women Workers of Great Britain and Ireland has issued a pamphlet on the National Health Insurance Act of 1918, which sets forth clearly and concisely the most important of the changes effected by the Act. Nurses who are insured under the Act would do well to obtain and study this leaflet. It is obtainable from Miss Norah E. Green, Secretary National Union of Women Workers, Parliament Mansions, Victoria Street, London, S.W. 1, price ½d. per copy, or 1d. post free, or 4s. 6d. per 100, post free.

The question as to whether hospital nurses who have latch keys are entitled to the Parliamentary Franchise is one upon which a decisive decision should be obtained, and we advise all nurses who are provided with latch keys to make a point of inquiring from the proper authorities whether or not they are entitled to a vote. We learn that the private nurses on the staff of St. John's House, Queen Square, Bloomsbury, each have the use of a latch key when in residence between their cases. What is the position in this case?

At Omagh Revision Sessions the claim of Miss L. H. Hayes, Matron of the Tyrone County Hospital, for a vote out of apartments in that institution was admitted, whilst the claims of Sisters Clarke and Brown, one of whom belonged to each side, were also ruled on without prejudice, but the claims of a dozen of the regular nursing staff were disallowed.

A contemporary says :—" If the service franchise does not apply to nurses, it is difficult to see to whom it would apply, and it is to be hoped that nurses in hospitals and institutions, if refused their vote by the local authority, will appeal to the county court."

It is stated that Lady Rhondda has definitely decided to claim a seat in the House of Lords as a peeress in her own right.

SUMMER SCHOOL OF CIVICS AND EUGENICS, 1918.

The above school, held in Oxford during the last fortnight in August, proved of the greatest interest to those few members of the nursing and midwifery professions able to attend, among them Miss Olive Haydon (lately Sister Olive of York Road), Miss Palmer (Senior Health Visitor for Brighton), Miss Tipper (Organiser for the National Council for Combating Venereal Disease), and several members of the National Union of Trained Nurses.

Beside the lectures, a considerable number of discussions—more or less informal—were held, on such subjects as " The Problem of the Unmarried Mother and Her Child," " Police Women and Women Patrols as regards Prostitution," " Treatment for Habitual Criminals," together with countless smaller discussions held on every opportunity by the " workers " themselves on their own particular subjects. And, as one nurse student remarked, " No matter what subject is under discussion, nursing seems to come into it ; one can always either give some special piece of information required, or get information oneself on some point that has puzzled one in dealing with social problems."

Certainly, one seldom has the opportunity of meeting so many intelligent and keen workers—all interested in the same great subject, namely, " The Betterment of the Race and how to obtain it." If one must select subjects which were of special interest to nurses, those on *Venereal Disease* and the great campaign to educate the civilian population ; also " *Fatigue and Efficiency* by Professor Stanley Kent, showing how long hours and insufficient rest affect the output of good work, came home to many a nurse. This subject had previously been dealt with in a " Psychology Lecture," showing a series of most interesting charts and experiments, given by Miss May Smith.

If one may criticise—" The Work of the Oxford Infant Welfare Association," though most interesting as given by Mrs. Wells, who openly stated she was only an amateur, made some of the professional nurses wish the lecture had been given by a leader on the subject—more especially as Sister Olive was amongst the audience ! .., }

Both Sister Olive, who spoke on the great need of an *expert* being in charge of and giving all the *advice* at all centres, and Miss Cancellor, who spoke of the value of the voluntary workers being trained and also encouraged to learn the management of infants, so that the centres could spread knowledge into the nurseries of the educated as well as the poor, made their points, and were asked many questions later by students interested.

Another interesting suggestion was made by Mr. Peake, *i.e.*, that both in the study of regional survey and in the collection of folk-lore, Health Visitors and District Nurses would find a great interest and also be able to collect many interesting facts ; he suggested that folk-lore societies would be very pleased to send particulars and forms to any nurses ready to take up this fascinating study.

The School broke up with a delightful impromptu party ; with " Story-telling " at its best, by Miss Elizabeth Clark, and lightning sketches of dream-creatures seen after the Biology Lectures, given by another talented student, Professor Laurie, who had given the lectures, joining in the laugh more heartily than anyone.

If the Summer School meets next year, nurses are most strongly advised to take this chance of meeting so many other workers and hearing all the most recent discoveries made on all social progress.

WAR NURSING.

An interesting book on War Nursing by Professor Richet, of the University of Paris, translated by Helen de Vere Beauclerk, is published by Messrs. Heinemann, 21, Bedford Street, London, W.C., price 3s. 6d. It deals with the elementary data of medical physiology, and the subjects discussed are anti-sepis, anæsthesia, foods, hæmorrhage, fever, and asphyxia. It is primarily intended for Red Cross Workers, and is admirably designed for this purpose.

A WORD TO THE WISE.

Nurses in the Marylebone district will be well advised to pay a visit to the establishment of Messrs. Gayler & Pope, Ltd., at 112–117, High Street, Marylebone, W. 1, where are to be found uniform coats and cloaks and bonnets to suit diverse tastes and purses. The present is an opportune moment for the renewal of uniform, both because the advent of September reminds us that it is time to think about winter garments, and also because prices are certain to mount higher than at present, and the wise are those who provide for their needs forthwith.

BOOK OF THE WEEK.

" CAPTAIN DIEPPE."*

It is a long time since we have enjoyed any long story from Mr. Anthony Hope's pen.

" Captain Dieppe " is a romance peculiar to his style, and written with his peculiar grace.

It is not perhaps on as high a platform of merit as some of his earlier works, but he cannot help being charming, nor can his characters fail to either attract or repel.

" Captain Dieppe " is full of improbabilities and impossible situations ; were it not so it could not be the product of Mr. Hope's pen. Its plot is elusive, and difficult to bring into the matter-of-fact atmosphere of criticism.

Who and what Captain Dieppe was doesn't seem to matter much, suffice it to say he was an attractive, so it is implied, gentleman in the thirties, who carried on his person papers of importance. Our readers will learn as much about him as we know ourselves from the following paragraphs.

Fresh from the failure of important plans, if not a fugitive, still a man to whom recognition would be inconvenient and perhaps dangerous, with fifty francs in his pocket, and his spare wardrobe in a knapsack on his back, without immediate prospect of future employment or replenishment of his purse, he marched up a long, steep hill in the glowing dusk of a stormy evening.

The Captain whistled and sang. What a fright he had given the ministers, how nearly he had brought back the Prince, what an uncommon and intimate satisfaction of soul came from carrying under his wet coat lists of names, letters and what not, all capable of causing tremors in high places. He broke off whistling to observe aloud :

" Mark this, it is to very few there comes a life so interesting as mine," and his tune began again with almost rollicking vigour."

Thus Captain Dieppe !

The drenched, but unquenchable Captain finds himself shortly afterwards entertained in a handsome house, and quite easily became the guest of the young Count Fieramondi.

" Stay with me," said the Count, " for to-night at least, and as much longer as you will. Nobody will trouble you. I live in solitude, and your society will lighten it. Let me ring and give orders for your entertainment."

Dieppe looked up at him. " With all my heart, dear host. Your only difficulty shall be to get rid of me."

He was accommodated in the " Cardinal's Room," which his host informed him he had himself until lately occupied.

" I left it owing to—er—circumstances."

" His Eminence is restless ? "

" I beg pardon ? "

" I mean—a ghost ? "

" No, a cat ! " was the Count's surprising answer.

---

* Skeffington & Son, Ltd. 6s.

And the cat was connected with a lady, and the lady was the Count's wife, and the relations between them were somewhat strained.

" My wife and I are not in agreement. She lives in the right wing with two servants, and I live in the left with three."

Captain Dieppe being of an enquiring turn of mind is not long before he makes (*sub rosa*) the acquaintance of the lady in the right wing, and the meeting is described in Mr. Hope's best inconsequent manner.

" Sir," said a timid voice at his elbow.

Dieppe shot round, and then and there lost his heart. One sight of her a man might endure and be heart-whole—not two. There, looking up at him with the most bewitching mouth, the most destructive eyes, was the lady he had seen at the end of the passage

" Madame la Comtesse ? " stammered the dazzled Captain.

" Yes, yes ; but never mind that. Who are you ? "

" My name is Dieppe, madame. Captain Dieppe at your service."

As the gallant Captain had surprised an interview between the lady and a young man, evidently of a secret nature, he is sharply rebuked for his blundering.

" Tell me what I must do," implored the Captain.

She looked at him kindly, partly because he was a handsome fellow, partly because it was her way, and she said with the prettiest, simplest air, as though she were making the most ordinary request and never thought of refusal :

" Will you give me fifty thousand francs ? "

To this modest request the Captain replied that he had but fifty in the world, but he set himself to retrieve the compromising papers from Paul de Roustache, by more exciting and decidedly less dull means than by merely paying the price in cash.

And these two went through a wild adventure to attain their object, and Dieppe having done his part handsomely found himself in the extremely awkward position of being deeply and profoundly in love with his host's wife.

And then comes the grand *finale*, when Dieppe discovers that his charming lady is not the Countess after all, but her cousin ; and that she and the real Countess have for involved reasons of their own been hoaxing both him and the Count.

" I am the happiest fellow in the world," he declared ; " and that," he added, as though it were a rare and precious coincidence, " with my conscience quite at peace."

As to the consciences of the two very ingenious young ladies—the Countess of Fieramondi and her cousin, Countess Lucia—the problem is more difficult. The Countess never confessed and Lucia never betrayed the secret.

What their secrets really amounted to we must beg our readers to discover for themselves.

H. H.

LETTERS TO THE EDITOR.

Whilst cordially inviting communications upon all subjects for these columns, we wish it to be distinctly understood that we do not IN ANY WAY hold ourselves responsible for the opinions expressed by our correspondents.

THE KING'S FUND FOR THE DISABLED. WHO WILL FOLLOW HIS MAJESTY'S LEAD?

To the Editor of THE BRITISH JOURNAL OF NURSING.

MADAM,—His Majesty the King has been graciously pleased to give not only his name, but also the magnificent sum of £78,000 to the Fund which was recently inaugurated to assist disabled officers and men of the Navy, Army and Air Force to become useful members of the community again.

We, the Trustees of the Fund, for whom I sign as Chairman, appeal to the humanity, the gratitude, of every one of your readers—man, woman and child—for a subscription which will help to find a new place in civil life for officers and men of His Majesty's Forces disabled in the War, and for the widows and children of officers and men who have given their lives for us.

"Why doesn't the Government do that?" some readers will ask.

Briefly, a State Pension scale must be hard and fast. Outside that scale there is a great human field which the King's Fund can cover in which the officer, the man, or the dependent can be put on his or her feet, and given a sound re-establishment in civil life.

A State Scheme must be a classification according to the type; the King's Fund passes beyond classification, and acts, not as a public official, but as a private friend.

The present facts are :—

We are receiving 600 applications a week. 2,500 cases have been dealt with thus far. Where the officer or man has been trained by the Ministry of Pensions or where there is a business given up for War Service, which he can restart, an adequate grant can be made.

The Fund is a Monument of Gratitude.

It will cheer our gallant fighters to see that monument rising to £3,000,000—the amount aimed at.

So let us, therefore, have the money—and quickly. Urgent cases are waiting.

The King leads off with his great gift of £78,000. Who will follow the King's lead?

Contributions should be sent to The King's Fund for the Disabled, Westminster House, Millbank, S.W. 1.

All cheques and postal orders should be crossed.

For the Trustees,
JOHN HODGE, *Chairman.*

AN INTERESTING COMPARISON.

To the Editor of THE BRITISH JOURNAL OF NURSING.

DEAR MADAM,—The paragraphs with regard to the Royal Air Force Nursing Service in THE BRITISH JOURNAL OF NURSING and F.S. Form 144 make a very interesting comparison and provide a very clear answer to why there is such a serious shortage of probationers. Most parents are now carefully considering such information and investigating conditions of service and possible chances in the professions open to their daughters.

The following information does not include the Matrons-in-Chief or highest officers in either department :—

OFFICERS OF WOMEN'S ROYAL AIR FORCE.

NURSING SERVICE AFTER THREE YEARS' TRAINING.

Matron	£75	Board and lodging provided and a yearly increment.
Supt. Sister	£60	
Sisters	£50	
Staff Nurses	£40	

GENERAL SERVICE AFTER THREE WEEKS' TRAINING

Area Inspector	£200	Quarters provided and £40 6s. deducted for board. Outfit allowance, £20. First-class travelling expenses and 15s. per day when on duty away from Headquarters.
Hostel Administrator	£175	
Deputy Hostel Administrator	£150	
Assistant Hostel Administrator	£120	
Technical Administrator	£150	
Assistant Technical Administrator	£120	

Is it any wonder that it is necessary to inform nurses in Military and Civilian Hospitals that they will not be accepted without permission from employers?

Yours faithfully,
INTERESTED.

AN AUSTRALIAN POINT OF VIEW.

To the Editor of THE BRITISH JOURNAL OF NURSING.

DEAR MADAM,—Please find enclosed postal note for subscription for BRITISH JOURNAL OF NURSING. I am always very pleased to get the Journal, as I consider it the most reliable nursing paper, all matters in it being handled by professional nursing experts not by lay people. I hope your State Registration Bill will soon go through, then your power as a woman voter registered nurse will be greatly increased. We are trusting our Bill will come on during the Session which opens soon. We think most of the members, both Liberal and Labour, are sympathetic in their views *re* our request.

Wishing your Journal continued success and power.

I am, faithfully yours,
GRETTA LYONS.
Melbourne, Victoria.

OUR PRIZE COMPETITION.

QUESTIONS.

September 14th.—What do you know of Ex-ophthalmic Goître, its symptoms, and nursing care?

September 21st.—What is the function of the blood? Why may hæmorrhage cause death?

The Midwife.

THE CENTRAL MIDWIVES' BOARD.

LIST OF SUCCESSFUL CANDIDATES.

At the examination of the Central Midwives' Board, held on August 1st, in London and the Provinces, 494 candidates were examined and 400 passed the examiners. The percentage of failures was 19.

LONDON.

British Hospital for Mothers and Babies.— D. A. Braithwaite, L. M. Stock.

City of London Lying-in Hospital.—D. M. Amos, E. M. Gaskell, M. Griffiths, F. A. Hewson, R. E. Langridge, C. F. Longstreeth, K. E. McConville, J. McDougall, M. A. Neville, A. F. Smith, B. Wade.

Clapham Maternity Hospital.—D. W. Adams, L. E. M. Bruno, I. J. Chilton, E. Doulton, A. W. Freke, L. M. Lott, P. A. Thorpe.

East End Mothers' Home.—M. Anderson, D. Bartlett, M. T. E. Collard, S. E. Derrick, E. Dickin, M. McR. Duguid, N. D. Jones, J. Llewellyn, D. L. Metzgar, A. M. Pape, E. Smalley, A. M. M. Stone, R. M. Strudwick, L. Welsh.

Elizabeth Garrett Anderson Hospital.—F. E. Nicholson, A. H. Turner.

General Lying-in Hospital.—C. Bream, R. E. Cole, F. S. Cox, M. C. Edwards, K. M. Forwood, M. E. Giles, A. L. Glover, E. I. Harker, J. E. Heywood, A. Husband, A. A. Kendall, F. E. Kewley, E. M. Lyth, C. Montrose, D. J. Mortimore, M. L. Newsome, H. Peate, N. Pleydell-Bouverie, F. E. Sampson, E. K. Seamer, R. O. Wall, J. Westnidge.

Greenwich Union Infirmary.—A. R. Halnan, E. A. Huggett, L. M. B. Nawells.

Guy's Institution.—J. Murray, E. M. Patrick, S. A. Taylor, L. D. Wharton.

Hackney Union Infirmary.—D. E. Martin, L. E. Townshend.

Kensington Union Infirmary.—N. Clogg, E. A. Haggett, M. P. Northrop.

Lambeth Parish Workhouse.—E. M. Bate, A. Stock.

London Hospital.—J. L. Abraham, G. M. Cook, M. E. England, M. M. Grand, A. John, A. H. Norrish, R. A. Thompson, M. J. Wilson.

Maternity Nursing Association.—L. K. Banwell, A. A. Curle, E. B. Dawson, E. Hurlstone, M. A. Joiner.

Middlesex Hospital.—D. M. Badock, H. M. Barber, D. W. Hay, M. Leaver, A. L. Read, M. Waterton.

Plaistow Maternity Charity.—E. Berson, F. H. Bridges, M. A. Broomfield, N. Dibble, A. H. Duffield, C. N. Golder, D. C. Hawson, M. A. Hill, M. E. Hughes, P. Isaac, E. C. Jackson, H. E. Jackson, J. Liens, E. Long, E. F. S. Mackenzie,

A. A. Martin, E. Meredith, M. A. J. Mills, M. Morgans, A. Newton, F. Oxtoby, E. G. Payne, G. M. Roberts, V. Roberts, E. A. Simmons, B. W. Smith, E. Tointon, E. A. Townell, E. True, M. A. Watson, N. A. M. Webb, M. W. Wellard, L. Booth.

Queen Charlotte's Hospital.—L. M. W. Bower, L. S. Church, M. G. Church, L. Coates, L. M. Cole, M. A. Cooper, O. M. Cooper, M. L. Gill, K. M. Hawkins, A. M. K. Hewitt, E. Hey, H. E. Jones, E. G. Kay, H. MacGregor, A. N. Menzies, M. K. Millard, M. J. Phillips, M. E. Simpson, D. Swain, A. M. Tester, W. P. Toleman, E. Wilkes, E. Williamson, N. Woodward.

Salvation Army Mothers' Hospital.—M. E. Drury, E. J. Finley, E. Long.

St. Thomas' Hospital.—J. A. Breach, H. D. Campbell, K. M. R. Carmichael, D. J. Cass.

University College Hospital.—G. Dale, D. Edenborough, A. J. M. Twine, C. A. Wetherspoon.

Wandsworth Union Workhouse.—W. B. Dunn, C. Walker.

West Ham Workhouse.—F. I. More, K. S. Whitehead.

Whitechapel Union Infirmary.—M. A. Brown, E. O'Connor, R. Willgrees.

PROVINCIAL.

Aldershot, Louise Margaret Hospital.—M. E. Nuttall.

Birkenhead Maternity Hospital.—E. Dugdale.

Birmingham Maternity Hospital.—M. A. Bailey, H. B. Campbell, M. Ellis, M. N. K. V. Hasse, W. A. Hyde, S. E. Jones, W. M. Lardieci, G. M. Oates, E. E. Thirkell, M. Wallis, K. A. Warren, A. H. Williamson.

Birmingham, Selly Oak Union Infirmary.—E. Beddoe. G. T. B. Leach.

Birmingham Workhouse Infirmary and Aston Union Workhouse.—E. E. Golby, A. M. Hall.

Birmingham Workhouse Infirmary.—A. M. Packwood.

Bradford Union Hospital.—H. Whalley.

Brighton Hospital for Women.—E. C. Cameron, G. Carter, M. Rist, J. Rook, I. G. Scott.

Bristol General Hospital.—D. M. H. Michell, D. A. Russell, L. M. A. Smith.

Bristol Royal Infirmary.—E. A. Butt, A. M. Farrant, H. K. Halls.

Cheltenham District Nursing Association.—A. Bradley, M. P. Cross.

Chester Benevolent Institution.—A. Griffiths, E. E. Owen.

Derby, Royal Derbyshire Nursing Association.—C. E. Baxter, H. M. Burnie, S. Evans, L. Heslop, E. Rose, E. S. Souch, L. J. Timms.

Devon and Cornwall Training School.—A. Batten, M. J. Brown, A. J. Gurrowich, E. B. Hilt, E. E. Mawdsley, L. Pethybridge, M. E. Striplin.

Devonport, Alexandra Nursing Home.—B. M. Dickson, E. M. Dunning, M. Hamilton, H. Sercombe.

Eccleshall Bierlow Union Infirmary.—E. Watson.

Gloucester District Nursing Society.—S. Collier, Lewis, S. Thomas.

Herts County Nursing Association.—C. Lister, . Tunwell, E. M. Vincent.

Huddersfield District Nursing Association and Huddersfield Union Infirmary.—M. E. Armitage.

Hull Lying-in Charity.—E. M. Petty.

Ipswich Nurses' Home.—C. Clark, E. Raven, A. B. Taylor.

Leeds Maternity Hospital.—F. Abbott, J. A. Bell, M. A. Carr, C. W. Cowan, D. S. G. Hirst, A. Holliday, E. Holmes, E. Johnson, M. E. Margerison, O. N. Musgrave, E. Oldfield, M. K. Parke, M. J. Rolling, E. Rowe, E. Southworth, L. C. Spice, M. A. Warlow, I. Woodall, I. A. Woodley, H. T. Young.

Leeds Union Infirmary.—E. Chippendale.

Leicester Maternity Hospital.—G. E. Barnett, J E. Bowen.

Leicester Union Infirmary.—L. M. Fudge.

Liverpool Maternity Hospital.—L. Alderdice, M. A. Bodey, F. Chadwick, L. Cragg, F. A. Ind, L. V. Johnston, A. Jones, A. D. Kinghorn, M. D. Macdonald, S. G. Newman, E. O'Callaghan, B. L. Rogers, M. A. Schoapper, M. A. Wadsworth, M. Yorke.

Liverpool Workhouse Hospital.—D. Girdlestone.

Manchester : St. Mary's Hospitals.—A. M. Barnes, E. A. Billington, M. Brocklehurst, E. A. Bruce, F. J. Burgess, H. Clegg, E. Cooper, S. S. Dixon, D. C. Jackson, M. Lewis, F. S. Mitchell, E. Shelmerdine, S. A. Watt, E. T. Wignall.

Northampton, Q.V.N.I.—G. A. Morrell, S. E. Preece, A. Weall.

North Bierley Union Infirmary.—M. Ash, E. Lee.

Nottingham Workhouse Infirmary.—F. T. Ford, F. Reeves, B. C. Roberts.

Portsmouth Military Families Hospital.—M. Russell.

Portsmouth Workhouse Infirmary.—E. M. Brown.

Preston Union Workhouse.—M. Murray.

Staffs Training Home for Nurses—M. E. Hughes, M. E. Kirkby, H. J. Mackenzie, M. Millward, E. M. Pile, A. F. Snedden.

Sheffield, Jessop Hospital.—M. D. Eastburn, S. Shillitto, F. A. Shuker, E. Thomas.

Sheffield Union Hospital.—E. Fleming.

Stoke-on-Trent Union Hospital.—E. Hulme, A. Taylor.

Wallsall Union Workhouse.—M. M. Mason, E. Riley.

West Derby Union Infirmary, Walton.—A. Clayton, E. Dunn, F. Dyke.

West Riding Nursing Association.—M. E. Lee, I. Ross.

Wilts Nursing Association.—E. A. Shaw.

Worcester County Nursing Association.—S. M. Davies, Z. V. Hamilton, A. Harris.

York Maternity Hospital.—A. Hare, H. M. Wilson.

York Union Hospital.—M. Garbutt.

WALES.

Cardiff Q.V.J.N.I.—E. Chapman, E. Evans, K. N. Jones, R. Rowles.

Merthyr Tydfil Union Infirmary.—M. Walters.

Monmouthshire Training Centre.—A. E. Comley, E. M. Evans, M. M. Gale, C. Harrison, A. Hughes, E. A. Morgan, M. Peters, M. Ware, M. Watkins, S. J. Winston.

SCOTLAND.

Dundee Maternity Hospital.—A. E. Davison, T. R. Mullan.

Govan Nurses' Home.—M. Costella, A. A. Ions, J. B. Leishman, M. Stoddart.

Glasgow Royal Maternity Hospital.—B. Melville.

IRELAND.

Belfast Union Maternity Hospital.—R. Beattie, M. Frazer, F. Thompson, J. A. Wiley.

Dublin Rotunda Hospital.—M. A. E. Andrew, M. E. Delahunty, H. M. Dixon, E. M. Gorman, E. J. Morgan, B. Mort.

Dublin : Coombe Hospital.—E. M. Jaques.

PRIVATE TUITION.

S. O. Allaway, A. J. Allison, C. H. Chappell, E. Coyne, L. Cross, F. Flint, E. W. Jones, M. G. Marles, E. M. Oxley, J. G. Raisbeck, M. E. Render, M. J. Roberts, S. E. L. Stowe, A. Ward, E. A. Whitworth, L. Wilkinson.

PRIVATE TUITION AND INSTITUTIONS.

Kensington Union Infirmary.—B. C. Babbage.

General Lying-in Hospital.—M. G. Bennett, A. Heatley, E. E. Hubbard, M. J. Kinsey, M. C. Stokes.

Mansfield Union Workhouse.—W. Barkinshaw.

Royal Derbyshire Nursing Association.—M. Cope, L. M. T. Fearn.

Essex County Nursing Association.—M. C. Crown, E. F. Davis, E. Rodgers.

St. Mary's Hospital, Manchester.—M. Davis.

Fulham Midwifery School.—G. L. Dobinson, A. E. Pellow, W. E. Turner.

Nottingham Workhouse Infirmary.—V. G. Gillmore.

Stoke-on-Trent Union Workhouse Hospital.—M. E. Grundy, E. Withington.

Birmingham Maternity Hospital.—E. B. Guest, C. Harris.

Jewish Maternity District Nursing Society.—E. Hyams, E. A. Kent.

Elizabeth Garrett Anderson Hospital.—M. J. McNeil.

East End Mothers' Home.—G. E. Parry.

Croydon Union Infirmary.—B. H. Pickering.

Liverpool Maternity Hospital.—M. E. Russell, L. E. Di Gennaro.

An interesting course of Elementary Lectures on Infant Care, to be held at 1, Wimpole Street, W., from 5.30 to 6.30 p.m. on Mondays from September 30th to December 16th, has been organised by the National Association for the Prevention of Infant Mortality.

THE
BRITISH JOURNAL OF NURSING
WITH WHICH IS INCORPORATED
THE NURSING RECORD
EDITED BY MRS BEDFORD FENWICK

No. 1,589.	SATURDAY, SEPTEMBER 14, 1918.	Vol. LXI

EDITORIAL.

THE WAR COUNCIL SHOULD TAKE ACTION.

It will surprise none of those who, at the outbreak of the war in 1914, desired to see the nursing service of this country put upon a war footing as a whole, that there is at the present time a very serious shortage of nurses and probationers in our civil hospitals. If thousands of nurses are taken out of these institutions to care for the sick and wounded it is evident that there will be many vacancies on the nursing staffs of such hospitals. But because the best must be available for our sick and wounded sailors, soldiers, and airmen, there is no valid reason why a comprehensive survey should not have been taken, with the object of filling these vacancies, or that it should not be taken even now in this fifth year of the war—late as it is to begin work that should have been inaugurated as soon as war was declared, in an international conflict which was bound to affect the furthermost ends of the world.

Had recruits been called for for our civil hospitals in the early days of the war, had the untrained enthusiasm of many ardent young women who desired to nurse our wounded soldiers been directed to hospital training as a means to attain this end, the probationary service in our civil hospital wards would not have been starved. As it was, short courses of a few weeks' instruction were inaugurated, and many young women were permitted at their conclusion to proceed on active service, whilst numbers of fully qualified nurses were turned down.

The National Council of Trained Nurses of Great Britain and Ireland presented a Memorandum on the Care of the Sick and Wounded to the Director-General of the Army Medical Service in December, 1914, prepared by the President, Mrs. Bedford Fenwick, which advocated the formation of an expert committee "representative of the various departments which are now engaged in organising the nursing of sick and wounded soldiers, and including independent experts on military nursing." Had such a committee been formed one of its first acts no doubt would have been to safeguard the sources of supply of military nurses, to see that the needs of the civil hospitals were met, as far as possible, while providing for the emergencies caused by the war. This statesmanlike course was not pursued, nor was it endorsed by the heads of the military services, and organisation proceeded in water-tight compartments. Unfortunately none of the heads of those departments had attended international conferences of nurses, or learnt what their colleagues of other nations were doing, and their outlook was very restricted.

One of the first acts of the nursing profession in the United States of America on the entry of that country into the war has been the formation of an expert committee composed of the heads of the naval and military nursing departments as well as other leaders of the nursing profession, with the result that attention is being directed to nursing as a field for national service, and 25,000 young women are asked for to join the United States Student Nurse Reserve, and thus to be ready, as trained nurses are drafted to the front, to fill up the ranks by entering the training schools as student nurses for the full term course.

This country might have led the way. It is now too late. But it is not too late to follow where the United States of America have led, and even now to organize a Student Nurse Reserve.

We hear of 600 nurses being needed in the hospitals of the Metropolitan Asylums Board alone, of wards in children's hospitals being closed for lack of probationers. There are still many employable women who are unemployed. Surely the need has only to be understood to be met.

The bureaucratic nursing committees in connection with the War Office have proved themselves totally incapable of elasticity of mind and action, and it is high time the Minister of National Service called in the aid of experts possessing creative faculty and power of organization.

OUR PRIZE COMPETITION.

WHAT DO YOU KNOW OF EX-OPHTHALMIC GOÎTRE, ITS SYMPTOMS AND NURSING CARE?

We have pleasure in awarding the prize this week to Miss M. D. Hunter, Section Hospital, Kineton, near Warwick.

PRIZE PAPER.

Ex-ophthalmic goître or Grave's Disease is due to excess of secretion of the thyroid gland. It is commonest in girls of from 18 to 25 years of age. The chief symptoms nearly always appear in the following order :—

(1) *The heart is quickened,* therefore these cases have a quick pulse due to the frequent heart action. Pulsation of the carotids will be noticed. Usually, too, there are sweats and hot flushes.

(2) *Protrusion of Eyeballs* is very noticeable, and this, ex-ophthalmos, suggested the name of the disease. It is supposedly due to dilatation of vessels and increased connective tissue and fat of the orbit. By holding up a finger and telling the patient to look at it while gradually bringing it lower, the eyelid will not quite follow the eye, but lags behind, thus proving " Von Graefe's sign " to be present. If there is weakness of the convergent muscles, it is known as " Mobius' sign."

(3) *Swelling of the Thyroid* occurs, but not till some months later than the two previous symptoms. If the hand is placed over it a thrill can be felt. The enlargement is quite symmetrical.

(4) *Fine Tremor* is present, and also extreme nervousness and excitability. The tremor is best seen by telling the patient to hold out her arms straight in front of her, when it will be easily detected in the fingers.

Other minor symptoms are headache and giddiness. The patient feels languid and has little appetite. She is usually anæmic and thin. The skin will feel quite moist, which is, of course, the exact opposite to that found in myxœdema. Nearly always there is acute constipation, and some doctors have a theory that this is the primary cause of the disease. The voice is often feeble. In rare cases vomiting occurs, and is a serious symptom, as it has been known to persist in spite of all treatment, thus eventually causing death from exhaustion.

The nursing care is likely to be very prolonged, as the treatment takes a long while. Rest in bed is essential, with plenty of fresh air and no excitements. In fact, a sort of modified rest cure is needed, but isolation is not necessary. Sometimes electrical treatment is ordered, consisting of prolonged daily applications of a moderate faradic current to the neck. Cold applications are best applied by Leiter's tubes, which in many cases are very effectual in reducing the thyroid swelling. Surgical interference is not generally recommended, as in mild cases medical treatment answers best, and in severe cases operative measures are so risky, and therefore inadvisable. The only operation generally possible is a partial re-section of the gland and ligaturing of two or three of the thyroid arteries. Feeding is very important, and plenty of milk must always be given—the constipating effects counteracted by suitable aperients. Tea and coffee should not be allowed, but cocoa is an excellent substitute. When possible, it is a good plan to give the patient the milk of goats from which the thyroid gland has been removed. The diet should be light, and fruit is generally allowed. As the most usual drugs given are arsenic or belladonna, the nurse should be well acquainted with symptoms of overdose. Belladonna is a great sedative, but if the patient complains of dryness of mouth, the medical man should be informed at once.

HONOURABLE MENTION.

The following competitors receive honourable mention :—Miss M. Cullen, Miss S. Simpson, Mrs. Farthing, Miss P. Thomson, Miss J. Robinson, Miss E. Bleazby.

Miss Cullen writes :—Anæmia, also debility, are present, and a feeble action of the heart. The stomach in many cases becomes irritated, causing vomiting, and sometimes diarrhœa. The urine should be frequently tested, as sometimes sugar and albumen are found to be present. This disease is most common in women between the ages of 20 and 30 years.

QUESTION FOR NEXT WEEK.

What is the function of the blood? Why may hæmorrhage cause death?

A VISION.

*" And they shall be mine, saith the LORD of
hosts, in that day when I make up my jewels."*
                —Malachi iii. 17.

Dawn stole again above the battle plain
When its mad din had ceased. Stretched at my
    feet
In all appealing silence lay the slain
Wrapt in the sunrise for their winding sheet.
And ONE arrayed in gleaming white, and
    crowned—
Each thorn point a lit star—stood at my side.
Awhile HE looked upon the stricken ground
Death's piteous dominion spreading wide—
Then turned and spake, triumphant eyes ashine,
" I have them now and all their souls are
    mine."
                     C. B. M.

August 26th, 1918.

NURSING AND THE WAR.

The King has been pleased to award a Bar
to the Royal Red Cross to the following lady,
for devotion to duty on the occasion of damage
by enemy action to a hospital ship :—

BAR TO THE ROYAL RED CROSS.

CASHIN, Miss A. E., R.R.C., Matron, Q.A.I.M.N.S.R.

Amongst the Honours and Awards for war
services, the *London Gazette* of September 4th
contained the following announcement :—

ROYAL RED CROSS.
SECOND CLASS.

FARRAR, Miss J. F., Nursing Sister ; PERDUE, Miss
F. L., Nursing Sister ; GROSVENOR, Lady A., Com-
mandant, Red Cross Hospl., Oakfield, Upton Heath,
Chester.

Captain W. Girling Ball, R.A.M.C.T. Surgical
Specialist in a General Hospital, B.E.F., somewhere in France, writes in an extremely interesting
article on "Some Experiences in a Base Hospital,"
in the *St. Bartholomew's Hospital Journal,* " I
cannot finish without referring to the great admiration which I learned to acquire for our sisters
in the nursing profession. In their hospital work
they are doing extraordinarily well, and no praise
of mine can be too high. Not only is this true of
those who have fulfilled their full training as
nurses in our own hospitals at home, but also of
those belonging to the V.A.D. The conditions
under which they have to live are the same as those
of the men, and it is a marvel to me that they
work as well as they do. The British Tommy has
much to be thankful for, if he really appreciates
all they are doing for him."

In a recent letter to a friend, Sister Gertrude
Lindsay, of the Scottish Women's Hospitals, a
daughter of ex-Provost Lindsay, Broughty Ferry,
gives a vivid account of the retreat from Villiers

Cotterets, where a hospital had been established,
of which she was acting Matron. This was an
offshoot from a now famous hospital.

In the days preceding the evacuation " the staff
was simply magnificent," she writes, " and not
even the youngest girl out from home was
' panicked,' they all went on doing their bit. We
were raided every night for three solid weeks
without fail, so there might have been an excuse
if anyone had been nervous."

" The attack started on May 27th, and from
that time until we cleared out on the 31st I do
not think anyone of the staff got a sleep.

" We had two thousand beds in our camp.
We were told to evacuate ; then came a counter
order to stay one more night, as they had no other
means of getting the wounded away. I shall never
forget that night. In the afternoon there was
a magnificent aeroplane fight just over our camp,
and the French brought down two German
machines. Then, as soon as it got dark, they
started in earnest. We had to put out all lights
and go on receiving a steady flow of wounded in
the darkness.

" About 2 a.m. I paid my visit round the wards,
and not a single girl seemed nervous ; they were
all so busy cheering the patients and comforting
the dying. One of the orderlies called me to come
to a man who was dying. I asked him if there
were anything he wanted, and he replied with a
smile, ' Oh, no ; I have a little mother sitting
beside me.' It was like that all night, with the
bombs crashing around us. Then a munition
train went on fire, and the whole town was a bright
target, to which the enemy came back and back.

" The next day we started to get away. The
Boches commenced shelling us about 4 o'clock in
the afternoon, but by that time we had all the
staff away except the Sisters. I got them off
about 8 o'clock, and left myself in an American
ambulance about 8.30. We raced from Villiers
Cotterets with tin helmets on, and by the time we
reached Senlis we had got into another raid. We
stayed in Senlis until next morning."

OUR ROLL OF HONOUR.
NURSING SERVICE.
WOUNDED.

BRAIN, Sister R., T.F.N.S.
DICKENSON, Miss D. M., V.A.D.
LARSEN, Miss A. O., V.A.D.
PLEYDELL-NOTT, Miss V., V.A.D.
WOOD, Miss H., V.A.D.

Miss Katherine Connelly, army nurse, who was
buried in New York recently, received full military
honours. This is the first military funeral ever
accorded to a New Jersey Irish woman. The body
was accompanied to the cemetery by a guard of
honour of seven army nurses, a band, an escort of
the State Militia, and a detachment of the Women's
Motor Corps. Miss Connelly was a graduate of
St. Elizabeth's Convent at Madison.

FRENCH FLAG NURSING CORPS.

Miss Alice Jane Harley Williamson has joined the French Flag Nursing Corps, and left for France on Saturday last. Miss Williamson is well known in Scotland as the Superintendent of the Training Home of the Scottish Branch of Queen Victoria's Jubilee Institute, Edinburgh, since 1913. She was trained at the Royal Infirmary, the Colinton Fever Hospital, and in district nursing, and at the Rotunda Hospital, Dublin, and was a member of the Colonial Nursing Association from 1909 to 1912.

Miss Williamson, therefore, is a very highly qualified nurse, holding certificates from leading training schools in general, fever, and district nursing and midwifery.

Miss Williamson is anxious, like so many patriotic women, to take part in military nursing during the great war.

Queen's Nurses attached to the three branches of the Jubilee Institute have won golden opinions in France as members of the F.F.N.C. Their district training, apparently, especially qualifies them to overcome the difficulties of initiation in a foreign land. If it were not hard upon our poor at home, we should urge more Queen's Nurses to join the Corps.

MISS ALICE J. H. WILLIAMSON, F.F.N.C.

Miss Grace Ellison is still suffering from the results of her very serious illness, and after a visit to Paris and Evreux, she has returned to Bagnolles for further treatment, from which it is hoped she may benefit considerably.

Miss Ellison, when sufficiently recovered, hopes to continue to work in France, so that her many friends will not lose sight of her.

LINDSAY.—On August 8th, abroad, of broncho-pneumonia, James Basden Lindsay, Sec. Lieut., A.S.C. (late Canadian Infantry), of Edmonton, Canada, brother of M. O. Lindsay, nursing sister, 8th Canadian General Hospital, France. (Canadian and Indian papers, please copy.)

AT THE FRENCH FRONT IN ITALY.

In Mr. Laurence Binyon's wonderful book "For Dauntless France," of which I have so far only seen reviews, there is, I fancy, one small section of Britons privileged to help the French who are *not* mentioned.

Our numbers are very few. I believe we could be counted on the fingers of one hand, but our work has a charm all its own. It is so unlike anything else. A French doctor patient recently said to the present writer : " Pour vous, Mademoiselle, puisque vous avez le goût des aventures et des langues barbares, il n'y a que vous proposer pour la Colonne Volante du Maroc !" Meanwhile there is a sufficient variety of material gathered together in this charming little Italian town (which must be nameless), and the medical section of a French ambulance provides varied and interesting work.

At first sight one would think it almost impossible to "overtake" the work, one nurse to 100 patients being quite usual, and the various wards will be tents, wooden huts, or rooms in a school, and may be scattered up and down stairs and all over the place, but the probationer work is all done by the orderlies (Infirmiers), who are also responsible for filling in the charts and diet sheets from the doctor's orders and making out dispensary, laundry and clothing store lists, all the clerking and copying work over which we have all wasted so many hours ; so that here we are really able to devote ourselves to the actual nursing and trying to make the patients comfortable and happy. They do not expect much. They and we have to do without a great deal that is taken for granted in an English hospital. Medicines are given in their ordinary tin drinking cups (or old Nestlé's milk tins), frequently preferred for the dose, with the remains of coffee or milk in them ! " N'importe," says the cheerful poilu. No knives are provided in hospital, and if he has not a clasp knife of his own he borrows his neighbour's, or tears up his meat with a spoon ! (The two Sisters, too, one French, one English, had only one tin plate each, one fork and one tin cup for all meals until a generous British Red Cross Depôt presented them with china tea cups for their morning coffee and actual knives and forks of their own, along with many other most welcome gifts.) In this particular ambulance there was a complete absence of dressing trays, bowls, forceps, probes, razors, syringes, scissors, &c. Lucky the Sister who had brought everything of her own !

Material of every sort is also lacking. When the doctor ordered a wet pack for a case of congestion of the lungs and very high fever, all the orderly could produce was an extra large and ragged sheet (which must on no account be divided) and a piece of mackintosh, stained all the colours of the rainbow, which had obviously already done its " Military service " and ought to have had several ribbons, certainly the one denominated " fatiche di guerra." Swollen ankles have to be swathed in wet bandages simply, and for an ordinary foment the only thing is to take the man's own towel, if he happens to have one and it is clean. Failing that, Sister must sacrifice something of her own. Socks might as well be served out singly. They never match either in colour or size, and always have holes. Handkerchiefs are non-existent, but a brilliant idea was to hand out to one ward of sick prisoners the calico squares in which the American packets of compresses arrive. "*Fala lepa*," the Croatian " thank you," echoed all around, and a request for "*igla i konatz*" (needle and thread) being complied with, they were soon all neatly hemmed, and even marked with the initials of the happy owners !

These so-called Austrian prisoners were found to be almost universally ignorant of the German tongue, but almost all—Bohemians, Hungarians, Bosnians, Poles, Roumanians and Croats—speak, or at least understand, the language of the last-named, which seems to be a kind of debased Russian, written in Latin characters, though, as, the present writer had, in the first instance, to acquire it without a book, that was little help !

To one to whom familiar ideas clothed in other languages are a never-ending source of delight, a morning which includes the following incidents is distinctly interesting.

On issuing from the parent hospital to do duty among the tents and barracks, one is met by a Croat ex-patient, now a prisoner on fatigue duty (which means sweeping up leaves and carrying buckets !), who explains that his shoes let in the water with which he is swilling the steps and hall. He has to be accompanied to the Vestiare, interpreted for and satisfied with a fresh pair (it would be a misnomer to call them new !)

Next, one meets that *rara avis*, a prisoner who really speaks German (he is a Hungarian). *His* grievance is that, having been discharged as a patient and retained at work, he is still on the *halbes-brod* which went with his " light diet " (petit-regime for " la diéte " in French hospitals means nothing to eat at all). This has to be translated to the orderly concerned and remedied.

Next comes one of the French cooks asking to have his ailments attended to before the day's work begins and probably two or three of his satellites, of varying nationalities—rush up with cut fingers, burns and other trifles. One of the Italian " chars," who corresponds to a ward-maid, has to be listened to while she explains at length how she had " febbre " last night and must positively have some remedy or she cannot work. If she receives the least encouragement she will probably ask for advice and free medicines for all her family, down to the latest grandchild. At last one gets to the wards proper and starts dressings and treatments. Sometimes out-patients come in, once or twice English chauffeurs or post office officials ; and the little French orderly paid the neatest possible compliment by exclaiming on the first occasion, with apparent genuineness : " Mais, mademoiselle, parle aussi l'Anglais, c'est qu'elle est *très* instruite."

The work itself is not very different to work anywhere else when one has become accustomed to the French medical procedure of treating everything with " piqures and ventouses."

To the simple Croatian and Bosnian, who had probably never been ill and certainly never been nursed before, it was a daily joy to feel his own and see his neighbour's back decorated with rows of little forcing glasses, which he gaily calls " chalitza " (the word is probably not spelt at all like that, but that is how it sounds !)

The prisoners are all painfully thin and give graphic descriptions of the hardships they have been through in the last few months and years ; and they enjoy their simple rations whole-heartedly. It was a middle-aged Frenchman, however, who asked the Sister anxiously whether the piqures of Cacodylate de Soude were to take the place of food !

The food in question, being mostly preserved, is dry and tasteless and sometimes none too plentiful, but that, and the extreme heat, and the smells and the insects are all hardships of war we will gladly endure as long as we are allowed to be useful in our present sphere.   H. T.

CARE OF THE WOUNDED.

The Queen, accompanied by the Princess Mary, visited the St. Andrew's Hospital, Clewer, last week. The hospital is under the charge of the Sisterhood of St. John the Baptist.

The Bishop of Peterborough last week dedicated his palace at Peterborough as a military hospital. Over a thousand pounds has been subscribed locally for the hospital equipment.

Captain Malcolm Ross, War Correspondent with the New Zealand Forces, in a message dated September 3rd, describing the scene at Haplincourt, says : " On the edge of our sector was a hospital hurriedly vacated two days ago. It was furnished with old beds and bedding left behind by the British in their last retreat. Two wounded Germans on stretchers were left. There was even a wounded German on the operating table."

AMERICAN RED CROSS HOSPITAL, TOTTENHAM.

The American Hospital, which has been established in the buildings of the M.A.B. Fever Hospital, known as the North Eastern Hospital, Tottenham, is now in full swing—at least so far as present capacity allows. The equipment of the former hospital, however, provided only for a thousand patients, and the present one eventually will accommodate three thousand—so that much strenuous effort is still needed before the additions can be completed. Those who are acquainted with M.A.B. institutions will be aware that their buildings maintain a high standard of efficiency, and the American staff now in occupation fully appreciate the nucleus which it is their part to develop to three times its original size. Though their occupation is still counted in weeks, the necessary work is in evident progress, and already the spacious tennis court is marked out for a staff mess room of formidable dimensions and the necessary operating theatre is in process of making in another part of the building. In addition to these, huts are to be erected to provide for the full complement of beds.

The Matron of this busy colony of buildings is Miss Laura A. Beecroft. She was trained at the Western Pennsylvania Hospital, Pittsburg. For eight years she was Superintendent of the Minnequar Hospital, Pueblo, Colorado. She was a member of the Colorado State Registration Examining Board for Nurses. This appointment is made by the Governor for five years, and Miss Beecroft was appointed a second time—ten years in all. She was also an Army Nurse for three years in the Spanish-American War.

The unit she has brought over is known as the Denver Unit (Colorado) Base Hospital 29. It has been fully equipped by the Denver Red Cross Chapter at a cost of 78,000 dollars. So far, however, none of its equipment has arrived in England, and the Matron awaits its perfect and

MISS LAURA A. BEECROFT, R.N.,
Matron, American Red Cross Hospital, Tottenham,
formerly Member of the Colorado State Registration
Examining Board for Nurses.

complete machinery with some impatience. Its medical staff are members of Denver University; and the nurses, numbering one hundred, are all graduates of Colorado State. In addition, there are 150 corps men drawn from the best families in Denver. These men correspond to our orderlies, and do the needful work in ward, kitchen, office and ambulance. The nurses are of one grade, and with the exception of one head nurse to each ward all work on equal terms. The uniform of matrons and nursing staff shows little variation, and is designed from a practical and economical point of view. The dresses are of grey linen with aprons made without waist-bands, and of a pattern easily laundered. The caps are of a modified "Sister Dora" type, with the Red Cross in the centre of the band. The wide turnover collars give a picturesque finish to the whole. Every nurse is provided by the Red Cross with a grey sweater, and we were reminded of the touch of autumn in the air by many of their number availing themselves of their comfort. Very necessary, too, when one remembers the long open-sided corridors.

Though it was a busy time in the morning on the occasion of our visit Miss Beecroft received us with great kindness and courtesy, and personally showed us the many interesting features of the hospital.

The nursing staff are enjoying the many domestic privileges which the M.A.B. had installed for their own staff— separate bedrooms, large and numerous bathrooms, comfortable sitting and mess rooms. The cubicles hitherto assigned to the domestic staff are now ear-marked for sick nurses. One hundred and fifty beds are told off for this purpose, as all sick nurses from the base hospitals are to be drafted here. We observed in the nurses' rooms that they had no use for bolsters, and these British articles were dressed up in ornamental coverings and were serving as chair cushions.

The kitchen is in charge of a lady dietitian, who is a graduate of Columbia University; they have also a skilled chef, and the food is pronounced "excellent." Here we noticed the "Corps" referred to before, busy in company with English domestics, attending to various culinary matters.

The wards have been coloured a delicate shade of green, very restful to the eyes. Some of them are furnished with the high American beds, while others still retain the British variety. One ward is entirely devoted to fractures, and here the surgeons were at work attending to their patients. Everywhere we noticed homely comfort and the absence of red tape and pomposity. Matron and staff and patients were entirely at their ease with one another. We were pleased to notice that the men were allowed to smoke in the wards, and so alleviate the tedium of their position. The contagious cases are nursed in cubicle wards, which plan appears to economise the nursing power. At present wards of forty beds are staffed by four nurses, but the Matron does not anticipate that the staff will be increased as the number of patients grow, so that the proportion of patients per nurse will be gradually increased. As there are *no* untrained women in the American Red Cross system, the trained nurses can entirely concentrate on their patients, and the result must be that more efficient work can be done in less time than where they have to be constantly supervising and undoing the work of the unlearned and ignorant. Would that this were the case in *all* Military hospitals. One could not be long in Miss Beecroft's company without realising that any work she had in hand would spell efficiency.

H. H.

THE MEDICAL TREATMENT OF DISABLED MEN.

Mr. John Hodge, Minister of Pensions, is hoping to introduce on the first day of the autumn session a Bill to give the Ministry of Pensions greater powers. One scheme he has in view is to enforce a certain degree of medical treatment on discharged and disabled men. Thousands of discharged men do not accept treatment—which is bad for themselves and for the nation. He considers they should only be discharged when the medical profession has done everything possible to restore them to their old condition.

Opening an exhibition showing the methods of treating disabled men at Birmingham on Monday, Mr. Hodge said he wanted to give every man who needed it a spare limb, so that he would have it to fall back upon when the first one was being repaired.

THE QUEEN'S HOSPITAL FOR CHILDREN, HACKNEY ROAD.

A letter in the press by the Bishop of London, drawing attention to the closing of two wards (twenty-four beds) at the Queen's Hospital for Children, Hackney Road, owing to the lack of probationers, and a paragraph in the press on the same subject, have resulted in applications for probationers' posts.

THE COLLEGE OF NURSING, LTD., AND THE EXAMINATION OF NURSES.

On behalf of the Executive Committee of the Society for the State Registration of Trained Nurses the following circular letter was addressed to the Secretaries of the principal nurse-training schools in the United Kingdom early in May last :

DEAR SIR,—Considerable apprehension is felt by nurses who have not yet qualified for their certificates in London and other training schools, at the rumour that in future their examination will be conducted by the College of Nursing, Ltd.—a Limited Liability Company which claims disciplinary powers over its nurse-members, and to the autocratic constitution of which many trained nurses take very strong exception —and not by their own training schools, or by a Statutory Authority set up by Act of Parliament.

My Committee would be obliged if you would, at your earliest convenience, inform me whether this rumour is correct, in so far as it applies to the probationers at ———.

I am, Dear Sir,
Yours faithfully,
MARGARET BREAY,
Hon. Secretary.

Replies have been received as follows :—

MR. THOMAS HAYES, St. Bartholomew's Hospital :—

"I have your enquiry of the 4th inst. and can only say that I have no knowledge of the rumour to which you refer.

"The training of Probationers here is, as it always has been, under the direction of the Governors of the Hospital, and the examinations for certificates will continue as hitherto to be conducted by the officially appointed 'Instructors of Probationary Nurses,' and the Matron."

MR. G. Q. ROBERTS, St. Thomas' Hospital :—

"The question you raise has not been considered by the Governors, but I venture to think that whatever the 'one portal' may be, there is no doubt that just as the students of our great Universities are able to take a University degree, in addition to their Conjoint Qualifications, so it will be perfectly consistent for nurses to qualify at the College of Nursing, and to hold the Nightingale Certificate which will be jealously guarded for the benefit of all probationers trained in the standard required to gain it."

There can be no analogy between an examination instituted by a Limited Liability Company which claims disciplinary powers over its nurse-members, and which is prohibited by its own constitution from conferring diplomas, and the honourable degree conferred by a great University. Were an examination leading to a degree inaugurated by a University the position would be entirely different.

SIR COOPER PERRY, Guy's Hospital :—

"I am directed by the House Committee to inform you that no proposals have been hitherto made either by Guy's Hospital to the College of Nursing, or by the College of Nursing to Guy's Hospital, for the holding of Nursing Examinations."

MISS M. HEATHER-BIGG, R.R.C., Charing Cross Hospital :—

"Our Secretary has given me your letter of May 9th. So far we have not been approached by the College of Nursing on the matter referred to in your note. No discussion has taken place on this matter."

MR. SIDNEY M. QUENNELL, Westminster Hospital :—

"In reply to your letter of yesterday's date, I find upon enquiry that the apprehension you mention does not obtain amongst the probationers training at this hospital."

MR. RICHARD COLES, King's College Hospital :—

I.

"I beg to acknowledge the receipt of your circular letter of the 9th inst. with reference to the examination of Probationers, which I will place before the Committee at their next meeting."

II.

"I am directed to inform you that there is no intention of changing the Nurses' Examination."

MR. WALTER KEWLEY, Middlesex Hospital :—

"I beg to acknowledge and thank you for your letter of the 9th inst. which will be submitted to my Board at its next meeting."

No further communication has, so far, been received.

MR. REGINALD R. GARRATT, Royal Free Hospital :—

"In reply to your letter of the 9th inst., I beg to inform you that so far as I am aware, no apprehension is felt by nurses with whom I am in contact on the subject to which you refer. It is fully realized by them that the College of Nursing will be of great value to the Nursing Profession, and will also be well able and desirous of protecting their interests in all respects."

In answer to this, the Hon. Secretary of the Society for the State Registration of Trained Nurses wrote :—

"I beg to acknowledge your letter of May 10th. I shall be obliged if you will be so kind as to answer the question contained in my former letter, *i.e.*, whether the rumour is correct that in future the examination of probationers at the Royal Free Hospital will be conducted by the College of Nursing, Ltd., and not by their own training school?"

Mr. Garratt replied :—

"Will you please inform me by what authority your Committee seeks the information referred to from the Board of this Hospital. It is not customary to supply information to unauthorized persons."

The letter addressed to Mr. Garratt was written on official paper bearing the names of the officers of the Society for the State Registration of Trained Nurses, the membership of which includes over 4,000 certificated nurses, presumably the unauthorized persons referred to by Mr. Garratt.

MR. A. BETTERIDGE, West London Hospital :—

"In reply to your circular letter, dated May, I beg to inform you that the examinations of probationers are still conducted by the hospital."

MR. J. COURTNEY BUCHANAN :—

"In reply to your circular letter I beg to say that the rumour is incorrect in so far as it applies to the probationers at the Metropolitan Hospital."

MR. GILBERT G. PANTER, Great Northern Central Hospital :—

"In reply to your letter of the 9th inst., I beg to inform you that no communication has been received from the College of Nursing by this hospital on the subject to which you refer."

No replies have been received from St. George's Hospital, the London Hospital, St. Mary's Hospital, and University College Hospital.

(*To be concluded.*)

APPOINTMENTS.

SISTER.

Children's Hospital, Hull.—Miss Florence Jones has been appointed Sister of the Medical Wards. She was trained at the Royal Infirmary, Halifax, where she held the positions of Sister of the Children's ward, and also of Night Sister. She has recently been Holiday Sister at the Children's Hospital, Hull.

Erdington Infirmary, Birmingham.—Miss Mabel Annie Barham has been appointed Maternity Sister. She was trained at the Dudley Road Infirmary, Birmingham, and has been Sister in a medical ward at the Erdington Infirmary.

Royal Infirmary, Truro.—Miss Gertrude Farrington has been appointed Sister. She was trained at the Lake Hospital, Ashton-under-Lyne, and has been Staff Nurse at the New Hospital for Women. She is a certified midwife.

QUEEN ALEXANDRA'S IMPERIAL MILITARY NURSING SERVICE.

Staff Nurse C. E. Bray resigns her appointment (August 24th).

AN APPRECIATION.

Widespread regret is expressed throughout the nursing world in Ireland at the resignation of Miss Lucy Ramsden, Lady Superintendent of the Rotunda Hospital, Dublin, which post she has held for over 20 years, for it means not only severing her connection with the hospital, but leaving Ireland. Only those who have worked intimately with Miss Ramsden on the several Boards and Associations of which she is a member can realise how great her loss will be. Her sound judgment and keen sense of justice made her an invaluable colleague, one not easily replaced. Her work in the Rotunda Hospital has had a world-wide influence, as candidates for training in midwifery come from all quarters of the globe. Some months ago Miss Ramsden was chosen as one of the representatives to act on the Central Midwives Board (Ireland), and her appointment was only waiting ratification by the Local Government Board. Miss Ramsden has now withdrawn her name and this new Board will suffer accordingly, as her experience and advice would have been invaluable. Miss Ramsden is an active member of the Irish Nurses' Association, of which she has been twice President ; also of the Irish Matrons' Association (twice President), a Director of the Nurses' Hostel, and a member of the Irish Nursing Board. Her name was found on every Committee that was formed in connection with nursing affairs, and no matter how busy she was, Miss Ramsden always found time for a "little more." Is it any wonder that the coming loss of such a faithful ally is deeply regretted ?

NURSING ECHOES.

At the quarterly general court of the Governors of the London Hospital last week the Committee announced that some beautiful gifts had been received for the sitting-room in the new Nurses' Home, including a bust of Edith Cavell by Sir George Frampton, who also collected engravings for the decoration of the walls from his private friends, and Mr. Foster, a member of the Committee, had given some fine reproductions of old masters.

The chairman, Mr. W. T. Paulin, also mentioned that the Committee had been informed that, as their nurses each occupied a separate room, they were entitled to have their names on the register, and to vote both in borough and Parliamentary elections.

If the nurses at the London Hospital are entitled to have their names on the Parliamentary Register, then the same must hold good for other nurses occupying separate rooms. We should advise all so qualified to make sure forthwith that their names are on the Register.

The pretty badge of the David Lewis Northern Hospital, Liverpool, may be purchased by any nurse who has successfully passed the final examination at the end of her third year. It is about the size of a florin, and is suspended by a gilt bar pin. The badge is enamelled white, and has a deep blue border edged with gilt, on which the name of the hospital appears in gilt letters. In the centre is a shield of alternate diagonal bars of red, gilt, and blue, effectively thrown into relief by the white background. A similar badge in gold and enamel is given as a first prize in the final examination held twice a year, and the nurse who has first place in the junior division receives a book or books to the value of 25s.

Miss Genevieve Cooke, R.N., of San Francisco, who is well known to many of our readers, writes that she has now moved from Leavenworth Street to an attractive lower flat at the north-west corner of Clay and Webster Streets, where she plans to give home nursing to convalescent patients, post-operative or others, in separate rooms, in addition to her Gymnasium work. Her sister, Mrs. Thompson, who is noted amongst her friends for the good meals she prepares, is with her, and in charge of the housekeeping. We wish them every success.

A WISE POLICY.

Sir Henry Morris will preside at a meeting of the medical profession at Steinway Hall, on October 1st, at 5.30, which will be addressed by Dr. Addison, Minister of Reconstruction. The object of the meeting is to secure the election of representative medical men to the House of Commons, so that expert advice may be available on vital questions concerning the national health.

CONFERENCE UNDER AUSPICES OF LABOUR PARTY.

At a National Conference of Women to be held under the auspices of the Labour Party in the Caxton Hall, Westminster, on October 15th and 16th, a resolution will be submitted demanding that the Government at once pass a Bill enabling women to be elected to the House of Commons, that further legislation admitting women to professions from which they are now excluded shall be passed, and that the Representation of the People Act be amended so as to give votes on a short residential qualification to all men and women of 21 years of age. Another resolution calls for the establishment of a Ministry of Health.

Mrs. Gwynne Vaughan, C.B.E., D.Sc., has been appointed Commandant of the Women's Royal Air Force, in succession to the Hon. Violet Douglas-Pennant. The new Commandant was a Professor at King's College before her appointment, and is one of the few women whose pre-war work is being kept open for her by a man. Let us hope, therefore, that she brings knowledge and administrative ability to deal with the task before her, and will command the confidence of those working under her. Experienced women workers, trained before the war in good methods of organization, find the task of working under women whose social influence is their chief qualification a heart-breaking one, and it is not surprising if they decline to make bricks without straw.

THE NATIONAL COUNCIL OF WOMEN OF GREAT BRITAIN AND IRELAND.

The Annual Meeting of the National Council of Women—the governing body of the National Union of Women Workers—will be held at Harrogate this year, beginning on October 8th. We shall refer again to the programme in a future issue.

WOMEN WAR WORK EXHIBITION.

An exhibition of women's war work will be opened at the Whitechapel Art Gallery next month, when every branch of women's activities in connection with the war will be shown—in hospitals, on the land, on relief funds, and on munitions.

Following a visit which the Queen paid to St. Mark's Court, St. John's Wood, the first block of flats for officers' widows and disabled officers provided by the Housing Association for Officers' Families, the King and Queen have each subscribed £100 to the funds of the association.

BOOK OF THE WEEK.

"THE HUNTER."*

" Louis Buttress was the nobody of Alamanca Creek. He was best described by his own remark, ' I'm a natural sort o' man.' " He lived near the water in an excuse for a cabin, which had cost about a dollar in the making, and he spent his life with the dumb creation.

Money-making had no pleasure for him at all; but the eyes of a coon, a fox, a ground hog or a mouse had power to arrest the whole man.

" Silvia Lake was the beauty of Alamanca Creek, and her father, Sylvester Lake, had endless callers at their home at Creek Point. He took the honour to himself, being an important feeling man; but Silvia had reason to know that she was the star for pony-riding boys to dream of." It seemed a far cry from pretty Silvia to Louis Buttress, but it is the unexpected that happens.

He came upon her one day inadvertently as she was bathing in the pool. " Plumb as the Almighty planned her."

" A water hen, disturbed by his intruding and unguarded feet, called loudly, and went into the lake. The girl looked in that direction, and her eyes met the man's just as a fox's eyes had done a minute ago.

" Her eyes reached him with their force, and she gave him her whole attention. Buttress put it in one word, ' trust.'

" Great God in Heaven, she's clothed from my poor eyes by that faith of hers," he said. He waved his hand to her and disappeared amongst the brush.

" 'Tis true," he said to himself, " I saw nothing but her beautiful soul after that first look when she was unknown of my presence."

Hitherto the wild hunter had known nothing of women; but from that moment he was obsessed with the thought of Silvia.

Silvia was under no illusion concerning Louis or his antecedents, when she decided to listen to his primitive wooing and run away and marry him.

Previously he had told her : " My father was a poacher in Lincolnshire. The vicar of the parish had said that he was ' cureless,' so he said to mother, ' You take father where poachin' is right, and thus you stop the sin. Father said he'd rather go once or twice to gaol and stop in England, but he says the Church and the woman were too much for any man to fight alone, and he found himself at last in U.S.A. But the queer thing is that father don't like it when it's lawful. ' Drat it, Louis,' he says to me, ' there's nothing to run up against, the hul thing's as stupid as a suet pudding.' "

The nature studies in the book are a most attractive feature.

" Sometimes Louis and Silvia sat outside the cabin watching evening as it melted into night.

The sky might be studded by stars; it might be swept by the moon; it might be soft and misty, with some orange-hued dusky cloud where the sun had set; but it was received with pleasure."

Married life with them began as an idyll, but tragedy was not long before it clouded their happiness. Silvia had been promised to Bill Din the pony boy before Louis swept her off her feet and she had neither told Louis of her entanglement with Bill, nor Bill that she intended to break faith with him. It was when Louis discovered what he had done to the man who was his friend that " he came slowly home with an indifferent listless movement, which even the shadows of evening could not disguise.

Silvia lit the lamp, putting it on the table. She looked at Louis after she had done it. The light showed the man's face, and his blue eyes were strange looking. His hair was dishevelled. He took up her crochet work and began to unravel it.

Silvia got the supper ready and put coffee on the table. Louis continued to unravel the work.

Silvia moved away from him and went to the door. Night had descended; the sky was brilliant with stars; the dog was barking."

All night these two kept vigil.

The cocks crowed at three o'clock, then stopped as if they had made a mistake; and did it again, with more life, at five."

Louis, like many gentle men, was implacable at the thought of her want of trust in him; and for a while they parted, but only for a while, for these two were predestined for each other.

She tells him " You gave me peace when I looked at you, even after I started to make mistakes. It got to be a prayer with me to hold this feelin' of beauty about why we was made different from each other, and how it was our part of God. I can't tell you how it came to be a prayer, but it grew out of the silence, and I wanted to make sure that the deep, deep voice was the real one.

" So I was a-watchin' for a man—watchin' with my soul dependin' on it, instead of believin' and waitin' on God to show me. That's how I started goin' with the boys. Yet there was no fire in them—no love of God's works. I wanted the man whose soul would rage when God's laws were mocked in either word or action. Creation ain't a crumpled leaf turned down to be hidden or despised. I wanted the man who thought it was a perfect law, because it was the law that created the best thing on earth—souls. And then, Louis, out of the silence of Ari-wa-kis North Bank spoke to South Bank. You were close by all the time. You were there, feelin' it perfect ! "

" It was God, Silvia."

" Don't I know it ! *You* was my answer."

" Silvia, paradise, ain't it ? "

A really refreshing book, which we can heartily recommend to all nature lovers.   . H. H.

* By Watson Dyke. (Putnam's Sons : 24, Bedford Street, Strand, London, W.C. 2.)

LETTERS TO THE EDITOR.

Whilst cordially inviting communications upon all subjects for these columns, we wish it to be distinctly understood that we do not IN ANY WAY hold ourselves responsible for the opinions expressed by our correspondents.

AN INTERESTING COMPARISON.

To the Editor of THE BRITISH JOURNAL OF NURSING.

DEAR MADAM,—I have been reading the most excellent and sensible letter in your issue of this week, under the heading of " An Interesting Comparison," and am now writing to take the liberty of suggesting that it should be sent for publication to the *Times* ; for in a general daily paper it would necessarily come to the notice of a larger number of readers than in a nursing paper. It deals with such a very important point that it is a pity it should not come before as large a number of people as possible.

Apologising for troubling you,

Believe me,

Yours very faithfully,

IRENE B. CUNNINGHAM.

Christchurch, Hants.

[We have advised the writer of the letter referred to to communicate with the *Times*.—ED.]

THE INFLUENCE OF COLOUR.

To the Editor of THE BRITISH JOURNAL OF NURSING.

DEAR MADAM,—I was extremely interested in the article on " The Influence of Colour " in last week's BRITISH JOURNAL OF NURSING, for I am quite sure that colour has a great effect on patients, though all may not be conscious of it. Most nurses, in this country, recognise it by the pains they take to obtain flowers for their wards, and the brightness and homeliness of our wards are much commented upon by visitors from abroad. The patients also appreciate the floral decorations, and so do their friends, for there are few who do not bring some flowers on a visiting day, while a former patient paying a visit to the ward will not unfrequently bring a flowering plant. So great indeed is the demand for flowers that on visiting days flower-sellers stand with their baskets outside the gates of hospitals and do a flourishing trade.

On the other hand very little consideration is given to the colour scheme for the decoration of hospital wards, and I do not think there will be much progress in this direction until we have women on hospital boards. Even the colour of the walls, if unobjectionable in itself, may clash with the colour scheme of quilts and screens and be a source of irritation and discomfort to a patient with an eye sensitive to colour harmonies.

Of the influence of colour from the therapeutic standpoint I, with I fancy most nurses, am very ignorant, but I can imagine it would be a fascinating study, and one that one might pursue with pleasure to oneself, and profit to one's patients. Perhaps the Journal will some day tell us more about it.

Yours faithfully,

A COLOUR LOVER.

THE ROYAL NATIONAL PENSION FUND FOR NURSES.

A CERTIFICATE OF EXISTENCE.

We have received a letter from Miss Christina Forrest, in reference to her last communication published in our issue of August 17th, desiring to have it made quite plain that, according to the letter of the Secretary of the Royal National Pension Fund for Nurses, which she quoted, it was September, 1919, and not this month, that it might be necessary to ask the policy holders for another certificate of existence.

The Royal National Pension Fund is an Insurance Society—and not a Pension Society—for which policy holders pay business prices. There is no reason, therefore, why they should claim to be exempt from business methods. We have always said, and shall still continue to hold the same opinion, that the title of the Society is misleading to the community.

KERNELS FROM CORRESPONDENCE.

Army Reserve Sister writes :—" Many of us have come to the conclusion that government by Matrons is not to our interest. We Reserve Sisters have to sign the ' Serf clause ' before we are eligible for a rise of salary and bonus, the Matrons on the Army Nursing Board agreed to it. Then the Matrons on the College Council have agreed to its penalising Constitution—to special facilities for the London Hospital sweating system, and to preference for V.A.D.s in Q.A.I.M.N.S. Also in the last draft of the College Bill the whole fabric of the three years' general training is undermined by the new Clause 4, providing for the setting up of Registers of Specialists, who of course can compete ' as registered nurses ' with the thoroughly trained. Seems to me the Matrons have betrayed our interests all along the line."

[Having closely watched for the past two years the conduct of business by the College Council we regretfully agree with the opinion that either through arrogance, ignorance or incapacity it has failed to protect the interests of the nursing profession ; but the nurse members of the College who join the institution without reading the constitution, and who permit rules and Registration Bills to be drafted without their being consulted, are just as much to blame, and their betrayal of the interests of their colleagues is equally reprehensible.—ED.]

OUR PRIZE COMPETITION.

QUESTIONS.

September 21st.—What is the function of the blood ? Why may hæmorrhage cause death ?

September 28th.—How would you recognize perforation in a case of enteric fever ? What immediate action would you take, and how could you temporarily relieve the patient ?

The Midwife.

THE CASE FOR A MINISTRY OF HEALTH.

The National Baby Week Council (27A, Cavendish Square, London, W. 1) have done wisely to place on record, in pamphlet form (Leaflet No. 13), the case for a Ministry of Health as stated in the House of Lords on July 17th by Lord Willoughby de Broke, and accepted by that House.

Lord Willoughby de Broke's resolution was :— "That this House urges His Majesty's Government to introduce at an early date a Bill to constitute a Ministry of Health."

In his foreword to the Leaflet Lord Willoughby de Broke says that the resolution was accepted by Lord Peel on behalf of the Government, and passed by the House of Lords without a dissentient. He continues :—

In its unanimous desire to create a Ministry of Health, the House of Lords is fortified by the large mass of enlightened public opinion. There is one voice that must be heard above all. The formation of a Ministry of Health in this country had long been the nearest project to the heart of Lord Rhondda. He has told us that the Prime Minister was heart and soul in favour of the movement. Had he lived, Lord Rhondda was to have introduced the Bill in the House of Lords.

The revision of the draft, after much postponement, has been completed, but Parliament has risen and the Bill has not been introduced; nor has Mr. Bonar Law mentioned it as part of the business after the adjournment. No one who wishes to see a Ministry of Health created will be wise to relax the utmost efforts until the Bill is introduced and passed. The chief difficulty is the adjustment of departmental authority. It may be natural that those who take pride in duties long and faithfully performed should be reluctant to abandon them to others. There may even be a legitimate rivalry between Departments for the honour of being associated with the Ministry of Health. But all this will surely give way to something more important. The true servant of the public will be the first to agree that the pathway of knowledge should not be barred by an entanglement of Red Tape.

The War has taught us that science has been given too low a place in the service of the State. It is hoped that this Bill will promote Medical Science and skill to the high places of responsibility and power, so that they may direct and prosper the most important aspect of National Welfare.

A CONFERENCE.

A Conference convened by the National Baby Week Council will be held on Wednesday, September 18th, at 5 p.m., at Bedford College, York Gate, Regent's Park, N.W., the chief object of which will be to provide speakers in the Autumn Campaign with the arguments for, and the possible solution of, the problems involved in the creation of a Ministry of Health. Amongst them, of course, the work of midwives finds place.

DEATHS OF INFANTS IN REGISTERED HOMES.

The fact that four infants have died in the course of a week at a home registered under the London County Council, in Courthill-road, Lewisham, was mentioned at Lewisham, on Saturday, when an inquest was held on the body of one of them, Bertha Pawfey, aged three weeks, the daughter of a parlourmaid.

Mr. H. R. Oswald, the coroner, said the death had apparently resulted from enteritis, but the cause of the trouble being uncertain, the people keeping the home were anxious for a public inquiry.

It was stated in evidence that on August 29th the baby was suddenly seized with sickness and died on September 3. She had been fed on milk and barley water like the other children.

Mrs. Johnson, certified midwife, who keeps the home, said the home was registered under the London County Council. Three children, she stated, including Bertha Pawfey, died after sickness, and another, two months old, from convulsions. There were five other children in the home, but they were not affected.

The coroner asked if there were many flies about, and witness replied. "We are rather bothered with flies, but I take special care that the milk is not contaminated by them."

Dr. R. V. Donnellan, police divisional surgeon, who made a post-mortem examination, attributed death to syncope following acute diarrhœa. He said at this time of year very rapid changes took place in the condition of milk, and although it might be sterilised and taste sweet it was difficult sometimes to detect mischief in it. If it were all curdled it would set up trouble in a very young infant. It might be that an unlucky consignment or two of milk had caused the trouble in the home.

Dr. I. P. Kelly, of Lee, corroborated Dr. Donnellan's evidence. He added that he had attended the children in the home, and when the second one died had sent the sample of the milk to the public analyst, but had not yet received his report on it.

The jury returned a verdict of death from natural causes.

Well deserved sentences of twelve months' and four months' imprisonment in the second division, were passed at Wood Green on Monday on James Ellsnore and Alice Hanley, alias Benson and Stanton of Westbury Avenue, Wood Green, who pleaded guilty to advertising for babies for adoption for a sum of money, and then readvertising them for other people to adopt for a smaller sum. In one case £45 was received with a baby, and on the same day it was surrendered for £15. In sentencing the prisoners, Mr. Biron described the fraud as most heartless and cruel.

THE
BRITISH JOURNAL OF NURSING
WITH WHICH IS INCORPORATED
THE NURSING RECORD
EDITED BY MRS BEDFORD FENWICK

No. 1,590.　　　　SATURDAY, SEPTEMBER 21, 1918.　　　　Vol. LXI.

EDITORIAL.

NURSES IN THE LAW COURTS.

The fact that twice within the last fourteen months trained nurses, or women assuming to be trained nurses, have been tried at the Old Bailey on a charge of murder affords evidence to the public, if evidence is needed, of the peril to which it is subjected through the lack of any system of State Registration of Nurses.

In the first of the cases referred to the capital charge was withdrawn by the Crown, but the women were sentenced to terms of imprisonment for offences committed under circumstances which demonstrated their unfitness for the responsibilities of trained nurses. In the most recent case, that of Eva Grace Thompson, indicted on September 13th, before Mr. Justice Darling, for the murder of two children at the Sydenham Welfare Centre, and with causing grievous bodily harm to two others, the prisoner was found guilty, but insane at the time, so as not to be accountable for her act. She was therefore ordered to be detained until his Majesty's pleasure be known, which, the Judge pointed out, meant detention as a criminal lunatic, and added that there was not the slightest doubt that she had brought herself to that pass by the continued taking of drugs, or that she had fractured the skull of one baby and killed the second. One of the best results of that inquiry would be to show a large number of people the state and the position to which they could bring themselves by drug-taking.

The case is specially important, because the victims of this drug maniac were helpless infants, and in view of the fact of the great increase in the number of institutions for the treatment and care of infants, a number which will certainly be augmented when a Ministry of Health is set up, it is most essential that the records of nurses to whom their care is entrusted should be readily available. Had an efficient system of State Registration of Nurses been in force, is it credible that a drug-maniac, with homicidal impulses, would have been able, with ease, to obtain employment in sole and responsible charge at night of a ward of sick babies?

So far as the published reports of the trial go, the police did not produce evidence of the professional training of the prisoner, but a police officer did state that he had received a report that from 1909 to 1912 she was in a home suffering from the result of drug taking. In the case of a registered nurse such an episode in her career would certainly be known. Moreover, the State Register, and the Official Directory based upon that Register, would be available to employers, and would also be at the disposal of every police court in the Kingdom as are the Medical Register and the Midwives Roll. We wonder how many sick people have been victimised by this criminal before her murderous mania brought her within the arm of the law. We understand that she was trained at a provincial fever hospital, and also for two years in a London hospital, the certificate of which she does not hold.

If public authorities in the near future are, as seems likely, to be increasingly responsible for the treatment and care of helpless infants and young children, public safeguards must be provided as to the competence and trustworthiness of the nurses in whose care, and at whose mercy, they are placed, and the foundation of such safeguards is the passage of the Nurses' Bill for their State Registration—opposed so bitterly and long by the Governors of Training Schools for Nurses.

OUR PRIZE COMPETITION.

WHAT IS THE FUNCTION OF THE BLOOD? WHY MAY HÆMORRHAGE CAUSE DEATH?

We have pleasure in awarding the prize this week to Miss J. G. Gilchrist, Gillespie Crescent, Edinburgh.

PRIZE PAPER.

The function of the blood is of a twofold nature—*i.e.*, absorption and distribution : (*a*) the absorption of oxygen necessary to the life or vital power of the body; (*b*) the absorption of nourishment derived from food materials for the growth and repair of the tissues of the body. This process of absorption has also the dual capacity of conveying to the tissues the material necessary for repairing the waste engendered by the work done by them, and removing from them the waste products caused by their activity. This balance of absorption and distribution is brought about by the circulation of the blood throughout the body through the medium of the heart and blood vessels, the complete circuit being made by the action of the heart sending the blood through the arteries to all parts of the body, and returning it to the heart through the veins, the connecting link between the arteries and veins being the capillaries, extremely minute vessels linking the smallest arteries to the commencement of the veins, and enabling the exchange of waste and repair products to take place. This process of absorption, or "osmosis," as it is technically called, also furnishes the various glands with the special secretions necessary to their particular functions, the relative lymphatic system collecting and storing up the surplus nourishment, to be gradually re-introduced into the blood stream by way of the thoracic duct. By the circulation also fluid (water) and heat is distributed equally throughout the body. The blood, if in a healthy condition, contains immune bodies, and the white corpuscles, called leucocytes and phagocytes, have the power of protecting the body from disease, and, when such is present, of combining in large numbers to attack and overcome the morbid processes brought about by foreign elements. The natural power of the blood to coagulate, to form a clot at the end of an injured blood vessel on exposure to air, is another function which protects the body from the possibly fatal results of hæmorrhage. In exceptional cases, known as "bleeders"—*i.e.*, persons having the hæmorrhagic diathesis or suffering from hemophilia—this protective power of coagulation is not present to a sufficient degree to arrest hæmorrhage, so that they bleed easily, even a very small wound making a fatal result possible.

The importance of hygienic living if the blood is to perform its function satisfactorily cannot be over-estimated, especially in regard to the allied systems of respiration and digestion; the necessity of breathing continuously fresh air, in the former, and of choosing a mixed diet, containing the elements of food which can be converted into nourishment in a simple form capable of assimilation through the blood stream, in the latter.

Hæmorrhage may cause death by actual failure of blood pressure and exhaustion of the nervous system. Thus serious hæmorrhage is treated by infusion or transfusion of a fluid, such as saline solution, to keep up the rush of fluid through the blood vessels, and so keep the heart beating. There are three kinds of hæmorrhage, each having a peculiar danger. Such are (1) arterial, (2) venous, (3) capillary.

(1) Arterial hæmorrhage is usually the result of a wound; the blood spurts out in jerks, and is scarlet in colour. The danger lies in the rapidity and violent nature of the hæmorrhagic attack. The force of the blood from the heart hinders the formation of clotting, so that direct pressure of the artery concerned against a bone between the heart and the bleeding part, and treatment is essential. It should also be remembered that the natural process of arresting bleeding is in this case that the heart beats less strongly after a time, which produces fainting. Therefore it is unwise to give stimulants, as such will cause the blood to flow again with increased force; rather employ cold, pressure and raised position.

(2) Venous hæmorrhage flows in a steady stream, is dark purple in colour. It may result from ulcer in the leg or varicose veins, when it is difficult to control, owing to the damaged vessels. The quantity lost may bring about heart failure, especially as it is usually unaccompanied by pain.

(3) Capillary hæmorrhage may be dangerous on account of the prolonged time the oozing of blood may last and the amount of blood lost. It may occur in ulcerated surface, such as cancer in the late stages, when the tissues have become softened. Capillary or oozing hæmorrhage is best treated by the application of ice with pressure.

HONOURABLE MENTION.

The following competitors receive honourable mention :—Miss Alice M. Burns, Miss R. E. S. Cox, Miss Clive M. Balderstone, Mrs. J. Gotlob, Miss J. Robinson.

NURSING AND THE WAR.

The King held an Investiture in the Quadrangle of Buckingham Palace on September 11th, when His Majesty conferred decorations as follows :—

ROYAL RED CROSS.

FIRST CLASS.

Queen Alexandra's Imperial Military Nursing Service.—Matron KATE ROSCOE, Sister HELEN DEY.

Territorial Force Nursing Service.—Matron SARAH COCKRELL, Sister JESSIE CARDOZO.

SECOND CLASS.

Queen Alexandra's Imperial Military Nursing Service.—Sister DORA GRAYSON.

Queen Alexandra's Imperial Military Nursing Service Reserve.—Sister LILY JENKINS and Sister MARY WEDDERSPOON.

Queen Alexandra's Imperial Military Nursing Service for India.—Matron MARION KNAPP.

Territorial Force Nursing Service.—Sister ANNIE GIBBINS.

Civil Nursing Service.—Matron ANNIE RASTALL, Assistant Matron EDITH COCKERAM, and Assistant Matron JEAN DUMBLE.

British Red Cross Society.—Sister LILY GRIFFITHS and Sister RUTH NICHOLAS.

Voluntary Aid Detachment.—Miss BERTHA CATTELL, Miss MAUDE EPPS, and Miss ELIZABETH SINCLAIR-WHITE.

Canadian Army Nursing Service.—Sister GWENDOLEN SPALDING.

THE MILITARY MEDAL.

Territorial Force Nursing Service.—Sister WINIFRED HAWKINS.

The King has awarded the Royal Red Cross, 2nd Class, to Miss Letitia Reeves, Australian Auxiliary Hospital, Welwyn, for valuable nursing services in the war.

Recently in a crowded motor-bus two wounded soldiers rose politely from their seats to offer them to two women, one in nursing uniform, who promptly took the place without even a word of thanks. The other, an elderly woman, exclaimed " No, not the seat of a man in blue. We ought to stand for you." We should have supposed that the nurse was merely one of the many women who don our uniform without the right to wear it ; but alas ! her uniform was that of the Territorial Force Nursing Service.

The headquarters of the American Red Cross has received from Havre an announcement that the Queen of the Belgians will apply a part of the gift of 1,000,000 fr. recently made to her by the American Red Cross, to the payment of the " household expenses " of a rest home for Belgian nurses, which Her Majesty will open at Cannes. It will be in the famous " Villa Henri IV," and the Queen has named it the " Royal Elisabeth Club." The fresh air and sunshine of the Côte d'Azur afford ideal surroundings for convalescing to wounded and overworked nurses.

An Army Order just issued states that the conditions governing the award of the Silver War Badge to disabled men (including officers) have been amended. Under the new conditions the Badge, subject to the consent of the Army Council, will be issued to the undermentioned persons (amongst others) who have served with the military forces subsequent to August 4th, 1914 :—

Female nurses and members of Voluntary Aid Detachments and Queen Mary's Army Auxiliary Corps who have been discharged or have relinquished their duties on account of physical disabilities, such as would render them permanently unfit for further service in their respective corps.

A friend writes from Paris : " Everything here is for the Americans. They are spending tons of money, and so well. Fancy, I have a little friend from the U.S.A. here in the Y.M.C.A. Bureau ; she has 600 francs a month for expenses The volunteer Red Cross Workers get 750 francs a month for expenses. No salaries ! None of them possess very extensive Continental experience.

" The American Red Cross are now calling upon the V.A.D. Department for workers in their hospitals in this country, as, owing to transport difficulties, it is impossible to bring the required number of workers from the United States. We wonder if they are to be paid at the same rate as in France ; for, if so, there will be an economic upheaval at Devonshire House. The high prices paid to American women working in France have caused a sense of alarm amongst those who fear this liberal recognition may be demanded by French women. In our opinion, anything which sweeps away the old miserable sweated rates for which European women were expected to work before the war will be a boon and a blessing ; and the first step to a higher moral standard of living throughout the community."

A contingent of Japanese nurses has been sent to Vladivostock by the Japanese Chapter of the American Red Cross.

FRENCH FLAG NURSING CORPS.

Miss Haswell and the Sisters have presented to Miss Grace Ellison a very charming handbag in green morocco and fitted with gold, accompanied by the following letter :—

" Miss Haswell and the Sisters of the F.F.N.C. beg Miss Ellison to accept the accompanying gift as a small token of their recognition and gratitude for all she has done for them. They regret extremely that her health compels her to withdraw from the active work of the corps, and they wish her a speedy recovery."

Naturally, Miss Ellison is deeply gratified by this mark of affection from her fellow workers.

THE ODYSSEY OF FRANCESCA.

PART I.

Francesca left Rome one night for a certain Italian port on her way to the Near East. Her manner of arriving at the port was a strange one, for she was promptly put under arrest and forbidden to leave the station. Some little cabalistic sign which should have been on her passport was missing, and the Italian authorities let loose vials of wrath on Francesca's innocent head. She was not perturbed—she felt no responsibility for that document. Had she not sat for hours at 83, Pall Mall waiting for that magic book in the chaste dark blue binding, which had been viséd by the Consul of nearly every country in Europe ? And had not the Powers that Be assured her that all was in order ? So she sat peacefully all day in the R.T.O.'s office (which was an empty railway van) and read the new book of Georgian verse, and lo ! by the evening all was well, and Francesca free to depart on her way.

Her destination for the next few days was a certain camp on the coast some miles away, and she went down to the quay and embarked on someone's picket boat to get there.

It was just getting dusk, and so warm and still one could not have believed it was December. As Francesca left the quay the sun was setting over the harbour and the sky was all afire with apricot colour and rose and gold. The sea was the deepest sapphire blue until it met the sky, and then it glowed with the reflection from it like the heart of a flame. Soon the sky faded into a warm velvety darkness powdered with stars. There were no lights anywhere, and the only sound to be heard was the throb, throb of the engine as the little picket boat made her way through the water. It almost seemed as though they were alone on the sea. They went on and on and Francesca began to experience that queer, uncanny sensation that one gets when one goes to an unknown destination at night. Presently they came to a tiny jetty and stopped. Francesca was landed, and began to climb a precipitous hill, stumbling along in the dark as best she could, not knowing where she was going. A sailor followed behind carrying her luggage. Ten minutes' walk brought her to the British Hospital Camp, where she was to stay, and the first sight of this prosaic institution dispelled at once all mystic dreams and visions. A long baraque with 28 beds all in a row and no other furniture save two iron camp washstands is enough to quench any romance. And, alas ! there were 27 other unknown females sharing this chaste retreat. Army Sisters are sometimes haughty and look down their noses at members of other units who are not of the elect as they, but those particular ones were very nice to Francesca and she enjoyed her sojourn with the British Army.

On the third morning a signal message came to say that Francesca was to be on the —— Wharf in half an hour's time, when a boat would convey her to a certain French transport which, in its turn, would take her to a certain Greek port. Francesca made her adieux, and presently the little boat pulled out and took her off to a great grey troopship which was lying outside, surrounded by her escort. She was crowded with French troops, mostly permissionaires returning to their units, and they were busy in trying on, with loud guffaws of laughter, the enormous life belts which had to be worn throughout the voyage. There were only eight officers on board—six French and two English. It is not permitted to describe how the ship was escorted, or where she went, but on the second morning Francesca found herself at anchor between the island of Corfu and the coast of Albania. No one was allowed to land, which was a great affliction. There was nothing to do on board but to eat, and this particular ship only rose to two meals a day—luncheon at 10.30 and dinner at 6.30—so however long they were spun out there were long gaps of time in between. Francesca would have been quite happy, but men are such restless beings that they probably infected her.

About 9.30 she was sitting on deck, watching the doings of the variegated crowd below, when a sailor brought a cow on to the lower deck. Francesca innocently thought they were going to milk it, and was not at all prepared for what followed. A blow, the flash of a knife, and the poor cow was no more. Some of the poilus standing round were also taken by surprise and were spattered with gore from head to foot.

Luncheon followed quickly on this sacrifice, but Francesca could not bring herself to look at the beefsteaks which had been walking about on deck an hour before. This ceremony was repeated every morning, but Francesca took care to be out of the way at that hour afterwards. The ship sailed away in a golden sunset mist, and the next morning found them again at anchor in a secluded little bay close to a rocky forbidding coast. A ship is like a village for rumours, and an interesting one spread quickly round that there was a submarine waiting outside, and that it might be a week before they could go on. So after lunch they settled down to a bridge party in the saloon, when suddenly they started, and presently were zig-zagging down the Gulf of Corinth. So much for rumours !

Francesca thought it incredibly beautiful. The coast-line, stretching away into space, could be seen on both sides. Far to the south the peaks of dream-like unsubstantial mountains caught the last rose rays of the setting sun. The sea was a deep ultramarine blue, just flecked with white, and there were fishing boats about, with russet sails and Greek sailors singing melancholy songs in the bows.

Just as it grew dark the ship approached the nameless port that was their destination, and Francesca was delighted to see a motor-boat at once skim out to meet them. It turned out to be for Lieut. X——, but he most nobly persuaded the captain to allow Francesca to go ashore with him, or she would have had to wait till the morning.

It is difficult to describe the thrill Francesca had when she first touched Greek soil. She did it quite consciously, putting down first her right and then her left foot, and saying to herself: " Now I am in *Greece*." It was quite dark then and she waited a long time alone on the quay while Lieut. X—— went to find the landing officer. The darkness and loneliness gave her a feeling of mystery which added to the joy of it. How she wished she hadn't forgotten all the little Greek history she ever knew. The very names of the places excited her beyond measure ; she seemed to taste them and turn them over on her tongue and enjoy their flavour. Friends seemed to spring up by magic at this place, which shall be nameless, and a kindly doctor whisked Francesca off to an empty cottage—which was available

CARE OF THE WOUNDED.

A regimental badge souvenir, embroidered by crippled South Africans at Richmond Park Hospital, has been accepted by Princess Mary, who sent a most appreciative letter of thanks to the givers.

———

No class of sufferers in this war require more skilled and tender treatment and care than those suffering from shell-shock. In our illustration is shown a group of convalescing shell-shock patients at the Seale Hayne hospital helping their nurse to gather in the beans for the day's supply.

———

What we enjoy about the Americans is their creative faculty, and whilst other nations go jogging on, or what they call " muddling through,"

SOLDIER PATIENTS WHO ARE RECOVERING FROM SHELL-SHOCK AT SEALE HAYNE
MILITARY HOSPITAL HELP A NURSE TO GATHER BEANS IN THEIR OWN GROUNDS.

for such waifs and strays—to spend the night. A fat, smiling British orderly turned up, made up a bed and produced bread, sardines and much strong tea for an evening meal.

And from her bed the next morning Francesca watched the sun rise over the peaks of Mount Parnassus. V. T.

(To be continued.)

———

The Ministry of Pensions has now decided to extend the benefits of the Country Host Institution for the treatment of war neuroses or of " shell shock," to pensioners in all areas of the United Kingdom. The success of the scheme, which originated in a letter to the *Times* about a year ago, is further shown by the fact that the Director-General of the Medical Department of the Navy approved of it some three months ago for undischarged naval ratings suffering from war neuroses.

the American evolves a good idea and puts it into practice. Quite simple things are often of immense value, especially in times of war. For instance, one difficulty of the walking wounded at the front is to determine the direction or location of the nearest first-aid station. The American Red Cross is furnishing to the American Army several thousand small cloth signs, the distribution of which will follow the advance of every American attack. Red Cross men, stretcher-bearers, and runners will carry them, and they will be tacked on trees and posts, or on the ground in the wake of the advancing men. The markers are of white cloth with a large Red Cross at one end and a red arrow at the other to indicate the direction. The American Red Cross has been told by Army officers that these markers will save untold suffering and even the lives of some men, as the seriousness of any wound depends largely upon the promptness with which it receives attention.

Royal British Nurses' Association.

(Incorporated by   Royal Charter.)

THIS SUPPLEMENT BEING THE OFFICIAL ORGAN OF THE CORPORATION.

THE HOUSEKEEPER'S DEPARTMENT AS A SPHERE FOR SPECIALISATION.

By Agnes Pavey, M.R.B.N.A.

Much has been written lately on the subject of what should or should not be included in the curriculum of a training school for nurses, in order that the instruction given in all branches shall be productive of the best possible results, and that the nurses may be fully equipped for appointments for which they may compete in the future. The career of a nurse should always receive a certain amount of consideration both from herself and those responsible for her training, so that the ever-widening scope for her abilities may be duly recognised and provided for.

Many of our leading hospital schools have, in recent years, given to suitable nurses, during the last year of training, a three months' course of work and instruction in the pathological laboratories or in some other department, not directly connected with nursing work, thereby stimulating an interest in some special branch of work which may prove of incalculable value to the nurse in the future. To the nurse who possesses a faculty for organisation perhaps the least help is given. She will probably become a ward sister and reach her zenith in training probationers, and perhaps she, more than anyone else, will influence the ideals and attainments of those who pass through her ward. All of us cherish memories of some Sister, all honour to her, who by her sweetness enabled us to retain our early ideals, and whose sterner qualities helped to develop an appreciation of the value of efficiency, method, and discipline. But what of the Sister herself? One hears much of the inadequacy of the remuneration paid to a Sister of a hospital ward, and the impossibility of providing for old age or a premature breakdown while " passing rich " on a salary of £40 a year. Be she the most devoted and altruistic of Sisters, it is still prob-

able that she must consider her financial position, and very often she is forced to the decision that she must seek another and a better post, and the one she is most likely to aspire to is a matronship. It is on arriving at this conclusion that she begins to realise her limitations, and there is perhaps no subject upon which she is so profoundly ignorant as hospital housekeeping and the management and training of a domestic staff. Yet to all who desire to attain to the higher posts in the profession such knowledge and experience is indispensable. How is the difficulty to be met and overcome? There are several hospitals in London where pupil housekeepers are received for a course of three or four months' training, but their number could be counted on the fingers of one hand, and the majority take only one pupil at a time. Yet where could one expect to learn better the administrative work of a hospital than in the administrative department itself? Why, therefore, should nurses not be allowed to have a certain amount of training there? It would tend to enlarge the scope of the profession, and would open up many administrative appointments, quite outside the hospitals, to nurses.

For the first week or two in the new department the nurse would probably do little more than weigh and give out stores, copy menus, and record tradesmen's deliveries. This, with all the bookkeeping involved, and the work of issuing from different departments foodstuffs, surgical stores, hardware, cleaning materials, &c., would be as much as she would grasp thoroughly at first. Later she could take a part in the management of servants, and success in this direction is sometimes only gained after long striving and many mistakes. Often it requires almost superhuman tact in these days to ensure the smooth working of the domestic machinery, and yet the most troublesome maid will often work the best when rightly handled, for it is frequently the one who has most character, energy, and latent possibility of better things who is the most hard to manage.

Towards the end of the course the nurse might be allowed to arrange all the menus and reckon out the cost per head. This involves considerable work and thought, for there are so many sections to be catered for—patients, doctors, the matron, sisters, day and night nurses, secretaries, and clerks, and sometimes a private staff.

The keeping of the various official books and accounts, and preparing reports, based on those, for the finance committees, would prove very valuable experience, and many nurses would welcome, as a part of their training, such a course of hospital housekeeping.

A USEFUL ASSOCIATION.

Princess Christian and the Duke of Connaught were patrons of the very successful carnival and fête held in the gardens of Belgrave Square on Saturday last, in aid of the Belgravia War Hospital Supply Depot, of which Her Royal Highness is President.

PRINCESS CHRISTIAN SETTLEMENT HOME.

A room is now available for one of the retired Members of the Association at the Princess Christian Settlement Home. Nurses who may decide to make application for this vacant room should write to the Secretary for the official printed form, which should be filled in and returned. A copy of the rules and other particulars will be supplied with this form.

APPOINTMENTS.

Miss Mary M. Smith, M.R.B.N.A., has been appointed Sister at Lagos Hospital, Southern Algeria. She was trained at Crumpsall Infirmary, Manchester.

Miss Elizabeth Todd, M.R.B.N.A., has been appointed Sister-in-Charge of the Military Hospital, Aylesbury; and Miss Bridget Weever, M.R.B.N.A., as Sister at the Military Hospital, Endell Street.

DONATIONS.

The Honorary Treasurer of the Corporation acknowledges with thanks a donation from the following :—

To the General Purposes Fund.—Miss Beatrice Kent, £1.

CORRESPONDENCE.

Whilst welcoming communications from its Members the Corporation does not hold itself responsible for individual expressions of opinion.

PROFESSIONAL WRITERS.

To the Secretary, R.B.N.A.

MADAM,—I should like to thank both Miss Atherton and Miss Sinzininex for their very able articles. Both of these ladies I have long known to be "past masters" in their own particular branches, and I am glad that such up-to-date articles do appear in the nurses' own paper—the only journal controlled and written by members of our profession. I hope that more and more we will learn to use the *B.J.N.*, therefore, as a medium for developing the profession of nursing. If I may be permitted to, I should like to ask Miss Atherton one question. Would not such an automatic obedience as her article seems to aim at, tend to stultify the child's ability to reason out points for himself, and prevent him, to a great extent, from acquiring a freewill of his own in the choice of right or wrong ? This is just a point that my interest in the article in question has aroused, and I should be glad to know Miss Atherton's views.

I am, &c.,

M. E. NASH.

THE NATION'S FUND FOR NURSES.

To the Secretary, R.B.N.A.

MADAM,—As a Scottish nurse I should like to protest against the hideous posters that line the London streets. Have the English nurses no spirit, no self respect, that they allow them to remain ? Quite apparently they have less of the sturdy independence of us who live over the border, for, so far, I have seen no such defacements in our Scottish streets. As a member of a great profession, I feel that I can never be indifferent to anything that affects its honour or its prestige, and I feel very strongly that the British Women's Hospital Committee and the College Company are insulting a self-respecting, hardworking body of women, never before regarded as objects for charity. "What does this appeal really mean ?" is a question I often ask myself, but I can find no definite answer to it. Am I myself or any qualified nurse a fitting object for charity ? Believe me, I am not against benevolence for nurses, but any appeal for benevolence should be issued in a proper and dignified way; our supposed poverty and dependence should not be paraded through the advertisement columns of the daily Press and the hoardings of the streets. Such an appeal should be strictly limited to the probable needs of the nurses who are in distress or ill-health. Again, I ask myself, how far does this appeal camouflage for the other object for which it is launched ? In other words, what proportion of the money collected is to go for buildings for the College Company, and what proportion to relieve sick nurses ?

Yours, &c.,

E. KELLY.

APPLICATION FORMS.

Application forms for Registration (5s.), Membership (Annual, 5s.; Life, £2 2s.), and the badge of the Corporation (4s.) can be obtained from the office of the Association, 10, Orchard Street, Portman Square, W. 1.

(Signed) ISABEL MACDONALD,

Secretary.

THE COLLEGE OF NURSING, LTD., AND THE EXAMINATION OF NURSES.

(*Concluded from page 170.*)

The following letters have been received by the Hon. Secretary of the Society for the State Registration of Trained Nurses in reply to the letter which we published last week enquiring whether the examination of nurses in the training schools concerned would in future be conducted by the College of Nursing, Ltd., which claims disciplinary powers over its members under a very autocratic constitution.

PROVINCES.

MR. A. H. LANEY, General Hospital, Birmingham.

" I have discussed your letter of the 16th inst. with Matron, and find that the rumour is without foundation so far as this hospital is concerned."

MR. HARRY JOHNSON, Royal Infirmary, Leicester.

" I have received your letter of the 9th inst., and beg to inform you that no suggestion has been made to the Board of Governors of this Institution for any alteration in connection with the examinations for Probationary Nurses on the staff of this Institution."

MR. FRANK G. HAZELL, Manchester Royal Infirmary.

" I am in receipt of your letter of the 9th inst., for which I thank you. I regret I have no information to afford you relative to the subject matter of your letter."

It will be remembered that the curt refusal by Mr. Frank Hazell, of the Royal Infirmary, Manchester, to afford any information on this matter of public importance was criticised on a previous occasion.

MR. C. AMASON, Royal Sussex County Hospital, Brighton.

" I am directed by the Board of Management to acknowledge receipt of your letter of May 9th in reference to the training of Nurses."

MR. J. G. HOWITT, Cumberland Infirmary, Carlisle.

" I am in receipt of your circular letter of the 9th inst. in regard to the examination of Probationary Nurses by the College of Nursing, Ltd., and in reply have to inform you that as far as this Infirmary is concerned no arrangements have been made. We are at the present time continuing the teaching and examination of our Probationary Nurses as formerly."

MR. SAMUEL COLE, Royal Devon and Exeter Infirmary.

" I am duly in receipt of your circular letter dated 9th inst., and in reply to your enquiry the rumour that Nurses not yet qualified for their certificates will have to be examined by the College of Nursing, Ltd., is incorrect as far as it applies to the Probationers at the Royal Devon and Exeter Hospital."

MR. FRANK INCH, Norfolk and Norwich Hospital, Norwich.

" In reply to your circular letter of the 9th inst., I beg to inform you that I have no knowledge of the rumour that in future the examination of Nurses who have not yet qualified at this Hospital for their certificates will be conducted by the College of Nursing, Ltd."

MR. FREDK. NEDEN, The County Hospital, York.

" In reply to your letter of the 9th inst., the report to which you refer has not reached us.

" The examination of our Probationers is undertaken by members of our Honorary Medical Staff and by a Matron of another Hospital, who visits the Hospital for the purpose, and there is no present intention of making a change."

MR. R. ORDE, Royal Victoria Infirmary, Newcastle-on-Tyne.

" I beg to acknowledge the receipt of your letter of May 9th, and in reply to inform you that we have no information on the subject referred to."

WALES.

MR. LEONARD D. REA, F.C.I.S., King Edward VII's Hospital, Cardiff :—

" In reply to your letter of 9th inst., I am able to assure you that the rumour is not correct, so far as applying to the probationers in this Hospital."

SCOTLAND.

MR. R. MORRISON SMITH, C.A., Glasgow Royal Infirmary :—

" I have received your letter of 13th inst., and in reply have to say that it is not contemplated in the meantime to make any change in our training or examination of nurses."

MR. J. MATHESON JOHNSTON, Western Infirmary of Glasgow :—

" I have to acknowledge receipt of your letter of 13th inst. At the Western Infirmary we have no knowledge of the rumour to which you refer."

MR. A. SCOTT FINNIE, Royal Infirmary, Aberdeen :—

" I have received your circular letter, dated 13th inst., with reference to the examination of nurses. As this is a matter coming within the Matron's department, I have sent the communication to her."

MISS E. EDMONDSON, Acting Superintendent, Royal Infirmary, Aberdeen :—

" In reference to your letter of the 13th inst., which has been forwarded to me, I beg to inform you that no definite communication has been received by the Board of Directors of the Aberdeen Royal Infirmary from the College of Nursing. I do not think the rumours which you mention are worth attention, as such examinations would only be compulsory for those who wish to become members of the College. The confidence of the trained nurses in the College is clearly seen by the large number of members at the present time "

MR. G. B. BROUGH, Royal Infirmary, Dundee :—

" No alteration is in contemplation on the existing arrangement by which the Dundee Royal Infirmary continues to grant certificates signed by the Hospital authorities to nurses who have satisfactorily completed their course of three years' training."

IRELAND.

MR. E. B. ARMSTRONG, Royal City of Dublin Hospital :

" In reply to your letter of the 13th inst., I beg to say that as far as this hospital is concerned, the rumour that in future nurses' examinations will be conducted by the College of Nursing, Ltd., and not by our own training school is unfounded and inaccurate."

MISS M. C. HILL, Matron, Adelaide Hospital, Dublin :—

" In reply to your letter with reference to the qualifying examinations to be held in future for probationers at the Adelaide Hospital, I am directed by the Nursing Committee to inform you that should the Nurses' Registration Bill, drafted by the College of Nursing, Ltd., become law, the probationers at this hospital will enter for examinations conducted by the Statutory Authority set up by that Bill. In the event of the Bill not passing into law, the nurses of this hospital will have the option of entering for the examinations of the College of Nursing, Ltd. The Board of Governors will retain the final qualifying examination of the hospital as at present conducted until such time as they deem it advisable in the interest of the nurses and the public that such examinations should be abrogated."

LIEUT.-COL. DEANE, Royal Victoria Hosp., Belfast :—
" *Re* State Registration of Trained Nurses : In reply to your letter of 13th inst. on the above subject, I beg to inform you that the matter you allude to has not been considered by my Committee, and as I do not know whether the report you have heard is correct or not, I am sorry I cannot give you any information about it."

No replies have been received from the Royal Infirmary, Liverpool ; the Royal Infirmary and the General Hospital, Bristol ; the General Hospital, Nottingham ; the Royal Hants County Hospital, Winchester ; the Royal Devon and Exeter Hospital ; the Royal Infirmary, Edinburgh ; Sir Patrick Dun's Hospital ; the Richmond Hospital ; the Meath Hospital ; and Dr. Steevens' Hospital, Dublin.

The Secretary-Superintendent of the Middlesex Hospital states : " Our nurses' examinations for the Hospital's certificate of training are conducted by the teachers of our own Training School." The enquiry of the Society for the State Registration of Nurses was, however, designed to ascertain the procedure in the future.

When the letter of the Society was sent out in May last, the then draft of the College of Nursing's Registration Bill compelled registered nurses to become members of the College, and to subscribe to its autocratic constitution as a condition of registration.

Some slight modification has been introduced into the seventh draft of its Nurses' Registration Bill, which does not make it compulsory for nurses to become members of the College in order to be registered under the Act, but the Memorandum and Articles of Association of the College are still to remain " in full force and effect."

Our contention is that the examination and registration of Trained Nurses should be conducted by an entirely independent body, under the authority of the State, and not by a Union of persons who train and employ nurses.

UNJUSTIFIABLE PRESSURE.

From all sides we hear of pressure being brought to bear by Matrons upon their young nurses to join the College of Nursing. They are handed application forms and told to fill them in, and, as far as we can gather, the Constitution of the College is never mentioned ; so these inexperienced young nurses sign a form to agree to Rules and Regulations—mainly framed by laymen—which they have never seen.

This unjustifiable pressure is for the second time

being brought to bear upon the members of the Guy's Hospital Nurses' League, to whom a printed letter is being sent, signed by S. A. Swift (past Matron), L. V. Haughton (past Matron), M. Hogg (Matron), and F. A. Sheldon (Lady Superintendent of the Guy's Hospital Nurses' Institution), from which the document is addressed. With the letter are included an Application Form, and Reasons for joining the College, but not a copy of its Constitution.

The gist of the letter is practically a demand upon the part of Guy's officials nominated on to the College Council, that an electorate should be provided amongst the nurses of the League. It is written :—" On the Council of the College, Guy's ought to be well represented amongst other hospitals, and the votes of Guy's nurses are needed to place their representatives there."

It is well known that the extremely autocratic Constitution of the College, which practically suppresses all professional liberty of the nursing profession as a whole, emanated from the reactionary policy of Sir Cooper Perry, the Medical Superintendent, and Miss Sarah Swift, the Matron of Guy's Hospital in 1905, when this Constitution was submitted to the Board of Trade, as suitable for a governing body for free British women, and was defeated by the progressive and conscientious supporters of the State Registration movement.

A special meeting of the College of Nursing, Ltd., to consider the formation of a London Centre, is to be held at the College of Ambulance, 6, Vere Street, on Wednesday, September 25th, at 7 p.m. Let us hope an opportunity will be afforded the members of discussing its constitution, and the Bill for their registration promoted by the College. No such discussion has, so far, been arranged for on these vital matters.

A local centre has been formed at Newcastle-on-Tyne.

APPOINTMENTS.

MATRON.

Cray Valley Hospital, St. Mary Cray.—Miss Jessie D. Milner has been appointed Matron. She was trained at the Hampstead General Hospital and the North-West London Hospital, and has been Sister of the Private Wing in the former institution, Sister at the King George Hospital, Stamford Street, as a member of Q.A.I.M.N.S.R., and Home and Housekeeping Sister at the Hampstead General Hospital.

Elder Cottage Hospital, Govan, Glasgow. — Miss Mary Taylor has been appointed Matron. She was trained at the Royal Infirmary, Edinburgh, and has held an appointment at the Military Hospital, York.

SUPERINTENDENT SISTER.

Queen Mary's Hospital, Carshalton, Surrey.—Mrs. Hilda M. Smerdon (*née* White) has been appointed Superintendent Sister. She was trained at the Evelina Hospital and at King's College Hospital, and has been Theatre and Ward Sister at the former institution and elsewhere.

NURSING ECHOES.

With the next issue Mrs. Bedford Fenwick will have acted as Hon. Editor of THE BRITISH JOURNAL OF NURSING for twenty-five years, so that the professional nurses of this country may have freedom of expression in the press. With three organs at the disposal of their employers, and many newspapers subsidised in opposition to their interests, how valuable such an asset has been will only be realised by a future generation of nurses.

We wonder if committees of district nursing associations have taken into consideration the cost of nurses' shoe leather. In the pre-war days the problem of keeping herself shod, in boots or shoes which were weather resisting, on the small salary she received, was a difficult one to many a district nurse, and now, with deterioration of materials, and prices soaring upwards, it is most acute. Yet, if nurses are to keep in good health, it is imperative that they should be well and comfortably shod, and committees, in arranging war bonuses, and increases of salary, will do well to take the question into consideration.

Strikes are in the air, and the asylums staffs in the London area recently notified the London County Council that unless their demand for an all-round advance of 25s. a week on pre-war wages, and other grievances were redressed, they would hand in their resignations. The women were said to be particularly determined in their attitude. We understand that substantial concessions have been made.

On Saturday the General Purposes Committee of the Metropolitan Asylums Board submitted a report, which was agreed to, dealing with staff petitions for increase of salary.

The first came from the male attendants at Tooting Bec Asylum, asking to be placed on the same scale of remuneration as that adopted for L.C.C. workers. The next was a similar petition from the National Asylum Workers' Union, representing the employees at other asylums of the Board; and the third a petition of the Municipal Employees' Association, representing the staff of the Board at all institutions except asylums, and asking for an increased war bonus, with a flat rate of £1 per week.

The Committee are reconsidering all scales of salaries, and will report to a meeting of the Managers on October 12th. As regards war bonuses, they advise the Managers to adopt an award made by the Conciliation and Arbitration Board for Government employees as applicable to Civil Servants with salaries not exceeding £500 per annum. They recommend that the bonus for the female staff should be at the flat rate of £18 per annum.

The strike of Asylum workers in two of the Lancashire Asylums was settled at the meeting of the Lancashire Asylums Board on Thursday in last week, when the matters in dispute were referred to arbitration.

The attendants and nurses at Prestwich Asylum had left work on Wednesday morning, and in the afternoon the Whittingham employees followed suit. On the Thursday afternoon, following a special meeting of the Asylums Board, which agreed to submit the demands to arbitration, the workers had returned to duty.

The following is a statement of the claims of the Asylum workers :—On January 7th last they made application to the Asylums Board for 5s. a week permanent advance in wages for all attendants and nurses; for a 60 hours' working week; for wages to be paid weekly instead of monthly; to be allowed to put union notices up in the messroom for the benefit of members; for the married staff who are called up to sleep in the asylum to be paid 1s. 6d. per night for doing so; for the outside artisans to be paid within a halfpenny of the district rate per hour; for men who earn the certificate for mental nursing to be paid £2 per year extra; and for the month's wages so far kept in hand to be paid up.

This was replied to in June, when 5s. per week bonus instead of an increase was given, and the month's wages kept in hand was paid up. No other concession was made.

At the present time (it is stated) the working hours average 72 per week. The staff is prepared to work overtime if necessary, provided overtime pay is forthcoming. The current wages worked out at about 6½d. to 6¾d. per hour for men, and 2d. to 3d. less for women.

On August 9th the original application was renewed, and the Asylums Board was given a 14 days' ultimatum. The reply to this was that the matter would be considered at the next meeting of the Finance Committee. This was not satisfactory to the Asylum union officials, as the Committee only meet quarterly, and about five months had elapsed between the application being made and the first reply.

Accordingly the strike began. The safety of the patients was seen to by a minimum staff being left on duty. The number of hours was said to be the greatest difficulty, as it happened not infrequently that men and women were kept on duty from 6 a.m. to 10 p.m., with 1¾ hours off for meals.

No complaint was made against the officials of the asylums; the whole of the workers' troubles were with the Board.

The Lancashire Asylums Board met in Committee last week at the County Offices, Preston, when Mr. Shaw, General Secretary of the National Union of Asylum Workers, was called in, and stated that the minimum on which his members would return to their duties was the acceptance by the Board of arbitration.

The Chairman, Sir Norval W. Helme, M.P., said that until the 9th of August, when the letter from the Union was received, the Board was not aware of any such feeling as unfortunately existed and had been developing amongst the members of the Union.

The Board had met in Committee, and considered the situation, and having a strong confidence in their own case, were prepared to ask the Board to formally approve a resolution accepting arbitration.

Replying to questions, Mr. Shaw said he was prepared, as far as it was possible for him to do so, to pledge his members to abide by the decision of the arbitrator and to resume their duties at once.

The Board then passed a resolution agreeing to the application of the National Union of Asylum Workers being referred to arbitration, the Ministry of Labour to be requested to appoint an arbitrator.

MEDALS FOR NURSES.

BRADFORD ROYAL INFIRMARY.

On Wednesday, September 11th, the annual interesting occasion of the presentation of medals to successful nurses took place. The Chairman, Mr. George Priestman, gave a short account of the year's work of the Nurse Training School, and said that it was a matter for congratulation that, despite many difficulties, the standard of training had been kept up and the necessary lectures had been given to qualify for the medals.

To obtain the gold medal, a first class must be obtained in each subject, with a percentage of at least 80 for the total number of marks gained. The silver medal is awarded to the candidate who obtains second highest marks. Nurse Kathleen Digney is this year's gold medallist, and Nurse Margaret Waterston was awarded the silver medal.

The Matron, Miss Davies, pointed out that since the re-organisation of the training in 1913 the gold medal had been awarded each year. She considered this very creditable with regard to the circumstances under which the nurses worked at present, and the small amount of time available for study. The best thanks of the nursing staff were due to Dr. West Watson for the able lectures he had given, in spite of the pressure of his professional work.

The Chairman then called upon Alderman Moorhouse to present the medals. Several nurses who had completed their training were also awarded certificates of merit.

ROLL OF HONOUR.

Louisa Charlotte Chamberlain, R.N.N.S.R., accidentally killed at sea, August 10th, 1918. Sister Chamberlain was trained at Bradford Royal Infirmary, where she was doing Sister's duty when called up to join the Naval Nursing Reserve in August, 1914.

OUTSIDE THE GATES.

THE NATIONAL COUNCIL OF WOMEN OF GREAT BRITAIN AND IRELAND.

The Annual Meeting of the National Council of Women of Great Britain and Ireland will be held in Harrogate on October 8th, 9th and 10th, at 10 a.m. and 2.30 p.m., when the Annual Report and Annual Statement of Accounts will be presented, and the Report of the Committee for the Revision of the Constitution. From this report, which has been circulated, we gather that it is proposed that the National Union of Women Workers shall become the National Council of Women of Great Britain and Ireland, and that the Governing Body shall be called the Representative Council of Women.

This Council is to meet annually to receive reports, transact business, and elect the Executive Committee. It is, however, proposed that the Resolutions for the Representative Council shall first be submitted to the Executive, which Committee " shall group the resolutions according to subjects, and shall select or draw up one resolution from each group." If the Governing Body may not discuss what resolutions it chooses without the permission of the Executive it is difficult to understand wherein government consists.

The subjects dealt with by Resolutions at Harrogate will be " Hostels for Mothers and Babies," " Solicitation Laws and the Equal Moral Standard," " Trade Unions," " Equal Pay for Equal Work," " Women on Government Committees," and " Laws of Naturalisation."

BOOK OF THE WEEK.

THE WEDDING GOWN OF "OLE MISS."*

This charming romance of Virginia makes a very wide appeal to the lovers of fiction, and is quite one of the most popular books of the hour.

---

* By Gertrude Griffiths. Skeffington & Son, Ltd., Southampton Street, Strand, W.C. 2. Price 6s.

It is based upon the war between the North and South for the abolition of slavery, and relates how Anna Maria is torn between her love for the South and her lover Drummond, whose conscience obliges him to fight for the North.

But the wedding gown is not directly connected with Anna Mar-ee-ah; it belongs to " Ole Miss " Agatha Talcot, who is holding the plantation in trust for Anna Maria until she comes of age. Her wedding gown was made for her thirty years before, when she was engaged to be married to Judge Standish. The wedding was postponed from one cause and another, but the Judge still remained the devoted admirer of the eccentric woman. " Ole Miss " was adored by her slaves, which gives the key to the fierce opposition to the Northerners on her plantation, although she was very unpopular in Virginia generally. Pansy, the little "handmaid ob Miss Agatha Talcot," is one of the prominent personages of the story.

She was an ingratiating little person, generally found with her ear to the keyhole or curled up in a corner feigning sleep, in order to acquire information, with which she proceeded to play the part of Providence.

Anna Maria threatened summary punishment when she found that Pansy had been spying on her and Drummond in the wood. " The soles of two little brown feet appeared as she fled in response to a furious glance from Anna Maria."

On finding her later under her own bed she dragged her out by the wool. "Pansy," she whispered furiously to the whimpering child, " if you ever tell you saw me to-day speaking to Master Drummond Hastie do you know what I'll do? I'll bang you over the head with my hairbrush as hard as ever I can."

" O lor! No, missy! " gasped Pansy, ashen with terror at this awful threat. " I'll nebber, nebber tell a blessed soul, honest Injun."

All the same, she promptly took herself to " Unk Tate," the seer of visions, and having related graphically the love scenes down his ear trumpet, " He wuz a kissin' her lyk dis," she removed her mouth a second from the trumpet and smacked the air violently by way of demonstration. " And den I heared dem say dee engage, and yo' should have heared how dee laugh at Ole Miss dee laugh and laugh at her."

" Dee laugh at Ole Miss," interrupted Tate angrily. " Dee dare laugh at Ole Miss. Lawk, I lyk to hab heared them. What fo dee laugh at her? "

" Coz she wear a yaller gown and green sunbonnet."

" Ain't green and yaller beautiful colours? " he cried indignantly.

Ole Miss wore her wedding gown after all, for the Judge, like the proverbial worm, turned at last, and threatened to propose to her enemy, Sophia Hastie. So, amid the amused glances of the congregation, Miss Agatha walked up the aisle attired in it, even though it was made in the fashion of thirty years before !

H. H.

LETTERS TO THE EDITOR.

Whilst cordially inviting communications upon all subjects for these columns, we wish it to be distinctly understood that we do not IN ANY WAY hold ourselves responsible for the opinions expressed by our correspondents.

MANY THINGS MAY HAPPEN!

To the Editor of THE BRITISH JOURNAL OF NURSING.

DEAR MADAM,—You will remember that a year ago I consulted you about my nursing career. I had worked for twelve months as a V.A.D., and felt that nursing was my vocation—that I was only learning rough and ready methods, and not really being properly grounded in a Red Cross Hospital, where very little discipline pertained, and as I come of military people, I prefer order.

You advised me to enter a good training school and prepare myself thoroughly for responsible work, and to be ready for service in Q.A.I.M.N.S. if found suitable. This I did, and now where do I come in under this new Instruction (No. 678), just arranged by the Army Council with the Red Cross? It seems to me that I shall be ineligible at the end of four years' first-class training because I have not been a V.A.D. for *two years*, and that all my colleagues to be certificated three years hence are also excluded from service in Q.A.I.M.N.S., as the two years voluntary workers are to have their names on a roll, and so block us out for years to come. What right has an Army Council in wartime to make rules to interfere with free promotion for the best nursing candidates when war conditions have passed? I am told the social influence of the Red Cross Society has managed this job— and it will not be the last, as it is not the first, which has injured the nursing profession through its social influence.

Yours very truly,

DONE BROWN.

[We advise you to devote yourself to your daily work for the benefit of the sick. "After the war" is a large order. Many things will be changed before you are certificated, and once soldiers and nurses have votes, even the War Office will be required to move with the times, and mandarins who draft " Serf Clauses " and other obnoxious Instructions will be swept into Whitehall with other impedimenta. By the by, do you belong to the R.B.N.A., and have you thus proved you are prepared to help yourself and your colleagues by strong united action? If not, join at once, and help to save the independence of the Nursing Profession, in the coming fight for a just Registration Bill.—ED.]

OUR PRIZE COMPETITION.
QUESTIONS.

September 28th.—How would you recognise perforation in a case of enteric fever ? What immediate action would you take, and how could you temporarily relieve the patient ?

October 5th.—How does puerperal septicæmia arise ? Describe the course and management of the disease.

The Midwife.

USEFUL APPLIANCES AT 50, WIGMORE STREET.

Maternity nurses and others interested in child welfare work will find innumerable useful appliances of every description at Messrs. Bell & Croyden's, 50, Wigmore Street. One of the most interesting is the apparatus for sterilising the baby's milk, by means of which ten 8 oz. bottles of milk can be sterilised at one time. The steriliser is easy to manage and by an ingenious arrangement the sealing of the bottles is ensured during the process of cooling so that the milk can be kept in them for days before it is used. By the use of this apparatus, too, the dangers which result for the baby from the over-sterilisation of milk are avoided. The most up-to-date feeding bottles can be procured from this firm and there is a large selection of teats, including that which is now so popular and is known as the Marylebone teat because it was first introduced at the Marylebone Dispensary. It is so designed that only those muscles are brought into play which would be used if the baby were breast-fed, and its form is such that there is little chance of even the most delicate baby becoming tired before it has had the food it requires. Those who contend that malformations in the teeth and gums may owe their origin to a badly-designed teat will admit that the risk is non-existent in the case of this carefully designed teat. The Marylebone Cream, now well known at all infant clinics throughout the country, can be procured from the firm, and this also was first used at the Marylebone Dispensary, having been introduced by Dr. Eric Pritchard. Owing to the ease with which it is digested and absorbed, it forms a valuable constituent in the food of even the youngest infant and should be much used in the nursery in these days when it is becoming increasingly difficult to procure the fats so important to the healthy development of children.

A very ingenious contrivance is that designed by Messrs. Clarke for heating the baby's food in the night. It does away with the necessity for maintaining a fire for this purpose, or for procuring methylated spirit.

It is almost unnecessary to refer to the accouchement outfits to be procured from Messrs. Bell & Croyden, except to emphasise the completeness of their equipment and the thoroughness of their sterilisation and sealing; tins opened after a long period of years have been found to be absolutely sterile. Nurses who obtain their supplies from this firm will, we feel sure, be thoroughly satisfied, particularly as the appliances and dressings easily bear comparison with articles procured from sometimes less reliable sources.

PENS FOR THE LAMBS.

One of the evils of institutional life for infants is, that owing to the lack of an adequate staff of nurses, healthy children often spend a large proportion of their time in their cots. It has been suggested that the high mortality rate of babies in institutions is partly due to the fact that they are cheated out of their fair share of dandling, which is their equivalent to exercise, and thus their livers are not sufficiently stimulated. The Pen should find its place in all institution nurseries when the babies can with safety be placed on mattresses and exercise their limbs to their hearts' content.

Where this plan is in vogue a great improvement will be observed in the health and contentment of the children without any extra labour.

CENTRAL MIDWIVES BOARD (IRELAND).

The Central Midwives Board for Ireland has now been constituted. The names of the appointed members are as follows :—

Appointed by the Local Government Board for Ireland.—E. C. Bigger, M.D., M.S., R.C., Irel.; L.M., K.Q.C.P., Irel.; D.S.M., R.C.P.S., Irel.; Medical Commissioner of the Local Government Board for Ireland.

Appointed by the Local Government Board for Ireland after Consultation with the County Councils and County Borough Councils.—H. T. Warnock, L., L.M., K.Q.C.P., Irel.; F.R.C.S., Irel.; Alderman J. McCarron.

Elected by the Registered Medical Practitioners Resident in Ireland.—Sir A. J. Horne, L.R.C.S., Irel.; F., L.M., K.Q.C.P., Irel. Sir W. J. Smyly, M.D., U. Dub.; L., L.M., K.Q.C.P., Irel.; L.R.C.S., Irel. Sir J. W. Byers, M.D., M.S., Q.U., Irel.; M.R.C.S., Eng.; L.M., K.Q.C.P., Irel.; Hon. M.A.O., R.U., Irel. Professor H. Corby, M.D., M.S., Q.U., Irel.; L.A.H., Dublin.

Appointed by the Local Government Board for Ireland under Section 3 (1) (c).—Miss J. H. Kelly, Matron, Maternity Hospital, Belfast; Mrs. M. Blunden, late Matron, Lying-in Hospital, Cork; Miss A. Michie, Superintendent for Ireland, Queen Victoria's Jubilee Institute for Nurses; Miss G. O'Carroll, Matron, Coombe Lying-in Hospital, Dublin.

Section (3) (1) (c) of the Act provides for the appointment of four women (referred to in the Act as midwives' representatives), of whom three shall be appointed after consultation with recognised nursing associations in Ireland.

After February, 1923, a midwives' representative must be certified midwife under the Act, and previous to that date must hold an approved certificate.

THE BRITISH JOURNAL OF NURSING

WITH WHICH IS INCORPORATED

THE NURSING RECORD

EDITED BY MRS BEDFORD FENWICK

No. 1,591.   SATURDAY, SEPTEMBER 28, 1918.   Vol. LXI.

TWENTY-FIVE YEARS' EDITOR.

THE LONG, LONG TRAIL.

There are milestones in the life of every profession, and soulful movement, where we like to call a halt, in order to take a survey of the past with the view of bracing ourselves to further efforts, and so go forward with increased courage and determination. We, therefore, invite our faithful supporters to look back with us, in imagination, to the year *1893*, for it marks the first milestone in the history of our own professional Journal. THE BRITISH JOURNAL OF NURSING, the only one in the world which is published weekly, which is also owned, controlled and edited by trained Nurses, and has the right, therefore, in this country, to claim to express professional opinion. Those of us who have created and sustained it may be proud of its status.

There can be no organisation without articulation. Realizing this truth, we assumed the Editorship of THE BRITISH JOURNAL OF NURSING (then *The Nursing Record*) in 1893, in order that trained Nurses might have a voice in the Press, without which no profession can be free and independent, or make any progress ; in fact, it is essential to its very *life*. In the year 1887—as is well known to our readers—the minds and hearts of a small group of women were stirred to bring about much needed reforms. We aspired, we laboured, we fought, we founded the British Nurses Association— now a Royal Association Incorporated by Royal Charter, the objects of which are well known.

The victory was gained only at the cost of tremendous and bitter opposition. This experience brought home to us forcibly the essential need of an organ owned and controlled by ourselves, if we were to succeed in the campaign of progress upon which we

had entered. In this connection, we may perhaps, be pardoned for quoting the words of an eminent American Nurse and Author, who has made a study of nursing conditions in this country and others. Speaking of THE BRITISH JOURNAL OF NURSING, she says :— " It rapidly came to be the foremost nursing journal in the world, and is the most complete record in existence of nursing affairs and progress in all countries. Fearless, and of consistent unwavering policy, it has been the advance guard of nursing interests all along the line."

In our survey of twenty-five years, we may reasonably claim that our journal has been a liberal educator ; it has imbued its supporters with professional enthusiasm and community of interests, which has carried the profession forward to a point of progress which it could not have reached without it. While deploring the unfair boycott of our Registration programme by the Public Press (with very few exceptions), it has taught Nurses the full value of an organ of their own.

THE BRITISH JOURNAL OF NURSING has ever been a consistent opponent to every form of injustice. It has fought many battles successfully, alike for the individual and for the profession. Looking down a long vista of achievement, we see with gratification and pardonable pride something of what we owe to our journal. 1. The establishment of our many organised, self-governing Nurses' Societies. 2. The founding of our National Council of Trained Nurses. 3. The founding of our International Council—that great Confraternity of Nurses of many countries. 4. The breaking down of stubborn prejudice, and the conversion of Parliament and the Public to the principle of State Registration and all it stands for— higher and sounder education, the protection of the public and the profession from unfair exploitation, and the freedom of conscience. 5. The defeat of many plots for the destruction of our economic independence.

In conclusion, we earnestly hope that our true and tried friends will lead others to understand and appreciate the benefits of a professional journal, which is free from commercial influence, because :—

"I hold every man a debtor to his Profession; from the which as men of course do seek to receive countenance and profit, so ought they of duty to endeavour themselves by way of amends, to be a help and ornament thereunto."

OUR PRIZE COMPETITION.

HOW WOULD YOU RECOGNISE PERFORATION IN A CASE OF ENTERIC FEVER? WHAT IMMEDIATE ACTION WOULD YOU TAKE AND HOW COULD YOU TEMPORARILY RELIEVE THE PATIENT?

We have pleasure in awarding the prize this week to Miss M. Cullen, Queen Mary's Hospital, Stratford, E.

PRIZE PAPER.

Perforation of the intestine is the most dangerous of all the complications of enteric fever. It most frequently occurs during the third week or a little later.

The onset may be acute. First symptoms consist of sudden sharp pain in the abdomen, with tenderness, hiccough, shivering, and vomiting.

The pain persists more or less continuously. The patient will lie with knees drawn up. The face becomes sunken, and is covered with cold, clammy perspiration.

There may be a rise or fall in the temperature, the pulse becoming rapid and feeble.

The only treatment which affords any chance of recovery is immediate operation; as soon as these symptoms are found to be present it must be reported at once to the doctor, who will decide whether the patient's condition will stand an operation. If so, then the abdomen is opened, and the hole in the intestine sewn up.

What has really happened to cause the peritonitis is that a minute opening will be found in the floor of an ulcer, which has been left after the separation of a slough from a Peyer's patch, and through this opening the contents of the bowel escape into the abdominal cavity and set up this inflammation.

If there is any special reason that the surgeon will not operate, he will probably order opium to check the motions.

The onset of perforation is not always so acute, and the symptoms may not be very marked, especially if the patient should be delirious or unconscious. It is therefore most necessary to observe the patient very closely, and to report immediately to the doctor any signs of abdominal pain and distension.

Meantime, to allay the severe pain, hot fomentations may afford some relief, with a few drops of laudanum sprinkled on. Or a piece of flannel wrung out of boiling water to which turpentine ʒi is added.

If there is much flatulence or distension, a long tube may be passed several inches up into the bowel, thus allowing the flatus to escape.

Treat the patient as for shock if very collapsed; raise the foot of the bed on blocks, apply hot bottles to the extremities. Give nothing by mouth.

Some relief may be afforded by a firm pillow placed under the patient's knees, as he will lie with the knees drawn up. The nurse must try to make him as comfortable as possible, and keep perfectly quiet.

He should not be moved more than absolutely necessary; if the bowels should act, a pad of absorbent wool placed on a mackintosh should be gently placed under him, and changed when needed. He must not be lifted on to a bedpan. Absolute rest must be given him.

In a very good Paper, Miss M. D. Hunter makes several points. She says: Some abdominal alteration will be noticed. There may be distension, or occasionally there is retraction, but in either case there is rigidity and marked tenderness. On palpation the pain is nearly always found to be more noticeable over the right iliac region. There will be immobility of the abdominal muscles during respiration, so that the movements are entirely thoracic. . . . There is sometimes frequent vomiting; often there is resonance instead of liver dulness, owing to the free gas in the peritoneal cavity.

Mrs. Gotlob writes : Diet must be carefully guarded during convalescence, as ulcers may still remain unhealed, and injudicious feeding may cause relapse. There are few conditions in which a patient's life depends so much upon the doctor and nurse.

HONOURABLE MENTION.

The following competitors receive honourable mention :—Miss M. D. Hunter, Mrs. J. Gotlob, Miss M. E. Thorpe, Miss C. L. Taplin, Miss R. E. S. Cox, Miss M. V. E. Davey, and Mrs. M. Farthing.

QUESTION FOR NEXT WEEK.

How does puerperal septicæmia arise? Describe the course and management of the disease.

NURSING AND THE WAR.

Better late than never! After four years of disorganisation, the *Pall Mall Gazette* inserts the following statement :—

" There is, I hear, much need for inquiry into the management of many of the smaller auxiliary hospitals for discharged soldiers throughout the country. The increasing number of these places has necessarily resulted in a serious shortage of really efficient matrons, and women quite unfitted by experience or temperament for such responsibility have been appointed.

* * *

" The very regrettable falling off in the number of voluntary workers in such institutions is also attributed to the treatment meted out to them by inefficient matrons. I have heard patients express the opinion that duly authorised inspectors could obtain much information if they sought for it in the proper quarters."

To be fair, the *Pall Mall Gazette* should have made it quite clear that these " inefficient matrons " are usually untrained women, belonging to the " governing classes " or the wealthy plutocracy. These women have been encouraged by the powers that be to dress themselves in fancy nursing dress, including pearls and pearl powder, and to assume charge of our sick and suffering men. Many of them of the " Dill-Binkie " class have never trained for an hour, and in their jealous self-sufficiency, employ only semi-trained nurses or V.A.D.'s to trifle with the lives of our men. This Society nursing matter is one of the big scandals of the war, and if the *Pall Mall Gazette* can buck up the present Director-General of the Army Medical Department and get him to put his foot down and stop the abuse, it will have done the best bit of war work for our sick and wounded the Press could do. It must begin at the top and clear out the Society clique on the Joint War Committee and its subservient officials " who will have it so."

As a Tommie said to us the other day, " Any old Duchess is considered good enough to mess me about."

Tommie knows the touch of a " Pucca Red Cape." Trust him.

There is no doubt that, when working in a French Military Hospital, being a member of the Roman Catholic Church has its advantages, as the large majority of the patients, their friends, and the staff are members of this Communion, and it is quite natural that such conditions make for harmony. Not that we have ever heard it reported that there has been any interference upon the part of the French authorities with the religion of British nurses. We do know, however, of some British nurses who have become Roman Catholics, and of more than one who has entered a religious community.

A friend writes :—" I have been staying in —— with little B's godmother. Poor child ! I cried bitterly all the way to Paris leaving her there in a dirty, insanitary hole, without a breath of air, just by the Cathedral. I turned up her dress and had a look at her ' undies.' My dear Editor ! that's enough to put anyone off being the Bride of Christ. But she is *so* happy. She is praying hard for the souls of the prostitutes at Woolwich, among whom she worked. They have to be saved. She was permitted to spend a day with me, and to eat with us. It did her a world of good, poor child, to fill her lungs with pure air. What I regret is her wasted training. I told her Confessor so. He was of my opinion, but she chose her own Order. I wish I could believe she was doing good, dear, sweet little Saint, and I hope her prayers for me will make me a less discontented woman."

THE SOB-SISTER.

Mrs. Gertrude Atherton, the famous American authoress, has addressed a warning to her compatriots of how the snivelling Hun will appeal for pity when he no longer possesses power to outrage decency and honour.

Mrs. Atherton says the poor starving children of the Teutonic Empires will be used as a peace weapon, and American mothers will be appealed to in " sweet reasonable voices " by German women in the States to listen to the wails of these darling ones—dying by inches—when peace with a conquered country would save millions of them."

Mrs. Atherton, who holds the German people, their system of Government, their craft, greed and cruelty, in abhorrence, writes : " Beware of the sob-sister appeal to save at any cost the lives of German babies that they may grow to manhood and compel our male babies of to-day to shed their blood in the death struggle of the United States of America."

There are many silly sob-sisters on this side, too.

Also speaking with a woman of gentle birth and apparent personal refinement, we were shocked to hear her say :

" It is a blessing in these days that we have got used to things. In the early days of the war bad news from the front and the sight of the wounded was almost more than one could endure. Nowadays we are all stoics."

A sad day for England if that were true, but it is not.

FRENCH FLAG NURSING CORPS.

Mrs. Bedford Fenwick will interview candidates for the F.F.N.C. on Wednesday, October 2nd, and on Saturday, October 5th, from 2.30 to 4 p.m., at 431, Oxford Street (first floor), London, W.

THE ODYSSEY OF FRANCESCA.

PART II.

(Continued from page 179.)

The next stage of Francesca's journey was by car. She thought it sounded opulent to be touring through Greece in an automobile, even though not a Rolls-Royce but a *very* joggly "tin Lizzie."

Their way led along the flat Crissian plain towards Amphissa. "Solid and heavy" had been the curses pronounced against whomsoever should till this soil by the Amphyctionic Council but now it looked fertile enough with vineyards, groves of cork oak and terraces of silver gnarled olives.

Presently, they began to climb the hill where Delphi lay hidden from profane eyes in the fold of a steep terrace under the stark grey cliffs of Mount Parnassus. Francesca was hoping to wangle time enough to visit the temples but to her bitter disappointment they turned off to the left on a forked road just a few kilometres from Delphi. There were two or three things about which she would have much liked to consult the Delphic Oracle. But the inexorable car went on panting up the steep hair-pin bends of the wonderful new road which in many places is blasted out of the solid rock with a sheer precipice below. Hundreds of peasant women and little girls of about seven years old and upwards were working away at the road. There ought to have been a glorious view from the top of the pass but clouds enveloped them with a clammy hand, on the summit an icy wind stung their faces, and as they went down the other side flakes of snow began to fall and Francesca began to freeze.

Her destination this time was a raw mountain camp knee-deep in mud and slush. Francesca was conducted to an icy leaking tent where she found four other females all in bed. They explained that it was much too cold to do anything else, but it was only two o'clock, so Francesca decided to be superior to these minor discomforts and go for a walk to warm herself. The sleet and the rain and the closing-in of the short winter afternoon soon drove her in again. There were no seats in the tent so she cowered on her bed, covering herself with everything she possessed. But she maintained her self-respect by refusing to *undress*. Those other depraved females had undressed altogether and got into their pyjamas, plus everything else they had with them.

The next day passed, and the next, and the next, and the mud and the snow were churned up ankle deep inside the tent. The cold grew colder, and the snow snew without stopping. Each morning they got up hurriedly, took it in turns to wash at the one tin basin, flew to breakfast and tore back to *bed*, got up reluctantly for lunch and returned triumphantly to *bed*. Got up to dinner and then retired finally for the night.

Habits grew primitive. The lady with the pink nose couldn't powder it any more, having dropped the box of powder into the mud on the floor of the tent, and the other with the lovely bronze hair bundled it up anyhow into a sort of penny bun. Francesca had lost her pocket mirror and couldn't see to do her hair at all, but being short it didn't much matter. Such big emotions as love or war seemed quite unimportant beside the thing that *really* mattered, such as getting one's hot-water bottle filled, or losing one's turn at the basin.

Francesca had lost all hope of ever going on, and had almost settled down to spend the winter there, when one morning, when they were still in bed, the Matron came in waving her permission to proceed. Francesca got up hastily while the other females cursed their luck at her getting off before them, but they were west and she was eastward bound. She fastened up her boots somehow with stiff, shivering fingers, threw her things into the kitbag, bid goodbye to the unhappy occupants of the tent, got into an ambulance, and was trundled away to a station. It was a glorious morning; it had stopped snowing and the sun came out in greeting for the first time in many days. Francesca's spirits went up with a bound.

The train did not start for several hours, as General Sarrail had announced his intention of travelling by it; but at last the great man appeared accompanied by his successor, General Guillemat.

The train presently began to climb, and they crept slowly up the mountain in front of them till they reached the top of the Pass of Thermopylæ, the plain laid out like a contour map far below their feet. Soon darkness came on and Francesca rolled herself in a rug and was about to compose herself to slumber when an officer from the next carriage—with whom she had made friends—marched in triumphantly, bearing a huge charcoal brazier. "Its getting frightfully cold," quoth he, "so I have wangled this for you for the night."

He deposited it on the floor and went away, and why Francesca wasn't burnt to death or suffocated by charcoal fumes, she never knew. The train swayed from side to side, and every now and then some burning embers escaped from the brazier's perforated sides and she had to jump up and stamp them out. As the brazier burnt down, she got very cold and kept lifting up one foot and then the other to thaw it by sitting on it for a while. She dozed off towards morning; and, just as the grey light was beginning to struggle in, the train stopped and she was wakened by her friend putting his head in at the window and saying: "Well, we have arrived in this heavenly spot." It was Salonika at last.

Francesca's first impression of Salonika was a rain-blurred sky, a misty grey sea, an icy wind that nearly cut one in half, noisy trams and streets, and, because it was Christmas Eve, everyone was rushing about buying presents at the little temporary booths that have been set up in Salonika since "The Great Fire" burnt out the centre of the beautiful eastern city.

(To be continued.)

UNITY OF EFFORT.

ANOTHER LESSON FROM THE U.S.A.

The extremely interesting and historic picture which we publish on this page, is that of the members of the Nursing Committee of the General Medical Board of the Council of National Defence in the United States of America, from which it will be seen that the foremost women in the nursing world in America have been commissioned to advise and act for the Council of National Defence in relation to nursing matters. We recently drew attention to the formation of this Committee, and this picture of its personnel emphasises its representative character most emphatically.

Organization for Public Health Nursing; Miss Hannah J. Patterson, Resident Director Woman's Committee, Council of National Defence; and Miss Pearl H. Braithwaite, Assistant Secretary of Committee.

Third row, left to right.—Colonel John M. T. Finney, Chief Consultant in Surgery, American Expeditionary Forces in France; Colonel William H. Welch, Surgeon General's Office; Colonel William J. Mayo, Chairman Surgical Advisory Board, Surgeon General's Office; Brigadier-General Robert E. Noble, Chief of Hospital Division, Surgeon General's Office; Lieutenant-Colonel Robert L. Dickinson, Medical Adviser, Operations Division, General Staff; and Dr. Franklin Martin, Member of Advisory Commission, Council of National Defence, and Chairman of Council General Medical Board.

NURSING COMMITTEE OF THE GENERAL MEDICAL BOARD OF THE COUNCIL OF NATIONAL DEFENCE
(at recent Conference with Col. J. M. T. Finney in Washington),

An Interdependent Service for the Sick
in National Defence.

Lower row, left to right.—Miss S. Lillian Clayton, Philadelphia, Pa., President National League for Nursing Education; Miss Annie W. Goodrich, Inspector-General of Nursing Service in United States and France and Dean of the Army School of Nursing; Miss Mary Beard, Boston, Mass., President National Organization for Public Health Nursing; Miss M. Adelaide Nutting, Chairman of Committee, Professor of Nursing and Health, Teachers' College, Columbia University, New York City; Mrs. John H. Higbee, Superintendent Nurse Corps, United States Navy; and Miss Dora L. Thompson, Superintendent Nurse Corps, United States Army.

Second row, left to right.—Miss Jane A. Delano, Director Division of Nursing, American Red Cross; Miss Clara D. Noyes, President American Nurses' Association; Miss Ella Phillips Crandall, Secretary of Committee, Executive Secretary National

MORALLY CRUCIFIED.

Mr. Edward Bok, an eminent American editor, has made a terrible indictment in the *Times*, on the appalling dangers of London streets. He says :—
"I have been in a great many large cities, but I have never seen a more disgraceful condition than is witnessed in the London streets every evening. Our boys are openly solicited, not only by prostitutes, but by scores of amateur girls."

He considers the precautions taken by the American Government "is of small avail if we send our soldiers clean-blooded and strong-limbed over here only to be poisoned and wrecked in the London streets. We should not be asked to send our boys here to be morally crucified. It is unfair to them; it is unfair to the great cause for which we are fighting; it is certainly unfair to the American mother."

We hope American women in London will take action.

HONOURS FOR NURSES.

ROYAL RED CROSS.

His Majesty has conferred decorations as follows, on Wednesday, the 18th inst., at Buckingham Palace :—

FIRST CLASS.

Queen Alexandra's Royal Naval Nursing Service.—Superintending Sister MARGARET GOODALL-COPESTAKE.

Queen Alexandra's Royal Naval Nursing Service Reserve.—Sister MURIEL HUTTON.

Royal Naval Auxiliary Hospitals.—Matron ELLEN FINNEMORE.

Territorial Force Nursing Service.—Matron KATHARINE MERRIMAN.

SECOND CLASS.

Queen Alexandra's Royal Naval Nursing Service.—Sister SARAH McCLELLAND.

Queen Alexandra's Royal Naval Nursing Service Reserve.—Sister VERA SPARK and Sister ZOE STRONGE.

Royal Naval Auxiliary Hospitals.—Matron MARGARET TOD, Matron ELSIE PHILP, and Matron ELIZABETH RITCHIE.

Queen Alexandra's Imperial Military Nursing Service Reserve.—Matron MELITA MARTIN, Sister HENRIETTA DALY, Sister EDITH DAVIES, Sister ANNIE ELLIS, Sister ANN GIBB, Sister FLORENCE HALE, Sister LIZZIE HAXELL, and Sister MAUD REYNOLDS-KNIGHT.

Territorial Force Nursing Service.—Sister CHARLOTTE KIRKPATRICK.

Voluntary Aid Detachment.—Miss BESSIE ERNEST and Miss SELINA LLOYD.

Canadian Army Nursing Service.—Sister MARY BLOTT, and Sister MILDRED PARKINS.

SPLENDID COURAGE OF CANADIAN NURSES.

MEDALS FOR MATRON AND SISTERS.

The King has been pleased to approve of the award of the Military Medal to the following ladies for distinguished services in the field :—

Matron Edith Campbell, R.R.C., C.A.M.C., and Sisters Leonora Herrington, Lottie Urquhart, Janet M. Williamson, Meta Hodge, and Eleanor J. Thompson, all C.A.M.C.

CENTRAL CHANCERY OF THE ORDERS OF KNIGHTHOOD, ST. JAMES'S PALACE, S.W. 1
ORDER OF THE BRITISH EMPIRE,

The appointment of Miss Emma Maud McCarthy, R.R.C., to be a Commander of the Most Excellent Order of the British Empire, announced in the *London Gazette* of the 7th June last, is hereby cancelled, and in lieu thereof the King has been graciously pleased to make the following appointment :—

TO BE A DAME GRAND CROSS OF THE SAID MOST EXCELLENT ORDER.

Miss Emma Maud McCarthy, R.R.C.

Miss M. A. Harvey, Matron of Base Hospital No. 1, who was formerly Matron of the 2nd Southern General Hospital, Bristol, before she went to France, is, says the *Lancet*, the first woman to be mentioned in Portuguese despatches.

CARE OF THE WOUNDED.

This is Italy's week. On Monday the very splendid Prince Colonna, Syndic of Rome, arrived in London, as the guest of our Lord Mayor. The Italian Carabinieri Band is here, and, as we go to press, Italy's Day is in full force. We hope piles of money will be gathered in for the Italian Red Cross, and thus help to comfort the stricken in war.

The Queen of Rumania, in an interview accorded to a representative of the Budapest paper *Az Est,* says :—

" The accusations that I have been working against the Central Powers do not trouble me at all. I have simply done my duty in encouraging my soldiers, in cheering up a defeated army, and in distributing food and clothes to a starving people.

" My conscience is clear, and I defy all calumnies. No one can rob me of the love of my people. Our common sufferings have but brought us more closely together."

It is to be hoped that this loyal Queen will soon have the happiness of sharing in the national rejoicings when her adopted country is wrested from the clutches of the unspeakable Hun. Queen Marie of Roumania has been the only European Queen of British blood who has shown its great qualities. Britain should have her specially in mind when it helps to dictate peace.

Sir Edward Ward is asking through the Press for winter comforts for the troops in France. Thanks to the loyal support of a large number of workers who have continued to knit during their summer holiday, he has already been able to meet the entire requirements for warm comforts of the Expeditionary Force in all other theatres of war. He writes :—" It needs but a small sacrifice for every knitter to send to the depôt of their local voluntary organisation or to the Comforts Depôt, 45, Horseferry Road, Westminster, S.W. 1, regular contributions of knitted comforts each week during the next three months. Such support will provide all the articles required and I am convinced our great home army of voluntary workers will see to it that ' nothing is wanting.' "

The hospital authorities in Salonika have sent urgent requests to V.A.D. Headquarters in this country for a considerable number of trained laboratory assistants, and also for several dispensers holding either the Pharmaceutical certificate or the Apothecaries' Hall certificate. The rates of pay are 39s. 6d. per week and 49s. 6d. for head dispensers, with a deduction in all cases of 14s. for board and lodging. Application may be made to the V.A.D., Department, 18, Devonshire House, Piccadilly, London, W. 1.

The interesting information subjoined is sent to the *Lancet* by its foreign correspondent.

TREATMENT OF GASSED PATIENTS.

The number of victims of enemy gas has become great, and the Under Secretary of the Service de Santé has reorganised completely the arrangements for their treatment in the sense of making it both more effective and more rapid. The therapy of gas cases is becoming better understood. As regards hyperite, which is the agent most frequently employed by the enemy, it is now known that if the victims can be douched within the first three hours, with lavage of the stomach and complete cleansing of the clothing, they are almost certain to recover. But the consecutive treatment of pulmonary and ocular complications is protracted. The need was felt of a mobile organisation to give at the close of a bombardment prompt aid at points where cases have occurred in great number, and of a special hospital service at the base to deal with all the cases evacuated after undergoing preliminary treatment up to complete recovery. The first object is attained by means of motor ambulances, a new model of which has recently been planned. Each consists of a lorry and a trailer. The lorry contains tent, portable flooring, douching apparatus, and other accessories. The trailer contains a stove to disinfect clothing. The whole installation can be set up in about a quarter of an hour. The routine is simple. Cases are received and undress in a part of the tent screened off from the douche. Their clothes are passed through the disinfector while the patients douche, and on returning they resume their clothes, which have been freed from all traces of hyperite. Each installation serves for the treatment of 100 men an hour. Forty men can be douched at a time, while the disinfector has a capacity of 40 complete equipments. Every combatant division is to be provided with one of these motor ambulances, and all the gassed cases thus treated are then to be evacuated to base hospitals in the rear, none remaining in the army zone. Numerous beds have been reserved in the Paris military hospitals in two sections, one to receive patients suffering chiefly from pulmonary symptoms, the other for burns of the skin, eyes, and mucous surfaces.

RECURRENT HÆMOPTYSIS DUE TO GUNSHOT WOUNDS OF THE CHEST.

M. Courtois-Suffit, in a study of hæmoptysis among soldiers who have been shot through the chest, states that a large number of cases relapse. Since this relapse may occur after a long interval he warns medical men against the tendency to consider such symptoms as necessarily pointing to tuberculosis, whether or not of traumatic origin. Radioscopy and examination of sputum are essential in each such case to control the information elicited on auscultation, or misleading statements will appear in the patient's discharge sheet.

OPEN LETTER TO THE STAFF NURSES OF THE TERRITORIAL FORCE NURSING SERVICE.

It has been proposed that the Staff Nurses of each T.F.N.S. hospital should sign a joint letter to Miss Sidney Browne, the Matron-in-Chief of the T.F.N.S., requesting that the title of " Nursing Sister " be officially recognised as the correct address for all Staff Nurses of the T.F.N.S., not merely " Nurse."

In most cases the T.F.N.S. works in conjunction with civilian hospitals, from which come drafts of probationers, T.P.'s and V.A.D. workers, who have to be trained by the T.F.N.S. nurses, who urge that their authority can neither be so powerful nor so useful without the befitting title. Nor is it advisable that qualified women—many of whom have held posts of high authority and great responsibility previous to " joining up "—should have the same form of address as these unqualified ladies, who are always addressed as " Nurse."

The Sisters by appointment could be designated as already recognised, viz., as Sisters-in-Charge. This, we believe, is done in all the Army hospitals and in Q.A.I.M.N.S. If all the Territorial Nurses who agree with this view will sign a letter to that effect, from any hospital to which they may be attached, and send it, not later than October 20th next, to Mrs. James, 3, The Pryors, Hampstead, N.W. 3, she would be glad to do her best to further the matter.

The letter must in each case be signed, " T.F.N.S. Staff Nurse."

" A WELL-WISHER."

We are pleased to insert this " Open Letter " from " A Well-wisher " of our profession, and to heartily endorse the claim of thoroughly qualified nurses to professional recognition in the Army Service.

When in 1901 we drafted a modern Constitution for the then Army Nursing Service, which was presented by a deputation to the Secretary of State for War by the Matrons' Council, and was almost in its entirety adopted in forming Q.A.I.M.N.S.—we laid stress on the value of rank, and provided that " Sister " should be the title of all regular ward nurses —senior and junior. We have never approved of " Staff Nurses " in military hospitals.

Military probationers and V.A.D.'s are products of circumstance—not, let us hope, to be permanently included in our Military Nursing Services in times of peace; and justice and good discipine demand that certificated nurses, who are not under tuition, should not be classed with young probationers. We advise military Staff Nurses to unite on this important question of rank, and if need be bring their just demands before the Army Council.

NATIONAL UNION OF WOMEN WORKERS AND THE COLLEGE OF NURSING, LTD.

At the June meeting of the Executive Committee of the National Union of Women Workers —which is practically the governing body of the National Council of Women.

Miss Macdonald moved :—

"That the request for affiliation received from the College of Nursing, Ltd., be granted."

Miss Eaton seconded and Miss Joseph supported.

Amendment moved by Miss Macmillan :—

"That it be remitted to the next meeting in order that members might report as to the constitution and the governing body."

Miss Wade seconded.

Mrs. Allan Bright pointed out that the present Council of the College was a preliminary one only.

The amendment was put and lost.

And the resolution was then put and passed.

It appears to us that several very vital principles in connection with the status of the Affiliated Societies are involved in this decision ; and as the revised Constitution of the Council is to be considered at Harrogate it would be well to define the constitution of societies eligible for affiliation.

1. We have always been under the impression that these conjoint bodies—the N.U.W.W. and the N.C.W.—are Women's organizations as expressed in their titles ; as we find Object 3 is to "co-ordinate women's organizations nationally and locally" ; and under "Membership" it is stated "Members shall be women."

THE COLLEGE OF NURSING, LTD.

The College of Nursing Company was founded by seven lay signatories (all men) who are called Subscribers and shall be perpetual members of the College of Nursing—(they are not even medical men !)

These seven signatories nominated men and women to form a Council, which nominated body has defined nursing standards and took power to make, alter and repeal bye-laws, rules and regulations as they think fit. The Memorandum and Articles of Association are autocratic in the extreme, and one alone, which takes power to remove a nurse's name from the Register, "as the Council may in its discretion think proper," without power of appeal, condemns the motives of the men who drafted it.

It is almost impossible to believe that the Executive Committee of the N.U.W.W., had it had a report on the Constitution before it, would have agreed to affiliate to a Woman's National Council, a Company so constituted, in spite of the partisan advocacy of certain members of the College who have seats on its Executive Committee.

Mrs. Allan H. Bright is in error in stating that "the present Council of the College was a preliminary one only." The College is governed by the Memorandum and Articles of Association which defines it ; and the nominated Council has defined all rules and regulations, standards for registration, and drafted seven impossible Bills without bringing them before the nurse members for discussion and approval. It is provided that one-third of these autocrats shall retire annually, but are eligible for re-election—and this year, at the first election, they all promptly sought re-election, and not one of the 100 Sisters, Nurses or independent candidates nominated had a real chance of election, as no Roll of Voters was printed and no candidate could appeal to an electorate !

But the question to which the self-governing Affiliated Societies of Nurses would like a straight answer is—Are Limited Liability Companies, promoted by men, of which every Signatory is a man, of which the Hon. Officers, Chairman, Hon. Treasurer and Hon. Secretary are men— which is calculated to very seriously interfere with the educational standards, the economic conditions, hours of labour, professional discipline and self-government of trained nurses, really "organizations of women," or qualified for affiliation with the "National Council of Women of Great Britain and Ireland ?" For, if so, it is imperative in the interest of truth and justice, that organizations and companies promoted by male employers, founded to control women workers, should be clearly included as eligible for membership of the National Council of Women in the revised Constitution. We hope there will be a clear pronouncement on this point at Harrogate. Self-governing professional women will then know where they stand. Personally, after twenty-five years' association with the National Council of Women of Great Britain and Ireland, we consider, as we always have done, that professional women should have expert representation on the Executive Committee, and until this principle is conceded, the Union will continue to fail in equitable action from lack of knowledge, not from lack of goodwill.

HONOUR TO WHOM HONOUR IS DUE.

The College of Nursing is starting a local centre at Cambridge. Miss Cowlin, who addressed a meeting of nurses there recently, had apparently never heard of the world-wide movement for higher education and State Registration of nurses until a quarter of a century after its inauguration, and so unselfishly supported by that noble woman Miss Isla Stewart, whose pupil Miss Cowlin had the honour to be.

THE ASSOCIATION OF POOR LAW UNIONS.

At a recent meeting of the Executive Council of the Association of Poor Law Unions of England and Wales held in London, " the Council agreed with the proposal of the Parliamentary Committee to appoint, as requested by Sir Arthur Stanley, Chairman of the College of Nursing, three members on the proposed Provisional Nursing Council, but this action is to be without prejudice to the future attitude of the Poor-Law Unions' Association in regard to provisions of the Parliamentary Bill about to be promoted by the College."

This Association of Poor-Law Guardians previously asked for much larger representation on the Council to govern trained nurses, but so many lay bodies have also demanded representation that if the College concedes these to each, the nurses will find themselves entirely suppressed as far as liberty of action is concerned.

NURSES' MISSIONARY LEAGUE.

The autumn re-union of the Nurses' Missionary League will be held on Wednesday, October 2nd. The morning and afternoon sessions (10.15 to 12.30 and 3–5) will be held at the Westminster Chapel, Buckingham Gate, S.W., and the evening meeting (7.30–9.30) at University Hall, Gordon Square, W.C. The subject for the day is " The City of God : the Citizen's Guide, Outlook and Service " ; and the speakers include the Rev. R. C. Gillie (morning), Miss C. Sharp (Sarawak) and Miss Ellis (afternoon), Miss Baker (Uganda) and the Ven. Archdeacon Sharp (evening). All nurses are cordially invited. Full programmes can be obtained from Miss Richardson, 52, Lower Sloane Street, S.W. 1.

APPOINTMENTS.

DEPUTY MATRON.

Cornwall County Asylum, Bodmin.—Miss Dorothy Jones has been appointed Deputy Matron. She was trained at St. Mary's Hospital, Paddington, where she acted as Sister. Miss Jones was also trained in mental work at Rubery Hill Asylum, and holds the Medico-Psychological certificate, and the certificate of the Central Midwives Board.

SISTER.

Bootle Borough Hospital, Derby Road, near Liverpool.—Miss Dorothy Lord has been appointed Sister. She was trained at the Dover Hospital, and has been Sister at the Stafford General Infirmary, Sister at Marlborough Hospital, Wilts., and has had charge of the Military Hospital, Harden House, Kent.

District Hospital, Newbury.—Miss Helen White has been appointed Sister. She was trained at the Royal West Sussex Hospital, Chichester, and amongst others has held the position of Children's Ward and Theatre Sister at the Infirmary, Harrogate, Sister at the Military Hospital, Kingston, and

Night Sister at the West Suffolk General Hospital, Bury St. Edmunds.

Royal Eye and Ear Hospital, Bradford.—Miss Louise Kingham has been appointed Sister of the Children's Ward and Outpatient Department. She was trained at the Lewisham Infirmary, and has been Sister at the S.E. Fever Hospital, at the Central London Ophthalmic Hospital and Birmingham Midland Eye Hospital. She has also been Matron of Hayes Cottage Hospital and Brentwood Cottage Hospital.

QUEEN VICTORIA'S JUBILEE INSTITUTE.

TRANSFERS AND APPOINTMENTS.

Miss Edith M. Epps is appointed to Plaistow as Superintendent. Miss Epps received general training at the Radcliffe Infirmary, Oxford ; district training at Westminster ; midwifery training at York Road Lying-in Hospital, and holds the C.M.B. certificate. She has held various appointments under the Institute, including that of county superintendent of the Notts. Nursing Federation and Inspector of the South Western Counties.

Miss Alice J. Buckle is appointed to Rotherham as Superintendent. Miss Buckle received her general training at the Royal Infirmary, Edinburgh ; district training at the Metropolitan N.A ; midwifery training at Cheltenham, and has the C.M.B. certificate. She has since held several appointments under the Institute, including that of Superintendent of Brighton D.N.A. and Nursing Superintendent for England.

Miss Edith Garratt-Jones is appointed to Nelson as Senior Nurse ; Miss Violet E. Hunt to Gillingham as Senior Nurse ; Miss Theresa O. Leonard, to Southfleet ; Miss Isabel A. Mainley, to Hazel Grove ; Mrs. Alice Mitchener, to Letchworth ; Miss Dora K. Mohun, to Chadsmoor ; Miss Alice Pearson, to Cheltenham ; Miss Mabel A. S. Esler, to Birmingham (Moseley Road) ; Miss Fanny Purseglove, to Birmingham (Summerhill Road).

MEDALS FOR NURSES.
BELFAST UNION INFIRMARY.

At the weekly meeting of the Belfast Board of Guardians on September 10th—the Chairman, Mr. Joseph Mitchell, presiding—medals were presented by Miss Clark to nurses who have taken first places in their final professional examinations : Nurse J. M'Auley Harkness, gold medal (presented by the Chairman) ; Nurse Rebecca Gleazer, silver medal (presented by Mr. A. Savage) and Nurse Dorothy Magowan, bronze medal (presented by Miss Florence Clark). Over 200 of the nurses trained in the Union have volunteered for service at the front.

THE PASSING BELL.

Miss Ashley, matron of Grimsby Hospital, who nursed the boy hero, Jack Cornwell, V.C., when he was landed wounded from the Jutland battle, has just died from an incurable malady. It was to her that he gave the immortal answer, " Oh, I just carried on, miss," when asked what he did after all his gun crew were killed.

NURSING ECHOES.

Queen Alexandra will visit Norwich on October 12th, the anniversary of the execution of Edith Cavell, to open the Cavell Memorial Home and to unveil the statue of her, both of which memorials have been subscribed for by the residents of Norfolk and the citizens of Norwich. Tombland, adjacent to the Cathedral, is the site of both the home and the statue. Miss Cavell spent the greater part of her life in or near Norwich.

Many nurses will learn with regret that the private nursing agency which has had so long and honourable a career at 123, New Bond Street, S.W., has now closed its doors. Its business has been transferred to the Belgravia Nursing Home at 50, Weymouth Street, W., formerly known as "Miss Pollock's Home," but recently taken over by the above Home, whose present Superintendent is Miss Shebbeare, but which was for many years under the superintendence of Miss Kimber.

A conference organised by the National Baby Week Council was held at Bedford College for Women, to inaugurate a propaganda campaign, in which trained nurses are invited to take part, in support of the immediate establishment of a Ministry of Health. Dr. Eric Pritchard, Lord Willoughby de Broke, Dr. Saleeby, Mr. G. P. Blizard, and others expressed the desire of the council to create a strong public opinion with a view to giving speedy effect to the promised introduction of a Ministry of Health Bill, and it was declared that the country would not tolerate the opposition of private or vested interests or departmental jealousies, to the immediate realisation of its demands and hopes. The following resolution was carried unanimously :—" That, in view of the declared intention of the Government to introduce early in the forthcoming session of Parliament a Ministry of Health Bill, the National Baby Week Council calls upon its members and local committees to pursue an active propaganda campaign in favour of such a Ministry, so that the weight of public opinion and the support of the electorate may strengthen the hands of the Government in giving speedy effect to its intentions." The National Baby Week Council has already organised various meetings in the provinces, and is prepared to find speakers to represent it and address such meetings, on application to the Secretary, 27A, Cavendish Square, London, W. 1.

In addition to a war bonus granted by the London County Council by resolution on the 30th of July last, the Council has now sanctioned additional war wages of 5s. a week for officers and employees under the direction of the Asylums and Mental Deficiency Committee, dating from the first pay-week following July 1st. All female officers and employees on the established staff under the direction of the Asylums and Mental Deficiency Committee who are receiving war wages of 7s. a week are eligible to receive this increase.

The remuneration of all temporary attendants under the direction of the above Committee is to be increased to 54s. a week, commencing from July 1st.

Mr. Samuel Whittaker, of Lytham, Lancs, whose estate has been proved at £21,051, left an annuity of £52 to his nurse, Miss Margaret Rossall.

A LOSS TO OUR NURSING SCHOOLS.

Miss M. Heather Bigg will retire from the Matronship of Charing Cross Hospital in December next, having completed sixteen years of service ; and the loss to our Nurse Training Schools will be irreparable—although we are glad to learn that the nursing profession is not to lose her active sympathy and invaluable practical help, of which it has never had greater need ; when Parliament is to be approached to sanction and appoint a Governing Body for the better organization of nursing education and general control through Bills promoted (1) by the workers, and (2) by their hospital employers. Needless to say, Miss Heather-Bigg has, with most unselfish courage, stood with her independent colleagues in support of the great principle of an independent Governing Body—for which they have fought a valiant fight—and has sacrificed much in her own personal interest in so doing. All the more honour is her due.

Charing Cross Hospital is by no means an easy charge, and during Miss Heather Bigg's term of office its empty wards were occupied by the Matrons and Nursing Staffs of the National Orthopaedic Hospital and the Cancer Wing from the Middlesex Hospital during the rebuilding of their hospitals. It is a feat worthy of recording that such a unique experiment was carried through with perfect accord, and the staffs of both Charing Cross Hospital and the other two hospitals parted with regret on the completion of the rebuilding. As President of the Matrons' Council, Miss Heather Bigg will entertain the members at the October meeting, when they will have an opportunity of expressing to her their affection and gratitude.

RELIGIOUS COMMUNITIES OF THE CHURCH OF ENGLAND.*

It is not often that one is fortunate enough to happen on a book which breaks new ground, dealing with a subject which is intensely interesting in a most interesting way, but all these conditions are present in the book before us, which is "the first attempt, historically, to bring together the data relative to the revival of the Religious Life among us" since the Reformation, though in "A History of Nursing" (Nutting & Dock) we have a most interesting survey of the Military Nursing Orders, the Rise of the Secular Orders, the later Mediæval Orders, and of St. Vincent de Paul and the Sisters of Charity.

For nurses who wish to understand the history of their profession some knowledge of that of the religious orders is essential, for many communities, both Roman and Anglican, have largely devoted themselves to the care of the sick, and have enriched the traditions of our profession by the example of saintly lives and the record of devoted service. The Duke of Argyll, in a most interesting preface to the book, writes :—"Have the readers of this volume ever pondered over that great list of Abbesses and Queens, 192 in number, all of the Saxon period, which appears in the Liber Vitae of Durham (Surtees Society). In that great Bede's roll, without any indication of what Abbey they ruled, or what Kings they had once been wedded to, flaming in gold and silver lettering, stand those strange Saxon names. Here and there we can identify one or two for certain, and that is about all. Of some we know the great Houses over which they once bore rule in Saxon England, others must be the otherwise unrecorded successes of Saints like Hilda, or of those whose very

·MOTHER CECILE,
Foundress of the Community of
the Resurrection, Grahamstown.

MISS E. A. BENNETT,
Foundress of the Order of
the Sisters of Bethany.

foundations may have vanished in the Danish invasions.

"Up and down the English realm stand countless reminders of England's sainted nuns and abbesses whose names are still remembered by entries in fading calendars. Oxford reveres the Abbess Frydeswyde as its special Patroness and Protectress. Far away on the Cornish headlands S. Ia raised a home of prayer by storm-sick seas. S. Bega did as much further north on the Irish Channel. Kent, the Garden of England, produced an extraordinary contribution to the number of S. Scholastica's daughters, for in an older Folkestone now beneath the waves stood the Abbey ruled by S. Eanswythe, daughter of the Kentish King. S. Sexburgha, Queen of Kent, built S. Mary's Abbey at Sheppey, and died as a nun at Ely, under her sister S. Ætheldreda. SS. Mildred, Eadburgha, and many more, all of royal blood, flourished in Kent and left sweet memories behind them which will last as long as history endures and pens remain to commemorate those early teachers of S. Benedict's Rule."

It is impossible to deal *in extenso* with all the sections of a book already so condensed. The first part includes an account of Sisterhoods, active and contemplative, and deals with the all-important question of "Vocation," or the call of God to a religious life. "The groundwork of such a life is the persuasion of each member that God has called her entirely to forego the claims of society and family, and devote herself wholly, entirely, and unreservedly to the work of God, whether actively or contemplatively, in the direction which He points out."

It is interesting that the first suggestion for the formation of a Sisterhood in England since the days of the "Tudor Pillage" was made by Rev. Alex. R. C. Dallas, in the interests of the sick. As curate of Woburn his intercourse with the poor led him to feel very keenly the lack of proper nursing

*The Faith Press, Ltd., 22, Buckingham St., Strand, W.C., 7/6 net.

and attendance in sickness. The doctor lived at a great distance, "the village nurses were deplorably ignorant, and Mr. Dallas having resided in France and having seen the superior nursing and the many advantages resulting from the system there carried on, of the ' Sœurs de la Charité,' devised a plan for the same system to be adopted in England.

"He appears to have impressed his views upon one who was in his day a great physician as well as philanthropist and philosopher, namely, Dr. Gooch. Like Dallas, Gooch had visited Belgium, and like Howard, the prison reformer, had been most interested in the Beguines and their works of mercy, their well-ordered hospitals, and their general efficiency in visiting and prescribing

nouncing it said that "any little objection the Archbishop had felt was now removed." This apparently refers to the change of title from "Sisters of Charity" to "Nursing Sisters."

The interesting and unique foundation of St. John's House—now in Queen Square, Bloomsbury—is described at some length. It was to her friend, Miss Mary Jones, Lady Superior of St. John's House, that Miss Florence Nightingale turned—and not in vain—when the Crimean War broke out.

The book abounds in most interesting and beautiful illustrations of the homes of religious foundations and also portraits of their pious founders. To mention only a few. There is the Community of the Holy Rood, at North Ormesby,

SOCIETY OF THE INCARNATION, SALTLEY.

for the sick poor. He published an account of his visit and experiences with the conclusions he had formed, directed to the advantage of a like system in England in *Blackwood's Magazine*, in December, 1825.

This was followed by a pamphlet by Mr. Dallas on "Protestant Sisters of Charity," "developing a plan for improving the arrangements at present existing for administering medical advice and visiting the sick poor." This resulted in much interesting correspondence with Mrs. Elizabeth Fry, who took up the plan advocated by Mr. Dallas to a large extent, and carried it out in the nursing establishment at Raven Row, Whitechapel, and afterwards in Devonshire Square. The Queen Dowager, through Earl Howe, lent her patronage to the scheme, and in the letter an-

where the good work done in the hospital which it nurses, is well known to our readers ; St. Mary's, Wantage ; All Saints', Colney ; St. Margaret's, East Grinstead ; and many more. By the kindness of the publishers, we are able to reproduce pictures of Miss E. A. Bennett, Mother-Foundress of the Society of the Sisters of Bethany, of the House of Retreat, Lloyd Square, E.C. ; Mother Cecile, who founded the Community of the Resurrection, Grahamstown, South Africa ; and a group of Sisters of the Society of the Incarnation of the Eternal Son, Saltley, founded by Mother Gertrude Clare, and some of the Poor Law boys in their charge. We most cordially recommend the book to the notice of our readers. To those who are interested in the work of Religious communities it will provide a fascinating study.

OUTSIDE THE GATES.

NURSES AND THEIR VOTES.

The vagaries of Registration Officers, judges and others in interpreting who may, and who may not, vote under the new Reform Act are so irreconcilable that it is time Nurses had a test case and fought it out. In one district hospital, nurses living in are denied a vote, whilst under exactly identical circumstances in another hospital they are granted the privilege.

At the recent quarterly Court of Governors at the London Hospital, in presenting the report of the House Committee, the House Governor stated that " they had been informed by the Registration Officer of the District that the nurses, as they occupied each a separate bedroom, were entitled to have their names entered on the Register and to vote both in Borough and Parliamentary elections. They therefore had to supply full returns of the nursing staff who fulfilled the conditions as to age and length of residence. They also had to supply returns of their resident medical officers."

This is definite and most satisfactory, as the rule for Whitechapel should hold good in each constituency.

We hope, therefore, the Matrons are compiling a list of eligible Sisters and Nurses in every hospital and asylum, and seeing that through the right authority their claims are put forward and their votes made secure. Bart's nurses of progressive proclivities should have quite an amusing time if the same old gentlemen stand again for the City. The Right Hon. Arthur J. Balfour always ignored their petitions for Registration Reform, and did not vote for their Bill in 1914, and Sir F. Banbury, Bart., as a professional blocker did not only help to block their Bill for years but was amongst the negligible minority who voted against it in 1914.

It is time the City of London was represented by young, liberal-minded men. Why should not the women put up a candidate of their own choice ?

One can imagine how all the nurses in St. George's, Hanover Square, would flock to his banner should the Right Hon. W. M. Hughes consent to stand for that constituency.

The Vote is doing a real national service in arousing public opinion on the iniquitous prosecutions under Regulation 40 D. Some more just method of dealing with venereal infection in the Army must be devised. Women voters have to tackle this question and save the health of both sexes. Such terrible tragedies we hear on all sides.

A TRUE TALE WITH A MORAL.

Young Wife of Officer : " Tell me the truth."
Medical Woman : " You are infected and need treatment."
Young Wife : " Oh ! I know what to do."
She did.
She went home and poisoned herself !

BOOK OF THE WEEK.

"THE PENDULUM."*

" If I was in my own country I'd be as good as a lord, and my wife would be Lady Sacre ; and if that d——d piece behind the bar there dared serve anyone else before us there'd be trouble, and of a very peculiar sort I can tell you." The speaker nodded his head portentously, darkling at the barmaid.

It was Morris Sacre who spoke, the son of Lord Sacre of County Clare, long since dead ; and how he came to be drunk in a low public-house near the Surrey Docks on the night in question needs explanation.

One point to be emphasised is that this was not an isolated occasion ; it had come to be his habitual haunt, and the company he found there had come to be adopted as his own class.

Neither his wife nor his children knew anything definite as to his origin. They knew him as Jim Sacre, and paid little attention to his boastful vaunts when he was in liquor.

Mrs. Sacre is a creation worthy of note.

A homely woman of the working class with a beautiful soul and a practical nature, calm and firm in the ruling of her difficult family. Her character shines out brightly, pervading and sweetening the whole history of her family.

A picture is given of her reception of her husband on his return on the night referred to, from the public-house in charge of little Michael.

" Mrs. Sacre was ironing. The little kitchen was full of the warm, sweet scent of it, while a folding horse, covered with homely garments, stood in front of the fire.

Mrs. Sacre had just taken an iron from the fire as her husband entered, and was holding it to her cheek to test the warmth ; but she put it down and stood motionless with her broad hands spread out on the table, her steady eyes lowered.

" Well, and how's her ladyship this evening ? "

She had waited his first words to gauge his mood. This was the mood she hated and dreaded above all else.

" I hate to see a woman for ever toiling and moiling. If I had my rights, and you had your rights, old girl, you'd never as much as soil your little finger," he went on, regardless of the fact that she was unlacing his boots as he spoke.

" Very well, Jim, very well," she spoke soothingly. Her children would not venture to sneer at their father. For all her quiet she had a sure and heavy hand.

It is with the boy Michael that the story is chiefly concerned. Michael, whose " finicky ways " were a throwback to his father's lineage, the strange intermingling of which with his sordid upbringing is the standpoint from which the story is written. Michael was the adored and the adorer of his lowly born mother. She had innumerable other offspring, and she was an admirable mother to all, but Michael was the apple of her eye.

* By Elinor Mordaunt. Cassell & Co., London.

A graphic picture is the following :—

" Saere's twelfth child was born that night, drew a few gasping breaths of the Thames fog and then passed on its way."

Mrs. Saere had what is known as a bad time, but she scarcely heeded the pain. She worried, poor soul, about everything but her own condition. Would Emily forget to keep in the kitchen fire, so that nurse might have hot water ? Would Maude get near it and tumble against the bars ? Would the burial man, who was calling that evening, be able to make anyone hear ?

Had anyone thought to tell Mrs. Sutcliffe she would be unable to come and do the washing that week " after askin' for it and all ? "

And then comes the alleviation.

" When the others have gone off out of our way, I'll get you a cup of tea," said Michael.

He always coupled himself with his mother— " our " and " us."

It was a little interval of peace that hour spent with little Michael, which had to be broken by the little boy being sent to the door.

" It's the burial man," said Mrs. Saere. " Now, if only nurse was here ! But you must go and see to him, Michael dear ; and mind and tell him it mustn't run into money, for I can't afford it."

How true a picture of the " lying-in " of the East-end mother, only those who have worked among the poor will appreciate.

The period of Michael's adoption by a wealthy mad woman is a terrible episode, and the murder of the unfortunate child Herbert is very " creepy " reading. It results, however, in the restoration of Michael to his own parents.

Young Michael grew into a clever, capable foreman in the wood-yard, and it was while on duty there that he was told off to show round some ladies—friends of Sir John Proudie, his employer. It was on this occasion that pretty Sallie exclaimed at his surname.

" My name's Saere," he said stiffly.

" There, now," said Sallie. " Isn't it extraordinary. I knew there was something. It may have been a pre—pre—what do I mean ? O, you know what I mean. A call of the blood ! "

There had always been a curious instinct in Michael's mother to put away from herself any tendency to believe her husband's boasting reference to the past. Where a vulgarer woman would have gloried in the mere possibility of well-born connections, she instinctively shrank from it. This trait in her character helped to baffle Michael's efforts to elucidate the truth.

There are many interesting passages in the book relating to labour disputes and social reform. Michael's family figure none too creditably in many ways, but innate refinement causes him to triumph over his many disabilities. The close of the book finds him at last, having established his father's claim. But although the way seems clear for him to marry pretty Sally, his happiness had still to be deferred.

The war claimed him.

" Sally, you'll have to look after Saere Court for

me—wait till I come back—if—if there's any chance for me, my dear—with all my folly, all you know of me."

This book is full of interest throughout, and the character of Mrs. Saere alone makes it worthy of attention.   H. H.

THE LAST PILOT.
(From a Hill-top in France.)

Overhead, in a tranquil sky, out of the sunset glow,
The stately battle-planes go sailing east, against the foe,
And the quivering air is all a-drone, like an organ, deep and low.

The sunset gleams on the old bell-tower and the roofs of the old French town :
Gleams and fades, and the shadows fall, as the night comes creeping down,
And the German line in the twilight glooms distant and dark and brown.

One by one, their duty done, the planes come back from the fight ;
One by one, like homing birds, back through the darkening night,
And, twinkling against the fading west, goes up their guiding light.

Hour by hour the light goes up, flashing the signal far,
But the Last Pilot heeds it not. His ship has crossed the bar,
And he has found eternal peace in the light of his Heavenly Star.

By Duncan Tovey.

COMING EVENTS.

September 30th.—Royal British Nurses' Association meeting of Consultative Committee, 10, Orchard Street, Portman Square, W. 3.15 p.m.

September 30th. — Inauguration of Course of Elementary Lectures on Infant Care (for Teachers, Infant Welfare Workers, Mothers, &c.), under the auspices of the National Association for the Prevention of Infant Mortality and for the Welfare of Infancy. 1, Wimpole Street, W. 5.30 p.m.

October 2nd.—Missionary Nurses' League. Autumn Re-union. Morning, afternoon and evening meetings. 10.15, 12.30, 3–5 p.m. and 7.30 to 9.30.

October 8th, 9th and 10th.—National Council of Women. Meeting in Harrogate. The Report of Committee on the Revision of the Constitution will be submitted. Conference.

October 12th.—Queen Alexandra will open the Cavell Memorial Home and unveil a statue at Norwich on the anniversary of Edith Cavell's execution.

WORD FOR THE WEEK.

You ask me how long this war must still go on. It will go on until our task shall have been accomplished, until our just cause shall have triumphed. For it is necessary that our dead should not have died in vain ; it is necessary that the Government of the People by the People and for the People shall have obtained the certainty that it will not be abolished off the face of the earth.

Abraham Lincoln.

LETTERS TO THE EDITOR.

Whilst cordially inviting communications upon all subjects for these columns, we wish it to be distinctly understood that we do not IN ANY WAY hold ourselves responsible for the opinions expressed by our correspondents.

CONGRATULATIONS.

To the Editor of THE BRITISH JOURNAL OF NURSING.

DEAR MRS. BEDFORD FENWICK,—We beg to convey to you the congratulations of the Royal British Nurses' Association on the completion of your twenty-five years as Editor of THE BRITISH JOURNAL OF NURSING, and to express the hope that before long the movement, of which it has been the earliest and leading literary protagonist, may be crowned with success by the passage of a Bill for State Registration, just to the nurses and calculated to foster and develop the Profession of Nursing.

We are,

Yours very truly,

(Signed) · C. E. THOMSON,

HERBERT J. PATERSON,

Hon. Secretaries.

Royal British Nurses' Association,

10, Orchard Street,

Portman Square, W. 1.

UNJUSTIFIABLE PRESSURE.

To the Editor of THE BRITISH JOURNAL OF NURSING.

DEAR MADAM,—All you have prophesied is coming to pass, and unless we obey orders and join the College we are made to realise "a chill."

I am a Guy's nurse and received the letter from the Matrons you allude to last week. The pressure I care nothing about, because after the manner trained nurses have been treated by the Red Cross nothing would induce me to join the College ; but it is shameful that four Matrons should sign their names to the document I received These ladies foot a statement which is, in plain English, a lie It is printed as the first reason why nurses should join the College :—

1. Because the Council of the College of Nursing has drafted a " Nurses' Registration Bill " [seven Bills—the last more dangerous to the personal and professional liberty of the Nursing profession than its predecessors.—ED.]—which provides that the Register already formed by the College of Nursing shall be the first Register under the Act. *If, therefore, you are on the College Register you will, automatically and without further fee, be placed upon the State Register when the " Nurses' Registration Bill " is passed.* I have italicised the words I consider a misleading lie.

Parliament has not dealt with this Bill, nor agreed to a College monopoly and is not likely to grant it.

But thousands of pounds have been taken from nurses by the College Council on this statement. In my opinion it is high time a public meeting was held to expose such indefensible tactics.

Nurses are very ignorant ; they believe statements made by persons in authority over them. The four Matrons ought to be made to refund every guinea paid by Guy's nurses. Who are they to pledge Parliament ? I would use much stronger language, only the last thing our Law Courts allow outside their sacred precincts is " the truth, and nothing but the truth."

A MEMBER OF GUY'S NURSES' LEAGUE.

KERNELS FROM CORRESPONDENCE.

" Old-Fashioned Hospital Nurse " says :—" All the medical staff, especially the juniors, are ' chortling in their joy ' that women medical students have been kept out, when so many other London hospitals are admitting them. At dinner, sad to say, this point of view was thoroughly applauded by the nurses. Many of them have worked with women medicos and say they have absolutely no knowledge of nursing etiquette and never observe it. They all think and act as if they were doctors plus nurses. This is sad."

" District Nurse " writes :—" After the war the millennium ! According to the *Leicester Post* the Government ought to shoulder a little of the burden of seeing that the nurses it will have no further use for shall have a good chance of maintaining themselves in comfort after their war duties are over.

" Very nice for the nurses who all rushed to the front trained and untrained, but how about us who have stayed behind ' in the dull,' often doing two women's work so that the poor should not suffer ? Are we to pay the rates and taxes to make it possible for these ladies to live in luxury ? It is time now to consider the future. Of course, the State should give generous pensions if nurses cannot work ; and when district nursing is a State service, we shall be pensioned when we have earned it, too."

REPLIES TO CORRESPONDENTS.

H. C. Sadleir.—The address of the Central Midwives Board is Queen Anne's Gate Buildings, Westminster, S.W. 1. The address has been in the Journal in the advertisement of the Board's Examinations, which appears the first week in the month.

OUR PRIZE COMPETITION.

QUESTIONS.

October 5th.—How does puerperal septicæmia arise ? Describe the course and management of the disease.

October 12th.—What is rabies ? How is it treated and nursed ?

October 19th.—Give instructions for making Anti-vermin Underclothing for the troops ; also for disinfecting soldiers' clothing at the Front.

OUR ADVERTISERS.

Do not omit to buy, as far as possible, everything you need from " Our Advertisers," and to recommend them to your friends. They are all first-class firms.

The Midwife.

THE EMPLOYMENT OF PREGNANT WOMEN IN MUNITION FACTORIES.

The question of legislation prohibiting pregnant women from wage earning within a certain time, both before and after their confinements, is one which should be approached with extreme caution. Dr. Mary S. Deacon, in a paper read at the Oxford Welfare Conference last month, shows how, far from having a prejudicial effect on the health of the mother, work is beneficial to her.

Dr. Deacon writes, in part :—

"The factory from which the following report was compiled is built on the site of a farm, in flat, open and well-drained fields ; there is an abundance of fresh air and sunshine. All the buildings are very well ventilated with cross and end-to-end through draughts, and the sanitary and bath accommodation is in excess of the Home Office requirements. The factory is particularly well managed ; the canteen is good ; the factory clothes are most suitable and made so as entirely to cover all the worker's private clothes.

"The factory is situated a mile from the station and tram terminus, and all workers have of necessity to walk this mile as there is no other way of reaching their work. The exercise is most salutary for them, and it is surprising to see the difference in their general appearance noticeable after about six weeks' work with us.

"A covered way is provided alongside the roadway for protection in rough weather, and this pathway has been well rolled so that it is always firm and dry.

"Our workers are of the usual city type—undersized, badly developed, with very bad teeth and often anæmic. About 50 per cent. are married and often these have their household duties to attend to after they get home at night. In spite of these drawbacks, after about six weeks' work—and hard work too—if they have the grit to stick it, they become more robust, less anæmic and much more healthy-looking in every way. I consider that this improvement is due to healthy exercise, well-disciplined work, the good and abundant food supplied in the canteen at moderate price, and above all to the abundance of fresh air which they are obliged to get when working in this factory. The fresh air and hard work make them hungry, and getting good money they can well afford to obtain sufficient food. During their meal hour they have amusement, some days they dance and on others concerts are arranged. All workers are medically examined before being engaged, and if found suitable but with bad teeth these are extracted by the factory dentist before work is actually started.

"During the nine months—June 1st, 1917, to February 28th, 1918—I have kept records with a view to finding out the effect of the work on any woman who may become pregnant. Of the total number of women workers engaged in that period (1,197), 575 were married and 622 single. The married women have been brought into the labour market for various reasons. Munitions factories have given them their opportunity and factory managers have no alternative but to engage them."

She then sets out the nature of the problem, and discusses it from the point of view of efficiency, the workers' point of view, and the question of maternal welfare.

THE WORKERS' POINT OF VIEW.

In regard to the workers' point of view, Dr. Deacon says :—

"From the workers' point of view it seems to me that most arguments must be entirely in favour of being kept on. The most cogent reasons are :—

"(a) The worker should not be turned away from work that she is quite able and competent to do because of her condition, excepting in cases where the work is very heavy, but as in our factory (and also, I should think, in most other factories) there is alternation of work, and as the same woman may do various kinds of work, some suitable employment can usually be found for her.

"(b) The worker will not be tempted to take drugs or to use other means to provoke miscarriage if she is free from the fear of losing work where she can earn a good wage, and being obliged either to drop out of the labour market altogether or to take on duller and less highly paid work because she cannot do without the money. I have heard of cases in which the worker, when dismissed from a factory because of her condition, has, in order to obtain bare necessities, gone rag-picking on some refuse heap and got into such a bad condition that both she and the child have been in great danger at the time of the actual confinement.

"(c) If the worker continues at her more highly paid work she can afford to save money for the time during which she will be laid by, and can also probably then afford to take a longer interval after the confinement, when the rest is all-important both to herself and the child.

"(d) During the pre-confinement period, if she earns good money, she can enjoy the better food which is so necessary to her condition. She shares the company and fellowship of her companions, so necessary to keep her cheerful, and by walking a mile to work obtains plenty of exercise and fresh air. The maintenance of the mother in a fit state of health and spirits is all-important to the health of the child to which she is to give birth. Several of the workers are reported as never having felt so well during former pregnancies or having had such good confinements or such healthy babies. In no case has the actual nature of their employment had the slightest detrimental effect."

THE
BRITISH JOURNAL OF NURSING
WITH WHICH IS INCORPORATED
THE NURSING RECORD
EDITED BY MRS BEDFORD FENWICK

No. 1,592.   SATURDAY, OCTOBER 5, 1918.   Vol. LXI

EDITORIAL.

THE RELATIONS OF WOMEN MEDICAL AND NURSING STUDENTS.

"Betty" is one of the few really brilliant young women who has been studying science, who is looking forward to a medical career, and who is entered for her hospital terms at a medical school which has recently admitted women students.

Over the teacups, we asked "Betty" about her future programme, and was interested in her reply.

"Next week," she said, "I begin my ward work, and I feel a bit anxious about it. They tell me the Sisters and nurses are just horrid to women students."

"But surely the duties of each are defined?" we remarked.

"It does not seem so," Betty replied. "For instance, take dressings—this is part of the work we are there to learn—in the past the nurses appear to have done most of them. But how can we learn to dress wounds unless we are taught?"

"But surely as dresser for a certain surgeon—work for which a student pays—you have a right to do the dressings, and the House Surgeon on duty will teach you your work."

"Yes, but the House Surgeon cannot be in every ward at once, and he has only time to attend to the big dressings, and then there are dozens of other things. What is the etiquette about taking temperatures, and all the practical applications such as enemas, and blistering and bandaging, and bed-making—all the interesting things appear to be nursing duties? There seems to be nothing left but urine testing, and note taking, and trotting after the surgeon and wandering round."

Then we reminded "Betty" of the manual drudgery and long years of training a woman had to put in, to learn all these "interesting things," and that as a Sister it became her duty to impart her wonderful knowledge to a succession of probationers who would carry on traditions and continually increase their knowledge and skill, and that what they learned and applied constituted the technique of the profession of Nursing. That in the past, very few male medical students had thirsted after a knowledge of nursing details, which should rightly be included in their first year's clinical curriculum, and in this lack of instruction they have been deprived of the basis of the practical application of much which constituted sound medical practice.

"Betty" is very intelligent, and whilst grasping these facts would prefer to enter upon her hospital duties without ambiguity. She loves peace and desires to ensue it; and rightly considers someone—she doesn't know who—is responsible that the position of women medical students, in so far as their relation to the Nursing Staff is concerned, should be clearly defined, and friction avoided.

Is Work in the Wards Defined?

With this point of view we thoroughly agree, and we have addressed the Wardens of the Medical Schools which have recently admitted women students, and asked them to be good enough to furnish us with a copy of the regulations adopted defining the curriculum for such students in the wards; and to kindly state if the trained sisters and nurses wait upon and instruct them in the application of dressings and other practical details; and if they have any remuneration either from the Medical School or the Hospital Board for these special duties?

A Hospital Sister's View.

We have also consulted an experienced

hospital Sister on the nurse's point of view, and here are a few of her conclusions :—

(1) "It is not exactly a question of sex, but, human nature being what it is, the masculine atmosphere brought into the ward by male students is wholesome and counteracts the somewhat narrow environment of a hospital ward and life in a nursing school. We are all the better for it.

(2) "Young women are more industrious than men of the same age. But they have not their initiative or vitality. They want to know more details, they require more waiting upon, and nurses have little time to spare.

(3) "For some unknown reason medical women take their professional position very seriously, and unfortunately do not realise that trained nurses have any. They do not recognise nursing etiquette. They do not appear to realise where medical duties end, or nursing duties begin. Their relations in war service have made medical women as a class very unpopular with trained nurses.

(4) "As usual the Sisters and nurses do not count. The hospitals which have admitted women medical students have done nothing to organise the situation and define the duties of medical and nursing students, and of course no suggestion has been made in the hospital to remunerate Sisters and nurses, for teaching medical students innumerable practical methods they should learn, if their clinical course is to be of real value to them."

OUR PRIZE COMPETITION.

HOW DOES PUERPERAL SEPTICÆMIA ARISE? DESCRIBE THE COURSE AND MANAGEMENT OF THE CASE.

We have pleasure in awarding the prize this week to Miss Mary D. Hunter, Section Hospital, Kineton, near Warwick.

PRIZE PAPER.

Puerperal septicæmia is due to infection of the uterus after child-birth by streptococcus pyogenes—either alone or with other organisms, especially bacillus coli. The infection is brought to the patient in two ways : from without—namely, on the hands or instruments of the attendant—or it already pre-exists in the body. The uterus, which is normally sterile, may be infected before labour (frequent vaginal examinations tend to infect), or the vagina may contain active organisms, such as gonococcus or streptococcus, which are carried up on the hands or instruments. The disease is nearly always due to failure of asepsis or carelessness on the part of the nurse or doctor. In many cases there is retained placenta in the uterus, which causes absorption of septic material. Failure of cleanliness on the part of the midwife is often a means whereby infection is carried, fæcal stains on the body or bed-clothes being quite sufficient to induce this, or unsterile sponges, towels, lubricant, &c., applied to the vulva. Anyone attending an obstetrical case should be thoroughly disinfected if they have been with an infectious patient or had to lay out a dead body, as infection is so easily carried to a puerperal woman. Prolonged labour, hæmorrhage, or albuminuria all favour infection. The disease starts with a rigor, and there may be repeated rigors. The temperature rises suddenly, usually about the third day, but sometimes earlier. This may fall, but if the pulse remains rapid it is not a good sign. The pulse is very quick, and becomes weak. Lochia is offensive, or may cease. The patient has no appetite, and her tongue soon gets dry and brown. At first there is often constipation, but in the majority of cases diarrhœa occurs later. The urine may contain albumin. Delirium may be present, and in many instances rashes appear on the skin. Great abdominal distension, insomnia, vomiting, or diarrhœa in the later stages foretell a fatal issue. Severe headache is generally complained of ; restlessness is frequently a symptom.

Septic pneumonia and toxic degeneration of the heart or liver are lesions of this disease, the infection spreading to other parts of the body by means of veins, lymphatics, and other natural channels.

Early treatment is most essential, and is nearly always operative. The patient is placed under an anæsthetic, and the uterus explored for retained debris. Curettage is frequently done. Vaginal douching is always employed, and requires the strictest asepsis. If catheterisation is needed it must be done carefully and aseptically, and in any case the vagina requires swabbing whenever the pad is changed. Great cleanliness in vaginal examination is essential as a preventative. The patient should always have plenty of fresh air, and no soiled pads, &c., should be allowed to remain in the bedroom. To promote drainage Fowler's position is useful. Saline injections, either subcutaneously or per rectum, are given, and a fluid diet, which would be gradually increased. Both the back and mouth require attention every four hours. If there is much flatulence and abdominal pain or distension a turpentine enema gives great relief. Alcohol and strychnine are the drugs most often ordered. The case must be treated with the greatest cleanliness and asepsis, sterile gloves being worn by the attendant, and all instruments, &c., thoroughly boiled. For insomnia, opium in some form is generally ordered by the doctor, and is often given in combination with atropin gr. $\frac{1}{160}$ to prevent vomiting and depression.

HONOURABLE MENTION.

The following competitors receive honourable mention :—Mrs. Farthing, Miss A. M. Burns, Miss M. Martin, Miss R. E. S. Cox, Miss C. T. Gaylor, Miss S. Simpson, and Miss E. Powell.

QUESTION FOR NEXT WEEK.

What is rabies? How is it treated and nursed?

OUR HEROINES.

MILITARY MEDAL.

We notified last week that His Majesty the King had awarded a Canadian Matron and five Sisters the Military Medal for distinguished services and splendid courage under fire ; we have pleasure in giving in detail the record of the special acts of gallantry for which they have been awarded the honour.

Matron EDITH CAMPBELL, R.R.C., C.A.M.C.—For gallantry and devotion to duty during an enemy air raid. Regardless of personal danger she attended to the wounded Sisters, and by her personal example inspired the Sisters under her charge.

N./Sister LEONORA HERRINGTON, C.A.M.C.—For gallantry and devotion to duty during an enemy air raid. She remained at duty the entire night, and by her excellent example and personal courage was largely responsible for the maintenance of discipline and efficiency.

N./Sister LOTTIE URQUHART, C.A.M.C.—For gallantry and devotion to duty during an enemy air raid, when four bombs fell on her wards. Regardless of danger she attended to the wounded. Her courage and devotion were an inspiring example to all.

N./Sister JANET MARY WILLIAMSON, C.A.M.C.—For gallantry and devotion to duty during an enemy air raid. When in charge of a ward badly damaged, she displayed exceptional coolness, and, regardless of personal danger, sustained her patients and ensured their evacuation.

N./Sister META HODGE, C.A.M.C., N./Sister ELEANOR JEAN THOMPSON, C.A.M.C.—For gallantry and devotion to duty during an enemy air raid. Although injured by a falling beam, these Sisters displayed great presence of mind in extinguishing overturned oil stoves, and later rendered valuable assistance in the removal of patients.

NURSING AND THE WAR.

Impressive ceremonies commemorated the installation of the first " Victory " syren on the roof of the Evans Building at Washington, U.S.A. The Victory or " Angelus " syren will sound each day the signal for noon-day prayer for victory for the American Army and the Armies of the Allies and for peace everlasting.

Pretty little Miss Irene Elliott Moore unveiled the syren—a typical, upstanding, smiling American beauty.

Let us imagine we hear that Angelus from across the Atlantic, and join silently in the petition for Victory and Peace.

We often wonder if the majority of people, comfortably housed and well fed, really realise the appalling amount of suffering the men of the Allied nations are daily going through so that all that makes life worth living may be secured to us—and how many of us are worth their suffering !

Take men who are gassed with the latest torture chemicals devised by scientific fiends, then ask yourself—What have I ever done in life to deserve that a fellow creature should meet death in the terrible form which thousands have endured and are enduring, so that the world may be a safe and cosy place for women to live in, and that, together with a future generation of men, they may stand straight upon their feet unbroken by tyranny and crime ? Just ask yourself every day—What have I done to-day to deserve it ?

We know of brave women who have only too gladly come to the rescue and tended these stricken men from the very earliest days of the war, whose tender hearts can no longer endure the sight of so much human agony, and who feel they will never during life forget it.

Here we have a true picture of war so seldom permitted to appear in print—for what reason we fail to fathom.

A Sister writes :—" I have had a particularly hard ten days, and have been on duty from a quarter past seven to nine at night. We have had a very bad convoy in, terribly burnt, and with their lungs in a dreadful state, and, in spite of all we could do, a great number died in terrible agony. We are, in a way, unfortunate to be placed where so many of the relations are able to come to see their husbands, brothers, or sons, and one feels that in so many cases it would be better that they should not do so. I have seen things here that I shall never be able to forget, and long to prevent the white-haired parents and young wives seeing them too !

" I have the small wards for the very bad cases, and the isolation-room for the dying, and since I have been here, particularly the last fortnight, I have felt as though I was living through a hideous nightmare, with visions of choking men, with blackened, burnt faces being held down by orderlies and attached to their beds to prevent them throwing themselves out of the window in their last struggles for breath.

"A great part of my work has consisted in persuading grief and horror-stricken relations to await the end in another room, to save them the pain of these tragic scenes, and in breaking the news to others that may have arrived too late to see their dear ones alive."

Another Sister supplements this terrible report. She says : "I am still working among the gassed cases. Very appalling it is to see the sufferings of the victims. The extent of the burns is hardly explicable—internally and externally in some cases—but, as ever, the brave, courageous poilu with never a murmur, is always cheerful and grateful when conscious."

And again :—" During my experience of war nursing (four years), this of the caring for the gassed cases is one, if not the most, fatiguing ; there is a continued indescribable feeling of tiredness, lassitude, and depression, and it is very sad —very sad—so many dying, and the death so agonising. And what to say to the poor heart-broken women, mourning their sons and husbands." What, indeed !

How one's heart burns to read of such torture ! For those who have caused it there must be just and adequate punishment, or there can be no real victory in this war, or future hope for humanity. We read with impatience the platitudes of politicians of alien descent in the Councils of the Nation, and turn with relief and hope to the robust mentality and plain speech of the men America has elected to power.

When one reads of the death of a nurse owing to a disturbance in a military hospital by black troops, one wonders who is responsible for the discipline of the institution, for evidently it requires twitching up.

An inquest was held last week on the body of Nurse McShane, aged 40.

Mr. William Henry Taylor, officer in charge of Belmont Road Military Auxiliary Hospital, Liverpool, said it contained black and white patients, the former being British West Indians. The

coloured men had been over-staying the time allowed them out of hospital. In consequence the military police guard was redoubled and the names and numbers of late-comers were taken. Wednesday, last week, a West Indian sergeant, named Demetrius, attempted to leave the hospital. He was stopped, but immediately drew a razor and slashed wildly with it. He was disarmed and

LITTLE IRENE ELLIOTT MOORE UNVEILING THE "VICTORY" SYREN AT WASHINGTON, U.S.A.

placed in a cell. Ten late-comers, all West Indians then appeared. Two of the number refused to go to their wards, and, being joined by four or five other coloured men, also late-comers, became very abusive. An attempt was made to take them to the cells, and fifty other West Indians joined in the affair, taking possession of the police lodge. Some 400 wounded British soldiers, who were at a concert in the hospital hall, came to the rescue of the military police. There was a struggle, in which crutches and sticks were freely used, and pots and pans were flying about. The police were reinforced and order was restored.

Unfortunately, Nurse McShane, while helping another girl, named White, a laundress, who had fainted, was caught in the rush of men. She was carried off her feet against a door that became unhinged, and was knocked down. She suffered from shock, but no severe injuries. Pneumonia developed, and she died four days later.

After hearing medical evidence the jury returned a verdict of " Death through misadventure "

THE ODYSSEY OF FRANCESCA.

Part III.

(*Continued from page 192.*)

Francesca was nothing if not intelligent. She had had the foresight to arrange to have an uncle on the British Headquarter Staff, and as she was not continuing her long journey up to the Serbian front till the evening, it was clearly her uncle's duty to take her out and show her what he could of Salonika.

Francesca, like everyone else, had heard of the Great Fire at Salonika, but she had not realised that the whole of the centre of the city, down to the very quays, had been destroyed. No doubt a finer and more sanitary city will rise on its ruins one day, but in the meantime little temporary booths or bazaars have been erected everywhere, and merchants who are for the most part Spanish Jews do a roaring trade at prices which only a millionaire or an up-country officer on two days' leave from the front could stand. Francesca particularly admired the colossal impudence of some of these ricketty little booths. For instance, a little wooden shanty with just room for one customer inside called itself " Galleries de la Fayette," and exhibited in its tiny lattice window three appalling hats at prices which would make even Paris stare.

Nevertheless, Francesca decided that Salonika is one of the Seven Sights of the world. No one who has not seen it can ever imagine the kaleidoscope it is of people of every nationality, jostling one another just like a crowd on the opera stage.

Francesca's uncle took her first to the White Tower, which is *the* place to have tea, hear music and see the world.

They found seats up in the gallery, and looked down on a great hall with hundreds of little tables occupied by representatives from every Allied Army who were consuming every known variety of drinks. There were Serb officers, tall, slim and good-looking, in khaki or *bleu d'horizon* and most magnificent shining top-boots ; French of every type, from the big blonde son of Normandy to the deep bronze of the Chasseurs d'Afrique, and in

every kind of uniform, as, for some reason known only to themselves, no two French officers ever wear the same dress. Red-tabbed British staff-officers abounded, Italians in grey green, French and English sailors, Colonial troops of every description, Albanian soldiers with khaki coats, British-looking khaki caps, dark blue breeches, long white stockings, finishing off at the feet with native shoes having long curled-up points. Women were conspicuous by their absence. The fair sex was represented by a few Sisters and other workers from the various hospitals, a fat Jewess dressed in a white piqué skirt, purple-brown boots and a mauve flowered silk dressing jacket ; and some frail beauties from the half world.

After tea they strolled along the quay and watched picturesque processions out of the " Arabian Nights " passing slowly up and down for our inspection. First came a grave Turkish gentleman in a blue dressing-gown and a red fez, riding on a donkey ; a Greek woman followed him in a gorgeous dress of blue velvet powdered with gold stars and edged with fur, and a bright green silk headdress lined with puce.

Two ambulances came tearing past, the first bearing the inscription " Presented to the B.R.C.S. by the British Residents in the Hawaian Islands."

Greek sailors were unloading casks of wine from Samos out of the gaily painted boats moored right up to the quay side, and slinging them on to the backs of poor little overloaded mules staggering under their weight ; ox-carts grinded slowly along the road piled high with evil-smelling hides. Then came a Greek funeral, the hearse going first, with the coffin open, showing an old man, yellow as wax, dressed in a black woollen cardigan coat and his bowler hat laid at the bottom of the coffin, a little open carriage, with five mourners, in deep crape, followed the hearse ; and behind them, another carriage contained three Greek popes in white surplices and tall black hats, who were going to perform the burial service.

After the funeral, the wedding. In a few minutes another little carriage appeared, in which a British " Tommy," grinning from ear to ear and looking more than a little sheepish, sat with a blushing Serbian bride beside him, a gipsy piper sitting on the box playing a native dance. Francesca wondered what they would do after the war. Would Tommy stay out in this country and present Serbia with little Anglo-Serbs to add to the *macédoine* of races already here, or would he take her back to England, where the customs, religion, speech and food are all strange to her ? And would it be a success ? What a toss-up a mixed marriage is, she thought—or any other marriage for that matter.

Francesca had only just time to get down to the station for the night train. And such a train ! Up to now she had travelled *de luxe* ; for the first time she began to realise that she was getting near the front.   V. T.

. (*To be concluded.*)

Royal British Nurses' Association.

(Incorporated by Royal Charter.)

THIS SUPPLEMENT BEING THE OFFICIAL ORGAN OF THE CORPORATION.

BUILDERS OF YOUR OWN PROFESSION OR PERSIAN KITTENS—WHICH?

The Registration Board meets, for the first time after the holiday recess, at the end of the forthcoming week, and nurses who have decided to place their names on the Register of the Corporation should send in their applications without delay, and thereby line up under the banner of the Royal Charter in the struggle to set the profession on surer foundations, and to attain to such organisation as will effectually safeguard the interests of the nurses and ensure real development and progress for their profession. Such development can never come by the easy paths offered by patronage and benevolence; it can only come from *within* the profession—that is, through the will and the effort of the nurses themselves. Unless the nurses are prepared to consider the present situation and to take some part, however small, in looking after their own interests, they will only have themselves to blame if the conditions under which they work continue to be dictated more by the convenience of the institutions than by any needs and claims of the workers.

In a letter, received just as we go to press, a very clear-headed and progressive Member of the Association tells of a call she had from a Member of the College of Nursing, Ltd. The latter lady was evidently blissfully ignorant of the actual principles involved in the present controversy, and kept reiterating her conviction that "we should all join up." As for the precise reason for arriving at this conclusion she was quite deliciously nebulous, her principal argument in support of her case being "everybody's doing it," a statement disproved by the existence and attitude of seven self-supporting organised societies of nurses. Apart from this inaccuracy, however, if her particular line of reasoning were, in itself, the correct one whereby to govern our lives, we should still have been cave dwellers, with an

intelligence a little higher than the brutes. Far too many people are content that, in their adult bodies, they shall retain but the child's faculty for reason and judgment; they are too lazy to think out courageously and independently those questions which concern them and their fellow-workers, but prefer to take the line of least resistance, to be mere reflections of those in whose environment they chance to be. In fact, they prefer to share among them a kind of group soul, which, at the present time, so far as nursing questions are concerned, they seem to have handed into the keeping of people outside the borders of the profession altogether —people much cleverer than themselves, who long ago recognised in a Royal Chartered Corporation of Nurses a prospective, potential antagonist, a power in the hands of the nurses. It therefore became their policy to use their influence to prevent the Association, if possible, from adding the strength of numbers to the powers it had won in the Charter. To any understanding authority, before which demands might be laid, there is a wide difference between a Royal Association of *Nurses*, incorporated by the most ancient and honourable form of incorporation, and a College of *Nursing*, incorporated under the Companies' Act. The latter can only claim to be a company started to deal with nursing education. But a Chartered Association of *Nurses* implies something quite different. It means a *living* organisation, built up by the nurses themselves, a body which, were it hundreds of thousands strong, could still move and act as one body. Under the Great Seal of the United Kingdom, the *Nurses* have been given the powers to build up such an organisation, a great combined body to voice their claims. Under the Sign Manual of a Sovereign of the Realm, they have been given the recognition and the authority for those claims to be heard if they come forward in sufficient numbers to show that they really desire progress for their profession, better salaries and more reasonable hours. It lies entirely with the nurses themselves to decide whether they will use the powers which have been granted to them by joining the Association or one of the Organised Societies affiliated to it.

COMFORTS FOR THE ARMY.

An appeal has appeared recently in the Press from Her Royal Highness the Princess Christian for comforts for a division of artillery serving at the front. Some years ago the members signified their wish to send work to Her Royal Highness' Hospital at Englefield Green and it has been suggested that Members of the Association and of the Societies affiliated to it might like to help this appeal for comforts for the soldiers. Articles sent to the office of the Association, 10, Orchard Street, Portman Square, will be forwarded to Her Royal Highness along with a list of the donors. Mufflers, woollen helmets, gloves and mittens are the comforts needed.

A POPULAR MEMBER OF THE AUSTRALIAN BRANCH.

Miss Mary Bennallack has resigned from Q.A.I.M.N.S. and is awaiting orders for transport duty to Australia. Miss Bennallack was formerly Secretary of the Australian Branch of the Association and was spending a holiday in England at the outbreak of war. She was granted extension of leave by her Committee in order to take up military nursing, and went to France in the early months of the war. In time it became impossible for the Australian branch to continue its work without a permanent secretary, and Miss Bennallack decided to resign that office. She has had very varied experiences indeed in the course of her military nursing, and was, at one time, seriously wounded during the course of a bombardment by the Germans. Miss Bennallack has been extremely popular among members of the home branch of the Association, and she takes their sincere good wishes back with her to the island continent.

CORRESPONDENCE.

Whilst welcoming communications from its Members the Corporation does not hold itself responsible for individual expressions of opinion.

THE NATION'S FUND FOR NURSES.
To the Secretary, R.B.N.A.

MADAM,—As an Irish Nurse I wish to support Miss Kelly's protest. I feel furious and ashamed when I walk along Whitechapel and see that insulting poster everywhere. I consider that the College of Nursing, Ltd., is using the gratitude of our patients to destroy our status and to get money for their own purposes and we will simply be reduced to a condition of serfdom if they can capture the "debt" which is due to us (the nurses), not to them. Had those on the Council

done anything for nurses in the past we might have had less anxiety but it is they and they only who are responsible for State Registration being too late to save us from the competition with the unqualified. There is another point of view, too. Only the other day I heard of a lady who openly said that she would support the Nation's Fund as, if there were a National Fund, the nurses would require smaller fees. We wish to retain our independence, to have just payment for what we do, and no charity. Please put my letter in the Journal also. Yours, &c., A. E. GOOD.

CHILD PSYCHOLOGY.
To the Secretary, R.B.N.A.

MADAM,—In answer to Miss Nash's letter in THE BRITISH JOURNAL OF NURSING of September 21st, I should like to thank her for the appreciation expressed in it. I certainly hope that there will be more articles by the nurses.

As regards her question, I must say that no child I ever knew was reduced to the state of submission she suggests. My recommendation, however, applied especially to children of a "negative" disposition. There are so many points to be considered and different dispositions require different methods of treatment; even when such methods are laid down we generally find that they are upset by the suggestions of the children themselves—suggestions that are often both interesting and instructive to us and often better suited than ours for their particular needs. As Dr. Saleeby so aptly said at the Baby Week Council Meeting, "Our highest aim must be to Guard, *Guide* and Teach." One could really give a lecture on Miss Nash's question.

Yours, &c., KATE C. ATHERTON.

[We regret that some letters are unavoidably held over.]

DONATIONS.

To the Fund for State Registration.—*Per* Miss Daisy Hobbs, £5 5s.; Dr. Clarke, £1 1s.; Mrs. Lawson, £1 1s.; Miss Gordon Brown, £1; A. Britten, 10s. 6d.; *Per* Miss Spearing, 9s.; Miss Bosworth, 5s.; Miss Mercer, 5s.; Miss Morgan, 5s.; Miss Owen, 5s.; Miss Puley, 5s.; Miss Crumpler, 5s.; Miss Fowler, 2s. 6d.; and Mrs. Moorhead, 5s.

Copies of the Royal Charter may be obtained from the Office at the cost of 1s., or 1s. 6d. post free.

Application Forms and other literature regarding the Corporation can be obtained from the office of the Association. The Secretary will be pleased to see any nurses who wish to have information regarding nursing questions, between the hours of 11 a.m. and 1 p.m., or by appointment.

(Signed) ISABEL MACDONALD,
Secretary to the Corporation.
10, Orchard Street,
Portman Square, W. 1.

THE MATRONS' COUNCIL OF GREAT BRITAIN AND IRELAND.

A Meeting of the Matrons' Council of Great Britain and Ireland will be held, by the kind invitation of the President, Miss Heather Bigg, R.R.C., at Charing Cross Hospital on Saturday, October 19th, at 3 p.m.

The President will be in the Chair, and several questions of interest appear on the Agenda for discussion. The report of Miss Helen Pearse, one of the delegates to the Meeting of the National Council of Women at Harrogate from October 8th to 10th, will be of special interest. Miss Steel, Matron County Hospital, York, and Miss J. Davies, Matron Royal Infirmary, Bradford, will also attend the Conference as representatives of the Matrons' Council.

POOR LAW INFIRMARY MATRONS' ASSOCIATION.

At a meeting, on September 28th, of the Executive Committee of the Poor Law Infirmary Matrons' Association, the following resolution was passed :—

"That the members of the P.L.I.M.A. learn with sincere regret of the retirement of Miss Stansfeld from the office of Chief Lady Inspector of the Local Government Board. They wish to record their deep gratitude and appreciation of her continued kindness and consideration to them, not only as Matrons, in their individual training schools, but also as members of the P.L.I.M.A. Miss Stansfeld from its earliest commencement has done all that was in her power to strengthen and encourage the Association, and her support has very considerably aided in its success. Their earnest hope is that Miss Stansfeld may long be spared to enjoy the rest which she so well deserves."

The Annual Meeting of the P.L.I.M.A. will be held at 3 o'clock on Saturday, October 26th, at the Eustace Miles Restaurant, Chandos Street, Charing Cross.

THE ROYAL RED CROSS.

The King decorated the following ladies with the Royal Red Cross, at Buckingham Palace, on September 26th :—

SECOND CLASS.

Queen Alexandra's Imperial Military Nursing Service Reserve.—Sister JANE TROTTER.

Territorial Force Nursing Service.—Sister LAVINIA TAYLOR.

Voluntary Aid Detachment.—Miss MARY FYNES-CLINTON, the Lady ARTHUR GROSVENOR, and Miss MARGARET RICHARDSON.

Miss Ellen Kate Finnemore, Matron, Queen Mary's R.N. Hospital, Southend, has been awarded the Royal Red Cross, 1st Class, in recognition of her valuable services in connection with the war.

OUR ROLL OF HONOUR.

Full military honours were accorded the funeral of Miss Dorothy Pearson Twist, at Aldershot. Deceased came from British Columbia to nurse, and died at Cambridge Hospital from pneumonia.

QUEEN VICTORIA'S JUBILEE INSTITUTE FOR NURSES.

EXAMINATION FOR THE ROLL OF QUEEN'S NURSES, SEPTEMBER 19TH, 1918.

1.—Describe how to peptonise milk and how to prepare (a) whey; (b) beef tea; (c) meat juice; (d) a saline injection.

2.—What conditions would lead you to suspect in a pregnant woman (a) gonorrhœa; (b) syphilis; and what advice would you give? What dangers would you seek to avert?

3.—What would you do if called into a case of a bad burn, or scald, in a child, before the arrival of the doctor?

4.—What is meant by putting a room in nursing order? How would you do it for (1) a case of pneumonia, and (2) a chronic case of paralysis, in a two-roomed house with two adults besides the patient?

5.—What advice, special and general, would you give a mother whose child is suffering from measles? What special precautions should be taken as regards (a) the child; (b) the family; (c) the nurse herself?

6A.—What advice would you give in order to assist a family, the members of which consist of (1) a soldier son blinded in the war; (2) a phthisical mother; and (3) a younger child, aged ten, with tubercular hip disease—the father being delicate, can only work half-time?

or

6B.—How would you act if brought into contact with a case of child neglect in your district?

APPOINTMENTS.

CHARGE NURSE FOR VENEREAL DEPARTMENT.

Leicester Royal Infirmary.—Mrs. Burnett has been appointed Charge Nurse for the Venereal Department. She was trained at West Bromwich Hospital, and has been Sister at the London Lock Hospital.

LADY NIGHT SUPERINTENDENT.

Belfast Municipal Sanatorium, Whiteabbey.—Miss Lillie Thompson Fitzgerald has been appointed Lady Night Superintendent She was trained at the Royal Victoria Hospital, Belfast, and has been Sister at Down County Infirmary, and Sister-in-Charge Belfast Charitable Society.

SISTER.

Queen Mary's Hospital for the East End, Stratford.—Miss Frost has been appointed Sister, She was trained at the Royal Hospital, Portsmouth. and has been Staff Nurse and Temporary Sister at the above hospital.

NURSING ECHOES.

The Editor wishes to offer her warmest thanks for the very kind and appreciative letters received during the past week from readers of THE BRITISH JOURNAL OF NURSING, many of whom have subscribed to it for the whole twenty-five years during which she has been responsible for its precepts and policy. The Editor intends to keep all these welcome *billets doux*, as she values them most sincerely, but she refrains from publishing them, as they estimate far beyond its merit the work she has done—although she has done her best!

The Editor is still convinced that the most valuable asset a profession can own is a free professional organ in the press, *an organ which is not to be bought.* She asks, therefore, as her reward that those nurses who love freedom will help to keep their JOURNAL alive and buzzing. This can be done by : (1) subscribing to it and supporting its policy ; (2) influencing others to do the same ; (3) contributing to it, and thus increasing its literary and public value ; (4) bringing it to the notice of high-class professional advertisers.

THE BRITISH JOURNAL OF NURSING has made great financial sacrifices for the professional principles for which it stands, and so long as the present Editor is in the Chair these principles will be paramount.

We have had some very instructive documents before us recently. How the demoniacal psychology of the Hun has influenced our nursing affairs in England for the past thirty years is almost incredible. Cash and craft, of course !

All the salaries of the various grades of the Nursing Staff at Charing Cross Hospital have been advanced 25 per cent., and the Committee, Matron, and Nurses are all to be congratulated.

At present Sisters receive per annum £45, rising £5 annually to £55.

Probationers—£16, £18, and £20, in first, second, and third years, and as Staff Nurses in fourth year's service £26.

Senior posts are remunerated as follows :— Sister Housekeeper, £70 ; Home Sister, £60 ; Maternity Sister, £65 ; and Night Sister, £50. Add 25 per cent. to these salaries, and we do not wonder the Nursing Staff are very well satisfied.

Board, lodging, washing and uniform are also provided, so that it will be seen such remuneration compares very favourably with the earnings of other professional women workers. We have no doubt if the right type of women is to be secured for training, all the hospitals and infirmaries must estimate their services at an increased value.

We hope to hear of banking accounts and the purchase of War Bonds.

The question of whether the Nurses' Home at the Staincliffe Poor Law Institution should be under the management of a housekeeper or a nursing sister was discussed last week at a meeting of the Dewsbury Board of Guardians. The Board had decided to fill a vacancy by again appointing a housekeeper, but the Infirmary Committee reported that in consequence of the receipt of a letter from the Sisters they had interviewed the Superintendent Nurse and two other nurses, and after hearing their representations they recommended the Board to rescind the previous resolution and to appoint a " home sister."

Mr. C. H. Appleyard, in moving the adoption of the committee's report, said it was understood that the unanimous desire of the seventy or eighty nurses was that their home should be controlled by a Sister. The committee supported the suggestion because they believed that if it was accepted a grievance would be removed, and the head of the home would have a better understanding and more sympathy with the nurses, who had difficult work to perform while on duty, as often happened, for twelve or more hours at a stretch.

The two Ossett members were not satisfied that a trained nurse would be qualified to undertake the duties of a housekeeper.

Mrs. Whitling replied that the duty of a home sister was to see that the cooks and other servants did their work in such a way as to ensure the comfort of the nurses. What was required was a woman of character to act as a " mother " to all the nurses, and especially to the younger girls who had just left their homes. Neither a housekeeper nor a home sister had to cook or clean, as some members seemed to think.

The Rev. J. E. Crabtree stated that he went to the committee meeting with an open mind, but after hearing the matter discussed he formed the opinion that it was desirable to appoint a home sister who would exercise more influence and secure better discipline than a housekeeper, who had not been a nurse.

Mr. G. Blacker said up-to-date nursing institutions were now being placed under the management of home sisters, and their appointment had been recommended by a lady inspector of the Local Government Board.

Eventually it was agreed, on the proposition of Mrs. Walker, seconded by Mrs. Hirst, to refer the matter back to the committee until the clerk had made inquiries as to the practice at similar institutions.

We are glad the Board is to give further consideration to this important matter. The Nurses' Home should be under the personal direction of a trained nurse, if good discipline, comfort, and happiness are to be maintained. Professional women are not amenable to the control of a lay housekeeper, whose personal interests are often at variance with the best interests of the Nursing School arrangements and domestic comfort of the staff. At the same time a Home Sister should have experience of domestic science and be a trained dietitian, otherwise the best standard of economy, together with efficiency, cannot be attained.

At a recent meeting of the Skipton Urban Council a letter was read from Dr. Bullough, the acting County Medical Officer, stating that Nurse Grainger, recently appointed health visitor for Skipton under a joint arrangement with the County Council and the local authority, was also to take charge of the maternity centre and clinic.

Mr. Farey moved that the letter be referred back, and characterised the arrangement as a deliberate betrayal of the intentions of the County Council and the Local Health Committee. That Committee had put its hand to the plough to suppress and extinguish phthisis, and they intended to carry out their task.

Mr. Hartly hoped the Council would support the maternity centre.

Both objects are good, but in our view they must not be carried out by the same nurse if justice is to be done to both. A Health Visitor's primary duty is visiting. She cannot, therefore, be on duty at the maternity centre and clinic.

There is the added risk of her bringing infection to the clinic, to which it should not be subjected. We agree with Mr. Jennings that a combination of the two appointments would probably end in the local authority having a nurse in theory only.

SAVE YOUR BOVRIL BOTTLES.

By desire of the Director-General of National Salvage all users of Bovril are requested to carefully save all empty Bovril bottles. The supply of Bovril this winter will largely depend upon the care which the public take in returning empty Bovril bottles.

OUTSIDE THE GATES.

The women's section of the Imperial War Services Museum is organising an exhibition to be opened at the Whitechapel Art Gallery on October 9th.

The Home Office will have a big section, organised by Miss Anderson, chief woman Factory Inspector, showing the substitution of women for men.

An important section will be that devoted to a memorial to the women who have lost their lives on war service. Their number is far greater than the ordinary civilian realises. A number of the medals won by women, which have been presented to the museum, will be shown, including Mrs. Harley's Serbian and French medals, and Dr. Elsie Inglis's Serbian medals. The memorial will be draped in black, and should prove both inspiring and impressive.

BOOK OF THE WEEK.

"THE LOVE OF AN UNKNOWN SOLDIER."*

FOUND IN A DUG-OUT.

Amongst the many pathetic documents which have been produced in connection with the war, none can make a more poignant appeal than the letters which are reproduced in this volume.

Mr. John Lane, who is the publisher, has himself written the "Explanation," and his reasons for publishing the volume.

He says : " The MS. was submitted to me by a young officer from the Front on leave. He explained that he had brought with him from France a bundle of papers which he had found in an abandoned gun position. There was no indication of the writer's name or his unit, and the name of the girl he loved was never recorded. His first impulse was to respect the dead man's privacy and destroy the papers ; but on second thoughts he recognised that they were the sacred property of the woman who had inspired such adoration and courage."

Mr. John Lane goes on to say that he was from the first impressed with the literary value of the MS. but " as I read on I became more and more deeply absorbed in its poignant human importance, especially in its importance to some American girl, who, all unknowingly, had quickened the last days of this unknown soldier's life with romance. I felt that she must be discovered and that the only chance of doing so was by publishing these documents."

This " explantaion " at once placed on the letters the *cachet* of their genuine character, and we know beyond doubt that we are reading the outpouring of a brave and gallant gentleman, to the woman he loved with a love so unselfish

---

* John Lane, Bodley Head.

and true that he counted his own happiness as naught in the balance. " So it is all over. It was only a dream which happened in my brain. We have said good-bye and I have not told you. We have come to our last night ; to-morrow I return to the Front, leaving you almost as much a stranger as when we met. And yet—yes, I am glad I said nothing. What right have I, who may be dead within a month, to speak to you of love ? To have done so would have been the act of a coward." Then he sums up the case to himself, " so that I may act strongly." " If I had spoken and you had loved me in return, what would have resulted—only suffering. . . . you all the time would have been lonely. . . Then I might have been maimed. I would not have held you to your bargain with a maimed man, for I might have to live to see you shudder. And then, I may die in this war. Who can tell ? If I had married you, I should have stolen your happiness, and left you deserted. No, I am glad I did not speak of love."

He goes on to describe his first meeting with her in America :

" I looked into your eyes. What did I see there ? Something haunting that I shall never forget. There you stood, a tall slim girl, like a rosebud on a stem with its petals unfolding. They said you were sailing for France with a unit that was going to take care of little children in the devastated district. I know devastated districts. I have helped to do the devastating. There are dead men mouldering in every shell-hole. I couldn't see you in that picture ; you, with your delicate, fashionable sweetness."

Fate decreed that he should meet her again in Paris. Fate ! He preferred to call it something else.

" Your footstep on the stairs. A gentle rustling. You were standing before me girlish and friendly, offering me the frailness of your hand. . . . The fun we had at the café where we went to lunch. Do you remember that ? Our laughter at the curious people. And who were we that we should laugh at others. We two, who by such strange chances had found each other from all across the world. When we left, it was snowing ; not hard, but in little puffy flakes, like jewels that settled on your hair and furs. . . . Since you will never read this, I will play a game. I will not send you what I write, but I will speak the truth to you on paper. If I live, perhaps some day when war is over, you will receive all your mail at once."

His last evening with her. " How the evening hurried. We were out in the Boulevard again " (after the opera). " Did you expect me to say anything in those last moments ? I heard myself talking commonplaces in a voice which did not seem my own. I would speak. I would tell you. We talked. It was too late. ' Good-bye,' you said. ' Good-bye,' I repeated. ' You won't forget to write.' "

You withdrew your hand and nodded. Turning, you ran upstairs.

I wonder, will you write ? When I asked you to do so, was that embarrassed nod of the head, a polite evasion of a refusal ?

I can see you now, as you ran upstairs. You didn't look back. Had you stayed a moment longer I might have spoken the words which were better left unsaid. I think you knew that."

She does write to him, but not so soon as his heart cries out for ; but it comes at last. " Such a jolly letter. So full of yourself. . . . "

" Military discipline has given me a purpose— to live bravely, dare cheerfully, and, if need be, to die gratefully. So you see how meeting you has upset my plans. You can't love a woman and not gaze into the future. You can't feel the need of her and be resigned to die. . . . I dreamed of you last night. It was the first time this has happened. We were in a garden full of sunshine and roses. You were leaning on my arm. We must have been married a long time, for there was no strangeness in our being together.

" You were intensely mine while the dream lasted, and then I awoke to find myself without you. . . . My dearest, I want to hold you and say nothing. I want——"

Here the letters end abruptly.

We feel that we are treading on holy ground as we read, almost as though we were desecrating some sacred place.

Will his " little American " recognise this message from " her man " ? Will it seem to her the " wild, wild talk " he feared it might ? Will the agony of the " might have been," or the joy of possessing for ever this chivalrous love outweigh in the balance ? " Those who have felt no pain have known no joy." Her lover has gone down into the silence which cannot be broken, but he has left her a record of tender chivalry which any woman would be proud to possess.

And yet—and yet—may she not echo his yearning words : " What I want is to feel your arms about me and your lips against my ears, whispering ' Mon petit.' "   H. H.

COMING EVENTS.

October 5th.—Irish Nurses' Association. Meeting Executive Committee. 34, St. Stephen's Green, Dublin. 8 p.m.

October 8th, 9th and 10th.—National Council of Women. Meeting in Harrogate. The Report of Committee on the Revision of the Constitution will be submitted. Conference.

October 12th.—Queen Alexandra will open the Cavell Memorial Home and unveil a statue at Norwich on the anniversary of Edith Cavell's execution.

OUR PRIZE COMPETITION.
QUESTIONS.

October 12th.—What is rabies ? How is it treated and nursed ?

October 19th.—Give instructions for making Anti-vermin Underclothing for the troops ; also for disinfecting soldiers' clothing at the Front.

LETTERS TO THE EDITOR.

Whilst cordially inviting communications upon all subjects for these columns, we wish it to be distinctly understood that we do not IN ANY WAY hold ourselves responsible for the opinions expressed by our correspondents.

A FREE PRESS.

To the Editor of THE BRITISH JOURNAL OF NURSING.

DEAR EDITOR,—Whilst offering my warm congratulations to you on the occasion of the twenty-fifth birthday of THE BRITISH JOURNAL OF NURSING with its record of unswerving service to the highest ideals of the profession, may I also offer a word of encouragement at a time when the struggle is perhaps harder than ever ?

Mr. Hilaire Belloc, in his recently published book, " The Free Press," testifies to the value of independent organs. Writing of two special periodicals, he says :—" We discover these papers with their limited circulation, their lack of advertisement subsidy, their restriction to a comparatively small circle, possessing a power which is not only increasing but has long been quite out of proportion to their numerical status." He writes very forcibly about the danger of advertisement to the freedom of the pen—a danger we have seen illustrated only too clearly in the case of the Nation's Fund for Nurses. He believes that the antidote to the advertisement-bribed press lies in " the formation of small, independent organs with their increasing influence." " It is now clear," he says, " that steady work in the exposure of what is evil, whatever forces are brought to bear against this exposure, bears fruit."

Had it not been for THE BRITISH JOURNAL OF NURSING there would have been no voice in the public press to uphold the cause of professional independence and progress.

May an ever-increasing number of nurses realise what this Journal is doing for them, and show their sense of indebtedness by supporting it in every possible way. We cannot be too grateful to its Editor for her clear vision and courageous stedfastness.

I am, yours faithfully,
E. L. C. EDEN.

The Grange, Kingston, Taunton.

NOT BEFORE TIME.

To the Editor of THE BRITISH JOURNAL OF NURSING.

DEAR MADAM,—From time to time suggestions have been made in the London press that the Nursing Staffs of civilian Hospitals are not receiving adequate remuneration.

We think that these suggestions are, in part, justified. The scale of nursing emoluments, none too high before the war, has now become very inadequate.

May we suggest that a Conference of the Chairmen of Metropolitan Hospitals should meet and discuss the whole matter of emoluments, holidays, and hours of work ? We think this would be the most satisfactory way of approaching matters.

Meanwhile the Council of Charing Cross Hospital have awarded an increase of 25 per cent. on the salaries of the Nursing Staff (which are on a level with most other London hospitals) to meet the additional cost of clothes and other living expenses, and we feel sure that the Council will have the full support of their subscribers in this movement.

We beg to remain, your obedient servants,
(Signed)   GEORGE VERITY,
Chairman of the Council.
HERBERT F. WATERHOUSE,
Senior Surgeon.
JOHN TOWER,
Vice-Chairman.

Charing Cross Hospital,
Agar Street, Strand, W.C. 2.

METHOD IN THEIR MADNESS.

To the Editor of THE BRITISH JOURNAL OF NURSING.

DEAR MADAM,—Can you explain this madness upon the part of the public for managing nurses ? Wherever I go it is the same, in town or country. No one appears to consider them capable of arranging their own affairs, and men are worse than women. I asked a patronising dame the other day why she did not try to run the shopgirls, or girl clerks, or even domestic servants ; but no, she must for ever be fussing and dictating to nurses, and, of course, they are all against a just form of legislation, and whenever the question is under discussion everyone flies into tempers. It must be a form of mania.

Yours truly,
A DISTRICT NURSE.

[If nurses were free to manage their own affairs they would become a rich and independent corporation. This their powerful employers are determined they never shall be. You will notice it is always their finances which must be so carefully kept under the control of outsiders. By the by, do you belong to the R.B.N.A., and have you thus proved you are prepared to help yourself and your colleagues by strong, united action ? If not, join at once, and help to save the independence of the Nursing Profession in the coming fight for a just Registration Bill.—ED.]

MANY THINGS MAY HAPPEN.

By an unfortunate printer's error the editorial replies to two correspondents were, on September 21st, included in one. The paragraph after the word " impedimenta " in reply to " Done Brown," should be attached, as it is this week, to a letter which was held over. As is well known the Royal British Nurses' Association only registers nurses who hold a certificate of three years' general training, the error of appearing to advise a *Probationer* to join the Association must be self-evident. —ED.

The Midwife.

THE SOLILOQUY OF AN UNWANTED BABE.

He never arsted to come. Bless 'is 'eart !

Somebody very big and large said that about me when I was born four weeks ago. It's the only sensible thing I have heard said since I *did* come for certainly I should never have 'arsted to come, and I only wish I knew the way to get back.

I don't understand anything here. A long time ago where I came from there were hundreds and hundreds of little creatures like me. Some were waiting to go to mummies and daddies who were waiting for *them*. How we knew about that I can't tell you, but we did. And every time a mummy finished a little gown or put another pair of boots in the bottom drawer, her little baby in the " Never Never Land " gurgled with delight because it knew the time was drawing nearer and nearer when it would go to its own real live daddy and mummy.

But in the corner of " Never Never Land," where I used to be, the little babies were sad because there did not seem to be any daddy for them, and very often their mummies did not want them to come.

Why do people have little babies if they don't want them ? Why do some daddies run away and hide, and often their mummies run away, too ? It seems very strange, because, as the big person said, we never " arsted to come." They must have " arsted " us or we should never have thought of it.

Where my mummy has gone I can't tell. She's gone a long way off. I think I heard the large somebody say, " Well, pore thing, she's out of 'er trouble now anyway. She's better orf, she is. She's been treated shameful, she 'as."

Well, of course, I don't know what that means at all. I wish she could have stopped with me. If she is out of her troubles, it seems to me I am only just beginning mine, and I feel very small and lonely.

I don't know what place this is where I am ; but I heard the large somebody say something about the workhouse being the best place for me, because, she said, " look at the price of milk and everythink, and then what a handful a baby is. You can't go nowhere nor do nothink with a baby to mind. And the washin' they makes no one could credit. Your own's bad enough, but you've got to put up with them whether you like it or not ; but other people's kids is different. Besides there aint no one reely 'sponsible for the money."

It's all very strange. What *did* she mean ?

So they brought me here.

There are no daddies and mummies here. It's a place for little babies who haven't got any.

Great, ugly people come and look at us now and then. They are called " Guardians." Its very funny as they are not in the least like the guardian angels who took care of us in the " Never, Never Land." You can't imagine *anything* more different.

These " Guardians " are very, very old indeed, and they say such *silly* things. I suppose they think we don't understand, but we do and we peep through our cots and laugh at each other. Of course, they don't see as they all wear great glasses over their eyes. Our guardian angels didn't.

" This is a beautiful nursery," they say. " 'Ow much better off the children are 'ere than in their own 'omes." (Silly old men !) " And so beautiful and clean too."

Its a great disadvantage not to be able to speak, and all I can do is to howl when they poke their great fingers in my soft little face. What I thought was this (for babies can *think* all sorts of wise things, though you mightn't imagine it to look at them) :—

" Old men, your nursery has the right amount of cubic air space ; your cots are the latest pattern ; your patent food is expensive ; your nurses do their duty, they feed us by the clock, they wash us night and morning, sometimes they kiss the prettiest of us. Do you really think, old men, that this makes up for not having a mummy of your own, even if she is not a very tidy or a very clean mummy ? Where I came from ' one baby one mummy ' was the rule. There, of course, real mummies say ' Diddums, diddums, my precious,' to their babies, and kiss them, and kiss them, and kiss them.

I should like to ask these old, old people, when they were babies (if they ever were), if they would like to have worn a little coarse " nightie " with a blue stripe in it, and not the teeniest, *teeniest* piece of lace round the neck—not the least like the little things we used to watch mummies putting in the bottom drawer when we were in " Never, Never Land."

Often the mummies would kiss the little gowns and sheets. I am sure no mummie would kiss these.

Well, I have finished my grouse, because it does not seem any use.

I think the next best thing to having a mummie and daddy of your own is for someone else's to have you. I hear it is sometimes done. *Real* mummies often love lonely little babies almost as much as their own.

I hope these old Guardians will board me out, I believe that is what they call it. I would rather make mud pies when I am older than be so dreadfully clean.

H. H.

THE
BRITISH JOURNAL OF NURSING
WITH WHICH IS INCORPORATED
THE NURSING RECORD
EDITED BY MRS BEDFORD FENWICK

No. 1,593.   SATURDAY, OCTOBER 12, 1918.   Vol. LXI.

EDITORIAL.

A MINISTRY OF HEALTH.

Those of us who for years have been advocating a Ministry of Health feel that at last in spite of " pull devil pull baker," public feeling on this greatest of national questions is apparently to be taken into consideration. Prominent politicians at various meetings have during the recess been making National Health a plank of their policy, and we are informed that the Home Affairs Cabinet, under the presidency of Sir George Cave, has nearly completed the Bill for the establishment of a Ministry of Health. It is probable that it will be introduced into Parliament after the resumption of the House next week, but whether any progress will be made with it depends on the date of the dissolution.

If the General Election takes place next month—as is not only possible, but even probable—the Bill will be, next to the conduct of the war and the terms of peace, the principal item in the Coalition's election programme.

Dr. Addison, the Minister for Reconstruction, when addressing a meeting of medical men at the Steinway Hall, assembled to urge the election of representative medical men to the House of Commons, remarked :—

" The point on which the nation has made up its mind is that we require a Ministry of Health to undertake the whole responsibility for the promotion of the physical well-being of the nation. Among many other lessons, the war has taught us how much can be done in the prevention of sickness and injuries. Nothing has been so wonderful as the massing together of these myriads of men under the most trying conditions and yet without any serious outbreak of infectious diseases. We need this beneficent supervision in normal times for the gradual improvement of the national health and physique."

" But what," asked Dr. Addison, " of the great army of the C3 class at home ? Is it possible to compute what these conditions represent to the men themselves, and to the nation in loss of energy, practicability, conduct, treasure and happiness ? If we are to reap the fruits of a successful fight for freedom in secured peace and progress, we shall certainly need the best effort that we are capable of for production and useful life. But this army of C3 men is the expression only in adult life of other armies coming onwards from the cradle. Questions affecting the home, workshop, school and its systems, personal habits, food, air, exercise, and many more, are involved.

" The Prime Minister told us the other day that we could not expect to run an A1 empire on a C3 population. We could not expect to get an A1 population out of C3 homes, habits, work places, or conditions. I suggest to you that your vision, experience, and responsibility, not as individuals only, but as an organised profession, extend to these things as they affect our public work, our laws and administrative efforts."

Mr. Hayes Fisher, the President of the Local Government Board, speaking on Public Health at Sheffield, was not too optimistic on the subject. He said we should be faced with a terrible shortage of doctors, nurses, and midwives—and especially we were likely to be short of well-trained physicians and surgeons for some years after the war. This was a problem that must be tackled.

Well ! let us tackle it. If conditions are fair, the nurses and the midwives will not be wanting. Let us remember that thousands of women now employed in war work must find a new sphere for their energies when war ceases, and blessed Peace is ours once more.

OUR PRIZE COMPETITION.

WHAT IS RABIES? HOW IS IT TREATED AND NURSED?

We have pleasure in awarding the prize this week to Miss E. A. Noblett, 2nd Northern General Hospital, Leeds.

PRIZE PAPER.

Rabies—hydrophobia, an acute specific disease due to the inoculation of a specific virus in rabid animals.

The disease is almost invariably contracted from the bite of a rabid animal, usually the dog; but the cat, wolf, and fox may also transmit it. The virus is in the saliva, which may be infective for a day or two before symptoms have developed. By no means all who are bitten are affected; wounds on uncovered parts are far more dangerous than wounds through clothing. Bites on the face lead to specially acute symptoms.

Since the Muzzling Order of Mr. Walter Long, the disease has become extinct in Great Britain and Ireland for several years. Recently cases of rabies in dogs have developed in Cornwall, and further development of the disease is being prevented.

The average incubation period is from six weeks to two months. It may be as short as a fortnight or as long as three months.

The main feature of rabies is hyperæmia and congestion of the central nervous system. There is also congestion of the pharynx, œsophagus, and stomach.

Symptoms.—The wound by which the poison was introduced, as a rule, rapidly heals, and for a time nothing happens to attract the patient's attention to the scar. In about six to eight weeks or so, the scar may become painful and nervous disturbances manifest themselves. The patient becomes sleepless, peevish, irritable, and experiences a choking sensation about the throat. When the disease is fully developed there are intense muscular spasms, the respiratory muscles and those of deglutition being specially involved. The features may be horribly contorted or wear an aspect of extreme terror; the saliva is not swallowed, and as it collects in the mouth, along with thick mucus from the congested fauces, it causes noisy attempts at ejection, attended with great difficulty.

The face is usually flushed or livid during the attacks, and there may be raving delirium, delusions, and hallucinations. It should be noted that, though the patient is very thirsty, he is afraid to drink, as any attempt at swallowing brings on the spasms at once; even the sound of running water will excite the attacks. After two or three days the patient may pass into the "paralytic stage," which, however, is more common in animals. He generally dies of exhaustion in from two to ten days after the development of the characteristic symptoms.

Treatment.—The bitten person or a bystander should at once suck the wound, and, if practicable, ligature the part above the injury. The wound should be cleansed and cauterised as soon as possible. The Pasteur treatment should be commenced whenever it is ascertained that the dog was rabid. It is practically certain to prevent the disease if begun within a week of the bite.

When the disease is developed, treatment is merely palliative. Morphia and chloroform for the spasm, and cocaine to diminish the sensitiveness of the throat, are the best remedies.

Pasteur's Method.—The virus is intensified by passage through a series of rabbits until a maximum degree of virulence is reached (virus fixe). The spinal cords of such rabbits gradually lose their toxic property by drying, and after fourteen days are no longer toxic. The virulence is in inverse proportion to the length of the exposure. Pasteur's treatment consists in the injection of an emulsion of spinal cord thus prepared, beginning with a cord which has been exposed for fourteen days, next day using one which has been less attenuated, and so on until a cord dried for only three days is used. In ordinary cases it takes nine days to reach this strength, and the treatment continues till the fifteenth day. When the incubation is likely to be short, as in bites about the head and face, an "intensive" treatment is employed. The details vary somewhat in different institutions, but the result is the same; the patient is rendered immune during the incubation period, and rabies does not develop. The treatment bears the same relation to hydrophobia as vaccination does to smallpox in those who have been exposed to infection.

An anti-rabic serum has also been used prophylactically, but does not replace the Pasteur method.

HONOURABLE MENTION.

The following competitors receive honourable mention:—Miss R. E. S. Cox, Miss S. Wild, Mrs. Farthing, Miss K. Jones, and Miss M. Fuller.

QUESTION FOR NEXT WEEK.

Give instructions for making anti-vermin underclothing for the troops; also for disinfecting soldiers' clothing at the Front.

CARE OF THE WOUNDED.

"Our Day," in support of the Red Cross work, will be celebrated on October 24th, and workers at street sales and collections, at stalls and depots and in every department are urgently wanted. Those who can help should offer their services to Miss C. May Beeman, 10, West Bolton Gardens, S.W. 5. The expenditure of the Joint War Committee now amounts to £100,000 a week, and it hopes for a million from London.

V.A.D. STRETCHER BEARERS.

The members of the Auxiliary Committee of the Y.M.C.A. will be grateful to receive gifts of footballs and football outfits for the men at the Base Camps in France, also any kind of indoor or outdoor games will be very acceptable.

Gifts of money and in kind should be addressed to Princess Helena Victoria, 74, South Audley Street, W. Envelopes should be marked "Base Camps Fund, Y.M.C.A." and inquiries made to the Hon. Secretary at the same address.

The Elsie Inglis Unit of the Scottish Women's Hospital participated in the victorious Franco-Serb offensive. The hospital camp, with its tent wards, operating theatres, and X-ray installation, situated in the mountains north of Vodena, is receiving the wounded of the Jugo-Slav divisions to which it is attached. A new transport camp has quite recently been established still closer to the fighting line, and from the camp, which serves as an advance dressing-station, and from the main camp the motor ambulances are doing heavy and indispensable work.

The King has granted unrestricted permission to Miss Jessie Anne Scott, M.D., Ch.B., D.P.H., to [wear] the Insignia of the Fourth Class of the Order of St. Sava, conferred upon her by his Majesty the King of Serbia, in recognition of her services as surgeon at the Scottish Women's Hospital at Ostrovo.

All United States soldiers, sailors, and civil employees who die in France will be buried in France until the end of the war, when the bodies will be brought back to the United States for final interment.

The lovely cemetery at Arlington, near Washington, where the soldiers who fell in the Civil War lie side by side, each little headstone numbered, may well be taken as a model for the God's Acre of American soldiers who have died for the liberty of the world.

Thanks to the energy of the American Red Cross organisation at Shanghai, a complete hospital unit, consisting of thirty-four doctors, and full equipment sufficient for 150 beds has been formed. The hospital has left for Vladivostock *en route* for the Volga Front.

We learn "Barts" has been in a "whirl," as it was suddenly decided to open all the top wards, which have been closed owing to raids. Abernethy, Lucas and Ophthalmic are to be given up for the care of wounded soldiers, as well as the present block devoted to them. It is right the premier Royal Hospital should be of the utmost service to the men who have probably helped to save it from destruction.

Owing to the scarcity of men, the women members of the Cornwall V.A.D. have taken up the duty of stretcher bearers for the cot cases at the Royal Naval Auxiliary Hospital, Truro, and their services have been greatly appreciated.

LYSOL, LTD.

Owing to the shortage of coal the supply of Lysol bottles has been cut down, and the firm has been asked by the Ministry of Munitions to endeavour to recover these bottles Will our readers, many of whom use Lysol, return their bottles to their chemist, who will make an allowance for them.

FRENCH FLAG NURSING CORPS.

For the first time for two years, Miss E. J. Haswe'l has been home on holiday. She returned to Paris on Monday. To have lived and worked in Paris during the past year, what with *avions* and " Big Bertha " continually disturbing one's equilibrium, and to remain calm, is no small feat of nerve power.

Miss Kathleen Bellamy, R.N.S., cert. Fulham Infirmary, has joined the Corps and left for France on Saturday, October 5th.

Miss Phyllis M. Cartmell, cert. Western Infirmary, Glasgow, will leave for France at the end of the week.

Sister Claudia Gaudin, who did such excellent work at Epernay, is now Madame Blanche, and we gather from a little gold-edged card that her home is at Rue Saint Nicolas, La Ferté Bernard, Sarthe, Jersey. Many years of happiness to Monsieur and Madame.

Another letter brings us the news from Bayeux that Madame Jamard (*nee* Hendric) is the " proud and happy mother of a fine baby boy." This first Franco-British grandson of the Corps weighed 9 lbs. at birth, and is each day gaining in weight. He must have a christening present from the F.F.N.C. Congratulations to " proud and happy " parents.

" For weeks I have made attempts at writing to you but the time was wanting. Since leaving N. on August 13th, we have had four moves; we seem to live on the road in more ways than one. But then the Hun has also moved so quickly; it has taken us all our time to keep up with him. We arrived here three days ago, eight days after the departure of the Hun destructors. Nothing can describe to you the utter ruin he leaves behind in each town and village. It is simply appalling. One specially destructed town we came through smelled strongly still of burning. We have lived in many queer places, one more shattered than the next. Our present abode certainly has four walls; and, after all, that is a great deal to expect these days. All the *mains d'œuvres* available has been put on, to try and get us a roof on, and we have had two nights of heavy storm without much roof. We just cover all we can with rubber sheeting. I am one of the fortunate ones to possess a sleeping-bag and I bless the donor each night, as once inside my bag, what matter what happens outside it. The water poured heavily all round and on me last night, but being dog tired after a pretty heavy day I slept in spite of everything. We have had a very busy and *very* interesting time. You would be more than amused could you have seen us visiting the abandoned trenches in search of furniture and utensils, and you would be surprised at the wonderful finds we made— enamel ware of all kinds, arm chairs, cooking stoves, pails, &c. As to war souvenirs, of course far more than we could possibly take with us. Coming across the battlefields of just—one might say—a few days ago, you come across wonderful things. The Bosches, having had to retreat so quickly, the whole place is swarming with his material. Bosches' hospitals just left everything and we are making use of a good deal of their stores. I have even a sterilising drum of his. But there is no use denying their ingenuity. We have come across string and rope made of paper, paper bandages and dressings; even their mattresses were covered with a canvas material made of paper. Our advance is going on well with comparatively few casualties and a good many prisoners. We are as near as we can be and do the sorting out of patients. The wounded come to us directly from the *poste de secours* (field dressing station), and we evacuate to the other centres, keeping only those who are too bad to go on. Oh! but we do need so many things urgently, and wish there was some way of getting supplies sent us by post. I am sending you a list and hope you can help us by asking Mme. de la Panouse, who has always been so good in helping us with supplies. I am marking one list urgent and the other for things which we need very much but can wait for. We have never left this ambulance, but when we left N. our surgeons were sent as special *equipes* to help, and as we belong to the surgeons we go where they go and work with them. So the ambulance, even while it is *en repos*, does not give rest to its surgeons. Naturally, it makes it very interesting for us and we have plenty of good work all the time. I was asked to assist our senior surgeon with his operations at the last place we were at, as it gave an extra *equipe*. Then I am running between the operating room and sterilizing room. There is always plenty of work for everyone."

A VISION.

We have received so many expressions of appreciation of the verse headed " A Vision," by C. B. M., which appeared on the 14th Sept., that it has been republished in card form. Those bereaved by the loss of dear ones in battle, to whom it has been sent, are greatly comforted by the beauty and feeling of the lines.

The cards, price 3d., can be obtained from Manager, B.J.N. Office, 431, Oxford Street, London, W. 1.

OUR ROLL OF HONOUR.
NURSING SERVICE.
DIED.

BAILEY, Mrs. W., V.A.D.
TOWNSEND, St.-Nurse M., Q.A.I.M.N.S.R.

THE ODYSSEY OF FRANCESCA.

(*Concluded from page* 209.)

It was a long goods train, taking up food, forage, and ammunition for the troops. Apparently, as an afterthought, a passenger coach was attached, composed of six unclean carriages with narrow wooden seats and a half partition between each two carriages, over which one could easily step. No lights were provided by the railway company, but Francesca had a candle and matches, and as the train went off she lighted up and had a look at her fellow-travellers. They were all soldiers returning to the front—one Negro, one Serb, and the rest French colonial soldiers. Being Christmas Eve they had already drunk liberally of that which gladdens the heart of man, and had brought

UNFRIENDLY LOOKING TENTS.

several bottles of wine with them, so Francesca looked forward to a lively night. It was cold, for there were no panes of glass in the windows, and one of the carriage doors flew open every quarter of an hour all night.

Before long the big Negro and one of the French soldiers began to have a furious quarrel and Francesca feared that blood would be shed, for the Negro was much more than three parts drunk by this time, and with threats and curses he brandished a long and evil knife, and certainly looked as though he proposed to use it.

The Serb soldier was a peacemaker, and at last persuaded them to sit down, while Francesca tried to propitiate them with offerings of oranges. It was long before they were quiet, but at last most of them went to sleep in horribly cramped positions, and Francesca looked out of the window at the new world she was going through. It was

a glorious night—still and cold and nearly as light as day. The train meandered slowly past desolate stretches of bare rock and wide lonely plains where the moon shone down on gentle-faced bearded shepherds watching their flocks, as they did on that other Christmas night so long ago.

After a time the ground grew hilly and broken and they began to climb slowly up a steep gradient. Then a long stop, and an extra engine was put on and they began to climb mountains which seemed as steep as the side of a house, panting up hills painfully and slowly through steep rocky defiles, short tunnels, over bridges and viaducts and deep dark chasms with valleys far below. It grew very cold as they climbed up, but it was wilder and more beautiful than anything Francesca had ever seen before. Once the train stopped for a long time and Francesca could see a town standing on a cliff, with slender white minarets gleaming in the moonlight.

About six in the morning the train stopped in a wide valley, a small shed alongside the railway the only sign of civilisation. The Serb soldier yawned and stretched himself, looked at Francesca and finally said " Voici, madame, c'est la gare Moharrem." There was no sign of life, but he helped Francesca out with her luggage, and the train went on and left her sitting on her kit-bag beside the railway line, wondering what to do next. A Greek brigand, who is station master and everything else combined, appeared at last from nowhere and made her understand that she must go over to the hospital camp, about a quarter of an hour's walk, and he would take care of her things meanwhile.

And then poor Francesca had *qualms* as she walked in the cold grey dawn towards some unfriendly-looking tents which she saw in the distance. She was sleepy and tired and cold and early morning-ish, and the glamour of the night had departed. Suddenly she felt better. A large red sun rose slowly and deliberately, and illumined a fairy white camp with thin blue curls of smoke rising lazily into the air, suggesting breakfast among other nice things. Behind the tents she saw tiers of mountains capped with snow at the top, and swathed with lilac mist lower down and in front were piled masses of rocks and hills of every colour—saffron, ochre, sage green and burnt siena. The bluest lake Francesca ever saw lay at her feet.

At the very entrance to the camp a sheep was

grazing with a magpie sitting on his back, darting his beak into the sheep's curls to find his breakfast and then putting his head back and gobbling it down with a self-satisfied air. " Surely *one* magpie means luck," remembered Francesca, and took it as a good augury for her future work.

THE END.   V. T.

NURSING AND THE WAR.

HOSPITAL HUNS.

Several of the nurses at a military hospital in South-East London have resigned because of the insulting behaviour of some of the Hun wounded who have recently been admitted. Is it not high time (asks the lay press) that the Huns in our hospitals were looked after by male nurses ?

Any way, it is time the silly sentimentalism of some women nurses was put down by the authorities. A trained nurse can do her duty when nursing the enemy without undue gush, which these barbarians do not understand, and we do not wonder nurses resign when they are expected to pamper men whose one aim in existence is to trample upon every decent instinct we possess.

HOW TERRIBLE THE COST.

" We have been very busy up to now. We have sixteen beds reserved for complicated head injuries, and this ward alone keeps us busy. They are terrible cases. Three have had tracheotomy done in addition to head injuries, some are blind, some are deaf, and there is hardly a man who can speak. Our poor mutilated men ! One of my poor men cried this morning because he cannot remember his own name—memory completely gone.

" Victory will come, but, alas ! how terrible the cost ! "

PRECAUTIONS NECESSARY.

Owing to the numerous cases of dysentery in Paris and the suburbs, the Prefect of Police has issued a notice to the public recommending that all milk should be boiled, no ice taken in drinks; no vegetables or fruit eaten raw, the hands washed carefully before eating, and flies kept from the food.

These precautions are very necessary, and nurses should try and have them carried out.

ANTI-INFLUENZA SERUM.

Tests with an anti-influenza serum, which have been conducted at several American Army cantonments, are reported to have given excellent results. Enough serum is now being produced to inoculate 50,000 patients daily. It is said to be specially potent in preventing cases of influenza from developing into pneumonia.

ROYAL BRITISH NURSES' ASSOCIATION.

ONE DAY'S CONFERENCE.

The Royal British Nurses' Association will hold a one day's Conference on Thursday, November 7th, at the Medical Society's Rooms, 11, Chandos Street, Cavendish Square, W., opening at 3 p.m. The meeting will adjourn for tea, and then hold an evening session.

The *raison d'être* of the meeting is to explain to members and others the difference between the two Nurses' Registration Bills drafted by the Central Committee and the College of Nursing, Ltd., and the reasons why the Royal Corporation is not in accord with the College. Four speakers in short addresses will compare the provisions of the Bills from the point of view of a doctor, matron, nurse, and member of the public.

The programme of the Conference will appear in the official Supplement of the R.B.N.A. next week.

NURSES' MISSIONARY LEAGUE.

The Autumn Reunion of the Nurses' Missionary League, held on October 2nd, was the occasion of much happy friendly intercourse between nurses from a number of London hospitals and representatives of various other branches of the nursing profession. Although there were opportunities for conversation during the interval in the morning and before the evening session, the special occasion for this was in the afternoon, when those present gathered round the little tea-tables and the three kind hostesses—Mrs. Drummond Robinson, Miss Bennett (Matron, Metropolitan Hospital), and Miss Jolly (Matron-in-Chief, R.A.F. Nursing Service)—did so much to make all feel thoroughly at home. Then the hum of friendly talk only died down when the three short addresses were given and when Miss Bruce Knight sang her beautiful renderings of " Mine Eyes have seen the Glory of the Coming of the Lord," " Oh ! Rest in the Lord," and other songs.

The morning session was largely devotional in character, the Rev. R. C. Gillie giving an inspiring opening address on the need for spiritual readjustment—readjustment towards God in the matters of sin and of sensitiveness to His will and call, and readjustment towards men, so as to be able to live in healthy fellowship with all with whom we live and work. The two subsequent addresses, by the same speaker, dealt with the Bible first as a progressive record of God's self-disclosure to man, and secondly as a record of man's response to God.

The chief features in the recent work of the Nurses' Missionary League were described in the afternoon by Miss J. Macfee, and in the evening by Miss H. Y. Richardson. They told of greater activity than ever before, greater interest in the hospitals, and increased numbers not only of members but of enquiries about work in the mission field. Two members—Miss Grist and Miss Dawson-Wilkes—had sailed during the summer for Africa; sixteen members had recently been able to return to their stations in various parts of the mission-field; and twenty-two members were waiting to go out as recruits as soon as permission could be obtained. Both these speakers—and also Major McAdam Eccles, M.S., F.R.C.S., R.A.M.C. (T.), chairman of the evening meeting—dwelt upon the great need and the many openings there will be for nurses in distant lands when the war is over and "demobi'ization" takes place.

Although there were no nurses among the speakers, the plea for nurses in far-off lands was perhaps more forcibly voiced by Miss C. Sharp (of Sarawak) and Miss Baker (of Uganda), both of whom, though untrained, had been forced into doing a nurse's work abroad. Miss Sharp told of the mother of three days who lay on bare planks in a small smelly room—the best "hospital" the place could boast; of the little child dying of small pox in the midst of her family; of another little child once thought to be deaf and dumb and covered with sores and bruises, but now cured and a helper in the school; of the woman dying and holding her hands when all her relatives fled. Each one she had tried to help— she, a teacher—and, as she said, "I apologize to you for doing it, but you were not there to do it for them!" And Miss Baker told of her station, with a population of half-a-million, with no doctor, no nurse, and how on itinerating tours as many as a hundred a day would crowd round seeking physical help, and dependent upon her and her few simple drugs for all the help they could get. Often the only way to reach them is by giving bodily aid, and the opportunities before a nurse in these lands are incalculable. Miss Baker struck a deeply impressive note as she dwelt upon the text, "Except a corn of wheat fall into the ground and die it abideth alone"; and a similar note was also sounded in the closing addresses of the afternoon and evening gatherings, when Miss Ellis spoke of the great and glorious task that lies before those who have known the Light; and Archdeacon Sharp dwelt upon the response of men and women to the challenge of the Kingdom of God.

NATIONAL UNION OF TRAINED NURSES.

There was a large and representative gathering of the nursing profession in and around Hull at a meeting held on October 5th, at the Swanland Club, to meet Miss Rimmer, Hon. Organising Secretary of the Union. Miss C. A. Little, Superintendent of the Hull Trained Nurses' Association, presided, and, in the course of a telling speech dwelt on the fact that the most important steps taken in the direction of organisation was taken twenty-five years ago, when they, in the face of strong opposition and nobly supported by H.R.H. Princess Christian, obtained for the British Nurses' Association the Royal Charter with which Association the National Union of Trained Nurses was affiliated. Miss Rimmer, in the course of her address, outlined some of the National schemes for reconstruction, as shown in the new Education Bill, the proposed Ministry of Health, Infant Welfare Work, &c., and emphasised the need for reconstruction in the nursing profession, and claimed that this could only be efficiently secured by the united efforts of the nurses themselves. In order to do this there must be self-organised societies with freedom of criticism, because, even when the much-needed State Registration Bill was passed, the administration of the law would be of great importance. This principle, she said, was embodied in the State Registration Bill promoted by the Central Committee for State Registration for Nurses, which had federated all the Trained Nursing Societies which had promoted the organisation of Nursing by the State, and which would continue their progressive work for "registered nurses." Miss Rimmer took exception to the autocratic bill proposed by the College of Nursing, Ltd., particularly to their provision for the keeping of supplementary registers of special and partially-trained nurses which would entirely nullify the value of the register of the fully-trained nurse.

We learn that Miss Rimmer's visit to Hull was greatly appreciated, and that she has left behind her much sound information, which should be productive of action in support of professional and free organisation amongst nurses in Hull—uncontrolled by lay interference and social patronage.

THE COLLEGE OF NURSING, LTD.

PERSONAL RESPONSIBILITY A DUTY.

It has been decided to form a "London Centre" of the College of Nursing, Ltd., and Miss Biggar, Sister St. Thomas' Hospital, has been appointed Hon. Secretary. There should now be no excuse for nurse members failing to have placed in their hands: (1) A copy of the Constitution, an agreement to conform to which the majority have signed *without seeing it*; (2) A copy of the Registration Bill promoted by the College, concerning which they have never been consulted. We call upon them to have this Bill explained to them, not only by their officials who drafted it but by members of the Central Committee for State Registration of Nurses, which promoted legislative reform for nurses and drafted a just Bill, when most of the College Council were actively opposing

State Registration, as they have done for years. We hope, therefore, that Miss Biggar and the secretaries of local centres will distribute copies and explanations of the Constitution of the Company, and make it quite plain that a nurse member's name can be removed from the Register, and herself from membership, in spite of her cash payments " as the Council may in its discretion think proper " *without any right of appeal.*

This autocratic assumption of power places the nurse in a most defenceless position ; for she practically agrees to be accused, tried, judged, and condemned, without the right to defend herself.

All the ladies who have taken office in connection with the London Centre must be called upon to state whether or no they are in favour of this type of tyranny. Those Matrons on the Council have condoned it, even if they were not consulted before it was in print.

The Secretary, Miss Rundle, has publicly expressed approval of the Council having the power (which this Clause gives them) to ruin a nurse's professional career without giving her the right to defend herself.

Our reason for requiring nurse members of the College to study and know something about their own affairs is that even if, through apathy, they are willing to sell their birthright of professional status for a mess of pottage, we are strongly opposed to their selling *ours.*

APPOINTMENTS.

MATRON.

Royal Victoria Hospital, Dover.—Miss Gertrude Vergette has been appointed Matron. She was trained at St. Bartholomew's Hospital, certificated in 1905, and has been associated with the hospital for sixteen years. Miss Vergette has for some years been Sister of the Massage Department, and has worked unceasingly and with wonderful success during the war in the Soldiers' Block.

Bath War Hospital.—Miss Maud E. Tate has been appointed Matron of the Bath War Hospitals in succession to Miss A. B. Hill (resigned). Miss Tate possesses the 1914 ribbon and the Serbian Order of St. Sava.

ASSISTANT MATRON.

Miss F. C. Wallen, Assistant Matron of the Islington Poor-Law Infirmary, who has discharged the duties of Matron of the Infirmary for the past six months, has been appointed permanently to the post of Matron.

NIGHT SISTER.

Dumfries and Galloway Royal Infirmary.—Miss Jean W. Wightman has been appointed Night Sister. She was trained at the Barrow-in-Furness Hospital ; and has been Sister at the Deaconess Hospital, Edinburgh ; and Night Sister at the Royal Infirmary, Perth.

QUEEN VICTORIA'S JUBILEE INSTITUTE.
TRANSFERS AND APPOINTMENTS.

Miss Caroline R. Sowden is appointed to Dewsbury as Senior Nurse ; Miss Edith Addis is appointed to Jewish Maternity and Sick Room Helps Society ; Miss Beatrice Avery, to Manchester (Salford) ; Miss Minnie Deverill, to Coventry ; Miss Alice M. Hopkinson, to Tottenham ; Miss Edith M. Symons, to Plaistow ; Miss Elizabeth A. Thornley, to Accrington.

A LOSS TO BARTHOLOMEW'S HOSPITAL.

The appointment of Miss Gertrude Vergette to the Matronship of the Royal Victoria Hospital, Dover, proves the acumen of the Committee of that institution, but will be a very serious loss to St. Bartholomew's Hospital.

Miss Vergette is one of the " old sort." By that we mean a woman devoted to duty and highly efficient in every detail of work she undertakes. In temperament, kind, bright, helpful, endowed with common sense and the courage of her own opinions, she is just the type of woman whose influence is of the greatest value in a Nursing School. We wish her the success she deserves in her future position, where we feel sure she will use all her best endeavours for the benefit of the hospital and the Nursing Staff.

SISTER TUTORS.

The Committee of the Nation's Fund for Nurses have established in connection with the College of Nursing, Ltd., three scholarships for training sister tutors at King's College for Women, London University, of £105 each. The successful candidates are :

Miss M. E. Abram, assistant matron, Royal Infirmary, Huddersfield ; Miss D. E. Bannon, sister surgical ward, and Miss D. M. Edgell, night charge sister, maternity ward, both St. Thomas's Hospital, London.

The Nation's Nurses have no control over this War Charity Fund raised in their name.

MY LITTLE IRISH NURSE.

She came to me so cheery—kind,
  Her steps so swift and light,
Her strong, warm hands drove fear away,
  And soothed me in the night.
Her voice is like the whisperings
  The angels send to earth.
Her presence is a peace—a rest—
  My little Irish nurse !

Her dark eyes hold a Faith that looks
  From a soul God knows is His.
Life's daily task fulfil a round
  Of beauty, mirroring this.
O, Service—sacred gift to heal
  An aching universe !
'Tis hands like yours lift the cooling draught,
  My little Irish nurse !
In the *Pacific Coast Journal of Nursing.*

NURSING ECHOES.

Major Chapple, M.P., and Mr. Morris, the House Governor of the London Hospital, are doing good service towards the economic emancipation of trained nurses by their correspondence in the press. The arguments for and against the exploitation of London Hospital nurses have been inserted in this JOURNAL for the past twenty-five years, so we need not allude to it further than to commend Dr. Chapple's sound arguments, and to ask Mr. Morris how he would enjoy being compelled to refund to the Hospital half his salary in support of the charity! Of course, "Members of the London Hospital Nursing Staff" write in support of serfdom; they always do, and in their ignorant self-sufficiency they appear entirely devoid of any sense of justice to the public, their colleagues, or themselves.

But, as we have remarked elsewhere, so long as degrading conditions only harm persons who prefer them, well and good, but when they injure one's neighbour, as the depreciation of our three years' standard of training, and the competition of semi-trained nurses in private practice do, that is the reason such conditions should not be tolerated by the public or by the nursing profession.

It is rumoured that a Private Nursing Department is going to be started at St. Thomas' Hospital. So far St. Thomas' has been content to charge fees for training, which in our opinion is quite justifiable, and has held aloof—as surely Miss Nightingale would wish it to do—from exploiting its trained Nurses. Let us hope if that rumour is true that the private staff will work on the co-operative system, as the day has gone by when hospital governors can make a cent. per cent. profit on nursing labour, as at the London Hospital, without the severest criticism and condemnation. That the Hon. Sir Arthur Stanley should have promoted the commercialism of Nightingale Nurses is almost incredible after all the College protestations that it is out for the economic benefit of the Nursing Profession.

We hear many "Nightingales" are strongly opposed to the new departure, as unworthy of their School, and calculated to affect its prestige.

Nursing Schools should discourage any scheme which curtails the freedom of individual private practice after certification. A few more hospital Nurse-Farms on London lines, and free private practice, whereby trained nurses take the fees they have earned, will be rendered impossible, as medical men educated at hospitals which run them are greatly influenced to support the finances of their Alma Mater by employing nurses attached to its Private Nursing Department.

But as so many "Nightingales" have been urged to join the College, and have signed an Agreement whereby their names can be removed from the Register of the Council—*without any power of appeal*—a Council on which the Treasurer, a lay member of the Nightingale Committee, the Matron, and a member of the medical staff have seats—we fear their objections are not likely to have much weight.

King Edward Order of Nurses in South Africa is doing good work as far as possible in these difficult times, and as the result of a discussion at the last annual meeting the Trained Nurses' Association has suggested to Lady Buxton that the good work the Order has already done might be greatly increased if special centres were established to train nurses already qualified in the duties of district nursing. The work is one for which very special qualifications are necessary, and the T.N.A. suggests that a Training Centre should be established by the Order in Cape Town or Johannesburg (or both), where applicants for district work, who must possess qualifications for general nursing and midwifery, should receive six months' special training in the duties of a district nurse, and at the same time study for the certificate of the Sanitary Institute, which she should be compelled to take.

We hope to hear this scheme has materialised. We are always pleased to note Trained Nurses' Associations offering expert advice, especially when they demand high and comprehensive standards of training. During the war, what with the interference of one ignoramus and another, and the subserviency of those who should stand firm for efficiency, we often wonder if, when peace comes, such a thing as skilled nursing will be found to exist.

Berthé Coutemache, a nurse at the Grey Nunnery Hospital at Montreal, who posed as a heroine in rescuing two children at the fire in which 65 infants perished and the lives of wounded soldiers were threatened on February 14th, has been arrested.

She has confessed that she set fire to the convent deliberately by burning newspapers in a cupboard. A month later she again set fire to the place, causing a small outbreak, which led to her arrest.

BOOK OF THE WEEK.

" UP AND DOWN." *

We must congratulate Mr. E. F. Benson on having abandoned his well-worn themes of prosperous villadom and country rectory and giving us instead a book that is more worthy of his pen, and which savours more of the writings of his brother, the late Monsignor Benson.

" Up and Down " takes the form of an intermittent diary between May, 1914, to April, 1917, but it is not primarily a war novel. Perhaps it is hardly correct to call it a novel at all. It has little to do with love in the popular sense, but it deals with the deep, close friendship of two men—the writer and one Francis—and for the rest it is chiefly about Italy, the attraction of which is charmingly described.

" Francis has been an exceedingly wise person in his conduct of life. Some fifteen years ago he settled, much to the dismay of his uncle, who thought that all gentlemen were stockbrokers, that he liked Italy much better than any other country in the world.

Having come across the Bay of Naples for the inside of a day, he telegraphed to the hotel for his luggage and stopped a month. After a brief absence in England, feverish with interviews, he proceeded to stop here for a year, and when that year was over to stop here permanently. In course of time he inveigled the writer to share with him the Villa Tiberiana. " It was too big for him alone, but if I felt inclined to go shares in the rent we might take it together. So when a fortnight ago I returned here, I made my return home not to Italy alone but to my home in Italy." They had some charming times, these two boon companions, in making their newly-acquired villa already described as an " amiable dwelling," a home after their own heart. It is Mr. Benson's charm that he can portray the little happenings in such an attractively descriptive manner.

" This island life is the busiest sort of existence, though a stockbroker would say it was the easiest and in consequence these social efforts give one a sense of rush I have never felt in London. The whole of the morning is taken up with bathing, and on the way up you call at the post office for papers and letters. The letters it is impossible to answer immediately, since there is so much to do and the pile on my table grows steadily, waiting for a wet day.

After lunch you read the papers. Then you have a good siesta, and so on till, as natural in the country, you go to bed early, and behold it is to-morrow almost before you knew it is to-day.

Francis asserts that he does an immense quantity of work in the winter. " I dare say that is so."

The approach of the sirocco broke up the *dolce far niente* of this attractive state of things.

" Pasqualino banged down the maccaroni on the table and spilled the wine and frowned and

shrugged till Francis told him abruptly to mend his manners, or let Seraphino serve us, on which for a moment the sunny Italian child looked out from the clouds and begged pardon and said it was not he but the cursed sirocco. And then, following on the cloud in the sky that had spread so quickly over the heavens, came the second cloud.

" Francis had just opened the Italian paper and gave one glance at it. " Horrible thing," he said " The heir to the Austrian throne and his wife have been murdered at Serajevo. Where is Serajevo ? Pass the mustard, please."

Francis is glad he is a denationalised individual. " If I have a motherland at all, it is this beloved stepmother land.

Damnable as I think war is, I think I could fight for her if any one slapped her lovely face."

But when the real need came, Francis was true to England.

" It's really such a relief to find that I didn't cling to what I had ; I was always afraid I might when it came to the point. But it wasn't the least effort to give it up, all that secure quiet life ; the effort would have been not to give it up."

" And when the war is over ? " I asked.

" Why, naturally, I shall go back to Alatri by the earliest possible train, and continue thinking."

Francis was not killed in the war, but died of malignant disease in his beloved villa at Alatri.

" To those who have loved the lovely and the jolly things of this beautiful world the day of little things is never over. . . ."

We talked of pleasant and humorous little memories of the past, and plans for the future, just as if we were spending one of the serene summer evenings the last time we were near here together.

We settled I should go back to Rome the day after to-morrow, and return if possible for Easter.

" For that," said Francis cheerfully, " will be about the end of my tether. The end, I mean, in the sense that I shan't be tethered any more."

At the end of those ten days there was a great change in Francis ; he had drifted far on the tide that was carrying him away.

At the end he bids his friend " go to the very top of Monte Gennaro to get the very biggest view possible, and stand there and thank God for everything there is. Say it for yourself and me. Say ' Francis and I give thanks to Thee for Thy great glory.' That's about all there is to say, isn't it ? "

" I can't think of anything else."

" Off you go, then," he said. " Oh, Lor' ! I wish I was coming too ; but I'll go to sleep instead. Good-bye."

Very early on Easter morning his friend returned to finish reading, as he had promised, the chapter in the Bible begun the evening before.

" I saw Francis sitting up." He was gazing with bright eager eyes to the entrance of the pergola, and in that moment I knew he saw there Him Whom Mary supposed to be the gardener.

H. H.

* By E. F. Benson. (Hutchinson & Co., London.)

THE
BRITISH JOURNAL OF NURSING
WITH WHICH IS INCORPORATED
THE NURSING RECORD
EDITED BY MRS BEDFORD FENWICK

No. 1,594.   SATURDAY, OCTOBER 19, 1918.   Vol. LXI.

EDITORIAL.

THE RED CROSS.

"Lest we forget" let us—at this appropriate time—recall the name and work of a great reformer, and one to whom the world at war owes so much. It is to Henri Durrant, a Swiss gentleman, that the Red Cross owes its inception. For some centuries, medical officers have been attached to armies in the field, and their services were deemed sufficient for all requirements. Florence Nightingale's mission in the Crimean war was the great innovation which roused the public from their apathy and ignorance to a realization of the misery suffered by sick and wounded soldiers without organized nursing. Notwithstanding the object lesson given, when the war of Italian independence broke out in 1859, the armies in the field were just as ill-equipped for the care of the sick and wounded as before. In the bloody battle of Solferino, when nearly 40,000 men were killed, Durrant served as a volunteer nurse, and the suffering he witnessed so affected him, that he was filled with an impelling desire to ease the burden of suffering in the future. He embodied his experiences in a pamphlet : "Souvenir de Solferino," which he published when the war was over. It was translated into many languages, and largely read and discussed. The Geneva Society of Public Utility invited M. Durrant later to submit some definite proposition. More than one meeting was held under the auspices of this Society. A Committee was appointed to start the work of organisation, which resulted in the International Congress being held in Geneva, in 1863, at which 14 countries were represented.

In the following year another Congress took place, the outcome of which was the famous Geneva Convention. The Articles provided for the neutrality of all hospitals, their personnel and equipment. It was not without much devoted work that Durrant roused the Governments of many European countries. Neutrality connotes impartiality, and it was laid down that members of the Society should be ready to serve all needing their succour, either friend or foe. We are all familiar with the red cross on a white field—the insignia of the Red Cross Society. It is the flag of the Swiss nation reversed, and it was a graceful compliment to the Reformer to adopt it. All civilized nations have joined this International Bond now ; and who shall tell the sum of suffering eased and prevented, and the lives saved by its inestimable work. Henri Durrant passed away five or six years ago. We can but be thankful that the great philanthropist did not live to see the day, when Germany, from whom he had received some of his greatest encouragement, should have so outraged humanity as to treat the sacred Geneva Convention as another "*scrap of paper.*"

The sight of unrelieved suffering on the battle-field would have been less of a shock to the tender-hearted man than the deliberate murder of the wounded and those ministering to them, by a barbarous foe solemnly pledged to succour them if needful. The cross has ever been an emblem of suffering in Christendom, but also an insignia of the *relief* of suffering. We know that both the Sisters and the Brothers of the Order of St. John of Jerusalem (the Brothers were the Knights Hospitallers), founded for the benefit of the sick pilgrims and wounded soldiers, in the time of the crusades, wore the beautiful eight-pointed white cross on their black habits ; the points being symbolic of the eight beatitudes. At the same period there were the Knights Templars, who wore a red cross on the shoulder, and were styled the "Knights of the Red Cross." Their duties were to protect the pilgrims to and from the Holy Land.

THE TREATMENT OF IRRITANT GAS POISONING.

Captain J. M. Lazenby, R.A.M.C., gives in the *British Medical Journal*, in the following notes, the treatment suggested. It applies to all cases of irritant gas poisoning when the symptoms are those of acute catarrh of the mucous membranes of the eyes and of the respiratory tract. With various modifications it has been employed on this ship for the past three months, and gives very satisfactory results. My experience is that success depends entirely on the care with which the method is carried out and the frequency of the treatment.

INSTRUCTIONS TO ORDERLIES.

1. Before embarkation begins furnish a dressing table with a throat spray, eye bath, Carrel syringe, vaseline, plain gauze cut to size, cotton wool, jaconet, bandages, and one pint of a warm solution of sodium bicarbonate—10 grains to the ounce. Cover with a clean towel.

2. After embarkation is complete, select all the severe eye cases whose eyelids are closed through photophobia or dried secretion, and place over the eyes a compress of gauze wet with solution. When the the milder cases have been dealt with the severe ones will be ready for treatment, the compresses having unsealed the eyelids and relieved the acute photophobia.

3. Bathe the margin of the lids till all the crusts can be wiped away with a wet cotton wool mop.

4. Fill the syringe with solution, and, taking a piece of cotton wool in the left hand, draw down with it the lower lid. Instil a few drops into the eye from the syringe, and close the lids. Repeat this till all the secretion has been washed away—about four times. Dry the skin with cotton wool.

5. In mild cases leave the eyes uncovered except by the eye shade. In severe cases put on another compress, cover with jaconet, and bandage lightly on.

6. In all cases it is better to smear a little vaseline on the skin to prevent irritation from the discharge.

For the throat (respiratory) cases proceed as follows :

1. Fill the spray half full with the solution.

2. The patient sits up and gargles his throat and mouth with the solution. He then opens his mouth wide and breathes in and out. The spray nozzle is held an inch from the mouth and the jet directed to the back of the throat. The patient *must* sit up and respire during spraying.

3. Cease when the patient wants to spit out, and repeat four times.

4. When patients are numerous, all cases who can see to use the apparatus should be instructed to carry out the treatment for themselves, using an eye bath for the eyes instead of the syringe.

5. Since success depends largely on frequency of treatment, patients must be dealt with every three hours. The last application should be made before lights go out at night, and in all severe eye cases the compress must be placed in position and secured with a bandage.

In a ward containing gas cases and other affections of the respiratory organs the former are kept on one side. When the percentage of gas patients is large the orderlies always suffer from irritation of the throat and cough. The other patients also cough more than they should for the same reason It is therefore advisable, when possible, to isolate patients suffering from gas poisoning

As regards results : Photophobia is either completely relieved or markedly diminished, so much so that patients coming on board unable to open their eyes are sometimes found, without their shades, looking at pictures and reading. The catarrh of the eyes still persists, but the pain is much relieved

In throat cases the immediate result is the expectoration of a large quantity of purulent mucus. The dry cough becomes loose and the pain in the chest lessened. The soreness of the throat usually persists. The chief benefit obtained is relief from the distressing night cough. These patients generally have a good night's sleep, and the whole ward is, in consequence, quieter.

Chronic cases of two or three weeks are not materially relieved by the treatment. Our most successful cases are from three to six days old. The treatment is cheap and simple, and is suitable for all cases in transit from the clearing stations to their destination in England. Since we have them for so short a time on board ship, I cannot say whether it is curative, but from the relief obtained I believe that if these cases were treated continuously from the beginning the period of convalescence would be materially shortened.

SPANISH FLU.

In our hospitals the Nursing Staffs have suffered severely during the past week from influenza, and in France hundreds of hospital workers have been attacked. The French Public Health Department orders doctors and nurses who come in contact with influenza victims to wear small gauze compresses, soaked in disinfectants, over the mouth and nose.

In a report on influenza the Public Health Committee of the L.C.C. states that in the June and July epidemic there were 16 000 deaths in London. As compared with earlier epidemics the incidence is higher between the ages five to forty-five, and lower at ages over forty-five.

Concurrently with the influenza mortality, there was a large increase in deaths from bronchitis and pneumonia, and as this increase cannot be accounted for by any abnormal climatic conditions by which these diseases are governed, it is reasonable to assume that the major part of the additional deaths from these causes are of influenzal origin.

Influenza is raging in Cape Town, and Bombay is suffering more from influenza than it ever did from plague. The daily mortality in the city from all causes rose from 110 on September 6th to 712 on September 30th. Plague and cholera are practically absent ; the increase is due to influenza followed by pneumonia which is sweeping away young and old among the poorer classes in particular.

NURSING AND THE WAR.

THE CAVELL MEMORIAL AT NORWICH.

Norwich gave Queen Alexandra and Princess Victoria a warm welcome, when, on Saturday last (the third anniversary of the execution of Edith Cavell), they visited that ancient city to open the Cavell Memorial Home for District Nurses, erected by the citizens of Norwich, and unveil the bust of the martyred nurse, the site of which is in Tombland.

The Royal visitors were received by the Lord Lieutenant, the Lord Mayor, and crowds of wounded soldiers, squads of nurses and ambulance units.

The Lord Mayor, in welcoming Queen Alexandra, said:—

Your Majesty will deem it fitting that in the chief city of Edith Cavell's native county, the home of Mrs. Cavell too, till her recent decease, some permanent memorial should be raised to this Norfolk heroine of whom we are so justifiably proud.

This city is already famous as the birthplace of Elizabeth Fry, and we desire to perpetuate the memory of this other noble woman, whose fame is also world-wide. In the splendid work which our nurses are doing, and in the knowledge that kind words and kind deeds can never die, we find reason to hope that the memorial to our martyred heroine will be lasting, for it depends not upon material things, but has for its foundation spiritual realities that are eternal. Edith Cavell rests from her labours and her works do follow her. This is the third anniversary of her death, bringing with it the promise of a lasting and righteous peace, and the hope that the cause for which Nurse Cavell gave her life is about to triumph.

THE BRONZE BUST OF EDITH CAVELL.

of Norwich to-day, not only because it is the capital of the county in which I live for a great part of the year, and which is endeared to me by the happiest and most tender associations, but because the occasion of unveiling this statue and opening the Nurses' Home has given me the opportunity of testifying my admiration and respect for the memory of a brave woman, Nurse Edith Cavell, who met a martyr's fate with a calm courage, an intrepid faith and a spiritual resignation that have made her name honoured and revered throughout the country and the Empire.

"No Home for Nurses could have worthier memories attached to it, and I should like, if it were possible, to see these homes established, as some, I am glad to say, have already been, throughout the Empire to perpetuate Nurse Cavell's memory and to preserve the traditions which she maintained in her life and upheld by her death. It is most fitting and suitable that the county to which Nurse Cavell belonged should have instituted this Home, which, I hope, may now be established on a permanent basis, and may remain, with the statue, as a lasting and historic memorial, erected by this City of Norwich in her honour."

Later, Her Majesty, with a gold key presented to her by the Lord Mayor, unlocked the door of the Home and afterwards inspected the building, which is under the superintendence of Miss Arnold with a staff of eight nurses. Queen Alexandra also visited the Red Cross Hospital at the Bishop's Palace, and the King Edward VII. ward of the Norfolk and Norwich Hospital.

After unveiling the bust, Queen Alexandra made the following reply: "I thank you, my Lord Mayor, for the welcome you have given me, and for the kindly expressions you have used with reference to my beloved husband, King Edward (who was so greatly attached to the County of Norfolk), and to myself. It has given me sincere pleasure to visit your ancient and historic City

QUEEN MARY'S HOSTELS FOR NURSES.

What has proved to be one of the most beneficent bits of war work has been the organization of Queen Mary's Hostels for Nurses, of which the Duke of Portland is President and Captain

Sir Harold Boulton, Bt., C.V.O., C.B.E., is the Chairman, and it is to the keen personal interest of the latter gentleman that much of the success of the scheme is due.

Hostel No. 1, at 40, Bedford Place, W.C., has earned for itself very special appreciation from thousands of nurses—mostly birds of passage, going to and from the various seats of war—who invariably receive the kindest welcome from Mrs. Kerr-Lawson, M.B.E., and who look upon this beautiful and happily conducted place as their very own home. We have visited the Hostel more than once, and always came away realising more and more what a real practical gift to military nurses this beautiful home is, and do not wonder that they hold it in sincere gratitude and affection.

Hostel No. 2, at 52, Russell Square, W.C., is equally useful to Red Cross Nurses, and they owe Miss K. S. Bankhead much for all her kindness; and No. 3, at 50, Warwick Square, of which Miss Francis Smith is Resident Superintendent, is arranged for the special convenience of nurses arriving at or leaving the railway termini, at which they stay for one night only, and where they are made to feel entirely at home.

Her Majesty the Queen has paid visits to all the Hostels and expressed her pleasure in and approved of the work. Princess Christian has visited No. 3.

We always turn to Balance Sheets with interest, and find upon examining that of Queen Mary's Hostels that last year it cost close on £8,000 to maintain the three Homes—which in these days, when prices are abnormal, proves that they have been managed with due economy. Donations amounted to £3,049 5s. 6d., and the Joint War Committee made a grant of £5,000.

The Committee, in issuing its report, takes the opportunity of putting on record their high appreciation of the devoted services of the Staff at the three Hostels—an appreciation, it is stated, which is endorsed in most glowing terms by the guests themselves in hundreds of letters received by the Chairman.

VICTORIA LEAGUE CLUB FOR NURSES FROM OVERSEAS DOMINIONS AND AMERICA.

Six months ago the Victoria League Club at 8, Rutland Square, Edinburgh, was opened for nurses from the British Overseas Dominions and America. It has proved such a boon to the many nurses who spend their well-earned furlough in Edinburgh that the present premises are far too small, and the Club is about to move to a much larger house in Drumsheugh Gardens, where it will be able to accommodate forty nurses. To reduce the heavy expense of furnishing the new club, it has occurred to the Committee that there may be some people willing to lend furniture for the period of the war, and for such loans Lady Linlithgow (President) is making an appeal. Any articles—*e.g.*, armchairs, sofas, tables, rugs, a sideboard, a piano, &c., also bedroom furniture—will be gratefully received and taken every care of; and will be fetched, returned and insured by the Victoria League. Offers of loan should be intimated to the Hon. Superintendent, 8, Rutland Square, as soon as possible.

FRENCH FLAG NURSING CORPS.

The Sisters attached to Ambulance 16/21 have share in the Special Order of Praise accorded the Ambulance by the Inspector-General, thanking the doctors, nurses and orderlies for the efficient way in which the service has been carried out.

This ambulance is right up at the front, surrounded by ruins and devastation, and as one Sister says, "it is truly a case of 'Marchons, Marchons.'" The Sisters are doing their own laundry, and tackling work just as it comes to hand for the well-being of the French heroes entrusted to their care.

The Sisters named in the Orders are Hilda Gill (Croix de Guerre), Mabel Jones, Helen McMurrich (Canadian Unit), Annie M. Hanning and Agnes Warner, whose devotion to duty has reflected so much credit on the Corps in France.

OUR ROLL OF HONOUR.
NURSING SERVICE.
DIED.

LIDDELL, Miss L., V.A.D., B.R.C.S.

MY MASTER HATH A GARDEN.

My master hath a garden, full-filled with divers
  flowers,
Where thou may'st gather posies gay, all times and
  hours,
      Here nought is heard
      But paradise-bird
      Harp, dulcimer, and lute,
      With cymbal,
      And timbrel,
      And the gentle sounding flute.

Oh! Jesus, Lord, my heal and weal, my bliss
  complete.
Make thou my heart thy garden-plot, true, fair and
  neat,
      That I may hear,
      This music clear,
      Harp, dulcimer and lute,
      With cymbal,
      And timbrel,
      And the gentle sounding flute.
        From "By-ways of Poetry"
      Compiled by Eleanor M. Brougham.

OUR PRIZE COMPETITION.

We regret that no papers were received in reply to last week's question. No Prize could therefore be awarded

HEROINES ON THE " LLANDOVERY CASTLE."

A Memorandum in pamphlet form has been issued and presented to the next-of-kin of the personnel of the Canadian Army Medical Corps who died in the performance of their duty on H.M.H.S. *Llandovery Castle*, destroyed at sea by enemy action, June 27th, 1918, with the high admiration and profound regret of the Director-General of the Medical Forces. We have to thank the Matron-in-Chief of the O.M.F.C. for a copy, which we greatly value.

Official verification of the facts surrounding the sinking of H.M.H.S. *Llandovery Castle* confirms two main points—the extreme devotion and valiant sacrifice of the medical personnel and the ship's company, whose courage and resignation were in keeping with the proudest traditions of the British Army and Merchant Marine Service ; the utter blackness and dastardly character of the enemy outrage on this defenceless institution of mercy—a crime surpassing in savagery the already formidable array of murders of non-combatants by the Germans. The story of the heroism of the fourteen Sisters who lost their lives is most touchingly told by Sergeant Knight. How magnificently they faced the final ordeal when their boat was carried towards the stern of the ship, when suddenly the poop-deck seemed to break away and sink, when the suction drew it quickly into the vacuum, when the boat tipped over sideways and every occupant went under.

" It was," concluded Sergeant Knight, " doubtful if any of them came to the surface again."

It is recorded that the whole eight minutes they were in the boat the Sisters were calm and collected. Everyone was perfectly conscious. There was not a cry for help or any untoward evidence of fear.

The following is the list of these heroic women of whom Canada and the whole Empire are so justly proud :—

NURSING SISTERS LOST.

N/S. Campbell, Christine
  ,,   Douglas, Carola Josephine
  ,,   Mussault, Alexina
  ,,   Follette, Minnie A.
  ,,   Fortescue, Margaret Jane
A/Matron Fraser, Margaret Marjory
N/S. Gallaher, Minnie Katherine
  ,,   McDiarmid, Jessie Mabel
  ,,   McKenzie, Mary Agnes
  ,,   McLean, Rena, R.R.C.
  ,,   Sampson, M. Belle
  ,,   Sare, Gladys Irene
  ,,   Stamers, Anna Irene
  ,,   Templeman, Jean

With the exception of six survivors—Major Lyon, Sergeant Knight, Privates Hickman, Pilot, Cooper, and Taylor—the list of casualties include the entire medical personnel.

OFFICERS LOST ON H.M.H.S. *Llandovery Castle.*

Lt.-Col. MacDonald, T. H.
Maj. Davis, G. M.
  ,,   Enright, W. J.
Capt. Leonard, A. V.
Capt. Sills, G. L.
Hon. Capt. and Chaplain
  Macphail, D. G. (attached).

The *South African Nursing Record* says : " The Hun has committed such revolting outrages that sometimes one wonders if one has any capacity for horror left ; but an affair like the sinking of the hospital ship *Llandovery Castle* was so unspeakable as still to bring a gasp of shame and surprise from all the world. Surely, there is nothing to do with a beast like that but annihilate him completely !"

CARE OF THE WOUNDED.

Every woman is asked to send now a knitted article for a soldier to a local Voluntary Organisation Depot, or to the Comforts Depot, 45, Horseferry Road, S.W. 1.

The Rt. Hon. John Hodge, M.P., Minister of Pensions, says Great Britain is to-day faced with the difficult problem of what to do with the hundred thousand officers and men discharged from the Navy and Army owing to tuberculosis.

Obviously it is not practicable to keep these consumptives in a sanatorium for the remainder of their lives. Nor would it be wise to allow them to return to their former occupations ; the risk of infection to other people is too grave.

We agree with Mr. Hodge that these men should work in the open, and the Ministry of Pensions and the Ministry of Reconstruction are two departments which must work hand in hand in rebuilding lives temporarily wrecked in the horrors of war. Disabled men must be given the chance to help themselves, under conditions conducive to their recovery. Where are the hundred thousand women prepared to help to pay their debts to these sufferers by giving time to solve this problem ? We hope they will come forward and help the Minister of Pensions. Thousands of them have lovely gardens—others land—let them see what they can do.

The atrocious murders on the high seas by our brutal enemies have inspired our loyal and patriotic seamen with the determination to pursue the only policy the barbarian understands, and his latest crime in torpedoing the *Leinster* and murdering hundreds of women and children in cold blood has added one more knot in the halter. The victims amount to 600, and a friend writing from Dublin says : " Dublin is in mourning to-day for her lost mail boat. Everyone feels very down about it. A large number of those saved have since died either from wounds or exposure. Whole families have gone. It has clouded all the good news from the front; it is so near home."

Where do the Huns secrete their petrol so that Irish waters become a death trap? That is what the Government should know and apparently does *not*. Also why did not the Board of Trade comply with the application of the City of Dublin Steam Packet Company for adequate escort for cross-Channel boats? One of the directors informs the *Times*: "For a long time past we have been made aware that the Huns have determined to get the *Leinster*. This information was conveyed to the authorities All that has happened is the carrying out of the threat to murder 500 persons." This is a very serious charge which the President of the Board of Trade or the Admiralty have been ca'led upon to explain.

PATRIOTIC NURSES TO SUPPORT MR. W. M. HUGHES.

Smouldering indignation on the question of the continued freedom of influential aliens of enemy blood, has culminated in the demand for further publicity, and upon the re-assembling of Parliament a great National Meeting will be held in the Royal Albert Hall on Tuesday, November 5th, at 7.30 p.m. Mrs. Dacre Fox will preside, and the principal speaker will be the Right Hon. W. M. Hughes, Prime Minister of Australia, whose courage in publicly denouncing the bribery and corruption by the Hun stands out as one of the most potent factors in the policy of victory.

The various Committees appointed to deal with the internment of enemy aliens have not so far announced that any wealthy German or Austrian of any social influence has been interned. Why not? A dozen "tinkers, tailors, and candlestick makers" count less in the espionage danger to the Empire than one wealthy German financier or burrowing journalist. These are the persons whose "hidden hand" scatters largesse in cash and kind, and who still retain positions of influence "on every front."

Many patriotic nurses will wish to support Australia's great Prime Minister in his public protest against this shameful evil, and will no doubt attend the Albert Hall meeting on November 5th. All information can be obtained from Mrs Dacre Fox, 3, Eastwood House, Emperor's Gate, London, S.W.

OUR DAY.

Our Day falls on October 24th, when throughout the country the Red Cross makes appeal for support. The king has sent £10,000 to the Joint War Committee, and the Lord Mayor of London is appealing for a million from the City. The activities of the Red Cross now cost £100,000 a week, and its needs grow and grow.

AN URGENTLY NEEDED REFORM.

JUNIOR SISTER, NOT STAFF-NURSE.

After the comparative failure of the Army Nursing System in the South African War, the Matrons' Council of Great Britain and Ireland presented to the Secretary of State for War in April, 1901, "Suggestions as to the formation of an Army Nursing Department at the War Office."

This comprehensive Report was published in THE BRITISH JOURNAL OF NURSING of April 27th, 1901, and dealt with Nursing Progress, Nursing Organization, Need of a Nursing Department, Standard of Training, Head Sister (Matron), Nursing Sisters, Senior Sisters, Junior Sisters, Night Superintendents, Increase of Salary, Orderlies, and an Army Nursing Service Reserve.

Queen Alexandra's Imperial Military Nursing Service was almost entirely organized upon these Suggestions.

After recommending the establishment of a Nursing Department in affiliation with the Medical Department at the War Office, superintended by a fully trained and experienced Administrative Nursing Officer and a Head Sister (Matron) in each Military Hospital, under the heading of "Nursing Sisters" the following suggestions were advanced :—

NURSING SISTERS.

The Matrons' Council would suggest that there should be two grades of Nursing Sisters, senior and junior.

SENIOR SISTERS.

The Senior Sisters should be in charge of wards, preferably containing not more than fifty beds. They should be responsible to the medical officers for carrying out all directions for the treatment of the sick and should be responsible to the Head Sister for the care of the ward linen and for the good order and cleanliness of their wards. They should personally superintend the service of food and should have authority to ensure the strict carrying out of medical directions with regard to dieting. They should also be responsible for the systematic clinical instruction of the Orderlies in practical nursing.

JUNIOR SISTERS.

The Junior Sisters should, when the Ward Sister is on duty, work under her direction. They should always be on duty in her absence from the ward. They should also be available for night duty and as special nurses on day or night duty.

The Senior Sister should report on their work to the Head Sister, and reports upon their efficiency and suitability should be forwarded by the Head Sister to the Nursing Department of the War Office. Their appointment as Senior Sisters, as vacancies occur, should rest upon the recommendation of the Principal Medical Officer and the Head Sister.

NIGHT SUPERINTENDENTS.

The Night Superintendents should rank with Senior Sisters, and it is desirable that their charge should not exceed 400 beds. Working under the night Superintendents should be a certain number of Junior Sisters and Orderlies as may be found necessary.

The value to discipline of the recommendation of the title of " Sister " being secured to every member of the certificated nursing staff in a military hospital was unfortunately not adopted, and the title of " Staff Nurse " was substituted. Actual practice has proved the wisdom of the recommendation in this connection by the Matrons' Council, and endless friction and dissatisfaction would have been avoided during this war if it had been adopted.

AN OPEN LETTER TO THE PUBLIC AND MEMBERS OF PARLIAMENT.

THE ORGANISATION OF NURSES.

MADAM,—A contemporary states that the efficiency of a Ministry of Health will largely depend on the work of nurses. The effectiveness of their work will again depend on the efficiency of their organisation. One of the main features of this organisation is a proper system of State Registration—a system that will give the proper measure of State control, and represent all the important interests involved, whilst leaving the members of the profession freedom for development and expression.

The pioneer, established promoter, and guardian of the movement for State Registration— the Central Committee for State Registration— has a Bill ready for Parliament, which has been merely awaiting a time when legislation of this kind could be passed without hampering urgent war activities. A recently formed body—the College of Nursing—has also drafted a Bill of its own, which is unfortunate, as all the bodies promoting State Registration had come to a complete agreement about the Central Committee's Bill, and this new one has aroused strong antagonism and plunged the nursing profession into discord.

The Central Committee has been patiently negotiating with the College for over two years in the hopes of putting an end to this harmful state of affairs, without the sacrifice of principle. As a result, the College Bill has been improved, and its latest draft provides guar-

antees that the qualification for the general register after the period of grace shall be a not less than three years' term of training and a central examination, and that registered nurses shall occupy seats on the Permanent Council to administer the Act.

Nominally also the principle that the nurses' societies shall be represented on the Provisional Council has been conceded, *but*—and it is a very big but—the value of the concession has been destroyed by the provision that the only duty which that Provisional Council can perform is to " forthwith " proceed to appoint the Permanent Council, on which the nurses' societies are not to be represented ! Their only function will, therefore, be to act as their own hangman !

A new and most dangerous provision is that empowering the Council to form as many supplementary registers as it pleases ; for instance, registers might be formed of Maternity Nurses, Children's Nurses, and many other partially trained women, thus undoing the value of Registration for the fully trained and upsetting the economics of the profession.

The draft also provides that the College of Nursing shall be specially recognised by the Act and its register of nurses accepted by Parliament. This is obviously unjust to many professional women, for there are registers of nurses and organised societies of nurses of much older standing, which have proved their worth by patient years of effective pioneer work. But, above all, such legislation is unwise for the future of the profession, for it grants a monopoly to one society, that society being largely under the influence of employers.

We ask that the Permanent Council which will control the affairs of the profession shall be independent and representative of all the interests concerned, as provided by the Bill promoted by the Central Committee, which is in charge of Major Chapple, and passed its first reading in the House in 1914.

I am, yours faithfully,

(Signed) E. L. C. EDEN.

The shortage of trained nurses and ward maids in civil hospitals and in private practice is acute, and the Dow. Lady Brassey is taking the Middlesex Hospital in hand, as its work is being hampered. A voluntary corps of women workers is being raised. A rota will be arranged to suit the convenience of members of the corps, who must be prepared to give four hours a day for two or three days a week. Women willing to join are asked to write to Lady Brassey at Middlesex Hospital.

Who says our Matrons have " cushey jobs " these days ?

Royal British Nurses' Association.

(Incorporated by   Royal Charter.)

THIS SUPPLEMENT BEING THE OFFICIAL ORGAN OF THE CORPORATION.

THE CONFERENCE.

FREE DISCUSSION ON PROFESSIONAL PROBLEMS.

Under the auspices of the Royal British Nurses' Association a Conference will be held on November 7th, at the Rooms of the Medical Society of London, 11, Chandos Street, Cavendish Square, W. 1. The first Session will commence at 3 p.m., when Her Royal Highness the Princess Christian, President of the Corporation, will take the Chair. "The Economic Position of the Trained Nurse" and "Some Phases of Modern Nursing" will be the subjects under discussion. Tea will be served before the evening session opens at 6 p.m. to consider "The Differences between the two Nurses' Registration Bills and why the Royal British Nurses' Association does not agree with the Bill of the College of Nursing, Ltd." Her Royal Highness has graciously promised to preside at the evening session if possible. Nurses, and particularly those who are Members of the Royal Corporation of Nurses, will deeply appreciate the support given to them by their President on this occasion, when they meet to confer on subjects of such great importance to them all. Should Her Royal Highness be unable to preside, the Chair will be taken at the evening session by Mr. Herbert Paterson, Medical Honorary Secretary of the Royal British Nurses' Association and Honorary Treasurer of the Central Committee for the State Registration of Trained Nurses.

The Executive Committee have invited Miss Pearse, Superintendent of the L.C.C. School Nurses, Miss Jentie Paterson, and Mrs. Collins to speak on "The Economic Position of the Trained Nurse."

Miss Marsters, Superintendent of the District Nurses of Paddington and Marylebone; Miss Sinzininex, A.R.R.C., Matron of Queen Alexandra's Hospital for Officers; and Miss Kate Atherton, Medallist of the Royal Sanitary Institute, will read papers on "Some Phases of Modern Nursing."

At the evening Conference Lieut.-Colonel Goodall, M.D., Mrs. Bedford Fenwick, and Miss Le Geyt will compare the Bills of the Central Committee and the College of Nursing, Ltd., from the point of view of the Medical Man, the Matron, and the Trained Nurse respectively. It is suggested that a Member of the public should also be asked to criticise the Bills.

The Conference will give to nurses the opportunity to discuss points which are of vital importance to them. If, in the future, there is to be progress and real liberty for members of the profession, the nurses must take an active part in the management of their own economic and educational conditions. Through this Conference the President and Executive Committee of the Chartered Corporation are giving publicity to claims for improving the conditions under which the nurses work and for free discussion on matters which closely concern them.

The Executive Committee of the Royal British Nurses' Association hope that there will be a large attendance of Members of the Corporation and of the Organised Societies of Nurses affiliated to it, to support Her Royal Highness and the Speakers. The programme of the Conference will be printed in the course of a few days, and can be obtained from the Secretary of the Royal British Nurses' Association, 10, Orchard Street, Portman Square, W. 1, or from the offices of any of the Organised Societies affiliated with the Corporation.

COMFORTS FOR THE SOLDIERS.

Sister Thompson very kindly writes, in connection with our recent appeal for comforts for a regiment of artillery at the front, that she is interested in a club for working girls and she will be very pleased to get them to do some work if any members care to forward to her the materials required. Sister Thompson's address can be obtained from the R.B.N.A. office.

HOSPITAL NURSES AND THE PARLIAMENTARY FRANCHISE.

As considerable uncertainty exists as to whether or not nurses resident in hospitals may have their names placed on the Parliamentary Register, the Executive Committee of the Royal British Nurses' Association have decided to take Counsel's opinion on the matter. The fact that the claims of the Nursing Staff at one London hospital have been allowed and their names placed on the Register, and that the claims of other nurses similarly situated have been refused, makes it imperative that Counsel's opinion should be obtained on this important question.

table invitingly spread for tea. The Governors' Room opens from the hall and a corridor leads to the beautiful little chapel, with its blue altar cloths, copies of one or two of the old masters which children can understand, and rows of small chairs. Upstairs we are joined by the Sister of that particular floor and inspect the bright wards with their rows of neat little beds, large windows, and tables bright with nasturtiums. The children greet us with happy smiles of welcome. Evidently they accept all visitors as their own particular friends and not as mere sightseers or journalists out to satisfy a lust for copy. Matron plainly has captured the hearts of these small people and their faces beam with delight as she asks this little person some question or addresses a teasing remark to the other. In one room the L.C.C. teacher is giving a lesson to the more convalescent

PRINCESS CHRISTIAN WARD, NORTHCOURT HOSPITAL FOR CHILDREN, HAMPSTEAD.

NORTHCOURT HOSPITAL FOR CHILDREN, HAMPSTEAD.

This is one of the best appointed hospitals of its kind and its beautiful surroundings add greatly to its attractions. As one enters the large oak-panelled hall with the wide staircase running up to the wards one gets an impression of light and space. Notice boards, printed rules and invalid chairs are conspicuous by their absence, and a pretty rustic settle takes the place of the usual narrow form. Evidently Miss Mackenzie Rose and those responsible for the hospital have decided that both surroundings and environment are important factors in the healthy development of children in the treatment of disease. From the hall we pass to the Matron's tasteful sitting-room, opening upon the conservatory, with a dainty

children, and from here we pass upstairs to another floor and see Sister Ray's pretty sitting-room and still more rows of little beds. We stop for a moment to admire Nancy's beautiful needlework. Surely never were there stitched so fine, lace inserted with greater precision, or more delicate drawn work on the finest of linen than that accomplished by these small fingers.

In a lift we descend to the kitchen department where a beautiful pantry with white marble floor and shelves must be the joy of the housekeeper's heart; and then lastly, we inspect the large kitchens and drying-room and feel constrained to congratulate the Matron on the order and efficiency which she has managed to maintain in spite of the difficulty in procuring suitable nurses.

(Signed)   ISABEL MACDONALD,
Secretary of the Corporation.

THE CENTRAL COMMITTEE FOR THE STATE REGISTRATION OF NURSES.

A Meeting of the Central Committee for the State Registration of Nurses will be held, by the courtesy of the British Medical Association, in its Council Chamber at 429, Strand, London, W.C., on Saturday, October 26th, at 2.30 p.m.

THE MATRONS' COUNCIL.

We are glad to hear that there is to be a good gathering of Members on the 19th inst. at Charing Cross Hospital, where, by the kindness of the Committee and the Matron, the Autumn Meeting will be held. We hope to have the pleasure of seeing some of our overseas friends, if they have time to accept the hospitality of the President to tea.

THE RELATION OF WOMEN MEDICAL AND NURSING STUDENTS.

The admittance of women medical students to some of our largest general hospitals, where part of their education will be carried on in the wards as medical clerks and surgical dressers, opens up questions in connection with the Nursing Department—whether the authorities have realised it or not—which we gather from the replies to our recent letters of enquiry to the Wardens of the London Medical Schools, have so far received no consideration.

LETTER OF ENQUIRY.

The following letter was sent out from our office, on October 2nd, to the Wardens of the Medical Schools attached to the London, Guy's, St. Thomas', Charing Cross, Westminster, University College, St. George's, and King's College Hospitals, and the following replies have been received from the Deans and Sub-Deans :—

BRITISH JOURNAL OF NURSING,
Editorial Office,
20, Upper Wimpole Street, London, W.
2nd October, 1918.

SIR,—May I enquire if the Medical School attached to the —— Hospital admits women Medical Students, and, if so, may I have a copy of the Regulations which define their ward work. Do these students receive any instruction in dressing minor wounds and other practical work, such as the administration of enemas, the passing of catheters, &c., from the nursing staff ; and, if so, do the members of the nursing staff receive any remuneration, either from the Medical School or Hospital Committee for such teaching ?

Awaiting your reply,
I am, Sir,
Yours faithfully,
ETHEL G. FENWICK,
Editor.

The Warden,
The Medical School,
—— Hospital.

REPLIES.

From the London Hospital.—" In reply to your enquiry, women students at the London Hospital do not receive any instruction such as you detail from the nursing staff." No copy of Regulations sent.

Charing Cross Hospital.—" In reply to your letter of the 2nd instant, I beg to say that the Charing Cross Hospital Medical School and the Charing Cross Hospital admit women medical students to all their courses of teaching without any restrictions whatsoever, other than those applying to men students.

They are eligible for all Prizes and all Appointments, resident and otherwise. Their instruction in Dressing and all other practical work is entirely in the hands of the Staff of the Hospital and is not deputed to the nurses. With regard to the remuneration of the members of the Nursing Staff, that is wholly in the hands of the Council of the Hospital.

I have pleasure in enclosing herewith a Prospectus of the School, and to add that any information contained therein applies equally and without notification to women as well as to men."

We have to thank the Dean for a copy of the " Prospectus and Directory of the Medical School."

From University College Hospital.—" University College Hospital Medical School does now admit women medical students. They are on exactly the same terms as men students. No instruction is given to either male or female students by any member of the Nursing Staff. The Teaching is entirely in the hands of the Honorary Staff with the assistance of the Resident Staff."

From St. George's Hospital.—In answer to your letter of the 2nd October, I have to inform you that a limited number of women students are admitted to this Medical School under exactly the same conditions as the male students."

At St. Thomas's and Guy's Hospitals we are informed that women medical students are not admitted.

From King's College and Westminster Hospitals the courtesy of a reply has not been extended to our enquiry.

IN THE OUT-PATIENTS'.

" Please, sir, could you give my little boy 'is medicine for a monfth ? "

" No, he must come every week till he's better."

" But I wants to take 'im 'oppin'."

" Well, I can't give him leave to do that."
(*Sotto voce* to nurse) : " He's 'oppin' enough now in all conscience."

IRISH NURSES' ASSOCIATION.

APPOINTMENT OF SECRETARY.

The Irish Nurses' Association have appointed Mrs. Lanagan O'Keefe as Secretary in place of Miss French, resigned.

Mrs. O'Keefe is the widow of a well-known Irish doctor, but before her marriage was a trained nurse. She received her training at St. Vincent's Hospital, Dublin, and Golden Square Throat Hospital, London. She has experience also in secretarial work, having worked in one of the Local Government Board offices for some time, and at present is supervising clerk in the office of the Mechanical Transport for Ireland. Mrs. Lanagan O'Keefe has kept in touch with nursing matters and takes a keen interest in everything connected with our profession.

ST. BARTHOLOMEW'S HOSPITAL, EXAMINATIONS.

At the recent examinations of third and first years' Probationary Nurses they passed in the following order :—

THIRD YEAR EXAMINATION.

1, A. D. Normandale (Gold Medallist) ; 2, Z. E. French ; 3, M. E. Moore ; 4, E. Everett ; 5, A. Cowell ; 6, M. Whitehead ; 7, C. Wilcox ; 8, J. Ingram ; 9, E. Aldous ; 10, F. M. Jupe ; 11, A. J. Barlow and D. Williams ; 13, M. Dingle ; 14, M. A. E. Smith ; 15, C. C. Duke ; 16, F. Young and L. G. Hughes ; 18, M. G. Carter and J. L. Procter ; 20, A. N. Martin and Kate A. Smith ; 22, E. M. Morgerrison ; 23, H. F. Pugh ; 24, N. M. Jackson ; 25, E. H. Holloway ; 26, O. Caldecourt ; 27, M. O. McLeod ; 28, E. G. Labey.

FIRST YEAR EXAMINATION.

Nurse W. F. Ledger passed first and was awarded the Prize of Books.

THE PASSING BELL.

We have to record with very sincere regret the sudden death on Friday of Dr. John Biernacki, Physician Superintendent of the Plaistow Fever Hospital, E.

Dr. Biernacki was for many years deeply interested in the higher education of nurses and a consistent supporter of the movement for the State Registration of Nurses. He did much to standardise the training of Fever Nurses, was a founder and a member of the Fever Nurses' Association, which Association he has represented on the Central Committee since its foundation in 1910 ; he was also a member of the Royal British Nurses' Association.

In the death of Dr. Biernacki the medical profession has lost a very eminent member and the whole nursing profession a sincere and helpful friend. He was a man of clear thought and steadfast purpose and will be difficult to replace in the councils of the Nurses' organisations with which he has been so long associated for their benefit.

APPOINTMENTS.

MATRON.

Munition Isolation Hospital, South Shields.—Mrs. S. C. Cowan has been appointed Matron. She was trained at the Royal Infirmary, Edinburgh, and has been Sister, Night Superintendent, and Home Sister at Belvidere Fever Hospital, Glasgow.

TEACHING SISTER.

General Hospital, Nottingham.—Miss Marie Vaughan Winters has been appointed Teaching Sister. She was trained under the able superintendence of Miss G. A. Rogers, at the Royal Infirmary, Leicester, and has held the following positions :—Theatre Sister, Royal Hospital for Sick Children, Edinburgh ; Ward and Theatre Sister and Assistant-Matron, Royal Infirmary, Sunderland ; Matron, 3rd Durham V.A. Hospital for Officers, Sunderland.

SISTER.

Aberdare and District General Hospital.—Miss Cecilia Toye has been appointed Sister. She was trained at St. Marylebone Infirmary, London, and has had experience in private nursing in connection with the Royal Sussex County Hospital, Brighton.

SUPERINTENDENT NURSE.

The Infirmary, Hillingdon. — Miss Gertrude Agnes Wickham has been appointed Superintendent Nurse. She was trained at the Stockport Infirmary, and has been Sister at several infirmaries, and assistant matron and night superintendent at the David Lewis Epileptic Colony, and assistant matron at the Union Infirmary, Edmonton.

RESIGNATION.

Miss Stansfeld, the Chief Lady Inspector of the Local Government Board, has resigned her important office after twenty-one years' service. Her courtesy and kindness to her fellow-workers has marked her association with all, and she has received some very charming tokens of their regard upon her retirement. Her many friends in the nursing work wish her many happy years of leisure after her long spell of public service.

V.A.D. CONTROVERSY.

A most instructive correspondence on the V.A.D. question is raging in the *Spectator*. We hope to boil it down to practical dimensions next week.

CLINICAL THERMOMETER ORDER.

The Minister of Munitions, in exercise of the powers conferred upon him by the Defence of the Realm Regulations, has ordered that no person shall sell, offer for sale, supply or deliver any clinical thermometer which has not been tested, approved and marked, in accordance with the rules, made from time to time by the Controller of Glassware Supply on behalf of the Minister of Munitions and for the time being in operation.

The accuracy of thermometers is a matter of great importance to the sick.

NURSING ECHOES.

Several hospitals are arranging to give the nurses one whole day off in seven. We quite recognise it is right, but how we should have hated it when we were young and had to be hunted off duty.

We learn there is no need for criticism that two of the three Nursing College Scholarships were given to Thomas' Sisters. Very few suitable candidates applied for them. This we regret to learn, as we like people to thirst after knowledge.

We hear the Charing Cross " rise " has aroused much discussion in hospital Board rooms, and that it is probable the precedent will be generally followed.

We are not quite sure of the system employed by the London Homœopathic Hospital in the training of nurses, which undoubtedly produces the very type of nurse required in private practice. We speak with many years of personal experience as Hon. Superintendent of the Registered Nurses' Society, upon which staff the " Homœos " have always been held in special esteem. Whatever the system, there is no doubt whatever that it produces the sort of nurse most popular with the patients, and we don't need to doubt just what characteristics are appreciated by sick people. Knowledge and skill, of course, but knowledge and skill applied along with the true nursing spirit, which finds a sympathetic environment in the sick room, and conveys as much to the patient. The Board of Management of the London Homœopathic Hospital have kept well up with the times. In 1911 they built, at a cost of £25,000, a fine Nurses' Home, providing each of the 70 nurses the privacy of a room for herself, and Recreation Rooms replete with every comfort. Very soon after the war the scale of remuneration of the Nurses was revised, and they now receive £17, £18, £20, and £28 for the four years' training.

The Board of the Royal National Hospital for Consumption, Ventnor, have much pleasure in announcing that Lady Madden has most generously placed her beautiful house, Southwold, St. Lawrence, at the service of the management as a temporary home for the nursing staff, so releasing a block of buildings hitherto occupied by the nurses, and increasing the accommodation at the hospital from 160 to 177 beds, to meet in a measure the great demand for treatment of sailors and soldiers invalided home from the war.

A new nurses' home is to be built immediately after the declaration of peace, and the Board appeals for funds for this good work.

We are glad to note the August *Nursing Journal for India* contains the very able letter, written by Miss Beatrice Kent on " British Nurses and their Fight for Professional Freedom." We hope Miss Kent will keep the professional nursing press throughout the world well informed on nursing politics at home, as so few nurses in these overpowering days have time to dive into economic matters, which so nearly affect the welfare of the nursing profession as a whole—and as social influence and cash count for so much in England, working women must not be led away by specious arguments and charity doles. If they wish to be independent they must pay their own way.

Our American cousins can no longer in justice call THE BRITISH JOURNAL OF NURSING " a voice calling in the wilderness," as they have so aptly done for so many years. All at once, after " a long, long wail " of 25 years, everyone to whom its policy was anathema for so long seems to be clamouring for the fulfilment of its programme—Organization of Nursing Education and Registration by the State, Better Home Conditions and Pay, Shorter Hours of Labour, More Thorough Practical Training, Sister Teachers educated for the purpose, Nursing Colleges (but no monopoly), International Amenities—all these professional privileges have been claimed by THE BRITISH JOURNAL OF NURSING for a quarter of a century, and now the " antis " and their press are just tumbling over one another (without acknowledgment, of course) to carry into effect our precepts—even if they are somewhat shaky about the principles. The one essential principle these people have yet to realise and concede is the right of the nurses to self-determination, self-expression, and self-reliance. We are now looking forward to the time when the pap feeding of " Pumblechook " will be recognised as conducive to professional decadence, and each nurse will be entrusted with her own knife and fork. Then indeed " the Voice " will have made itself heard in the wilderness to some effect, and the special characteristic of our race—tenacity of purpose —be proved once more an unconquerable asset.

OUTSIDE THE GATES.

NATIONAL COUNCIL OF WOMEN OF GREAT BRITAIN AND IRELAND.

At its annual meeting held at Harrogate last week, the National Union of Women Workers adopted as its title " The National Council of Women," as suggested a quarter-of-a-century ago, when Mrs. Mary Wright Sewell, the founder of the International Council of Women, proposed to Mrs. Eva Maclaren, that such a council should be founded in the United Kingdom. Another " long, long trail " !

Much time was given to the revision of the Constitution, the most important innovation adopted being to eliminate sex, from Object 3 of the Council, which ran : " To co-ordinate women's organizations nationally and locally " The word "women's " has been eliminated in the new Constitution, so that for the future, societies governed by men, although having women members, are eligible for affiliation. Women alone can be delegates and members of committees, but as delegates are instructed how to vote, men-managed societies will have real power in the National Council of Women. Self-governing women's societies, at least, those composed of wage-earners, will certainly object to this innovation, and, we think, to be accurate, the new title should make it clear that it affiliates both sexes as provided under No. 3 of Article IV, in defining membership.

The President, Mrs. Ogilvie Gordon, suggested that messages of congratulation should be sent to General Foch and to Sir Douglas Haig. The proposal was enthusiastically endorsed, with a further suggestion that the services of the Navy and Air Force should be likewise recognised.

Many resolutions in support of useful reforms were agreed to.

WOMEN AND LABOUR.

The National Conference on Women's Civic and Political Rights and Responsibilities, organised by the Labour Party, at the Caxton Hall, Westminister, on the 15th and 16th inst., brought together some remarkable women. Amongst chairs and speakers, Dr. Ethel Bentham, Miss Susan Lawrence, L.C.C., Mrs. Sidney Webb, Miss Mary Macarthur, Dr. Marion Phillips, Mrs. Salter and Miss Margaret Bondfield were prominent. They discussed with eloquence and feeling " The Civic Rights of Women," " Ministry of Health and Maternity and Child Welfare Act," " Housing," " The Political Organisation of Women," " The Prevention of Venereal Disease," and " Food Problems after the War."

Many women's societies did not accept the invitation to send delegates owing to the participation of pronounced pacifists in the Conference.

WELCOME TO "ROBERTA."

The Home Office has decided to recognise a force of Women Police in London. We wish " Roberta " every success.

BOOK OF THE WEEK.

"THE SOUL OF SUSAN YELLAM."*

War from the point of view of a country village is the theme that Mr. Vachell has chosen for his latest book, and war more especially from the point of view of Susan Yellam.

" Sunday after Sunday Susan Yellam sat bolt upright in her pew. Her son, Alfred, sat beside her. Mother and son were never guilty of missing a response or of looking behind them, or of failing to contribute something in copper to the offertory plate. If a stranger happened to be conducting the service, and if he was so lost to decency as to display an unseemly haste, Mrs. Yellam's voice might be heard loud and clear setting the proper pace. At the end of every prayer her ' Amen ' came to be accepted even by the young and thoughtless as a grace and benediction."

Always she wore decent black, as became a woman who has buried, in the churchyard outside, a husband and three children.

Her clothes were not the least part of her personality.

Authority exuded from every pore in her skin.

She possessed the British cocksureness which so endears us to foreigners. The parson, Mr. Hamlin, observed of her that she was temperamentally incapable of detecting the defects of her great qualities.

Alfred was what the French term " *un celibaire enduri.*" And he was made extremely comfortable at home.

But he had passed his thirtieth year, and of late his mother had hinted discreetly that her cottage, larger than most, could accommodate three persons or more.

Alfred, who was the village carrier, met his fate when he brought Fancy Broomfield to her first place at the vicarage in his cart. He left her and her modest box at the door. She thanked him demurely, and asked him how much she owed him. Alfred was tempted to demand a kiss in payment, but a glance at the virginal face restrained him. He said instead, " One shilling, please, Miss." When he found himself alone he transferred the shilling to another pocket, wondering furtively if he were making a fool of himself.

But with the engagement came the other problem, for it took place at the outbreak of the war.

The slow working of Alfred's bucolic mind is well described, but the wrestling with his love for his mother and Fancy and his duty to his country do not tempt Mr. Vachell to stray from the path of sober realism.

" He said heavily—

" I ain't one for argument. I only know this, dear, if I go, others go too. And the men are wanted, Captain Lionel says. And if he says so, 'tis so. I feel I ought to go if you approve. When

---

* By Horace Annesley Vachell. Cassell & Co., London.

it coms to mother, I'm weak-kneed. If I leave her out, Fancy, 'tis because I know what's tearing her —the thought of the graves in the churchyard. 'Taint in mother as 'tis in you to stand hand-in-hand with me and forget her dear self."

Susan Yellam's faith was not strong enough to support her in those terrible days of the war and now, and Fancy would be vouchsafed a glimpse at an indurated heart. She had noticed that Mrs. Yellam avoided any direct reference to the Deity, Whose name had been so often on her lips before the war.

"One day Fancy said :

"God will be with Alfred."

Mrs. Yellam said quickly—

"He be wi' the Kayser too, seemin'ly."

She no longer discussed the sermon which had been her favourite mental exercise. One that made a special appeal to her she dismissed with—

"'Twas a notable sermon, but he ain't been tried as I have."

It was after the news came that "Alfred" was missing that his child was born. Mrs. Yellam tells her brother Habbakuk—

"She be low, but I be fightin' for her. Oh! there's so little of her—and no milk for the baby."

"Lard preserve her dear life !"

Susan frowned.

"'Tis milk that be wanted."

"You be right. Bottle babies suffer crool wi' colic."

"Not if I wash the bottles. Fancy have chosen the names. 'Tis queer Fancy keeps on a-sayin' to me, ' Alfred'll come back ! ' "

"Maybe he will, maybe he won't. Parson be prayin' in church for Alfred. 'Twould seem more respectful if you joined in wi' your loud voice."

At once Mrs. Yellam's face hardened.

"I bide at home till Alfred comes back."

Fancy's frail body slipped its moorings before the baby was many days old, and at her death she who had always been something of a seer had a vision of Alfred.

"I hear you as plain as plain. You had to come for both our sakes—mother's and mine. And such a night ! You ain't a bit wet neither. Afraid, Alfie ? With you holding me as tight as tight. Oh, no ! "

Susan Yellam heard a trickle of laughter. After that Fancy sighed twice, and her small body relaxed.

In Alfred's child, Susan Yellam recovered her soul.

H. H.

———————

COMING EVENTS.

October 19th.—Matrons' Council of Great Britain and Ireland. Meeting Charing Cross Hospital, 3.15 p.m. Tea, 4.15.

October 24th.—Society for the State Registration of Trained Nurses. Meeting Executive Committee, 431, Oxford Street, London, W. 4 p.m.

October 26th.—Central Committee for the State Registration of Nurses. Meeting, Council Chamber, British Medical Association, 429, Strand, London, W.C. 2.30 p.m.

LETTERS TO THE EDITOR.

Whilst cordially inviting communications upon all subjects for these columns, we wish it to be distinctly understood that we do not IN ANY WAY hold ourselves responsible for the opinions expressed by our correspondents.

PRECEDENCE FOR "THE MAN IN BLUE."

To the Editor of THE BRITISH JOURNAL OF NURSING.

DEAR MADAM,—May I be allowed to remark on a small writing which appeared in the JOURNAL of September 21st, and say how truly disgraceful I think it is that any woman should remark adversely upon "A man in blue" offering a Territorial his seat, and she accepting the same ?

I take it that the man in question would be well on the way to recovery before being allowed to be absent from hospital and take rides on 'buses.

Probably the "elderly woman" had never done a day's work in her life, and very probably not sacrificed any comfort, &c., during the present crisis, or endured any hardships, whereas the nurse has more than likely stood on her feet for the best part of the past four years, not taking into consideration her previous hard life, viz., "her training."   Yours truly,

A TERRITORIAL NURSE ON ACTIVE
SERVICE, ITALIAN FRONT.

[The following is the "par" to which our correspondent takes exception :—

"Recently in a crowded motor-bus two wounded soldiers rose politely from their seats to offer them to two women, one in nursing uniform, who promptly took the place without even a word of thanks. The other, an elderly woman, exclaimed ' No, not the seat of a man in blue. We ought to stand for you.' We should have supposed that the nurse was merely one of the many women who don our uniform without the right to wear it ; but alas! her uniform was that of the Territorial Force Nursing Service."

We cannot believe that the above member of the T.F.N.S. expresses the feelings or opinions of her colleagues. We feel sure that with very few exceptions, our military nurses would promptly offer their seats in any vehicle to "the man in blue." Personally we constantly elbow the pushing public aside at 'bus stopping stations so that the "man in blue," often weak and crippled, shall have the first chance of a seat inside. "Wounded first, wounded first "—called out in no uncertain voice—generally brings the " 'bus hogs " to their senses. It is a pity conductors have not the right to give precedence to the " man in blue."—ED.]

COLLEGE OFFICIALS SHOULD STUDY NURSING HISTORY.

To the Editor of THE BRITISH JOURNAL OF NURSING.

DEAR MADAM,—I was recently at a meeting in support of the College of Nursing, Ltd., and should like to have corrected several of Miss Cowlin's statements, but evidently we were only there to listen and agree. Miss Cowlin said : " Had such an organization as the College of Nursing existed before 1914, it would have been possible

THE BRITISH JOURNAL OF NURSING

WITH WHICH IS INCORPORATED

THE NURSING RECORD

EDITED BY MRS BEDFORD FENWICK

No. 1,595.　　　SATURDAY, OCTOBER 26, 1918.　　　Vol. LXI

EDITORIAL.

VICTORY IN VIEW.

Now that after four years of war, of a magnitude and horror unknown in the history of the world, the victory of the Allies, and the triumph of right and justice are in sight, none rejoice more than trained nurses, who from their intimate association with the wounded in the clearing stations and close behind the firing line, realise most poignantly the splendour of the valour of the allied troops, whether fighting with the enemy, or maimed and wounded enduring the results of the conflict in hospital wards.

And of the nurses none are able to enter into the joy of the victorious troops more than those in the invaded districts in France and Belgium now liberated from the grip of the Hun. No personal pain or disablement can dim the joy that illuminates the faces of the dauntless poilus and the "braves Belges," who stand once again on the soil of their dear native land, theirs once more, at the price of the life blood and agony of many thousands of brave men and women, and of the sacrifice even of innocent children.

It was inevitable that sooner or later British valour, French gallantry, and American prowess in war should overcome barbaric methods of war.

Now that the valour of the sailors, soldiers and airmen of the Allies have placed victory within our grasp, let us hold it tenaciously. As we read of the suffering endured in these four years of German domination in Lille and the devastated districts of France, in Courtrai, and the liberated towns in Belgium, as we thank God that that reign of terror is over, let us vow that by every means at our disposal we will ensure that the terms of peace made by the Allies are such as to deprive Germany for ever of the power to enslave the free peoples of the world ; and that they secure to the smaller nations that national independence which is their heritage and their birthright. Justice demands not only the suppression but the punishment of crime.

Meanwhile our hearts throb at the news of the King and Queen of the Belgians at Ostend; of the Armies of the Allies, led by King Albert, liberating town after town of gallant Belgium, of the thanksgiving service in the cathedral in Courtrai, of the Abbé who celebrated it (who, when the Germans entered the town, refused to leave a sick woman, though threatened with death by shooting if he did not do so), and of the joy bells ringing out from the Belfry of Bruges. Those who know and love this mediæval city, and have noted how its docks have again and again been bombed by Allied airmen, have scarcely dared to hope that ever again they would look on the beauty of its Belfry, or hear its carillon chiming the hours.

Longfellow's lines as he stood on the summit of the Belfry at dawn come irresistibly to mind :—

In the market place of Bruges stands the belfry old and brown ;
Thrice consumed and thrice rebuilded, still it watches o'er the town.
As the summer morn was breaking on that lofty tower I stood,
And the world threw off its darkness, like the weeds of widowhood.
　*　*　*　*　*
Then most musical and solemn, bringing back the olden times
With their strange, unearthly changes rang the melancholy chimes.

Long may the Belfry watch over Bruges, and as we listen to its melodious bells, may they be to us the symbol of those harmonies which underlie the beauty of human life in a world at peace, after the discord and horror of war.

NOTES ON NURSING IN FRANCE.

THE HÔPITAL ÉCOLE (RED CROSS), SQUARE DES PEUPLIERS, PARIS.

This School—Hôpital École de la Société de Secours aux Blessés Militaires—is attached to a beautiful Red Cross Hospital, erected some twelve years ago in the Square des Peupliers, Paris, and is a surgical *clinique*.

From the inception of the war, as Hôpital 12, it has been used for the care of the wounded, and many Red Cross workers have eagerly availed themselves of a short course of practical instruction for war nursing.

The elementary instruction to qualify for the simple Diploma after one year's work is exceedingly practical, the full term of training for a "Diploma Supérieur" is two years.

The school is superintended by a highly experienced Directrice, Mlle. Génin, who received me with delightful courtesy and herself conducted me over the whole institution.

Mlle. Génin is *maîtresse femme*, and her wonderful power of organisation was apparent to the professional eye in every department of the hospital, notably in the order and cleanliness of the wards, the disciplined demeanour of the nursing staff, and the evident comfort of the patients. The stairs, walls, floors, all were pure white and speckless. In the beautiful little chapel dim lights were burning and nurses knelt in prayer.

We visited all the domestic offices, and found every department in order, so essential for the comfort and happiness of the inmates of a hospital.

From her little bureau on the ground-floor it was evident that the whole direction of the institution was effected by "wireless."

The extensive grounds surrounding the hospital were beautifully laid out in gardens, or thriftily cultivated for use.

Situated in a very poor district this fine open

MLLE. GÉNIN, Directrice.

space with the heights of Bicetre in the near distance permits a sufficiency of light and air. The sunset as seen from the windows was amazingly beautiful.

With Mlle. Génin I exchanged opinions on the difference of nurse-training in England and France, taking into consideration national temperament and idiosyncrasy.

I gathered that women's paid work was not yet held in the same honourable esteem in France as in England and America. Thus nursing as a paid profession for gentlewomen was yet in its infancy in France.

Mlle. Génin is herself a voluntary worker but is in favour of encouraging respect for women's paid services, especially those of such inestimable value to the community as the work of the trained nurse.

She would also eagerly embrace an opportunity of adding medical and obstetric training for the nurses to the surgical branch already provided at the Peupliers, thus providing a thorough training for the "Diplôme Supérieur" under central control. To effect this extension new blocks and a Nurses' Home must be built, and for this at the present time money is not forthcoming in France.

I was introduced by Mlle. Génin to the Marquise de Montebello, a leading Red Cross worker, who has taken the trouble to study the nursing question in France and England, and who is deeply and intelligently interested in the progress and evolution of nursing in France.

With her I visited the fine wards arranged for the care of the wounded in the magnificent École Diocésaine at Conflans, by the grace of the Archbishop of Paris, where a nursing staff trained by Mlle. Génin have established a well-ordered service.

The same standard of order and cleanliness prevailed as at the Peupliers, and many of the new scientific treatments brought into practice during the war were being used for the relief and cure of the patients.

Mme. de Montebello was also good enough to show me something of Red Cross activities in Paris, to which she devotes her wonderful energy and talents.

In spite of some of the defects in the system of nursing in France, I observed a marked improvement in the wards and personnel since 1907 when I made a former tour of inspection.

Let us hope that in the next decade still further progress will be made.
                                                    E. G. F.

CARE OF THE WOUNDED.

The King and Queen and Princess Mary paid a visit to the American Base Hospital, No. 37, in

OUR ROLL OF HONOUR.

It is with deep regret that we record the death from influenza and pneumonia, on Friday, October 18th, of Miss Kathleen Stewart, Matron of the Welsh Hospital, Netley.

Miss Stewart was trained at the Royal Infirmary, Sunderland, and for some years held the position of Housekeeping Sister at Charing Cross Hospital, then that of Assistant Matron at the Royal Hospital for Sick Children, Edinburgh, and from there was appointed Matron of the York County Hospital (where she was Commandant of the Military Section). She was a member of the Matrons' Council and one of its delegates on the Central Committee for State Registration of Nurses.

Miss Stewart, who was appointed Matron by the

PUPILS IN THE GARDEN. HOPITAL ÉCOLE DE LA SOCIÉTÉ DE SECOURS AUX BLESSÉS MILITAIRES.

the neighbourhood of Dartford, on the 17th inst, and evidently by their simple kindness greatly impressed the patients. In the schools of the great republic kings and queens are represented as very dangerous beings indeed ; they have not yet forgotten the stupidity of poor old George III.

George V and the Queen Mary gave the American patients a very different impression of real royalty, and left amidst their ringing cheers, one man remarking that " they made the patients feel as much at home as their own President could have done, and," he added, " we have heard so much about your King and Queen, and are tickled to death to meet them like this."

The hospital accommodates 2,000 patients, and will shortly have room for 4,000. The staff is from the King's County Hospital at Brooklyn, and all the supplies have been provided by the generosity of Brooklyn citizens.

Welsh Hospital Committee last June, took over her duties on July 15th. In the brief period during which she held her office she quickly made her influence felt, winning without effort the confidence and trust of all the staff, and the gratitude and friendship of the patients, both officers and men, whose hearts she won by her warm and tactful sympathy.

Her fine and sterling character and example, the loss of which are so deeply felt in the Welsh Hospital, had already gained for her honourable distinction during her period of service at the York County Hospital, and must surely have carried her, had she been spared, to a leading position in the profession to which she was so intensely devoted.

The interment took place on Wednesday, October 23rd, at Blair Atholl, a memorial service also being held in the Garrison Church at Netley.

THE ROYAL RED CROSS.

The King held an investiture at Buckingham Palace on October 19th and conferred decorations as follows :—

FIRST CLASS.

Australian Army Nursing Service.—Matron ETHEL DAVIDSON, Matron CLARA ROSS, and Head Sister CLARICE DICKSON.

SECOND CLASS.

Territorial Force Nursing Service.—Sister GERTRUDE THOMAS and Sister BEATRICE THOMPSON.

Australian Army Nursing Service.—Head Sister ALICE DOUGLAS.

MILITARY MEDAL AWARDS.

For distinguished services in the field during air raids the following women have been awarded the Military Medal. We warmly congratulate them upon the recognition of their fine national service :—

Dr. PHŒBE CHAPPLE, R.A.M.C., att. Q.M.A.A.C.—During an air raid she attended to the wounded regardless of her safety.

Assistant-Administrator ELIZABETH S. CROSS, Q.M.A.A.C.—After a bomb fell she was knocked down, but got up at once and worked with the doctor while the raid was going on.

Forewoman Clerk ETHEL GRACE CARTLEDGE, Q.M.A.A.C.—Although both her shoes were blown off and she received injuries on one foot, she went on with her work.

Sister ETHEL FRANCES WATKINS, Q.A.I.M.N.S. (R.).—During an air raid lasting four hours she was wounded by shrapnel, but made light of her injury, and set a magnificent example to others.

Staff Nurse AGNES JACK PARKER, T.F.N.S.—Her ward was badly damaged, but she was exceptionally cool, and comforted the patients.

Miss MARY STUBBS, F.A.N.Y.—While getting patients out of a hospital a bomb dropped within thirty yards of her car, and stretcher-bearers who were loading another car called to her to take cover in a dug-out. Regardless of her own safety, however, she stayed in the open with two wounded and finally got them unloaded and to a safe place. During the unloading a second bomb fell on the hospital.

Sister JANE ELIZABETH TROTTER, Q.A.I.M.N.S. (R.).—In a night raid she visited all the wards to reassure the sick and the wounded. Her orderly was killed while standing by her in one of the wards.

FRENCH FLAG NURSING CORPS.

We learn that the Service de Santé, the authority under which the F.F.N.C. works in France, would use many more Sisters if they could be supplied. Now that the Comité Britannique C.R.F. have an active centre in Paris, the Service de Santé turns to it for British nurses, and when a good nurse is asked for it adds : " *All* the F.F.N.C. Sisters are *serieuse,*" which is indeed a very great compliment.

NURSING AND THE WAR.

Miss M. F. Billington, President of the Society of Women Journalists, is acting as Hon. Secretary of a Committee of women formed to bring together, at a Luncheon, a representative assembly of women whose guests will be the Matrons-in-Chief of Queen Alexandra's Imperial Military Nursing Service at home and in France, of the Territorial Force Nursing Service, and of the Canadian, Australian, and New Zealand Nursing Services, in recognition of the magnificent work done by the Military Nursing Services of the Crown.

The Luncheon will take place at the Trocadero, Piccadilly Circus, on Wednesday, October 30th, at 1.15 p.m. It is hoped H.R.H. Princess Louise, Duchess of Argyll, will preside. Mrs. Humphry Ward will write the address of appreciation that will be offered.

We think it is a pity that the Head Sister of Queen Alexandra's Royal Naval Nursing Service, and the Matron-in-Chief of the Nursing Service of the Royal Air Force have not been included as guests of honour on this occasion. Surely those responsible for the care of our heroic defenders on Sea and in Air are equally worthy of recognition with the ladies who superintend our Military Nursing Services of the Crown. We feel sure, had the Nursing Profession been represented on the Committee as the V.A.D.'s are, this omission would not have occurred.

Miss Gladys Slade has been awarded the Special Silver Insignia of Merit instituted by the Military Health Department of the French Republic, on May 1st, 1917. This has been conferred in recognition of long-continued devotion to wounded soldiers under the most trying circumstances. Miss Slade has been nursing the French wounded since March, 1915.

We regret the loss of the following young lives, so usefully employed in the service of their country.

Probationer-Nurse Michael, of Glasgow, who, with Nurse Evans, of Carmarthen, died from influenza, which they contracted while nursing patients at a military hospital, were buried on Saturday last in the Heroes' Corner of Tottenham Cemetery with full military honours. Nearly a dozen nurses at the hospital are on the sick list.

BARRETT.—On the 10th Oct., 1918, drowned through the sinking of the R.M.S. Leinster by a German submarine, when returning to duty in France, Sophia Violet, V.A.D., younger daughter of the late Samuel Barrett, J.P., Ballintava, Co. Galway, and beloved niece of Mrs. W. H. Wilson, Carrickmines House, Carrickmines.

THE WOMEN'S SENIOR WAR SERVICE.

THE SHORTAGE OF V.A.D.'s.

Under the above heading there has appeared in the *Spectator* during the month of September an interesting correspondence and series of articles on the important question of the shortage of V.A.D.'s or Auxiliary Nursing Service members, for our Military and Red Cross hospitals both at home and abroad, due to the competing and superior attractions of the three new war services for untrained, or non-*ad-hoc*-trained women—Queen Mary's Auxiliary Army Corps (Q.M.A.A.C.), Women's Royal Naval Service (W.R.N.S.) and Women's Royal Air Force (W.R.A.F.), which, both for officers and members, provide a much more inviting field for girls who have to consider the problem of earning their living, or supplementing slender means.

It is pointed out that not only has recruiting for Voluntary Aid Nurses under the British Red Cross practically ceased, but that much of the already existing *personnel* is being drained away from what is woman's first and most essential war work, because it is the work that is universally admitted she can do *better* than men, whereas the newer services were avowedly called into existence in order that women might temporarily fill men's places, and set them free for service in the fighting line.

It is quite clearly recognised that the V.A.D.'s are not trained nurses, but constitute material for the dilution of skilled labour, and the failure in the supply of this material, leading to the closing of Home Hospitals, or the impossibility of opening new ones abroad (actual instances of both these dangers are given) will be, in the opinion of the correspondents, a national disaster.

Various commandants and other Red Cross officials give their experiences of the enormous difficulty of finding a continuous supply of competent women to fill the posts in what is an arduous and monotonous occupation leading nowhere, carrying no pay except in the doubtful guise of a compassionate allowance to the really needy, and no reward except the vague one of "a diffused sense of general self-sacrifice."

It is stated that V.A.D. members employed in subordinate positions in military hospitals do receive a small salary, but it is less than that of the newly-recruited soldier; there is no prospect of a rise, and these workers have no definite standing and no hope of real promotion.

Sir George Beatson, who speaks with the authority of the Red Cross Council, points out that this failure in supply is due to various factors.

Firstly, Voluntary Aid Detachments were originally raised, organised and trained to do temporary First-Aid Ambulance work near their own homes. The pre-war Red Cross regulations show this, for it is laid down that members working away from home shall receive suitable military grading and pay, but this provision was apparently entirely lost sight of when war actually broke out.

When the V.A.D. members had to be used to supplement, in however humble a capacity, the insufficient supply of trained labour in hospitals, the support and approval of the nursing profession was not first obtained and friction inevitably arose. Sir George Beatson writes that following on this difficulty came the further hardship that, not being a recognised part of the Military Nursing Service, no official grading nor promotion was possible. He advocates the immediate formation of a Red Cross Nursing Reserve by which a definite though subordinate position would be given to the partially-trained nurses, and full use made of them. He considers that in this he could safely count upon the approval and support of the Military and Civilian Nursing Services. The body thus formed would have a definite standing, and promotion in its own ranks would be possible.

The Spectator itself goes much further, and wishes to see the formation of an entirely new War Service, to be called the Women's Auxiliary Army Medical Service (W.A.A.M.S.) to take rank *above* the other three new forces, on the ground that not only is there no war work for women superior to that of Nursing, but none in any way equal to it, in importance or dignity.

All members of this Service would be duly enlisted by the Government, under definite contract, would wear the King's uniform, receive pay and be eligible for promotion; the officers to be appointed by the Military authorities, receiving pay and allowances suitable to their rank, as in the other recently formed women's Services, with which the Auxiliary Nursing Service would then be able to compete on equal terms, and, by offering the same advantages, would retain the material now being drawn away from it.

The Spectator suggests that this matter be taken up without delay, in order to retain material for the work of keeping the hospitals fully staffed, thus enabling them to fulfil their functions in "the maintenance of man-power, the mending of men, and the restoration of the soldier to the fighting line," which, in the long run, is the only way to end the war.

REMARKS.

It is interesting to note these views on the V.A.D. question, and some of the opinions expressed are sound. But the root of the evil has not been made clear, and that is that the organisation and management of this auxiliary branch of the work of tending the wounded was most disastrously shifted by the War Office on to the shoulders of the inexpert. The initial mischief was done in pre-war days. The V.A.D. movement was fostered and managed by lay people. It was practically a Society movement; the professional point of view was not taken into consideration, in spite of the representations made by various societies of trained nurses who foresaw the danger and endeavoured to get the authorities to avoid it. When war broke out there was not a single nurse on the Council of the Red Cross nor of the Order of St. John, and they had no reserve of trained nurses, such as the Red Cross societies of other nations possessed. In spite of this, the War Office delegated to them the great responsibility of organising the nursing of auxiliary hospitals and the diluting of skilled work. The consequence was that the supply of trained nurses available and keenly desirous of serving in the early days of the war was never given its opportunity, that V.A.D.'s were allowed to undertake work for which they were unfitted, and that trained women were put under the command of amateurs. The result was that, in spite of the splendid devotion of all grades, the work of the Nursing Service has not been carried through with the unfailing enthusiasm and efficiency which comes from skilled organising.

Is it too late to hope that the War Office may yet shoulder the responsibility which it can never morally lay down, and organise an Auxiliary Service to assist in the work of hospitals, which shall be controlled by experts and be thoroughly representative of the nursing profession? Such an organisation would be just to the profession which it undertakes to temporarily dilute, as well as to the workers in its ranks and to those whom they serve.

Private generosity will always find ample scope in the provision of comforts, but the financial responsibility (from which control is necessarily inseparable) must remain in the hands of the State.

We should much like to hear what our professional sisters have to say on this suggested scheme. The present organisation as a supplementary Nursing Service for War, organised by amateurs has failed, as was inevitable.

A *sine qua non* of any such organisation must be professional control, and until that fundamental principle is conceded, muddle and waste will continue.

AFFILIATION OF THE TRAINED NURSES' ANNUITY FUND AND THE BENEVOLENT FUNDS OF THE R.B.N.A.

An arrangement has been made whereby the Trained Nurses' Annuity Fund and the Helena Benevolent and Settlement Funds of the Royal British Nurses' Association will be managed by a Conjoint Committee; the Council of the Royal British Nurses' Association and that of the Trained Nurses' Annuity Fund still retaining control of their own Funds.

The Council of the Trained Nurses' Annuity Fund have received with deep regret the resignation of Dr. Ogier Ward as Hon. Secretary. Miss Isabel Macdonald was appointed Hon. Secretary at a recent meeting of the Council, and donations to any of the above-mentioned Funds should be sent to her at 10, Orchard Street, Portman Square, W. 1. Subscribers should state to which they wish any amounts sent to be allocated.

THE MATRONS' COUNCIL OF GREAT BRITAIN AND IRELAND.

By the kindness of Miss Heather-Bigg, the President, the quarterly meeting of the Council was held in the Nurses' Home, Charing Cross Hospital, on Saturday afternoon, October 19th. Thirty-five members attended, and many sent letters of regret at inability to be present. In her opening remarks from the Chair the President said that she desired in the name of all present to assure Mrs. Fenwick of the pleasure they all felt to see her with them again after her recent severe illness. All felt deeply indebted to her for her strenuous and devoted work of many years for the preservation of the rights and liberties of nurses, which a just Bill framed by the Central Committee for State Registration would secure to them.

Miss Heather-Bigg then asked Mrs. Fenwick's acceptance of a beautiful bouquet of golden chrysanthemums, a gift for which Mrs. Fenwick expressed sincere appreciation.

The Minutes of the last meeting were then read and confirmed. A number of letters of regret were read by the Hon. Secretary from those unable to attend. A large amount of correspondence was dealt with, which aroused most interesting discussions.

NEW MEMBERS.

Nine new members were elected.

THE MIDWIVES ACT AMENDMENT BILL.

Among other matters of interest, the question of the Midwives Act Amendment Bill for England now before Parliament was brought forward. Mrs. Fenwick, who raised the question, said that she and Miss Breay had been in communication with members of Parliament, and had urged that the following Amendments should be proposed, if not incorporated in the Bill :—(1) Direct representation of the midwives on the Board; (2) legal assistance for midwives who may be required to appear before the Central Midwives Board, to enable them to defend themselves.

In Mr. Hayes Fisher's sympathetic speech, upon introducing the Amendment Bill into the House of Commons, he had stated that "it will be possible, if it is thought desirable, to give the midwives themselves direct representation upon the Board," and she gathered that Clause 7 in the Bill, which allows the Central Midwives Board to pay the expenses of any midwife who may be required to appear before the Board to defend herself, would include the expenses of a lawyer. The Board itself, when enquiring into accusations made against a midwife, employ a solicitor, and every midwife should be provided with legal assistance when defending herself before it.

Mrs. Fenwick proposed that an Emergency Resolution should be drafted by the Hon. Officers of the Matrons' Council, thanking Mr. Hayes Fisher for defining a liberal and just policy for midwives on these two points.

This was seconded by Miss M. Winmill.

Miss Marsters proposed the following addition :—" That the Matrons' Council approves of Clause 12 as it stands, which provides that the inspection of midwives should be the duty of County Councils, without power of delegation to District Councils."

It was unanimously agreed to incorporate this amendment with the original resolution.

NATIONAL COUNCIL OF WOMEN.

Miss Helen Pearse gave an interesting report of the Conference of the National Council of Women held recently in Harrogate.

The meeting then terminated.

By the courtesy and kindness of Miss Heather-Bigg the guests were most hospitably entertained to tea, including the following American military " Chief Nurses " now on duty in London—Miss Leonard, Miss Shillaburger, Miss Minnette Hay, and Miss Porter. " Over the cups " tongues were loosed, and a very enjoyable afternoon, both of business and pleasure, was passed. But there—Miss Heather-Bigg was hostess ! Some of the guests gladly availed themselves of the kind permission to visit the wards, which were greatly admired.

ANNIE E. HULME, *Hon. Secretary.*

ROYAL BRITISH NURSES' ASSOCIATION.

The Programme of the Conference to be held on Thursday, November 7th, at the rooms of the Medical Society of London, 11, Chandos Street, Cavendish Square, and at which Her Royal Highness Princess Christian, the President, will preside, can be obtained from the Secretary R.B.N.A., 10, Orchard Street, Portman Square, W. It will be found on page ii of our cover this week.

The Conference will be opened at 3 p.m. First Session. Subjects for Discussion : " The Economic Position of the Trained Nurse " and " Some Phases of Modern Nursing."

Tea will be served, and the Second Session open at 5.30 p.m., when various speakers will compare the two Bills for the State Registration of Nurses drafted by the Central Committee and the College of Nursing, Ltd.

Free discussion and questions are invited.

AN IMPUDENT GAMBLE.

We publish below a " Prize Drawing " Scheme in conjunction with the Dublin Stock Exchange, purporting to be in aid of " The Nation's Tribute to Nurses." A greater insult has never been offered to the dignity of the Nursing Profession, and we hope Lady Cowdray and her supporters are now satisfied that the indignant protest of the independent members of the Nursing Profession in objecting to widely-advertised charity upon their behalf has ample justification.

PRIZE DRAWING.
218 MONEY PRIZES.
1,000 TICKETS.

The above Drawing in conjunction with the Dublin Stock Exchange, is in aid of

The Nation's Tribute to Nurses.

(For all Irish Certificated Nurses.)

The price of the first Ticket drawn will be one penny, the second twopence, the third threepence, and so on, until the maximum is reached for the last Ticket, No. 1,000, £4 3s. 4d.

The Tickets then participate in a further Draw for the undermentioned Prizes —

1st Prize	..	..	£250 0 0
2nd Prize	..	..	£100 0 0
3rd Prize	..	..	£50 0 0
5 Prizes of	..	..	£20 each.
10 Prizes of	..	..	£10 each.
50 Prizes of	..	..	£5 each.
150 Prizes of	..	..	£1 each.

Applications for Tickets to be made through Members of the Stock Exchange only, and these applications must be received not later than Friday, October 18th.

The Final Drawing will take place on Thursday, October 31st, and winning numbers published in *Irish Times* on Saturday, November 2nd.

The above scheme appears to us a peculiarly barefaced gamble for personal profit, and hardly the type of Tribute the Nation's Nurses will appreciate, as the Scheme exploits their splendid national work with cruel disregard of their professional self-respect. Stripped of camouflage, it is a simple method of obtaining about £2,000, one thousand of which is to be gambled for by the public. Presumably what is left over when the prizes have been pocketed is to be added to the Nation's Fund as an expression of its appreciation and admiration of the certificated Nurses' services ! It is an abominable insult, and we call upon the London County Council, which has registered this " War Charity," to make searching enquiries into the conduct of the business of " The Nation's Fund for Nurses " and to stop these gambling scandals in connection with it.

Our attention has been drawn to the fact that London is plastered with " illegal " posters referring to this Fund.

THE COLLEGE OF NURSING, LTD.

Unjustified Pretensions.

The Council of the College of Nursing, Ltd., announces throughout the Press "That it has had under consideration the question of salaries in the Nursing Profession, and is setting up a small representative Committee of Nurses to deal with the subject."

We do not know by what right the College of Nursing, Ltd., presumes to speak in the name of the Nursing Profession, or to dictate to it concerning its economic affairs. So long as it is content to be dominated by lay authority and supported by charity it is the very last organisation which can inspire confidence in the thousands of self-supporting trained nurses who strongly object to its unsound methods of finance.

But this assumption of authority over the whole Nursing Profession requires action upon the part of trained nurses who are not under the control of members of the College Council, and we are glad that at the Session of the Royal British Nurses' Association Conference, at which "The Economic Position of the Trained Nurse" is to be discussed, on November 7th, its members and the members of its affiliated societies will be given an opportunity for free discussion on their own affairs, and of defining a policy.

The Danger of Supplementary Registers.

The leaflet in the first instance advertising the Bazaar in support of the Nation's Fund for Nurses to be held in Manchester in November omitted the notice required by the law; but the attention of Dr. Oswald, the Hon. Treasurer, having been drawn to the illegality, it has now been rectified. But in this little printed slip we note another ambiguity. In specifying the objects of the College of Nursing, Ltd., which the Fund proposes to endow, it is stated that (c) is "To have One Portal system of examination into the profession."

The College Bill provides that, as well as the General Nurses Register, there are to be any amount of Supplementary Registers of persons "trained under conditions approved by the Council." The institution of Supplementary Registers, other than for male and mental nurses, means the professional depreciation of the General Register of three years' trained nurses, and we fail to see, therefore, how the College Council can claim that their Bill provides for "One Portal system of examination into the profession." It does no such thing, but specially takes power to institute Supplementary Registers of specialists "trained under any conditions" its Council chooses; and practically undermines the three years' standard of general training as the present College regulations permit. It is these disingenuous methods employed by the men who manage the College and the Matrons who support them, that fill the intelligent members of our profession with indignation and distrust.

APPOINTMENTS.

MATRON.

St. John Aux. Military, "A," Hospital, Morecombe. —Miss S. G. Nobbs has been appointed Matron. She was trained at the General Hospital, Auckland, New Zealand; and has been Matron of Opotilha General Hospital, N.Z; General Hospital, Cook's Islands; and of Ramsgate and Chigwell Aux. Military Hospitals.

Walton Sanatorium, nr. Chesterfield. — Miss Winifred Mason has been appointed Matron. She was trained at the Derbyshire Royal Infirmary, and has been Staff Nurse at King Edward VII Sanatorium, Midhurst; Sister, Royal National Hospital, Ventnor; and Matron, Salterley Grange Sanatorium.

Penarth Isolation Hospital.—Miss Elma J. M. Davies has been appointed Matron. She was trained at the City Hospital, Bristol, and County Hospital, Hertford; and has been Matron of the Caerphilly Urban District Isolation Hospital; and School Nurse under the Glamorgan County Council.

OUT-PATIENT SISTER.

Garrett-Anderson Hospital, Euston Road, W.C. — Miss E. P. Scrase has been appointed Out-patient Sister. She was trained at St. Bartholomew's Hospital, including massage. She has held the positions of Assistant House Sister, and was, in 1916, appointed Assistant Out-patient Sister in the Throat and Ear Department.

SISTER.

Samaritan Free Hospital, London,—Miss Dorothy Metzger has been appointed Theatre Sister. She was trained at St. Mary's Hospital, Paddington, where she has acted as Holiday Sister.

Sandon Red Cross Auxiliary Hospital, Weston Stafford.—Miss Anna F. Hobbs has been appointed Sister. She was trained at Adelaide Hospital, Dublin, and has been Sister and Masseuse at the Anglo-American Hospital, Cairo; and at the Military Hospital, Seaford.

The Hospital, Newcastle, Co. Wicklow. — Miss Mary Kennedy has been appointed Sister. She was trained at the City Infirmary, Belfast, and has been on duty at the Third Western General Hospital, Newport.

HEAD NURSE.

Lichfield Union Infirmary. — Miss Alice Rhead has been appointed Head Nurse. She was trained at Ancoats Hospital, Manchester, and has been Sister at the Lichfield Nursing Home.

QUEEN VICTORIA'S JUBILEE INSTITUTE.

Transfers and Appointments.

Miss Eva W. Owen is appointed to Warrington, as Superintendent. Miss Annie Mannion to Derbyshire C.N.A., as Assistant County Superintendent. Miss Gladys K. S. Robson to Dorsetshire C.N.A., as Assistant County Superintendent. Miss Mildred M. Stephens to Gloucestershire C.N.A., as Assistant County Superintendent and Health Visitor. Miss Annie Aldridge to Woolwich;

Miss Hannah F. Barniston to Fullerton Hospital Denaby Main ; Miss Ethel Daniells to Taunton ; Miss Sarah B. Rowland to Taunton ; Miss Wilhelmina Mathieson to Watford, as School Nurse ; Miss Millicent E. Tunsley to St. Austell ; Miss Edith Webster to St. Austell.

PRESENTATION.

Miss M. G. Vergette, appointed Matron of the Royal Victoria Hospital, Dover, has been presented by her colleagues at St. Bartholomew's Hospital, with whom she is exceedingly popular, with a charming Georgian silver tea-service, on which has been engraved the date of her resignation, the crest of the hospital, and her initials. We feel sure when in use it will remind her of many happy years spent with her dear friends at Barts.

RESIGNATION.

Miss E. M. Byles, who, since 1901 has been Matron of the Lambeth Infirmary, has, owing to ill-health, resigned that position. The work of hospital matrons has, since the beginning of the war, become more and more arduous and difficult. Miss Byles feels the necessity of a rest, at least for a time. She will be greatly missed at Lambeth by both nurses and patients, where she has laboured unceasingly for the benefit of both, and where she has raised the status of the Nursing School to one of the best attached to a Poor Law Infirmary.

IN MEMORIAM.

Queen Alexandra has graciously accepted a copy of the " In Memoriam " card of the death of Edith Louisa Cavell written by Miss Henrietta Hawkins, and expressed her thanks for the " beautiful lines." Nothing more exquisite has been written on the splendid death of Edith Cavell than this wonderful poem.

The Prince of Wales sent £3,000, the Queen £1,000, and Queen Alexandra £500 in support of " Our Day," October 24th, when the great Red Cross appeal was made at home and abroad.

Nurses can do good service by urging those with whom they come in contact to save all the shells of hard-shell nuts for the National Salvage Council. They are very useful in the manufacture of charcoal for gas-masks. Now is the time to begin putting them aside until there are enough to make a creditable showing for the National Salvage Council.

TRUE TALE WITH A MORAL. 1930.

Granddaughter : " What did you do in the Great War, grannie ? "

Grannie : " I escaped without a decoration ! "

NURSING ECHOES.

" Do tell me," said a lady whose *bottines* were irreproachable, " do hospital Sisters only get paid 13s. a week? It sounds an outrage considering all the hard work they do. I have a friend at the —— Hospital, and the Matron called her over the coals for wearing shabby shoes ! Fancy having to dress, pay for holidays—and supplement food—and stamps, and buses, and a whole floor full of things on 13s. a week ! No wonder there is a shortage of hospital nurses ! "

At a recent meeting of the West Ham Guardians a letter was received from the Ministry of Labour, stating that the Board's probationer nurses had asked for an arbitration on the question of their salaries, and that an arbitrator had been appointed for the purpose.

A question arose as to whether the Board should be represented at the inquiry, and Mr. Shreeve asked if it was proposed to go there and oppose the nurses' application. They ought not to do that, in his opinion, but they might take the opportunity of trying to get all these increases " shoved " on to national funds. They were purely a war charge.

Mr. Ward said the scrubbers at the infirmary received nearly double the wages of the nurses in charge of whole wards.

The Chairman pointed out that this was not correct when board, lodging, and other emoluments were included.

The Acting Clerk stated the normal remuneration of the scrubbers was 14s. for seven days. The new scale included a war bonus of 12s. 6d. a week, and if they added the 10s. paid in lieu of rations, it came to more than 33s. The commencing salary of staff nurses was £36, war bonus £15 a year, residence, and uniform value £5.

The Chairman said that in Committee he was in favour of nurses rising to £150. He added that he desired to see the status of nurses raised, but he did not want to let Mr. Ward's statement pass unchallenged.

It was agreed that five members of the Board should officially represent it at the arbitration.

The House Committee of Queen Mary's Hospital for the East End has raised the salaries of all grades of the nursing staff. Probationers' salaries start at £12 a year and rise to £35 ; ward sisters, £45 to £60 ; night sisters, £50 to £70 ; massage sister, £60 to £70 ; out-patients sister, £50 to £70. In addition, when circumstances permit, extra off-duty and holidays are to be granted.

From July 1st, 1919, a Pension scheme will come into force. Nurses with 25 years' service will be given at least £52 annually upon retirement, and, further, if any member of the nursing staff of not less than ten years' service, through no fault of her own, breaks down in health so as to render her unfit for further work, the Committee may award her such pension or gratuity as they might think fit.

———

Great changes have been made in the Nurses' conditions at the Prince Alfred Hospital, Sydney.

To enable the nurses to state their point of view with respect to any matters relating to the conditions and duties of the nursing staff, a Conference was held at the hospital, when representatives of all the grades on the staff, from first-year pupil nurse to Sisters, met the Medical Superintendent, Secretary, and Matron, and presented various points for consideration.

These matters were submitted to the Board in concrete form, with recommendations from the executive officers, and the Board has now given its decision upon various points, which we are sure will be for the benefit of all concerned.

The salaries for fully qualified nurses shall be as follows :—

Sisters, for first year £100, for second year £110, for third year £120; Charge Nurses, £80.

The appointment of Charge Nurses shall be for one year, and if then appointed as Sisters they will serve for a term of three years, at the end of which period they will be eligible for re-appointment for a further term, but need not necessarily be re-appointed.

More leave is to be allowed, and evening leave is permitted without a late pass till 10 p.m.

VISCOUNTESS RHONDDA AND THE MINISTRY OF HEALTH.

At a meeting of the National Baby Week Council held on October 15th, Major the Hon. Waldorf Astor was elected chairman in succession to the late Lord Rhondda, and Viscountess Rhondda was elected vice-chairman. In taking the chair, Lady Rhondda proposed the following resolution, which was carried unanimously :—

"That in view of the general and keen support for the proposed Ministry of Health already afforded to the propaganda efforts of the National Baby Week Council, and in view of the acute problems of health

and disease which demobilisation will bring, this Council reiterates its urgent demand upon His Majesty's Government to introduce without delay the Bill for the Ministry of Health into Parliament.

Lady Rhondda referred to the work of her father whilst at the Local Government Board, in urging the introduction of a Ministry of Health Bill as a war measure, and spoke of the opposition which was still being shown among certain vested interests in commerce and in politics. She said that it could not be allowed that such interests should stand in the way of lives. Lady Rhondda gave the opinion that the Ministry of Health would be well advised to get into touch with the women, who were the lay section of the community which took the most vivid interest in all questions of health, and if the Ministry of Health was to be a success it had got both to educate the women of the country and to keep in touch with them. Any Bill which was to achieve everything which the Council asked it should achieve must institute machinery by which women had a large place in the Ministry of Health, and some scheme by which they were kept in close touch with it. Lady Rhondda referred to the excellent propaganda work being done by the Council in London and the provinces to strengthen the hands of the Government in regard to the Ministry of Health.

OUTSIDE THE GATES.

WOMEN IN PARLIAMENT.

On the 15th inst., Mr. Jowett asked the Prime Minister in the House of Commons whether the Government had considered the initiation of legislation to allow women to stand for Parliament; and whether he would give time for debate on a private Member's motion on which the House might record its wishes in this matter ?

The Chancellor of the Exchequer (Mr. Bonar Law) replied that in the opinion of the Government this, like similar questions which arise in connection with the Franchise Bill, is one which ought to be left to the House, and that he would arrange to give an opportunity for its discussion.

———

Mr. Herbert Samuel gave notice of a motion affirming the desirability of a Bill being introduced making women eligible as members of Parliament, which is being debated in the House of Commons as we go to press.

It is understood that the Labour Party have a Bill drafted which will be introduced at once if the opinion of the House indicates a favourable reception. Several women candidates have been selected should the Bill become law.

OUR PRIZE COMPETITION.
QUESTIONS.

November 2nd.—Describe the treatment of fractures by massage.

November 9th.—Give the nursing of a case after removal of kidney, and state the complications that may occur.

LETTERS TO THE EDITOR.

Whilst cordially inviting communications upon all subjects for these columns, we wish it to be distinctly understood that we do not IN ANY WAY hold ourselves responsible for the opinions expressed by our correspondents.

EFFICIENCY BEFORE CHEAPNESS.

To the Editor of THE BRITISH JOURNAL OF NURSING.

MADAM,—The country is beginning to realise that a Ministry of Health is necessary. City Corporations, Town Councils and other governing bodies are already bestirring themselves to look after the mother and infant within their boundaries. Unless, however, we are to become a " C 3 " Empire a more thorough realisation of the situation is necessary.

It is lamentable that so many of these public bodies have decided to do their work " on the cheap." Their only apparent desire is to show they are " doing something," without increasing the rates ; yet the care of Mother and infant, as shown by the Local Government Board in their Circular of 1918, is one of the most important branches in Reconstruction. It should secure the best workers, most experienced, best educated and consequently most highly paid. To ensure good work good workmen must be obtained, and for good workmen good money must be paid.

Despite this accepted axiom, one is constantly reading of Corporations advertising for " A Lady holding the Central Midwives Board's Certificate or a Health Visitor's Certificate "—the former is generally essential. Both certificates are excellent and necessary, but should be held in conjunction with a certificate of three years' general training.

The salaries offered suggest the Sweating System in the highest degree. To ask any woman competent to undertake duties of such national importance to work, lodge, board, dress, pay for coal, laundry and annual holiday, and provide for old age on £85 to £100 per annum is a scandal. Sometimes the advertiser offers as further inducement £3 to £5 in lieu of uniform, well knowing it cannot be provided for that sum. When, moreover a *trained Nurse* is preferred, " with C.M.B. Certificate, Health Visitor's Certificate, Maternity and Child Welfare Certificate and others," and the *same salary* is offered we need not wonder that Mr. Hayes Fisher deplored the scarcity of Nurses and midwives as being one of the great obstacles in the way of the Ministry of Health.

There are plenty of trained women eminently qualified for this sphere of work who are forced to remain in posts which, though under paid offer board and lodging. Public Authorities should pay a salary in proportion to the work to be undertaken—£200 per annum, rising by increments—for a fully qualified women, and these nurses would be able to offer their services to the community.

The Royal Air Force rightly pays £200 to Women Area Inspectors, £175 to Superintendents of their women's hostels, plus quarters, outfit allowance £20 and other extras. This after *three weeks' training.* Yet the country remunerates Nurses—or does without them—who undertake greater responsibilities and have spent years and money acquiring knowledge and skill with less than half the amount considered necessary for work requiring much less training.

The Local Government Board, on page 7 of its Circular on " Maternity and Child Welfare," after enumerating the duties and necessary qualifications of Health Visitors, to assure the local Authorities obtaining the Board's Grant towards incurred expenses, suggests that the Health Visitor be paid not less than £120 *per annum,* whether she be a trained nurse or not. We need hardly wonder at the salaries offered by local Authorities when an Advisory Board makes such incompetent and unfair suggestions.

I am, yours truly,
JENTIE B. N. PATERSON.
Member National Union of Trained
Nurses.

KERNELS FROM CORRESPONDENCE.

Another T.F. Nurse : " I can hardly believe a ' Territorial Nurse on Active Service ' could express such an opinion on the ' Man in Blue ' in 'buses. It seems to me nursing etiquette, no matter how tired she is, for a Territorial Nurse to refuse to take the seat of a patient. The ' bus hog ' is indeed becoming a blot on the community and I have seen men in mufti, and women, sitting whilst the wounded have to stand, and pushing and jostling against arms in splints and leg stumps, &c., when getting in and out. I have also said an indignant word in season."

" Independent Nurse " : " I enclose the Petition to the Premier, signed, asking for the direct representation of the organised societies of nurses on the Provisional Governing Body authorised by Parliament to frame the Rules and Regulations in a Nurses' Registration Bill. I note in the Seventh Draft of the College Bill that it is *specially provided* to *exclude* the representatives of the nurses' societies from participating in this responsible duty. It is scandalous. May I urge every certificated nurse trained at my old school— University College Hospital—to look into this matter, and sign the Petition."

COMING EVENT.

October 26th.—Central Committee for the State Registration of Nurses. Meeting, Council Chamber, British Medical Association, 429, Strand, London, W.C. 2.30 p.m.

OUR ADVERTISERS.

Do not omit to buy, as far as possible, everything you need from " Our Advertisers," and to recommend them to your friends. They are all first-class firms.

The Midwife.

THE MIDWIVES BILL.

A BILL TO AMEND THE MIDWIVES ACT, 1902.

On Tuesday, October 15th, the day on which the House of Commons resumed after the Adjournment, the second reading of the Midwives Bill was moved by Mr. Hayes Fisher, President of the Local Government Board, in the words, " I beg to move, ' That the Bill be now read a second time.' "

Mr. Hayes Fisher said that he could perform this duty in a very few sentences. He explained that the Bill was introduced in the House of Lords, on behalf of the Privy Council, early in the Session, and passed that House with only one important Amendment. When it came to the House of Commons a lynx-eyed member detected in some of the Clauses an infringement of the privileges of the House of Commons. These Clauses were held to contain a public charge. That being so, the Bill should have been introduced into the House of Commons instead of the House of Lords ; therefore it had to be laid by. He consequently introduced it precisely in the same form in which it passed the House of Lords.

THE ACT OF 1902.

He then explained that the basis of all legislation in relation to midwives was the Act of 1902, which set up a Central Midwives Board and required that after a certain time women should not act as midwives unless they were duly certified by that Board. The Act applied to England and Wales only. After some years' experience of its operation, a Departmental Committee made valuable recommendations as to amendments which might fittingly be brought into the Act by subsequent legislation. When Scotland and Ireland obtained the benefits of a Midwives Act, the principal recommendations of the Departmental Committee were incorporated in those Acts.

THE CINDERELLA OF MIDWIFERY LEGISLATION.

So it came about that England and Wales became, as it were, the Cinderella of midwifery legislation. The whole object of the present Bill was to assimilate the law relating to the midwives of England and Wales to that which obtains in Scotland and Ireland.

THE IMPORTANCE OF THE CLAUSES.

Mr. Hayes Fisher went on to explain the importance of the Clauses of the present Bill.

Clause 1, he said, provides machinery by which the constitution of the Central Midwives Board can be altered, with proper safeguards, by an Order in Council. *Clause 2* endeavours to make an equitable apportionment of any deficit ; the present system appeared to penalize the more active authorities as against the negligent ones. *Clause 6* amplifies the provisions relating to suspension ; in this Clause, Sub-section (2) introduces, for the first time, the principle of compensation.

Clause 7 allows the Central Midwives Board, if they think fit, to pay the expenses of any midwife who may be required to appear before them to defend herself ; whilst *Clause 8* empowers the Central Midwives Board, in removing from the Roll the name of any midwife, also to prohibit her from attending maternity cases in any other capacity.

Clause 10 introduces provision for the reciprocal recognition of certificates granted by the Central Midwives Board in this country, and of midwives certified by similar bodies in other parts of His Majesty's Dominions where the training is equivalent. *Clause 11* empowers Local Supervising Authorities to contribute to the training of midwives in conformity with the resolution passed by the County Councils Association. *Clause 12* repeals Section 9 of the principal Act (Delegation of Powers by County Councils to District Councils).

Mr. Hayes Fisher pointed out that this proposal gave rise to a division of opinion in another place, and said he thought it probable that, in the Committee stage, some objection might be taken, he should be only too glad to listen to all those capable of advising him as to the best form this proposal ought to take.

Clause 14 provides a simple machinery for the payment of medical assistance summoned by midwives in cases of emergency, and makes it obligatory to summon a doctor in typical cases of emergency.

EFFECT OF THE BILL.

In conclusion, Mr. Hayes Fisher said : " It only remains to be said that the Bill embodies the principal recommendations of the Departmental Committee, and that it brings the whole of our legislation connected with midwives in England, Wales, Scotland and Ireland all on the same footing. We are all most anxious to do everything we can to promote maternity, and anything that relates to child welfare. If we can pass such a Bill as this, which improves the status of midwives and removes some of the difficulties under which they suffer, I feel that we shall have done something to diminish the suffering of motherhood, and we shall have done something to attract more women, and possibly a better class of women, to that ancient and honourable profession. By this Bill we shall take an important step forward in one branch of the public health which endeavours to see that everything is done for the strengthening of the health and the general improvement of the vitality of both mother and child."

DEBATE.

MR. GEORGE THORNE said he rose to refer to one point relating to Clause 12 to which reference had already been made. He understood that the Right Honble. Gentleman wished to reserve discussion on this point to the Committee stage, but, if he were able to make any statement at this stage, it might considerably reduce the time required for the Committee stage. He pointed out the memorandum of the Bill distinctly indicated that the measure was proposed in such a way that all contentious matter was avoided. The question raised in Clause 12 was a distinctly contentious matter. The County Councils very strongly objected to Clause 12, which robbed them of the power they at present possessed of delegating their powers to District Councils, and he hoped the Right Honble. Gentleman would be able to indicate that he did not intend to proceed with that Clause, and so avoid discussion on the Committee stage.

SIR JOHN HARMOOD-BANNER endorsed the remarks of the previous speaker. He urged that the Memorandum said all contentious matter was avoided, yet Clause 12 was contrary to the very strongly expressed opinion of the Municipal and County Council Associations of the Kingdom, and that it was rather curious to call the measure non-contentious when that was the position. The representatives of the County Councils and Municipal Associations had a strong view upon this question, and they did not like to have the opinion of the House of Lords foisted upon them by stating that this was a non-contentious question when, as a matter of fact, these Associations all disapproved of it.

CLAIM FOR MORE WOMEN ON MIDWIVES BOARD.

MR. HANDEL BOOTH supported the view of the previous speakers. He drew attention to Clause 1, and wished to have it clearly understood that the word " person " in that Clause included women. As things were developing at present there was a general recognition that women must more and more be called into the counsels of the nation. If they could have an assurance from the Government that they contemplated, under Clause 1, having the freedom to appoint more women—he suggested possibly a midwife, providing a suitable candidate came forward—he thought the House would regard it as a distinct step in advance.

MAJOR HILLS said, in relation to Clause 12, that the House must not assume that all the arguments were on the side of his hon. friends who had spoken. There was a very strong case the other way which he and other members of the House were prepared to make at the proper time. Since the Memorandum had been referred to, and stress laid on the fact that it stated contentious matter had been withdrawn from the Bill, he directed the attention of the House to the fact that the Memorandum also stated that the Bill brought the law of England and Wales into line with the law at pre-

sent in force in Scotland and Ireland, and that that uniformity could not be effected unless Clause 12 remained in its present form.

MR. HAYES FISHER'S REPLY. DIRECT REPRESENTATION CONCEDED.

In reply to Mr. Handel Booth, Member for Pontefract, MR. HAYES FISHER stated that under Clause 1 it would be quite possible to increase the number of women now on the Central Midwives Board. He said further : " I entirely share his view that in all this maternity and child welfare legislation we shall need more and more the services and special knowledge of women.

"It will be possible, if it is thought desirable, to give the midwives themselves direct representation upon that Board."

In regard to Clause 12 he expressed himself as having a very open mind, but indicated a certain preference in his own mind, not on this subject only, but upon many other subjects. He thought generally it was wise to give a discretionary power, subject to the sanction of the Local Government Board. He did not think it wise to close the door altogether upon the power of delegation by these local bodies, but he assured the House that he had a very open mind on the question and that he had purposely kept it open until they debated the whole matter in Committee.

The Question was then put and agreed to.

The Bill was accordingly read a second time.

THE MIDWIVES BILL PASSED IN THE HOUSE OF COMMONS.

On Monday, on the Committee stage of the Midwives Bill, Mr. Hayes Fisher said, in the House of Commons, it was the intention of the Privy Council to include midwives as representatives on the Central Board. The first 11 clauses of the Bill were passed rapidly, but there was a discussion on the 12th clause for the repeal of section 9 of the Act of 1902, which enabled county councils to delegate their powers and duties under the Act to district councils.

SIR J. BOYTON moved an amendment to ensure that the right of the London County Council to delegate its powers to the metropolitan borough councils would be continued. SIR R. ADKINS, who preferred the clause as it stood, suggested that in no case ought delegation to be permitted, except on the initiative of the county council and with the approval of the Local Government Board. CAPTAIN BARNETT argued that borough councils ought not to be deprived of the powers which they now possessed.

SIR C. HOBHOUSE said that in every rural area where delegation had been put in force there had been a failure of the Act. After further discussion the amendment, having been opposed by Mr. Hayes Fisher, President of the Local Government Board, was withdrawn, and on a division clause 12 was carried by 60 votes to 38. The remaining clauses and the report stage were agreed to, and the Bill was read a third time.

THE
BRITISH JOURNAL OF NURSING
WITH WHICH IS INCORPORATED
THE NURSING RECORD
EDITED BY MRS BEDFORD FENWICK

No. 1,596. SATURDAY, NOVEMBER 2, 1918. Vol. LXI.

EDITORIAL.

A MINISTRY OF HEALTH.

One of the imperative needs of the immediate future is the Ministry of Health long promised and overdue. This is acutely emphasised by the epidemic of influenza now raging, and the fact that there is no central authority whose primary business it is to deal with the outbreak, though the Local Government Board has stepped into the breach, and called a special Conference of medical representatives of all the Departments concerned, including the Army Medical Department, and the Medical Research Committee.

There is no doubt that the fact that influenza is not one of the notifiable diseases makes cases much more difficult to locate, and the epidemic to control, and it is quite possible that, in the near future, the notification of this disease may be made compulsory.

Meanwhile laws of health well known, but not universally practised, should be strictly observed. Dr. Leonard Hill, F.R.S., Director of the Department of Applied Physiology of the Medical Research Committee, and a Member of the Army Medical Advisory Board, in a letter to the *Times*, points out the very great importance of breathing cool open air, and of exercise, which amplifies the breathing in promoting the defensive mechanism of the respiratory membrane, for many people unwisely seek to keep themselves and children in rooms which are over-warm and humid. The defence depends on the volume of arterial blood passing through the membrane, and on its being kept in a taut state and well washed with its watery secretion. He estimates that the water evaporated from the respiratory membrane out of doors, on a cool winter day, when exercise is taken,

may be at the rate of a pint in the 24 hours, while in a crowded room or ship, with the air saturated and over-warm, the water evaporated will not be more than a third of a pint. Similarly the total heat lost from the respiratory membrane by vaporization, and in warming the inspired air, will be about six times greater on the cool day out of doors, when exercise is taken, than in the over-warm room or ship."

Facts such as the foregoing would be most usefully crystallized and disseminated by a Ministry of Health, one of the first duties of which must unquestionably be the creation of a strong medico - scientific department, and while this department would be employed in investigation and research, the professions of both medicine and nursing would apply the laws of health framed as the result of the knowledge thus acquired, to the treatment and care of epidemic and other diseases.

It is certain that nursing must have a prominent and honourable place in any Health Department established by State Authority if the work of that Department for the community is to be effective, and the Public Health services of Nursing and Midwifery should be co-ordinated under its control, while still leaving individuals the right to practise their professions independently.

Nurses, owing to the fact that their appeal for State Organization has been ignored, are at present subjected to patronage, exploited, and sweated, but their trained, expert services are an invaluable national asset which should be standardized through a Nurses' Registration Act. Registered Nurses, whose knowledge would be of a tested and ascertained quality would then be available for enrolment in Government Services, including the Ministry of Health, the establishment of which, in the near future, the nation awaits.

OUR PRIZE COMPETITION.

DESCRIBE THE TREATMENT OF FRACTURES BY MASSAGE.

We have pleasure in awarding the prize this week to Miss E. O. Walford, Maldon Road, Colchester.

PRIZE PAPER.

In describing the treatment of fractures by massage no fixed rule can be laid down, as naturally the treatment varies according to the bone injured and the position of the injury; also the instructions of the various surgeons will differ, and, of course, the masseuse must always be careful to carry out the directions given by the medical man in charge of the case. The earlier massage is ordered the better, but in many cases the bone has been fractured some time before the patient is put into the hands of the masseuse. Most surgeons do not think it advisable to give passive movements to the joint involved till one to seven weeks have elapsed, according to whether a small or a large bone is fractured; adhesions will not form for at least a week, while, if movements are commenced too soon, in addition to the risk of displacing the fragments, an excess of callus may be formed and permanent stiffness result.

The object of massage for fractures is to lessen the pain by relieving muscular spasm, and by promoting the absorption of the blood, serum, and lymph which are pressing on the nerves; to prevent wasting and weakness of muscles and the excessive formation of callus; to keep the ends of the bone in good position by relaxing the muscular spasm which tends to draw them apart; to render the joints mobile; and to stimulate the blood, nerve, and lymph supply to the injured part, and thus aid repair and shorten the time the limb is " out of action."

Unless otherwise instructed, the limb, which is generally on a splint if the fracture is a recent one, should be carefully unbandaged, but left resting on the splint; steady the limb in a good position with the left hand, and with the right give gentle effleurage, starting a little distance *above* the fracture. This movement should be repeated several times, and then commenced *below* the fracture, passing very gently over it. For at least four days, and longer where large bones are concerned, effleurage should be the only movement given; it is a very important one, and will :—

(1) Help the circulation, and thus relieve swelling.

(2) Soothe the nerve endings, and by so doing relieve the muscular spasm, which is liable to draw the two bones apart.

(3) By improving the circulation help to maintain the nutrition of the tissues.

Very gentle passive movements of the neighbouring joints may in some cases be given from the first, and these, by moving the tendons passing over the joint, will act as internal massage, increasing the circulation and preventing the formation of adhesions.

After four days (or longer) very careful petrissage and frictions may be added to the effleurage, starting as with the latter, first above and then below the fracture, and always beginning and ending the treatment with effleurage.

Passive movements should gradually be given to the joint involved, and as healing becomes firmer active movements should also be employed.

The splint must not be removed till permission is given; also, should the fracture be compound, the wound must be kept covered to avoid any risk of sepsis.

HONOURABLE MENTION.

The following competitors receive honourable mention :—Miss R. E. S. Cox, Miss N. Hutton, Miss J. Robinson.

QUESTION FOR NEXT WEEK.

Give the nursing of a case after removal of kidney, and state the complications that may occur.

INFLUENZA PRECAUTIONS.

The widespread epidemic of influenza in this country, and its serious results—septic pneumonia often supervening—make it incumbent upon nurses, whose services are in such demand, to show the way in the recognition of its contagious nature, and in taking precautions to protect themselves and others from infection. In France this is recognized, and we hear from nurses in attendance on influenza cases that they wear a medicated mask over nose and mouth, besides gargling the throat with an antiseptic lotion. Nurses in this country will be well advised to take similar precautions. If they are to do their part in stemming the epidemic they must conserve their own health. Nurses will not need to be reminded that the best safeguards are an abundance of fresh air, and the avoidance of crowded meetings and ill-ventilated rooms. The general standard of health should also be maintained at as high a level as possible.

NEW JOINT NURSING BOARD.

The Secretary of the War Office announces that the two Advisory Boards, which have, respectively, dealt with Queen Alexandra's Imperial Military Nursing Service and the Territorial Force Nursing Service, have been reconstituted as a joint board, under the title of "Queen Alexandra's Army Nursing Board," with Her Majesty Queen Alexandra as President. The joint board has been formed to secure greater uniformity of administration in the two nursing services. The services themselves remain distinct as heretofore. The constitution of the Board is as follows :—

The Director-General, Army Medical Service (Chairman).

The Matron-in-Chief, Queen Alexandra's Imperial Military Nursing Service.

The Matron-in-Chief, Territorial Force Nursing Service.

A Representative of the Voluntary Aid Detachments.

Six Laywomen and six Matrons of Civil Hospitals.

The following ladies have been appointed members of the new Board :—

The Dowager Countess of Airlie (Vice-President).

Lady Ampthill (representing Voluntary Aid Detachments).

The Countess Roberts.

The Countess of Minto.

Lady Codrington.

Lady Knox.

Miss E. S. Haldane, LL.D.

MATRONS OF CIVIL HOSPITALS.

Miss R. Cox-Davies, R.R.C. (Royal Free Hospital).

Miss A. Lloyd-Still, R.R.C. (St. Thomas's Hospital).

Miss A. B. Baillie, R.R.C. (Principal Matron T.F.N.S.) (Royal Infirmary, Bristol).

Miss H. Gregory Smith, R.R.C. (Western Infirmary, Glasgow).

Miss E. S. Innes, R.R.C. (General Infirmary, Leeds).

Miss M. G. Montgomery (Middlesex Hospital).

HONOURS FOR NURSES.

The King held an Investiture at Buckingham Palace on October 23rd, when the following decorations were conferred :—

THE ROYAL RED CROSS (SECOND CLASS).

Q.A.I.M.N.S.: Sister Isobel Whyte. Q.A.I.M.N.S.R.: Sisters Sarah Bowe, Annie Duncan and Frances Spedding. T.F.N.S.: Sister Helen Drinkwater. B.R.C.S.: Sister Annie Walker. V.A.D.: Miss Muriel Batey, Mrs. Frances Crawshaw and Miss Hester Trimble.

THE MILITARY MEDAL.

First Aid Nursing Yeomanry: Miss Muriel Thompson.

NURSING AND THE WAR.

H.R.H. Princess Louise, Duchess of Argyll, presided at the Luncheon at the Trocadero, Piccadilly, given in honour of the Matrons-in-Chief of the Military Services under the Crown, on the 30th inst. Queen Alexandra desired to be kept informed of the arrangements, and sent the flowers to decorate the tables.

Now that the day of the deliverance of Belgium is at hand, the nurses who worked for its people in their hour of agony are rejoicing with them. Our picture on page 266 shows a group of British nurses who worked in a hospital in Flanders.

Sister Jane Elizabeth Trotter, Q.A.I.M.N.S. (R.), who, as reported, has been awarded the Military Medal for distinguished service on the field, belongs to Leicester. During a night air raid, which lasted four hours, she visited all the wards reassuring the sick and wounded, and her orderly was mortally wounded while standing by her in one of the wards. Before the war Sister Trotter was for some years a valued member of the nursing staff at the Leicester Royal Infirmary. She volunteered for foreign service in the early days of the war, and has been serving abroad four years. At the outset she was nursing in a hospital at Brussels, remaining there up to the time of its evacuation by the Belgian Army. She was awarded the Mons Star and was twice mentioned in despatches. While she was at home on furlough the King decorated her with the Royal Red Cross. Sister Trotter formerly had nursing charge of the casualty department of the Leicester Infirmary, where she received her training as a nurse.

An eminent nurse from America writes :—" We are all very thankful for the encouraging fortunes of the war, and we get most thrilling letters from the nephew, who is still flying over the French lines. I hope and trust your beautiful little family are still intact. I have ardent hopes that the Hohenzollern and Hapsburg dynasties will be cast down into utter oblivion and that a self-governing free grouping will arise in the places so long crushed under these robber barons. How often one realises that we are just at the very dawn of civilisation—just emerging from the Dark Ages ! Old England herself has just lately outgrown those bad habits. Now she must not fail to do with Wilhelm and Karl what she did with Napoleon.

" I am posting to you the pamphlet showing what is being done in our Congress to get army rank for nurses. The War Department has done something, but not enough, and can go no further without Act of Congress. I enclose a letter to visualise to you the most charming and capable woman lawyer who is trying to get the Act through. A splendid example of women's work for women, and not least I must mention that for two months in the beginning she stayed in Washington at her own expense to work it up.

We were exceedingly delighted to handle the enclosed letter signed " Helen Hoy Greeley," who is a member of the New York Bar, and as Counsel for the Committee to secure rank for Nurses in the American Army delivered an astoundingly brilliant Statement in April last before the Committee on Military Affairs, House of Representatives, U.S.A., on Suggested Changes in the Nurse Corps, published in the *Johns Hopkins Nurses Alumnae Magazine,* which we regret we have not space to republish in full.

Mrs. Greeley stated that the only incidents of absolute rank which the relative rank, contem-

It is as sound in the case of the nurse and her orders as in that of the second lieutenant."

That reminded us of our last glimpse of " Francesca "—no longer in the Nursing Service. She was attired as an officer of the Women's Royal Air Force, and was bubbling over with *esprit de corps.* The daintily smart uniform of " air blue " gabardine, brass buttons and gold lace, and a charming felt hat with badge to match, and across the left breast the ribbons of the 1914 Star, the Russian " George," and the Military Medal made a *tout ensemble tout à fait ravissant.* " Francesca " is quite sure that the " Rank " accorded this Women's Corps will soon make it the most popular, as it will be the most efficient Corps

BRITISH NURSES IN FLANDERS.

plated in the amendment, would confer were :—

1. The dignity incident to the name of rank.
2. The right to wear the insignia thereof.
3. The eligibility to exercise authority within limits set forth in the law which provides that as regards medical and sanitary matters and all work in the line of their duties, nurses shall have and shall be regarded as having authority in and about military hospitals next after the medical officers of the Army.

Amongst the wise arguments used, Mrs. Greeley said, " Prompt obedience to orders is the root of military efficiency. The best insurance of prompt obedience is a badge on a uniform. One gold bar on a shoulder strap is worth two regulations in a book. This is military psychology.

in the service of the Crown. On all sides we hear of loyalty to the new Commandant, Mrs. H. C. I. Gwynne Vaughan, C.B.E., who is apparently the right woman in the right place. We all realize " being in the air " no longer signifies futility, but the most effective environment for national progress.

OUR ROLL OF HONOUR.

It is with deep regret that we record the sudden death, from influenza, of Sister Helen Cole, at the First London General Hospital, Camberwell. Sister Cole was trained at St. Bartholomew's Hospital, and her death has caused widespread grief amongst her colleagues. The funeral service which was of a military character and largely attended took place at the Hospital on Tuesday last.

We regret to record the death of Miss R. Stanley, who was trained in children's nursing at Queen Mary's Hospital, Carshalton, and afterwards at St. Bartholomew's Hospital, London, where she obtained her certificate in 1915. She has recently been working at Queen Mary's Hospital, Roehampton, and last week was warded at St. Bartholomew's, where she died on Sunday last.

———

BAKER.—On October 17th, of pneumonia, at No. 15, Canadian Hospital, Tap'ow, Nursing Sister. Miriam E., eldest daughter of the late George W. Baker, K.C., of Winnipeg, Canada. Canadian papers please copy.

———

FRENCH FLAG NURSING CORPS.

GRIPPE ESPAGNOL CONTAGIOUS.

A Sister writes :—" In the meanwhile we have turned into a medical ambulance and we are receiving ' grippe Espagnol ' cases. For the first time since the beginning of the war we are doing medical nursing and our surgeons, leaders as they are, have now to turn their attention to the treatment of these cases. As this disease is supposed to be contagious we wear special gowns, overalls for the wards, and also we are obliged to have masks, which contain a strong-sme ling disinfectant. Many of our cases are very serious—bad pneumonia—in fact, nearly all of them have complications of the lungs, and in many cases it turns quickly into pneumonia. We seem to be in a little world of our own in this château, surrounded by a big wooded park. The news from the front is always good. We are living in wonderful times. The end seems to be in view, but I think we need all our courage and endurance. This last year of the war seems to press heavily on everybody."

Another Sister says :—" We have had a terrible time fighting the Spanish grippe. It has been a ghastly time. Three of the nurses apparently dying at the same time, the pharmacien died, and many of the youngest and apparently the strongest of the *blessés* ; the surgeon down with it, so Sister C. had entire charge of the surgical cases ! Though running temperatures we Sisters held on and weathered the storm, *and showed them what the English can do*, and taught them the meaning of ' carrying on.' It was a stiff time—no ward-maids, no *infirmiers*, no kitchen staff—but the *blessés* who were well enough worked and cleaned and cooked and were just splendid !"

That is the way to win the war.

A CHRISTENING GIFT.

Madame Jamard writes from Bayeux :—" Many, many thanks for your very kind letter and all good wishes. I do think it so very kind of the Corps wanting to give baby a christening gift, and I cannot tell you how much I appreciate the very kind thought. It will be his most cherished gift, for it represents the Corps with which I worked so long and was so very, very happy. Here in France they christen babies very early, so ours was christened when his father was on permission, and has been named Douglas Edmond Charles. Please accept our united warmest thanks for this very kind thought."

The gift is to be a pretty silver cup bowl and spoon, suitably inscribed as follows :—

" Presented as a Christening Gift, to Douglas Edmond Charles Jamard by the French Flag Nursing Corps, in recognition of his mother's devotion to his sick and wounded compatriots in the Great War."

———

WORDS OF COMFORT FOR THE SUFFERING.

We have received a copy of " One Minute Readings for Nurses and Patients," a little book arranged by Fanny K. Kindersley, with a Foreword by the Bishop of Worcester, who writes : " How to lead the soldiers in prayer when they come to us ill and convalescent has proved a difficulty, for in many cases no clergyman is constantly available. Commandants at the little hospitals have expressed this to me, knowing how precious a quiet time may become to the men, if properly handled."

To meet in some measure this need, Miss Kindersley has arranged " One Minute Readings for the Nurse," when all is put ready for the night ; and it is suggested that she shall reverently stand, or kneel, and slowly read one of these portions, which takes one minute. They are composed of a few appropriate verses from the Bible and from well-known hymns, calculated to give comfort, and inspire the sick with hope, " The entrance of Thy words giveth light." The readings are prefaced by

" THE NURSES' PRAYER."

Lord, dost Thou need a human hand,
    Sad pain to stay ?
Oh ! use my hands, and through them deign
    Thine own to lay
On the sick ones, who need Thee so
    On earth to-day.

And, as I work, grant that my faith
    Discerning Thee,
Veil'd in these weak and suff'ring forms,
    May give to me
A tender rev'rent touch, a deep
    Humility.

Oh, wondrous thought ! That glorious hope
    To mortals giv'n !
That when I see Christ face to face,
    All doubts forgiv'n,
He'll own it then as done to Him,
    My King in Heaven.

            F. K. K.

We are informed that this little book has been much appreciated by nurses and patients, and we are pleased to bring it to the notice of others. It is published by Elliot Stock, 7, Paternoster Row, London, E.C. Price 6d.

Royal British Nurses' Association.

(Incorporated by   Royal Charter.)

THIS SUPPLEMENT BEING THE OFFICIAL ORGAN OF THE CORPORATION.

THE CONFERENCE.

Members of the Royal British Nurses' Association, its affiliated Societies and others are reminded of the Conference which is to be held on November 7th, at 3 p.m., at 11, Chandos Street, Cavendish Square, W. 1.

No speakers with a more comprehensive understanding of the subjects before the Conference could have been found than those which the Association has secured for its platform, and the Council cordially invite all trained nurses to attend, and to share, if they care to, in the discussion on problems which vitally concern their future prospects.

MEETING OF THE GENERAL COUNCIL.

The Quarterly Meeting of the General Council was held on 24th ult. Mrs. Campbell Thomson, and later Dr. Kenneth Stewart, occupied the Chair. The Report sent up from the Executive Committee was read. dealing with the arrangements for the Conference and other matters relating to the work of the Consultative Committee, the Central Committee, and the Registration Board. The Treasurer's Reports for the Quarter were also laid before the Meeting.

A Resolution was passed expressing the regret of the Council on learning of the illness of Her Highness the Princess Victoria, and asking Her Royal Highness the President to be graciously pleased to convey to the Princess their hope that she might have a speedy recovery.

The death of Dr. Biernacki was reported, and a Resolution was passed placing on record the appreciation of the Council of his whole-hearted efforts to promote the interests of all trained nurses, and of sympathy with his relatives.

Miss Helen Todd was elected to fill a casual vacancy on the General Council.

Certain amendments were made on the Rules governing admission to the Princess Christian Settlement Home, and questions relating to the amending Bill of the Midwives Act and other matters were discussed.

SOME R.B.N.A. MEMBERS "AT HOME."

On learning of the affiliation of the Trained Nurses' Annuity Fund with the Benevolent Funds of their own Association a number of R.B.N.A.

nurses decided to entertain, at 10, Orchard Street, the Members of the three Funds. Invitations were promptly sent out, but as (particularly in the case of the first-mentioned Fund) large numbers of the Members lived at a distance, a difficulty presented itself as to how people, living in the three parts of the United Kingdom, could join in a " tea party " in London. The problem was solved by mentioning in the invitations that if, as was probable, those at a distance could not come to town, cakes, &c., would be forwarded, which were to be eaten at the same time as that at which the London Members gathered at 10, Orchard Street. A few nurses therefore met during their off-duty time on Saturday morning, packed and posted their boxes. Just as they were doing so a box arrived for themselves, which, when opened, was found to contain lovely country chrysanthemums from the oldest of the T.N.A.F. Annuitants. They were sent with a view to decorating the nurses' tea tables, but, as one nurse remarked, " They seemed to come like beautiful, friendly thoughts, from one who had given a long life to the service of others, for those who had taken up her work when she laid it down."

It gave to the nurses, and particularly the R.B.N.A. Members, no small amount of pleasure when the Chairman of the Annuity Fund and Mrs. Price accepted their invitation and came in, in the course of the afternoon.

Her Royal Highness the Princess Christian, President of the Royal British Nurses' Association and of the Trained Nurses' Annuity Fund, personally telephoned a message to the nurses giving them her remembrances and expressing her hope that they were enjoying themselves. This gave much pleasure, and one nurse, who said that she was now over eighty years of age, in a happy little speech moved that the thanks of the Members of the Benevolent Schemes be sent to Her Royal Highness, with assurances of their loyalty to her person. (This Resolution was telegraphed to Her Royal Highness from the office.) This Member also said how much it pleased them all to meet Mr. Price, the Chairman of the affiliated Funds, and thanked him warmly for his kindness to nurses. Next, on behalf of all the guests, she thanked the hostesses of the afternoon. She was one of the earliest Members of the R.B.N.A., and it gave her great pleasure to welcome the Members of the affiliated Funds to the first of their meetings with one another. She had loved the R.B.N.A., and, as one of its oldest Members, urged her young hostesses to be " steadfast and true " to it always, and all would be well with the nursing profession.

Mr. Price, on behalf of Her Royal Highness, thanked the members present for their message of loyalty, and, in speaking of the Benevolent Schemes, very strongly urged the nurses to take an active part in developing these themselves. In this connection he referred to the splendid manner in which the military nurses were doing so, and expressed the hope that the civil nurses would soon follow this example by taking a very active part in developing their own Benevolent Funds. His hope was that all the Benevolent Funds of the Nursing Profession would ultimately be self-supporting.

A Member of the Princess Christian Settlement Home then spoke, saying that she felt she could not leave without saying something of her appreciation of the kindness of her fellow-Members of the R.B.N.A. in maintaining such a nice Home. " My room there has been my greatest joy."

Old and younger nurses exchanged hospital reminiscences, and told many amusing stories of their experiences. One nurse " told fortunes," as only a nurse can, with teacups and cards. " The Astronomer " from the Settlement Home, an old nurse of Lord Lister's, gave an interesting little lecture on astronomy, and told of comparisons made by herself and Professor Ball, when, on retiring from nursing work between the ages of sixty and seventy, she invested some of her savings in a fine telescope and boldly started the study of astronomy. Mrs. Price won her heart immediately by promising to visit the Settlement Home one afternoon in order to participate in astronomical investigations!

The little gathering broke up with warm feelings of good will between those who were, many of them, pioneers of the nursing profession, and others who are doing their best to uphold its great traditions and promote higher educational standards and professional organisation.

LECTURES.

In accordance with the request of a number of Members of the Association the Executive Committee are arranging a course of lectures on lines very similar to those given last winter. Some who, on the afternoon of 25th inst., had the pleasure of hearing Mr. Price Bell lecture in the Hall of Bedford College, will learn with pleasure that he has undertaken to give a lecture for the Association also. His beautiful thoughts were clothed in beautiful language, in words prophetic of a grand new world freedom, of the liberty and possibilities for the individual which would arise yet out of the great world struggle. This brilliant American speaks with the force and clearness characteristic of his nation, and we look forward with no small degree of pleasure to his lecture at

11, Chandos Street, Cavendish Square, on December 5th, on " America and the New World Order.'

On December 19th Miss Annette M. B. Meakin, F.R.G.S., will lecture on " Bokhara and Samarkand." She is the only traveller who has studied the women of these countries in their own homes. Later Mr. Herbert J. Paterson, F.R.C.S., will lecture on " Scottish Wit and Humour," and Professor Flinders Petrie on " Ten Thousand Years of Civilization." Professor Selwyn Image (Slade Professor of Modern Art) has also promised to lecture, but we have not yet been informed as to the subject on which he will speak. It is proposed that the lectures shall be given on alternate Thursdays, and nurses who wish to attend should notify the Secretary, who will have pleasure in forwarding to them the syllabus when this is complete.

OBITUARY.

It is with deep regret that we have to report the death of Mrs. Mary Hopkins. She was one of the earliest Members of the Association, and well known to large numbers of our Members, as she and her sister, Miss Hatton, have rarely been absent from its General Meetings.

On hearing of the death of Mrs. Hopkins, Her Royal Highness the President graciously telephoned her commands that a message be sent to Miss Hatton expressing the sorrow of Her Royal Highness and her heartfelt sympathy with Miss Hatton in her irreparable loss. Young Members of the Association have united with those who joined the Association in earlier days in sending to Miss Hatton expressions of deep sympathy.

DONATIONS.

The Hon. Treasurer acknowledges with thanks donations from the following to the Fund for State Registration :—

First List.—Per Miss Daisy Hobbs, £5 5s.; Dr. Clarke, £1 1s.; Mrs. Lawson, £1 1s.; Miss Gordon Brown, £1; A. Britten, 10s. 6d.; per Miss Spearing, 9s.; Miss Bosworth, 5s.; Miss Mercer, 5s.; Miss Morgan, 5s.; Miss Owen, 5s.; Miss Puley, 5s.; Miss Crumpler, 5s.; Miss Fowler, 2s. 6d.; and Mrs. Moorhead, 5s.

Second List.—Per Miss Wallis, £1 2s. 6d.; Nursing Staff, Isleworth Infirmary, per Miss Davis, 14s. 9d.; Nursing Staff, Princess Christian Hospital, Englefield Green, per Miss Sumner, 13s. 6d.; Miss Talbot, 10s. 6d.; Miss Blizard, 10s.; Miss Terry, 10s.; Miss Vidler, 10s.; Mrs. Lyster, 1s.

Application forms for Registration (5s.), Membership (Annual, 5s.; Life, £2 2s.), and the badge of the Corporation (4s.), can be obtained from the office of the Association, 10, Orchard Street, Portman Square, W. 1.

(Signed) Isabel Macdonald,
Secretary to the Corporation.
10, Orchard Street,
Portman Square, W. 1.

THE CENTRAL COMMITTEE FOR THE STATE REGISTRATION OF NURSES.

A meeting of the Central Committee for the State Registration of Nurses was held, by the kind permission of the British Medical Association, in the Council Chamber at its offices, 429, Strand, W.C., on Saturday, October 26th. Mr. T. W. H. Garstang was voted to the chair. Major Chapple, M.P., who is in charge of the Bill, was present, and there was a large attendance of members.

Before the meeting was opened sympathetic reference was made to the recent deaths of two members of the Committee, Dr. John Biernacki and Miss Kathleen Sinclair Stewart, A.R.R.C., both of whom had died since its last meeting. The members of the Committee then rose while a vote of condolence with their relatives was passed.

IRISH NURSING BOARD.

A letter was read from Miss Carson Rae, Secretary of the Irish Nursing Board, enclosing the names of the five delegates nominated on to the Central Committee as follows :—

Col. Sir Arthur Chance, F.R.C.S., Chairman of the Board.

Col. William Taylor, M.D.

Miss Ramsden, Rotunda Hospital, Dublin.

Miss O'Flynn, Children's Hospital, Temple Street, Dublin.

Miss McArdle, The Castle Red Cross Hospital, Dublin.

LETTER FROM THE COLLEGE OF NURSING, LTD.

A letter was also read from the Secretary of the College of Nursing, Ltd., in connection with which Major Chapple made an explanatory statement, and action upon it was deferred until the Report of the Executive Committee on the College Bill had been discussed.

THE REPORT OF THE EXECUTIVE COMMITTEE.

The Report of the Executive Committee on the Seventh Draft of the College of Nursing Nurses' Registration Bill was presented by Lieut.-Colonel E. W. Goodall, who moved that it should be received. It stated that, in pursuance of the instruction given to it by the Central Committee at its meeting on July 6th, 1918, the Committee carefully considered the re-drafted Bill of the College of Nursing, Ltd., together with an accompanying letter from Major Chapple, M.P. This draft was the seventh draft, and was dated June 20th, 1918. The Committee compared this (the seventh) draft put forward by the College of Nursing

with the fourth draft which was considered by the Central Committee on a previous occasion.

RESOLUTIONS.

Five Resolutions drafted by the Executive Committee were adopted.

COUNTING OF VOTES.

1. Relating to the counting of the votes in the election of the Council.

TERM OF OFFICE OF FIRST COUNCIL.

2. " That a period of two years be named in the Bill as the term of office of the First General Nursing Council."

NOTIFICATION OF DEATHS.

3. " Every Registrar of Deaths in the United Kingdom, on receiving notice of the death of any person registered under this Act, shall forthwith transmit by post to the Registrar of the General Nursing Council a certificate under his own hand of such death, with the particulars of time and place of death, and may charge the cost of such certificate and transmission as an expense of his office."

NO AUTHORITY TO PRACTISE MIDWIFERY.

4. " Nothing contained in this Act, or in any rules made thereunder, shall confer any authority to practise medicine, surgery, or midwifery."

CENTRAL COMMITTEE TO PROCEED WITH ITS OWN BILL.

5. The Committee then passed the following Resolution, which was presented by Lieut.-Colonel Goodall, as a unanimous recommendation from the Executive :—

" That in the opinion of the Executive Committee the present Bill of the Central Committee, amended as suggested in Resolution G (relating to the counting of the votes in the election of the permanent Council), Resolution H (two years' term of office for the Provisional Council), Resolution N (duty of a Registrar of Deaths to notify a registered nurse's death to the General Nursing Council) and Resolution O (the addition of midwifery to medicine and surgery in the Clause which states that the Act does not confer authority to practise these professions) is a better Bill than that drafted by the College of Nursing and should be adhered to."

Lieut.-Colonel Goodall then moved that the Report be adopted, which was agreed.

COLLEGE OF NURSING INVITED TO SUPPORT CENTRAL COMMITTEE'S BILL.

It was then resolved :—

" That it is the considered opinion of the Committee that the Bill drafted by the Central Committee for the State Registration of Nurses should be presented to Parliament, and that the College of Nursing, Ltd., be formally invited to agree to this Bill, and join in getting it passed."

REPRESENTATION OF THE ROYAL BRITISH NURSES' ASSOCIATION AND THE COLLEGE OF NURSING, LTD.

Mr. Herbert Paterson moved that the Royal British Nurses' Association, incorporated by Royal Charter, and the College of Nursing, Ltd., should be included amongst the Bodies which nominate representatives on the General Nursing Council. This was agreed to, and the following Clauses dealing with their representation on the First Council were adopted in relation to subsequent Councils :—

" Two persons to be appointed by the Royal British Nurses' Association, one of whom shall be a registered medical practitioner and one a nurse.

" Two persons to be appointed by the College of Nursing, Ltd., one of whom shall be a nurse."

DIRECT REPRESENTATION FOR NURSES IN WALES.

It was proposed by Miss E. L. C. Eden, and agreed, that an alteration be made in Clause iv 1 (*g*) as follows :—

" Eighteen registered nurses to be elected as the direct representatives of the women nurses on the General Register; eight to be elected by the nurses registered in England, and two by the nurses registered in Wales."

BRITISH SUBJECTS ONLY ELIGIBLE FOR REGISTRATION.

It was proposed, and agreed, that only nurses who are British subjects shall be eligible for registration.

LETTER FROM SECRETARY OF COLLEGE OF NURSING, LTD.

Lieut.-Colonel Goodall moved, and it was resolved, that the receipt of the letter (previously referred to) from the College of Nursing, Ltd., be acknowledged, and a statement of the decision arrived at by the Committee, together with a formal and official invitation to support the Central Committee's Bill, be sent to the College.

The meeting concluded with a vote of thanks to the Chairman, and to the British Medical Association for the use of the Council Chamber.

———————

A beautiful wreath was sent by the Matrons' Council of Great Britain and Ireland, and laid on the grave of Miss Kathleen S. Stewart at her funeral on October 23rd at Blair Atholl.

IRISH NURSING BOARD.

(APPROVED BY THE ROYAL COLLEGE OF SURGEONS IN IRELAND.)

A meeting of the Board was held on October 23rd in the Royal College of Surgeons of Ireland. Colonel Sir Arthur Chance, Chairman of the Board, presided, and there was a good attendance. Five delegates were selected to sit on the Central Committee for State Registration, viz., Colonel Sir Arthur Chance, Colonel William Taylor, M.D., Miss Ramsden, Miss O'Flynn, Miss McArdle. The following resolution was proposed by Colonel Taylor and unanimously adopted, that : " After July 1st, 1918, any person who had failed to register may have her case specially considered by the Executive Committee, and if they think fit, may have her name placed on the Register for a fee of £1 1s."

Mrs. Lanagan O'Keefe was appointed secretary to the Board. The usual routine business was transacted and the Board were pleased to hear the Register was " growing in strength."

————◆————

SCOTTISH MATRONS' ASSOCIATION.

A meeting of the Scottish Matrons' Association was held in Edinburgh, on Saturday, October 19th, Miss Gill, R.R.C., in the chair. There was a representative attendance.

The minutes of the last meeting were read and signed ; also the minutes of the Edith Cavell Memorial Fund Committee meeting, held on April 19th, in Edinburgh.

The Chairman intimated the decisions made by the Executive Committee on various communications dealt with at their meeting on April 19th, in Edinburgh.

An address, which was very much appreciated, was given by Mrs. Chalmers Watson, C.B.E., M.D., on the work of the National Council for Combating Venereal Disease. She spoke of the special points emphasised by the Royal Commission ; of the progress made in discovery and treatment during the last twelve years ; and of the most hopeful lines along which improvement might be looked for in preventing the heavy toll taken on the efficiency of the nation by venereal disease.

A vote of thanks was proposed and heartily responded to by Mrs. Chalmers Watson.

Three new members were elected to the Association : Miss White, Q.V.J.N.I., Superintendent Scottish Branch ; Miss Cumming, Longmore Hospital, Edinburgh ; and Miss Crichton, Dumfries and Galloway Royal Infirmary.

Two members resigned : Miss Simbert, Cripple Children's Home, Edinburgh, on giving up Matron's duties for the present ; and Miss Scott, Schaw Memorial Home, Bearsden, Glasgow, on retiring from work.

Miss Graham, Hon. Sec., gave a short account of the proceedings of the N.C.W.W. annual meeting, held in Harrogate, to which she had been elected a delegate of the Association along with Miss Thomas, City Hospital, Edinburgh, and Miss Gregory Smith, Western Infirmary, Glasgow.

Notice was given of a proposed alteration in Clause II of Constitution, to be submitted at next meeting.

THE NATION'S FUND FOR NURSES.

The Fund has moved its office from Duveen's antique shop, in Old Bond Street, although it is still advertised in blue letters a foot high—omitting of course the notification that it is "registered under the War Charities Act, 1916," an illegal proceeding in connection with many hoardings, for which the promoters of this Fund are apparently not held responsible. We wonder why. It is specially impertinent, as it was the Red Cross Society which agitated for the Act, so that money given by the public in support of war charities should have some redress if they were exploited by bogus appeals. We advise Lady Cowdray, Hon. Treasurer of the Fund, who is the prime advocate of this war charity for nurses and for the plutocratic methods of appeal which self-respecting members of our profession most heartily detest, to conform to the provisions of the War Charities Act, which directs that the words "Registered under the War Charities Act, 1916," shall appear on every appeal.

COMPARATIVELY FEW.

Speaking in Manchester in support of the charity, Mrs. Martin Harvey, an actress, in paying tribute to the work of the V.A.D.s in France, drew attention to the great strain which had been put upon the "comparatively few" trained nurses at the front, and suggested that the secure establishment of the College would prevent anything of the kind in future.

Comparatively few ! We wonder what the 20,000 trained nurses, who have, by their devotion, saved thousands of lives, and attended the sick and wounded men of all allied nations with knowledge and skill, think of that. No wonder they fear the institution of a V.A.D Register of which there are so many rumours, and which, under Clause 4 of the College Bill is practically provided for. We advise members of the College to look into this question *before it is too late.*

LEAGUE NEWS.

LEICESTER ROYAL INFIRMARY NURSES' LEAGUE.

The nurses of the above League held their Autumn Social Meeting in the Nurses' Home of the Royal Infirmary, on the afternoon of Friday, October 25th. The President was unable to be present. In her absence, the chair was taken by Miss Pell Smith. Many members wrote regretting their absence from illness and other causes, and sent best wishes for the success of the meeting. An interesting address was given by Miss Prior, Organizer and Lecturer to the Leicester Health Society (Schools for Mothers). After the meeting the members greatly enjoyed tea, most kindly arranged for by Miss Vincent, R.R.C. (Vice-President), who was also unable to be present.

THE ROYAL VICTORIAN TRAINED NURSES' ASSOCIATION.

CONGRATULATIONS.

We offer our heartiest congratulations to the Royal Victorian Trained Nurses' Association on the election of Miss Gretta Lyons as their President. Except for a few months the Association since its foundation in 1901 has had a medical President, and it is surely fitting that this position should be filled by a trained nurse, more especially now that women are enfranchised citizens of the State.

No happier choice for the Presidency could have been made than that of Miss Gretta Lyons, who has for many years worked to secure the registration of trained nurses on self-governing lines in the State of Victoria, and to improve their professional and economic status.

Miss Lyons, who was trained at the Alfred Hospital, Melbourne, has kept in touch with nursing politics, both in the United Kingdom and in the United States of America, and is a leader of whom the Victorian nurses may well be proud. We hope that during her term of office the State Registration of Nurses will become an accomplished fact. Of this there seems considerable prospect as the Bill before the House is stated to be satisfactory, and to have, if some small amendments are incorporated, the approval of the Association.

APPOINTMENTS.

LADY SUPERINTENDENT.

Dr. Steevens' Hospital, Dublin.—Miss Alice Reeves has been appointed Lady Superintendent. Miss Reeves was trained in the Adelaide Hospital, Dublin, where she held the post of Sister. For the past ten years Miss Reeves has been Matron of the Royal Victoria Eye and Ear Hospital, Dublin, where she has brought the hospital to a great state of perfection and where she is deservedly popular and will be immensely missed. Miss Reeves is well known in Ireland as one of its foremost leaders in nursing. She is Vice-President of the Irish Nurses' Association, which owes much to her spirited support, Hon. Secretary of the Irish Matrons' Association, a member of the Irish Nursing Board, and a delegate of the Irish Nurses' Association on the Central Committee for the State Registration of Nurses, a reform for which she has worked with single-minded devotion for many years. Miss Reeves carries the good wishes of all her colleagues for success in her new and influential sphere of work.

We heartily congratulate Dr. Steevens' Hospital on its choice of a Lady Superintendent.

WARD SISTER.

West Ham Sanatorium for Consumption, Dagenham, Essex.—Miss Leonora Davison has been appointed Ward Sister. She was trained at the Union Infirmary, Sunderland, and has been Staff Nurse at Barrasford Sanatorium, Northumberland, and Sister at Mowsley Sanatorium, North Kilworth, Rugby.

NURSES.

Anglo-American Hospital, Cairo. — The following appointments have been made to the staff of the above hospital :—

Miss A. M. Pearson, trained at the Infirmary, Kingston-on-Thames. She has been Sister at the Military Families Hospital, Devonport, and is at present Night Sister at the Kingston Infirmary. She is a certified midwife.

Miss M. A. Lake, trained at the Royal Infirmary, Manchester, and late Matron of the Cottage Hospital, Crowborough. She is a certified midwife.

Miss K. Mee, trained at the Edmonton Infirmary, N., and for two years a member of the British East African Nursing Service. At present Sister at the V.A.D. Hospital, Corsham, Wilts.

THE PASSING BELL.

We regret to learn that Miss Ball, the Matron of the Colwyn Bay Council's Isolation Hospital, at Bronynant, died at Walthamstow, on Tuesday last week, from pneumonia, two days after being attacked by influenza. Miss Ball was to have been married next week, and was retiring from her appointment under the Colwyn Bay Council. Before her appointment at Colwyn Bay, Miss Ball served for six years on the nursing staff of the Llandudno Council's Isolation Hospital. She was a passenger in the express train which was derailed at Ditton Junction some years ago, and, being herself uninjured, she rendered very valuable service to the injured passengers before the arrival of the doctors. In recognition of this the directors of the London and North-Western Railway gave her an honorarium and sent her a letter of thanks, signed by all the members of the Board.

HUMOURS OF THE OUT-PATIENTS.

Enter a stout lady with a violent squint, and her hat set rakishly at an angle.

She beams genially at the dignified, bearded physician and addresses herself in a friendly fashion to the nurse.

" Ain't that queer now ? I dreamt last night I should see a strange gentleman with whiskers."

NURSING ECHOES.

The Annual Open Meeting of the Ladies' Association of the Great Northern Central Hospital was held in the Board Room on October 24th, when the work of the members during the year was exhibited. The Acting Chairman, Miss Amy Hill, who occupied the Chair, referred to the activities of the Association generally. The Hon. Mrs. Lawson Johnson congratulated the members upon their splendid work during the year, and Miss M. F. Roby urged that the Association should be made more widely known in the West End. Mrs. Norman Moore, Hon. Secretary of St. Bartholomew's Women's Guild, and Mrs. Blinco, of the North Islington Welfare Centre, also spoke. The Matron, Miss A. N. Bird, R.R.C., thanked all members who had kindly made and given garments during the year, and for the help always accorded to her. The display of clothing was excellent, and included garments suitable for all classes of patients, the woollen articles for babies being particularly admired. There was a large attendance, which included representatives of Ladies' Associations of other Hospitals.

We have received from a correspondent the following notes by Mr. Waynman Dixon, who was for nearly forty years chairman of the House Committee, North Ormesby Hospital, the following interesting appreciation :—" The Sisterhood, or Community of the Holy Rood, North Ormesby, recently celebrated the 60th anniversary of its foundation and its service for the North Ormesby Hospital—the first cottage hospital in this or any other country—and all who know and love the noble work carried out by them will be glad to congratulate and wish them long-continued prosperity in their work of Christian charity. The writer, then a schoolboy (in 1859), lodging in Albert Road, well remembers that, looking out from his bedroom window, he saw some half-dozen men with bandages, slings, and crutches in the backyard of the cottages opposite, who, he was told, were Miss Jaques's cripples. This good lady, afterwards known as Sister Mary, had, at the request of Mr. Jordison, come to the rescue a year before, on the occasion of a terrible boiler explosion at works in the town (then of 15,000 inhabitants), the victims of which had to be treated in overcrowded lodgings, some of them even on straw in dirty stables, over an open sewer. Miss Jaques, having had some training as nurse, herself hired two cottages in Dundas Mews, and not only gave her services, but bore all the expenses of the good work. Others voluntarily joined her, and a Sisterhood of seven members was formed to continue the work, Mrs. Newcomen, of Kirkleatham, being the head as Mother Superior of the community. Shortly afterwards the hospital at North Ormesby, containing 20 beds, was built by public subscription, and in the course of 60 years has been extended to the present noble institution with 110 beds.

———

"The first sister in charge," continues Mr. Waynman Dixon, "was Sister Elizabeth, who for thirty-five years superintended all the work, and was really 'The Angel in the House.' Her stately presence, sympathetic nature, and winning smile so won the hearts of the working men of Middlesbrough that they soon arranged that at all the works in the neighbourhood one penny per week should be deducted from each man's wages towards the support of the Hospital. These good ladies of the Sisterhood, with their successors, in 'weariness and painfulness and in watching oft,' have continued the work up to the present jubilee, and in the course of sixty years have treated over 100,000 patients. From what small beginnings do great things grow. Their influence on the life of the working men community is untold, for not only have they healed the wounds, but mended the lives of countless numbers of their patients. When an extension was required for out-patients in 1892, the workmen of Middlesbrough 'got up early one morning and built a hospital before breakfast'—that is to say, every workman contributed a quarter-day's pay, and thus raised a sum of £750 towards the cost. All the original members of the Sisterhood have gone to their rich reward, but the community goes on, and there are still those who have been in the work for forty years, assisted by three head nurses of very long standing."

———

The annual sale of work for the Norwich District Nursing Association at Tombland, now known as the Cavell Home, was held last week at the headquarters. The maintenance of district nursing associations is a very serious business in these days of increased expenses in all directions, and the institution was never so much in need of funds as at the present time.

Amongst the stallholders were the Lady Mayoress, who sold fancy work and glass, and the Matron and nurses were kept busily employed in connection with their stall of miscellaneous articles.

THE ROYAL SANITARY INSTITUTE AND THE MINISTRY OF HEALTH.

For more than 40 years since the Public Health Act of 1876 came into operation the Royal Sanitary Institute has been co-operating with the Public Health Service of the country, and has noted the steady progress made in methods and organisation both official and voluntary for improving the health of the people.

At a recent meeting of the Council the progress made with regard to the Bill for the establishment of a Ministry of Health was under consideration and the following resolution was passed :—

The health of the people being of paramount importance in the progress of the nation, the Council of the Royal Sanitary Institute have noted with great satisfaction the progress that has been made and the valuable work accomplished during the past fifty years by the various departments dealing with public health.

The rapid development under present conditions of the many subsidiary factors affecting the question, and the complexity of the interests involved make it essential, for the effective continuance and development of the work, that so far as possible all matters relating to public health should be co-ordinated in one department as a Ministry of Health.

The Council therefore desire to urge that the matter is one of pressing public importance, and trust that it may receive the early attention of His Majesty's Government.

———

A HISTORETTE OF PUBLIC HEALTH PROGRESS IN NEW ZEALAND.

We have pleasure in publishing the following Historette of Public Health Progress in New Zealand from Miss H. Maclean, who is an expert in all matters of Health, Nursing, and Midwifery in the Dominion :—

DEPARTMENT OF PUBLIC HEALTH, HOSPITALS, AND CHARITABLE AID.

Wellington, N.Z.,

July 30th, 1918.

DEAR MADAM,—In the account of the first of a series of lectures on Infant Care in your issue of May 11th I read in the concluding paragraph under "National Baby Week Council," the following :—

The death-rate of infants under one year in New Zealand has been reduced from 80–50 per 1,000 by Dr. Truby King, who has been instructing the people in mothercraft for eight or nine years.

While giving every credit to Dr. Truby King, with whose work I am thoroughly familiar, for a large share in the reduction of the infant death-rate in New Zealand, I would like to give some prominence to the even earlier commencement of decrease in the death-rate attributable :

1. To the work of the Department of Public Health, which has improved the sanitary condition

of towns. New Zealand was the first part of the British Empire to establish a Ministry of Public Health, in 1900.

2. The Midwives' Act, passed in 1904, under the superintendence of the late Dr. MacGregor, Inspector-General of Hospitals, and his assistant, Mrs. Grace Neill, a trained nurse and midwife.

3. The establishment of training schools for midwives and hospitals for maternity patients, from which thousands of women have gone forth, some as midwifery nurses, into all parts of the Dominion, some as mothers, taught how to properly care for their infants and impressed with the importance of breast-feeding and fresh air.

New Zealand was the first part of the Empire to establish State Maternity Hospitals. This was one of the great life works of the Right Hon. Richard John Seddon. Himself born at St. Helens, Lancashire, the hospitals were all named "St. Helens." He was also responsible for labour laws which, tending to produce good social conditions, are certainly responsible in a good measure for decrease of infantile death-rate.

4. Midwifery Nurses trained in the State Maternity Hospitals, many of whom are now Plunket Nurses, have undoubtedly had a large share, and through them their training schools, in the reduction of Infantile Mortality.

Ante-natal and post-natal teaching has been given to mothers in these Institutions since 1905, when the first hospital was opened, three years before Dr. Truby King started his campaign, and a year ago special ante-natal clinics and free ante-natal advice and treatment for mothers were established in connection with each State Maternity St. Helens Hospital.

When the fact is considered that New Zealand is for the most part a rural country with no real slum areas, even in her largest cities, that poverty such as prevails in the old world is unknown, and that food is cheap and plentiful, it will be seen that the problem of the reduction of the infantile death-rate is a very different matter in the Old Country.

I am, yours truly,
H. MACLEAN,

Assistant-Inspector of Hospitals; Deputy-Registrar of Nurses and Midwives; Officer-in-Charge, St Helens Hospitals, &c.

A NEW LEAGUE.

As we go to press, a meeting is being held in the Nurses' Home at the Fulham Military Hospital, Hammersmith, W., to discuss the formation of a Nurses' League of nurses trained at the Fulham Infirmary. Amongst other matters which will come up for consideration is the establishment of a journal. Nurses trained at the Fulham Infirmary, if unable to attend, are asked to write to Miss L. A. Wallace, Assistant Matron at the Hospital, and give their opinion on the above subject, the amount of subscription to be paid and kindred questions.

PROFESSIONAL REVIEW.

FOODS AND DIETARIES.

Dietetics are concerned with a branch of professional knowledge of which nurses can scarcely absorb too much; firstly, because suitable, nourishing, and well-prepared food is one of the great essentials to recovery in any patient of whom they have charge; and secondly, because the selection and administration of food are frequently left to the nurse, whose knowledge of food values is usually most superficial and inexact, even if the subject is not one of which she is totally ignorant. It is only comparatively recently that a short course of sick room cookery has been included in the curriculum of some of our nurse training schools, and few nurses have any adequate knowledge of the science which underlies the presentation of a well-balanced and appetising meal, suited to the needs of the individual patient.

Nurses who are desirous of increasing their knowledge of this subject will find in "Foods and Dietaries: a Manual of Clinical Dietetics," by Sir. R. W. Burnet, K.C.V.O., M.D., J.P., a book which will furnish them with a large amount of information in a readily assimilable form. It is published by Messrs. Charles Griffin & Co., Ltd., Exeter Street, Strand, at the modest price of 4s. The fact that it is now in its fifth edition is proof of its popularity. As the author remarks: "Sick-room cookery is now much better understood than it used to be, but it is to be feared that many nurses and attendants on the sick, not to speak of medical men, hardly yet appreciate fully the help that attention to such details will bring to those under their care."

The plan followed by the author is to arrange his chapters in relation to different diseases. Thus the first chapter deals, broadly, with "Diseases of the Stomach," and its general contents include Chronic Gastric Catarrh (Chronic Gastritis; Irritative Dyspepsia; Inflammatory Dyspepsia), Atonic Conditions of the Stomach (Atonic Dyspepsia), Ulcer of the Stomach, Hæmatemesis, Inflammations of the Stomach (Acute and Subacute Gastritis; Acute Gastric Catarrh). The symptoms of these allied diseases with their origins and causes are enumerated and the correct dietary given. Other diseases and their dietaries are dealt with in the same way. If, therefore, a nurse is in doubt as to a suitable diet in a given case, she has only to turn up the disease in her "Foods and Dietaries," which she can readily do with the aid of the admirable index, to receive sound and expert advice on the point.

A valuable chapter is that on "Prepared and Pre-digested Foods," and the great advance made in "prepared foods," by the addition of malt, —mainly on account of the action of the diastase it contains in converting starch into dextrine and sugar—is emphasised. In this connection, "Liebig's Food for Infants and Invalids," Allen & Hanburys Malted Food, and Kepler's Extract

of Malt, are given as typical instances.
The value of the book is materially increased
by the appendix for " Sick-Room Cookery," in
which a number of useful recipes are given.

OUTSIDE THE GATES.

Already the extension of the franchise to
women is fruitful in results. By the overwhelming
majority of 274 votes to 25, the House of Commons,
on October 23rd, recorded, " That in the opinion
of this House it is desirable that a Bill be passed
forthwith making women eligible as Members of
Parliament."

It is probable that shortly the House of Lords
will follow suit, and that the peeresses in their
own right will take their seats in the Upper
House.

Then, on the motion of Colonel Sir James Craig,
the House declared, " That this House is in
favour of all available galleries being opened to
men and women equally and impartially, and
requests Mr. Speaker to make arrangements
accordingly." This was done, and on Monday
last, for the first time, a number of ladies took
their places in the Strangers' Gallery, and a
momentous change was effected without any fuss
whatever !

GREAT UNITED PROTEST.

The great united Protest against Regulation 40D
of the Defence of the Realm Act which is to be
held in the large Queen's Hall on Wednesday,
November 6th, at 7.30 p.m., promises to be an
impressive demonstration of the ever-increasing
volume of public opinion rising against this
Regulation.

The fifty societies co-operating with the Association
for Moral and Social Hygiene represent not
only social and religious bodies, but the industrial
and professional organisations of both men and
women.

Mrs. Henry Fawcett, LL.D., presides.

Free tickets can be obtained from the Association
for Moral and Social Hygiene, 19, Tothill
Street, Westminster, S.W. 1.

BOOK OF THE WEEK.

"THE BURNING GLASS."*

It is not always that the title of a book shows
much relation to the story within its covers, but
Miss Marjorie Bowen, in the following quotation,
shows that this is no unmeaning choice.

" What is the Beloved to the Lover ?

" A Burning Glass, through which the rays of
the Sun of Love do concentrate. Sometimes the

———————————
* By Marjorie Bowen. Collins & Co., London.

heat breaketh into flames and consumeth that on
which it falleth."

Here is summed up the result of the unhappy
love, or rather loves, of the fascinating Julie de
Lespinasse, who was literally consumed by the
fires of her passionate heart.

Miss Bowen has devoted the whole of the volume
to this theme alone, and has clothed it with vivid
realism and intense vitality.

Julie is portrayed with a wealth of detail that
makes it impossible to quote adequately in a short
review ; for, as is usual with Miss Bowen's personalities,
they are not only sumptuous in themselves
but are set in environment equally glowing
and desirable.

Briefly, Julie was forty years old. She was
possessed of a figure and carriage of unusual
beauty and distinction, and, though her face had
always been plain and was now disfigured by the
smallpox, it appeared in no way to hinder her
fascination for fastidious men many years younger
than herself. She lived in Paris in lodgings that
the generosity of her many friends enabled her to
sustain. She managed her affairs badly, having
very little interest in them, and spent extravagantly
on clothes. Her minute establishment was
that of a great lady. She kept two women
servants, a lackey and her tire-woman. Her
apartment was a nobleman's hotel in miniature.
Her tastes were fine, luxurious, exquisite. She
was famous, very sought after, and generally the
centre of brilliant company."

She was a disciple of Voltaire, and was addicted
to opium.

The period to which this story belongs is that
preceding the French Revolution, and, needless to
say, Miss Bowen uses to the full the romance and
colour of the time.

Julie, when the story opens, is an entirely
virtuous woman, although her friendship with the
famous philosopher, M. D'Alembert, was misunderstood
by some. The passion that consumed
her was not for this humble, great man who
blindly adored her, but for a young Spaniard,
while her affection was given to M. de Mora,
who was far advanced in consumption, and
who reciprocated her love to the full. But the
circumstances of her birth stank in the nostrils
of his proud family, and every obstacle was placed
in the way of their union.

When M. de Guibert came across her path, he at
once exercised a strong attraction for her which in
time obsessed her, and to which in spite of her
better nature she succumbed.

From thenceforward she is torn between her
passion for one man and her love for the other.

Though de Guibert was no libertine he possessed
the easy morals of his day, and in truth the infatuated
Julie, with her undeniable fascination,
must have been hard to resist.

" To-night he could think of nothing but Julie
de Lespinasse. She was an incomparable creature,
she loved like some heroine of antiquity—not like
the boudoir women of the day. But—she would
want everything, and could he give—anything ?

She was tempestuous, uncontrolled, a woman who would make scenes. She was pledged to another man and loathed her infidelity.

No softness, no laughter, no ease, was to be expected from the tragic love of Julie de Lespinasse."

With the death of M. de Mora, who had never suspected her defection, and who had died with her name on his lips, and with the marriage of de Guibert, Julie's stormy heart touched the height of misery.

Her naturally frail body enfeebled by drugs succumbed to the same disease that had slain her lover.

It fell to the lot of her faithful friend D'Alembert to arrange her affairs and to sort her papers They revealed to him what would have seemed quite obvious, that he had held no place in her love.

" I wasted for her sixteen years of my life," he said. She never loved me. Among all her letters had she kept one of mine ? She belonged to the world sooner than to me. I am sixty years old."

To read Miss Bowen is a real refreshment especially at a time when the world is drab coloured.   H. H.

COMING EVENTS.

November 2nd.—Irish Nurses' Association, Meeting Executive Committee, 34, St. Stephen's Green, Dublin. 8 p.m.

November 7th.—British Committee French Red Cross, French Embassy, Albert Gate, S.W. The Lord Mayor of London will, through His Excellency, hand over to the British Committee, F.R.C., the proceeds of France's Day appeal. 12 noon.

ROYAL BRITISH NURSES' ASSOCIATION.

November 7th.—Royal British Nurses' Association Conference, at the Rooms of the Medical Society of London, 11, Chandos Street, Cavendish Square, London, W. Chair, Her Royal Highness Princess Christian. First Session, 3 p.m. (1) The Economic Position of the Trained Nurse. (2) Some Phases of Modern Nursing. Interval for tea. Chair, Herbert J. Paterson, Esqre., F.R.C.S. Second Session, 5.30 p.m. The Differences between the Two Nurses Registration Bills, and why the Royal British Nurses' Association does not agree with the Bill of the College of Nursing, Ltd."

LETTERS TO THE EDITOR.

Whilst cordially inviting communications upon all subjects for these columns, we wish it to be distinctly understood that we do not IN ANY WAY hold ourselves responsible for the opinions expressed by our correspondents.

AS FAR AS VANCOUVER.

To the Editor of THE BRITISH JOURNAL OF NURSING.

DEAR MADAM,—I beg to enclose subscription for one year. THE BRITISH JOURNAL OF NURSING is an inspiration, and especially in the way it is

holding out against the dangerous constitution of the College of Nursing, Ltd.

If I were home again I would gladly rejoin its fighting ranks. One of Mrs. Bedford Fenwick's letters in the Journal was read at our last Association Meeting, and I was proud to think her influence was felt all the way to Vancouver.

Yours truly,
INA M. COLE, R.N.,
Assist. Superintendent.
Victorian Order of Nurses,
Vancouver, Canada.

[We also are proud that the influence of THE BRITISH JOURNAL OF NURSING is felt " all the way to Vancouver." The fact is that in our free Dominions the nurses have always been warm supporters of the Journal's policy, and professional programme, and have in many instances adopted it greatly to their advantage, and of the sick public, whose helpers they are.—ED.]

INFORMATION REQUIRED.

To the Editor of THE BRITISH JOURNAL OF NURSING.

DEAR MADAM,—Could you help me to find out particulars about an article which appeared in your Nursing Record a week or two ago ? It was headed " Makeshifts," spoke about flies being blind to certain colours, especially blue. In a country like this, where flies abound in the hot weather, it would be invaluable to know if blue blinds would be a protection against flies, and what the shade of blue should be. I wonder also if having the walls painted or papered blue would help. . . . I get your paper regularly and appreciate it very much, and also the work you are doing in trying to get registration for nurses. I have just read the article about Miss Elizabeth Asquith and her wax doll, it really makes one's blood boil !

Yours very truly,
MARY BALMER.
Native Mission,
S. Africa.

[We shall be greatly obliged if the writer of " Makeshifts," a most interesting article, will be good enough to reply to this question through the Journal, so that others may benefit by it.—ED.]

We regret that several letters are unavoidably held over.

OUR PRIZE COMPETITION.
QUESTIONS.

November 9th.—Give the nursing of a case after removal of kidney, and state the complications that may occur.

November 16th.—What complications would you watch for if nursing a patient suffering from an injury to the spine ?

November 23rd.—What precautions would you take if nursing a case of septic pneumonia following influenza ?

November 30th. — What do you know of " mustard gas " burns and their treatment ?

The Midwife.

THE MIDWIVES BILL.

We briefly announced last week the result of the Debate on the Committee stage of the Midwives Bill in the House of Commons, when Mr. Hayes Fisher stated that " it is the intention of the Privy Council which governs this matter to give direct representation to midwives on the Board."

THE DIRECT REPRESENTATION OF MIDWIVES.

It is very essential that a definite statement should be made on behalf of the President of the Local Government Board as to the meaning of the term " direct representation " which the House of Commons decided on Monday, October 21st, should be granted on their governing body to certified midwives. Speaking in the representative Chamber, during the Committee stage, on the clause of the Bill which he presented, the Right Honble. Gentleman said :—" It is the intention of the Privy Council which governs this matter to give direct representation to midwives on the Central Midwives Board. There are already, I believe, two women on this Board, and it is intended to increase the number and to have direct representation of midwives upon it." The question was then put, and the clause under consideration agreed to.

The House of Commons therefore unquestionably granted to midwives the right to send representatives elected by themselves to their governing body—the Central Midwives Board.

At a later stage in the debate a new clause was proposed by Mr. Watt as an amendment to Section 3 of the principal Act as follows :—

" The following sub-section shall be added after sub-section (3) of section 3 of the principal Act :—

" (4) Three persons, who shall be certified midwives, to be elected for a term of three years by the certified midwives practising in England."

In moving the second reading of this clause, Mr. Watt said :—

" It provides that three certified midwives should be elected on the Central Midwives Board. When the 1902 Act was passed, the Board had power to deprive midwives of their livelihood, and I believe this Board still has the same power. It is the opinion of my honourable and gallant friend (Major Chapple), who placed this new clause on the paper, that the midwives themselves should be represented on the Central Midwives Board."

The President of the Local Government Board said, in reply : " I am informed by the Privy Council that this proposal would necessitate setting up very cumbrous and expensive machinery and I think it would be better to deal with this question of representation of midwives through the first Clause, which provides machinery by which that can be effected. I am told that this proposal would result in a very haphazard and unsatisfactory representation of the midwives, and I see no reason for setting up machinery of this kind which is not in the Scottish and the Irish Acts. I think we should be satisfied with the provision in Clause 1, which enables us to provide for the representatives of the midwives on the Board."

But the question remains whether, the House of Commons having granted direct representation to midwives, it is not the duty of the President of the Local Government Board, who has charge of the Bill, to provide the machinery to give effect to that mandate. Nobody is in a better position to understand what is meant by the term " direct representation " than the House of Commons. There is further the precedent of the medical profession, which has secured the highly prized right of electing five direct representatives on the General Medical Council.

It cannot with any logic or justice be argued that midwives nominated to seats by their governing body—the method provided for in the first Clause of the Bill—are the direct representatives of the class governed. It would be equally just to say that workpeople nominated by their employers to sit on a board to discuss their mutual relations are the direct representatives of the employees.

The effect of Clause I of the Bill is to place the future revision of the Constitution of the Central Midwives Board in the hands of the Board itself :—(1) " The Central Midwives Board may at any time represent to the Privy Council that it is expedient to modify the constitution of the Board either by (a) increasing or diminishing the number of persons appointed by any body or person, or (b) abolishing the power of appointment by any body or person, or (c) conferring on any body or person a power of appointment of one or more persons, or (d) altering the term of office or qualifications of any members.

(2) The Privy Council before considering such representation shall cause it to be laid before both Houses of Parliament."

Unless either House of Parliament presents an Address to His Majesty within forty days declaring that such representation, or any part thereof, ought not to be given effect to, the Privy Council may report to His Majesty that it is expedient to give effect to the representation, when this may be done by Order in Council. It will be realised, therefore, that the controlling voice as to its constitution is practically given to the Central Midwives Board.

RECIPROCAL TREATMENT OF MIDWIVES CERTIFIED IN OTHER PARTS OF HIS MAJESTY'S DOMINIONS.

On the motion that Clause 10, dealing with the reciprocal treatment of midwives, should stand part of the Bill, Sir Archibald Williamson enquired why, seeing it was intended to allow women trained in Canada to practise in this country, the same privilege was not to be extended to women trained in the United States. He asserted that nurses in the United States got an excellent training as midwives, and there seemed to be no reason for admitting nurses from Canada to practice here while refusing those from the United States the same privilege, in the event of the privilege being reciprocal.

Mr. Hayes Fisher replied : " This opens a very wide question. The Clause provides that a midwife who produces satisfactory evidence of having been trained as a midwife, and being certified in any other part of His Majesty's Dominions shall be allowed to practise as a midwife in another part of His Majesty's Dominions. My hon. friend wants to extend that to certificated midwives whose training may have been quite as excellent in the United States. I do not know whether it would be possible to entertain a proposal for reciprocity as between this country and the United States, unless we also have one for reciprocity between this country and France or some other country ; I have never seen legislation founded on those lines. It opens up indeed a wide international question.

I should advise this House not to make precedent, but to follow precedent, and to content itself with extending to midwives properly trained in one part of His Majesty's Dominions the right to practise in another part of His Majesty's Dominions." This was agreed.

Sir Archibald Williamson showed an extraordinary ignorance of midwifery conditions in the United States, and had the House supported his proposition he would have led them into an *impasse*, as the midwives practising in the United States are mainly foreigners practising among the foreign population, the care of maternity cases being in the hands of trained nurses acting under the direction of medical practitioners, including a large number of medical women. Training schools for midwives have never been organised in the United States, and the class for which Sir Archibald Williamson desired to legislate is practially non-existent ! He further apparently overlooked the fact that Canada owes allegiance to the British flag, whereas it is a matter of history that the United States of America prefers to frame its own legislation under the Stars and Stripes.

THE MIDWIVES BILL IN THE HOUSE OF LORDS.

On Tuesday last the Order of the Day in the House of Lords was the second reading of the Midwives Bill, which was moved by Viscount Peel, who said :—" The Bill was introduced in another place in the same form as that in which it left the House, and the united intelligence of another place was unable to make any improve-ment in the handiwork of your Lordships. The only change they did effect was to insert ' January 1st ' in the blank space which your Lordships left open for the date."

The Bill was read a second time and committed to a Committee of the whole House.

NATIONAL MATERNITY HOSPITAL, DUBLIN.

At the annual meeting of the National Maternity Hospital, Dublin, the Lord Mayor, who presided, said that the Government which could afford to spend millions of pounds daily for war purposes should help to save life by supporting a deserving institution like the National Maternity Hospital. He announced a subscription of £500 from Archbishop Walsh.

ABORTION IN LORRAINE IN THE EIGHTEENTH CENTURY.

Dr. A. Satre, of Grenoble (says the *British Medical Journal*), has found a collection of old decrees in an ancient manor house of Lorraine where he was quartered (*Paris méd.*, September 11th, 1918). Among them is an ordinance against concealment of pregnancy and delivery by unmarried women or widows by Leopold " by the Grace of God Duke of Lorraine and Bar, King of Jerusalem, Marches, Duke of Calabria, Gueldres, Montferrat, Charleville," &c., with a string of other titles recalling those of the Earl of Shrewsbury in " Henry VI." After calling attention to the prevalence of abortion and infanticide in the Duchy he enunciates the principle that, although a child born out of wedlock is the fruit of incontinence, it is nevertheless a citizen of the commonwealth and as such it is the interest of the State to afford it protection against violence by parricidal (*sic*) hands. Women when brought before the magistrate plead that the child was stillborn, and the law provided no definite penalty for the offence ; it was therefore deemed expedient to lay down an inviolable rule for the future. Wherefore, says the Duke, " on the advice of our Council and of our sure knowledge, plenary power and sovereign authority we declare, ordain," and so forth, that a woman who has been seduced and become pregnant shall report her condition to the official authorities, a record of which statement shall be signed by her if she can write, or if not by the judge or his clerk. This must contain the name of the father and an undertaking to take care of the child. The mother must be attended by a midwife, and while she is in the throes of labour the chief officer of justice shall be present and press for a declaration on oath of the name of the father. If women are delivered without assistance, and the child is born dead or dies immediately after birth, it shall be presumed to have been murdered by suffocation or otherwise, and they are punished with death. Women convicted of having attempted abortion by means of drinks or drugs shall be liable to such penalties as the judge may think fitting ; if abortion has actually been induced, this may be death. Exposure of the child on the highway, at a church door, or elsewhere in such manner as to endanger its life, either by weather or the voracity of animals, is punishable by flogging at cross roads and branding on the shoulder with a hot iron by the public executioner. Accessories are liable to a similar penalty. If an exposed child dies by accident or want of food the mother or other persons convicted of having exposed it shall be punished by death.

THE
BritishJournal of Nursing
WITH WHICH IS INCORPORATED
THE NURSING RECORD
EDITED BY MRS BEDFORD FENWICK

No. 1,597. SATURDAY, NOVEMBER 9, 1918. Vol. LXI.

EDITORIAL.

A CORPORATION WITHOUT A SOUL.

"The War Office is a corporation without a soul." That is the accusation brought against it in the House of Commons by Captain Charles Craig, M.P., speaking with the experience of a prisoner of war in Germany for two years, and few who read the report on the debate on the motion for the adjournment of the House—moved by Colonel Sanders on October 29th, in order to raise the question of the treatment of our prisoners of war—will have any wish to qualify the statement.

General Sir Ivor Philipps, who opened the debate, declared that "right from the beginning of the war our whole treatment of this question of prisoners of war has been most unsatisfactory. . . . There was a feeling at the beginning of the war that there was something of contempt to be felt for a prisoner of war. There is not," he said, "the slightest doubt in my mind that the War Office took this line, and I am not certain that even to-day they have quite got rid of it. . . .

"There would," he continued, "have been no starving prisoners, or going to charity, or need to have young ladies of the Red Cross touting for prisoners up and down Bond Street, simply to feed your prisoners if you did your duty. . . . You made a contract with the soldier that you would feed, clothe and pay him, and you have done none of these things. You have left it all to charity. These men, some of the finest soldiers we have got, would have starved—you have said so yourself—if it had not been for the noble work of numbers of men and women who throughout the country have done their best to help."

And Captain Charles Craig spoke equally sternly. "I regret," he said, "that the first thing that I have to do when I come home,

after two years in Germany, is to level as strong an indictment as I possibly can against the Government for their treatment of this prisoners of war subject, during the last three or four years. I wish I could tell the House that my experiences assure me that the Government have done all that they could for the prisoners of war. Unfortunately I have to say the very reverse. As far as my experience goes, they have done little or nothing for us. I have to say, further, that they could have alleviated our lot to a very considerable extent. If they had done their duty as they ought to have done, they could have made the lives of those thousands of men I will not say happy but comparatively easy, instead of which they have been lives of unutterable misery all these years."

It is a grave indictment, especially when we know that the brutality with which even sick and wounded prisoners have been treated in Germany is proved up to the hilt, and we regret to observe Sir George Cave's statement that even among German nurses "many are found who, far from helping suffering prisoners, have stooped to inflict insult and injury upon them."

His Majesty's Forces on active service, or as prisoners, are not objects of charity. They are the servants of the State, and it is the duty of the State to provide for their upkeep, their well being, and their protection. The War Office has shirked the responsibility for which it is paid by the Nation, and left the financing of many of its duties towards the Army to the amateur efforts of charitable persons.

It is this principle against which we have persistently inveighed in the treatment of the sick and wounded from the beginning of the war, and we hope the womanhood of the country will make it perfectly distinct to would-be legislators that no shirking of duty in Government Departments will be permitted in the future.

OUR PRIZE COMPETITION.

GIVE THE NURSING OF A CASE AFTER REMOVAL OF KIDNEY, AND STATE THE COMPLICATIONS THAT MAY OCCUR.

We have pleasure in awarding the prize this week to Miss E. A. Noblett, 2nd Northern General Hospital, Leeds.

PRIZE PAPER.

Nephrectomy—excision of kidney. The dressing should not be so voluminous that it makes a mass uncomfortable to lie on. Temporary drainage is in the renal space. In bed the patient is surrounded by heaters, and symptoms of shock and hæmorrhage attended to as they appear. Uncomplicated, the sutures should be out on the tenth day; the patient is allowed up when the remaining kidney seems to have assumed its doubled function.

If the nephrectomy has been for tuberculosis of the kidney, the ureter is usually followed down and removed. In the wound, therefore, if there is any question of tuberculosis remaining, it is treated later by repeated applications of tincture of iodine, as in tuberculous wounds elsewhere.

Complications and Sequelæ.—Suppression of Urine.—After-care of nephrectomy, as in nephrotomy, should be at first directed toward encouraging the other kidney to rise to its increased labour. It seems probable that uræmic suppression is due to the concentration of blood containing too much matter to be excreted. The posturing of patients for nephrectomy is important. Of course, an extension of the iliocostal space greatly facilitates operation. This is ordinarily secured by bags of sand underlying the opposite antero-lateral region of the abdomen. When by such an arrangement the spine is sufficiently flexed to extend the operative field, the pelvis is nearly lifted from the table and the pyramidal support thus bears a considerable part of the total weight of the body. This pressure impinges upon a yielding surface immediately about the sound kidney, and the organ may be heavily compressed against the spine, with deleterious consequences. This evil is avoided by the use of a nephrectomy table.

Nitroglycerin and adrenalin, which cause a rapid rise in arterial tension, are avoided if possible. Strychnine, with digitalis or strophanthus, is given to overcome the shock of operation.

Hæmorrhage.—If this occurs, particularly with rising pulse, and it is known that every reasonable effort was made to control bleeding by direct ligation at the time of operation, the patient should be turned over on the good side, the wound opened, and tightly packed with iodoform or other chemically treated gauze. In packing a capacious cavity of this sort one should leave the end of each strip which has been introduced protruding from the wound, in order that later, when the packing is removed, nothing may be left.

Saline adrenalin solution—made by adding common salt (1 dram) and adrenalin solution (2½ drams) to 1 pint of sterile water—should be injected under the breasts as soon as the patient is in bed, and should be given to the limit of capacity of both breasts. Salt solution should also be started by the slow method per rectum, and kept going twenty-four hours. Tincture of digitalis or strophanthus may be added to the enema, if it seems best, and strychnine given subcutaneously ($\frac{1}{30}$ gr.) every one to six hours if indicated. The patient must be kept warm to the extent of mild perspiration, and must be encouraged in every way to drink.

For nourishment during the first week milk should be the main resource. After that start soft solids, leading to a rapid resumption of ordinary diet.

The amount of urine, day and night, separately, should be carefully noted from the first.

HONOURABLE MENTION.

The following competitors receive honourable mention :—Miss Amy Morris, Miss Janet Lawson, and Miss Mary Flower.

QUESTION FOR NEXT WEEK.

What complications would you watch for if nursing a patient suffering from an injury to the spine?

THE INFLUENZA GERM ISOLATED.

A Salamanca physician, Dr. Maldonado, has, says the special correspondent of the *Times*, after several weeks' research succeeded in isolating what he believes to be the specific microbe of the so-called Spanish influenza, which continues to spread through the country with devastating results.

Contrary to the usual belief, this germ is not the Pfeiffer bacillus, but one approximating in character to that of the bubonic plague. If this theory, which has been extensively examined by the epidemological section of the National Institute of Hygiene, is confirmed, it would explain the extremely severe and, in many cases, rapidly fatal symptoms of the epidemic. The morphology and colouration of the cultures of the new bacillus are almost identical with that of the bubonic plague, but its difference is proved, according to Dr. Maldonado's theory, by its failure in pathogenic action on animals of known susceptibility to the bubonic germ.

Other authorities here incline to the opinion that there are two epidemics—one the ordinary influenza and the other this far more serious disease which has the symptoms of septic pneumonia and frequently proves fatal in 12 hours.

It is now spread over the whole country. The schools are closed, and the authorities are issuing what advice they can with regard to sanitation and hygiene, but, if anything, the disease is on the increase.

OUR ROLL OF HONOUR.

NURSING SERVICE.

We greatly regret to record the following deaths of nurses, which are reported in the official list of casualties :— DIED.

Queen Alexandra's Imperial Military Nursing Service.—Nurse S. Danaher.

Queen Alexandra's Imperial Military Nursing Service Reserve.—Sister S. Hilling, Sister A. Gledhill, Staff Nurse H. E. Wright.

Voluntary Aid Detachments.—Miss E. M. Tonkin, Miss V. C. Hackett, Miss E. Richards, B.R.C.S.

Australian Army Nursing Service.—Staff Nurse E. A. Clarke.

Canadian Army Nursing Service.—Sister V. B. Hennan.

South African Nursing Service.—Staff Nurse I. R. Wattkins, M.C.

DROWNED.

Voluntary Aid Detachment.—Miss S. V. Barrett.

JACK.—At 1st Birmingham War Hospital, Rubery Hill, on 22nd ult., on service, Sister Christina Jack, R.R.C., Q.A.I.M.N.S.R., daughter of Donald Jack, Princes Street, Thurso.

As a member of Q.A.I.M.N.S. Reserve, Sister Jack has done excellent work, first at Alexandria, then on the hospital ship *Valdivia*, and lastly as Night Superintendent at the 1st Birmingham War Hospital, where she was justly beloved, for she was full of sympathy, devotion to duty, and self-sacrifice. She was awarded the Royal Red Cross in June last.

CAREW.—On the 3rd November, at 11, Berkeley Square, of pneumonia after influenza, Margaret Carew (V.A.D., Coulter Hospital), beloved only daughter of Mrs. Henry Carew and the late Rev. Henry Carew, of Mattery, Devon.

HOBBES.—On the 10th May, at sea, Sister Narrelle Hobbes, Q.A.I.M.N.S.R., late 32nd British General Hospital, Amara, also Military Hospital and St. David's, Malta, daughter late I. T Hobbes, P.M., and Mrs. Hobbes, Balblair, Cremorne, Sydney, N.S.W.

WOODS.—On the 30th October, from influenza, Kathleen Felicia Devereux, second daughter of Inspector-General Henry C. Woods, R.N., of Lisnamandra, Alverstoke, and member of the Alverstoke Relief Hospital Voluntary Aid Detachment, St. John Ambulance Association.

THE ROYAL RED CROSS.

The King held an Investiture in the Ball Room of Buckingham Palace on October 31st, when the following ladies were decorated with the Royal Red Cross :—

SECOND CLASS.

Territorial Force Nursing Service.—Matron Emmeline Wilding.

Voluntary Aid Detachment.—Miss Daisie Buffard, Miss Lucy Purcell.

Canadian Army Nursing Service.—Sister Hilda MacDonald.

NURSING AND THE WAR.

THE MILITARY NURSING SERVICES OF THE CROWN.

The luncheon at the Trocadero Restaurant, on October 30th, in honour of the Matrons-in-Chief of the Nursing Services of the Crown, arranged by a Committee of representative women, was a very interesting function. Her Royal Highness Princess Louise Duchess of Argyll presided, and a number of well-known women were present.

The tables were decorated with lovely roses, sent by the King from Windsor, and trails of smilax, and the vases were filled with chrysanthemums and autumn leaves given by Queen Alexandra, who also sent grapes from Sandringham, which, by desire of the guests of honour, were subsequently sent to Queen Alexandra's Hospital for members of the Imperial Military Nursing Service in Vincent Square.

The representatives of the nursing profession included Mrs. Bedford Fenwick, President of the National Council of Trained Nurses of Great Britain and Ireland; Miss S. A. Swift, R.R.C., Matron-in-Chief Joint War Committee, British Red Cross; Miss Leonard, Chief Nurse American Army Nurse Corps, and Miss Torrance, Chief Nurse of the American Red Cross in this country; and Miss M. Breay, representing THE BRITISH JOURNAL OF NURSING.

After the loyal toasts had been proposed and honoured, Miss M. F. Billington announced that a telegram had been sent to the Queen expressing loyal appreciation of Her Majesty's " constant solicitude for our wounded and stricken men," and the following message had been received :—

THE QUEEN'S MESSAGE.

I am commanded by the Queen to request you to convey her sincere thanks to the president and representative women assembled at luncheon in honour of Matrons-in-Chief, Military Nursing Services of the Crown, for their telegram, and for the loyal assurances to which it gives expression.

Her Majesty fully realises the splendid work which has been achieved by nurses throughout the Empire, and it is a great satisfaction to the Queen to know that their untiring efforts on behalf of our wounded soldiers are being so deservedly recognised by you to-day.　　EDWARD WALLINGTON.

THE PRESIDENT'S SPEECH.

Princess Louise, who, on rising to speak, was warmly applauded, said :—" We are met together here to-day to do homage to the matrons of our hospitals at home and abroad. The nursing organisation, combined with our marvellous achievements in surgery, undoubtedly form the greatest development which science owes to this terrible war. On the matron centres all the working of the hospital—on the matron's tact, knowledge, experience, patience, on her sympathy and true womanliness, on her fearless untiring devotion, cheerfully given to the great charge entrusted to her. Not only does she need these attributes, but she must have the intellectual capacity to make practical use of her gifts. We are indeed thankful that our Empire has given us women who have been able to fulfil this trust and bear this great trust so nobly. We ask them with all our hearts to accept from us our gratitude, thankfulness, and our true appreciation."

An address of appreciation was then read by Mrs. Humphry Ward, who said that they were there to do honour to the heads of the great nursing profession in the British Empire. Everywhere the nursing women of the Empire have followed in the wake of their men, comforting, tending, saving, and so, for these most sufficient reasons those present—whose dear ones had suffered and died in this war—brought their homage and gratitude to the Matrons who were their guests.

Dame Ethel Becher, R.R.C., responded on behalf of herself and her colleagues, and a vote of thanks to the Princess for presiding brought the proceedings to a close.

QUEEN ALEXANDRA'S MESSAGE.

The following message was subsequently received from Queen Alexandra :—

Queen Alexandra asks you to thank the Matrons-in-Chief and the representative women assembled in their honour for their kind telegram of loyal greetings, which Her Majesty greatly appreciates.

Queen Alexandra is always glad to hear of any mark of esteem paid to members of the nursing staffs, whose services throughout the war have won them universal praise and gratitude.

　　ARTHUR DAVIDSON.

It was reported at the quarterly meeting of the Sheffield Royal Hospital that the Matron, Miss A. L. Earle, had been awarded the Royal Red Cross (First Class) in recognition of her services in Mesopotamia. It is nice to see committees appreciating the national services of their matrons.

Everyone will be reading the Memoir of Dr. Elsie Inglis, by Lady Frances Balfour, and we hope to do it justice at an early date. " From first to last she was a woman nobly planned." In these words Lady Frances sums up the great heroine of the Scottish Women's Units. In 1916,

hearing of the lack of arrangements in Mesopotamia, she determined to get there. She approached a departmental chief, and the historic sentence was uttered : " My good lady, go home and sit still." In that utterance lay the germ of the inspiration which was to carry the Red Cross and the Scottish women among the nations.

Dr Elsie Inglis after fine service in Serbia and Russia, returned, fatally ill, in November, 1917, and died, deeply lamented, by a world at war.

In aid of the Imperial Club for Nurses, 2, Old Steine, Brighton, a most interesting loan exhibition has been on view at the Chapel Royal Hall, Brighton. The club is non-residential and is open from 10 a.m. till 10 p.m. for the use of fully and partly trained nurses, V.A.D. nurses, masseuses and dispensers, who pay a small subscription. Notepaper and magazines are provided, and members are entitled to bring friends to the club and tea-room. Money is needed for necessary expenses beyond the members' subscriptions, and a piano is a great want. The club is very largely used by nurses from the local hospitals for recreation in their off duty time. What is really hoped is that the scheme may be developed into a residential club, where Imperial nurses may come for rest by the sea. As an expression of gratitude towards members of the nursing profession, Brighton will do its best to provide them with a residential club. The sum of £2,000 is needed to cover all initial expenses (furnishing, &c.) and to help with the upkeep until the club is self-supporting.

As a practical result of the Conference of British Women War Workers held in Paris in the summer, monthly meetings are now arranged, so that the work in which the various organizations are engaged can be reported and a helpful exchange of experience and opinion result

On November 7th, Mrs. Charles Scott convened a meeting at which the chief speakers were Mlle. Chaptal for France, Miss E. J. Haswell for England, and Miss Stimson for America. All these ladies are well known as earnest workers for the sick and wounded, and are interested in the wide field of social reform and reconstruction.

We much regret to hear that the splendid Astoria Hotel in the Champs Elysées, Paris, which was converted into a lovely hospital in the early days of the war, has been bought, and the proprietor wishes to use the fine building for its original purpose as an hotel. Thus Miss C. C. du Sautoy and the fine band of nurses she has gathered round her have to " demobilise " at very short notice. This is a thousand pities, but " coming events cast their shadows before them," and peace will mean fewer hospitals will be needed for which let us thank God ; and the old order must be reconstructed. Many nurses are now beginning to consider : " What shall I do after the war " ?

Nurses' Aids, and lay women helpers are now being sent from the United States to France for work under the Red Cross. Upon arrival in France they may be assigned to French military hospitals, to hospital hut service, canteen service, work among the civilian population, or in any capacity where extra hands or heads are needed to carry out relief work.

These workers must have had the course in elementary hygiene and home care of the sick, and if suitable, must take the 240 hours' practical experience in a classified hospital.

Applicants are warned of the physical strain to untrained women in France, and, if possible, should be able to pay their own expenses.

The Americans have started in earnest an immense amount of social reconstruction work in France in connection with the care of infants and children, visiting, nursing, and the welfare of those who have suffered so terribly in the devastated districts, and like ourselves, the average American trained nurse knows little French. This organisation necessitates interpreters, and we learn now that she is convalescent, Miss Grace Ellison is helping forward with her intimate knowledge of France and its beautiful language the work at Lyons, where a corps of *visiteuses d'enfants* is being organized. We hear of a charming chief nurse who is drafting rules for the corps. These young French women are to have a four months' course—two theoretical and two practical—after which they are to visit mothers in their homes and help them with their children. Medical lectures are given. Miss Ellison opened the first session with " A Lay Woman's Point of View on Nursing," giving just praise to " all the nursing heroines." Then all the following lectures are to be written by the Chief Nurse—translated into French and delivered by Miss Ellison. This is a very interesting experiment. We hear the *B. J. N.* and its ethical standards and policy received due recognition—for which many thanks.

FRENCH FLAG NURSING CORPS.

" The news is glorious these days," writes a Sister. " Our poor gallant poilus are wild with joy, and so proud of their chiefs. It is now their turn to rejoice and the Boche to weep ; but I have no pity to waste on them—only for their victims."

Two Sisters on leave congratulate themselves on having met most of the great French Generals. " Magnificent men, who treated us like queens," they report with pride.

A Sister, following the flag on the western front, writes :—" This is a deserted village, the gardens wildernesses, but with wonderful flowers hidden amongst the weeds." There is a lesson there. The season of weeds will pass with the barbarian, and these gardens soon bloom in all their old beauty—tilled by man at peace.

RED FOR SAFETY.

A TALE FROM SUVLA BAY.

When it became known that I had orders to join a hospital ship, many were the gifts which reached me. I became stocked with necessities to meet every conceivable need, especially as it was being whispered abroad that events were about to become lively in the Dardanelles.

My old Highland nurse brought me her offering with an apologetic look on her dear old face.

" My dear, what will you be thinking when I tell you that your daft old Nannie has brought you red ribbon when she kens fine you canna abide the colour ? "

" It is lovely ribbon, Nannie ; I like it very much."

The old woman smiled wistfully.

" My lassie, I went by the steamer to Oban to get you blue ribbon to tie your hair at nights, and when I got to the shop my gift of second sight began to trouble me sore."

" Oh, Nannie, I am sorry."

" It was like this. I got to the shop, and just as I was going to ask for blue ribbon I found I couldna do it."

" How was that ? " I queried.

" It sounds gey foolish you'll be after thinking, but as sure as death something kept hammering in my brain driving me to ask for *red* ribbon. I tried that hard to ask for blue ribbon, but my tongue went back on me, so after making queer-like faces, and kenning fine that the young woman was taking me for a gowk, I heard myself asking for twelve yards of good red ribbon one inch wide."

" That was very strange, Nannie."

" Aye, it was that. The second sight was on me right enough : for why, the dear knows. I thought at the latter end I'd no' give you the red ribbon, but something just drove me to do it, and now "— with a sigh of relief—" you have got it."

My protestations that I loved red ribbon did not deceive the old lady in the very least, and when we parted she whispered : " You'll forgive your old Nannie, my bairn ; I had to go by the sign."

The Army Sister does not usually care for the colour red. It borders her uniform cape, and she often gets as tired of it as of being hedged round and round by red tape.

The whispers concerning our destination were justified. We went straight to Gallipoli, of tragic fame, and did our part in the transport of sick and wounded to Egypt, Malta, and sometimes Blighty.

On one precious week of leave I saw my old nurse. She was concerned over my bleached appearance, and wept when I told her of the bravely borne sufferings of our men. At our farewell she whispered : " Do you wear the ribbon ? "

I fear my reply was inaccurate. The roll of ribbon lay at the bottom of my cabin trunk. I disliked the colour intensely. It reminded me too vividly of blood which dripped and dripped when our brave men were shot in the boats, and thus wounded afresh on their way to the hospital ships —their sole sanctuary.

Our good old ship never returned empty on its eastward way. We usually carried the staff and equipment of a hospital to meet the ever-growing urgency in Alexandria.

On this occasion we carried over 200 medical officers and a smaller number of nursing sisters. The latter we disembarked at Alexandria. The medical officers were bidden to remain on the ship to receive their orders later. Conjectures were rife. Whispers of another attempted landing went round the ship.

We were bound for Mudros, to get fresh orders there. I was on night duty, as some orderlies had gone sick. On this particular day sleep was for me an unknown quantity. The Sisters appeared to be rummaging in their boxes in the neighbouring cabins, and murmurs of " I was quite sure I had *some* red, but, of course, I never wear any, so I only have a scrap."

" I haven't got any at all; looking is just a forlorn hope."

" They seem red mad for some curious reason," I murmured, trying desperately to sleep.

In the afternoon a white-capped head peeped through my porthole.

" Oh, good; you are awake. Have you any red ribbon or any red material? "

" Yes, I have some. What is all the fuss about? "

" You know the medical officers are bound for Mudros without definite orders, and that there are rumours of another landing? "

" Yes."

" Well, you know how stupid men can be. Out of 200 doctors, less than fifty have the white armlet with the red cross, as they mostly imagined they were bound for Egypt. They may have to land on hostile ground, and they *must* have armlets. We Sisters have stolen white linen from the stores and have been making them like mad, but the red stuff on the ship is practically nil, and we have over a hundred armlets short of the red cross."

I dressed quickly, and fishing out the long-neglected red ribbon from my cabin trunk, unrolled it so that it might appear to the best advantage, and hurrying on deck I gladdened the eyes of over a hundred men by the delirious sight.

All the time Nannie's wistful face was before my eyes, and her words came back to me : " As sure as death something kept hammering in my brain driving me to ask for *red* ribbon."

Someone queried : " How ever did you come to have such lovely *red* ribbon by you? " and then I told old Nannie's tale.

" Scotland for ever! " shouted an exuberant voice. " Let us all drink the health of your Highland nurse to-night."

The landing at Suvla Bay has passed into a memory, but a bitter one for those whose dearest paid the price.

On my next few days' leave I saw my old nurse again, but I left her one of the proudest dames in Scotland. The glad memory will always abide with her that *she* provided the red ribbon which marked over a hundred red cross armlets—the only means of safety carried by a devoted band of men who wrestled with the death by wounds which threatened such numbers of our volunteer men at Suvla Bay.

ANNA M. CAMERON.

PREMONITION.

" If I should fall, do not grieve for me. I shall be one with the sun and the wind and the flowers."— *Leslie Coulson.*

If I should fall, my presence may be sought
  In all the teeming beauty of the earth.
With every lovely thing that God has wrought
  I shall be one, and find in it new birth.
Therefore within the shadow of the wind
  Upon green meadows, or in April grass
And flowers, who wills my presence still might find,
  Which shall inhabit these until Time pass.
Seek in the gold and purple of the west,
  Seek in the sunshine of a summer's day,
Seek in the ocean's silence and unrest
  If you would find me ; and, while seeking, say :
" He loved all these—he loved all lovely things :
  And from them now his living spirit sings."

    2nd Lieut. Robert S. Lasker,
                        Royal Air Force.
From *Windsor Magazine.*

This gallant boy was brought down in enemy territory and is now reported dead.

SOCIETY FOR THE STATE REGISTRA-TION OF TRAINED NURSES.

A meeting of the Executive Committee was held at 431, Oxford Street, London, W. 1, on Thursday, October 24th, to compare in detail the two Nurses' Registration Bills (1) promoted by the Central Committee, and (2) the Seventh Draft of the Bill promoted by the College of Nursing, Ltd.

The Committee, after considering the College Bill, strongly disapproved of the following provisions :—

(1) The incorporation of a lay company (the College of Nursing, Ltd.) in a Nurses' Registration Bill, the Memorandum and Articles of Association of which provide for autocratic control of the nursing profession.

(2) The power to institute any number of Supplementary Registers of Specialists (other than of Male and Mental Nurses), which registers must inevitably lead to a many portal

—instead of the *One Portal*—system of admission to the nursing profession, and thus depreciate the standard of three years' general training.

(3) The inclusion on the State Register without further fee of registered members of the College of Nursing. Registered members of the R.B.N.A. and other nurses' organizations demand equal treatment, during the term of grace, for all nurses who conform to the standard of training approved by the First General Nursing Council.

(4) To the regulation dealing with the Constitution of the General Nursing Council, as the number of representatives each body is to nominate is omitted.

(5) To the immediate dissolution of the Provisional Council, on which the Organized Nurses' Societies are to have representation through the Central Committee, as it is to be "forthwith" disbanded after having prepared for the Privy Council the rules regulating the constitution of the General Nursing Council, which latter body will prepare and present all the Rules and Regulations to which the registered nurses will have to conform.

The Committee agreed that the Petition to the Prime Minister safeguarding the rights of organized nurses in this connection should therefore be pushed forward with all energy, as their exclusion in the Seventh Draft of the College Bill from participating in framing the Rules they have to obey, is one more proof of the determination of the nominated College Council to override professional opinion in the future, as they have done in the past.

(6) To the control of "registered nurses" by the Nurse Training Schools, which have no responsibility for them, unless in the employment of hospitals to which such schools are attached.

(7) The establishment of Local Boards in parts of the United Kingdom, other than Boards national in character, in England and Wales, Scotland and Ireland.

(8) The omission of any special provision for reciprocal training to qualify for registration.

The Executive Committee considered that the Bill drafted by the Central Committee, which is the outcome of many years' thought and collaboration of those who have promoted the State Registration movement, is a better Bill than that drafted by the College of Nursing, Ltd., and it unanimously decided to support it and to further its promotion in Parliament.

After the election of new members, the meeting terminated.

MARGARET BREAY,

Hon. Secretary.

POOR LAW INFIRMARY MATRONS' ASSOCIATION.

The annual meeting of the Poor-Law Infirmary Matrons' Association was held on October 26th at the Eustace Miles Restaurant. Miss Gibson occupied the chair.

Miss Barton, on behalf of the Association, presented Miss Stansfield with a handsome bag as a small token of its great gratitude for her continual kindness and sympathy, her helpfulness to all the members of the Association, and their very real regret at her retirement.

Miss Stansfield, in thanking the Association for their gift, spoke with appreciation of the work which had been done by the Infirmary Matrons, and of the pleasure her association with them had always given her.

Miss Gibson read the result of the ballot for the hon. officers of the Association, which was as follows :—*President :* Miss Barton, R.R.C., Matron, Chelsea Infirmary ; *Hon. Secretary :* Miss Alsop, Matron Kensington Infirmary ; *Hon. Treasurer :* Miss Inglis, Shoreditch Infirmary. *Committee :* Miss Bodley, Matron Selly Oak Infirmary, Birmingham ; Miss Clark, Matron West Ham Infirmary ; Miss Dodds, R.R.C., Matron Bethnal Green Infirmary ; Miss Dowbiggin, R.R.C., Matron Edmonton Infirmary ; Miss Hannaford, O.B.E., Matron Poplar and Stepney Sick Asylum ; Miss Musters, Matron Leicester Infirmary ; Miss Mowatt, Matron Whitechapel Infirmary ; Miss Myles, Matron Brighton Infirmary ; Miss Emma Smith, Matron City of Westminster Infirmary, London ; Miss M. Smith, R.R.C., Matron West Didsbury Infirmary, Manchester ; Miss Williams, Matron Cardiff Infirmary ; Miss Seymour Yapp, Matron Ashton-under-Lyne Infirmary.

Miss Helen Todd gave a very interesting account of the work which she has been doing temporarily in connection with the Royal Army Flying Corps. This was illustrated by some very beautiful photographs, which were handed round. After some hearty votes of thanks, those present were entertained to tea in the Restaurant, the guests included Miss Amy Hughes, Miss Wilde, and Miss Leigh.

NURSES' MISSIONARY LEAGUE.

A Sale of Work in aid of the Nurses' Missionary League will be held on Saturday, November 9th, at Sloane Gardens House, 52, Lower Sloane Street, London, S.W. 1, from 10 a.m. to 6 p.m.

In spite of the many claims made upon everyone at this time, the Committee of the Nurses' Missionary League earnestly invite help. The past year has brought the League fresh and increased opportunities for usefulness, and it depends largely upon the Annual Sale for its income.

Useful or fancy articles, especially undergarments and children's clothes, comforts for the troops, biscuits, soap, or money will be gratefully received, and should be sent to Miss H. Y. Richardson at the above address.

Members and friends of the League are asked to help to make the Sale widely known.

For any who are unable to come on the 9th, goods left over will be for sale in Miss Richardson's room at Sloane Gardens House, all day, on Saturday, November 16th.

THE NATION'S FUND FOR NURSES.

"THE CRUMBS."

Under the heading "The Nation's Tribute to Nurses" the Stock Exchange, Dublin, notifies in the *Irish Times* that the winning numbers in the gamble for £1,000 will appear on the 16th November, as the original drawing has been postponed. After the ticket holders have been paid, if there is anything over we presume it will be handed to the Nurses' Fund. The only thing Lady Arnott and her Committee can do, in decency, is to refuse to support this scandalous method of exploiting trained nurses by declining to accept the "crumbs."

COLLEGE TO PROTECT V.A.D.'s.

At a recent meeting at Huddersfield in support of the Nation's Fund for Nurses, the Mayor, who presided, said :—"One feature that appealed to him was that they were not going to do an injury to that noble army of women, the V.A.D.'s. We should never know what we owed to those ladies, who, in a great emergency, had come to our help, and he believed one of the conditions of the College was that no injustice should be done to them."

How about the trained nurses, for whom the Fund appeals?

NURSES MISLED.

Miss Sparshott, Matron of the Royal Infirmary, Manchester, said :—"The College of Nursing was organised and managed by trained nurses, with the help of a few laymen, but these gentlemen had nothing to do with administration."

This is the type of misleading statement the College officials are constantly making at meetings of nurses ignorant of the College constitution—and is absolutely untrue. Not only are the seven Signatories of the Company laymen, but they have taken power in the Articles of Association they drew up to make themselves "perpetual members of the College of Nursing."

Also of the five Hon. Officers who manage the affairs of the College four are men and only one a woman. The Hon. Sir Arthur Stanley, M.P., is Chairman, Sir Cooper Perry Hon. Secretary, the Hon. Sir William Goschen (of Früling & Goschen) and Mr. Comyns Berkeley are Hon. Treasurers. These gentlemen practically administer the College, and, as far as our experience goes, the business of the Council is in their hands. To say that they have "nothing to do with the administration" is an astoundingly inaccurate statement.

WHY NURSING HOMES ONLY?

Miss Alison Garland, a one-time suffrage lecturer, urged from past experience the necessity for steps being taken in this matter now before enthusiasm for the work of the soldiers and nurses had evaporated. She specially emphasised the necessity for safeguarding the uniform in order to avoid scandals that had arisen through nurses with insufficient training obtaining positions in some nursing homes.

Why nursing homes only? What of the hundreds of untrained women who during the war have been masquerading as Matrons and "Sisters" in our uniform? We never hear of *their* delinquencies. Why not?

APPOINTMENTS.

SUPERINTENDENT.

Queen Victoria's Jubilee Institute, Scottish Branch.—Miss Mary M. Miller has been appointed Superintendent of the training home in Castle Terrace, Edinburgh. She has recently held the office of First Assistant in the Home.

NURSE MATRON.

Ellen Badger Cottage Hospital, Shipston-on-Stour.—Miss Elizabeth Gillies has been appointed Nurse Matron. She was trained at the Royal Infirmary, Glasgow, and has been Matron of the Cottage Hospital, Bromyard.

NIGHT SUPERINTENDENT.

The Infirmary, Shaw Heath, Stockport.—Miss Annie Maude Shepherd has been appointed Night Superintendent. She was trained at Stepping Hill Hospital, Stockport, and has been Ward Sister at the Union Infirmary, Rochdale, and Night Superintendent at the Union Infirmary, Keighley; she is also a certified midwife.

SISTER.

Royal Hospital for Sick Children, Aberdeen.—Miss Ella Menzies has been appointed Sister of Surgical Wards. She was trained at the Royal Infirmary, Edinburgh, where she has also held the position of Sister, and has been Sister-in-Charge in Burcote House Private Hospital, Berks.

QUEEN VICTORIA'S JUBILEE INSTITUTE FOR NURSES.

Her Majesty Queen Alexandra has been graciously pleased to approve the appointment of the following to be Queen's Nurses to date October 1st, 1918 :—

ENGLAND.

Fanny Purseglove, Evelyn I. Gallacher, Muriel Trayner, Margaret Heritage, Essie Sharman, Mary J. Dillon, Mary Rowe, Lily Perrin, Alice M. Hopkinson, Elizabeth Rogan, Elizabeth A. Thornley, Edith Matthews, Dora C. Hawson, Margaret A. S. Kinsman, Edith Calton, Emily J. Allen.

WALES.

Kathleen Clifford, Ellen Davies.

SCOTLAND.

Margaret L. Anderson, Martha M. Jack, Rachel McLellan, Mary Macmillan, Agnes Malcolm, Sarah Ann Watson, Sarah J. Woods.

IRELAND.

Leonore Ellison-Doherty, Kathleen Hall, Sarah C. Hendron, Elizabeth Allen, Dora Rebecca Black, Martha Matthews,

PRIZES FOR NURSES.

The Annual Prize-giving to the Nurses recently took place in the Board Room of the East Suffolk and Ipswich Hospital.

The Chairman of the Board, Mr. John D. Cobbold, presided, and was supported by Miss Deane, the Matron, Miss Collet, Assistant Matron, and the medical staff. In a few well-chosen words Mr. Cobbold eulogised the services of Miss Deane and Sister Collet, which evoked the great enthusiasm of the nurses and others present. Mr. Cobbold then proceeded to distribute the prizes, handing books of medical and surgical interest to the following :—

1st Division, 1st prize, Nurse Booth.
1st Division, 2nd prize, Nurse Palmer.
2nd Division, 1st prize, Nurse Mayes.
2nd Division, 2nd prize, Nurse Rogers.

With regard to the medals he had then to present, Mr. Cobbold explained that the position each nurse gained was this year based upon the marks won at the two examinations conducted by Mr. Russell Howard, M.S., F.R.C.S., and for general efficiency. The following were the winners :—

Gold Medal—Nurse Saunders.
Silver Medal—Nurse Sinclair.
Bronze Medals—Nurses Shephard, Bingham, Scarfe, Cracknell, Sayer, Buck, Denny, Singleton, Francis, Wright, Nunn, Parr.

Great applause greeted each recipient of a prize or medal, and at the conclusion Mr. Cobbold called upon Miss Deane for her annual report.

Miss Deane, on rising, received an ovation from all present, and commenced her address with a feeling reference to one of the most promising members of her staff (Nurse Kirkland), who had been taken ill and passed away recently. The Matron's address to the nurses was one full of interest to those who heard it. Dealing with her own special prize, Miss Deane set forth very clearly to the nurses present the qualities that were necessary to win this, and it was evident that her frank but kindly explanation met with warm approval. Having concluded her remarks, she announced that the Matron's Prize was awarded to Nurse Buck, to whom, amid a scene of great enthusiasm, the Chairman then handed a travelling clock.

A vote of thanks to the Matron for her address, and cheers for her and for Sister Collet, brought the proceedings to a close.

HOSPITAL WORLD.

Princess Christian presided at a meeting held, by the invitation of the Duchess of Portland, at 3, Grosvenor Square, in connection with a special jubilee effort to help the Shadwell, East London, Hospital for Children. Her Royal Highness spoke of the ready help extended as our duty to wounded fighting men, but urged the claims of civil hospitals, particularly those for children. A matinée in aid of the institution will take place at the New Theatre on November 25th, and the Queen has promised to be present.

NURSING ECHOES.

The Right Honble. C. Addison, M.D., M.P., Minister of Reconstruction, received the Executive Committee of the Association of Approved Societies—which represents some 2,500,000 insured persons—which had invited information on the Ministry of Health Bill, at his office, Queen Anne's Buildings, on Friday, 1st inst. Mrs. Bedford Fenwick, as President of the Trained Women Nurses' Friendly Society, and a Vice-President of the Association, was invited to attend. Miss B. Kent, who is a member of the Executive Committee, was also present. The delegation was introduced by the Right Honble. J. H. Thomas, M.P., and exceedingly interesting, but confidential, information was placed before it.

The Nursing and Midwifery professions, together with the Medical profession, will be entrusted with so important a part in giving effect to a Health Act, that now is the time for those who are drafting it to realise that the *personnel* of these all-important Departments must receive due consideration, and that the old system of organizing nursing and midwifery services for the people by amateur and aristocratic persons at sweated rates, must no longer be tolerated either by the workers or the State. If we are to have an efficient State Nursing Service under the Ministry of Health, as we have so often advised, we must have sufficient expert advice available to make it the valuable asset it ought to be for the community.

One thing enfranchised nurses bitterly resent is the assumption of authority over their professional affairs by rich, titled and leisured women, who have no knowledge of the ethics of self-support, and who have proved in the past incapable of respecting the rights of the wage-earner, culminating in the offensive "Serf Clause," to which they have, as members of Nursing Boards, subjected military nurses. We warn our legislators that for the future skilled professional nurses do not intend to submit to "class" government, and that if, after the war, the old "Society" control is to be continued in State Departments, they intend to rise and sweep it away without further ceremony. Forewarned is forearmed.

At the quarterly meeting of the Scottish Council of the Queen Victoria's Jubilee Institute, the report for the past three months' work was submitted. It showed that the Council were directly responsible for the maintenance of seven Queen's Nurses and twenty-two candidates receiving instruction in the Training Home. Eight candidates had completed their training during the period, six of whom were now engaged in district work at Ellon, Lochgilphead, Vale of Teith, Tollcross (Glasgow), Edinburgh (temporary), and Wick. The nurses' work in sixty-nine affiliated districts had been inspected, and reports thereon submitted to the Executive Committee. 1,061 cases had been nursed in Edinburgh by the nurses from the Training Home, involving a total of 18,463 visits. Donations received during the quarter amounted to £116, and subscriptions to £239.

We regret to learn that the nursing staffs in the hospitals of the Metropolitan Asylums Board have suffered severely in the influenza epidemic. Over three hundred nurses and ward attendants have been attacked by the disease, and the death roll is eleven.

NATIONAL UNION OF TRAINED NURSES.

Under the auspices of the National Union of Trained Nurses a Meeting to consider the influence on the Nation of a Ministry of Health will be held at the College of Ambulance, 3, Vere Street, Oxford Street, W., on Saturday, November 23rd, at 2.30 p.m. The Rev. H. R. L. Sheppard, rector of St. Martin's-in-the-Fields, will be in the Chair, and the speakers will be Dr. Saleeby and Miss H. L. Pearse.

Dr. Saleeby will speak on What a Ministry of Health can do for : (a) The Babies of the Nation; (b) The Children of the Nation; (c) The Workers of the Nation.

Miss Helen Pearse will speak on " The Need of the Co-operation of the Trained Nurse in the effective working of a Ministry of Health."

All interested are cordially asked to attend and to bring friends. Entrance free.

The Employment Bureau of the N.U.T.N. assists Nurses in finding permanent posts, and now that demobilisation is within sight it should have a very busy time.

The N.U.T.N. is bringing its " Statement " on " Nurses' Salaries " issued in 1916 up to date. The notes in connection with this Statement touch on the economic conditions of the nursing profession. It is the aim of the Union to help to raise the salaries to such a level as will make them correspond with the value of the work done by the nurses.

THE GAS INDUSTRY AND PUBLIC SERVICE.

At the seventh Annual General Meeting of the British Commercial Gas Association, held at the Royal Society of Arts, John Street, Adelphi, W.C. 2, on Wednesday afternoon, October 16th, the President, Sir Hallewell Rogers, J.P., in introducing the incoming President, Lord Moulton, P.C., K.C.B., F.R.S., Director-General of Explosives Supplies, said that apart from its prompt action in meeting the need for explosives in the early days of the war and in releasing men for the fighting forces, and experts for the laboratories, the gas industry had done invaluable work for the country in the quick improvisation of depots, canteens, hospitals, and other establishments of the militant army, and of factories and workshops for the industrial army. It had set itself to providing fuel oil for the Navy ; had furnished the farmer with cheap and indispensable fertilisers ; had been an important source of ammonia supply ; and, last, but not least, had furnished enormous supplies of gaseous fuel to munitions works of all kinds, as well as in increasing quantities to all branches of industry and to the homes of the people.

THE SURGICAL MANUFACTURING COMPANY.

A visit to the Surgical Manufacturing Company's show rooms at 83 and 85, Mortimer Street, London, W. 1, by those desirous of securing invalid furniture and appliances will be well repaid, for the firm are the makers of the goods which they supply, and thus can secure the quality of the materials used, and supervise the workmanship which means so much in fashioning articles of this kind.

A special advantage offered by the firm is that invalid furniture, spinal carriages, bath chairs, water beds and cushions can be had in the first instance on hire, and, if purchased subsequently during the first month, they will be charged at the List Price, less any amounts paid in advance for hire. The advantage of such an arrangement is apparent. Private nurses, for instance, often hesitate to ask a patient's friends to buy an expensive appliance which after all may not meet his needs, or may not be wanted for long, but if it can be hired at a moderate cost with the option of purchase, they will often do so.

We were particularly struck by a rest chair made for American Convalescent Hospitals at the low cost of 30s. Back and arms are both at an angle which is most restful and, when not in use, the chair folds up and can be tucked away. A bed table, costing 10s. 6d., also packs flat when not required. We must not forget to mention that the establishment is open day and night, and that operation outfits (with which dressings are included) can be hired for 25s., and an operation table for 7s. 6d.

'Mustard Gas' Burns

A New Treatment
having remarkable results in hospitals.

Relief from pain is assured from the first application of this treatment, and complete recovery is effected more quickly than by any other treatment.

TREATMENT.
'Mustard Gas' Burns should be thoroughly sprayed with Chlorcosane Solution of Dichloramine-T 5%. Then apply to the burns melted 'No. 7 Paraffin' with a large camel-hair brush, to form a wax glazing (or covering). On this wax glazing quickly place a *thin* layer of cotton wool. Afterwards cover the cotton wool with more melted 'No. 7 Paraffin,' giving special attention to the edges to ensure an air-tight dressing.

DAILY DRESSINGS.
For the first few days the dressing should be renewed every 24 hours. Later it can be left for 48 hours.

'No. 7 PARAFFIN' (Burnol Brand).
'No. 7 Paraffin' is the name adopted by the Army Medical Service and Military Hospitals for a preparation containing Beta Naphthol, Eucalyptus Oil, Paraffin Molle, Paraffin Durum, and Olive Oil. The word 'BURNOL' is the registered trade mark for a standardised preparation of 'No. 7 Paraffin,' which is prepared under analytical control in the laboratories of Boots Pure Drug Co. Limited, Nottingham.

SUPPLIES.
Chlorcosane Solution of Dichloramine-T 5%, in 20oz. bottles   ...   .   price **12**-, post paid.

Special Spray for the purpose ...   .   price **6/6** extra, post paid.

The Burnol Brand of 'No. 7 Paraffin,' in 4oz. cakes,   price **9**- per dozen, post paid.

The Burnol Brand of 'No. 7 Paraffin' is also supplied in combination with Flavine or Scarlet Red, in 4oz. cakes   ...   ...   price **12**/*- per dozen, post paid.*

LARGE STOCKS ALWAYS ON HAND.

□ □

BOOTS PURE DRUG CO. LIMITED

Head Offices: Station Street, NOTTINGHAM.   ::   SIR JESSE BOOT, Managing Director.

Telegrams: DRUG, NOTTINGHAM. ———————— *Telephone: 3160 Nottingham.*

BOOK OF THE WEEK.

"WASTRALLS." *

Cornwall is always associated with romance, and brings with it an atmosphere of primitive men and women. This story brings out the flavour of that fascinating county, and has an additional attraction in its originality and dramatic force. That it is also creepy and even gruesome in parts is a natural outcome when one remembers that the Cornish are a race that is superstitious and imaginative to a high degree.

There are some priceless characters in this volume, and we venture to think that Sabina is a creation. We do not remember to have met her before, and certainly it would be unwise for any one to attempt to re-dish her up in any future story. The pattern should be destroyed, she is quite unique.

Sabina was the vital bright-haired child of a vague, colourless mother, who died shortly after her birth. For lack of a son, Freathy had taken his daughter with him about the farm. By the time he died she had gathered a little store of experience, had indeed been farming Wastralls for over a year.

" Freathy, intending to re-marry and leave hearty sons, had not troubled to make a will, and the girl of one-and-twenty succeeded to an unencumbered freehold of five hundred acres, the manor house and what remained of the old Squire's savings." As the neighbours said " to give the maid her due, hers a first-rate farmer."

When Byron Leadville, the waif, washed up by the sea, but reared in the immediate neighbourhood of Wastralls, returned from his voyaging, he found that Sabina, big, fair, ripe, a woman who might have stepped out of an Elizabethan age reigned at Wastralls.

In outward seeming the man was not unlike the people among whom he lived. A little more swarthy, with a more sombre expression in his dark eyes, a broader chest than was often seen, he might have passed for a Cornishman. The difference was one of temperament, and the difference was so great that never to the end of his life was he to be other to them than a " foreigner."

It was not Sabina that he wanted but Wastralls. " Asking no more than to spend his passion on the land he found consent in Sabina's awakening interest."

After he was safely married to her he had the surprise of his life. Sabina flatly refused to allow him to farm the land.

" What's the good to let you 'ave it, you dunno nothing about farmin'. Yo bin to sea most all yer life."

" 'Avin married you, the farm's my due."

Sabina sat very straight in her chair. " Now once for all," said she, " let's settle this matter. Wastralls is mine, and I dare you to so much as lay a finger on it."

* By C. A. Dawson-Scott. London : Heinemann.

Byron's surprise at her attitude was so intense that he stared at her in helpless silence, until she clinched the matter by saying in her hearty, fresh-air voice, ' 'Tis no good for ye to think any more about it.'

He entreated, she smiled ; he blustered, she laughed ; he cajoled, she warmed to him, but though she warmed she did not weaken."

The break up of the situation was due to an accident.

Sabina was thrown from a trap, and her injuries were so severe as to necessitate the amputation of both legs.

But if Byron imagined that this was to be the end of Sabina's activities he was doomed to disappointment. She invented for her use a self-propelling trolley, and on this made a triumphant return to the farm, for she was much respected and beloved by the neighbourhood.

Byron lifted his eyes as the beflowered cortège rolled into the yard. The trolley, with its basket work cone, was an unpleasant surprise ; while his wife, in brightly-coloured gown and pink sun bonnet, swelling out of it like some monstrous fruit, completed his dismay. She was a figure of fun, a queer oddity, repellent as something out of Nature, Sabina had returned to farm her land with undaunted will if with diminished activities.

We are not disposed to retail the " creepy " parts for our readers, but we can promise them that if they read the book for themselves they will be glad of a candle to " light them to bed."

But we cannot conclude without a reference to dear Mrs. Tom, a delightful woman, Sabina's life-long friend and kinswoman, and the mother of a long " tail " of pretty girls.

" Wastralls " is a work of high literary merit and a story of unusual power that everyone should read.   H. H.

OUTSIDE THE GATES.

The Qualification of Women Bill, which was contained in one clause, passed its second reading in the House of Commons on Monday night without a division, giving a woman, married or single, the same right as a man to sit in the House of Commons.

Lord Robert Cecil, who was in charge of the Bill, confessed that he was in favour of its being extended to the House of Lords, but he indicated technical difficulties which might make such a clause prejudice its chances.

There are now twenty peeresses in their own right, and we have no doubt they will soon grace the crimson benches in their " Lordships' House."

A WORD FOR THE WEEK.

" Political liberty is a part of the whole. Liberty is the development of the personality along moral lines towards moral ideals, the setting free, in each individual and throughout the State, of a great flood of creative energy."

COMING EVENTS.

November 21st.—Central Midwives Board Meeting, Queen Anne's Gate Buildings, S.W.

November 23rd.—National Union of Trained Nurses. Meeting to discuss the proposed Ministry of Health. Speakers : Dr. Saleeby and Miss H. L. Pearse. Chair, the Rev. H. R. L. Sheppard, 3, Vere Street, Oxford Street, W. 2.30 p.m.

November 29th.—Annual Meeting of the Grand Council of the National Council of Trained Nurses of Great Britain and Ireland, 431, Oxford Street, London, W. 4 p.m.

LETTERS TO THE EDITOR.

Whilst cordially inviting communications upon all subjects for these columns, we wish it to be distinctly understood that we do not IN ANY WAY hold ourselves responsible for the opinions expressed by our correspondents.

A GREAT NATIONAL DANGER.

To the Editor of THE BRITISH JOURNAL OF NURSING.

MADAM,—In view of the rapidly changing European situation the immediate internment of all persons of enemy blood, naturalised or un-naturalised, and *the removal of all such persons from every Government and public office* becomes a matter of the most urgent necessity, for these people, active in time of war on behalf of their own country, will be doubly active as peace approaches. Their influence will be used, with all its subtlety and persistence, to operate in favour of every step which will be advantageous to Germany in the coming critical months, and unless drastic steps are taken to eliminate this influence, Great Britain and her Allies lie open to the danger of a moderate policy towards the Central Powers, which will lead to a negotiated peace with the enemies of civilisation.

Yours truly,

NORAH DACRE FOX.

3, Eastwood House,

Emperor's Gate, S.W. 7.

[No class of the community realises this danger more than we nurses do. It has been brought home to us in a very intimate manner. So long as persons of enemy blood are free and have patronage and money to distribute the danger is very real—amongst those in whom self-interest is the paramount instinct.—ED.]

NOT A NATIONAL FUND.

To the Editor of THE BRITISH JOURNAL OF NURSING.

DEAR MADAM,—Can you inform me whether the Nation's Tribute Fund for Nurses is giving any portion of the money subscribed to it to the Trained Nurses' Annuity Fund or any such old-established society for the benefit of nurses ?

I am frequently asked the question and have been unable to give an answer.

Yours faithfully,

A SUBSCRIBER.

[We have no knowledge of how this Fund is distributed. Its Committee is in no sense national, and is in the hands of a few unrepresentative women who have absolutely no right either to appeal for, or to distribute charity in the name of the Nursing Profession. We should advise you to communicate with the London County Council, which body is responsible for having registered this fund as a "war charity" under the War Charities Act, the regulations of which the Committee constantly ignore.—ED.]

A GRIEVOUS LOSS.

To the Editor of THE BRITISH JOURNAL OF NURSING.

DEAR MADAM,—It is with great sorrow that we communicate to you the death of our beloved and highly esteemed member, Jeanne van Lanschot Hubrecht.

After a short illness of only ten days we lost her, who has done so much for our organisation.

We hope that the ties between your organisation and ours, which were kept strong mainly through her influence, will not be suffered to relax.

For the Board of *Nosokomos,*

C. LIGTELIJN,

First Secretary.

[We deeply regret to receive this sad news as we go to press, and shall refer to the work of this leading Dutch nurse in our next issue.—ED.]

KERNELS FROM CORRESPONDENCE.

A Matron writes :—" Some of your readers appear to think that all Matrons join the College from choice, and approve its policy. I can assure you this is not so ; but my lay Committee were very nasty because I preferred not to join, and I was prepared to resign if pressure was put on me to do so, and make my reasons public. Most of the Matrons in this town have done as they were ' advised,' as they do not want to lose their posts. They have never seen the Constitution—anything for peace ! "

Irish Matron writes :—" I am glad you exposed the scandalous gamble on the Stock Exchange here, to make money in the name of the Nation's Tribute to Nurses. Recently Major General Fry inspected aeroplane workers and shell workers in a pageant symbolical of women's work in the war in aid of the Nation's Tribute to Nurses, which was held in Viscount Iveagh's grounds, Dublin. Personally, I cannot see why industrial workers should be utilized to raise money for professional women like trained nurses, and have several letters from Irish nurses protesting against this form of charity. It is no use arguing that all this begging does not lower our status —*it does.*"

OUR PRIZE COMPETITION.

QUESTIONS.

November 23rd.—What precautions would you take if nursing a case of septic pneumonia following influenza ?

November 30th. — What do you know of " mustard gas " burns and their treatment ?

The Midwife.

CENTRAL MIDWIVES' BOARD FOR SCOTLAND.

The Examination of the Board, on October 28th and 29th last, held simultaneously in Edinburgh, Glasgow and Dundee, has concluded with the following results :—

The following are the successful candidates —

EDINBURGH.

Misses Jessie L. Barber, Janet A. C. Bell, Mrs. Kathleen Burleigh, Misses Annie Coghlan, Annie M. Fraser, Kate V. Fromman, Williamina Garrow, Margaret G. Gerard, Ada D. M. Kerr, Jean W. Low, Nancy A. Macadam, Mrs. Annie H. MacDonald, Misses Catherine McKay, Ellen McLellan, Mary McPhee, Jessie Martin, Mary C. Nicholson, Jeanie P. Pollock, Christina M. Reid, Jane Robertson, Janet Spence, Margaret S. Swanson and Marian Walshe.

GLASGOW.

Misses Gwendolen A. Arthur, Mary A. Baird, Marirete Beaton, Mrs. Joannie R. Binnie, Miss Catherine L. C. Backwood, Mrs. Martha Burke, Misses Elizabeth Carruthers, Mary M. Edgar, Margaret S. Falconer, Alice Fisher, Mary K. Gardiner, Mrs. Mary M. R. Graham, Miss Margaret N. Harley, Mrs. Annie T. Hickie, Mrs. Helen Hughes, Misses Helen C. Keegans, Catherine C. King, Margaret Leightley, Janet Macalister, Flora MacGillivray, Mrs. Medling MacIver, Mrs. Agnes McLuskey, Misses Madeline Miller, Marion N. Montgomery, Mrs. Jessie O. Morrison, Mrs. Elisabeth Muir, Misses Janet Muir, Jeanie S. Neilson, Mrs. Louisa O'Flynn, Miss Helen G. Sharp, Mrs. Madeline K. Sharp, Mrs. Mary Shephard, Mrs. Ethel Spark, Mrs. Margaret Sturdy, Miss Jamesina C. Thomson, Mrs. Marion Watt, and Miss Elena Winlow.

DUNDEE.

Misses Jemima Cameron, Ida W. Cowan, Annabella Christie, Agnes H. Crockett, Mrs. Jane T. T. MacIntosh, Misses Margaret McKenzie, Barbara G. Serlie, and Alice Sutherland.

EXAMINATION PAPER.

The following are the questions set for candidates at the examination :—

1.—Define the terms : Presentation, true conjugate, internal rotation, lochia, and puerperium.

2.—A patient, 3½ months pregnant, has continuous dribbling of urine. What is wrong with her and what treatment will be necessary ?

3.—What are the varieties of asphyxia neonatorum ? How would you treat them ?

4.—Give the diameters of the fœtal head. What is meant by the caput succedaneum ? What other swelling of the fœtal head may be discovered at birth and how would you treat it ?

5.—Breech case. At what stage of a breech case does the danger to the child begin ? Describe how you would manage the labour after the breech is born.

6.—Under what conditions occurring in newly-born children is it specified in the Rules of the Central Midwives Board that a midwife must advise that a registered medical practitioner be sent for ?

THE EMPLOYMENT OF PREGNANT WOMEN IN MUNITION FACTORIES.

In a recent issue we published in part a paper read by Dr. Mary S. Deacon at the Oxford Welfare Conference, on the above subject, in which the writer expressed the view that in no case has the nature of their work had the slightest detrimental effect on pregnant women in a munition factory under her observation, and several of the workers were reported as never having felt so well during former pregnancies, or having had such good confinements, or such healthy babies.

Miss Maria Drysdale, of Rawtenstall, writes that her experience of mills and factories is vastly different. With the exception of about two and a half years of nursing experience in London hospitals she has been able to keep in touch with mill life and mill workers, and has a fairly intimate knowledge both of the mill life and the home life of the worker. She writes :—

" For several years strenuous efforts have been made to educate the working classes in Lancashire, particularly with a view to making them good citizens. More and more have Lancashire folks, at any rate, realised that the mother's place was in the home, and a true moral and intellectual standard could only be maintained when the family life had a safe pivot around which it could revolve.

" Under exceptional circumstances it may be possible to employ pregnant women in factories without immediate ill effects. From a psychological point of view it is the worst thing that can happen to a family. When the mother has to be the bread-winner life is a drudgery, and the children, nine times out of ten, a nuisance, and any observant or thoughtful person will see at once that it is impossible for anyone, man or woman, in that condition of mind to cope with children.

" If the war has put us so many years behind the knowledge we had already gained the struggle will wear a good many of us out before we attain more than a fraction of that for which we are striving.

" The strength of England depends on the home life more than ever it did in the past. . . . Surely we ought to diffuse knowledge more widely than ever, and to do our utmost to strengthen the bulwark of English life—the Home."

THE BRITISH JOURNAL OF NURSING
WITH WHICH IS INCORPORATED
THE NURSING RECORD
EDITED BY MRS BEDFORD FENWICK

No. 1,598.　　　　　SATURDAY, NOVEMBER 16, 1918.　　　　　Vol. LXI.

EDITORIAL.

VICTORY.　JUSTICE HAS WON.

" On make Thou us, through centuries long,
In peace secure, in justice strong ;
Around our gift of freedom draw
The safeguards of Thy righteous law ;
And, cast in some diviner mould,
Let the new cycle shame the old ! "

The universal rejoicing when it became known on Monday morning that the Armistice had been signed, and the sword sheathed for a definite term, was the measure of the repression of over four years which our splendid people have endured with fortitude. But, when the hand of time pointed at length to the hour of victory their gladness overflowed, and in true British fashion they celebrated one of the most memorable days in the history of the world.

The first general intimation of the signing of the Armistice was given by the maroons. The effect was electric, tools were downed, and away raced the people into the open, where without ceremony it was possible to express their joy, and it was a stupendous joy, which made magnificent music from millions of throats, and drums and pipes, hooters, tooters and dancing feet.

Just to be in the crowd made one feel a thousand years young.

Then the crowds surged to Buckingham Palace, and called for their King. The King and Queen throughout the four grim years of war have been in the midst of the people, strengthening, comforting, sympathizing wherever they found trouble, pain and sorrow, and instinctively the heart of the people turned to their Sovereign in their joy.

The great ovation which greeted their Majesties as they appeared on the balcony of the Palace (hung with crimson and gold), was not only that of people loyally acclaim-

ing their Sovereign on the declaration of Victory, but of a more intimate and personal quality. The King and the People had been through deep waters together, and together they exulted that at length they had come to the desired haven.

Their Majesties' appearance was the signal for the band to play the National Anthems of the Allies, followed by " O God our help in ages past " and " Now thank we all our God " and " Land of Hope and Glory."

The King struck the right note as he spoke to the People.

" With you I rejoice, and thank God for the victory which the Allied Armies have won, which have brought hostilities to an end, and Peace within sight."

In his message to the Empire's Armies His Majesty wrote :

" I desire to thank every officer, soldier, and woman of our Army for services nobly rendered, for sacrifices cheerfully given, and I pray that God Who has been pleased to grant a victorious end to the great crusade for Justice and Right will prosper and bless our efforts in the immediate future to secure for generations to come the hard won blessings of Freedom and Peace."

Crowds also flocked to St. Paul's and to Westminster Abbey, where thanksgiving services gave expression to the deep joy of the Empire, while in the street merriment and high spirits were in happy contrast to the repression of the last four years.

And if we in this country are filled with thankfulness and relief that the war cloud has at length lifted ; what must be the feelings of our brave French and Belgian Allies whose countries have been invaded, and their inhabitants brutally treated. To them the Peace foreshadowed must indeed come with healing in its wings.

As Justice has won—we must have a Just Peace to crown a glorious Victory.

THE BACTERIOLOGY OF "INFLUENZA."

By A. KNYVETT GORDON, M.B.Cantab.

In order to understand the apparent vagaries of the present epidemic it is necessary to go to the root of the matter, and look upon it as just one of the numerous battlefields on which the eternal war between the microbe and the man is being waged.

This conflict is always going on between the opposing armies. That of the microbes is composed of many military units—some of them are famous regiments, have won their spurs, and are known as formidable foes; the organisms of tubercle, diphtheria, and enteric fever are good examples. When a patient is attacked by one of these we are not surprised, as we know his microbe of old, and can often defeat him by methods with which we are also familiar.

Sometimes, however, we are faced with the activities of what the general public—and especially the sensation-mongering section of the daily press—hastens to call a new disease. It usually goes on incidentally to affix such sensational titles as "the scourge in our midst," "the terror that flieth by night," and so on. Furthermore, the public is more impressed by the fact that a disease has killed the local mayor than by any accurate conception of what it can and cannot do in the way of destruction or damage.

An epidemic, however, is simply the bringing into action by the enemy of a microbial unit that has not recently seen much fighting, and to get a clear view of its activities it is better to look at large maps. Otherwise we are in danger of not being able to see the wood for the trees.

Let us carry the military analogy a little further. A fighting force does not consist merely of one arm. For infantry, for instance, to be effective, they must have the way prepared for them by artillery fire, and their rations and ammunition brought up to them by the transport. So it is in an epidemic. There is the microbe that actually delivers the attack, and is always found in the tissues of a patient suffering from the disease, but it is accompanied by other germs whose function is to weaken the patient generally, or to damage some particular organ, so that on the whole the patient's power of resisting the principal germ is lessened or destroyed altogether.

Thence comes confusion. When the bacteriologist gets to work, he may find numerous organisms in his patients, sometimes one,

sometimes another, and until he has had the opportunity of examining a fair number of cases, he is often unable to work out the precise function of each microbe.

But the general public has no such difficulty. One newspaper says the " pestilence " is due to a streptococcus—if it is able to spell it—while another trumpets the rival claims of a pneumococcus, until the effusions remind one of the Eatanswill election. Occasionally they become lurid by summoning alien bacilli altogether, such as those of plague, spotted fever, and goodness knows what besides, to their aid, if there are signs that the public is getting tired of their previous microbial claimant.

All this, incidentally, is not merely inaccurate or ridiculous : it does great harm by actually lowering the resistance of those who are impressed by it, so that they are more likely to succumb than those who keep not only a healthy body, but a sane mind also.

Let us, however, come back to influenza. There are really two kinds of "influenza," one that is and one that is not. The latter is the type that a man has, or says he has, every year, and is due not to the Bacillus Influenzæ, but to another organism altogether, the Micrococcus Catarrhalis. Personally, I dislike the term influenza when it is applied to an illness for which the old name "feverish cold" is much more appropriate, as it is quite sufficiently accurate.

This epidemic, however, is true influenza, that is to say, it is due to the bacillus influenzæ, or, as it used to be called, Pfeiffer's bacillus. If one examines any particular patient, or if you like, any particular half-dozen patients, it is quite possible that the bacillus influenzæ will not be found in one's cultures, but it does not follow that it is not present in the patient. As a matter of fact, the bacillus influenzæ is rather difficult to cultivate. For one reason, in a swab containing a mixture of other organisms with it, the bacillus influenzæ is apt to be choked out by the more rapid growth of the others. Then it will not grow at all unless the culture medium employed exactly suits it. It prefers human blood to any other food, and in practice one often succeeds in cultivating it on an agar tube that has been streaked over by blood shed from a finger prick. Curiously enough, some people's blood seems to be more use than others in this respect. I remember, for instance, that I could more often succeed when I punctured my own finger than when I performed a similar human sacrifice on a certain laboratory assistant !

If then a large number of patients are taken, and suitable media employed, the bacillus influenzæ can be obtained in a sufficient number of instances to justify one in saying that it is the cause of the disease. Definite proof, however, is obtained from the fact that it will reproduce the disease when it is injected into a suitable experimental animal. In appearance it is a very minute, thin rod.

At the onset of the disease it grows in the throat and nose, where it gives rise to the well-known catarrh, with which the attack starts. The toxins or poisons which it then forms are absorbed into the blood and produce the rise in temperature and prostration, while later on the organism itself may spread downwards into the lungs, where it gives rise to bronchitis and not infrequently to a disease which has the characteristics of a broncho-pneumonia, with the distribution of the lobar variety, or upwards through the Eustachian tube into the middle ear, where it is particularly liable to set up mastoid disease.

The microbes with which the bacillus influenzæ is often associated in this epidemic are usually a streptococcus or the pneumococcus, or both—and there can be no doubt that they are both responsible for many of the fatalities which have occurred. The reason is that many organisms grow better—both in culture media and in the body—when in association with others, just as one can imagine a soldier fighting better when he has his friends alongside him. The phenomena is known as " symbiosis," and one occasionally takes advantage of it in a laboratory when one wants to grow a particularly virulent strain of a microbe. In the preparation of diphtheric antitoxins, for instance, a much more luxuriant growth of the diphtheria bacillus can be obtained if one adds some bacillus podigiosus to the cultures.

The pneumococcus-influenza combination seems to be particularly liable to attack the lungs, and the addition of staphylococcus appears to increase the severity of the initial toxæmia, and of suppuration such as mastoid abscesses.

Coming now to treatment. As regards the patient himself, we try both to kill the microbe direct and to increase the bodily resistance, so that he is able to manufacture antibodies to the germ for himself. As regards the first, we cannot do very much. There is no drug taken internally that will kill the microbe, but there is some evidence that irrigation of the nostrils with a weak solution of permanganate of potash is able to retard the growth of the germ

in the nose. The measures adopted to keep up the resistance of the patient are common to most infectious diseases, and comprise nursing, good food, tonics, stimulants, &c., but the two most important are bed and more bed. I need not dwell on these now.

Secondly, can we do anything in the way of preventive treatment? Apart from obvious essentials of sanitation, such as free ventilation and disinfection, together with prompt isolation of those suffering from the disease, the general public is asking us to inoculate them against it. They have a sort of idea— for which I am afraid we must blame some over-enthusiastic bacteriologists—that we can now " inoculate " against anything from a chilblain to the plagues of Egypt; that all we have to do is to collect the germ, kill it, and inject it under the skin of a healthy person in order to prevent him from contracting the disease.

I wish we could do that. There would soon be no more disease of any kind, and most of us could sell our microscopes and buy a farm !

Unfortunately, however, the problem is by no means so simple. A vaccine is like a sharp scalpel, and is capable of doing almost unlimited harm in the hands of an unskilled person, or when improperly used.

As regards the present epidemic, it is easy enough to prepare a vaccine containing a mixture of bacillus influenzæ, streptococci and pneumococci, but the trouble is that its use is followed by a marked " negative phase," as it is called, that is to say, that for a variable period after inoculation, the patient's resistance to influenza is actually lowered. It is true that this is followed by a prolonged rise in his defensive powers, but as he may go down in the negative phase, it is usually undesirable to inoculate during an epidemic : we should wait for it to subside, and then try to immunise the patient for the future. It is probable that a course of about twelve injections is required for success in this respect. The vaccine may appropriately contain b. influenzæ, streptococcus and pneumococcus.

MINISTRY OF HEALTH BILL.

Dr. Addison introduced the Ministry of Health Bill into the House of Commons on November 7th. Keen interest was evinced in his speech. Under the Bill the Minister of Health will have the powers of all present Departments that deal with health. Treatment of the sick and infirm will *not* be part of the Poor Law.

Our Poor Law Infirmaries should become State Schools of Nursing.

NURSING AND THE WAR.

Miss Julia C. Stimson, R.N., Chief Nurse of the American Red Cross in France, has just been appointed Chief Nurse of the Army Nurse Corps of the American Expeditionary Force.

Miss Stimson's appointment is a most popular one. It will be remembered that prior to America entering the war she came over to this country with the Missouri Unit which formed the Nursing staff of Base Hospital No. 21 of the United States Army, the members of which were drawn not only from St. Louis, but from Kansas City, and Hannibal. Miss Stimson was trained at the New York City Hospital, under Miss A. W. Goodrich, and holds the appointment of Superintendent of Nurses at the Washington University Training School, St. Louis.

"ABCÈS DE FIXATION."

"The influenza epidemic, generally taking the form of septic pneumonia, has been raging with unexampled fury on the Italian Front. In various places the following heroic remedy has met with a certain amount of success :—That a general inflammation sometimes cures itself by sudden local suppuration is well known ; the method of Fochier is founded upon this principle, and aims at artificially producing the necessary suppuration in the form of an abscess.

"The irritant medium employed is spirit of turpentine, of which 1 cubic centimetre is injected into the cellular tissue of the loin, thigh or leg. Should no painful reaction follow within twelve hours from the time of the first injection, another must be made at a different spot, and this may be

A HAPPY FAMILY.   KING, QUEEN AND WAR WORKERS.

A Sister on the Italian Front writes :

"Since I have been back we have been fighting a most terrible outbreak of Spanish Influenza, and our death roll has been ghastly. It seems now as if the scourge were abating slightly. Perhaps the general cheerfulness of the news has something to do with it. This medical annexe is warned to go forward, so if I get anywhere very interesting, and the censor passes it, I will send you some account. I hear that the Austrians had left behind completely installed hospitals, full of equipment and patients, but with no *personnel*, so I hope we may soon get there and be able to do something for them. I enclose a brief note of what was to me quite a new treatment—the C.C.S. doctors here rejected it as too brutal.

repeated a third or even a fourth time, though the "prognostique" is not very favourable if a second has been made without result, the probability being that in this case the patient's vitality is so much lowered by the course of the disease that no further leucocytic reaction is capable of taking place. It is, therefore, important that recourse should be had to this remedy before it is too late, though naturally from the extreme painfulness of the process, doctors are unwilling to employ it if a cure can be obtained or reasonably hoped for by ordinary means. (In the case of children pure turpentine must not be employed, but diluted with 60 per cent. of sterilised oil, it can be tolerated fairly well.)

"The result expected and desired from the turpentine injection is that within a few hours, generally six or eight, redness, swelling and intense pain appear in the whole limb. These conditions tend to localise with more or less rapidity (septic symptoms elsewhere at the same time subsiding), pus is formed and a large abscess results, which must be treated with hot fomentations, both to assist maturation and to control the pains. It must be opened, with the usual aseptic precautions, at the critical moment, just before it bursts, probably in from five to six days ; not too soon, or the full benefit will not be obtained. If, on the other hand, it appears to open prematurely of itself, and the pus begins to trickle away while the general inflammatory condition continues, a second abscess must be induced in another place.

" The pus in these abscesses smells strongly of turpentine, and is in itself aseptic, but the wound remaining after the abscess has been drained is highly susceptible of infection, and the utmost precautions must be taken to keep properly sterile dressings constantly in place ; often a most difficult matter with delirious patients for each of whom a special nurse cannot be detailed, and unavoidable secondary infection has sometimes taken place with fatal results. In favourable cases, the abscess having been satisfactorily drained and kept aseptic, begins to heal, and the whole process is over in eight or ten days. If the patient's strength can be maintained, there is then a very good chance of recovery.

" As may be imagined, this method is not very favourably regarded by the patients, who groan over, " *l'abcès du médecin. Comme si je n'avais pas assez de mal sans cela !* " If indeed they are in a condition to speak.

" If, however, life is to be saved, it is worth it."

Miss Torrance has been appointed Chief Nurse of the American Red Cross in this country in succession to Miss Carrie M. Hall, who is now in France. The headquarters are at 40, Grosvenor Gardens, S.W. 1.

ROYAL RED CROSS.

On Saturday last the King decorated the following ladies with the Royal Red Cross :—

FIRST CLASS.

Queen Alexandra's Imperial Military Nursing Service Reserve.—Sister ELIZABETH ROGERS.

Territorial Force Nursing Service.—Assistant Matron FLORENCE CARTER and Sister MILDRED OAKLEY.

Civil Nursing Service.—Matron ALICE REEVES.

SECOND CLASS.

British Red Cross Society.—Assistant Matron MABEL WOODFIN and Sister CHARLOTTE ROBERTSON.

Doughty White Unit.—Nursing Sister FLORENCE PERDUE.

Voluntary Aid Detachment.—Mrs. FRANCIS ROBERTS, Miss EDYTH TAYLOR, and Mrs. BELLA TAYLOR.

THE MILITARY MEDAL.

Miss MOYRA CAVANAGH.

HYMN FOR PEACE.

OH, God of all, within Whose guiding hands,
The issue lies of warfare and of peace,
In mercy look on these divided lands,
And bid the conflict of the Nations cease.

Oh, Prince of Peace ! Whose tender human tears
O'erflowed in pity for a world in pain ;
We need Thee now as in those far off years,
Take up Thy sceptre, Lord, and reign again !

Oh, Dove of Peace ! unfold Thy healing wing,
O'er lives forlorn, who call on Thee to bless ;
Bring each within Thine overshadowing,
And give Thy creatures of Thy loveliness.

Be Thou their strength where'er our soldiers stand,
Where'er our ships, Oh ! God, their Pilot be,
If Thou be near, by farthest sea or land,
So surely may we leave the end with Thee.
Amen, Amen.
C. B. M.

PEACE, THE SONG OF THE ANGELS.

" Peace " was the song the angels sang
When Jesus sought this Vale of tears,
And sweet the heavenly prelude rang
To calm the wondering shepherds' fears.

" Peace " was the prayer the Saviour breathed,
When from our world His steps withdrew ;
The gift He to His friends bequeathed,
With Calvary and the Cross in view.

And ye, whose souls have felt His love,
Guard day and night this rich bequest ;
The watchword of the host above—
The passport to their realms of rest.
Sigourney.

PEACE.

Turn, turn, wide sea of Peace
And flood the shore . . .
Down thou all yesterdays, and hide
My soul for evermore.

Cleanse, lave me, sea of Peace,
And may no tide
Recall thee, may no winds disturb
The depth where I would hide.

Lull, heal me, sea of Peace ;
My listening heart
Slow, slowly sinking down in thee,
Far from the world, apart,

The music of thy wave
Like some faint bell
Repeats :—then rests in thy deep bed
As lies the murmuring shell.
—From Trackless Regions,
By G. O. Warren.

Royal British Nurses' Association.

(Incorporated by Royal Charter.)

THIS SUPPLEMENT BEING THE OFFICIAL ORGAN OF THE CORPORATION.

THE CONFERENCE.

The Conference convened under the auspices of the Royal British Nurses' Association, on November 7th, at the Rooms of the Medical Society of London, 11, Chandos Street, Cavendish Square, W. 1, was extremely well attended, notwithstanding the fact that the nursing profession at the present time is working to the limit, and almost beyond the limit of its powers, in caring for our sick and wounded soldiers, and grappling with the " influenza " epidemic. The yellow chrysanthemums and beautiful autumn leaves sent by the Society for the State Registration of Trained Nurses (one of the Societies affiliated to the Association), gave a charming touch of colour to the platform.

AFTERNOON SESSION.

The disappointment of the afternoon was the announcement made from the chair by Miss M. Heather-Bigg, R.R.C., Vice-Chairman of the Association, that Princess Christian, President of the Corporation, was unavoidably prevented by medical advice from being present. She then, by command of Her Royal Highness, read the following letter :—

To the Members of the Royal British Nurses' Association and the organized Societies of Nurses affiliated to it.

It is a very great disappointment to me that circumstances over which I have no control should have arisen to prevent my presiding at your Conference to-day, a pleasure I had so much looked forward to. I had particularly wished to be with you all to-day, because I feel that the subjects before the Conference are of such real importance to each one of you, and that such a Conference must have a very far-reaching influence indeed on the development of the profession of nursing. That profession has now reached that stage, and *I congratulate you on this*, when help from outside its ranks can avail you little. If your profession

is to go forward, and hold its own amongst the foremost of those open to women, if the remuneration paid to our nurses is to be more in line with the magnificent services rendered by them to our Empire and the State, if we are to attain to the goal for which we are striving, viz., State Registration of Trained Nurses, on lines just to the interests of the Nurses and public alike, I am convinced that the effort must come from the ranks of the profession itself.

May I therefore appeal to you all to decide that the burden of organizing your profession, of protecting and promoting your interests, shall not be laid on the shoulders of the few, but that you will individually realize the powers you possess, and take a real active part, each one of you, in the management of the affairs of your profession. I feel this very strongly, and have done so for a long time.

May I take this opportunity of reminding you how much you can help by influencing your fellow nurses to join my Association, or one of the organized societies of nurses affiliated to it.

By combining in this way, and yourselves helping to bring the force of numbers behind your Royal Charter, and the powers which it gives you, there is nothing within reason that Nurses could not attain to for themselves and their great profession.

It is my deep and warm interest in Nurses and the nursing profession which has prompted me to write these lines and to speak thus frankly.

I send you all my very best wishes for a most successful Conference.

Helena,
Princess Christian,
Princess of Great Britain and Ireland,
President of the
Royal British Nurses' Association.

Miss Heather-Bigg said that before proceeding to the business of the Conference, she felt sure the members would wish to send a message in reply to Her Royal Highness' letter. She then proposed from the chair the following Resolution :—

RESOLUTION.

" That the members of the Royal British Nurses' Association and the organized Societies of Nurses affiliated to it desire to express to Her Royal Highness the Princess Christian their sorrow on learning that she is unable to preside at their Conference, and their sincere hope that she may speedily recover. Also they wish to convey to Her Royal Highness assurances of their loyalty and their deep sense of gratitude for the support which, as President of the Royal British Nurses' Association, she has given to them in their efforts to organize the nursing profession on lines which are just to the liberties of the Nurses."

This was carried by acclamation.

THE ECONOMIC POSITION OF THE TRAINED NURSE.

Miss Heather-Bigg then called on Miss Helen Pearse to present the first paper.

THE PROFESSION MUST BE SELF-SUPPORTING.

Miss Pearse said that the trained nurse of to-day is the sufferer from the " vocation " of trained nurses of thirty years ago ; at that time there were very few openings for the employment of educated women, and a woman who entered a hospital for training took no thought of proper remuneration for her work. She was supposed to be above such sordid ideas, and she therefore saddled her on-coming sisters with many struggles, and, to the hospital authorities she gave a chance to run the institution on cheap labour.

The result of this self-sacrifice was that her attempts since then to make her profession self-supporting had been (until the last year or two) systematically opposed by various authorities, the work of which had been to train nurses.

The speaker then pointed out that had the efforts of pioneers to obtain the State recognition of their profession, as advocated by Mrs. Bedford Fenwick been attained, we should not have had the present wretched economic position of nurses.

The nurse was handicapped throughout her career by the late period at which her training began, and the one-sided contract which she was asked to sign, in which the safeguards were on the side of the hospital.

She then discussed the nurse's chance of making a fortune, when fully trained, in private nursing, district nursing, or public health work, and from the statistics which she gave the likelihood seemed remote.

Referring to Public Health Work Miss Pearse said that if the trained nurse is to obtain a position of responsibility in health work she must be given a better economic position, and her long and careful training must be given its proper value.

Poor salaries made poor nurses—poor, because unable to give themselves good lodgings, food, or holidays, so essential to anyone's growth in usefulness.

The profession must be self-supporting, and be given a chance to make provision for early retirement, for one of the disabilities of nursing was the comparatively early age at which members of the profession were " too old " for further use.

If the earning life was so short, so much the more should it be well paid, and then we should be independent of appeals in the streets, and on posters, to give charity to the poor nurses ; that was not the way to repay them for their sacrifices, yea, even to the death, in the cause of freedom.

Let people learn to value the trained nurse for her devotion to duty, her carefully acquired skill, and her conscientious work, and give her a just remuneration while she could make use of it, rather than please themselves by exploiting her dependent economic position. (Applause.)

THE HOSPITAL SISTER.

Miss Jentie Paterson dealt specially with the hospital sister, viewed from an economic standpoint. She pointed out that hospital authorities realize that the nurses they appoint as Sisters should have special qualifications but there was no evidence that they were prepared to pay for such qualifications ; in fact, the remuneration specified in advertisement columns was often less than that offered for domestic servants. To fill the post of Sister the authorities aimed at choosing one whom, by reason of education and manners they termed a lady, who would prove herself capable of performing nursing duties in the most efficient and advanced manner, who would be capable of and interested in the training of probationers, realizing that their future greatly depended on her activities, and that the prestige of the hospital as a nursing centre and a training-school was in her hands.

The medical staff expected to find in charge of their wards a woman to whom they could safely depute the duty of carrying out their directions, to whose discretion they could entrust the more responsible duty of modifying treatment should the occasion arise ; they relied on her to observe and report on their cases, and, often, to help them when engaged in research work. The surgeon, when he had proved his Theatre Sister, relied on her entirely. The Sisters' responsibilities involved life and death, and the pittance they received in this country for the forethought, tact, and work involved in running one hospital department for a day, worked out at £40 a year —the average Sister's salary—at 2s. 2¼d. a day, or at £50, at 2s. 9d. a day. True she got board, lodging and uniform ; domestic servants got the two former though not always the latter. Over and over again women eminently suited for the post of Sister were forced by economic reasons to resign and try private nursing. On £40 you could not save for old age, and such a post was only comfortably tenable if the Sister possessed some private means. This should not be so.

THE CANKER AT THE ROOT.

For years the most suitable girls had passed over nursing in their choice of a career. Could we wonder, in view of the long hours, hard work, and undefined duties and standards of training ? Hospital governors in this country employed probationers more with the view of carrying out the nursing of the sick and the working of the hospital, than with the aim of training and turning out efficient nurses. The canker at the root was the exploitation of cheap labour. Economy in running public institutions was an admirable quality, but, when it was replaced by meanness, the outcome was shortage of labour and closed wards and the sick directly suffered.

SEEING RED.

Miss Paterson declared that to urge that nursing was a vocation and that, therefore, nurses objected to put pressure on employers for better conditions made her see red. She had no patience with those who claimed that nursing was a vocation and not a profession. Did the British public expect their poor to be nursed on the cheap by women with a vocation ? If a hospital could not be supported by its subscriptions, don't let it be run at the expense of the nursing staff.

HANG UP THE HALO !

Let us hang up the " halo " and realize that the aims and ideals of the nurse were not lowered because she was working for her living and fighting for a strong economic position. Our terribly low economic position to-day was due to the facts that the probationer could not afford to risk her certificate nor the Sister her post. Moreover, one had very little energy left to rebel after twelve hours' daily work, and well the employers knew it. Any sign of reform (rebellion it was called) was quickly squashed by the Matrons, who, fearful of their own positions, had missed a glorious chance of organizing and leading their nurses out of the slave market into the purer economic atmosphere enjoyed by our Colonial and American Nursing Sisters.

MATRONS DESERT RANK AND FILE.

There were exceptions, splendid ones, said Miss Paterson, turning to the chairman (an incident acclaimed by a round of applause), but it would be a long time before we could forgive those who had deserted the rank and file in their fight for better conditions and gone over to the employers' side during the present crisis. The College of Nursing Company, Ltd., were the employers. The economic position of the hospital Sister would not be improved by them ; the Company was formed when they saw a chance of the nurses improving their position at their employers' expense.

Nothing struck the Colonial nurses more than our lack of status. Perhaps the hospital Sister might be accorded a degree more than the private nurse, but we had all suffered from the patronage of the aristocratic " ward visitor," who tried to run our ward for us ; from the untrained Commandant, placed by virtue of her bank balance or birth over the trained woman working for a salary ; and last, but not least, from the association of women who plead for charity on our behalf under the name of the Nation's Fund for Nurses. One and all, we were exploited and patronised to a degree the Colonials failed to understand.

The speaker contrasted the salaries of Sisters in this country with those in our Dominions. These are, in New Zealand, for Staff Nurses and Sisters £50–£100 (where the former have an eight hours' day ; in Australia, with an eight hours day, £50–£96. Lately they have been under revision, and, at the Prince Alfred Hospital, Sydney, Sisters' salaries now range from £100–£120 ; in Canada the average is £120–£144, in one large hospital the head theatre Sister drawing £180 and all found.

These figures might make us gasp, but we could do more than gasp, we could earn the same by making a stand. The nurses had won a Royal Charter. The Conference was held under the auspices of the only nurses' society that could use the word Royal. Possessing the Charter, let them, as the Americans say, " get busy "—use it. We must strengthen the nurses' societies now affiliated under the Charter, force the Nurses' (not the Employers') Bill for State Registration through Parliament, set up an independent Nursing Council to arrange our profession and settle our salaries. Then, and not till then, could we hope to have the same professional and economic status as the nurses of the Colonies ; but we should get nothing by sitting still and letting employers of nurses arrange our affairs, rather we should soon lose the little we already have.

Miss Paterson concluded by saying that as a probationer she fought, as a Sister she fought, and she intended to go on fighting until we attain our goal. (Applause.)

THE PRIVATE NURSE.

Mrs. Ernest Collins, who spoke from the standpoint of the private nurse, said that if the scale of salaries in institutions was what it ought to be there would not be overcrowding in the ranks of private nurses, and, consequently, there would be less competition and fewer of the long and expensive intervals of waiting between cases which made private nursing work anything but the pathway to affluence which so many people believed it to be.

She thought a great deal could be done to improve the prospects of private nurses if they would loyally stand by one another. The experience of most private nurses was that there was no cohesion to strengthen their position. Each nurse was more or less a law to herself, and far too often nurses had to accept conditions as to hours on duty, the fees charged for their services, &c., simply because the nurse first put in charge of the case had established certain precedents.

By a little more co-operation they might get more definite regulations established in private nursing practice generally. Of course, well managed private nursing staffs had definite regulations which were communicated to the patient, but her experience was that there was much too great a tendency to regard these as quite elastic.

She thought certain aspects in the present position of affairs in the nursing world affected the economic position of the private nurse very seriously indeed. (Applause.)

COMPETITION FROM THE V.A.D.s.

First there was possible competition from the V.A.D.s. She alluded to this in no spirit of criticism, but asserted that professionally, the V.A.D. could not claim to be on a footing with those who had undergone years of strenuous training to qualify themselves for all branches of general nursing work. We had already heard of cases where she had come into the field to undersell the fully trained and qualified nurse. She had no wish to appear " dog in the manger-ish " in raising this point, but it was a very serious menace to the private nurse, and must be recognised and discussed. To her it always appeared the strangest thing that, though nurses seemed to be alive to the competition they might look for from the V.A.D.s, many of them were ready to turn to the V.A.D. chairman when he offered to organize them. By what strange logic they made their selection of a leader she was unable to explain, but she had never yet met a nurse who had read the Memorandum and Articles of Association or the Registration Bill promoted by the College of Nursing, Ltd. The leader they had chosen might be quite an amiable gentleman, but he was neither a doctor nor a trained nurse, and did not understand the position of the working nurses, neither did his advisers. The only means by which trained nurses could protect themselves from the partially qualified was through a *one portal* system of State Registration.

Another development which she regarded as serious for private nurses was the establishment of the so-called Nation's Fund for Nurses. It was *not* a National Fund, but a Fund to develop one particular organization, and that the newest and most untried of all—a Limited Liability Company representative of the employers of nurses and their officials.

She would not deal with the appeal, as it affected our honourable and independent position in the community, to see the streets lined with posters begging for us. Would the medical profession ever submit to have their benevolent funds financed by such methods. They were bound to undermine our status. Moreover, wherever you got a body of workers provided for by any national charity on a large scale you were bound to have depreciation in the scale of salaries of the workers. Already she knew of two cases in which the public said they approved of a national appeal for the nurses because they would require smaller fees in the future.

NATION'S FUND A DOUBLE APPEAL.

This aspect was the more dangerous because the appeal of the Nation's Fund was a double one, and there was no indication as to what proportion of the money collected was to be used for benevolence, and what for equipment, buildings, and travelling expenses for the College of Nursing, Ltd. She was not against benevolent funds for nurses, but she considered when any appeal for benevolence was launched its precise purposes should be clearly stated, it should be strictly limited to the probable needs of the profession, and it should be promoted with some degree of dignified reserve ; otherwise it was bound to have an effect upon the economic position and status of the independent working nurses.

PRIVATE NURSING AND THE HOSPITAL SCHOOLS.

Another difficulty nurses must be alive to was the growing tendency of hospitals to organize private nursing staffs of their own—a more serious thing than many people realized. There was not the slightest doubt that a very large proportion of private nursing practice would become more and more the monopoly of the hospital schools, and the sooner the nurses woke up to these dangers and came together to protect their own professional interests the better it would be for them. Unless private nurses took a very active interest in their own professional affairs there were serious times before them. She would like to see some informal conferences between private nurses arranged by the Association, and some scheme evolved whereby their interests and independent practice might be more protected. They should combine and use their Charter, use their organized societies, use their *professional* press, and use their own brains to protect their own interests. (Applause.)

DISCUSSION.

The CHAIRMAN then invited discussion, when MISS BEATRICE KENT inquired why the nurses were so full of fear. The rank-and-file were afraid of the Matrons, and the majority of the Matrons afraid of their committees.

Nurses had been coerced into joining the College by Matrons, who handed them their certificates with one hand and an application form for membership of the College with the other, and the nurses were afraid of losing posts if they did not accede. Why this lack of courage? The President, Princess Christian, had told them, in her letter read by the Chairman, that there was nothing within reason which nurses could not attain to, for themselves and their great profession.

AN EPIDEMIC OF FEAR.

The epidemic of fear was spreading at a most alarming rate. It vitiated character and stultified ideals. They must stand for higher educational standards and a higher appreciation of corporate responsibility. She appealed to those who were not members of the Association to join it forthwith. Was it right to let a small group of their colleagues work year in, year out, while they stood aside, whether from apathy or craven fear?

MRS. GLOVER said one reason why nurses were afraid was that they feared they would not get testimonials if they did not conform to the wishes of the Matrons.

Mr . Bedford Fenwick pointed out that it was the nurses' own fault that their economic conditions were so unsatisfactory. They had had a Royal Charter since 1893 and had made very little use of it. She supported the contention of the previous speakers that they must co-operate if they hoped to manage their own affairs and raise their status. Nurses needed a wider outlook; in the past they had been too genteel for a trade union, and had not shown sufficient courage for a strong professional union. They should make it impossible for their employers to intimidate them. She advised the nurses to go away from the Conference and rebel against wrong.

SOME PHASES OF MODERN NURSING.

The second part of the Afternoon Session was devoted to the consideration of " Some Phases of Modern Nursing," dealt with by Miss Marsters, Miss Sinzininex, A.R.R.C., and Miss K. Atherton It is proposed to report this next week, and to devote the rest of the available space to the Evening Session.

At the conclusion of the Session tea was served, and a very enjoyable half-hour spent.

EVENING SESSION.
THE REGISTRATION BILLS.

The Differences between the Two Nurses' Registration Bills, and Why the Royal British Nurses' Association does not agree with the Bill of the College of Nursing, Ltd.

At the Evening Session the chair was taken by Mr. Herbert J. Paterson, F.R.C.S., Medical Hon. Secretary, Royal British Nurses' Association, and Hon. Treasurer of the Central Committee for the State Registration of Trained Nurses, and there was a crowded meeting of Matrons and nurses. The following members of the Council of the College of Nursing, Ltd., were present:—Professor Glaister, Miss Sidney Browne, Miss Lloyd Still, Miss Hogg, Miss Cox-Davies, and Miss Barton, Miss Rundle, and Miss Cowlin, Secretaries.

The CHAIRMAN said that in the afternoon they had considered the economic position of the trained nurse. This was closely bound up with a just Registration Bill, and a subject on which much light was needed. He hoped there would be a good discussion.

The first speaker was LIEUT.-COLONEL GOODALL, M.D., Hon. Medical Secretary of the Central Committee, who began by saying that they might wonder why a man should address a meeting concerned chiefly with women's affairs. But the professions of Medicine and Nursing were intimately bound up. He would leave Mrs. Fenwick to deal with the Memorandum and Articles of Association of the College, as she was more thoroughly acquainted with them than he was.

In a lucid and logical speech Colonel Goodall then explained why any Act for the Registration of Nurses must concern the Medical Profession, and said that the British Medical Association, which included half the medical practitioners in the country, had taken great interest in the Bill, and from the beginning had furthered endeavours to get an Act of Parliament.

DIFFERENCES IN BILLS.

Contrasting the two Bills Colonel Goodall explained that the Central Committee's Bill had been in existence for nine years, and was promoted conjointly by a number of Societies. Previous to 1910 there had been two or three Bills before Parliament, and the supporters of Registration were faced by the position that the authorities were of opinion that they should decide which Bill they wished to have. Consequently the Central Committee was formed, a lot of trouble was taken, delegates from England, Scotland, and Ireland met in conference and adopted a Bill, which had been varied from time to time to meet the varying situation.

At a later date the College of Nursing, Ltd., was formed. In the first instance it was not eager to promote State Registration, but when it found it would get no large support unless it did so, it promoted a Bill. Communications had taken place between the Central Committee and the Council of the College of Nursing, Ltd., in an endeavour to get a joint Bill, but these negotiations had not led to agreement.

There were several important points to which the Central Committee took exception, the first being that the College of Nursing made provision that the College, without the word " limited," should be included in the Bill. The College was a limited liability company, and it might be very desirable for it to drop the word " limited," but there were other ways by which this might be effected. The Central Committee objected to its being dealt with in the way proposed. The General Nursing Council set up under the Act was to administer it, and it was undesirable that any other body should be included. The General Medical Council might as well have incorporated the College of Physicians. There was no reason why any particular body should be mentioned in the Bill. He did not know why the College wished to be put in. If they joined with the Central Committee and supported its Bill they would have no difficulty in getting rid of the word " limited." The Central Committee recognized the useful function of the College as an educational body.

In regard to the incorporation of the Memorandum and Articles of Association in the Bill, the Central Committee most strenuously objected. It was not in the interest of the nurses. If the College was recognized in the Bill and received the approval of Parliament the Memorandum would have the force of an Act of Parliament behind it.

Colonel Goodall then dealt with the setting up of the General Nursing Council.

Under the Central Committee's Bill the First General Nursing Council was differently constituted to subsequent Councils, and it was charged with the most important duty of framing the Rules and Regulations which the nurses would have to obey. The College of Nursing had a different arrangement. It proposed to appoint certain persons to form a Provisional Council, and that they should forthwith prepare and present to the Privy Council the Rules to be made for setting up the General Nursing Council. The Central Committee thought that would be done in too much of a hurry. The Electorate in that case would be formed of members of the College. There should be a longer time from the setting up of the First Council for the formation of the Register.

In regard to Supplementary Registers the Central Committee only provided for those of male and mental nurses. How many the College proposed to set up was not known. But the provision in the College Bill in regard to such registers was a blow against the one-portal system, which was the chief point of the Central Committee's Bill. Supplementary Registers opened back doors and side doors to the nursing profession. (Applause.)

These were points which would very seriously affect the working of the Act. The Central Committee wanted the registered nurses to have control of their own affairs.

The CHAIRMAN then called on Mrs. Bedford Fenwick to address the meeting.

MRS. FENWICK'S EIGHT POINTS.

Mrs. Bedford Fenwick said Colonel Goodall suggested that she should refer to the Memorandum and Articles of Association of the College of Nursing, Ltd.

Briefly in 1905 a scheme for Promoting the Higher Education and Training of Nurses was launched by the officials of Guy's Hospital, and an application made for its incorporation by the Board of Trade without the word "Limited." This scheme included clauses for the registration of nurses, and was opposed by the British Medical Association, and the Royal British Nurses' Association, and the Society for State Registration (which had Nurses' Registration Bills before Parliament), and other organized societies of nurses in England, Scotland, and Ireland. Indeed, when the objectors appeared before the Board of Trade the pile of documents in opposition were over a foot high.

The application was not granted, but its consideration deferred " until the Bills now before Parliament for the Registration of Nurses have been disposed of." No more was heard of the project until 1915, when the scheme for the promotion of the College of Nursing, Ltd., was proposed by the Chairman of the Red Cross Society, upon the suggestion of the same people, notably Sir Cooper Perry, Medical Superintendent, and Miss Swift, late Matron Guy's Hospital. Comparison of the two Constitutions showed that they were almost identical.

This scheme in 1915 for the control of the nursing profession was not addressed to it, but to the Chairmen and Governors of hospitals, and to Poor Law Guardians, and one of its proposals was the formation of a Consultative Board, representa-

tive of the interests of employers, which, if everyone invited had responded to the invitation, might have consisted of some 2,000 lay persons.

The proposition was that Registration of Nurses should be carried out by a voluntary body, and it was astounding that such a recommendation, substituting a voluntary scheme for legal status, should have been supported by professional men and women. During the many years in which independent trained nurses had been advocating and working for State Registration in this country, many of our overseas Dominion Governments had effected such legislation, and by 1915 forty-two States in America had passed Nurses' Registration Acts. We in this country had been working and paying for this reform for twenty years, and it was an outrage to the intelligence of the trained nurses in this country to attempt to offer them a voluntary instead of a legal system of registration.

When, however, the promoters of the College found that they would get little support unless they advocated State Registration, they adopted that principle, and had these anti-registrationists been really converted to the principle, and desirous of supporting self-government for nurses, they would have approached the Central Committee, which had already drafted a Bill, upon which much conscientious expert thought had been expended, but they did no such thing, but themselves drafted a Bill—a mere skeleton of legislation, an action lacking both in courtesy and consideration towards the organized members of the nursing profession; since which time there had been seven successive drafts of that ineffective Bill, in which principles of good government inserted in one had been eliminated from the next!

There were certain fundamental principles for which the Central Committee stood firm throughout subsequent negotiations, and which we still demanded should be incorporated in any Bill to which we could give our support.

THE EIGHT POINTS.

Mrs. Fenwick said we had heard a great deal lately of the fourteen points. There were eight points in connection with the differences in the two Bills drafted by the Central Committee and the College, to which she wished to briefly allude.

AN INDEPENDENT GOVERNING BODY.

1. The incorporation of a lay Company (the College of Nursing), as proposed in its Bill. Independence of outside influence, in any Statutory Authority set up by Parliament to govern the nursing profession, was essential. The medical colleges were not incorporated in the Medical Acts which provided for the Registration of members of the medical profession, nor did these Colleges attempt to enforce discipline, or define educational standards, throughout the medical profession. That was the function of the General Medical Council—an independent Governing Body. Again the great public voice of the medical profession was expressed through the British Medical Association. The nurses could not do better than follow the policy of the inter-dependent profession

of medicine, and the Bill of the Central Committee accordingly provided for an Independent Governing Body. (Applause.) It was a very dangerous provision that the Constitution of the College should be incorporated in the Bill. The College Constitution, as defined in its Memorandum and Articles of Association, was a very drastic one, and had been turned down by a concensus of medical and nursing opinion in 1905. The powers over nurses claimed by the College and incorporated in its Constitution proved that those who drafted it were not fit to govern the nursing profession. It not only took power for the Council to remove a nurse's name from the register without power of appeal—(Shame)—but whilst posing as a Collegiate Body had actually taken power *not* to grant Diplomas! So terrified were the promoters of this scheme of giving nurses honourable professional status that they had actually taken power to stultify their educational pretensions!

THE DANGER OF SUPPLEMENTARY REGISTERS.

2. The College had widely advertised its adoption of the principle of the One Portal system, or entry by equal training and examination to the General Register; while in recent drafts of its Bill it had made provision to institute as many Supplementary Registers (presumably of specialists) as it chose, thus opening many doors to semi-trained persons, a back stairs cut to registration which would inevitably depreciate the General Register, and greatly confuse the public.

Moreover, these Supplementary Registers constituted a grave injustice to the women who would be registered as specialists, and had been instituted to placate institutions, such as children's hospitals, fever hospitals, &c. Nurses so trained had been excluded from membership of the Nursing Services of the Crown during the war, and could only nurse our sick and wounded in a subsidiary position, usually under an untrained Commandant. (Shame.) These Supplementary Registers were a sop to cheap labour. What right had the College to induce nurses to join its ranks upon the distinct provision that it stood for the One Portal system, and then to open the door to inefficient and partially trained nurses, who might include V.A.D.'s?

The Central Committee's Bill provided for a statesmanlike system of reciprocity of training, so that special clinical experience could be included in varied curricula.

PREFERENTIAL TREATMENT ON THE FIRST REGISTER.

3. The College Bill provided for the inclusion of all nurses on its Register on the State Register, without discrimination or further fee. This pledge had been made to its nurse members by the College Council. It had no right to make such a promise, and no power to enforce it. It was pledging Parliament on a financial arrangement—what the registration fee should be—a right on which the House of Commons was exceedingly tenacious. It had recently snubbed the House of Lords and held up the Midwives Act Amendment Bill on a much less serious violation of its financial supremacy.

But why were nurses registered by the College Company to have precedence of those on the Register of the Royal Chartered Corporation—or on any other list of nurses? Nothing could be more unjust. The College was attempting to make a corner of registration for those nurses who had paid it a guinea.

The Central Committee's Bill provided for a three years' term of grace, during which time all nurses would have the right to register, under certain defined conditions; and it was not likely that Parliament would permit preferential treatment for a few nurses to the detriment of those who objected to the College Constitution and declined to subscribe to it.

NUMBER OF GENERAL NURSING COUNCIL MUST BE DEFINED.

4. Then in the Constitution of the General Nursing Council the numbers of the nominees of the various bodies it was proposed should be represented were not defined. The number should be stated in each case. This was done in the Central Committee's Bill.

IMMEDIATE DISSOLUTION OF PROVISIONAL COUNCIL.

5. Provision was made in the College Bill for the dissolution " forthwith " of the Provisional Council set up under the Act, on which the trained nurses' societies were represented, immediately it had prepared for the Privy Council the Rules regulating the Constitution of the General Nursing Council, so that all the Provisional Council had to do was to commit suicide. It would have no time to make the Rules and Regulations to which the nurses had to conform, or in which to establish an *independent constituency* of registered nurses to elect the Council empowered with this responsibility. The scheme was to adopt the College Register, and forthwith constitute its members the electorate for the whole Nursing Profession. To this suggestion the Central Committee took strong exception. Under the Central Committee's Bill the First Council would have a two years' term of office, as it would take quite that time to frame Rules and form a representative and independent electorate.

NO CONTROL BY NURSE-TRAINING SCHOOLS.

6. It was difficult to imagine that any body of British people would deliberately define such a system as that incorporated in the College Bill, but we were not concerned with motives, but with the letter of the law. We claimed the right of self-determination and self-government when trained and registered, and were not going to submit to be controlled by the Nurse Training Schools, governed by laymen and their officials, which had no responsibility for trained nurses unless in their employment.

LOCAL BOARDS. THE VILLAGE PUMP.

7. The College had introduced into its Bill provision for the establishment of Local Boards in various parts of the United Kingdom, other than Boards national in character in England and

Wales, Scotland and Ireland, as provided in the Central Committee's Bill, a form of legislation calculated to glorify the village pump. Parochialism was very undesirable in this connection, and might interfere with the nurses' personal liberty and economic independence.

RECIPROCAL TRAINING.

8. Further, there was no provision for reciprocal training to qualify for registration in the College Bill, by means of which the valuable clinical material in well-managed special hospitals could be co-ordinated and utilised, and nurses qualified for a wide field of professional usefulness, as in the Central Committee's Bill.

CONCLUDING REMARKS.

Mrs. Fenwick said that it was not reasonable to expect persons such as the members of the Central Committee, who had spent so much time in carefully considering these questions, to conscientiously support a Bill which omitted the fundamental principles which they considered vital.

The Central Committee, after a careful comparison of its own Bill and that of the College of Nursing, Ltd., had come to the conclusion that its own Bill was the better Bill, and had therefore formally invited the Council of the College of Nursing to support it, and help to get it through Parliament. (Applause.)

CLEAN-CUT PRINCIPLES.

The third speaker was MISS GLADYS LE GEYT, a member of the Executive Committee of the Society for the State Registration of Trained Nurses, who said that the members of the Royal British Nurses' Association had in their keeping the honour of their profession, and powers sufficient to annihilate any attempt to force unjust legislation upon them. We needed, to achieve our purpose :—(1) An ever-increasing membership; (2) clean-cut principles; and (3) a policy embodying the same. We could truthfully say we possessed these essentials, but our concern at the moment was to prove the soundness of our policy.

The Royal British Nurses' Association staunchly supported the principle of State Registration through its delegates on the Central Committee, and had given valuable assistance during the past eight years in drawing up and revising its Nurses' Registration Bill, which was ready for presentation to Parliament at the earliest opportunity.

She had by her a precious, thumb-marked copy of the Bill, and could vouch that not a paragraph of its contents had been hastily drawn up, or any Clause inserted without serious thought and judgment. Here also was her copy of the seventh draft of the Bill for Registration drawn up by the College of Nursing, Ltd., all crisp and fresh from the printer, and its contents ill devised and indiscriminately strung together, alien to the fundamental reasons which underlie our long-drawn-out struggle for registration, both for the public who employ trained nurses and the safeguarding of our own interests.

Miss Le Geyt then supported the demand of the Central Committee for an Independent Governing Body, untrammelled by any connection with the Memorandum and Articles of Association of the College of Nursing, Ltd., or any other body. She said that the College offered Registration, without reserve, to every name on the Company's Books at the passing of the Act. The Register which we meant to acknowledge was one that would be formed after the passing of the Act, and in accordance with that Act. There should be no side entrance or back doors into the Nursing Profession, but the rights of all nurses eligible for registration should be equal.

She emphasised the provision in the College Bill that the first General Register under the Act should include, without further fee, the registered members of the College of Nursing, Ltd. This opened up an unpleasant vista for the rest of us, who, according to Clause 10 of the same Bill, would have to pay the General Nursing Council " such fee as may be prescribed by the Rules." We might therefore be expected to pay such sums as would adequately cover the expenses of the Register, while members of the College Company were to have the right to registration without further fee. What fair dealing could we look for at the hands of the College Council after such a Clause?

THE COLOSSAL FLAW.

From the trained nurse's point of view the colossal flaw in the College Bill was the loophole left for the introduction of Supplementary Registers, other than those of male and mental nurses; such a Clause would literally undo all the good that the title of " Registered Nurse " was to confer, and leave the public in as great a dilemma as to what constitutes a trained nurse as at the present time, and, by covering the title " Registered Nurse," would create appalling possibilities for fraudulent practice in nursing.

It was not sufficient to think of Registration from the academic and institutional standpoint only. We must bear in mind the relations in which we stood, and the duty we owed to the public who employed us, generally at a time of great crisis to themselves.

After touching on the question of the Provisional Council, and drawing attention to a new Clause in the College Bill in relation to the registration of deaths, Miss Le Geyt concluded : " I would venture to suggest to the supporters of the College that they intimate to their Council that they waste no more time drafting Registration Bills, but give proof of their sincerity by uniting with all speed in supporting the Registration Bill which is promoted by the Central Committee for the State Registration of Nurses." (Applause.)

DISCUSSION.

The CHAIRMAN then invited discussion, when PROFESSOR GLAISTER, of Glasgow, a member of the Council of the College of Nursing, Ltd., said he had been associated with Mrs. Bedford Fenwick in drafting the Central Committee's Bill, and had spent a great deal of time in North Britain in promoting the State Registration of Nurses. But we got no nearer while we were engaging ourselves in minor disputes. He was out for State Registration.

Everyone would wish to be quite fair. The College Bill had undergone evolution; the Central Committee's Bill had also been amended. The Clause criticised by the previous speaker, regarding the notification of death, followed the lead of the Medical Acts, and had been adopted by the Central Committee.

In regard to the Supplementary Registers, he was the last person in the world to try to admit people by side doors. The Royal College of Nursing [*not* Royal, the meeting reminded him] did not propose to do more than take powers to establish Supplementary Registers.

HOLD HATS WHILE THE FUR FLIES.

In regard to the duties of the Provisional Council, Professor Glaister did not consider these afforded ground for differences, but if so, then someone must " hold hats while the fur flies."

As to the constitution of the General Nursing Council, Professor Glaister asserted that under the College Bill, as well as under the Central Committee's Bill, control would be in the hands of the nurses. There were only " little differences " between the two Bills.

NO POWER OF APPEAL.

MISS JENTIE PATERSON drew attention to the power given in the Memorandum of the College to remove a nurse's name from its Register without opportunity of appeal.

This was defended by PROFESSOR GLAISTER, who said, however, that Clause V (3) of the College Bill was as clear as daylight. Nothing in the Memorandum and Articles of Association inconsistent with the Act could remain in force.

MRS. SHERLIKER, MISS KENT, MRS. GIBSON, MRS. LAWSON, and others also took part in the discussion, the last-mentioned remarking that, with the College, education came first and registration second.

PROFESSOR GLAISTER inquired: " Why fight about unimportant details ? "

MRS. BEDFORD FENWICK : " We are standing for fundamental principles."

The discussion then ceased, and the CHAIRMAN invited the speakers to reply.

COLONEL GOODALL said that the Central Committee desired a proper State Registration Bill. In the Supplementary Registers the College took powers to open the doors to all sorts of people.

They had not heard why they should have the College in the Bill, but one of its supporters had acknowledged that it placed registration second and education first. The organization of nursing education should be carried out by the State, by an authority appointed by the State.

The Clause providing for the framing of the Rules and Regulations was one of the most important in the Bill. They were for the protection of the nurses, and they should have a share in framing them.

MISS COX-DAVIES asked leave to suggest that the College did not put education first and registration second, but hand in hand.

NO BLANK CHEQUES.

In closing the meeting the CHAIRMAN said they were much indebted to the speakers, and expressed the opinion that there was too much permissive legislation in the College Bill. It wanted a blank cheque. The Central Committee desired regulations laid down definitely.

The Conference concluded with votes of thanks to the Chairman and speakers.

(Signed) ISABEL MACDONALD,
Secretary to the Corporation.

THE CENTRAL COMMITTEE AND THE COLLEGE OF NURSING, LTD.

As reported, a correspondence has recently taken place between the College of Nursing, Ltd., and the Central Committee for the State Registration of Nurses. Naturally the officials of the Central Committee consider such a correspondence confidential, until the reply from the College has been placed before its Executive Committee.

The ethical standards of business apparently differ in the opinion of the College officials, as the hon. officers of the Central Committee have been informed by the Secretary of the College that " by the instruction of the Chairman (Hon. Sir Arthur Stanley, M.P.), this correspondence has been sent for publication to the Nursing Press this week " !

It will, of course, not appear in THE BRITISH JOURNAL OF NURSING until the Executive Committee of the Central Committee has authorised its publication.

Further comment is superfluous !

THE IRISH NURSES' ASSOCIATION.

A few of Miss Ramsden's friends gave a farewell supper to her at 34, St. Stephen's Green, Dublin, on Friday last week. Owing to the epidemic of Influenza, many of her friends were unable to be present, but all greatly regret her departure from Dublin. A quiet but pleasant evening was spent, and only " Au Revoir " was said, as Miss Ramsden has promised to come back often, and will try to time her visits so that she may sometimes attend the meetings of the various Nursing Societies of which she will remain a member. Miss Ramsden has received very handsome gifts from the Nursing Staff (past and present), and also from the past and present Masters of the Rotunda Hospital. The Governors have also generously recognised her devoted work for the Hospital and midwifery and maternity schools during the 27 years of service.

The British Journal of Nursing.

APPOINTMENTS.

MATRON AND LADY SUPERINTENDENT.

Charing Cross Hospital, W.C.—Miss Florence Tice has been appointed Matron. She was trained at St. Bartholomew's Hospital, and subsequently held the position of Sister at University College Hospital. Since 1905 she has been Matron of the Samaritan Free Hospital, in the Marylebone Road, London.

Edith Cavell Home of Rest for Nurses, Winton House, Church Road, Richmond.—Miss Margaret Carruthers has been appointed Lady Superintendent. She was trained at the Cumberland Infirmary, Carlisle, and has held the positions of Sister at the General Infirmary, Macclesfield; Sister and Home Sister at the Manchester Children's Hospital, Pendlebury; and Matron for fourteen and a half years at the Kensington Dispensary and Children's Hospital.

Edith Cavell Home of Rest for Nurses, Haslemere.—Miss Julia Hurlston has been appointed Lady Superintendent. She was trained at St. Bartholomew's Hospital, London, and has held the positions of Sister at St. Peter's Hospital, the Victoria Hospital for Children, London; has had experience of Private Nursing as a member of the Registered Nurses' Society, London, and in Egypt. Sister-in-Charge, Muirfield House, Gullane, attached to the Royal Hospital for Sick Children, Edinburgh, and Matron of Military Auxiliary Hospitals since 1915.

Rotunda Hospital, Dublin.—Miss Winifred A. Todd has been appointed Matron and Lady Superintendent. She was trained at Guy's Hospital, London, and at the Rotunda Hospital, Dublin, and holds the certificates of Guy's Hospital, the Central Midwives Board, and the Incorporated Society of Trained Masseuses. Miss Todd has had a wide and varied experience of nursing. She has been temporary Sister at the Royal General Hospital, Newport, Mon., Ward Sister and Assistant Matron at the Rotunda Hospital. In 1914 she went to France as a member of the French Flag Nursing Corps, from 1915–16 she was on the Reserve of Q.A.I.M.N.S., and has been Superintendent of the Women's Legion attached to the Army Service Corps.

Cottage Hospital, Ballymena, Co. Antrim.—Miss Ethel McMath has been appointed Matron. She was trained at the Royal Victoria Hospital, Belfast, and has been Sister at the Fitzroy Private Hospital and at the Ulster Volunteer Hospital in the same city.

QUEEN VICTORIA'S JUBILEE INSTITUTE

TRANSFERS AND APPOINTMENTS.

Miss Alice Hulme is appointed to Todmorden as Senior Nurse; Miss Edith E. Bitten, to Manchester (Ardwick); Miss Alice M. M. Corns, to Sale; Miss Olive Carpenter, to Littleborough; Miss Aukje Saüerhoff, to Littleborough; Miss Muriel Trayner, to Wilmslow.

PRESENTATION TO MISS ROW.

FORMER MATRON OF EAST LONDON HOSPITAL FOR CHILDREN, SHADWELL.

It was peculiarly fitting that the Board Room at the East London Hospital for Children, Shadwell, which is decorated with many mural tablets commemorating the good services and munificent acts of various deceased hon. officers of the Board of Management, should have been chosen as the scene of a very interesting little ceremony on Wednesday, November 6th. The room was further adorned with flowers and ferns to do honour to the occasion. Miss Adelaide Row has lately retired from the post of Matron of the hospital, which she had held for thirty-five years. It was to give practical proof of the esteem in which she is held and of appreciation of her splendid services that a meeting was called in order to make the presentation. A handsome sum of money was collected among her many friends, the bulk of which was invested in War Bonds, and the surplus presented to her in the form of a cheque. Mr. Machin, Chairman of the Board, made the following graceful tribute :—

" Miss Row,—In offering you this gift, I want to ask you to accept it as a token of the very high esteem in which you are held through your thirty-five years' devoted service in the most noble profession any lady can adopt. You have earned the unbounded gratitude of the whole neighbourhood. We heartily appreciate your generous services while living in one of the poorest districts in London.

" I trust you may be spared for many years to enjoy the health you so richly deserve."

Miss Row, in replying, said it was impossible for her to express what she really felt, but she was extremely touched by the kind words uttered by the Chairman. She added that she had thoroughly enjoyed her work in the Children's Hospital, and modestly disclaimed any right to the praise so kindly expressed. She spoke warmly of the friends she had made in that time, many of whom were present; also many of her nurses. The meeting then terminated, and the guests were hospitably entertained to tea.

WEDDING BELLS.

On November 9th, at Garforth Church, near Leeds, Lieutenant-Surgeon Hamilton, Royal Naval Auxiliary Hospital, Gravesend, was married to Sister A. Howson. The bride was trained at Beckett Street Infirmary, Leeds, and subsequently became Staff Nurse and Sister. On leaving her training school Sister Howson was presented by the Matron with a silver tea service with the heartiest and best wishes from the Infirmary staff for future happiness. Illness on the staff unfortunately prevented the Matron and some of the Sisters attending the ceremony at Garforth.

ASSOCIATION OF NURSING SUPER-INTENDENTS OF INDIA.

Miss M. Bonsor, Matron of the Indian War Hospitals in Karachi, has been elected President of the Association of Nursing Superintendents of India. Miss Bonsor is one of the earliest members of the Trained Nurses' Association of India, and at one time acted as its Secretary.

The Nursing Journal of India announces the appointment, and in offering Miss Bonsor a warm welcome, publishes a charming picture of her, and expresses the opinion that she will assist the growing process of the Associations.

These professional Associations are affiliated to the International Council of Nurses, and have always been represented by delegates at the Triennial Meetings, who have contributed to their professional value and prestige.

OUTSIDE THE GATES.

On Wednesday, November 6th, the Bill making women eligible to be Members of Parliament passed its third reading in the House of Commons amidst cheers Attempts to confine it to women over thirty, to enlarge it so that women may sit in the House of Lords, or to prevent a Peeress from sitting in the Commons were negatived.

TRUE TALES WITH A MORAL.

Doctor : Well, Nurse, now you have a vote I suppose you will be running a woman candidate for Parliament.

Nurse: Quite the reverse. No more bossing by women for me. I have learned my lesson under the untrained commandant. Never again !

COMING EVENTS.

November 21st.—Royal British Nurses' Association. Lecture, " Ancient Egypt," illustrated by lantern slides, by Miss Murray, Assistant to Professor Flinders Petrie, Botanical Theatre, University College, Gower Street. W.C. *Chair,* Mrs. Latter. 2.45 p.m. After Lecture, personally-conducted tour of Egyptology Department. The collection, which is said to be second to none in the world, comprises the concrete remains of the entire civilisation, from the finest examples of art, down to the simplest domestic utensils. The lecture will be open to all nurses.

November 23rd.—National Union of Trained Nurses. Meeting to discuss the proposed Ministry of Health. Speakers : Dr. Saleeby and Miss H. L. Pearse. Chair, the Rev. H. R. L. Sheppard, 3, Vere Street, Oxford Street, W. 2.30 p.m.

November 29th.—Annual Meeting of the Grand Council of the National Council of Trained Nurses of Great Britain and Ireland, 431, Oxford Street, London, W. 4 p.m.

LETTERS TO THE EDITOR.

Whilst cordially inviting communications upon all subjects for these columns, we wish it to be distinctly understood that we do not IN ANY WAY *hold ourselves responsible for the opinions expressed by our correspondents.*

OPEN CONFESSION GOOD FOR THE SOUL

To the Editor of THE BRITISH JOURNAL OF NURSING.

MADAM,—I was at the meeting of the R.B.N.A. on Thursday, and was most interested in all that was discussed. This is the first time I have ever heard the Bills discussed at an open meeting. Perhaps it was unfortunate that the only attempt to explain the College Bill was that of Professor Glaister ; he evidently had a long paper to read and quite rightly could not expect the same time as the original speakers, but I think that the College—in the interests of the nurses—should arrange with your Association to have a meeting at which *each* side would *read* papers. I was disappointed that the Army Matrons present, whom I understand are College members, did not air their views, but left it to " the man from Scotland." Surely Englishwomen with a vote should not require to receive aid from Scotland to uphold and explain the aims of the Company they have joined and which they urge their nurses to join. I myself am a Scotchwoman and I wondered when Professor Glaister pleaded for a longer hearing because he had come from Scotland, whether, like myself, he had travelled third at his own expense, or first class on the guineas of the nurses. Personally, I have not joined the College, the Scottish Nurses' Association, or the Royal British Nurses' Association — being Scotch I look before I leap—but I have very little doubt since the meeting into which camp one ought to leap— the one that can afford to hold an *open* meeting.

I am, yours truly,
GLASGOW BRED AND BORN.

KERNELS FROM CORRESPONDENCE.

Huddersfield Nurse.—Can you tell me if a paid suffrage lecturer, who is now going about lecturing on the Nation's Fund for Nurses, is also paid for this job ?

[We do not know, but strongly object to political lecturers—actors and actresses, &c.—presuming to dictate to professional nurses about their economic affairs of which they know nothing. Enquire of Lady Cowdray, 16, Carlton House Terrace, as the prime mover in this objectionable campaign.—ED.]

OUR PRIZE COMPETITION.

QUESTIONS.

November 23rd.—What precautions would you take if nursing a case of septic pneumonia following influenza ?

November 30th. — What do you know of " mustard gas " burns and their treatment ?

The Midwife.

A TEXT-BOOK FOR MIDWIVES.

The ",Text Book for Midwives," by Dr. J. S. Fairbairn, F.R.C.P. (Lond.), first pub'ished in 1914, met with the reception it deserved ; and a second edition has now been published by the Joint Committee of Henry Frowde and Hodder & Stoughton, at the Oxford Press Warehouse, Falcon Square, London, E.C., price 20s. net. In spite of the war and the cost and difficulty of production, the edition is a sumptuous one, beautifully printed on paper which is both thick and fine, and with three plates and 113 illustrations—five of which are in colour.

Dr. Fairbairn needs no introduction to midwives. As physician and lecturer to midwives at the General Lying-in Hospital, York Road, S.E., many owe much to his teaching ; and he is also an examiner to the Central Midwives Board.

He tells us in his preface to the first edition that his reasons for adding another to the many text books from which the midwife can make her choice are twofold. First, that the book has special characteristics of its own ; and second, that what special features it may possess represent an experience of the needs and aspirations of midwives acquired by over twelve years' association with them as "teacher, examiner, post graduate lecturer and medical colleague." He says further, "This text book contains more than has hitherto been considered necessary for midwives and is open to the criticism of going beyond what is required by them and of them. On this score, however, those who know the more advanced school of practising midwives will make no demur. That school is possessed with an insatiable thirst for knowledge, and is rarely content with what has hitherto been given it in books written solely for midwives. Formal medical books are in constant use, and my hope is that the scope of this book has been made wide enough to render the purchase of such unnecessary.

"There is, however, another and a better justification for a comprehensive book. A more educated class is now coming forward to qualify as midwives. . . . This book is my contribution towards meeting the legitimate aspirations of the midwife for a higher professional education."

In the second edition the text has been carefully revised in accordance with the changes in the Rules of the Central Midwives Board, and points of difficulty in the chapters on the Physiology of Labour and on Delayed Labour have been cleared up. The most important addition is a fresh chapter on Antenatal Care, which has been added in view of the part the midwife may be called on to take in schemes for Maternity and Child Welfare.

THE CARE OF THE PREGNANT WOMAN. ANTE-NATAL HYGIENE AND TREATMENT.

We agree with the author that " ' antenatal ' and ' prenatal ' as applied to the pregnant woman are not satisfactory terms as they mean ' before birth,' and suggest an application to the child only." The Hygiene of Pregnancy would probably be a more exact description. Antenatal, however, is the term in general use.

" Antenatal care involves the close observation of the pregnant woman up to the birth of her child, and aims at keeping her in health in body and mind, preserving the pregnancy to term, avoiding preventable difficulties and complications in labour, and thus diminishing the maternal and infantile mortality at childbirth. Antenatal treatment is therefore almost entirely preventive.

"What part the midwife may be called on to play in this crusade is not easily determined, owing to the divergent views held as to what and how much antenatal care should mean, and to the differences in the provision made for it in different localities. Some would magnify it so far as to have the notification of pregnancy made compulsory, as if it was an infectious disease and every pregnant woman under continuous medical supervision, but probably between this extreme and the other of entirely neglecting it, some intermediate course will be taken till time and experience of its results have decided its true worth and importance as a branch of preventive medicine.

" As the prevention of abortion is so large a factor in antenatal work, and as abortion is most frequent in the early months of pregnancy, it is evident that if success is to be obtained, the pregnant woman must come early under observation. Patients should be encouraged to engage their midwife and make arrangements for their confinement as soon as they know, or even suspect that they are pregnant. The loss of population from the high abortion-rate is quite as great as from the high infant mortality, and to lower it, and to diminish the invalidism and incapacity following on neglected abortions, it is essential that the midwife should use her influence to induce her patients to report their pregnancy early."

Again, " overcrowding, slum life, and bad housing conditions in the big towns are more than anything else the cause of the high infant mortality rate, and therefore all efforts to combat it, whether antenatal, natal, or postnatal are largely a social problem."

A chapter is devoted to venereal disease, a subject upon which it is very essential the midwife should be informed.

The book is one which should be in the library of every training school for midwives, and individual midwives who purchase it will be well recompensed for the outlay.

THE BRITISH JOURNAL OF NURSING

WITH WHICH IS INCORPORATED

THE NURSING RECORD

EDITED BY MRS BEDFORD FENWICK

No. 1,599.   SATURDAY, NOVEMBER 23, 1918.   Vol. LXI

EDITORIAL.

THE LIBERATION OF THE NURSING PROFESSION.

A VICTORY THANK OFFERING.

The rejoicing of the world that at length the end of the war is in sight, and that the tyranny and brutal domination of an arrogant Empire has been broken on the wheel of justice, is taking concrete expression in the organization of various thank-offerings in commemoration of this event of soul-stirring magnitude.

Liberty, self-expression, self-determination, for the small as well as the great nations of the world, will henceforth be safeguarded by the victorious Allies, who recognize that might is not right, and that the weaker nations have an inalienable right to individuality.

When we, as nurses, consider what form our Victory Thank Offering shall take, let us remember the battle which has been waged by the Society for the State Registration of Trained Nurses for over sixteen years, to secure for the nursing profession just those blessings which the flower of mankind has gone into battle to uphold, and thought life itself not too high a price to pay in order to secure.

Never have those nurses who have stood so faithfully for the principles of freedom and self-determination in the organization of their profession been confronted by so serious a situation as at the present time, when the employers, who have for years so bitterly opposed the effective co-operation of the Nursing Profession, are enlisting, in their bid for domination, the aid of wealth and social influence in forcing dangerous and obnoxious legislation upon the rank and file. We therefore ask those who have so generously supported the Society for the State Registration of Trained Nurses in the past to make their Thank Offering for Victory a donation to its funds, to enable it to carry on the campaign for the liberation of the Nursing Profession from its very dependent position.

The record of the successful work of the Society since its inception in meeting, and defeating, all past attempts to subjugate trained nurses will be found in historical sequence in the Statement on page ii of our cover; and we feel sure our readers will agree that it is a record of which the organizers of this Society may be exceedingly proud.

The co-operation (through the Central Committee for the State Registration of Nurses) of all the societies which had been working for the higher education and registration of nurses, through an Act of Parliament, rendered the situation in 1914 hopeful in the extreme, and, had time been given by the Asquith Government for the consideration of the Bill, unquestionably it would have been placed on the Statute Book before the war. The time asked for was not conceded, and now the clear issue is again complicated by an opposition Bill drafted by the College of Nursing, Ltd. When the new Parliament comes in, however, let us hope it will settle the question in a generous and honest spirit, having due regard to the dignity of labour.

It is going to be difficult after the war for nurses to counteract the domination which social influence, and the money at the disposal of those who have monopolised the wealth of this country, can exercise. But we have had in the war a magnificent object-lesson in the all-conquering power of right, when faced with the dastardly methods of might, and those who have on previous occasions saved the profession from subjugation are quite prepared to fight its battle once again. They have every hope, moreover, that the awakened spirit of the new Parliament will see justice done to the workers.

Propagandism, with an inimical press, is very costly, and we therefore ask our readers to support those principles which the Central Committee has incorporated in its Bill, by sending their Victory Thank Offering to the War Chest of the Society for the State Registration of Trained Nurses.

OUR PRIZE COMPETITION.

WHAT PRECAUTIONS WOULD YOU TAKE IF NURSING A CASE OF SEPTIC PNEUMONIA FOLLOWING INFLUENZA?

We have pleasure in awarding the prize this week to Miss Maude Cullen, West Ham Hospital, Stratford.

PRIZE PAPER.

Nurses who are attendant on cases of septic pneumonia following influenza, should be most careful to minimise the risk of taking the disease, as well as of conveying it to others with whom they come in contact.

A mask may be worn over the nose and mouth, soaked in some non-poisonous disinfectant. Gargles must be frequently used. Plenty of fresh air is essential. Ill-ventilated rooms and crowds are to be avoided.

In nursing a case of this sort, the chief point to bear in mind is to isolate the patient whenever possible, and to try to prevent the spread of the sepsis by the disinfection of the mouth and nose. Permanganate of potash, in a saline solution, for gargling and sniffing up the nose, is useful, also tincture of iodine in boiling water, quantity ʒi, to water Oi, is excellent as an inhalation, and preferable for children.

Another method which has been tried effectively is continuous inhalations of oxygen from a gas-bag which has a soft rubber nose-piece passing up into the nostril.

Numerous organisms are present in the nose and also may be found in the mucus membrane. Gargling should be frequently resorted to, especially if the person attacked is accustomed to breathing through the mouth. Teeth must be well brushed and kept scrupulously clean. If the patient is too ill to do it himself, then it must be done for him. The tongue and whole of the inside of the mouth and gums must be well swabbed with glycerine and borax, or peroxide of hydrogen (diluted), three or four times daily, if necessary, also especially before and after feeds. Precautions must be taken to guard against chills. The room must be well ventilated and kept at an even temperature of 65° Fahrenheit, or 70° Fahrenheit.

A steam kettle and tent have often proved of great benefit, if continued until the temperature is down to normal. This has been very effectual in some hospitals.

There is a vaccine now prepared which consists of the bacilli of (1) influenzæ, (2) streptococci, (3) pneumococci. It has disadvantages. It lowers the patient's resistance in taking the disease, certainly for some time after. It is best to wait till the disease subsides, and then give several injections to prevent any further attacks.

The inoculations so far against the influenza bacilli have not proved very remedial. There has been in several instances next to no reaction, and the dose has been repeated two, or three, or four times without more effect. The ward or room wherein the patient is nursed should be thoroughly sprayed, or washed all over with some disinfectant daily, all feeding utensils duly marked and kept, and washed up separately. Everything possible must be done towards trying to avoid the spreading of this highly contagious disease.

It is in the nose and mouth chiefly where this bacilli thrives, therefore aseptic measures must be employed as thoroughy as possible.

HONOURABLE MENTION.

The following competitors receive honourable mention :—Miss Lucy C. Cooper, Miss M. Brent, Miss J. Robinson.

QUESTION FOR NEXT WEEK.

What do you know of " mustard gas " burns and their treatment?

THE ROYAL RED CROSS.

On Saturday last the King decorated the following ladies with the Royal Red Cross :—

FIRST CLASS.

Matron Vida MacLean, New Zealand A.N.S.

SECOND CLASS.

C.N.S. : Sisters Winifred Bimson, Jessie Reid and Ethel Robinson. V.A.D. : Mrs. Marjorie Monks. New Zealand A.N.S. : Sisters Mary Christmas, Jean Dodds, Rose Fanning, Matilda Fricker, Emily Nutsey, Alice Ingles, Florence Siddells, Mabel Wright and Carrie Young.

The King has awarded the Royal Red Cross to the undermentioned ladies of the Nursing Services in recognition of valuable services in connection with the war :—

FIRST CLASS.

Miss A. Bennet, Matron, Aust. A.N.S. ; Miss A. E. Dowsley, Matron, Aust. A.N.S. ; Miss T. J. Dunne, Matron, Aust. A.N.S. ; Miss L. B. Dunwoodie, Lady Superintendent, Q.A.M.N.S.I. ; Miss I. H. McNally, Senior N. Sister, Q.A.M.N.S.I.

SECOND CLASS.

Miss W. M. Aldridge, Acting Senior N. Sister, Q.A.M.N.S.I. ; Miss E. B. Butler, Senior Sister Aust. A.N.S. ; Miss E. Dalyell, Senior Sister, Aust. A.N.S. ; Miss E. L. Horne, A. Matron, Aust. A.N.S. ; Miss V. I. Lamb, Senior Nursing Sister, Q.A.M.N.S.I. Nursing Sister Florence Perdue, whose decoration was notified in our last issue, belonged to the Doughty Wylie Unit.

FRENCH FLAG NURSING CORPS.

OUR SECRETARY.

Many women who have during the four years of war done unobtrusive yet invaluable work for the country have never been heard of beyond the immediate sphere of their particular usefulness. They come and go quietly, without fuss and without ulterior motives. We do not see them dressed up in uniforms they have no right to wear, posing as heroines before the camera, their names in all publicity pars.

One of these real workers is Miss Isabel Hutchinson, the Secretary almost from its inception of the French Flag Nursing Corps, who has performed all her clerical duties with so much kindness and tact— well known to many of the Sisters as a good friend at home.

Miss Hutchinson has artistic talent, and studied drawing at South Kensington and in Germany, and specialised in design. The Corps owes to her the charming Badge of the French Flag, so greatly admired at home and abroad, and her beautiful book-covers, we learn, are greatly appreciated by the best publishers. Miss Hutchinson learnt typewriting to help her father, Colonel Hutchinson, in his work as Hon. Secretary of the Royal Artillery Charities, and as she is devoted to music, she has been Secretary of "The Oncomers Association."

Olga is the name of the devoted and very clever little doggie friend which appears in the picture on this page.

MISS ISABEL HUTCHINSON,
Secretary French Flag Nursing Corps.

Miss Hutchinson's great interest in the welfare of the Corps has done much to make it the very great success it is acknowledged to be, and her work is much valued by the Hon. Superintendent, Mrs. Bedford Fenwick, with whom she has been closely associated for the four years of the war.

LE SOLEIL DE LA VICTOIRE.

The Sisters send accounts of the wonderful joy of the "poilus" and their thankfulness for Victory and Armistice. The sun shone brightly that wonderful 11th November, 1918. "C'est le soleil de la Victoire," acclaimed one poetic soldier. What a glorious triumph! All the horror and tyranny of the German conquest of 1870, and the brutal terms of peace, swept away let us hope for ever. Joy bells rang everywhere calling the people to prayer, and our Sisters took part with their brave charges in many a solemn service of praise and thanksgiving. From Paris we learn that the joy was indescribable. Happy patriots of all ages, dancing like children, in their fields Elysian. The stolen provinces Alsace and Lorraine are home again after all the bitter years of alien rule. What a whirligig of time!

We deeply regret to record the death of Madame Delord (Mlle. de l'Epine), the only trained French member of the Corps. Her end seems very tragic. She was soon to be a mother, and has died quite suddenly, only forty hours after leaving her sister to rejoin her husband, and just as Sedan was to be again free, where her mother had been interned by the Huns from the beginning of the war. Now, alas! she regains her liberty to find her dear daughter has passed away.

Madame Delord was trained at St. Thomas Hospital, London, and joined the Corps early in the war. She was one of the Sisters so happily attached to the ambulance at Verneuil, where she met her husband, who was Med. Chef. They were parted during the terrible attacks on Verdun where he worked for months amidst great tragedy, and on our visit to Verneuil last autumn Mlle. de l'Epine was spending a few days with the Sisters. We well remember her brightness as she chatted with the old postman over the wall, and the grace with which he offered her "the last rose of summer." Then we wished her many happy years with her future husband "after the war," and now, when peace is with us, such wishes are all in vain.

OUR ROLL OF HONOUR.

NURSING SERVICE.
DIED.

Miss G. Llewellyn, V.A.D., B.R.C.S.; S. Nurse E. H. Watson, Q.A.I.M.S.R.
Staff-Nurse D. Bernstein, South Afr. M.C.

NURSING AND THE WAR.

We think it is high time trained nurses who have given four years' devoted service to the sick and wounded and their country began to wake up to the necessity of looking their economic prospects in the face. We hear of no effective organisation to provide them with well-paid work, excepting through the office of the National Union of Trained Nurses, which has throughout the war carried on a most successful " Professional Nurses' Bureau " at 46, Marsham Street, S.W. The Red Cross and V.A.D. Committees are looking well ahead and are determined to protect the interests of their V.A.D. nurses. For instance, as we have reported, Army Council Instruction No. 678 of 1918 has ear-marked all posts in Queen Alexandra's Imperial Military Nursing Service for V.A.D.s who complete three years' training in a general hospital, thus excluding for many years to come regular probationers who are compelled to give four years' service for the same certificate, and now we learn from Lady Quill in the *Weekly Dispatch*, that the training of V.A.D.s who wish to qualify in various other branches of Health work is to be paid for. Lady Quill (a well-known woman journalist) says on this important matter.

" Now with peace and reconstruction no one fears for the great army of women. Hundreds of doors tightly closed before are wide open for the ambitious, enterprising woman. Her four years' training have taught her what she can do best or they have taught her how to find out what she can do best, and she is going to be more needed than ever before, for the peace world is to be a world of hard work for men and women alike.

" For V.A.D.s"

" Devonshire House, the headquarters for V.A.D. workers, is as busy a place as ever. ' We shall want V.A.D.s for at least a year,' Lady Oliver told me yesterday. ' Some of the girls, those who interrupted university careers to work for us, will come straight home and take up their own work. For other V.A.D.s we have a great scheme in progress and £50,000 to start it working. We intend to give all V.A.D.s who show the inclination and aptitude a chance to train for the Public Health Service.

" ' Any V.A.D. may write to us, and we will see that her application is attended to. We feel that these girls who have their years of war service as groundwork will be of the greatest service to the State. We shall see that they are trained as sanitary inspectors, health visitors, nurses, midwives, &c., and with the co-operation of other organisations plenty of work will be found for them along these lines.' "

EVERYONE SHOULD READ IT.

A report has been issued by Mr. Justice Younger's Committee on the treatment of British prisoners of war in coal and salt mines in Germany. It leaves no doubt of the unrestrained brutality which Germany has habitually practised towards defenceless men.

OUR CHRISTIAN DUTY AND NATIONAL OBLIGATION.

Susan Sinclair was left a widow in her youth with one baby boy and no pennies.

But she had genius, and for twenty years she worked early and late, a perfect and devoted mother. Johnny grew and thrived, and did her credit. They were more like brother and sister than mother and son.

Then came War.

Johnny, as became a son of Susan, was in khaki in the first flight of valour.

Later he went " over the top," was crashed down, and weeks later notified a prisoner in a German camp.

Then the heart of Susan Sinclair became as water.

In spite of the Government policy, which cast a veil for years over the deadliest infamies of the Hun—the systematic " breaking of brave English hearts " by humiliation, starvation, and base and bestial ill-treatment of the nation's sons in captivity—this mother realised its fullest horror. All day long and half the night she spent herself for the prisoners; she pinched and screwed in food and fuel and clothing, and dwindled into grey middle age.

One day we met. Could this pale flitting figure be bonny Susan?

" Whither—whither? " I cried, catching her sleeve. " How is Johnny? "

She stood vibrant.

" Burned alive," she whispered hoarsely; " just a rat in a trap. A hell hole—a locked door—a barred window. Mercifully the sentry cracked his skull with a carbine—*I'm hoping, hoping all the time the flames did not reach him in time, but I can never be sure.*"

Then she turned away her withered face, and clutched my arm.

" Come and dine," she said; " no starvation these days. Do you realise we have been informed that it is our Christian Duty, our National Obligation, to feed these murderers? "

As we linked arms, no doubt she noticed my startled heart and the scalding tears that dripped and dripped.

" Happy women who can weep," she sighed.

We stumbled towards her charming home, always before the war gay and beautiful; a bower of flowers, so snug and bright and warm, with a dog and cat, the best of friends; and Johnny—(oh! brave boy Johnny!)—thumping discords on a fine piano to improvised songs out of tune!

During War all had been hushed and dark and colourless.

" Every penny for prisoners, my dear—*every* penny."

We arrived. The old brightness and sweetness prevailed. Glorious fires burned in the grates.

By and bye a couple of spectres in khaki came in. I was introduced to " two brave unbroken English hearts, prisoners of war since Mons."

We dined sumptuously, as in Johnny's day.

" Behold my ' Christian Duty,' " cried Susan, toasting spectre No. 1, " and my ' National Obligation,' " bowing to No. 2. " Here is to the 140,000 prisoners coming home from the Torture Camps of the Hun. Women of Britain, see to it that these ' brave English hearts ' have every available bit and sup they need before one crumb which falls from their table is handed to the Hun."

We clinked glasses and vowed a vow.

E. G. F.

NATIONAL COUNCIL OF TRAINED NURSES.

The annual meeting of the Grand Council (Delegates) of the National Council of Trained Nurses will be held at 431, Oxford Street, London, W. 1, on Friday, November 29th, at 4 p.m.

Nominations for one Vice-President and two Directors, who retire annually, should be sent to the Hon. Secretary at 431, Oxford Street, London, W. 1, before that date. Each affiliated Association has the right to depute two Delegates to serve on the Grand Council; Associations of 400 members three Delegates, and over 600 four Delegates, after which there is no increase of representation.

OFFICE BEARERS AT PRESENT.

President.—Mrs. Bedford Fenwick.

Vice-Presidents.—Miss Elma Smith, Matron, The Infirmary, Hendon; Mrs. Strong, President, Scottish Nurses' Association; Miss A. M. Macdonnell, R.R.C., Matron, War Hospital, Perth.

Directors.—Miss M. Heather-Bigg, R.R.C., Miss H. L. Pearse, Miss A. Dowbiggin, R.R.C., Miss S. A. Villiers, Miss J. W. Davies, Miss Carson-Rae.

Hon. Treasurer.—Miss Christina Forrest.

Hon. Secretary.—Miss B. Cutler.

Ex-officio.—The Presidents of the Matrons'

Council, the Irish Nurses' Association, and the National Union of Trained Nurses.

The business before the meeting will be of professional importance. As events are framing, it is probable that the International Council of Nurses may be convened for 1920, instead of in this year of war, 1918, when it was due to meet. If so, it will be none too soon for the National Council of Great Britain and Ireland to begin to consider this great event.

NATIONAL UNION OF TRAINED NURSES.

We are glad to hear the Meeting organised by the N.U.T.N., " To consider the Influence on the Nation of a Ministry of Health," promises to be well attended and very interesting. It is to be held at the College of Ambulance, 3, Vere Street, Oxford Street, W., and Dr. C. W. Saleeby and Miss Helen Pearse are to speak. The Rev. H. R. L. Sheppard will be in the chair, and we hope there will be a lively discussion. The work of Trained Nurses should be recognised at its true value in any Health scheme for the community, and it is to be hoped that they will not stand silently by and permit the Service to be largely composed of women with a superficial knowledge of sanitary science and home nursing. The pushing amateur is ever in our midst, and often commands higher remuneration from public funds than the skilled worker. We all know the cheap and inefficient standards of nursing offered to the poor, especially in rural districts. Of course nothing will alter that but State Authority and the escape of our profession from plutocratic patronage. We must see that under a Health Ministry the poor get the right thing, and the N.U.T.N. means to do its part to bring about this happy consummation.

NURSES' MISSIONARY LEAGUE.

A Quiet Day for Prayer and Meditation will be held on St. Andrew's Day, Saturday, November 30th, at St. Michael's Church, Chester Square, W.1, conducted by the Rev. Cecil White, M.A., and the Rev. J. Gough McCormick, M.A. 6 a.m., and 8 a.m.: Holy Communion, 10.30–12.30: Addresses by the Rev. Cecil White, M.A. " To Strengthen Such as do Stand " (1) By a clearer vision, (2) By a Brighter hope, (3) By a stronger faith. 3–4.30: Special Thanksgiving Service and Intercession. Address by Rev. J. Gough McCormick, M.A., " To Beat Down Satan under our Feet." Fellowship of Silence. There will be periods for Prayer and silent meditation after each address.

Courage for the great sorrows of life and patience for the small ones, and then, when you have laboriously accomplished your daily task, go to sleep in peace. God is awake.—*Victor Hugo.*

Royal British Nurses' Association.

(Incorporated by Royal Charter.)

THIS SUPPLEMENT BEING THE OFFICIAL ORGAN OF THE CORPORATION.

THE CONFERENCE.

(*Concluded from page 308.*)

SOME PHASES OF MODERN NURSING.

The second part of the Afternoon Session at the Conference convened by the Royal British Nurses' Association at 11, Chandos Street, Cavendish Square, 1, on November 7th, dealt with " Some Phases of Modern Nursing."

MODERN NURSING AS IT AFFECTS DISTRICT NURSES' TRAINING.

MISS MARSTERS, Superintendent of the Paddington and District Nursing Association, who presented the first paper, said that in looking back on twenty-two years of district nursing in London one must realize the enormous change in the condition of the people among whom the district nurse works.

Twenty years ago nursing amongst the poor was indeed slum work, and very strenuous it was; nothing to make use of in the homes, and it was a frequent occurrence to have no towel, soap, or basin for washing or dressing purposes; the nurse had to improvise in nearly every case she attended.

If the housing were bad now (which it was in many places), what was it then? Underground cellars, and back to back houses, houses in back yards to which the only entrance was through another house, abounded.

Thanks to the sanitary authorities many of these evils had been done away with, and with them many of the diseases the district nurses were constantly asked to attend—typhoid, diphtheria, &c. There was not hospital accommodation for all these, and many were nursed in their own homes.

A number of serious cases were still nursed on the district, but the character of the work, and the class of patient in large towns was changing. The work of district nurses to a great extent was becoming preventive. The patients were much better off, and it was seldom that they could not procure what was required in the way of dressings, &c., so that it was comparatively easy for an operation to be performed at home.

Amongst the branches of work undertaken by district nurses were nursing for the Public Health authorities of such diseases as measles, whooping-cough, ophthalmia neonatorum, tuberculosis, and she hoped soon the *nursing* of maternity cases.

Again, there were the school work, and minor ailment centres for school children, infant welfare work, ante-natal clinics, dispensaries for the prevention of consumption and for venereal disease, &c. This was all a part of modern nursing, and for the fully trained nurse to do this work well she must receive instruction during her training in these varied branches of work; also a course of lectures in sociology.

To nurse the poor successfully in their own homes a nurse must understand their ways and the available means of helping them.

The Queen Victoria Jubilee Institute gave instruction in the above subjects to nurses taking up district work, and, as we progressed in preventive nursing, fully trained nurses would specialize in these subjects.

It was not now sufficient when a nurse attended a member of a family for her to simply nurse the patient; she must also observe the manner in which (if there were one) the baby was fed, washed, and clothed, where it slept, whether it attended a welfare centre, the state of the mother's health and teeth, and her ante-natal symptoms, and in the event of there being children under school age, whether they were attending a welfare clinic.

Although there was no glamour about district nursing, and no honours given, it was worth a great deal more to hear a poor mother say, as was often said to her: " Matron, I do not know what I should have done without nurse. She saved baby's life. I shall never forget her."

THE PLACE OF THE TRAINED NURSE IN PREVENTIVE WORK.

MISS K. ATHERTON, Medallist of the Royal Sanitary Institute and Educational Organizer of the Hampstead Council of Social Welfare, spoke of the work of the trained nurse in infant welfare centres, and said that the underlying principle of all work of this kind was to get the mothers to bring their children regularly to the centre while they were well. Then the onset of various diseases, such as malnutrition, anæmia, spinal curvature, rheumatism, strained heart, or nervous system could be early detected by the medical officers, and the mother could be gradually educated and brought to the realization that all her children could not be treated alike, but must be studied individually.

Everyone, said Miss Atherton, was talking about infant welfare centres just now. They were the present fashion, for it was realized that the preservation of child life and health was all-important, not only to the child, but to the nation.

All such work was very costly, requiring special equipment of all kinds—special training and experience on the part of the doctor and nurse, and the very best equipment for the Clinics, embracing, as they often did, ante-natal and dental departments. It was only by having the very best that the best results were obtained. The doctors were often specialists in women's and children's diseases, and the nurses usually had some qualification in public health, as well as the usual hospital training, and were preferably midwives.

The children dealt with were of the ages of one to five years, when their case papers, and charts of weight and height, were handed on to the School Medical Officer, and were invaluable as a complete record of health. Formerly no special attention was paid to children of this age. It was not considered necessary to fill their teeth, and discharging ears were supposed to be the natural result of bad teeth. Now the tiniest holes were filled, thus preserving the permanent teeth. The teeth of the mother also received attention; at some Centres the rule was that all mothers attending dinners must first have their teeth put in order.

Miss Atherton then dealt in detail with the work of the Ante-Natal Clinics, and said that if they could only get a mother with her first baby, they could probably lay the foundation of a large and healthy family.

Home visiting was an important department of the work. The regular visitor—trained, though possibly a voluntary worker—gained a very intimate knowledge of the family, and watched the growth and progress of the children.

In the discussion which followed, MISS MARQUARDT inquired the qualifications of the Home Visitors, and was told that they often had the certificate of the Royal Sanitary Institute.

MODERN DEVELOPMENTS IN SURGICAL NURSING.

MISS ISABEL MACDONALD, Secretary to the Corporation, then read an interesting paper prepared by Miss Sinzininex, A.R.R.C., on the above subject. The present day developments of surgical nursing were not, the writer said, merely those of ordinary progress, but were special developments due to conditions arising out of the war. They were wide in the extreme, and it was only possible in a short time to deal with one chiefly, and perhaps to touch on one or two others. She confined herself, therefore, to the one she had had most experience of—the variety of compound fractures met with in these days. The paper dealt with much the same subjects as the one by Miss Sinzininex published in a recent issue of this JOURNAL.

(Signed) ISABEL MACDONALD,
Secretary to the Corporation.

In connection with the high salaries earned by Sisters in Canada, Miss Jentie Paterson desires to make it plain that uniform is not usually provided, but she thinks they are well able to provide that item from their generous emoluments.

OFFICIAL CORRESPONDENCE BETWEEN THE COLLEGE OF NURSING, LTD., AND THE CENTRAL COMMITTEE FOR THE STATE REGISTRATION OF NURSES.

At a Meeting of the Executive Committee of the Central Committee held on Thursday, November 14th, it was agreed that the following correspondence between the Central Committee and the College of Nursing, Ltd., be published in THE BRITISH JOURNAL OF NURSING, as it had already been sent to the press by the Secretary of the College by direction of the Hon. Sir Arthur Stanley, M.P., Chairman of the Council of the College :—

THE NURSES' REGISTRATION BILLS.

THE COLLEGE OF NURSING, LTD.
6, Vere Street, London, W.,
14th October, 1918.

DEAR MADAM,—At the last Meeting of the Council of the College of Nursing the Chairman informed the Council, on the authority of Major Chapple, that your Committee had received copies of the 7th Draft of the Bill for the State Registration of Nurses, and that it was under their consideration. I was instructed by the Council to write and ask whether your Committee agrees to the introduction of this Bill by Major Chapple as a joint measure.

My Council further instructed me to say that if your Committee feel that any difficulty is caused by Clause 5 (3) they would be willing to delete that Clause if this is the only objection felt by your Committee to the Bill as now presented to them.

As my Council meets next Thursday I shall be grateful if you will let me have an answer before that date.

I enclose two copies of the 7th Draft of the Bill.
I remain, yours faithfully
M. S. RUNDLE,
Secretary.

FROM NURSE HON. SECRETARY, CENTRAL COMMITTEE FOR STATE REGISTRATION OF NURSES, TO SECRETARY, COLLEGE OF NURSING, LTD.

19th October, 1918.

DEAR MADAM,—I have received your letters of 14th and 18th October.

The former, as corrected, will be submitted to the Central Committee for the State Registration of Nurses at its Meeting on October 26th.

Yours faithfully,
ETHEL G. FENWICK,
Hon. Nurse Secretary.

CENTRAL COMMITTEE FOR THE STATE REGISTRATION OF NURSES.
431, Oxford Street, London, W. 1,
November 1st, 1918.

DEAR MADAM,—The letter of the College of Nursing, Ltd., of the 14th ult. was placed before the Central Committee for the State Registration of Nurses at its meeting on October the 26th last. The Committee considered the letter in connection with a report presented by its Executive Committee, upon the 7th Draft of the College of Nursing Bill. As a result of its deliberations, the Committee passed a Resolution to the effect that its own Bill is a better Bill than that drafted by the College of Nursing, and should be adhered to.

We were instructed by the Committee to acquaint your Council with this decision, and at the same time to ask your Council whether it would be willing to support the Bill framed by the Central Committee as a joint Bill. The Committee is unable to support the Bill proposed by the College of Nursing, Ltd., even if Clause 5 (3) were deleted, and for the following reasons :—

1. The Committee is of opinion that it is most undesirable that any particular body should be included in the Bill, in the manner in which it is proposed to incorporate the College of Nursing. It would equally object even if the body were any other body—say the Royal British Nurses' Association or the Society for the State Registration of Trained Nurses—because it is of the opinion that the General Nursing Council should be free and independent of any such influence as would certainly prevail in it were it so intimately associated with an incorporated body as is proposed by the College Bill.

As regards the College of Nursing, Ltd., in particular, the omission of Clause 5 (3) from the Bill will not prevent the Memorandum and Articles of Association of the College from remaining in full force and effect; and with these Articles and Memorandum the Central Committee does not feel itself able to agree. If the College is taken under the protection of an Act of Parliament, its Memorandum and Articles of Association will, by that fact, receive the approval of the Legislature.

2. The Committee objects to the proposed immediate dissolution of the Provisional Council provided for in the College Bill. According to the scheme laid down in that Bill there will be no constituency to elect the General Nursing Council except the nurses on the College Register at the time the Bill becomes law. In the view of the Committee the First (provisional) General Nursing Council should draw up not only the rules provided for in Clause 5 (1) (a) of the College Bill, but all the remainder of the rules, and it should not go out of office till sufficient time has elapsed for the growth of a constituency of Registered Nurses sufficiently extensive and independent.

3. The institution of Supplementary Registers, other than those of Male and Mental Nurses, is, in the opinion of the Committee, certain to lead not only to a many-portal system, instead of the one-portal system which the Committee has always considered to be one of the most essential features of State Registration, but also to a shorter period than the three years which is the minimum period the Committee believes to be necessary for the training of a nurse.

Lastly, the Committee feels bound to state that

it fails to see the necessity of providing for the College of Nursing or any other body in the Registration Bill. It has no objection to offer to the College as an educational institution; but, as such an institution, the College will be but one amongst many, and why should the College be singled out for special favour?

The Committee recognise the educational importance of the College, and, on that ground, is quite willing to provide for its representation on the General Nursing Council.

As the Resolution referred to above states, the Committee is of opinion that its own Bill—which is the outcome of many years' thought and collaboration on the part of a number of societies which are interested in matters connected with the nursing profession—is a better one than that drafted by the College of Nursing, and therefore it invites the College to co-operate with it in its promotion in Parliament.

The Committee's amended Bill is in the hands of the printers, and copies will be forwarded for the information of your Council as soon as they are received.

We are, dear Madam,
Yours faithfully,
ETHEL G. FENWICK,
Hon. Nurse Secretary.
E. W. GOODALL,
Hon. Medical Secretary.
To Miss M. S. Rundle, R.R.C.,
Secretary, College of Nursing, Ltd.

FROM SECRETARY, COLLEGE OF NURSING, LTD., TO HON. SECRETARY, CENTRAL COMMITTEE FOR STATE REGISTRATION OF NURSES.

2nd November, 1918.

DEAR MADAM,—I beg to thank you for your letter of the 1st inst., which shall be placed before the Council of the College at its next Meeting.

I remain, yours faithfully,
M. S. RUNDLE, Secretary.

THE COLLEGE OF NURSING, LTD.
6, Vere Street, London, W.,
9th November, 1918.

DEAR MADAM.—Your letter of the 1st inst. was considered by the Council of the College on Thursday last, and I am directed to say at once that no Bill for the State Registration of Nurses will receive the support of the College which does not provide for the inclusion on the first Legal Register (without further fee) of all Nurses on the College Register at the time of the passing of the Act, and, further, for the election of two-thirds of the General Nursing Council by the Nurses upon the General Register under the Act.

Neither of these essential provisions, to which the College is fully pledged, is found in the Bill framed by the Central Committee. Under these circumstances the Council of the College has decided to proceed without delay to promote their own Bill, of which copies have been already furnished to you, with such modifications, if any, as they may judge expedient.

The Council think it right that you should immediately be informed of what they propose to do, without thereby precluding themselves from making a fuller reply to your letter when they have received from you a copy of the Central Committee's Bill with the latest amendments.

I remain, yours faithfully
M. S. RUNDLE, Secretary.

FROM SECRETARY, COLLEGE OF NURSING, LTD., TO HON. SECRETARY, CENTRAL COMMITTEE FOR STATE REGISTRATION OF NURSES.

11th November, 1918.

DEAR MADAM,—I think you should be informed that, by the instruction of the Chairman, we are sending to the Nursing Press this week the correspondence which has lately passed between the Central Committee for the State Registration of Nurses and the Council of the College of Nursing, Ltd.

I remain, yours faithfully,
M. S. RUNDLE, Secretary.

FROM HON. NURSE SECRETARY, CENTRAL COMMITTEE FOR THE STATE REGISTRATION OF NURSES, TO SECRETARY, COLLEGE OF NURSING, LTD.

12th November, 1918.

DEAR MADAM,—I beg to acknowledge your letter dated November 9th, which will be placed before my Committee at its next meeting; also your second communication, dated November 11th, informing me that, by direction of your Chairman, you have sent the recent official correspondence between the Central Committee and the College of Nursing to the so-called Nursing Press, before my Committee has considered your letter of November 9th, and, as courtesy demands, has given its consent to such publicity.

I remain, yours faithfully,
ETHEL G. FENWICK,
Hon. Nurse Secretary.

Having considered the correspondence, the Executive Committee passed unanimously the following Resolution, and directed that it should be sent to the Council of the College of Nursing, Ltd. :—

RESOLUTION.

The Executive Committee of the Central Committee for the State Registration of Nurses desires to express to the Council of the College of Nursing, Ltd., its strong disapproval of official correspondence between the two Bodies having been sent to the press for publication, before the Executive Committee of the former has had time to receive and consider the letter from the Council of the College of Nursing, Ltd., dated November the 9th, in reply to the important communication from the Central Committee dated November 1st.

Our readers will learn from this correspondence that the Central Committee for State Registration of Nurses, and the College of Nursing, Ltd., will now proceed to support their own Bills.

DANCING ON THE DEAD.

What is known as the "Hulton" press, which owns the *Daily Sketch,* the *Evening Standard,* and other papers in the North, is widely advertising the scheme of a "Victory Ball," to be held at the Albert Hall on November 27th, in aid of the War Charity, the Nation's Fund for Nurses, and nearly every paper in the Metropolis is flooded with advertisements. We professional nurses can hardly conceive such an outrage to our ethical standards possible at the present time, even by the Committee of the Fund and their supporters, who continue to ignore the dignity and sensibilities of our profession, in spite of indignant protests.

The Nation's Nurses are still engaged in the sacred and often heartrending duty of attending the Nation's Sick and Wounded, broken in battle and in the torture camps of the enemy, and that Society and the Drama should dare to make our honourable work the excuse for their heartless pleasure and diversion, before the corpses of our valiant dead are cold in the grave, is an unendurable offence against decency we shall not easily forgive.

We call upon the galaxy of duchesses who are giving their patronage to this function, to realise, if possible, the injury not only to the Nursing Profession, but to their own "Order" in the opinion of the "common people" of unerring instinct, who are still mourning their dead, and who are heartbroken at the sight of the returning mad and mutilated prisoners, who are "bone of their bone and flesh of their flesh."

We do not live in times when it is safe for the callous rich to ignore the convictions of those whose moral ideals and work form the basis of a solvent State. Already the warning is writ large upon the wall.

NOT A NATIONAL FUND.

DEAR NURSES,—During the past week I have met many Nurses who one and all, have expressed indignation and strong disapproval of the scheme promoted by the Committee of

The Nation's Fund for Nurses, viz. :
"A Victory Ball
At the Albert Hall."

This ball, according to the promoters' programme, is to raise funds for "The Nation's Nurses."

I undertook, on behalf of indignant members of the nursing profession, to call at the Office of the Nation's Fund for Nurses in North Audley Street, and to voice the Nurses' very justifiable protest against the action of the Committee in begging on their behalf and without their consent at a time like this, when our prisoners are still abroad and starving, and our Hospitals at home still filled with the wounded and the dying.

I think the readers of THE BRITISH JOURNAL OF NURSING may like to hear what occurred at the interview.

I informed the secretary that the Nurses, on whose behalf I spoke, were grieved and distressed to think that our prisoners and wounded should come home and find (at a solemn time of thankfulness like the present) Society women revelling to raise money for Nurses, who object at all times to being held up as objects for patronage and charity and especially at the present juncture.

The Secretary disagreed with me.

She considered it was just the time when the officers were returning from the front to have an entertainment for them, and that a very influential section of the nursing profession approved of the scheme, including Miss Sidney Browne, who must be a good judge.

I replied that Miss Sidney Browne was only an official *under orders* and *not* an independent Nurse and that the Nurses whose opinion I voiced were members of organised Societies of Nurses who were free women.

Another official then appeared from behind a screen, and expatiated on the support the College of Nursing received, &c., &c.

I had, however, uttered my protest and fulfilled my mission, so I wished them Good Morning with this parting remark :

" I think you will get into trouble before long if you continue to beg for a *National Fund*, as your Fund is only registered to provide Funds for the members of The College of Nursing, Ltd."

One of the ladies replied :

" Oh, if you choose to stay *outside* the movement we cannot help that."

I came away thoughtful but triumphant !

Nurses are to be coerced and bribed by promises and doles to enter the College of Nursing, Ltd., and many do so and hug their chains !

And what of the independent spirits who remain outside ?

There is one possession left to them, and it is a " Pearl without price."

Liberty of conscience !

Freedom to fight for the right !

And we have just seen in this worldwide conflict Might collapse before Right.

A FRIEND OF NURSES.

WEDDING BELLS.

Members of the Staff of the Registered Nurses' Society will congratulate Miss J. Thomasina Grant, one of their number, on her approaching marriage to Lieut. J. E. Reid, 18th Essex Regt.

The wedding will take place on December 4th at St. Luke's Church, West Norwood. We wish bride and bridegroom every happiness.

AN IMPUDENT GAMBLE.

We are glad to learn that the Lottery started by the Dublin Stock Exchange in the name of " The Nation's Tribute to Nurses," whereby those who bought tickets stood to win large money prizes amounting to £1,000 before any benefit to the Nurses accrued has been stopped—we hope by the Committee of the Fund, although we hear the police played a part in this discreditable affair.

The " Nation's Nurses " are the sport of every notoriety hunting climber ; but when it comes to exploiting, not only their professional work, but hard cash, it is time to call a halt.

An Irish Nurse writes : " The lottery has been stopped ! and there are great lamentations in certain quarters. It was a scandalous business. Those of us who required accurate information concerning ' the gamble ' could not get it. Anyway it has been squashed. The Nation's Tribute has brought in roughly £10,000. Trustees are to be appointed to invest the money. Irishmen and women also will see it is kept in Ireland. A Committee will be formed for its distribution. It is rumoured that now war is over the College of Nursing, Ltd., is to start a great campaign to induce Irish nurses to join it. It may succeed in Ulster, but will only arouse contention and ill-feeling in other parts of Ireland, as the country is much more disturbed than the papers say, and Irish nurses mean to have professional Home Rule as the doctors have, and will fight for it. For English Matrons to attempt to govern Irish nurses from London is doomed to failure, and shows a lamentable lack of tact, perception and knowledge of history."

PRIZES FOR NURSES.

Viscountess Allendale distributed the prizes and certificates to the probationer nurses at the Poor Law Infirmary, Newcastle-on-Tyne. The prizes were awarded by the Heath Trust to successful nurses in each of their first, second and third year of probation.

The following were the successful nurses :—
Certificates for three years' training : Nurses Herdman, Brinton, Turnbull, Blyth, Spenceley, Armstrong, Forrest, McKinley, Redpath, Hall, McReady, Davidson. Heath Prizes : Third year. 1, McKinley ; 2, Davidson ; 3, Hall. Second year.—1, Harrison ; 2, Lowerson ; 3, Lawson. First year.—1, Gordon ; 2, Connelly ; 3, Park.

A Tribute Sale in aid of the Elizabeth Garrett Anderson Hospital (the New Hospital for Women) will be held on November 21st, 22nd, and 23rd at the Grafton Galleries, Grafton Street, W., with the object of raising funds towards the completion of the endowment of the various beds already started under the Garrett Anderson Memorial Scheme. Subscriptions will be gratefully received by the Secretary, Miss Imogen H. Murphy, at the Hospital, 144, Euston Road, N.W. 1.

THE PASSING BELL.

Miss Edith Mary Harrison died at the post of duty from influenza, following pneumonia, during a serious outbreak of influenza at York County Hospital, where she was training as a nurse. Miss Harrison had nearly completed her second year of training. She had taken the third place in her first examination, and was a great favourite with the staff and the patients on account of her unfailing energy and great kindliness of heart. A beautiful cross of carnations and violets was sent by the nursing and resident staff to Whitby, where Miss Harrison was buried.

Miss J. C. van Lanschot Hubrecht, whose death was announced in our issue last week, was one of the leading progressives in the Dutch Nursing World, and through her letters to this JOURNAL,

The Late MISS J. C. VAN LANSCHOT HUBRECHT.
A Pioneer Worker for State Registration of Nurses.

the part she took in helping to build up the International Council of Nurses, and her presence at its meetings, was well known to many British nurses, who will sincerely mourn her loss. For years she was a member of the Board and Hon. Secretary of the Dutch Nurses' Association, and worked steadfastly to secure the State Registration of Nurses in Holland, and was also closely connected with its paper, *Nosokomos*. She also acted as Hon. Secretary of the International Committee on Nursing Education which presented a report on " Preliminary Training " at the Cologne Meeting of the International Council of Nurses in 1912. Miss Lanschot Hubrecht was trained at the Children's Hospital, Amsterdam, and in the Training School of " La Source " at Lausanne. We offer to our Dutch colleagues our sincere sympathy in the loss they have sustained.

This country is indebted to the Dutch Nurses for much kindness in the care of interned and wounded soldiers, and for their work on hospital ships, and we hope when the International Council of Nurses holds its next meeting that our gratitude will find some public expression.

APPOINTMENTS.

MATRON.

Fusehill War Hospital, Carlisle. — Miss S. G. Dalziel has been appointed Matron. She was trained at the Kilmarnock Infirmary, Ayrshire, and held the position of Charge Nurse at the City Hospital, Hull. She is a member of the Territorial Force Nursing Service, and has worked both in Home Hospitals and at Salonika. She has held the position of Night Superintendent at the Fusehill War Hospital, and has also had experience of private nursing.

SUPERINTENDENT NURSE.

Union Infirmary, Bromsgrove. — Miss Leah Lillie Simmonds has been appointed Superintendent Nurse. She was trained at the Dudley Road Infirmary, Birmingham, and has held the position of Superintendent Nurse at the Northampton Union Infirmary, and at the Oswestry Incorporated Hospital.

QUEEN ALEXANDRA'S MILITARY NURSING SERVICE FOR INDIA.

The following ladies have been appointed members of the above Service :—Miss E. E. Bott, Miss Vera Francis, Miss G. Harvey James, Miss F. G. Warren, Miss A. L. Blomfield Dickson, and Miss E. M. McPherson.

LEAGUE NEWS.

The Winter General Meeting of the League of St. Bartholomew's Hospital Nurses will be held in the Clinical Theatre on Saturday, December 14th, at 2.30 p.m. The President, Miss H. Todd, will give an account of the work she has been doing for the Women's Royal Air Force, and Miss Heath (Sister Ophthalmic) will tell of her work for the past eighteen months for the Italian Red Cross.

The Social Gathering and tea will be held in the Nurses' Sitting Room, where there will be music by members of the Nursing Staff, arranged by Miss Bostock.

A SEQUEL.

Little Daughter : " What did Mummie die of Daddy dear ? "

Daddy : A broken heart."

Little Daughter : " Who braked it ? "

Daddy : " I did."

Little Daughter : " Poor, poor Daddy ! *How* misfortunate. Mummie loved you best of best— and so do I."

NURSING ECHOES.

Bath is going to raise £2,000 in support of the Nurse Cavell Homes of Rest for Nurses. A room will be called after Bath, and the local committee will have power to nominate a certain number of nurses to occupy it. There are now Homes at Haslemere, Bridport, Market Drayton, Wellington, Tewkesbury, Bristol and Richmond, which will meet the needs of 600 nurses. At present the Homes are full.

A monument to Nurse Edith Cavell and Canadian nurses killed during the war is to be erected at Ottawa by public and private subscription.

It was announced at a recent meeting of the Lincoln Guardians that the Mayor had written stating that the trustees of the Bromhead institution having intimated that for financial reasons they would be unable to carry on after December 31st next the work of district nursing in the city, he had been asked to call together those specially interested in the matter to consider what steps should be taken to ensure that the deserving poor of Lincoln should continue to have available in case of illness the assistance of trained nurses. It was agreed that Mr. Harley and Miss Nevile should represent the Board in the matter.

There is little doubt that Lincoln will make arrangements to organize and continue the benefits of district nursing for its poor, and perhaps on a more modern basis than that which has pertained hitherto. A high standard of training is most essential in this particular branch of nursing. We always resent the semi-trained nurse for the poor.

At the annual meeting of the Dunblane Nursing Association, it was reported that the number of cases attended by Nurse George was 229, and the number of her visits 4,233. The income of this Association was stated to be £130 0s. 9d., and the expenditure £125 14s. 5d. A reverend gentleman described the reports as "most gratifying." He said, "They were greatly pleased with the diligence of the nurse." A second minister remarked that "without such an Association as theirs at the present time, he did not know how Dunblane could exist." The Rev. D. R. Alexander ventured to throw out a suggestion that the nurse should be more highly remunerated. A Mrs. Stewart concurred, but pointed out "that the nurse was paid as much as any nurse they knew of." Colonel Arthur Hay

Drummond, the Chairman, expressed the opinion that "with regard to their finances, he thought they were in a very secure position, and that a church collection was not actually required!"

We are not a bit good at sums, and the report failed to say how much of the munificent sum of £125 14s. 5d. was paid to Nurse George for her 4,233 visits (think of the shoe leather—or brown paper, as the case may be), but in our opinion the committee of the Dunblane Nursing Association is guilty of sweating in connection with their admirable nurse, whose salary alone should certainly not be less than £3 a week.

The State Cabinet in Melbourne has been reviewing a question of concern to the nursing profession—the hours and the working conditions of nurses in public hospitals. The sweating conditions and the starvation wages paid have amounted to a public scandal, says the *Age*. Following on indignant protests in Parliament last March, and the case stated by the Australian Women's Association to the Chief Secretary in April, the Cabinet directed Mr. T. E. Meek, chief clerk of the Treasury, to carry out an investigation. Mr. Meek's report is in the Premier's hands, and it is understood that a reduction of hours is urged, if not the institution of the eight-hour day sought for nurses. The Cabinet's decision to direct reform could be enforced, it is observed, through the influence of the Government subsidies.

Nursing questions have been to the fore recently in the House of Commons at question time.

On November 6th Lord Henry Cavendish-Bentinck inquired of the Secretary for Scotland the names of the prisons and Polmont institutions in which trained nurses are employed, the number of such nurses, and the qualifications possessed by each; also what provision is made for sick prisoners in institutions in which no trained nurses are employed.

Mr. Munro had to admit that "trained nurses in the professional sense are not employed on the Scottish prison staff, but in the mainland prisons there are male and female officers trained and certified after examination to be qualified for simple nursing. He also stated that medical officers are authorized to engage trained nurses when required, and that there is power to remove serious cases to hospital.

The fees paid to masseuses was also the subject of a question by General Page-Croft.

CONTROL OF NURSES.

The Association of Poor Law Unions (a federation of Poor Law Guardians) will hold its twentieth annual meeting in London, on November 21st and 22nd, and will, of course, discuss the burning question of a Ministry of Health. In this connection the *Poor Law Officers' Journal* states, under the heading of "Control of Nursing":—

Another question connected with the Ministry of Health in regard to which there can be no difference of opinion is raised in the report on a resolution forwarded by the Chichester Board of Guardians. The Guardians, "in view of the proposal to institute a Ministry of Health, which will tend to create a demand for additional nurses, and in view of the action of the College of Nursing and the Central Committee of State Registration, which will tend to diminish the supply of nurses, asked the Association to petition the Local Government Board to institute a Register of Nurses to be subject to such curriculum, training and examination as may be prescribed, and which will be applicable to all Poor-Law Infirmaries where nurses are trained at present or where superintendent nurses are engaged." Many months ago, when the College of Nursing first proposed to acquire powers for the Control of Nurses and Nursing, we contended here that a proper method would place this public matter in the charge—as a central authority—of the Local Government Board which, as a Government Department, is the Ministry of Health. Any further development of central authority in the direct establishment of a Ministry will strengthen the argument in favour of such a system of control, nursing being an indispensable adjunct to the treatment of sickness for the purposes of restoration to health. A Ministry of Health could not divest itself of the central control of nursing. Concurrently, the Ministry would or ought to work locally through the several Local Authorities which provide nursing as a part of the whole organization of public health. A wise disposition of Local Authority would, as regards the poor or necessitous, allot this to the Assistance Authorities—the Guardians of the Poor. These contingencies appear to be so logical in their consecutive application to local public duty that we ought not to look farther for a new plan. Unfortunately, however, it is not the simple and direct method which always finds most favour.

We venture to think that there is a very widespread difference of opinion on this resolution—we take the strongest exception to the suggestion that a Ministry of Health should "control" the whole Nursing Profession—and then delegate its powers to lay Assistance Authorities—the Guardians of the Poor!—or that Nurses trained in Poor Law Infirmaries should be registered as a class apart. Trained Nurses have at last got the bit between their teeth, so far as "control" is concerned—and they intend to push forward in Parliament (now that many are enfranchised citizens) for a Bill to "control" themselves. That one of the first duties of a Ministry of Health will be to organize a State Service of Nursing for the poor there is little doubt; but no State Department has a right to deprive the Nursing Profession as a whole of self determination. Thousands of nurses will not be employed by a Ministry of Health—which will be in no way responsible for nurses it does not pay.

We have just won political liberty, and we must remember that liberty is the development of the personality along moral lines towards moral ideals, the setting free, in each individual and throughout the State, of a greater flood of creative energy.

Our Nurses' Registration Bill provides an outlet for this great flood. Any such suggestion as that to which we have alluded dams it at its source.

OUTSIDE THE GATES.

We are to have a General Election, and, of course, there are very diverse opinions on its necessity and efficacy. Parliament is to be prorogued this week; on November 25th the proclamation summoning a new Parliament will be read; December 4th is Nomination Day, December 14th Polling Day, the votes will be counted from December 21st to 28th, and according to the Coalition if their candidates are returned we shall be happy ever after! We wonder.

The truth is that the Coalition of both the old Parties, by which arrangement they have agreed to divide power, will practically disfranchise many ardent women voters, as, of course, progressives will not trouble to vote for the one reactionary candidate, and vice versa. The irony of fate—after their monumental efforts to wring the power from Parliament to support their political convictions.

A few women candidates have been nominated by various Parties for Parliamentary honours. It will be interesting to see what support they get from their own sex. We hope they will be loyally supported, and their right to help to make laws to which women have to conform will be vindicated at the polls.

A WORD FOR THE WEEK.

Marshal Foch, in a speech at British Headquarters on Sunday, said that it was, above all, the hammer-blows of the British Armies that were the decisive factors in the great and final defeat of the enemy.

BOOK OF THE WEEK.

"JOAN AND PETER."*

When Mr. Wells starts out to discuss a subject, he at least does it thoroughly; one must anyhow admit that, even if one does not agree with him. He calls the story of Joan and Peter a story of an education—and it begins with Peter's birth—before Joan's—ends with their marriage, and they are being educated all the time; at least Peter is, and Joan so soon as we

---

* Cassell & Co. London.

are introduced to her, which is at a very tender age.

Peter's father was an artist and he designed the little low-browed house with an enormous and very expensive roof of green slates, where Peter was born. His nursery was a perfect room in which to hatch the soul of a little boy. Its walls were done in a warm cream-coloured paint and upon them Peter's father had put the most lovely pattern of trotting and jumping horses and dancing cats and dogs and leaping lambs and a carnival of beasts. There were many other delectable points about his nursery. There was nothing casual about the early years of Peter.

His first impressions of the universe are as amusing and understanding as Mr. Wells is apt to be.

Peter could not remember a time when Joan was not in his world. From the beginning it seemed the chief fact was Mary. " Nanny," you called her, or " Mare-*we*," or you simply howled till she came. She was omnipresent or just round the corner night and day. Other figures were more intermittent—" Daddy," a large, loud, exciting, almost terrific thing ; and " Mummy," who was soft and made gentle noises, but was, in comparison to Mary, rather a fool about one's bottle.

Arthur, Peter's father, had a theory that children should not be solitary. From their earliest years children must be accustomed to co-operation. Mary used to watch the proceedings with a cynical and irritating expression.

" Peter's tower," Peter would propose.

" *Our* tower," Arthur used to say.

" Dadda not put any more bricks, Peter finish it."

" Na-ow," from Joan, in a voice like a little cat. " *Me* finish it."

Mary's way was quite different. With a piece of chalk she would draw a line across the floor.

" That's your share, Peter ; and that's yours, Joan. Them's your share of bricks, and them's yours. Now don't you think of going outside your share either of you, nowhow. Nor touch a brick that isn't yours." Whereupon there was peace once more.

Peter's father and mother were drowned under circumstances that we have not space to describe. As we have intimated, Peter and Joan were not brother and sister ; Joan was what Peter's aunt, Lady Charlotte, termed in their hearing a " Bye-blow."

" Which is the Bye-blow, my dear, the boy or the gel ?"

Peter made a note of " Bye-blow "—it was a lovely word. " Can't we go into the garden, now, Auntie, and play at Bye-blows ?"

Mr. Wells, in attacking the present educational system and the moral training of boys, is no doubt perfectly justified, but does he imagine that to abolish a religion that has stood the test of the ages and to substitute his own theories is to resolve the problem ? If he wishes to destroy simple faith, let him at least offer something to take its place. When Mr. Wells has long since been forgotten, the old religion will exist, none the worse for his attacks.

It goes without saying that there are many interesting and arresting people in the story of Joan and Peter. Aunts Phyllis and Phœbe added their quota to the educational scheme.

" Never let Peter touch meat in any shape or form," said Aunt Phœbe. " Once a human child tastes blood the mischief is done."

" Surround him with beautiful things. Accustom him ——"

She winced that Arthur should hear, but spoke as one who has a duty to perform. " Accustom him to the nude from his earliest years. Associate it with innocent amusements. Retrieve the fall." At this point Peter found his aunts over stimulating.

" He must be almost entirely lungs," said Aunt Phœbe when her voice could be heard. " Other internal organs will no doubt develop later."

When one has disentangled the story of Peter and Joan from the maze of Mr. Wells' theories and new theologies, one decides that they are both quite lovable young creatures.

Joan had some trouble to make her dear "Petah" discern that she wasn't his sister, and had no desire to be. We are glad she succeeded.

Of course the book had to end up with the war ; how could it do otherwise these days ?

Some of our readers will be a little bored if they attempt to read from cover to cover.

Mr. Wells is a capital novelist, but not much of a theologian, and he should stick to the former, where he is both powerful and convincing.

H. H.

COMING EVENTS.

November 23rd—National Union of Trained Nurses. Meeting to discuss the proposed Ministry of Health. Speakers : Dr. Saleeby and Miss H. L. Pearse. Chair, the Rev. H. R. L. Sheppard, 3, Vere Street, Oxford Street, W. 2.30 p.m.

November 25th.—West London Hospital, Hammersmith. Opening Abercorn Home for the Nursing Staff by H.R.H. Princess Arthur of Connaught. 2.30 p.m.

November 29th.—Annual Meeting of the Grand Council of the National Council of Trained Nurses of Great Britain and Ireland, 431, Oxford Street, London, W. 4 p.m.

November 30th.—Nurses' Missionary League. A quiet Day, St. Michael's Church, Chester Square, W. 1. Apply Miss H. Y. Richardson, 52, Lower Sloane Street, S.W.

OUR PRIZE COMPETITION.
QUESTIONS.

November 30th. — What do you know of " mustard gas " burns and their treatment ?

December 7th.—Describe the management of a newly born infant for the first week of life.

LETTERS TO THE EDITOR.

Whilst cordially inviting communications upon all subjects for these columns, we wish it to be distinctly understood that we do not IN ANY WAY hold ourselves responsible for the opinions expressed by our correspondents.

MAKESHIFTS.

To the Editor of THE BRITISH JOURNAL OF NURSING.

DEAR MADAM,—I must apologise for delay in replying to your correspondent in the issue of November 2nd, but in my present sphere of work we are so busy celebrating Italian victories and peace that English posts and papers reach us very rarely, and after long delays! I hope, however, that as she belongs to the half of the world with its summer before it, my information may still be useful. The highly-developed optical organ of the common fly and of some other insects is blind to the blue rays of the spectrum. I will not be so foolhardy as to try to explain why this is so. The exact tint of blue does not matter, but what is generally employed is the full "royal blue," of the shade used for old-fashioned glass salt-cellars. (The most hygienic spittoons are made of this glass, to prevent the dissemination of their infectious contents by visiting flies.) If one has quite a free hand in doing up a sick room or hospital ward for the fly season the best plan is to colourwash the walls and ceiling of as rich a blue as possible; ordinary dry paint, mixed with the whitewash; this makes a most restful "ambiente," as we say in this country. Then drape or cover your windows with net or muslin, dyed blue. This is easily managed with Dolly dyes or their equivalent; it is actually sufficient if you veil the upper part of the window, particularly if it is of the sort that comes down to the ground. If the windows are half shut, colourwash them also; but, as the plague of flies is usually with us in hot weather I am supposing that all the air possible is to be allowed to enter the room or tent, for the colour scheme is of course equally practicable with the latter. If the floor can share in the prevailing tint so much the better, as the wandering fly will then see what appears to him to be a pitch-dark cavern and so will turn his attention elsewhere.

I am, yours faithfully,
THE WRITER OF THE ARTICLE.

Montecchio Maggiore,
Forces Françaises en Italie.

THE MISCHIEF OF MEDDLING.

To the Editor of THE BRITISH JOURNAL OF NURSING.

DEAR MADAM,—In your issue of November 2nd, I note that you say that in speaking " of the charity," namely, the Nation's Fund for Nurses, in Manchester, I drew attention to the "comparatively few" trained nurses at the front. This is not so. What I said was that had the V.A.D.s been more efficiently trained, the strain would have been considerably less for the trained nurses, and that I strongly advised any V.A.D. who thought of taking up nursing as a profession

to go in for regular and efficient training, in addition to the experience gained during the war. I would also like to point out that I particularly emphasised that the College of Nursing and the Tribute Fund attached to it *was in no way a charity,* but a tribute due to those nurses who had done such splendid work. I know nothing whatever of a "V.A.D. Register," and in speaking of the proposed College for Nurses I have regarded it as the highest tribute to a profession for women which I honour beyond any other.

I would be glad if you would kindly correct the misstatement in your next issue.

Believe me, yours faithfully,
N. MARTIN HARVEY.

New Theatre, Cardiff.

[We made no " misstatement " in our report of Mrs. Martin Harvey's speech at Manchester, in our issue of November 2nd. Our correspondent's account concerning the " comparatively few " trained nurses at the Front, to which she alluded, in eulogising V.A.D.s, also appeared in the *Manchester Guardian* of October 18th, and so far has not been contradicted, and Mrs. Harvey's statement " that the establishment of the College would prevent anything of the kind in the future," also appears in that leading paper.

Mrs. Martin Harvey writes: " I should like to point out that I particularly emphasised that the College of Nursing and the Tribute Fund attached to it *was in no way a charity.*" We have before us the registration certificate by the London County Council under the War Charities Act 1916, of " The Nation's Fund for Nurses," established 2nd July, 1917, the objects of which are defined " To provide Endowment and Benevolent Funds for the College of Nursing, Ltd." One is prompted to ask Mrs. Martin Harvey why she attends meetings of nurses, and particularly emphasises an untrue and misleading statement calculated to allay the objections of many nurses who may be present to the begging of alms upon their behalf. If Mrs. Martin Harvey has not taken the trouble to acquaint herself with the facts as to the constitution of the College of Nursing and its " charity " fund, we consider it quite inexcusable of her to interfere with the professional and economic affairs of trained nurses, and in so doing mislead the unwary. We nurses who object to all this noisy chatter concerning our work by persons who know nothing about it, cannot be blamed for protesting against the disastrous results of it.

How would Mrs. Martin Harvey and her fair colleagues of the dramatic profession like a band of trained nurses to form themselves into a Committee and stump the country advocating their eleemosynary control by a Council of Actor-Managers authorised by Act of Parliament? If we know anything of these spirited women, they would soon expose the danger and absurdity of such a situation. Then, why should actresses and society women hold our honourable profession up to public commiseration and incidentally help to find the funds to enable our " managers " to control our professional and personal independence ? We consider the situation equally false and absurd. We advise Mrs. Martin Harvey to acquaint herself with the true inwardness of the misnamedFundshe advocates and no further meddle therein.—ED.]

THE AWAKENING.

To the Editor of THE BRITISH JOURNAL OF NURSING.

DEAR MADAM,—The Royal British Nurses' Association is to be congratulated upon the success of the Conference held under its auspices on November 7th. It was my privilege to attend both sessions. The speakers did full justice to the important and interesting subjects dealt with. One impression gained was that the nurses are at last beginning to wake up and take an intelligent interest in their own professional affairs, and to realize that no battle can be won by the generals alone, the rank and file must fight, too, if professional freedom is to be secured and *deserved.*

It was refreshing and edifying to hear the nurses speaking up and giving their views upon a matter of such importance as a Bill for the State Registration of Trained Nurses. It was a happy idea to provide a special session to explain and compare the two Bills. It was quite obvious that the one drafted by the Central Committee was the one to which the audience gave its support. Another impression I gained was that if Professor Glaister came from Scotland at the expense of the College of Nursing Co., Ltd., to speak on behalf of the Bill drafted by that body, it was a great waste of the company's money. To call vital principles insignificant " trifles " is not the way to convince an enlightened audience. I was pleased to observe three military Matrons present, who also, apparently, supported the Bill of the Central Committee ; at least,they gave no support to Professor Glaister.

A " PICKER UP OF LEARNING'S CRUMBS."

A GREAT BENEVOLENT FUND FOR THE NURSING PROFESSION.

To the Editor of THE BRITISH JOURNAL OF NURSING.

MADAM,—In a recent issue, you draw attention to the vulgarity of a poster begging for subscriptions for Lady Cowdray's Fund for Nurses. It is, indeed, sad to reflect that Matrons connected with the Fund should have submitted to this public degradation of their profession.

But there are still greater evils covered by this poster which appeals for funds for the College of Nursing and the Tribute Fund for Nurses.

The following resolution, adopted by the Council of my Society in May, 1918, expresses the opinion of all those who care for the independence and dignity of the nursing profession :—

" The Council of the National Union of Trained Nurses protests against the methods by which the British Women's Hospital Committee is raising Funds for providing annuities for nurses, for the following reasons :—

" 1. It objects, as being inconsistent with the dignity of the profession, that appeals for charity should be made by means of advertisement in the Press and by posters placarding the streets.

" 2. It maintains that such a Benevolent Fund should not be coupled with an Endowment Fund, especially for an unrepresentative body such as the College of Nursing, Ltd., which has as yet no established claim to confidence.

" 3. It urges most strongly that the British Women's Hospital Committee, whose feelings of sympathy for the nursing profession it fully appreciates, should place the management of the Nation's Fund in the hands of a reallynational and representative body.

" For this purpose the Council of the National Union of Trained Nurses suggests that a joint committee should be formed of the existing benevolent funds, such as the Trained Nurses' Annuity Fund, the Royal British Nurses' Association Benevolent Fund, the Queen's Nurses' Benevolent Fund, the Edith Cavell Homes, the Junius Morgan Benevolent Fund, and any other that may appear suitable."—I am, yours faithfully,
EVELYN L. C. EDEN,
Hon. Adviser to the National Union of Trained Nurses.
46, Marsham Street, S.W. 1.

REVERENCE FOR THE DEAD: IS IT REALLY TRUE?

To the Editor of THE BRITISH JOURNAL OF NURSING.

DEAR MADAM,—This is the question I asked of the pleasant-mannered Secretary of the British Women's Hospital Committee, at her office a few days ago. Her reply was that it was perfectly true ; a " Victory Ball " was to be given at the Albert Hall, on November 27th, in aid of " The Nation's Fund for Nurses," to celebrate victory. She was very surprised at my indignant protest. In the first place, peace has not been proclaimed, technically, therefore, the war is not over. An armistice means a *temporary* cessation of hostilities. Surely the dominant thought in the mind of all true patriots in this connection is that this large measure of victory has been won for us by the incomparable valour of our sailors and soldiers—wounded and otherwise—and *above all* by the " great sacrifice " of those unconquerable souls who fell in their tens of thousands on the battle-field. Was there ever such a strange way of celebrating their passing ?

If people like to dance on such an occasion they are, I suppose, at liberty to do so ; but they are *not* at liberty to do so in the name of and much against the wishes of patriotic nurses (some 400 of whom have also made the great sacrifice). It is an act of sacrilege towards the dead, and an insult to the great profession of nursing. This was the substance of my conversation with the lady, who could not see my point of view. We are certainly entitled to rejoice, but our hearts are full, and we incline more towards the giving of unbounded thanks to the " only Giver of all victory," for the conquest of an evil power in the world.
REVERENCE FOR THE DEAD.

The Midwife.

BABY WEEK COUNCIL.

On Monday, November 25th, National Baby Week Council is organising a Meeting at the Armitage Hall, 224, Great Portland Street, W. at 5 p.m., to discuss "The Ministry of Health Bill: Our Hopes and Fears." The following have already kindly consented to speak :—" Why We Need a Ministry of Health," Major Waldorf Astor, M.P.; "The Responsibility of Voters," The Viscountess Rhondda ; "The Ministry of Health and the Poor Law," The Rt. Hon. Lord George Hamilton ; "The Ministry of Health and the Racial Perils of Peace," Dr. C. W. Saleeby, F.R.S.E.

Admission to the Meeting is free, and all interested are cordially invited.

WORKERS' SECTION, ASSOCIATION OF INFANT WELFARE AND MATERNITY CENTRES.

A conference will be held on Wednesday, December 4th, at 5.45 p.m., at 24, Underwood Street, Vallance Road, E. *Subject.* — The Ideal Health Visitor for Infant Welfare Work, and the Qualifications Needed. *Chair.*—Miss Macdonald, Secretary, Royal British Nurses' Association. *Speakers.*— Miss H. Walters, and others. 'Bus 25 and Aldgate Station. Tea at 5.30.

EXTRA COAL RATION FOR MATERNITY CASES.

Mr. W. H. Gaunt, Secretary of the Coal Mines Department of the Board of Trade, has informed Miss Halford, Secretary of the National Association for the Prevention of Infant Mortality, that a claim could certainly be submitted for an additional allowance of coal on the ground of illness in the case of childbirth, and would be allowed for a reasonable period thereafter.

The maximum quantity of fuel that may be granted on such a claim is 5 tons, but the decision as to the actual quantity granted must depend on the circumstances of the particular case.

A "FREAK" OF NATURE.

Miss Amelia M. Burke sends us from Bombay the picture of an Indian baby with a patch of white hair. No reason for this "freak" is forthcoming, although it has caused a fair amount of interest.

TREATMENT OF ANTE-NATAL AND POST-NATAL SYPHILIS.

Mr. John Adams, F.R.C.S., Medical Officer in Charge of the Thavies Inn Venereal Centre for Pregnant Women (the only hospital of the kind), gives an extremely interesting account of the results of the first year's work in the *British Medical Journal*, in the course of which he says,

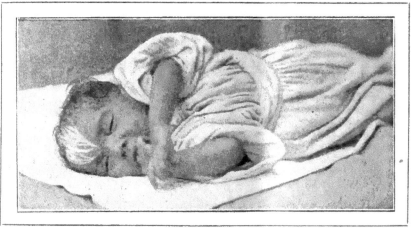

A FREAK TUFT OF WHITE HAIR. AN INDIAN BABY.

in regard to the children, "the results are most encouraging. But the future treatment of ante-natal and post-natal syphilis cannot be allowed to remain where it has been in the past; and the treatment which is being adopted to-day will be improved on to-morrow. I am certain that the lives of thousands of syphilitic children have been lost unnecessarily in the past, while it would have been a blessing to themselves and humanity if many of those who have survived had never lived in misery to be a burden to the State. In the future such children may be made healthy and useful members of the community. . . .

"If I were to criticize my year's work I should say that, had the drugs been in bigger doses, the results would have been still better; but one had to tread with caution the unknown paths of research in the case of these newly born children, and, on the whole, I am of opinion that the means adopted are only the beginning of still greater progress in the future treatment of ante-natal and post-natal syphilis."

THE
BRITISH JOURNAL OF NURSING
WITH WHICH IS INCORPORATED
THE NURSING RECORD
EDITED BY MRS BEDFORD FENWICK

No. 1,600.   SATURDAY, NOVEMBER 30, 1918.   Vol. LXI.

EDITORIAL.

A DANGER OF DEMOBILIZATION.

One of the dangers apprehended when demobilization takes place in the near future is the increase in venereal diseases, and none know better than trained nurses the ill-health and sorrow which these bring in their train, and no section of the community should, therefore, be more on the alert to assist in enforcing such preventive precautions as are indicated by expert knowledge and sanitary science.

In a letter to the press Lord Sydenham, the President and other officers of the National Council for Combatting Venereal Diseases, on its behalf, urge that unless strong measures are taken there will be grave danger to the public health.

It is understood, they say, that there will be about 300,000 men of the Army and Navy under treatment, and infective, on demobilization. The incidence of venereal disease in the Army where instruction, treatment and discipline combine to reduce infection, is put at only 2 per cent.; in the adult civilian population, where these influences do not obtain, it is estimated at nearly 20 per cent., and it is urged that immediate steps must be taken to prevent the spread of disease to wives, families and others.

The Committee ask the public to support the following plan of action.

That the Local Government Board should authorize the appointment of whole-time venereal officers (a man and a woman) on the staffs of the medical officer of each county or county borough. That the present hospital accommodation should be supplemented by *ad hoc* clinics under the supervision of such venereal officers in every town of 10,000 inhabitants, and also in the county boroughs. Such clinics to open for continuous and early treatment both for men and women, and to be available early in the New Year.

Over a dozen other recommendations are made, amongst them the appointment of women police, and an adequate number of voluntary women patrols, but throughout these recommendations there is no word to suggest that the co-operation of trained nurses is desired, or that it is essential to success in the war against venereal diseases. Yet, when there was still a conspiracy of silence as to the ravages of these diseases the trained nurses were on the alert, and drawing attention to the necessity for dealing with their effects, instead of concealing and ignoring them.

Speaking in support of the Ministry of Health Bill, and its relations to problems of Reconstruction, at the Armitage Hall on Monday last, Dr. Saleeby stated that venereal disease had increased during the war, and said that " the real danger was the infection of hosts of healthy men who had fought for us, on their release, by exposure to the greatly extended area of infection among our young women at the present time." Better were it for our brave men that they should die on the field of honour, than infected and infectious drag out a miserable existence, and transmit a horrible disease to their wives and children.

Small wonder that nurses who know the misery entailed by even one case and its consequences, are appalled at the prospect of widespread infection, and desire to be effectively associated with any schemes for its prevention.

The work of nurses is not primarily to fight the disease on moral grounds, but certainly the moral side needs emphasising and such a campaign would have widespread support among nurses.

OUR PRIZE COMPETITION.

WHAT DO YOU KNOW OF "MUSTARD GAS" BURNS AND THEIR TREATMENT?

We have pleasure in awarding the prize this week to Miss Marjorie E. Thorpe, University War Hospital, Southampton.

PRIZE PAPER.

Mustard gas (Dichlorethyl sulphide) derives its name from its odour, reminiscent of mustard. It is an oily liquid, and when released it slowly evaporates.

The fluid may be scattered on clothing, rifles, and on the ground, &c., and may thus become infective through direct contamination of the skin.

The gas attacks the mucus membrane and the skin. The principal symptoms take from four to twenty-four hours to develop. The burns start with widespread erythema and local vesication. The commonest sites are the axillæ, genitals, and back, but any area may be attacked. The surfaces affected show very marked pigmentation. Deep burns sometimes occur.

Laryngitis, pharyngitis, and bronchitis may occur in from twenty-four to forty-eight hours. The degree of the lesion varies from a simple irritation to an ulceration of the mucous membrane of the whole passages, followed by infection of the raw surfaces. Vomiting and epigastric pain also occur if the mucous membrane of the stomach and œsophagus is affected. Conjunctivitis is the first symptom to appear. Intense photophobia results and swelling of the eyelids.

Treatment (Skin).—The slighter burns heal perfectly with some non-irritating protective application, *i.e.,* boric ointment, Lassar's paste, &c.

Severe burns are generally indolent in healing. If there is suppuration, repeated hot boric fomentations give relief.

If the burns are extensive and dressings painful, hot alkaline baths may be given. The patient may be totally submerged for twenty minutes or half an hour. The dressing may then be painlessly removed, and a liquid paraffin dressing applied. In later stages of healing, ung. eucalyptus, boric, or Lassar's paste may be applied.

For uncomplicated cases, a dusting powder of boric acid, starch and zinc oxide may be applied freely.

Eyes.—If pain is severe, fomentations over the eyeballs give relief. If inflammation is severe, the patient may wear a shade or dark glasses, or the room may be darkened.

The eyes may be irrigated with boric lotion, and liquid paraffin (which is not irritant, and acts as a lubricant) should be instilled into the conjunctival sacs three times daily.

When inflammation subsides, drops containing zinc sulphate, boric acid and adrenalin are beneficial.

The laryngeal condition is best relieved by inhalations of menthol and benzoin. For the throat and nose, warm alkaline washes at least three times a day are necessary.

Functional aphonia of varying degree is often present, and may be cured by breathing exercises and a brisk rubbing of the pharyngeal wall with a laryngeal mirror. The cough, which is a very distressing later symptom, may be relieved by cough mixtures and by heroin gr. $\frac{1}{8}$. If the respiratory organs are very severely involved, the oxygenation of the blood is interfered with, and the patient dies through suffocation. In this case oxygen may be given as a palliative treatment, and the patient should be left in the open air.

HONOURABLE MENTION.

The following competitors receive honourable mention :—Miss E. F. James, Miss Phillips, Miss P. Robertson.

QUESTION FOR NEXT WEEK.

Describe the management of a newly born infant for the first week of life.

THE ROYAL RED CROSS.

SECOND CLASS.

On Saturday last, at the Investiture at Buckingham Palace, the King decorated the following lady with the Royal Red Cross.

Sister Jessie Ferguson, South African Military Nursing Service.

FOR COURAGE IN THE FIELD.

The King has been pleased to approve of the award of the Military Medal to the following ladies for distinguished services in the field :—

Miss Rosa Brain (S./Nurse), T.F.N.S.—For exceptional courage and devotion to duty during a hostile air raid, when bombs were dropped on the hospital. One of the bombs wrecked the hut in which she was on duty, and, with the greatest coolness, she attended to all the patients in the ward, though she herself was wounded.

And to the following members of the First Aid Nursing Yeomanry Corps :—

Miss Evelyn M. Cridlan.
Miss Gwendolyn Garrish Peyton Jones.
Miss Mary Devas Marshall.
Miss Rachel Gertrude Moseley.
Miss Ellen Russell.
Miss Christina Margaret Urquart.

NURSING AND THE WAR.

When we nurses celebrate Victory and Peace let it be with quiet thankfulness and homage. Let it be a holy day, rather than a holiday. The Royal British Nurses' Association and its Affiliated Societies should be ready to celebrate Peace in a nurse-like spirit and not by any frivolous function calculated to give the public an entirely wrong impression of our real feelings. War may cease, but what true nurses have faced and suffered during this tragic time will not be effaced from their hearts or their memories for many years to come. The agony has been so intense and world-wide, many of us will never be the same again ; and it is not well that we should be.

The authorities of the Edmonton Military Hospital, where four nurses have died from influenza, which they caught while nursing wounded patients, have received the following letter from the War Office :

" The Director-General wishes it to be known in all military hospitals in the Eastern Command how much he appreciates the unselfish devotion to their duty of the members of the Nursing Services at this time of emergency.

" He is aware that they are being much over-worked, and regrets that in spite of all efforts which have been and are being made to procure more nurses, it is quite impossible, owing to the wide-spread epidemic of influenza, to send the necessary help.

" The admirable spirit of devotion to duty of all ranks of the Nursing Service will be brought to the notice of the Nursing Board of the Army Council."

The letter is to be reprinted in the form of a Christmas card and distributed to the nurses at the Edmonton Military Hospital.

We have heard of many deaths of young nurses during this really serious epidemic of illness which has not yet been surely defined. No doubt the general health has for months been undermined by overwork and the unnourishing food on which we are existing, although we hear from many private nurses that the tables of the rich are still loaded with every luxury, in spite of the profiteering of the provision dealers. We are glad to note that this question of food prices may receive attention after the Election.

SISTER WATKINS:

Sister Watkins, who has been awarded the Military Medal for bravery during the bombardment by the enemy of a casualty clearing station in France, was trained at Guy's Hospital, and went to France under the British Red Cross Society in 1914, joining the Army Nursing Service in 1915. Sister Watkins remained at her post until wounded in the leg, and was later sent to London and admitted to hospital. She hopes shortly to return to duty in France.

We are indebted for our portrait to the courtesy of the Editor of the *Oxford Chronicle*.

The Burdett Press exclaims :—" We are all looking with expectation to Sir Arthur Stanley, G.B.E., promptly to put himself at the head of a Great Free Will Movement, which we have no doubt would produce two hundred and fifty thousand pounds without delay." This large sum is to be expended in controlling the Nursing Profession, but we are not enlightened as to where the " Free Will " comes in. How heartily sick we are of all this fuss-potting upon our behalf by the proprietors of newspapers (charity ads. are very lucrative), and of climbing plutocrats who hanker after proximity to the *tabouret !* We long to be left alone to work out our own salvation on self-supporting and independent lines. That is the only great Free Will Movement as far as trained nurses are concerned which matters.

It now appears that the beautiful hospital established at the Hotel Astoria in Paris is to be closed down forthwith, so that it may be used as offices by the British Government during the Peace Conference. Our legion of representatives will be located at the Hotel Majestic, so that there should be ample room for Mr. Hughes and the other Dominion Premiers. We should feel safer about those German Colonies if he were there.

Miss Muriel Gladys Hutton, daughter of Alderman W. L. Hutton, J.P., of Moss Bank, Aughton, who was recently invested by the King with the Royal Red Cross (first class) decoration, has been further honoured by the presentation of the Granton Nautical Button by Admiral James Starton, at Edinburgh, " in token of the appreciation of her courtesy and kindness."

FRENCH FLAG NURSING CORPS.

DEVOTED SERVICE RECOGNISED.

The French Ministry has asked for the names of all the Sisters who have served in the Corps for two years and upwards, and have thus devoted themselves to the sick and wounded in military hospitals under the French medical authorities.

The French Flag Nursing Corps is the only Service of British Nurses working under the direct authority of the French War Office which throughout the war has maintained the minimum qualification of a Certificate of three years' training in general nursing, thus its members well deserve the honour which the French Government proposes to award them, the " Médaille de la Reconnaissance Française."

We have been having more compliments, and we will just repeat what an important official at Paris in the Service de Santé said :—" I do not wish to be complimentary nor yet flattering, but the Service de Santé has found the nurses of the F.F.N.C. the most satisfactory of all the nurses—English, French, or American—who have worked under its formation in point of view both of discipline and work, and should any of them care to remain on, after the signing of peace, we shall be only too pleased to place them in their various formations." Isn't that some reward for three and four years' real work, and recognition of the value of the standard of three years' general training of the members of the Corps?

We as Hon. Superintendent are specially gratified with the recognition by the Service de Santé of the value of discipline—the more especially as it has been maintained throughout the four years on duty by mutual understanding between officials and Sisters, and without the sinister support of a Serf Clause !

Several of the ambulances to which the Sisters are attached are on the march to Germany.

A Sister writes :—I wish I could describe to you the sights on the road, especially when crossing the line—terrible devastation and death—many German corpses lying just where they were killed—caught in acts of destruction and pillage.

A Sister writes from Paris : " I had not seen any mention of the ' Victory Ball ' till I read my *B.J.N.* It sounds horrible. How I wish I could take some of these heartless women and dump them in some of the hospitals for the gassed cases—where the death struggles and agony of these poor stricken men will never be effaced from one's memory—or let them see the returned French and British prisoners who have crawled to the line, before they have been cleansed and fed. If they feel like dancing after such heart-rending sights, then indeed they could ' Dance on the Dead.' "

THE WEST LONDON HOSPITAL, HAMMERSMITH.

OPENING OF THE NEW NURSES' HOME.

The Abercorn Home, which is otherwise the Nurses' Home for the West London Hospital, was formally opened on Monday, November 25th. Some disappointment was felt at the unavoidable absence through illness of H.R.H. Princess Arthur of Connaught, who was to have performed the ceremony, but her place was gracefully taken by Lady Evelyn Farquhar, who, in the name of Her Royal Highness, accepted the silver key of the Home, and received the address in the recreation room before a large audience.

The Chairman, Mr. G. F. Marshall, in presenting the latter, said the Home was a memorial to their late President, the Duke of Abercorn, who had always had this scheme at heart.

Lady Evelyn then read Princess Arthur's address, in which she expressed her pleasure at being asked to perform the ceremony. From her personal knowledge she could appreciate the benefit that such a Home would be to the nurses. Since the war much attention had been drawn to the needs of this skilled body of workers.

The Prayer of Blessing was then offered by the Chaplain, the Rev. Nelson Walshe, who asked that this Home might be for the mental rest and bodily refreshment of those for whom it was provided, and that it should be used for their comfort and God's glory.

Sir William Bull said that this Home was a model of what a Nurses' Home should be, as everything had been carefully studied to give the maximum of comfort. Different sitting-rooms for various grades of nurses might appear a small matter, but a little thought would show how, if a junior nurse were comfortably toasting her toes before the fire and her senior entered the room, etiquette would oblige her to give place to her.

The Home would repay the authorities a hundred times (not in money) by making the nurses happy and comfortable.

The Chairman then moved a vote of sympathy with Princess Arthur of Connaught in her indisposition, and said he was proud to think she had seen her first surgical operation in the wards of the West London Hospital.

The visitors were then free to inspect the charming arrangements. Tea was provided in the various sitting-rooms, and organised so that there was no overcrowding.

A tablet in the entrance hall of the Home, placed there by the Board of Managers, notifies that the erection was largely due to the generous benefaction of Dan Mason, Esq., who also gave the land upon which it stands. The Home is fortunately placed, inasmuch as there are open spaces near by. It also has a garden of its own, and a lady who has made a study of the flowers and shrubs which will grow in London soot, and has undertaken its supervision, anticipates that something will be flowering all the year round.

The Home contains 104 bedrooms, and it is the pride of the Matron, Miss Florence Nevile, and the joy of Sisters, nurses, and maids that each one has a separate room. The building is heated by radiators, so that it is very warm and comfortable. There is a bathroom to five bedrooms, and shampooing-rooms are provided with electric dryers, which will dry the thickest head of hair in fifteen minutes.

All the clocks in the building are timed by the control clock in the hall, which is kept in order by the Standard Electric Time Company. The floors are of dolament, a material smooth in texture and deep red in colour, which, polished with Shell Brand Polish, presents a most attractive appearance.

All the principal meals are served in the hospital, but the nurses can make tea from 8.30 to 9.30 at night, boiling the water on gas-rings provided for the purpose, as well as at other off-duty times, when they may receive "cousins from the Front" and other visitors in rooms which are at their disposal. There are also reading, writing, and sewing rooms, with the free use of a sewing machine and electric irons.

The sick rooms, daintily furnished and with glowing fires, must be most attractive to a tired nurse. The night nurses' quarters are cut off with doors from the rest of the building, so that quiet is assured. Lastly, mention must be made of the flat roof, provided with four teak seats and eighteen deck chairs, which is sure to be a very popular rendezvous in summer. The Matron will be pleased to show the Home to other Matrons or to former nurses any afternoon between 2 and 4 p.m.

M. B.

NATIONAL COUNCIL OF TRAINED NURSES.

We hope for a full Meeting of the Delegates on Friday next at 431, Oxford Street, W. International questions will be considered, and they are of a somewhat delicate nature just now. Tea at 4 p.m.

A VICTORY THANK OFFERING FOR STATE REGISTRATION.

Our Appeal for funds to promote our State Registration Campaign, which will be found on page ii of the cover, is meeting with success, and offerings large and small will be equally welcome.

The sister of the Editor has given £50 " for propaganda through THE BRITISH JOURNAL OF NURSING, and as a protest against the most unfair boycott of the press of the Trained Nurses' just demand for self-government and independence, hoping others will help this just cause according to their means."

CENTRAL COMMITTEE FOR THE STATE REGISTRATION OF NURSES.

The amended Bill is now in print, price 3d. and postage. Copies can be obtained from the Office, 431, Oxford Street, London, W.

This is a just Bill. All nurses should study it—and join a Society which supports it. Times are critical. The profession is faced with great danger to personal liberty at the present time under the College Constitution. God helps those who help themselves.

HOMAGE TO EDITH CAVELL.

Now that Belgium is once again free from the heel of the oppressor one of the first acts of the Military and Civil Authorities is to honour the graves of its martyrs.

The Belgian Councillor of Justice, M. Moordecker, and the French Captain Benoit Stein, who is attached to the Staff of the Military Administration accompanied the members of the Communal Council last week to the Evere Cemetery to lay wreaths on the graves of Belgian soldiers.

The party then went to the spot where Nurse Edith Cavell is buried. There they saluted the dead, 41 others shot by the Germans being buried close by.

" They knelt with deep emotion at the grave of the British national heroine, Miss Edith Cavell who rests among the Allied martyrs," says a telegram sent by the Military Governor of Western Flanders to the vice-president of the Imperial Graves Committee at the British Headquarters.

The Soldiers' Council in Brussels has decided to send a report to the German Government on the situation in Belgium, demanding the punishment of those responsible for the execution of Nurse Cavell and other crimes.

Royal British Nurses' Association.

(Incorporated by   Royal Charter.)

THIS SUPPLEMENT BEING THE OFFICIAL ORGAN OF THE CORPORATION.

LECTURE—ANCIENT EGYPT.

The Members of the Association who were able to be present at the Lecture given to nurses at University College on 21st inst. agreed that they had rarely spent a more delightful afternoon.

Mrs. Latter, who presided, said that it required no words of hers to emphasise the privilege of being able to listen to a lecture by Miss Murray, whose name was so well known to all who were interested in Egyptology. The civilization of Egypt dated back thousands of years, and in this ancient civilization were to be found all the aims and ideals of the nineteenth century.

Miss Murray, in commencing her lecture, of which we can only give a short synopsis, said that the Egyptian civilization may be said to end where our own commences; roughly speaking, we can find traces of this ancient civilization back to six thousand years before Christ, but probably the Egyptians were civilized at even an earlier date. Miss Murray put several examples of ancient hieroglyphics on the screen and explained those, saying that the ancient Egyptian writing was certainly the most beautiful in the world. She drew attention to the lining and beautiful grouping of the picture words, and explained the meaning of certain of them. Pictures were also shown throwing light on the religious beliefs of Ancient Egypt; according to one of those, when an Egyptian died he divided into seven different parts : body, soul, mind, heart, shadow, Ka, and name. Many very wonderful pictures of kings of the various dynasties were put on the screen, and those present were amazed to find the amount of character portrayed in those faces carved in stone, particularly in the lower portions of the face. A picture of the Sphinx was shown, Miss Murray adding, at the close of her description of this, that she considered it one of the most impressive things to be found in Egypt; the "Father of Terrors" it had been called in olden times. Next came pictures, all carefully explained, showing the various things found in the tombs, and put there by the friends of the dead in the firm belief in a future life. There were utensils of all sorts, game, jewels, and different kinds of games, some of the latter very similar evidently to those of the present day. In another picture the lion and the unicorn were shown playing chess, and, as the lecturer remarked, it was evident from the expression of the lion that he was winning. In another view there was the portrayal of a lady preparing

for some feast or dance, and engaged in touching her lips with a colour brush. Pictures were shown indicating the custom of killing the animals which had belonged to the dead person, in order that he might not be lonely when he " crossed the bar." Miss Murray pointed out a remnant of this custom in these later days, in which the charger of a chief or an officer is frequently led behind his coffin, although it is not now slaughtered.

A most beautiful slide was shown representing the arm of a mummy with gorgeously coloured jewels. Miss Murray told of how this was discovered by Professor Flinders Petrie. The tomb must have been robbed in ancient times, and the thieves had been discovered or at least interrupted, and this arm had been hidden away in a crevice in the rock. The tomb was explored at different periods, in one case as early as 600 B.C., but the jewelled arm was not discovered then nor on any of the later dates at which there is evidence that the tomb was entered, until a few years ago when Professor Petrie was engaged in research work in Egypt. His servant came to tell him that he had discovered something bright, and when he examined the object the Professor saw the bright central jewel of an ornament. He cut up the covering, and disclosed the arm weighted with its wonderful bracelets. Several views of ancient temples were also shown, Miss Murray remarking that curves were never found in the architecture of ancient Egypt.

A fresh treat awaited the nurses after the lantern lecture, for Professor Flinders Petrie, Miss Murray, and others took them round the great Egyptology Collection of the University College, which is second to none in the world. It has not quite so many large specimens as the collection at the British Collection, but there is far greater variety, and one gazed with amazement at the beautiful pottery, the vases carved in rare stone materials, the dainty sculptured heads, the perfect enamelling of certain tiles, and many other beautiful and wonderful things. The perfect, graceful curves of some of the vases carved in stone were greatly admired, and one realized the marvellous control which those ancient Egyptians must have had over their muscles to produce such perfect work. In one case we saw the scent-bottle of the mother of the Princess who found Moses; it was of a beautiful cream stone, adorned with bands of lovely gilding, fresh as the day when it was put on many thousands of years ago. Many of the necklaces were very beautiful, and, as Miss Murray pointed out, it was interesting to note that they were mostly of a colour which suited the dark complexion of the Egyptians. Those beads might almost be said to take one through an entire civilization, from four little iron specimens of a very early period and others of wonderful lustre and representative of lost arts, down to the decline of the Egyptian dynasties, when the beads gradually became much coarser and more vulgar in appearance. Two nurses had brought rings with ancient Egyptian carvings or stones in them, which they showed to Professor Petrie, who said that one belonged to a period three hundred years before Christ, and another to one fifteen hundred years before the Christian era.

COURSE OF LECTURES.

The following lectures, of which particulars will be given later, will commence on December 5th. On that date Edward Price Bell, Esq., M.A., the famous American Journalist and Editor, will lecture on "America and the New World Order," at 11, Chandos Street, Cavendish Square, at 2.45 p.m. Those who had the privilege of listening to Mr. Price Bell a few weeks ago at Bedford College will look forward with great pleasure to this lecture, and we urge all our members to make every effort to be present ; Miss Meakin, Fellow of the Royal Geographical Society, will lecture on "Bokhara and Samarkand," on December 19th ; Mr. Herbert Paterson, F.R.C.S., on "Scottish Wit and Humour"; Professor Flinders Petrie on "Ten Thousand Years of Civilisation"; and Mr. Selwyn Image, late Slade Professor of Fine Art in Oxford University, on "Two Famous Diarists of the Seventeenth Century" (John Evelyn and Samuel Pepys). Mr. James Berry, F.R.C.S., will lecture on "Land and Peoples of the Lower Danube." All these educational subjects have been carefully chosen and as a relief from professional questions.

APPOINTMENTS.

Miss H. C. Sadleir has been appointed Matron of the Harrow, Wealdstone and District, War Memorial Maternity Hostel, 10, College Road, Harrow, Middlesex, to be opened on December 7th. Miss Sadleir has been a member of the R.B.N.A. since 1895. She was trained and certificated at the Royal Free Hospital, and at Kensington Infirmary for Midwifery, and holds Certificates in Gynaecology and Monthly Nursing, and C.M.B. She has done many years of private nursing, and taken Sisters' holiday duty at several V.A.D. Hospitals in Harrow.

Miss Edith Robinson has been appointed Assistant Housekeeper at St. Mary's Hospital for the East End. Miss Robinson was trained at the Royal Hants County Hospital, and became a Member of the Corporation in 1913.

A PROFESSIONAL PROTEST.

The following letter was sent from the Office last week to certain ladies patronising the Victory Ball promoted by the *Daily Sketch* in the name of "Nation's Fund for Nurses," as it was felt they could not have been informed of the natural indignation felt by thousands of the Nation's Nurses, that such a function was to take place during a period of mourning by those who have lost their dearest, and whilst sick, wounded, and prisoners are still suffering as the cost of Victory :—

MADAM,—At the urgent request of Members of this Corporation, and of the organised societies of Nurses affiliated to it, I am to express to you their deep regret on hearing that you have given your support to the Victory Ball at the Albert Hall in aid of the so-called Nation's Fund for Nurses.

They have pointed out to us that they freely gave their services to their King and Country, and that, to use their own words, " Some have made sacrifices even to the death." It is with feelings akin to horror that they realise that, while the sufferings they have witnessed are still fresh in their memory, while the casualty lists are still appearing in the press, while our men, on their march back from the German prison camps are undergoing the most terrible hardships and, according to some reports, dying by the wayside, and while the cloud of sorrow and bereavement is still hanging over so many homes, the Members of the Profession of Nursing are to be made the excuse for a charity ball.

Moreover, the nurses maintain that the public do not understand the precise purpose of the appeal, which purports to be an appeal for the Nation's Nurses, but which, according to its Registration Certificate under the War Charities Act, is secured for one section of nurses only, namely the College of Nursing, Ltd.

I am, Madam,

Yours very truly,

ISABEL MACDONALD,

Secretary.

DONATIONS.

The Hon. Treasurer acknowledges with thanks donations from the following :—

General Purposes Fund.—Miss Bainbridge, 5s. 6d. ; Miss Mitchell, 2s. 6d. ; Miss E. Hall, 2s.

Fund for State Registration.—Miss C. J. Cowie, £2 18s. 6d. ; Mrs. Bartlett, 10s. ; Miss E. Hall, 5s. 6d. ; Miss A. M. Burfield, 5s.; Miss M. Stein, 5s. ; Miss A. James, 4s. ; Miss Cobbett, 2s. 6d. ; Miss E. R. Diver, 2s. 6d. ; Mrs. Findlater, 2s. 6d. ; Miss H. Halsall, 2s. 6d. ; Miss E. H. Kenny, 2s. 6d.

Helena Benevolent Fund.—F. F. C., £1 1s. ; Miss H. L. White 5s.; Miss Neighbour, 2s. 6d. ; Miss Barry, 1s.

(Signed) ISABEL MACDONALD,

Secretary to the Corporation.

10, Orchard St., Portman Sq. W.

NATIONAL UNION OF TRAINED NURSES.

CONFERENCE TO DISCUSS PROPOSED MINISTRY OF HEALTH.

A largely attended Conference, convened by the National Union of Trained Nurses, was held on Saturday, November 23rd, at the College of Ambulance, 3, Vere Street, W., to discuss the proposed Ministry of Health. In the unavoidable absence of the Rev. H. R. L. Sheppard, the Chair was taken by Miss M. Heather-Bigg, R.R.C., and the audience was evidence of the wisdom of the policy of consolidating the self-governing societies of nurses through affiliation with the Royal British Nurses' Association, and with the prestige conferred by its Royal Charter, for it included many members of these societies, as well as of the general public, which was well, for it is highly important that the public should hear the nurses' point of view on matters which vitally affect them.

The Conference was opened by a brilliant speech by Dr. C. W. Saleeby, who paid a high tribute to the work of the late Lord Rhondda at the Local Government Board in promoting a Bill for the establishment of a Ministry of Health, and said that the Bill introduced by Dr. Addison last Session was the product of much hard work. There was not a vested interest which had not been consulted, and there was not time to discuss the Bill in detail clause by clause before the end of the Session. It was important that the Bill should be introduced as early as possible next Session.

In essence the Bill was a small thing out of which, as such, nothing proceeds, but it was the germ of a good thing. Its aim was to get rid of our ridiculous muddling in Whitehall by co-ordinating in one department the health activities of a number of departments. Lord Rhondda had found fourteen Government Departments exercising control in this connection, but that was not final, and the Admiralty was now engaged in starting a maternity department. (Laughter.) The work must be done in a logical and coherent way.

The Ministry of Health was bound to be a feature in electioneering speeches, and candidates for Parliamentary honours were, said Dr. Saleeby, writing to him to know what it meant. He put the position thus. There is poverty in the world, and there are also great resources. The State ought to function as a Ministry of Health.

But it was possible to deal with the question so that the more help was supplied the more help would have to be given.

The foundations on which such a Department should be built were four square. They were—

To learn and to teach ;
To guard and to help.

1. *To learn.*—The Ministry must set out with the function of learning the facts of life and death, availing itself of medical learning and research, of demographic research, and must continuously observe the conditions affecting the health of the people.

2. *To teach.*—The Ministry must be responsible for the teaching given on health subjects and must itself teach. On the whole, teaching in this country was very bad. North of the Tweed they were much in advance of England, where the virtues inculcated were pluck, luck and muddle through. A Ministry of Health should immediately raise the standard of education for the professions, including doctors, dentists, nurses and midwives.

It was not our way to put things in the hands of experts, and the fellow feeling of the Government made it tender to quackery of every description.

All who knew the difference between knowing their job and not knowing it must hold together, and exact that those employed under the Ministry of Health should be trained for their work. There might be geniuses, but even a heaven-sent nurse was improved by training, and the notion that amateurs were as good as experts was a pernicious one. All who had sat down and swatted, because it was the only thing to be done if they were to learn their work thoroughly, knew that it was simply monstrous.

But we had tradition south of the Tweed against us, and we should have hard work to secure the recognition of the expert, but we were right and we had got to win.

3. *To guard.*—It would be the duty of the Ministry of Health to guard the country against disease. It was for the most part borne into our bodies by the channels which conveyed to them the necessaries of life, such as air, water and food ; all these were liable to convey disease. The Ministry of Health must prevent them from conveying the germs of disease.

4. *To help.*—There were cases, however, in which from the nature of the case help was required. The mother and infant were cases in point. It was monstrous that in England and Wales, 3,000 mothers should die annually from puerperal fever. The country of Lister and Florence Nightingale should not know the disease. But the deaths were not all ; there was also the damaged motherhood and damaged infancy. The need of the mother and infant was a biological law. They must have a special service. If ever knowledge were wanted it was wanted here. A highly qualified woman should be highly placed in the mother and baby department.

Dr. Saleeby also advocated the formation of a special department dealing with adolescence, which should include a section of recreation to teach the young—amongst other things—how to use their leisure without doing themselves damage, and how to avoid the racial poisons, such as venereal disease and alcohol. At present, the only people who studied recreation were those who knew how much money could be got out of it. If adolescence were to be protected recreation must be provided ; it was a physiological necessity.

Dr. Saleeby concluded by emphasising the four points he had laid down, and said that the proposals for a Ministry of Health might be perverted unless disinterested people kept them on the right lines.

Miss Isabel Macdonald pointed out the danger of the tendency to put health work into the hands of the incompetent, and said that the training she had found most useful for work of this kind was that given in the wards of a hospital. Health workers should have a full nursing qualification in addition to training in hygiene. Preventive nursing was even more important than curative.

Mr. Williams emphasised the need for expert knowledge on the part of welfare supervisors in factories, and Mr. C. H. Wigington spoke strongly of the need for nurses in factories where the work was of a dangerous character.

THE NEED OF THE CO-OPERATION OF THE TRAINED NURSE IN THE EFFECTIVE WORKING OF A MINISTRY OF HEALTH.

Miss Helen Pearse, who regarded the co-operation of the trained nurse as essential to any effective Ministry of Health, impressed upon her hearers the value of training in helping them to preserve their own health, and consequently the good temper so important in a nurse. Training also helped a nurse to estimate facts, to give proof of knowledge, to attain accuracy, and to condense and write down the result of her observations for the benefit of others. In connection with the administration of public health work nurses were essential and she considered that a trained nurse should be head of any Maternity and Child Welfare Department. She spoke of the value of the work of School Nurses, and said that district nurses were a credit to private endeavour. She emphasised the fact that only women who had expert knowedge could effectively supervise others. It was sometimes asserted that nurses were not organisers. Nothing could be more ridiculous. From the moment a probationer entered a hospital she was obliged to organise in order to get through her work.

Miss Cancellor gave a personal account of public health work for which she considered desirable not only general training, but fever training, a knowledge of the manifestations of skin diseases and venereal diseases, as well as the certificates of the Central Midwives Board and the Sanitary Institute. She hoped that fully-trained nurses would help to administer the Ministry of Health Act; they knew they would have to help to work it.

Miss Beatrice Kent spoke of social work done at the Massachusetts General Hospital, the system employed, and the educational standard of the nurses and had with her for inspection the beautiful charts illustrative of the hospital's activities in this connection.

Miss Jentie Paterson expressed the view that women who had not had three years' training were employed as nurses by the London County Council, and were taking the pay which should be reserved for the fully-trained nurse. It was not right that this should be so.

Mrs. Bedford Fenwick said that when we had a Ministry of Health, she concluded that Dr. Saleeby anticipated it would exercise the same powers that the General Medical Council and the Central Midwives' Board which the Privy Council now did. He had not mentioned a General Nursing Council or a State Nursing Service, both of which were urgently required.

The Minister of Health would be faced with the question, " What is a trained nurse " ? No uniform standard had ever been defined.

Trained nurses must endeavour to get a Nurses' Registration Bill passed without delay by the new Parliament, they had suffered severely from lack of organization during the war, and it was time that those who passed successfully through the recognised training should have the hall mark conferred by a State Register.

It was a fundamental necessity, if a Ministry of Health was to be a success, that a standard of training should be established for nurses as well as doctors and midwives, otherwise when a Minister of Health came to deal with nursing in relation to his Department he would have nothing to guide him.

Miss Macdonald warned trained nurses not to permit their legitimate work to be usurped, and mentioned that in several factories welfare supervisors, with no training, were earning from £400 to £800 per annum, while trained nures were working under them at salaries of from £70 to £130. It lay with nurses to be alive to this danger. They must protect their own profession—no one else would do so.

RESOLUTIONS.

Dr. Saleeby then moved the following Resolution which was carried unanimously.

I.

That this meeting of the National Union of Trained Nurses welcomes the introduction of a Ministry of Health Bill by the Minister of Reconstruction, and, in view of the grave delay of the past eighteen months, and the danger of racial infection during demobilization, urges the Government to proceed with such a measure, as the foundation of racial, and therefore of all reconstruction.

Mrs. Bedford Fenwick proposed the following Resolution, which was seconded by Miss Jentie Paterson, and carried unanimously.

II.

That this meeting of the National Union of Trained Nurses urges upon the Government the need for the State Registration of Trained Nurses, and of a General Nursing Council as an indispensable corollary of the establishment of a Ministry of Health.

It was agreed that copies of these Resolutions, should be sent to the Prime Minister, Dr. Addison, Sir Auckland Geddes, Sir Robert Morrant and the Press.

The meeting closed with a vote of thanks to the chair and speakers, proposed by Miss Cancellor and seconded by Miss Marsters.

On either side of the entrance in the street, as the meeting assembled, a trained nurse, wearing the patriotic colours, stood, bearing a placard inscribed—

DANCING ON THE DEAD.

"**Patriotic Nurses protest against money being raised in their name by a Victory Ball before our splendid men are cold in their graves.**"

In the unfair fight between the employers with the power of wealth behind them, and the under-paid and overworked trained nurses, the former can secure the interest and support of the press at sumptuous luncheon parties and teas organized for the purpose; the nurses cannot employ this method of placing their case before the public, for their scanty salaries in most instances barely suffice to supply their needs, but personal service they can and do give, and the public are with them. While many expressions of sympathy were heard, as men and women stopped to read the posters, not one voice was raised in defence of the heartless section of society in making the nursing profession their excuse for this ill-timed festivity.

APPOINTMENT.

MATRON.

The Welsh National Hospital, Netley. — Miss Helen Mary Akerigg has been appointed Matron. She was trained at Addenbrooke's Hospital, Cambridge, and has been Matron of Clayton Court Auxiliary Hospital, Liss, Sister at the 1st Southern Hospital, Birmingham, as a member of the Territorial Force Nursing Service, Matron of the Cottage Hospital, Fleet, Hampshire, Acting Matron of the Cray Valley Hospital, and Sister at St. George's Hospital, London.

PRESENTATION TO MISS M. HEATHER-BIGG, R.R.C.

On Tuesday evening last the Sisters and nurses of Charing Cross Hospital assembled in the Lounge of the Nurses' Home at 9 o'clock, to present their Matron, Miss Heather-Bigg, with tokens of the affectionate regard of members of the past and present Nursing Staff, on her retirement.

Sister Annie (Miss Pike) made the presentation, comprising a silver-plated tray, suitably inscribed, with coffee pot and milk jug, and a silver sugar basin, with a morocco-bound book containing the names of the subscribers, and a box of goodies.

In thanking them warmly for their beautiful gift, Miss Heather-Bigg said that the high standard set during her 16 years tenure of office had been greatly due to the good work and feeling of the nursing staff; they had never had any disagreeables but had always worked together for the good of the patients.

She counselled the nurses always to receive and treat the patients as they would their own mothers and sisters, and to be true to themselves, and not to evade rules because they thought they would not be found out, but to be good women and good nurses.

She then presented to Sister Annie a fitted writing case, with the love and affection of the donors, and spoke warmly of the help she had received from her in the work.

Tea, by invitation of the Sisters, was then served, and a pleasant ceremony concluded with three cheers for the Matron, followed by three for Sister Annie.

Other gifts on view were a pewter card basket from the Secretary, Mr. Alvey; a beautiful week-end case from the outside workers; an attaché case from Miss Rees (a war probationer); and a black cat, made and presented by the soldier patients in Worcester Ward. The clerks, domestics and charwomen are also presenting a fitted work-box and a thermos flask.

PRESENTATION OF MEDALS AND CERTIFICATES.

At the Whipps Cross Infirmary, Leytonstone, on November 13th, the annual distribution of medals and certificates took place. The Chairman of the West Ham Board of Guardians—Mr. A. Lewis Evans—supported by members of the Board, was in the chair, and gave a short history of the training school, founded when the new Infirmary was built thirteen or fourteen years ago.

The medals and certificates were then presented by Lady Simon to the following recipients :—

Gold Medal and Certificate (awarded for the highest marks) : Nurse Bertha Jane Maddock.

Silver Medal and Certificate (awarded for the second highest marks) : Nurse M. E. Marsh.

Bronze Medal and Certificate (awarded for the third highest marks) : Nurse W. O. Clarke.

Certificates : Nurses Austin, Ayton, Bailey, Baker, Barker, Blackmore, Boddington, Buffee, Chapman, Cooper, Cornwell, Courts, Cullen, Curtis, Dabbs, Foley, Foster, Garner, Gudgin, Hansford, King, Lafferty, McArd, McKeller, Page, Pratt, Richardson, Riley, Soames, Stokes, Taylor, West.

THE PASSING BELL.

At St. James' Church, Brighton, on November 15th, a Requiem Service was held for Sister Daisy Ethel Cox, Assistant Matron at the Brighton and Hove Hospital for Women. She was beloved in the district where she had done midwifery for years, and much appreciated by the Committee as a valuable member of the hospital staff. The service was conducted by the Vicar, the Rev. W. Breton, and was attended by many members of the nursing staff of the hospital. The funeral took place on Monday, November 18th, at Chard, in Somerset.

THE DEPRECIATION OF PROFESSIONAL ETHICS.

Fleet Street agrees that the *Daily Sketch*, one of the group of the " Hulton " newspapers, has made a fine " scoop " in utilising the unfortunate Nursing Profession as the *raison d'être* of its Victory Ball at the Albert Hall, and what the public and the nurses have a right to know is, will the huge amount spent in advertising the *Daily Sketch* Ball be paid direct by the London Publishing Company. Anyway, Fleet Street agrees the whole move is good " biz."

By the bye, the victimised Nursing Profession have had a lesson in the value of loyal co-operation, second to none, over this distasteful affair, which they may well take to heart.

Mr. Hilton Carter, the manager of the Albert Hall, refused to let it for a Labour Conference. By way of reprisal the members of the Kensington Branch of the Electrical Trades Union arranged to cut off the light in the middle of the Victory Ball (imagine the flutter in frivolous society circles!) Members, however, were too impatient and removed the links from the box in front of the hall on Friday last, greatly to the inconvenience of the manager. On the recommendation of the Labour Minister the Hall is now at the disposal of victorious trades unionism, for their meeting next Saturday, and Society will trip the light fantastic toe as we go to press, from 10 p.m. till 5 o'clock in the morning—in the name of the Cinderella of working women, the Trained Nurse! According to Mr. George Lansbury, who has been in politics for forty years, now is the time to keep the safety-valves wide open and have perfect freedom of discussion. He wrote to Mr. Lloyd George and the Home Secretary when the Hall was refused, and both declined to intervene.

" Now," says Mr. Lansbury, in the *Weekly Dispatch*," when the men cut off the electric light the Minister of Labour intervenes and we get the Hall.

" This is a bad lesson to teach the workers. The Government has conceded to Fear what they would not concede to Reason."

EMPLOYER AND EMPLOYED.

As it is intimately concerned with the right of professional co-operation amongst trained nurses, we shall deal fully, next week, with the exchange of opinion in the press between the representatives of the Nurses' Organizations and Sir Arthur Stanley, M.P., Chairman of the British Red Cross Society, Treasurer of St. Thomas' Hospital, Chairman of the College of Nursing Company, and, incidentally, the largest employer of nursing labour at the present time.

Believing that shuttle kissing in cotton mills spreads infection and is largely responsible for the influenza epidemic, the Blackburn Weavers' Association has appointed a deputation to wait on the Medical Officer of Health.

PRESENTATIONS.

Nurse Harlock has been presented by the residents with a cheque for £114, upon her retirement after thirty years' service as district nurse at Egham.

The *Leeds Mercury* announces that the district nurse at Hebden Bridge has received the special badge of the Queen Victoria Jubilee Institute for Nurses, in recognition of twenty-one years' continuous service. We wonder if our contemporary is not acquainted with the name of this devoted nurse who spent nearly a quarter of a century in the service of the poor of Leeds.

COOK'S FARM EGGS.

One of the greatest problems which confront the housekeeper in these days, whether in private houses or institutions, is how to provide nourishing and attractive dishes now that the price of eggs is prohibitive.

Cook's Farm Eggs (Dried) come therefore as a boon to the worried housewife, for, while they are really new laid eggs, from which the moisture has been removed by a new patent process—and which can be restored by the addition of water as directed—the cost of the eggs is within reach of all. Thus in cartons of twelve eggs the cost is 24s. per dozen cartons, or of twenty-four eggs 44s. per dozen cartons. They are obtainable wholesale only from Donald Cook & Son, Ltd., 35-37, Bermondsey Street, London, S.E. 1. When purchased in single cartons from grocers, in the ordinary way, the cost is 2s. 6d. per carton of one dozen eggs. Certainly hospitals, infirmaries and nursing homes should make a point of procuring supplies of these dried Farm Eggs, and so not only effect a necessary economy, but procure a thoroughly satisfactory and reliable article. For making custards, omelettes, scrambled eggs, puddings, cakes, buns and scones these eggs (which are guaranteed absolutely pure) may be used with the assurance of success if the directions are carefully followed.

WORD FOR THE WEEK.

" The British Empire is one of the few Empires that in its greatest material prosperity has never lost its high regard for moral force, and stands forth as one of the greatest craftsmen of moral law."—*Echo de Paris.*

COMING EVENTS.

November 30th.—Nurses' Missionary League. A quiet Day, St. Michael's Church, Chester Square, W. 1. Apply Miss H. Y. Richardson, 52, Lower Sloane Street, S.W.

December 5th.—Royal British Nurses' Association. Lecture: " America and the New World Order," by E. Price Bell, Esq., M.A. Chair, Herbert Paterson, Esq., F.R.C.S. Rooms of the Medical Society of London, 11, Chandos Street, Cavendish Square, W. 2.45 p.m.

LETTERS TO THE EDITOR.

Whilst cordially inviting communications upon all subjects for these columns, we wish it to be distinctly understood that we do not IN ANY WAY hold ourselves responsible for the opinions expressed by our correspondents.

THE DEEP SIGHING OF THE POOR.

To the Editor of THE BRITISH JOURNAL OF NURSING.

MADAM,—Have we reverted to something akin to the old state of things ?

"Rattle his bones over the stones,
He's only a pauper whom nobody owns."

I refer to the conditions of affairs existing at this moment in the East End, where large numbers of dead have been lying unburied for an unseemly length of time.

Would not the problem have been grapp'ed with long ago if such indecency had been experienced by influential members of the community ?

One whose long life has been spent in intimate touch with the poor asks : " Why were not soldiers experienced in trench digging released in order to dig graves at this crisis ? "

Similarly one might ask, " and carpenters to make coffins ? "

Will the proposed Ministry of Health provide against a recurrence of such callousness towards the helpless ?

" It is well it is cold weather," said my saintly old friend, significantly. She lives in the slums, you see—*and knows.*

HENRIETTA HAWKINS.

PUBLIC HEALTH NURSES MUST ORGANIZE.

To the Editor of THE BRITISH JOURNAL OF NURSING.

DEAR EDITOR,—At the Conference of the Royal British Nurses I was greatly interested in the observations made by the speakers, but I must say I differed when the lady who spoke upon the subject of Infant Welfare described voluntary visitors who had attended a course of lectures as being " highly trained."

It does not seem to me as if the best aspect of Infant Welfare was put forward. Would it not be better for the Association to advocate the provision of fully trained nurses, with the C.M.B. certificate, for visiting, and advising mothers? It is nothing to go into a house and find people seriously ill or dying. People who have to deal with emergencies like that need to have had experience in recognising symptoms of illness.

Mothers are often in need of advice about the care of themselves and the feeding of their babies. I think only the trained nurse is suitable for that.

It seemed to me rather waste of time to be talking about boot-mending when the more pressing problems are the provision of suitable homes for motherless babies, the provision of good cow's milk, and the appalling ignorance among all classes of people about the feeding of babies and the real duty of a mother towards her home.

Some of the Infant Welfare Centres are not really giving the right teaching to the people. The sale of patent foods is advocated far too much. I know of one where the principle of feeding babies on tinned milk was run for years.

Is it possible to have a gathering of fully trained nurses engaged in public health work, with a view to getting up a really good public health section and putting forward good papers at the Conferences ?

I should be glad to help if there was anything to be done.

Yours truly,
C. MARGARET ALDERMAN.

Westcliff.

[We are in favour of these views, and would urge trained nurses engaged in Public Health Work to form a League and formulate a sound policy for the future.—ED.]

KERNELS.

Writing on paper, headed " British Red Cross Society " and " The Order of St. John of Jerusalem in England," Miss May Beeman replies to a nurse's protest against the Victory Ball in the name of the Nation's Nurses, as the " kick up " is in aid of the College of Nursing, Ltd., and it has no authority to speak for the profession generally or to associate our profession with this type of entertainment.

" I have received your letter protesting against the appeal of the Nation's Fund for Nurses. I cannot understand any member of the profession protesting in this way. Surely it must be plain to all that a College of Nursing on the same lines as the College of Physicians and Surgeons must go a long way to raise the nursing profession to the position it ought to hold in our national life. I mean to devote every effort to raise half a million of money, so that there may be a good endowment fund and pension fund, and incidentally a College of Nursing."

[This is the type of reply a professional woman may expect from a lady who knows absolutely nothing of our educational or economic condition—whose life is now spent in collecting for Charity schemes.

It is quite plain to a professional nurse that the College of Nursing, Ltd., is not " on the same lines as the College of Physicians and Surgeons." If it were, it would not attempt to monopolise the duties under *one lay Corporation* of the Colleges aforesaid, the General Medical Council and the British Medical Association—all composed of members of the medical profession, and therefore expert professional bodies.

The colossal ignorance of these professional philanthropists concerning nursing organization is one of the most serious dangers to which our work has ever been exposed ; and it will be quite time for them to buy up our independence and hand it over to a lay Corporation when we are willing to submit. At present we resent the impertinent interference of Miss May Beeman and her associates in our affairs, as we hope to prove effectively in the near future.—ED.]

The Midwife.

CENTRAL MIDWIVES BOARD.

THE MONTHLY MEETING.

The Monthly Meeting of the Central Midwives Board was held at the Board's Offices, 1, Queen Anne's Buildings, Dartmouth Street, Westminster, S.W., on November 21st, Sir Francis Champneys in the Chair.

REPORT OF STANDING COMMITTEE.

The Committee reported that a further communication had been received from the Acting Registrar of the General Medical Council with reference to the action of a medical practitioner who had given a certificate to an uncertified woman certifying that she was "quite capable of undertaking the duties of an ordinary midwife."

A letter from the Local Government Board asking the Board to consider the advisability of framing a new rule, E. 22 (1) (f), in terms similar to the corresponding Rule of the Central Midwives Board for Scotland, which requires a midwife to notify the Local Supervising Authority "whenever under Rule 19 (b) she has advised the substitution of artificial feeding for breast feeding." The Board decided to reply that they were prepared to submit such a Rule for the approval of the Privy Council.

The case of a candidate for the Board's examination of November 1st, who had presented a birth certificate which had been tampered with, was further considered, and it was decided not to admit her to any examination prior to that of May 1st, 1919.

The Board decided to reply to an applicant for admission to Examination by a Norwegian subject that the time has not yet arrived for the admission to the Board's Examination of candidates who are neither of British nor of Allied nationality.

A letter was considered from the Secretary of the Four Boroughs Maternity Clinics bringing to the notice of the Board a scheme for the payment of midwives for ante-natal visiting. The Board, in acknowledging the letter, expressed the fear that any scheme by which additional payment was made to midwives for bringing patients to a Clinic could hardly fail to be utilized for the notification of pregnancy, and therefore to prevent early engagement of midwives. It was strongly in favour, however, of promoting the co-operation of midwives in ante-natal and maternity care.

A letter was received from the Secretary of the National Poor Law Officers' Association asking the Board to amend Rule C. 1 (2) (b) by deleting the words "and maintaining a Resident Physician or House Surgeon and a Matron or Superintendent Nurse." The Board replied that it was not prepared to amend the rule in the sense suggested.

Permission was given to a nurse on the staff of the Notts Nursing Federation about to undergo a course of midwifery training to count three of the four months' training she had received at the Jessop Hospital, Sheffield, as part of the qualifying period of six months required to admit her to the Board's Examination.

A similar privilege was granted to an applicant who in 1915 underwent a course of three months' training as a Maternity Nurse at the Clapham Maternity Hospital, and now proposes to take a course of midwifery training under an approved midwife at Paget House, Loughborough Park.

A letter was received from the County Medical Officer of Health for Derbyshire, asking that a pupil who had undergone a portion of her training at the Birmingham Maternity Hospital might be allowed to complete it with the Royal Derby and Derbyshire Nursing Association. The Board decided to reply that, having regard to the refusal of the Matron of the Birmingham Maternity Hospital to sign on behalf of the applicant the certificates of training required by the Rules, it had no power to facilitate her admission to the Examination.

APPLICATIONS.

For Appointment as Examiner.—Dr. Harold Clifford and Dr. William Fletcher were added to the list of examiners for the Manchester and Liverpool Centres.

For Removal from the Roll.—The applications of sixteen certified midwives for removal from the Roll were granted.

For Approval as Lecturer.—Dr. Mabel Eliza May was approved as a lecturer, and Dr. Thomas Gibson *pro tem.*

For Approval as Teacher.—The following certified midwives were approved as teachers :—Annie Brownlie Edington (No. 28617), Helena Gertrude Summerbell (No. 37367), Gertrude Smith (No. 37070), and Martha Hannah L. Wilson (No. 32557).

REPORT.

It was agreed that the Report submitted by the Secretary on the work of the Board for the year ended March 31st, 1918, be approved and adopted, and forwarded to the Privy Council.

THE MIDWIVES BILL.

The Secretary reported that the Midwives Bill had passed both Houses of Parliament, and had probably at the time he was speaking received the Royal Assent in the words "Le Roi le veult." The Act would come into force on January 1st, 1919.

The Chairman reported that he had received and replied to a telegram of congratulation from Sir Halliday Croom, Chairman, Central Midwives Board for Scotland, on the passing of the Midwives Bill, 1918, facilitating reciprocal arrangements between the three kingdoms.

NOVEMBER EXAMINATION.

At the Examination of the Central Midwives Board held in London and the Provinces on November 1st, 450 candidates were examined and 346 passed. The percentage of failures was 23.1.

THE
BRITISH JOURNAL OF NURSING
WITH WHICH IS INCORPORATED
THE NURSING RECORD
EDITED BY MRS BEDFORD FENWICK

No. 1,601.   SATURDAY, DECEMBER 7, 1918.   Vol. LX

EDITORIAL.

"THEIR NAME LIVETH FOR EVERMORE."

By order of the King, British officers have carried a number of floral tributes to the cemeteries of Paris to be placed on the graves of French soldiers who have fallen in the war, and in so doing His Majesty interpreted the feelings of every person of sensibility in the Empire, whose first instinct is to pay homage to the glorious dead.

"With a great price obtained I this freedom." As we think of the seven hundred thousand British soldiers who have paid that price, those of us whose freedom was purchased at the cost of their lives realize the magnitude of their sacrifice, and pray that we may be worthy of it, for its splendour and its wonder surpass our comprehension.

The small seasoned army whose business in life had been soldiering led the van, and thousands fell as heroes fall, face to foe, fighting for freedom and honour. Then without hesitation there leapt into the gaps the young manhood of the Empire, fresh from the public schools, debonair and unafraid, from city offices, from the slums of the great towns, from country homesteads, from the furthest outposts of Empire.

Shoulder to shoulder they made of their flesh and blood a living barrier against which the hordes of Huns flung shell and shot and poison gas in vain. They too died gallantly in their thousands, so did the heroes of Gallipoli, and other gallant men, under tropical suns in Mesopotamia and Africa, and on many another battle front and "some there be who are perished as though they never had been," but "their name liveth for evermore."

Nor do these 700,000 dead British soldiers complete the toll taken of brave young lives. Our hospitals are still filled with the aftermath of war, we cannot walk abroad without meeting men maimed, or disfigured or blinded, and, as to their lives' end they will bear the burden of their gallantry, so we too, for whom they made the great sacrifice must, if we have any sensibility, share their burden, and feel its weight—a weight of suffering so great that it oppresses the world. Our thankfulness that at last the holocaust of butchery and rapine has ceased will be marked by the sober joy of those whose freedom has been bought with a price, and who cherish in their hearts the remembrance of the sacrifice of countless dead. We are compassed about by so great a cloud of witnesses, that we instinctively walk reverently as if on holy ground.

Grief hears the funeral knell; hope hears the
    ringing of birthday bells on high;
   Faith, hope, and love make answer with soft
    singing,
Half carol and half cry.

So will we cherish the memory of our dead, and in days to come beautify the graves where their bodies hallow the countryside where they fell. The inscription selected for their sleeping places by Mr. Rudyard Kipling, "Their name liveth for evermore," will keep fresh in our minds our obligation by lofty purpose, and high endeavour, to walk worthy of the heritage bequeathed to us by those who died that we might live.

When a Sovereign of these Realms is gathered to his fathers, the accession of his successor is proclaimed, and then a period is set before the Coronation and accompanying festivities, a custom which we recognise as seemly and fitting.

Would it not also be decorous, in a country in which there is hardly a house which has not mourned one near and dear, that after the proclamation of Peace, a period of public mourning should be officially proclaimed in honour of our dead?

OUR PRIZE COMPETITION.

DESCRIBE THE MANAGEMENT OF A NEWLY-BORN INFANT FOR THE FIRST WEEK OF LIFE.

We have pleasure in awarding the prize this week to Miss Dorothy M. Clarke, the Infant Welfare Centre, Sydenham, S.E. 26.

PRIZE PAPER.

The management of a newly born infant must be divided into two classes :—

(*a*) The child born at full term.

(*b*) The child born prematurely.

(*a*) At birth the child is covered with a greasy substance, the *vernix caseosa*. This is removed by applying olive oil, and then washing with warm soapy water. The temperature of the first bath should be 100° F., gradually reducing the heat to 80° F. A strong healthy baby should be, from the beginning, bathed twice daily.

Great care must be taken with *the eyes* of a new-born baby. They should be bathed night and morning with warm boracic lotion, being careful to use a fresh swab for each eye, and bathing from the inside, outwards. At the least sign of discharge, a doctor must be sent for.

Baby's mouth must not on any account be cleaned out—there is no need. Baby has a natural mouth wash, its own saliva, and although this is present, only in a very minor degree, in the newly born child, it is sufficient to be a satisfactory mouth cleanser. The poor baby who has his mouth carefully cleaned out with boracic, &c., is almost sure to be a victim to thrush, because the delicate lining to the baby's mouth becomes injured and the thrush parasite can do its worst.

A healthy baby should be out of doors as much as possible, from the very beginning. Windows should be kept open and the room at a temperature of 55° to 60°. A delicate baby should be out on fine warm days, well wrapped up, and a hot bottle to its feet. The temperature of the room in which it is should be 60° to 65° F.

Baby's clothes should be loose and warm. The only clothes needed for the new-born baby are :—A woollen vest, flannel binder until the navel is healed, a napkin, pair of booties, and a woolly coat. When baby is not in his cot, he should have a light, warm shawl.

Before putting on the napkin, it is advisable to put vaseline on the buttocks, because the first stools consist of a dark greenish substance, the meconium, which is very sticky. Baby should be put to the breast every four hours from the time it is born. Even before the mother has anything for the child, it is good for both mother and child that it should be put to the breast very regularly.

Baby's day could be divided as follows :—20 hours' sleep, 1 hour 30 minutes feeding (six feeds 15 minutes each), 2 hours 30 minutes to be spent in kicking, being nursed, crying (the crying at intervals is good, it helps to expand the lungs), and ablutions.

(*b*) The premature baby should, as far as possible, have its pre-natal conditions imitated for it—warmth, quietude and darkness.

The baby born before full term should not be bathed. It should be oiled twice daily with warm oil and wrapped in cotton wool, and should have a cap of cotton wool made for its head. The child should be either kept in a cot with hot-water bottles, an incubator, or an electric cot, the latter being the most practical, as, without any difficulty, the child is kept at an even temperature. The bed should be made by lining the cot with a full-size blanket, and then putting in the mattress, &c. The two sides of the blanket can then be folded over the child, and it is in this way protected from draught. Electric wires are now fixed from any light in the room and brought on either side of the cot (outside) where two long bulbs (as used for a heating radiator) are fixed. A thermometer should be kept inside the cot, and the light turned out should it rise above 70°.

The room should be kept darkened and quiet. No visitors should be allowed.

The child should be put to the breast, or have the milk drawn off and be fed, if too feeble to suck, three-hourly, and as it gets stronger, four-hourly.

———

The above method of managing a baby's mouth represents modern, and no doubt, sound teaching. We are learning to leave Dame Nature alone as much as possible, realizing that she knows what is best for her children.

But we cannot agree that a baby who has his mouth "*carefully* anointed with boracic, &c." (glycerine and borax for choice), "is almost certain to be a victim to thrush." Experience proves the contrary. A maternity nurse should always ascertain the wishes of the physician-in-charge on this point.

HONOURABLE MENTION.

The following competitors receive honourable mention :—Miss Isolen M. Moore, Miss E. Ford, Miss Catherine Wright, Mrs. M. Farthing, and Miss Alice M. Burns.

QUESTION FOR NEXT WEEK.

Describe your method of disinfecting after an infectious case in a private house, (*a*) the patient's room, (*b*) yourself.

NURSING AND THE WAR.

Miss Constance E. Todd, who has received the much-prized Military Medal, is Matron of the Brigade Hospital maintained by the Order of St. John of Jerusalem in this country, which was first established at Etaples, and suffered so severely in the deliberate bombardment of that colony of hospitals by the Huns. Not only were buildings and equipment provided so generously through the self-denial of many members of the Order, destroyed, but, more precious still, wounded men as they lay in their beds were done to death, with the heroic Sisters who remained at their side. As the bombs were falling and shells bursting, Miss Todd went from ward to ward, cheering the patients and encouraging the nursing staff. Later the hospital was rebuilt at a greater distance from the Front. Miss Todd was trained at Guy's Hospital, and when selected as Matron of the Brigade Hospital, was Matron at St. James' Infirmary, Wandsworth.

It was a great pleasure to see Miss Helen Scott Hay, R.N., and Miss Robinson, R.N., lately Chief Nurse of the American Ambulance in Paris, when they spent a day in London last week on their way to the Balkans, where they will be engaged in all phases of relief work in connection with the Balkan Commission of the American Red Cross at Salonika. The party, which is going out under the leadership of Colonel Anderson, includes six women — three trained nurses one dietitian, one social worker, and one interpreter. Later it is hoped that Miss Rachel Torrance, at present Chief Nurse of the American Red Cross in Great Britain, will join the party.

Miss Hay is eminently qualified for this work. It will be remembered that in September, 1914, she took a party of American Red Cross Nurses to Russia, and afterwards worked in the Balkans, principally in Bulgaria, helping the late Queen Eleanore. She has recently been associated with Miss Anna W. Goodrich in the organisation of the Army School of Nursing, and she relates with

Photo]   *[Elliot & Fry*

MISS CONSTANCE E. TODD, M.M., R.R.C.

some pride that when the mental capacity of the accepted candidates was scientifically tested the large proportion were of a very high average.

Miss Hay is looking forward with great pleasure to her new sphere of work.

The special correspondent of *The Matin* at Brussels has succeeded (says the *Central News*), after overcoming countless difficulties, in discovering the grave of Edith Cavell. It is situated in a field at Brussels which had been a firing range, but which the Germans had transformed into a great cabbage patch. The grave bears the number 6 and lies close to that of Philippe Bacq, who was shot on the same day. For three months the German commander refused to permit any name to be inscribed on the cross which indicates the sepulchre of the British nurse. Burgomaster Max has been to the spot to pay homage to the dead martyr, and a monument will commemorate her glory at the very spot where, with her companions, she faced the firing party.

Those who have worked for, and are interested in Russia, should read General Gourko's great book, "Memories and Impressions of War, 1914-1917." It is a perfectly fascinating record of a terrible tragedy; but do not let us condemn Russia until we have realized her heroic efforts before the reign of Bolshevism—by which heroism France was saved if Russia was cast into the abyss.

Writing from Lyons, where she was helping the American Red Cross, Miss Grace Ellison says: "The Nurses of the S.T. Zone here, of which Lyons is the chief city, send you their congratulations on the 25th anniversary of your control of the BRITISH JOURNAL OF NURSING, and wish you every success in your campaign. It is a very great surprise to them all here that the British Nurses are not registered, and they wonder if it is not a little the nurses' fault that they have not got registration, as in America it is only too evident to laywomen that it is for their own protection. Every nurse in the A.R.C. is a graduate and registered, and no one has the right to wear her uniform, which she must wear throughout her military or overseas service. We certainly are behind the times ! "

FLORENCE NIGHTINGALE COLLEGE OF NURSING.

The American Red Cross have invited Mrs. Bedford Fenwick to accompany Dr. Anna Hamilton of Bordeaux, as its guest, on a mission to New York to collect funds for the Florence Nightingale College of Nursing, and new hospital it is hoped to build at " Bagatelle." What a delightful proposal ! but alas ! duty to the profession at home makes it imperative at this crisis that Mrs. Fenwick should remain at her post. Dr. Hamilton leaves France for America on December 7th, and the hearty good wishes of her friends in England for the success of her appeal will go with her across the Atlantic. It is to be hoped she will return with a pocketful of money and that the erection and equipment of a beautiful and up-to-date hospital and Nursing School, the desire of her heart, will materialise for the benefit of France.

HONOURS FOR NURSES.

For Distinguished Service.

The following notice appeared in the *Leader* :— " For distinguished service rendered during the East African Campaign numerous decorations have been conferred upon the British troops by King Albert of Belgium." Then follow nine classes of decorations, including—

Croix de Chevalier de l'Ordre de Leopold (Sixth Class).—Mrs. Eva O'Hagan, Hon. Nurse, East African Service.

Croix de Chevalier de l'Ordre de la Courranne (Seventh Class).—Miss Constance Watney, Senior Sister, Uganda Medical Service. Miss Watney was trained at St. Bartholomew's Hospital, and has for years been on the Staff of the C.M.S. Hospital at Mengo, Kampala, Uganda, British East Africa.

CARE OF THE WOUNDED.

Lieut.-Colonel Sir Henry Webb, M.P., of Dean Rise, Newnham, Gloucester, has given £25,000 to the King's Fund for the Disabled. This Fund is not registered as a War Charity.

Asserting that he wished to see " how the trick was done," Driver J. E. Scott, a Cleethorpes artilleryman, decided to be chloroformed while blood was transfused from his body to that of an apparently dying comrade. The operation was successful and last week-end Scott and the man whose life he had saved travelled home together on convalescent leave. General Sir H. Rawlinson,

Commanding the Fourth Army, warmly commended Scott's self-sacrificing act. These men of ours can't help being heroes !

ANGLO=FRENCH SERVICE BAR.

(Authorised by the British War Office and the Ministère de la Guerre, Paris.)

To be Awarded to men and women—British Allied or Neutral—whose work has been carried out in England or abroad.

(1) With the Anglo-French Certificate or the Pink Certificate of the British Committee of the French Red Cross.

(2) Otherwise in the service of the British Committee of the French Red Cross.

(3) In the service of other organisations recognised by the British Committee of the French Red Cross, working for the French, who do not hold either Anglo-French or Pink Certificates, on productions of certificate of service from the said organisation, signed by the head of it.

1. One bar will be awarded on the completion of one year's whole-time service, which may include the regular periods of leave (the total duration of which may not exceed one month in every twelve), any additional leave to be deducted.

2. The bar to be of saxe-blue cloth, similar to this forming the facings of the regulation Anglo-French uniform, and to measure 2 ins. long by $\frac{1}{2}$ in. wide (50 m/m by 12.5 m/m). To be placed horizontally on the left upper arm of the tunic sleeve, three inches from the point of the shoulder.

3. A further bar will be awarded for every subsequent six months' service completed, such additional bars to be of the same material as the first year's bar, but half the width (2 ins. long by $\frac{1}{4}$ in. wide, 50 m/m by 6.25 m/m). To be placed parallel to the first year's bar, and $\frac{1}{8}$ of an inch (3.12 m/m) below it.

4. Service bars may only be worn by those possessing permission in writing from the British Committee of the French Red Cross, signed by the Présidente or Director-General, whose decision on all points shall be final.

5. " Service Abroad." The qualifying time to count from the date on which the worker leaves England for abroad, until the date of reporting on return to England, as shown by the endorsements on passports and by the records of the British Committee.

6. Application for chevrons to be made to the British Committee of the French Red Cross, 9, Knightsbridge, S.W. 1 ; envelopes to be marked " Chevrons."

French Flag Nursing Corps.

Application is being made through the office for chevrons for the Sisters to whom they are due, so Sisters need not apply individually. What a fine row of bars may be worn by those who have served four years !

NATIONAL COUNCIL OF TRAINED NURSES OF GREAT BRITAIN AND IRELAND.

The Annual Meeting of the Grand Council, composed of the Delegates of Affiliated Societies of Trained Nurses, was held at 431, Oxford Street, London, W., on Friday, November 29th, at 4 p.m. The President, Mrs. Bedford Fenwick, was in the chair. The majority of the affiliated societies were represented. The absence of Miss B. Cutler, Hon. Secretary, owing to indisposition and absence from town, was much regretted, and the Council welcomed Miss Christina Forrest, the Hon. Treasurer, from Bournemouth.

BUSINESS REFERRED TO IN MINUTES.

The Minutes having been read and confirmed, the President said, as referred to in the Minutes, the Hon. Secretary had sent the following letter to the Presidents of the Royal Free Hospital Nurses' League and the President of the Chelsea Infirmary Nurses' League, upon the retirement of these Leagues from the Council :—

NO CHANGE IN THE PRINCIPLES OR POLICY OF THE NATIONAL COUNCIL OF TRAINED NURSES.

431, Oxford Street, London, W. 1,
February 2nd, 1918.

DEAR MADAM,—At the annual meeting of the National Council of Trained Nurses of Great Britain and Ireland, held on December 15th, 1917, your letter, notifying that the League of Royal Free Hospital Nurses had decided to withdraw from affiliation, owing to the attitude adopted by the Council towards the College of Nursing, was read and directed to be recorded.

In notifying you of the fact, I was desired to say that the position of the National Council towards the question of the organisation of the Nursing Profession, and the State Registration of Nurses, is the same as when the League of Royal Free Hospital Nurses joined it. It has supported the Central Committee for the State Registration of Nurses in its demands for :—

(1) An Independent Governing Body for the organisation of the educational standards of the Nursing Profession, and the State Registration of Trained Nurses, on which they themselves have direct representation.

(2) The representation of the self-governing Societies of Nurses on the Provisional Nursing Council created under a Nurses' Registration Act, which Council will frame the rules which the Registered Nurses will have to obey.

(3) A One-Portal System of Registration after a three years' term of training in a hospital, or hospitals, and a central examination.

These principles for the organisation and good government of the Nursing Profession are incorporated in the Nurses Registration Bill, introduced into the House of Commons by Major Chapple on behalf of the Central Committee, to which are affiliated several of the most important Nurses' Organisations in the National Council.

That the Council of the College of Nursing, Ltd., has deliberately omitted these great principles in the Bill it has drafted is deeply to be regretted.

Beyond its support of the consistent policy of the Central Committee the National Council, as such, has, since the College was incorporated, taken no part in the controversy, as the interests of the nurses have been safeguarded by other organisations ; but the Council is aware that many of its members are strongly opposed to the policy of the College of Nursing, Ltd., as tending to economic dependence, and, through a charitable appeal of a committee of actresses, to place trained nurses in an exceedingly dependent and invidious position.

Charity, resulting in economic dependence, is calculated to degrade any body of working women, and cuts at the very root of the principles of their self-support and solidarity in the body politic.

If these great principles are not recognised by the Council and exclusively male executive, which govern the College of Nursing, Ltd., as apparently they are not, then it would appear the management of the College requires drastic reform.

I was requested to ask you to place this letter before the next General Meeting of the League of the Royal Free Hospital Nurses.

I am, yours faithfully,
BEATRICE CUTLER,
Hon. Secretary.

Miss Isobel Yule, Hon. Sec.,
League of Royal Free Hospital Nurses.

REPORT FROM THE PRESIDENT.

The President said she had written no formal Report. Owing to the war the activities of the Council had been in abeyance, and it had taken no part in the Nursing Controversy as a whole, as several of its component Societies were actively engaged in guarding and fighting for the true interests of the Nursing Profession, and were supporting, as self-governing organizations, the progressive and just legislation proposed for the profession by the Central Committee. There were now two Bills ready to present to Parliament, and, owing to the isolated action of the College of Nursing, Ltd., we had unfortunately reverted to the lack of unity in which the profession found itself in 1909 before the promoters of the three Bills came into touch, and, with reasonable good sense and expert knowledge, agreed upon one Bill, and harmoniously supported it. There was no doubt that, had the College not thrown the apple of discord into the nursing arena, the Nurses' Registration Bill, supported by English, Scottish, and Irish nurses, and the British Medical Association, would have become law in the last Parliament. The reactionary element which evolved and controlled the College was entirely to blame for depriving the State Registrationists of the fruit of their long years of work for the benefit of the public and the nursing profession—work for which the nurses had paid thousands of pounds out of their own slender remuneration. The College Bill was not a Bill for the State Registration of Trained Nurses, but (1) a Bill to incorporate the College of Nursing and its drastic Constitution ; (2) to secure for its own members (and not for the Nursing Profession as a whole) the power to form the First Register to elect the Council which had power to frame the Rules ; and (3) to constitute as many Supplementary Registers as this Council chose, to register specialists, and thus depreciate the value of the General Register of thoroughly trained Nurses and open innumerable portals to the Register, instead of the One Portal it promised its members. The Central Committee's Bill provided for an independent Governing Body, equality of opportunity for all trained nurses, two Supplementary Registers only—one for male and one for mental nurses—and the One Portal, after three years' general training in hospital wards, to the Women Nurses' General Register. The Central Committee intended to oppose privileged legislation calculated to injure the nurses who refused to join the College, and to work energetically for their Bill, designed to benefit the whole Nursing Profession.

FINANCIAL STATEMENT.

The Hon. Treasurer (Miss Forrest) presented the Financial Statement, which showed expenditure of £4 7s. 6d., and a Balance in the bank of £22 4s. 11d. The Statement was adopted.

CORRESPONDENCE.

1. A letter was received from Miss Hulme, Hon. Secretary of the Matrons' Council, notifying that Miss Lucy Ramsden, formerly Matron of the Rotunda Hospital, Dublin, and Miss Bushby, Matron of the Queen's Hospital for Children, Hackney Road, E., had accepted nomination as Delegates on the Council. The nominations were approved.

NATIONAL BABY WEEK COUNCIL.

2. A letter from Miss S. F. Musson, inviting the Council to appoint a representative on the National Baby Week Council, was received. The appointment of the President was confirmed. Mrs. Bedford Fenwick said the Council was doing very useful work, especially since the appointment of Miss S. F. Musson as Secretary, and its activities would be increased under a National Health Ministry.

MINISTRY OF HEALTH WATCHING COUNCIL.

3. A letter was received and considered from the Viscountess Rhondda, inviting the Council to send a representative to a Meeting of the Ministry of Health Watching Council, to enlarge its scope to include not only Infant and Maternity Welfare, but women's interests generally; as a Council which could really be said to represent Women's Organizations would carry great weight at the present time, and might be of very great value.

ADVISORY COUNCIL OF WOMEN.

The following resolution would be considered at the Meeting :—

Resolution.

" That the Watching Council adopt as part of its policy to press for an Advisory Council of Women at the Ministry of Health, elected on democratic lines, and in an analogous position to

and with the same rights, privileges, and powers as any other Advisory Council."

A copy of the proposed Constitution was enclosed. It was agreed to send a representative to the Meeting.

The President in this connection reminded the Meeting how important it was that trained nurses should have access to the Ministry of Health, as it was proposed that the medical profession should have. Trained Nurses and Midwives would be called upon to do most of the practical work in connection with such a Ministry, and, if precedent were followed, certainly the most laborious and ill-paid work. But as their trained skill was of paramount importance to all classes in the prevention of and care of disease, they must be alive to the best interests of the community by refusing to agree to any system which forced semi-trained or amateur workers on the sick poor—at salaries far in excess of their value. There would be responsible positions under such a Ministry, and the trained and skilled workers should be appointed to them.

In the past lay women's organizations had shown a lamentable lack of appreciation of the powers and status of the trained nurse. After association for upwards of twenty years with the National Council of Women, the affiliated nurses' societies were still without direct representation on its Executive Committee, so that decisions were arrived at on nursing affairs without expert advice. For the future it was imperative that in all questions referring to legislation and the economic conditions of trained nurses that they should present their own case, and she advocated an Advisory Council of Nurses as admissible in the Ministry of Health Bill.

RESOLUTION.

The following resolution was proposed from the chair, and it was passed unanimously :—

" That this Meeting of the National Council of Trained Nurses of Great Britain and Ireland urges upon the Government the urgent need of an Act for the State Registration of Nurses, providing for an independent General Nursing Council, as an indispensable corollary of the establishment of a Ministry of Health."

QUESTIONS FOR PARLIAMENTARY CANDIDATES.

4. A communication was received from the Hon. Secretaries, Legislation Committee of the National Council of Women of Great Britain and Ireland, enclosing the following list of questions, suggesting that some or all might be included among the questions to be addressed to candidates for the Parliamentary Election.

1. Are you in favour of removing the disqualification of women being admitted and practising as solicitors (and as Law Agents in Scotland)?

2. Are you in favour of abolishing the existing practice of penalising married persons by taxing their incomes together?

3. Are you in favour of making parents the equal joint guardians of their children?

4. Are you in favour of providing that in any change in the Divorce Laws the equality of the sexes should be recognised?

5. Are you in favour of legalising the adoption of children, with proper safeguards?

6. Are you in favour of granting to women the right to retain British nationality on marriage with an alien (a right enjoyed by them under the laws of the United Kingdom until 1870), and that she should be given the same choice of nationality as a man?

7. Would you support legislation to increase the responsibility of the father for his illegitimate child?

All the questions were approved. Further information *re* No. 5 was desired, and it was agreed to draw the attention of the Legislation Committee N.C.W. to the omission of any reference to the important national question of the State Registration of Trained Nurses, and to invite the N.C.W. to include the following question in its list :—

8. Are you in favour of legislation for the State Registration of Trained Nurses, providing for an independent Governing Body with adequate representation of the Nurses themselves?

Women as Members of Parliament.

5. A letter was received from Mrs. Vulliamy, Cambridge, Chairman of a Committee formed to promote the candidature of independent women as members of Parliament, in which she wrote :—
" We feel that any reforms which Societies exist to promote or any subjects on which women's opinions are organized, would gain immensely by having an independent M.P. always on the alert to watch their interests and to remind the Government of its importance.

We shall be very glad if you will consider the policy of running a candidate and working for her through your Society, and if so will give you any advice or help that is in our power. We wish to point out that even if the candidate is unsuccessful, an election campaign would give an opportunity for more effective propaganda than any other means now available.

You have probably heard that two nurses have been returned to the Canadian House of Representatives, and a nurse would undoubtedly be a popular candidate just now."

This letter was received with evident pleasure, all present agreeing that National Health and Nursing questions would receive more consideration in the House of Commons if in charge of an expert.

A Nurse M.P.

Miss Wade then proposed and Miss H. L. Pearse seconded the following Resolution :—

" That the National Council of Trained Nurses, in Annual Meeting assembled, hereby invite Mrs. Bedford Fenwick, President, to stand for election as a Member of Parliament to represent the interests of the Nursing Profession."

Mrs. Fenwick said she felt much gratified by this mark of confidence of the Council. She

feared it was too late to stand as a candidate in the present election, but she would accept nomination on the Nursing and National Health Ticket when a suitable constituency could be found.

This decision was greeted with much applause.

Election of Hon. Officers.
Vice-President.

As no Vice-President was elected in 1915, it was agreed that there should be no change until next year.

Directors.

Miss Carson Rae's term of office having expired, Miss Lucy Ramsden was nominated in her stead.

Hon. Secretary and Hon. Treasurer.

Miss Beatrice Cutler and Miss Christina Forrest were unanimously re-elected to office for the ensuing year, and the thanks of the Council expressed for their valuable services.

The Presidents of the Matrons' Council, the National Union of Trained Nurses, and the Irish Nurses' Association were confirmed as *ex officio* members of the Council.

The Royal British Nurses' Association and the National Council.

A courteous communication was received from the Royal British Nurses' Association notifying that a Consultative Committee had been formed in connection with the Chartered Corporation, and extending to the National Council an invitation to affiliate with it.

The intimation that the Royal British Nurses' Association was co-ordinating Nurses' Organizations was received with pleasure, and it was reported that the four largest Nurses' Societies in the National Council had accepted the invitation—the Matrons' Council, the Society for State Registration, the National Union, and the Irish Nurses' Association—and to avoid duplication it was agreed that for the present it might be better for the smaller societies to take independent action, and thus avoid any suspicion of coercion—to which the self-governing Leagues of Nurses so strongly objected. The National Council would work in complete harmony with the Royal British Nurses' Association, and hoped that the Royal Corporation would take an active interest in its International programme.

The International Council of Nurses.

A letter had been received from Miss L. L. Dock, Hon. Secretary of the International Council of Nurses, pointing out that owing to the war the triennial Meeting due this year must be postponed, and it was improbable that it could take place until 1920. Those present expressed the opinion that international intercourse between the nurses of various countries was of the utmost benefit to all, and the proposal to hold an Interim Meeting in 1919, as had been done in 1901 and in 1907, was warmly received. It was agreed that Trained Nurses had covered themselves with glory all over the world during the war, and a gathering of the nurses of the Allies in Conference would have a significance all its own.

It was agreed that such a Conference was to be arranged if possible.

With votes of thanks the exceedingly interesting Meeting terminated.

MARGARET BREAY,

pro BEATRICE CUTLER,

Hon. Secretary.

STO ET STABO.

We have to thank an unknown host of kind friends for their individual approval, and support, of the action taken by the National Council of Trained Nurses, at the annual meeting on November 29th, in inviting by resolution the Editor of THE BRITISH JOURNAL OF NURSING to stand for election in the interests of the Nursing Profession; especially for their expressions of confidence in our ability to " stand for our principles " and " not to betray the rank and file."

Some compensation these letters for many tugs of war.

TRUE TALES WITH A MORAL.

College Matron No. 1 : How do you manage about THE BRITISH JOURNAL OF NURSING ? It seems to give the nurses *ideas.*

College Matron No. 2 : I skim through it, and if there is anything in it I do not consider the nurses ought to read, I just don't send it down.

In Nurses' Sitting Room.

Nurse No. 1 : *B.J.N.* come down this week ?

Nurse No. 2 : Not yet.

Nurse No. 1 : Ah ! then there is something we ought to read. I'll bring it in when I go out.

WHO NEEDS A MINISTRY OF HEALTH ?

Mother (to Poor-Law Guardian) : " You'll excuse me speaking to you, Miss, but when I see you comin' down the street, I was rather *antici-pated*, as I thought you was come to tell me as my little girl was going to be discharged from the infirmary. I should be very sorry if she 'ad to come 'ome now, as they 'ave done wonders for 'er —they ' ave give her outward massage with cod liver oil, which she could never take inwardly, which no 'ospital 'as ever done for 'er. She is quite 'eavy to lift now, so it stands to reason there must be some transformation in 'er inside, don't it ? "

USEFUL WORK.

The National Food Reform Association, Danes Inn House, 256, Strand, is putting a series of questions to Parliamentary candidates, as it did at both elections in 1910. The subjects include Milk Supply, Food Adulteration, Health and Temperance, &c. Copies may be had post free, 1½d.

THE RANYARD NURSES.

(25, Russell Square, W.C. 1.)

The Ranyard Nurses have been quietly cele-brating their Jubilee Year, the first three or four nurses having been placed in London districts in 1868.

The celebrations were brought to a close by a concert on behalf of the Nurse Fund, at the Æolian Hall, on November 22nd. Very grateful thanks are due to those who gave their services— Miss Margaret Balfour, Miss Audrey Richardson, Miss Irene Scharrer, and Mr. Plunket Greene.

The programme was a delightful one and very much appreciated by the audience, and a sum of £128 was realised. During the interval the Archdeacon of Westminster spoke of the work of the Ranyard Nurses, who number eighty-three, referring to the friendly co-operation which now exists between the various Nursing Associations of London, helped by the Central Council for District Nursing, which meets at the Local Government Board. He appealed for more sup-port, mentioning a gift of £50 which had just been received from H.R.H. the Princess Louise, Duchess of Argyll, with the assurance that the helpful work of the Ranyard Mission has Her Royal Highness' sincere sympathy.

The Archdeacon also appealed for more workers. There is great need and many opportunities for developing the Nursing Service of London, and it is hoped that many who have been giving their services for special war work will in future dedicate their services to the poor of London.

District Nurses are wanted to play their part in the schemes for the welfare of the nation by helping to make the homes healthier and happier, and so more worthy of the heroes who have fought and died for them. This work calls for a true spirit of adventure and a grip of social problems, as well as a heart of sympathy and understanding.

Ranyard Nurses must have had three years' General Hospital Training and be women of vision, seeking to serve not only in obedience to the example of Christ, but in the strength of His power.

"HOME RULE" IN HEALTH.

A movement is afoot in Scotland, promoted largely by insurance interests, for the creation of a separate Ministry of Health for Scotland, entirely free of any control from London. The advocates of this " revolution " want to see the Scottish Health Ministry swallow the Local Government Board, the Education Department, the Registrar-General's Department, and the Commissioners of Scottish Insurance. This is a pretty big bid for Home Rule in health matters (says a correspondent in the *Weekly Dispatch*), and is attracting much attention in Scotland.

How about a Scottish College of Nurses ? We have always advocated the devolution of educa-tional facilities for Scottish and Irish Nurses, as well as for English Nurses ; and the Irish mean to have it.

ANOTHER "GAMBOL" IN SUPPORT OF THE COLLEGE OF NURSING, LTD.

The hot indignation of the independent members of the Nursing Profession, and the very widespread disgust at the exploitation of its prestige by the *Daily Sketch* Victory Ball, would need little further comment on the part of this JOURNAL, were it not for incidents connected with it that require our criticism. Suffice it to say that at this most untimely "gambol," thousands of the most frivolous section of the community danced and romped at the Albert Hall, on the 27th November, from 10 p.m. until 5 o'clock on the following morning, that drink flowed freely until such time as it was considered advisable to notify that it had "run out," and that when the doors at last closed, the riotous mænads continued their dizzy gyrations in the public thoroughfares! Best draw a veil—as we note many of the daily papers considered it wise to do.

"Eye-Witness" reports, "The best people were not there—but the wrong 'uns were," and the lack of patronage from the Royal Family was as significant as it was decisive—so far as the "right thing" was concerned. We are informed that the statement made by the *Evening Standard* (Hulton press) on November 15th, that "the Victory Ball has the complete approval of the King and Queen," was quite unauthorised, and we consider that this statement was calculated to place Their Majesties in a totally false position in the opinion of thoughtful members of the community.

In this connection we must intimate to the Hon. Sir Arthur Stanley, the Chairman of the Ball; to the Viscountess Cowdray, and other persons who inflicted it upon us, that what is not good enough for Royalty is not good enough for the self-respecting members of the Nursing Profession. We must now direct our readers' attention to the following correspondence :—

A PROTEST AND THE REPLY.

A Protest against the holding of the Victory Ball at the Royal Albert Hall was issued by Isabel Macdonald, Secretary of the Royal British Nurses' Association; Mildred Heather-Bigg, R.R.C., President of the Matrons' Council of Great Britain and Ireland; Ethel G. Fenwick, President of the Society for the State Registration of Trained Nurses; and M. L. Rimmer, Hon. Secretary of the National Union of Trained Nurses. In their protest the signatories say :—

We, representing many thousands of professional men and women, beg to offer a whole-hearted protest against the so-called Victory Ball to be held at the Albert Hall on November 27th; especially we protest because it is declared to be given on behalf of the Nation's Fund for Nurses. The organised Societies of Nurses have never been consulted; they thoroughly disapprove, and have repeatedly protested. We know, better than most people, by what awful suffering the measure of victory we are enjoying—and it is not complete—has been won. This ball, held at such a time, seems to us like dancing over the graves of the dead, and we object to its being associated with the Profession of Nursing.

Sir Arthur Stanley communicated to the press the following reply to the Protest :—

SIR,—My attention has been drawn to the letter issued by officials of four associations, claiming to speak on behalf of the nurses of Great Britain and Ireland, protesting against the holding of the "Victory Ball." To those who know that the high-sounding titles of the societies which these ladies claim to represent, cover a very small and insignificant minority of the nursing profession, the protest carries no weight. The College of Nursing, in aid of which the ball is being held, numbers at least three, and probably four, times as many nurse members as all these four associations put together. It should also be remembered that a large part of the proceeds of the ball will go to the Tribute Fund, which is being established to help all nurses—not only those belonging to the College of Nursing, as has been falsely stated, who are sick or suffering or have fallen on evil days.

Those of us who are responsible for the College of Nursing—the only body that can fairly claim to speak in the name of the nurses—are accustomed to those protests, which occur with almost wearisome regularity from the same quarters whenever any effort is made by the College to raise funds which will be for the benefit of nurses, who have done so much for others, and who take so little thought for their own welfare. The Council of the College of Nursing approves the holding of the ball; that the public approves the objects for which it is held is shown by the fact that all the boxes and tickets have already been sold.

Yours faithfully,
ARTHUR STANLEY,
Chairman of the Council of the College of Nursing, Ltd.

The professional women who signed the Protest did not, as Sir Arthur Stanley states, "claim to speak on behalf of the Nurses of Great Britain and Ireland." In their official capacities they presented the views of the members of the Organized Nurses' Associations—which comprise the intelligent and independent wing of the nurses—and they protested against this War Charity, the Nation's Fund for Nurses, being associated with the Profession of Nursing of which they are members, at this time, when thousands of our people are still mourning their dead. The cheap sneers of the autocratic Chairman of the College of Nursing, Ltd., who informs the public that those who are responsible for his Company are "the only body that can fairly claim to speak in the name of nurses," is as ridiculous as it is misleading, but when he adds that "the Council of the College of Nursing approves the holding of the ball," then it is time for the members of the profession at large to estimate the danger of the College policy at its true economic value. For it means that the Matrons of the Nurse Training Schools originally nominated by Sir Arthur Stanley to form his Council, and who are largely responsible for the tone and discipline of the nurses of the future, are content that our profession should be based on charity obtained by reprehensible methods, controlled by laymen, and the whole fabric of its prestige reduced to dust and ashes. Alas! how are the mighty fallen! Surely such a betrayal of our hitherto high ethical standards is enough to make Florence Nightingale turn in her grave!

" THE PROTEST CARRIES NO WEIGHT."

To quote Sir Arthur Stanley further, he tells the public that the opinion of those trained nurses who refuse to subscribe to the dangerously autocratic Constitution of his College Company, which has taken power to remove a nurse's name from its register—*without power of appeal*—" carries no weight." That has yet to be proved, when the organized workers come to grips with their employers, in their coming struggle for legal status and freedom from tyranny, in the House of Commons.

But enough said.

The result of the Protest was instant and extraordinary, to judge from our post-bag, and sympathy with the " insignificant minority " produced immediate effect.

The Labour Party, which has always most loyally supported the claims of the organized nurses for State Registration—and voted for their Bill to a man when introduced into the House of Commons in 1914—at once grasped the economic significance of the Protest, " Nurses do not want Charity and plutocratic control—they ask for Justice," and that " funds to finance their Employers' Union through such a method as the Victory Ball was an insult, not only to the working nurses, but to the dead and mutilated men, whose intense suffering and heroic sacrifices the best nurses have shared with them all the years of the war."

THE LABOUR PARTY AND PLUTOCRATIC WASTE.

Having been denied the use of the Albert Hall for a few hours in which to hold a meeting, members of the Socialist wing of the Labour Party attended the Victory Ball to judge what sort of people were to be permitted to disport themselves there *all night*. Why this extravagant waste of light, coal, food and drink for the leisured class, when thousands of poor people are deprived of a mere sufficiency? Also, " a mother of men killed in battle " threatened, " if the Queen or any of the Royal Family are present, I will make a protest." Suffice it to say that what these visitors saw added fuel to the fire of their discontent, and one described as " sacrilegious " an " abandoned female wearing the honourable blue suit of the wounded soldier, with crutches all complete."

WIPING OUT THE INSULT.

On Saturday and Sunday last overflowing meetings of the Labour Party were held at the Albert Hall, and where a few days before " light London" had capered to finance the College of Nursing, Ltd., a Protest was offered from the platform from Matrons and Nurses against the notorious function organized by the *Daily Sketch.*

" Nurses," it was stated, " do not want Charity. They ask for Justice and your help in passing their democratic State Registration Bill, now before the House of Commons in charge of Major Chapple." At the words, " Nurses do not want Charity," the huge audience broke into such tumultuous and sympathetic applause that the final words of the speaker could not be heard.

It was the sound of the tocsin so far as the *ancien régime* in relation to Nursing is concerned.

APPOINTMENTS.

MATRON.

Kensington Dispensary and Children's Hospital, Church Street, Kensington.—Miss K. M. Moore has been appointed Matron. She was trained at St. Bartholomew's Hospital and subsequently held the position of Sister at the Hospital for Sick Children, Great Ormond Street, W.C., Matron of its Convalescent Branch at Highgate, and Matron of the Children's Hospital, Nottingham

Samaritan Free Hospital for Women, Marylebone Road, N.W. 1. — Miss Winifred Tice has been appointed Matron. She was trained at St. Bartholomew's Hospital, London, and, as a member of Queen Alexandra's Imperial Military Nursing Service Reserve, was Sister-in-Charge of a Clearing Station in France and at the Military Hospital, Colchester.

Eltham and Mottringham Cottage Hospital. —Miss Mary Young Thomson has been appointed Matron. She was trained at Addenbrooke's Hospital, Cambridge, and has been Theatre Sister in a women's surgical ward, and Assistant Matron at the General Infirmary, Worcester, and Sister at the Royal Herbert Hospital, Woolwich, and in connection with the Salonika Field Force in connection with Queen Alexandra's Imperial Military Nursing Service Reserve.

Bideford and District Hospital, North Devon.— Miss Jennie Jones has been appointed Matron. She was trained at the General and Eye Hospital, Llanelly, and has held positions of responsibility in the same institution, at the Cancer Hospital, Fulham Road, S.W., and at the Aberystwyth Infirmary and Cardigan General Hospital.

Isolation Hospital, Malvern.—Miss J. E. Gilbert has been appointed Matron. She was trained at the City Hospital, Colinton Mains, Edinburgh, and the Royal Berks Hospital, Reading, and has been Ward Sister and Deputy Matron at the Infectious Diseases Hospital, Huddersfield, Sister in-Charge of the Sankey Sanatorium, Warrington, and Superintendent of Nurses at the Fever Hospital, Blackburn.

ASSISTANT MATRON.

Royal Hants County Hospital, Winchester. — Miss Margaret L. Adams has been appointed Assistant Matron. She was trained at the Royal Hospital for Sick Children, Edinburgh, and at King's College Hospital, London, and has done war service with the Scottish Hospitals at Royaumont and Villers Cotteret. She has also been Night Superintendent at the Empire Hospital, Vincent Square, S.W.

Royal Hospital for Sick Children, Aberdeen. —Miss Christian B. Lumsden has been appointed Assistant Matron (temporary). She was trained at the Royal Infirmary, Dundee, and has been Sister at the Royal Hospital for Sick Children, Aberdeen ; Assistant Matron at Morningside Asylum, Edinburgh ; Matron at the James Murray

Royal Asylum, Perth ; and Sister at the first Scottish General Hospital (Territorial), Aberdeen.

Royal Asylum, Glasgow.— Miss Florence M. Gordon Duff has been appointed Assistant Matron. She was trained at the Epsom Infirmary, and has done private nursing.

Miss Eva Cuthbert has also been appointed to a similar position. She was trained at the Belfast Infirmary.

SISTER-IN-CHARGE,

Maternity Home, Edinburgh. — Miss Laura Bruford has been appointed Sister-in-Charge of the Maternity Home attached to the Royal Scottish Nursing Institution, Edinburgh. She was trained at the General Hospital, Cheltenham, and has had experience both in fever and maternity nursing, having been on the staff of Queen Charlotte's Hospital for nearly three years. For the last four-and-a-half years she has been on the staff of the Registered Nurses' Society, part of which time she has acted as Sister-in-Charge of the V.A.D. Hospital, Thame, Oxon.

THEATRE SISTER.

Children's Hospital, Sheffield.—Miss Mary Stanley has been appointed Theatre Sister. She was trained at the Swansea General and Eye Hospital, and has been Staff Nurse and Temporary Theatre Sister in the same hospital.

HOME NURSING.

Under the above heading a handy little book, entitled " Home Nursing," has been published at St John's Gate, Clerkenwell, E.C. 4. It has been compiled at the request of the Ambulance Committee of the Order of St. John as the official Home Nursing Handbook of the St. John Ambulance Association chiefly from the manuscript of Miss Mildred Heather Bigg, R.R.C., whose name it bears on its title page. The book follows the plan adopted in the official First Aid Manual and is in the square form used by the Association bearing its seal, with the eight-pointed Maltese Cross on the cover. We commend the book to the notice of nurses.

PRISON FOR BOGUS NURSE.

For giving false information as to her identity at the Abbotsford Hotel, Russell Square, where she registered herself as " Sister D. P. Gordon," Annie Jarrett, 22, was at Bow Street Police Court sentenced to six months' hard labour.

When arrested she was wearing the uniform of a Red Cross Nurse, badges, and the Military Medal and D.C.M. ribands. She carried one of her arms in a sling and walked with a limp, supported by a crook stick, but there was nothing the matter with her. She also pleaded guilty to stealing a lady's golf cape from the Mid-Surrey Ladies' Golf Club at Richmond.

We regret to note several bad cases of theft amongst nurses from Nursing Institutions in Torquay. Careful investigation before engagement should protect private patients and fellow-nurses from this danger.

NURSING ECHOES.

The second birthday party of the Nurses' Imperial Club, Ebury Street, was celebrated on Friday afternoon, when the additional new bedrooms were on view. The guests were warmly welcomed by Miss Mayer, the popular Lady Superintendent. Quite early in the afternoon the table of birthday gifts was burdened with useful and ornamental donations to the Club. Pictures to adorn the new rooms, hot-water bags, candlesticks, soap, pickles, salad oil, made a motley collection, and showed that the donors were in the secret. Another table showed a collection of articles left by former guests, who apparently had an *embarras de richesse*, as there were many desirable things in this lost property department.

The new bedrooms are snugly and tastefully furnished, and only require some of the new birthday gifts to complete their attraction, although we understand from Miss Mayer that any further offers of pictures and ornaments would not be despised. The cosy drawing-room looked very alluring, in contrast with depressing climatic conditions without.

An excellent tea and music, to which latter Miss Mayer contributed some delightful piano-forte playing, helped to make this second birthday of the Club most enjoyable.

We are glad to observe that the Committees of County Hospitals are considering the question of raising the salaries of their nursing staffs.

At the County Hospital, York, the salaries have been revised and the following scale sanctioned :—*Assistant Matron*, £70; *Night Sister*, £60; *Ward Sisters*, commencing salary £50, rising by annual increment to £55 and £60. Further increase at the Matron's request.

At the Royal Victoria and West Hants Hospital, Bournemouth, the Finance and General Purposes Committee have recently authorized the following increases in the salaries payable to the Nursing Staff :—

Ward Sisters, from £50 per annum, to First Year, £50, Second Year £55, Third Year £60 per annum, together with an allowance of £3 for uniform.

Staff Nurses are to receive £40 per annum, increased to £45 after one year's service as Staff Nurse, with £2 10s. per annum for uniform.

The salaries of probationers have been increased, First Year from £10 to £15, Second Year from £15 to £20, Third Year from £20 to £28, with £3 10s. allowance for uniform for the first year, and £3 per annum for the second and third year.

Departmental Sisters receive various additions to the salaries laid down for Ward Sisters.

Lady Stirling Maxwell (President) presided at the twenty-fifth annual meeting of the Glasgow and West of Scotland Co-operation of Trained Nurses in Charing Cross Halls, Glasgow, on November 21st, when Dean of Guild Hunter, in moving the adoption of the reports, said that seventy-three of the Nurses of the Co-operation had gone to France and were doing magnificent work. Dr. A. E. Maylard referred to the resignation of Miss Helen M. Rough, to whom the Co-operation owed its inception, and to the appointment of Miss E. E. Taylor, who had had wide professional experience, as her successor.

BOOK OF THE WEEK.

"THE MIRROR AND THE LAMP."*

" But, mother," said the little boy, firmly, " you are pretty *now*; you are the prettiest person I have ever seen."

And perhaps then, for who can say what tiny tortuous paths will one day make the widest roadway to a woman's heart ?—Mrs. Churchill, for the first time, was plainly aware that she loved this boy more tenderly than the other two.

Neither Tom nor Charles could have made such an answer ; neither could as yet have dimly guessed that out of all the possible things that might be said, this was the right thing to say— the only thing that from boy to man, would at that moment give exquisite pleasure. Edward was more sensitive than the other two, a finer organism, a more complex instrument that responded to fainter stimulus—he was going to be very clever and to make his mother very proud.

It was Mrs. Churchill's earnest wish that her beloved son should enter the ministry, and when after a certain service at the cathedral Edward announced that he had heard the call, she could hardly speak for joy. " You crown my life with gladness," she told him.

And that night she made their supper a feast. She wore her finest dress, put on one of her poor little ornaments ; looked radiant, grand and at least ten years younger than before.

Edward's ideals were of the most lofty. He

* By W. B. Maxwell. London : Cassell & Co.

dreamt of a slum parish with his darling mother as his life-long and best-loved companion. His first curacy found him located in the vicarage of a poor parish in the neighbourhood of East India Docks. Inside the vicarage, from roof tree to the basement, its inmates were always busy, always trying to do more than was humanly possible—knowing that it was so, yet still trying.

Edward's first shock was the defection of his mother, who shattered his dreams—both of his own happiness and his faith in her perfection— by marrying a stout, vulgar, albeit worthy man, named Battersby.

She spoke about the furniture. " It was as though I had cheated you, dear ; I led you to expect it ; of course, you have been counting on the furniture."

He bowed his head so that she should not see his eyes, and there came from his throat a sound that was half a cough and half a sob. He was stifling the words that had nearly said themselves : " I was counting on you mother more than on your furniture."

" All ties of family were broken and not a single personal affection was left to him. But the blank must be filled that was a necessity. Mankind in the mass was surely large enough to supply what had been withdrawn by a few individuals."

It would have been well had our friend Edward stuck to the mass, but his sympathies became enlisted in the ill-used young wife of the loud, blustering Vickers, and pity soon changed into love. The primitive man in him was roused to fury at the evidence of Vickers' brutality on this frail young creature, and, after a violent scene, in which he thrashed the bully, he took Lilian under his protection. Henceforth, he, of course, had to renounce his sacred office, and, at the same time, he renounced his faith.

It was not until some years after that the death of Vickers enabled Edward to make Lilian his wife. In the meantime he had become successful as a novelist, and had further been made independent by various legacies. But it is not until the close of the book that he is reinstated by the bishop to his office.

His return to his faith is very gradual and is marked by no dramatic incident.

" I don't think I should care to go to church regularly, perhaps scarcely at all a—I mean, no more than in the past."

He said to himself : " I will belive all that I can ; I will believe all that I *can't* for their sakes (his wife's and Allan Gate's). Love can make me believe, perhaps, as nothing else can." The kindly Bishop, when he lifts the ban, makes his resumption of office possible to Edward's flickering faith by giving him a position that carried with it little responsibility and no emoluments. But the reader is left with the comfortable certainty that, in course of time, Edward will take up work once more with his old ardour and his old faith.

This is a powerful sketch of an unusual personality showing both the force of temptation to a good man and the long and painful process of his restoration. H. H.

OUTSIDE THE GATES.
OUR POLICY.

Don't forget that December 14th is Polling Day, and if possible before that date interview the Parliamentary candidates in your constituency and ask them a few pertinent questions as follows:

1. Are you going to work for a just peace with indemnities for the cost of the war, damage made good, to hold what we have in hand in German colonies, the banishment of Germans from our shores for years to come—in fact, Britain for the British—so that our race may not be further contaminated by the criminal strain of the Hun ?

The deplorable flabbiness of the attitude of the average politician towards a treacherous and savage foe makes it the more imperative that true patriots should be very firm on these points. It was Coventry Patmore who said, "Nations die of softening of the brain, which, for a long time, passes for softening of the heart."

2. Are you heart and soul in favour of a Health Ministry, so that there may be fresh air, pure water, unadulterated food, a good house, a bit of garden, plenty of coal, light and transport for all, also of a practical education and plenty of work, so that it may be possible for women to bear and rear children without heartbreak ?

Don't forget that we have a higher percentage of physical unfits than any belligerent country !

3. Will you support the just Bill for the State Registration of Nurses, promoted by the Central Committee, so that their educational and economic conditions can be defined and protected to enable them to take their place in the general scheme for raising the standard of the nation's health, free from grinding poverty and unskilled competition ?

If the candidate is in sympathy with these demands, vote for him or her, as the case may be

COMING EVENTS.

December 7th.—General Hospital, Birmingham. Nurses' League. Autumn Meeting at General, Hospital, Birmingham. Address by Miss Bartleet on "Local Government Work." 3 p.m.

December 7th.—Irish Nurses' Association. Meeting Executive Committee, 34, St. Stephen's Green, Dublin. 8 p.m.

December 14th.—League of St. Bartholomew's Hospital Nurses' League. Winter General Meeting, Clinical Theatre, St. Bartholomew's Hospital. 2.30 p.m. Social gathering, Nurses' Sitting Room. Tea, music.

December 19th.—Royal British Nurses' Association. Lecture : "Bokhara and Samarkand" (fully illustrated by lantern slides) by Miss Annette Meakin, F.R.G.S. Chair : Miss Mildred Heather - Bigg, R.R.C., Vice - President. The Rooms of the Medical Society of London, 11, Chandos Street, Cavendish Square, W. 1. 2.45 p.m.

LETTERS TO THE EDITOR.

Whilst cordially inviting communications upon all subjects for these columns, we wish it to be distinctly understood that we do not IN ANY WAY hold ourselves responsible for the opinions expressed by our correspondents.

"THE UNTRAINED COMMANDANT."
To the Editor of THE BRITISH JOURNAL OF NURSING.

DEAR MADAM,—I have read so often the unkind and unjust criticisms of V.A.D. Commandants, that I feel bound to protest.

Why, when these ladies undertake the duties of a commandant, should they be expected to be trained ?

Surely, in that case, their duties would lie in the *nursing*, not the administration, of a hospital ! One does not expect the chairman of a hospital to have the qualifications of a physician or surgeon. I have worked under our Commandant now for over two and a-half years, and under her management of clear judgment, justice, firmness and great understanding, our hospital has been run in all its branches—office, wards and kitchen, in perfect harmony and unison.

Our patients (now numbering over 1,100) well fed and well cared for, are always happy and very well behaved. The whole staff, both in kitchen and wards, have always been very happy and contented in their work, their only regret being the fact that in the natural course of events our hospital must soon close.

If the many hundreds of posts held by the hardworked and long-suffering Commandants in the past four years had been held by highly trained and efficient nurses, who would have nursed our wounded soldiers ?

The " Untrained Commandant," I presume !
SISTER-IN-CHARGE.
56, Herts.

[We are glad to hear of a Commandant who apparently does not interfere with the professional duties of the Sister-in-Charge, but according to her charge she has the right to do so—and in hundreds of Red Cross Hospital engages the Nursing Staff, and controls—or fails to maintain discipline ; moreover the Commandant wears the cap and apron of the professional nurse. Why ? Chairmen of hospitals do not don the surgeon's operating gown.

During the war we have constantly been applied to for Nurses by Commandants, and all correspondence concerning these professional nurses is conducted by them, even if there is, which often there is not, a Sister-in-Charge. Moreover, we have before us testimonials written by Commandants, expressing opinions concerning the *professional qualifications and work of trained nurses*—and in many instances they practically act as Matrons and interfere with the nursing of the patients, of which they know nothing. Some have the effrontery to attempt to control the medical officer. To quote : " Can you find me a working nurse ?   I myself shall act as Matron—*don't send a dragon ;* our V.A.D.s are very efficient.'

" I want a trained nurse to take the lead ; but I prefer she should not be called Matron, as our duties might clash."

Trained nurse writes : " Please recall me from this hospital.   I am the only trained nurse, and have to be on call at night for fear the V.A.D. on duty requires help ; moreover the Commandant arranges all off duty times and I never know who will be on duty from hour to hour."

" I have been Matron in two Red Cross Hospitals, and the Commandants have both been awarded the R.R.C.   Where do the nurses come in ?"   And so on by the yard ; the system is wrong.— ED.]

FREEDOM OF SPEECH BY UP-TO-DATE METHODS.

To the Editor of THE BRITISH JOURNAL OF NURSING.

DEAR MADAM,—As the " Free Press " is *not* free, we, independent freedom-loving members of the nursing profession, having proved on various occasions that posters in the open streets are a most effectual method of protest, sallied forth (those of us who had time) on November 26th, adorned with posters bearing the following words : " Dancing on the Dead— Patriotic Nurses protest against money being raised in their name by a ' Victory Ball,' before our splendid men are cold in their graves."   We walked up and down in front of the Automobile Club (now being used for overseas officers) and the offices of the British Red Cross Society.   The hour and the place favoured our enterprise.   It was a scene of cease-less activity, of coming and going of the military and civic population of men and women.   Eyes, which were opened wide, were expressive of many emotions : scorn, amusement, indifference, anger, kindness and sympathy.

Civilian : " I admire you for coming out to protest in such a manner.   It is more fitting at this time to be on our knees with thankfulness than to *dance.*"

Poster Paraders : " Thank you, sir, for your sympathy " (with a few more words of enlighten-ment).

Officer (reading thoughtfully) : " Oh, I thought this ball was under the auspices of the Red Cross Society."

This remark illustrates in the clearest manner the wrong done by the promoters of the " Victory Ball," in using this sacred symbol to cover their advertisement for a purpose which has no con-nection whatever with it.   Have not Britons often bewailed indignantly the Huns' *misuse of the Red Cross ?*   The difference is only one of degree, not of *principle.*

We made our explanations to the officer who left us an enlightened man.

A Lady : " What is this protest ? "

We explained.   She showed sympathy and understanding.

Porter of Automobile Club : " A lady inside says you must not stand here."

We !   We do not recognise her authority ; we intend to remain, and we *did !*

A POSTER PARADER.

JUSTICE NOT CHARITY.

To the Editor of THE BRITISH JOURNAL OF NURSING.

MADAM,—My attention has been drawn to Sir Arthur Stanley's reply to the protest issued by the Secretary of the Royal British Nurses' Associa-tion and the President of the Society for the State Registration of Trained Nurses, &c., &c.   The protest is a valuable one, and Sir A. Stanley's remarks about these societies are *not* correct and also appear to be very ungentlemanly.

Mrs. Bedford Fenwick has represented the Nursing Profession for many years.   She has con-sistently pressed for State Registration of Nurses and for better salaries.   She is indeed a " Pioneer " in their cause.   She has exceptional knowledge of nurses and their status and salaries.   It is a well-known evil that trained nurses have always been paid insufficiently in institutions of all kinds, having regard to the skilled work they are required to undertake.   They *do not ask for charity ; they ask for justice,* and one hopes that with the " new order " of things, viz., the Women's Vote in the future, they will attain this.

Yours faithfully,
DORA H. COLMAN,
Commandant " Surrey 100."

KERNELS FROM CORRESPONDENCE.

Disgusted Private Nurse : My patient is still in danger, but both mother and daughter attended the Victory Ball.   Nothing was discussed but fancy dress for days, and a sum which would have kept a sick soldier for a year, or taught him a trade was lavished on their get up.   They were simply furious at the Nurses' Protest in the Press (guilty conscience as one son was killed in the war).   As you know, my dear brother is still missing and all this frivolity in *our name* is most hurtful.   I had a good cry over it."

" *A Nurs* " *writes :* " I went to 52, North Audley Street to make a protest against the Victory Ball.   Whilst in the shop, someone dressed in a Red Cross uniform (with white shoes and stockings) asked the saleswoman if men in evening dress would be admitted, and it was suggested to her ' the man might borrow khaki ! ' "

" *Military Nurse* " : " Here Victory Ball tickets were sent to the Mess and young officers were urged to buy them by the colonel, who had had them sent for disposal—' for a good cause, our broken-down military nurses,' as he explained.   What a shame to make these young men waste £3 3s., even over us broken old war nurses !   Also Sisters and nurses in this hospital are told by the Matron they must join the College *or it will be most serious for their future,* and they may pay the guinea in instalments.   How about Kaiser-ism ?   Is our boasted liberty all ' pot-calling-kettle ' ? "

[We regret to hold over a number of interesting letters.— ED.]

The Midwife.

CENTRAL MIDWIVES BOARD.

LIST OF SUCCESSFUL CANDIDATES.

At the examination of the Central Midwives Board, held on November 1st, in London and the Provinces, 450 candidates were examined and 346 passed the examiners. The percentage of failures was 23.1.

LONDON.

British Hospital for Mothers and Babies.—E. Francis, L. Nield, I. E. Wilson.

City of London Lying-in Hospital.—E. C. Anderson, E. Bettinson, M. L. Goulding, M. G. Leader, E. A. Maxwell, E. L. K. Moore, M. A. Robertson, A. C. Smith, F. M. Webster, L. M. Wright.

Clapham Maternity Hospital.—E. M. Campbell, A. Child, S. A. M. Kent, E. J Markham, A. Roberts.

East End Mothers' Home.—M. Alexander, E. A. Camp, E. R. James, M. M. Picken, L. L. Standley, G. Watkins.

General Lying-in Hospital.—A. F. Barnes, G. Browne, W. Burt, D. Cohen, E. B. Creasy, A. Edwards, S. M. Jones, E. Lambert, D. A. Leak, J. M. Pinhorn, M. Pipe, H. M. Richer, A. M. Sadlier, B. M. Scott, M. Senior, A. E. Stubbs, A M. Williamson, M. E. Wilson.

Guy's Institution.—G. L. Olley, E. M. Shephard, M. W. Sparkes, G. B. Thomson.

Kensington Union Infirmary.—A. Gifford, L. Heading.

Lambeth Parish Workhouse.—E. O. Price, J. M. Watson.

London Hospital.—D. Baker, R. W. Derrick, M. Pring.

Maternity Nursing Association.—D. E. Bee, O. Cozens, C. Earnshaw, A. E. Roughton.

Plaistow Maternity Charity.—E. Barker, A. L. Bennett, E. A. Brooke, E. Cantrell, E. M. Cook, F. E. Cummings, M. E. Davies, A. B. Delaine, M. F. Dier, C. Dixon, I. Edmonds, J. M. Ferguson, S. A. Garner, E. G. Gough, M. J. Hand, M. E. Hudson, M. M. Jessop, C. J. Jones, M. Legg, L. Lunn, F. M. May, A. Nuttall, M. G. Owen, R. Parry, M. E. Pritchard, A. Purser, L. E. Rowles, L. B. Spencer, J. Tough, K. Troop, A. Turner, C. Wallbank, A. J. Wilson, F. Wood, A. Wylie, E. Jones.

Middlesex Hospital.—L. F. Hartley, E. Letters.

Queen Charlotte's Hospital.—W. E. H. Bell, M. L. Berger, G. C. Bickerstaff, T. E. Bowman, W. C. Chapman, F. E. Chubb, F. Colson, I. M. Cooper, C. M. A. Curtis, L. M. Dyne, E. A. Eacott, J. Fraser, E. E. Hayman, I. M. Hopkins, R. H. Hopkins, M. F. James, K. Jones, B. M. Lewis, W. A. Lintott, M Manger, F. M. Masters, F. L. Morrison, M. E. Packer, D. A. Parker, M. F. Parker, E. C. H. Purvis, R. N. Singer, M. Stewart, A. F. Thomas, E. Webb, M. M. Williams, E. L. Wolsey.

Salvation Army Mothers' Hospital.—A. E Carter, R. A. Castle.

St. Marylebone Workhouse Infirmary.—K. Reed, E. G. Vallance.

St. Pancras South Infirmary.— D. Driver.

St. Thomas' Hospital.—B. K. Newill, E. K. Servêtopoulos.

PROVINCIAL.

Aldershot, Louise Margaret Hospital.—N. Gregson, G. Johnstone, E. Lazenby, F. M. Wheatley.

Birkenhead Maternity Hospital.—E. Adams, M. E. McCabe, E. Quinn.

Birmingham Maternity Hospital.—C. Barber, M. Burghall, A. E. Charnley, E. M. Coxon, A. M. Derrick, L. Gold, E. E. Hamilton, E. Herring, H. A. Mead, L. Palfreyman, B. M. Parry, W. M. Prince, H. Roberts, R. Sedgwick, S. I. Sewart, K. Sheridan, E. Stuttard, L. Wright.

Birmingham, Selly Oak Union Infirmary.— Emily Brayne.

Bradford Union Hospital.—J. Marshall.

Brighton Hospital for Women.—M. E. Darbyshire, G. Ede, C. E. Hilton, K. A. Moore, H. M. Nash, D. D. Sharpe, L. Willey, A. Wolsey.

Bristol, Eastville Workhouse Infirmary.—E. M. Dawe.

Bristol General Hospital.—A. D. Bermingham, N. J. Bryant, L. M. Lawrence.

Bristol Royal Infirmary.—F. G. Clarke, M. A. A. Henley.

Cheltenham District Nursing Association.—E. Leigh, E. M. Reid.

Coventry Union Infirmary.—M. Pilkington.

Derby, Royal Derbyshire Nursing Association.— B. M. Bevan, I. Morton, M. E. Pendlebury, B. M. A. Wilson.

Devon and Cornwall Training School.—M. Barker, J. Barnes, R. K. Sharp, E. E. Tremlett.

Devonport, Alexandra Nursing Home.—E. M. Crichton, F. Davis, A. T. Hailes, A. S. Lovely.

Gloucester District Nursing Society.—F. R. Beazer, S. E. M. McKenna, R. N. Wheeler.

Halifax District Nursing Association and Huddersfield Union Workhouse.—E. M. Sands.

Hastings District Nursing Association.—L. Fifield.

Hartlepool Union Infirmary and Newcastle-on-Tyne Union Hospital.—E. Elstob.

Huddersfield District Nursing Association and Huddersfield Union Workhouse.—E. Taylor.

Kingston-on-Thames Union Infirmary.—M. M. Kemp.

Leeds Maternity Hospital.—E. Booth, F. J. Dale, E. M. Lloyd, E. E. Robson, A. Slee.

Leicester Maternity Hospital.—E. Carter, M. C. Chappell, L. Woolley.

Leicester Union Infirmary.—E. M. Bamley, K. Tipper, F. E. Wood.

Liverpool Maternity Hospital.—E. Barlow, B. Bracewell, F. Cardwell, B. M. Dubberley, C. H

Ferguson, L. H. Foale, L. Hall, E. P. M. Harlow, E. Heald, M. Hindley, S. E. Jones, M. A. Lewis, M. O'Keefe, E. C. Parry, M. E. Peacock, H. M. Robertson, D. M. Vickers.

Manchester, St. Mary's Hospitals.—E. L. Ashworth, E. M. Barlow, S. A. Bradshaw, M. Collins, H. Graydon, M. Jones, A. Pickles, M. Popplewell, A. A. Roscoe, M. E. Smethurst, M. E. Tetlow, S. Walker, S. A. Wilson.

Manchester Workhouse Infirmary, and St. Mary's Hospitals.—I. Burrill, E. Halliday, N. Hawkins, E. Taylor, N. Tranter, J. Watkinson, M. Whitehurst.

Newcastle-on-Tyne Maternity Hospital. — C. Lupton, E. Price, M. Robinson.

Newcastle-on-Tyne Union Hospital.—I. Mackenley, A. Young.

Northampton Q.V.N.I.—H. Hollies, E. J. Page, J. Trueman.

Nottingham Workhouse Infirmary.—H. Widdowson.

Oldham Union Infirmary.—E. M. Bulley.

Preston Union Infirmary.—R. Mackenzie.

Preston Union Workhouse.—M. A. Wilson.

Sheffield, Jessop Hospital.—G. Allchin, G. W. Hickson, L. Pilkington, E. Smith, A. Thorne, F. I. Vieler.

Sheffield Union Infirmary.—E. Upton.

Staffs Training Home for Nurses.—A. Brown, M. J. F. Challoner, G. Davies, M. Duffy, E. E. Redhead, J. Watkin, J. Weaver, E. Wilcox.

Steyning Union Infirmary.—K. Penfold.

Walton, West Derby Union Infirmary.—G. M. Sellar.

West Riding Nurses' Home.—D. E. Beeton, N. Matthews.

Wilts Nursing Association.—E. Crabb, A. M. E. May.

Wolverhampton District Nurses' Home.—S. Bakewell, E. J. Griffiths, C. H. Lovatt.

Wolverhampton Union Infirmary.—H. E. Cooper, F. M. Finn, F. Mason, C. M. B. Smith.

Worcester County Nursing Association.—Alice Tranter.

York Maternity Hospital. — H. F. Cook, F. C. Sedgwick, M. A. Shipley.

WALES.

Cardiff Q.V.J.N.I.—R. Johns, N. Lewis, A Mills, E. Tunley.

Monmouth Nursing Association.—M. A. Brown.

Monmouth Training Centre.—A. Adams.

Swansea District Nursing Association.—L. G. M. Thomas.

SCOTLAND.

Dundee Maternity Hospital.—I. E. Bodin, E. Hinchcliffe, A. Lake, C. Wilson.

Edinburgh Royal Maternity Hospital. — E. M. Baxter, Douglas S. Wetherell.

Glasgow Royal Maternity Hospital.—J. T. Taylor, M. Tindal.

Govan Nurses' Home.—M. Jackson.

IRELAND.

Dublin, Rotunda Hospital.—E. M. Barczinsky, C. A. Fisher, S. S. Iredale, V. A. Peel.

Belfast Union Maternity Hospital.—M. Getty, R. Glazier, S. Kennedy, S. E. Smyth.

Dublin, Coombe Hospital.—K. Hartley.

PRIVATE TUITION.

A. M. Brown, M. M. Chin-Chen, C. Collins, E. M. Deverell, F. M. Evans, J. A. Geers, G. Jones, S. Mills, A. M. Morris, E. Stubbs, E. Swift.

PRIVATE TUITION AND INSTITUTIONS.

Preston Union Workhouse.—H. S. H. Burton.

Birmingham Maternity Hospital.—E. L. Chinery, E. A. Owen.

General Lying-in Hospital.—S. Clark, E. L. Shinnie, M. E. Thorold.

St. Mary's Hospital, Manchester.—M. A. Hall, E. Leigh, E. Leyland, E. Rigby.

Newcastle-on-Tyne Union Hospital.—M. Hall.

Fulham Midwifery School.—A. C. Hubbard, F. M. Palmer, M. A. Scovell.

East End Mothers' Home.—J. M. Lundy.

Birkenhead Maternity Hospital.—M. Metcalfe.

Liverpool Maternity Hospital.—C. P. Morgan.

Belfast Union Maternity Hospital.—M. E. Robinson.

Jewish Maternity District Nursing Home.—S. A. Virgo.

───────

PENAL CASES.

A Special Meeting of the Central Midwives Board was held at 1, Queen Anne's Gate Buildings, Westminster, on Thursday, November 21st, for the hearing of the charges alleged against six certified midwives, with the following results :—

Struck off the Roll and Certificate Cancelled.—Midwives Mary Austin (No. 2207), Mary Corbishley (No. 1622), Frances Davies (No. 18829), Charlotte Etherington (No. 20154), Rose Hannah Keaveney (No. 1557) ; also Elizabeth Conley (No. 2050) and Charlotte Major (No. 41223), whose cases had been adjourned for judgment.

Sentence Postponed.—In the case of Lucy Smith (No. 30861) C.M.B. Examination, the Board found the charges, with one exception, proved, but postponed sentence, and asked for a report from the Local Supervising Authority in three and six-months' time. If they found she was contumacious, she would be removed from the Roll. If not, nothing further would be done.

In this case it transpired that the Register of Cases kept by the midwife had been signed by eleven people in two years, and that these were members of the Committee of the Kenilworth Maternity Nursing Association. The Chairman said the Board disapproved, they must not sign its official Register. The books should be signed by the inspector. The Nursing Committee had no business to sign them. They must leave the Board's books alone.

Harriet Eliza Garnett (No. 34531) was restored to the Roll.

───────

PENAL BOARD.

The next Penal Board is fixed for Thursday, December 19th, at 10.30 a.m., the same day as the Monthly Meeting.

THE BRITISH JOURNAL OF NURSING
WITH WHICH IS INCORPORATED
THE NURSING RECORD
EDITED BY MRS BEDFORD FENWICK

No. 1,602.　　　SATURDAY, DECEMBER 14, 1918.　　　Vol. LXI.

EDITORIAL.

THE QUEEN'S MESSAGE TO THE WOMEN OF THE EMPIRE.

The Queen has addressed the following message to the women of the Empire :

"Buckingham Palace.

"A few months ago, at the height of our anxiety and strain, I sent a message in the name of the women of our lands to our men fighting for us across the seas. Now, in an hour of thankfulness and hope, I should like to give a message to the women of the Empire. During the war they have been given the high privilege of service, they have risen to the great opportunity, and have proved their courage, steadfastness and ability.

"I have been allowed to watch and appreciate their work in many parts of the country, and my heart is full of admiration and gratitude for what I have seen. I earnestly trust that, though the thrill and glamour of war are over, the spirit of self-sacrifice and helpfulness which it has kindled will not wane in the coming days. A new era is dawning upon the world, bringing with it many difficulties, fresh responsibilities, and serious problems to be faced.

"Parliament has secured for the whole country greater opportunities of more thorough and varied education, but it will depend upon the parents whether these opportunities are used to the full. We all rejoice that plans are afoot for bringing to an end the existence of such bad and crowded housing as makes home-life almost impossible.

"To-day, more than ever, the Empire needs her daughters, for in the larger world of public and industrial work women are daily taking a more important place. As we have been united in all our work, whether of head or hands, in a real sister-hood of suffering and service during the war, let us go on working together with the same unity of purpose for the resettlement and reconstruction of our country.

"Mary R."

Her Majesty's message, which will be gratefully received by every woman who has striven to do her duty during the four years of war, reminds us of the fresh responsibilities which we shall have to face.

For the great gift of citizenship, which is the Christmas gift to the women of the Nation this year, places upon them, for the first time, the deep responsibility of helping to fashion the destinies of the Empire at a time when the direction of its policy is a matter of more vital importance than ever before in the national history.

As the Prime Minister reminded us at the great meeting at the Queen's Hall, on Monday, it is the duty of every woman who possesses a vote to record it at the polling booths on December 14th. Especially he reminded his audience of the great social programme of the Government which commanded general acceptance. If women rose to their responsibilities the whole of their sex would be lifted to a higher level of well being, and they would be able to exercise a sacred trust for the advancement of the race.

CHRISTMAS GREETINGS.

The Christmas greetings of the Nursing Profession go forth with this issue to the Men of the Navy, Army and Air Service—the men who have saved the Empire and in conjunction with our Allies have delivered the world from militarism. To the Prisoners of War returned to this country our heartfelt thanks go out. May they spend the happiest Christmas they have ever known.

And to every Nurse striving to maintain the high ideals of her profession we heartily wish Christmas joy.

OUR PRIZE COMPETITION.

DESCRIBE YOUR METHOD OF DISINFECTING AFTER AN INFECTIOUS CASE IN A PRIVATE HOUSE—(a) THE PATIENT'S ROOM; (b) YOURSELF.

We have pleasure in awarding the prize this week to Miss Isolen M. Moore, Registered Nurses' Society, 431, Oxford Street, London, W. 1.

PRIZE PAPER.

(a) To disinfect a room after an infectious case the following method may be adopted.

After the patient has vacated the room all cheap books, toys, and valueless clothing should be burnt in the bedroom grate. Bedding, blankets, and eiderdowns should be rolled up in a dust sheet and sent to be stoved. If there is no stoving room in the district, then they must be spread out over the bed and chairs in the bedroom while it is being fumigated. All drawers or wardrobes containing clothing should be opened.

Washable articles, such as sheets, towels, or cotton garments can be soaked in lysol 1 per cent., and afterwards boiled for ten minutes before being sent to the laundry.

Crockery should be washed and put into lysol 2 per cent.; eating and drinking utensils kept separate from toilet crockery, and sterilised by boiling.

The carpet, if not previously removed, should be rolled up loosely and left in the room. Window curtains, ornaments, and all superfluous furniture ought to have been removed before the occupation of the room, but if they have not been taken out, then they must be left until after fumigation.

The fire is extinguished, and the fireplace and windows sealed over.

The cleanest and one of the best disinfectants is formalin, and this can be procured in a very convenient form in a McDougall's vaplamp. This should be lighted and placed on a tin in the middle of the room, the door hermetically sealed, and the room left so for twenty-four hours.

After that it should be thoroughly aired by opening doors and windows.

Where it is impossible to have the bedding, &c., stoved, it is always wise to have mattresses and pillows recovered.

The carpet, after being put out into the sun for some hours, should be sent to be cleaned.

The bedroom can now be spring cleaned, and, if possible, re-papered.

(b) To render myself free from infection and to prevent the infecting of others I should take a bath containing sufficient permanganate of potash to make it a pale pink, and wash my hair in hot soapy water to which a little lysol was added.

For the hands the best and most efficient disinfectant is scrubbing with soap and water, and afterwards steeping in carbolic 1-40.

The nails should always be kept cut short when nursing infectious cases.

For the mouth and throat frequent gargling is very necessary, and for this Listerine—an excellent disinfectant—and Formamint tablets slowly dissolved in the mouth are most useful preventives.

All clothing worn in the patient's room must be laundered before being worn again. If a dressing-gown or soft slippers were worn in the patient's room, these should be stoved.

Before going to another case the nurse must go into quarantine for the prescribed time.

HONOURABLE MENTION.

The following competitors receive honourable mention :—Miss E. Tipton, Miss James, Miss F. Barnes, Miss B. O'Connor.

QUESTION FOR NEXT WEEK.

Describe the nursing care of a case of double pneumonia.

"DR. WISE ON INFLUENZA."

Under the auspices of Sir Auckland Geddes, President of the Local Government Board, a kinematograph film has, says the *Lancet*, been prepared by Mr. Jos. Best, B.Sc., on influenza. The film, which takes about 15 minutes to show, is entitled "Dr. Wise on Influenza." The doctor on the screen lectures to the audience on the precautions to be adopted by a person suffering from influenza, in the patient's own interest, as well as the interest of those he comes in contact with. The exhortations of the doctor are emphasised by the kinematograph pictures in a popular vein, designed with the intention of leaving a marked impression on the audience. The film is prefaced by an appeal from Sir Auckland Geddes to the public to assist the health officials by adopting the precautions indicated. The Board have a certain number of copies of the film, which they are prepared to lend to medical officers of health for exhibition purposes. Application for the loan of a film should be addressed to the Medical Officer of the Board.

FRENCH FLAG NURSING CORPS.

Wedding Bells.

Sister Helen Canning, of the French Flag Nursing Corps, who has been a member of the Corps for three years, and did much good service at Caen, has recently resigned upon her marriage to Mr. G. Taylor. Mr. and Mrs. Taylor live in London, and we unite with many of her colleagues in wishing both a very happy future.

Thanked God.

The Sisters with Ambulance 12/2, who so coolly escaped by the back door as the Huns rushed in at the front, during those terrible days of the retreat, are again passing through exciting times.

FOLLOWING THE FRENCH FLAG.
SISTERS' QUARTERS IN THE BACKGROUND.

The Armistice was announced amidst intense excitement and joyous acclaim—" Vive la France "—" Vive l'Angleterre," and then all the Sisters went to *l'Eglise* and thanked God for glorious victory. " It is exactly four years since we all left Scotland together," writes a member of this ambulance, " and little did we think that we should have to wait so long for victory, but we knew it would come at last." And so it has.

En Avant.

Ambulance 16/21 thanks its stars that it is always " *en avant*." " We hope soon to cross into Germany," writes a Sister. " Isn't it wonderful ; just like a dream ? We have had some civilian prisoners in our hospital, their condition is truly pitiful. Covered with vermin, just skin and bone. Their joy at being with us and having decent food to eat was enough to reduce one to tears. How they must have suffered,!"

Another Sister writes :—" We are on the way to ' Bochie,' as the Poilus call it. Our army corps has been in the thick of everything, and all the most interesting events of the last few weeks have occurred on our bit of the front ; we are close to where the ' pourparlers ' came across, and it makes us very proud to be with this corps. For the first time for many months we are in a village undamaged by ' German Kultur,' and also for the first time amongst French civilians in a town which the Germans have had under their vile rule for four years. The stories of their captivity are terrible. One wonders how ever they survived such hardships. Of course, the Germans had mined the roads and railway all round here, and the explosions are tremendous at times. The story goes it was the intention to blow up the whole town, but two Alsatian soldiers cut the wires and so saved the town and some 25,000 people — extraordinary how devilish these Boches are even when whining for peace. More of their atrocities when we meet. Our work now consists of looking after sick soldiers (those needing surgical care) and also surgical women. The civilians under the Huns have been horribly neglected ; they just cried with joy when they came to us. One poor lad had suffered for two years. The Boches even left their own dead unburied in the hospital we are now in ; the corpses were found by civilians—twenty-five of them ! We can hardly believe these things. These poor people have had no meat for two years, other food almost uneatable, and had it not been for the American relief they would have starved. What work there is facing the Allies, especially for France ; not only rebuilding the towns but relief for the people. The devastation is complete. You can buy nothing ; all the shops have been depleted of everything, also private houses. Everything was stolen and taken to Germany—mattresses, furniture, blankets, clothing ; even shoes were commandeered for the ' Sisters.' One wonders what sort of nurses they could be who could wear shoes snatched from these poor people. We believe we are going to C——; it will be a great pleasure to me to see Germany under opposite circumstances to 1914! Altogether, these last six months have been a wonderful time for us. I only wish I could write it all down."

"There was a great ceremony to-day," says another Sister. "Two of our doctors were decorated with the Croix de Guerre, and the General made some charming speeches. We were told we were to follow the corps wherever it went; and, as it is forming part of the ' troops of occupation,' we expect ere long to be camping on the borders of the R——. We are all, of course, very anxious to enter Germany."

"CHEZ EUX."

" Our dear, brave Poilus are absolutely overwhelmed with joy at the prospect of soon going ' Chez eux ' once more. I shall never forget my experience of them, their gratitude, their manliness, their splendid cheerfulness, courage and fine moral. . . . Thanking you for all the good you have established for us at the Front, and for having so well looked after our welfare through thick and thin all these past eventful four years."

RECOGNITION BY FRENCH GOVERNMENT.

Certain information is required by the French War Office, in reference to the recognition of the services of the Members of the French Flag Nursing Corps who have served for two years and upwards under its authority. Mrs. Fenwick will be obliged if the present address of Miss Beatrice Ackroyd, Cert. Brownlow Hill Infirmary, Liverpool, and of Miss Florence Morris (Canadian Unit), Cert. General Hospital, Vancouver, can be communicated to her at 431, Oxford Street, London, W., without delay.

OUR ROLL OF HONOUR.

Staff Nurse Bessie Coltman, who died recently at Lenzie, was buried with military honours at Alloa. Miss Coltman transferred from a civilian to a military hospital at the outbreak of war, and had seen service abroad, both in East and Central Africa and at Malta. For devotion to duty she was awarded the M.B.E. a few months ago.

REPLY TO BIRTHDAY MESSAGE.

Queen Alexandra, replying to a birthday message from " all ranks of the British Armies in France," sent by Sir Douglas Haig, said :—

" With a deeply grateful heart I thank you and all our splendid and brave Army in France for kind wishes on my old birthday. Accept all my heartfelt congratulations for your splendid and glorious achievements and peace."

TRUE TALE WITH A MORAL. 1930.

Another little grand-daughter : " What did you do in the Great War, grannie ?"

Grannie (triumphantly) : " I married twice."

NURSING AND THE WAR.

Miss Winifred Wood has been appointed Matron of the Royal Air Force Convalescent Hospital at Swanage, a beautiful, breezy watering-place on the south coast, where the gulls which frequent the cliffs and sweep over the bay, will afford many a lesson in the art of flying. Miss Wood, until recently, has been Head Sister at the Royal Air Force Hospital in London.

All the service patients capable of moving or of being moved, and practically the entire staff of Princess Patricia Military Hospital, Bray, assembled at the railway station to bid *au revoir* to Sister McIlroy, who had relinquished her appointment after two years' service at the Institution. The affection in which Sister McIlroy was held was given tangible expression in an attaché case and gold brooch from the staff, and gold signet ring and gold bracelet from the patients.

Miss Torrance, recently Chief Nurse of the American Red Cross in Great Britain, has left London to join the Mission to the Balkan States, in which from previous experience she is deeply interested. American Mission Nurses undoubtedly led the van in such work before the war—especially in China and in the Far East—and have now immense scope for pouring oil on the troubled waters after months of war. We hope our own trained nurses, especially those who have been attached to Pioneer Corps, whose experience is of great value, will be encouraged to go far afield and help bind up the world's wounds by carrying the teaching of the prevention of disease, and skilled nursing, into many insanitary and malodorous places.

We are glad that attention is being drawn in the Press to the arrangement that Australian nurses on active service may be granted leave without pay, prior to their leaving for Australia. It is pointed out that a soldier's pay is not stopped when he gets leave, and neither should that of the nurses be. *The British Australian* says:— "Their work is as laborious as that of any soldier— much more so than that of an officer— and very often they have shared the same dangers. Throughout the war the conduct and devotion of the military nursing staff have called for nothing but admiration. This has been accorded freely enough, but praise is cheap, and, if unaccompanied by justice, paltry."

"POT-POURRI FROM AN EDITH CAVELL GARDEN."

Anyone wishing to help an Edith Cavell Home of Rest for Nurses can do so by purchasing potpourri made from an old recipe (1804). All the proceeds are given to the Home. Apply to Hon Mrs. Corbet, Raven House Edith Cavell Home, Adderley, Market Drayton.

THE COMMANDANT.

By the Surgeon.

She was a lady of boundless energy and a newly acquired title, and she had a husband who, having supplied the money, devoted most of his time to laborious efforts to efface himself in the triumphal march towards the distant peerage, the pace of which was being so skilfully forced by his more capable spouse.

When war broke out she decided to run a hospital, and gave up one of her five " country seats " for the purpose. As she said, " All of my houses have marble floors, so they can easily be disinfected afterwards."

I was the surgeon—at least, I suppose I was —but before the craze for being " interested in the war " had passed off, and the hospital had therefore been closed, I came to the conclusion that I was rapidly qualifying myself mainly as an expert in the dark and devious ways of diplomacy.

Some of the incidents in the career of the hospital are sufficiently amusing to be recorded, but when the final closing down took place I felt a little out of breath, and rather as if I had been acting as referee in a North Country cup tie. I emerged much battered as to reputation, and with a plentiful increase of grey hairs.

The equipment of the place was gorgeous— in many senses. When the problem came up for solution, the third footman (it was before the days of conscription) was sent to bring up three weighty surgical catalogues which had just arrived, and the process of selection took place. This was simple, because the Commandant not only selected all the most expensive items in each section, but also ordered many of them in duplicate, or even in half-dozens, while I stood by and gasped. She even went up to Town to choose the instruments herself, and I shall never forget the arrival of what was apparently the entire contents of about three instrument makers' shops—a collection of useless ironmongery dating from the ark to the present time. Much to her regret, there was no time to have her crest engraved on the handles of the scalpels.

Then the uniforms! We had a nucleus of very capable sisters and qualified nurses, who saved the patients from destruction, and the surgeon from an untimely grave, and they flatly refused to be camouflaged in any way; but there was a long procession of " helpers " —Heaven save the mark !—each of whom did " duty " for about three hours a day—when there were no social functions to be attended

outside. As the Commandant wanted as large a " staff " as possible, and none of her numerous friends had any objection to wearing, or being photographed in, the extremely decorative uniform which she had designed for them, recruiting was not attended with any obvious difficulties.

Oh, those uniforms ! They were carried out in a groundwork of some white, silky-looking stuff, with a bordering of various colours, each of which was repeated in the shoes and stockings. The principle of free ventilation was emphasized in the " blouse " part, and the skirts were exiguous. Red crosses were stuck on every available square foot of space, and the caps reminded one of a Breton " Pardon." The situation was aptly summed up by a dear old " brass hat " who inspected us one day. As I was conducting him round the wards, a sort of procession gradually formed of all the available " helpers " in the building. The great man grew more and more perplexed and fidgety, until at last he broke cover with : " If you will kindly shift that beauty chorus a little further off, we shall be able to discuss the treatment of the patients." After his tour of inspection he had to be revived with what the text-books call a " diffusible stimulant " before he could go on to the next hospital on his list.

By a process of mixing up what was, with what was not, I managed to keep the peace in a sort of triangular duel between the Commandant, the sisters, and the helpers, and to get a fair amount of work done in the intervals between entertainments for the patients and the constantly recurrent photographings of the staff, but I never knew what was coming next, or when I would be myself crushed between the upper and nether millstones of surgery and diplomacy.

The first surprise came when I arrived in the theatre just in time to begin on a " list," and found the Commandant sitting there in a uniform (devised for the purpose) resembling that worn by the fashionable contralto when she sings " The Rosary " in costume at a music-hall. She had come as a spectator of the morning's procedure ! The sister managed to whisper as she was tying on my mask that it *wasn't* her fault and what *was* she to do, but she was obviously much perturbed. I am afraid that my solution of the problem was somewhat brutal. I had intended to begin with a nerve suturing, but started instead with the amputation of an especially septic leg, which resulted in hasty retreat and sounds of internal commotion in the passage outside !

For a short time at the beginning some of the numerous male staff of the house helped in the work, and I shall never forget the wooden face of (I think) the third footman, who had been delegated to wheel the dressing trolley, as he said to me : " Will you take cyanide gauze or plain, Sir? " He joined up, incidentally, almost immediately afterwards, and was killed, poor fellow, in an act of great gallantry later on.

I shall never forget one incident. It happened when we were expecting a fresh convoy, and all the patients were up and about except an abdominal section case, who thus had the wards to himself in the daytime. " Her ladyship " thought she would entertain him with a little music, so a procession was formed, consisting of herself, " vested " in uniform (number six or thereabouts), the second footman carrying the gramophone, and the butler bringing up the rear with some records. The patient was a little rat-faced man hailing originally from the slums of a northern town, and he listened stolidly and without moving a muscle to " Abide with Me," enlivened by the " Bing Boys." At the conclusion the Commandant asked him how he liked the music, but the only reply was : " We've got a bigger one than that in our 'ouse." She subsequently told me that she thought he was not quite a nice man !

I have poked gentle fun at this good lady, and I suffered daily attacks of what Army forms call " D.A.H." in efforts to avoid putting a patient into a new and completely unsuitable splint which she had seen in an instrument maker's catalogue, and had promptly bought because it was so expensive, but when the place closed down, and the last photograph had been taken (and sent to the *Sketchler*), and the last patient had gone off, blushing from the effusive compliments of the " helpers," I found I had a real liking for her after all. Mainly, there was nothing she would not do for the patients. She got their wives and families up, even from the regions of the Isles of Skye, clothed and fed them, and put them up in the town, and to this day has kept in constant touch with every man who had passed through the hospital and got his discharge. In her view, nothing was too good for any man who had fought, and the ostentatious ironmongery was not purely swagger. All honour to her, anyhow, for she had a big heart underneath her parti-coloured uniforms. But whatever nerve centres are involved in the process known as " keeping a straight face " have, in my case, almost succumbed to over-work, and I still feel as if I had been acting in the " Pantomime Rehearsal."

RHYMES OF THE RED TRIANGLE.

Mr. John Lane, of the Bodley Head, Vigo Street, W., and of the John Lane Company, New York, has published for our enjoyment a series of " Rhymes of the Red Triangle," the verses being from the talented pen of Hampden Gordon and the pictures by Joyce Dennys, whose inimitable portrayal of the V.A.D. in " Our Hospital A.B.C.," and of " Our Girls in War Time," has earned for her a distinguished place amongst war-time artists.

The opening verse propounds the following :—

A RIDDLE.

" What is it that can spread its limbs to reach
    From Euston Square to fabulous Baghdad :
That has a thousand arms, and lends with each
    A helping hand to cheer the fighting lad :
That follows fast where Freedom's forces go,
    Through dust-storms of the desert, Afric rains,
The mud of Flanders, Macedonian snow,
    The palpitating heat of Indian plains :
Whose growth keeps pace with ev'ry changing need
    And flourishes the most where battle rages ?

    *   *   *   *   *

The answer, if you'll stop, and look, and read,
    Lies (somewhat camouflaged) within these pages."

The picture which we here reproduce (reduced) is a sample of the quality of those contained in the " Rhymes of the Red Triangle " (the sign of the Young Men's Christian Association Huts). It illustrates the following rhyme, and appears on page 367 :—

UNSKILLED LABOUR.

" The Duchess at the Maytair Hut
    Made cocoa for a ' Wounded Boy.'
She said : ' I can't come often, but
    I love to see their smile of joy.'
As Tommy's smile of joy grew louder,
    She grasped the tin was marked
        ' Knife Powder.' "

Our space only permits us to quote one other verse.

MOVIES.

" You'll meet all the fighters to-night, boys,
    At the Eagle American Hut,
The sailor man back from the Bight, boys,
    The Londoner lately at Kut.
From Boston, from Auckland, from Devon,
    From Melbourne, the Rockies, the Rand,
They're meeting for ' Movies ' at seven
    Along down the Strand."

Other subjects dealt with by pen and brush are Concerts, Night Patrol, Breakages (Penelope, you'll drop them ! Yes, you will !), Letters Home, and many more besides. The cost of the book is 4s. 6d., and it should be secured without delay, as it will make a delightful Christmas gift. It will no doubt be quickly out of print.

OUR CHRISTIAN DUTY AND NATIONAL OBLIGATION.

The return of our prisoners from torture camps and starvation in Germany is now well in hand, and thousands of these men, who have suffered intolerable misery and insult (all for us) are

UNSKILLED LABOUR.

returning home. The Queens and Princesses have done themselves honour in meeting prisoners on their arrival in London, and letting them know how every woman's heart has grieved over their sorrows. Now is the time to try and make it up to them by every means in our power ; and if every grateful woman does her bit, organized help should quickly and materially restore these martyrs to happiness, and, let us hope, to health.

We fear there is very little doubt that a certain number of our poor suffering men wounded in the war have become " drug addicts," and one would urge nurses to keep a sharp eye on any patient who may be suspected of the drug habit, and help them by every means in their power to overcome it. Gallant men who have fought and suffered for us have been given morphine to alleviate their intolerable sufferings. Many do not realise its insidious and demoralising influence. It is up to our nurses to help those addicted to it to overcome the craving.

Is it too much to hope that the dear animals who have suffered so terribly for want of food during the war, may, at least, have a real feast on Christmas Day. The saddest sight in our streets—next to that of our mutilated men—is the *ribs* of the horses. This evidence of their privations and weakness makes one's heart sick.

" Christie " is going to sell the thirty graded pearl necklaces by auction, on December 19th, in support of the Red Cross, and they will be on view from the 16th inst. No doubt they will bring a handsome sum—as no self-respecting society woman can afford to be minus pearls. We recently saw a wealthy peeress wearing a sham pearl necklace in the morning ! We hope she will now treat herself to the real thing.

THE NURSE.

Dear, tender-hearted woman, full of rare
Rich qualities ; a spendthrift in your care
    Of those who greatly need,
Searing your heart by contact with their pain,
Be comforted, for never yet in vain
    Was done a kindly deed.

SHOULD NURSES STRIKE?

In reply to the question, Do you consider any conditions justify a strike of nurses? we reply " No." But offer the following expression of opinion for what it is worth.

This is supposed—we only say supposed—to be a free country, and if every worker were loyal to her cloth and to her *soul* there would be no need for strikes. People usually find themselves in unendurable positions because they have acquiesced in wrong-doing and have failed in moral courage. Nurses in hospitals are often extraordinarily cowardly. Why? Because their sense of self-interest, as apart from a sense of justice, is so strong. We can imagine no conditions which can excuse a woman for submitting to injustice and indignity—at the worst in protesting she may s ffer personally, then take the risk.

Our experience of life leads us to the conclusion that human beings are reasonable animals, however ignorant and wanting in sensibility, and that even the most selfish are greatly influenced by right if a fellow human declines to endure a wrong. In nine cases out of ten in which nurses complain to us of unjust methods of control, and bad conditions of institutional life, they are themselves to blame. Grumble—yes, but how many will go straight to the Matron, or the Committee (if the Matron herself is a weak woman), and just quietly place the case before them?

That is what we did in every hospital in which we ever worked in the good (or bad) old days, and *never once did we fail to have the wrong rectified.* Nottingham, Manchester, the London, Barts—we could a tale unfold. Some day when we have time we will recall a few interesting incidents in this connection. And in no instance were we penalised. A Pro. at the Children's, Nottingham, 1st April, 1878. (Mother, who hated careers for girls, pronounced it a very suitable date to enter for training.) Matron, Barts, 1st April, 1881. Three years' combat, but no lack of promotion. Then six years' strenuous reform work, yet perfect concord and happiness all the time. No necessity for a strike on any issue, but no wrong condoned, and every issue satisfactorily attained. Often on duty sixteen hours out of twenty-four—that, of course, would be unpardonable in these enlightened times. Even so long ago as 1879 we remember being taken to task by an old Sister at the " London " for " never sitting down, and exposing the older Sisters, who looked to remove their cap-tails for a nap in the afternoon, to odious comparison."

NURSING ECHOES.

We have received from the General Infirmary, Leeds, a most interesting and important Report of a Sub-Committee appointed on July 5th last to examine the conditions under which the nursing of the Infirmary is carried on, to formulate any improvements which they deem necessary, to estimate the extra cost involved in such improvements, and to report to the Board. The inquiry was undertaken in consequence of a report from the Lady Superintendent of Nurses that the Infirmary was understaffed with Nurses, and that the individual Nurses were underpaid.

The special importance of the Report is that it intimates that the Committee further requested the Sisters and Nurses to formulate any recommendations which they might be able to make for the improvement of their condition, and to appoint four Sisters and eight Nurses to meet the Committee and discuss their recommendations. Individual Matrons have done wonders with the material at their disposal, but, knowing the need for economy, it is not surprising that they hesitate to recommend a large increase in the way of expenditure in regard to salaries. In this connection it is quite the right thing that, as the preliminary to considering the revision of salaries, the views of those chiefly concerned should receive consideration.

The shortage of private nurses has resulted in the death of many civilians, especially the stricken children, during the pneumonia epidemic, and we hear of no offer of help from V.A.D.'s or other " patriotic " laywomen for these sufferers, whilst we learn that the officers' hospitals in London have a very full complement of trained and untrained nurses.

There is no doubt that in this country drastic reforms as to salaries and hours of work will have to be made at an early date. And if parents are unable to pay for their daughters' nursing education, as they pay for medical education, then the State must step in and subsidize our nursing schools. At present many are schools only in name. Thorough education is costly, and the present lack of standards can no longer pertain. Women of culture and education paid for their training in the 'seventies and 'eighties. What is to hinder them from doing so now? But the *quid pro quo* must be worth their while.

For the future the " cottage helps " attached to the Ipswich Nurses' Home, sent out to those who cannot afford a private nurse, are to be known as " home nurses." Is this fair, either to the poorer patients or the trained members of the staff? Not in our opinion. Surely it is high time lay Committees running Nursing Associations realised that it is the severity of the illness and not the fatness of the purse which should decide the standard of nursing required. Let us hope the new Ministry of Health will go carefully into nursing conditions so far as the poor are concerned, and evolve a co-operative scheme for providing a high standard of nursing for all classes. And do not let us forget there is or ought not to be any " class " distinction in sickness.

In lamenting the death of Queen's Nurse Sowerbutts, who for five and a half years had laboured with so much devotion for the sick at Haywards Heath, the chairman, Mrs. Holgate, said the Association will have the greatest difficulty in filling her place. Mrs. Holgate states that rich and poor alike shared the benefit of her willing service, and she pleads for a Nurses' Home, whence nurses of various qualifications could deal with the needs of the surrounding neighbourhood. We hope this does not mean that there is to be one standard of nursing for the poor—and another for the rich ! Indeed, we strongly disapprove of Queen's Nurses being used by persons who can well afford to pay for their service, just because they give a trifling subscription to the charity. This is often done without the well-to-do paying anything like the cost of skilled service. But in any scheme for raising the health of the community generally, co-operative nursing for the middle classes will have to find its place.

Arrangements are being made at Lincoln to form a district nursing association, to be operated from the Bromhead Institute, for the benefit of Lincoln and Boultham.

The monthly meeting of the Committee of the Queen Victoria's Jubilee Institute for Nurses, Rutland Square, Dublin, showed the extraordinary amount of work done by the nurses in visiting the sick poor in their own homes during this awful epidemic of influenza. In the month of October six nurses visited 317 cases, and paid 3,444 visits—269 of these cases were influenza and pneumonia. Two of the nurses contracted the epidemic, leaving the burden still heavier on the remainder of the staff. The only outside help was from two

V.A.D.'s, who came to their assistance. St. Lawrence's Home should have a staff of twelve nurses at least, but want of funds has obliged the Committee to reduce the number to six. If only the public would give more help to the Committee, the work could be extended indefinitely to the great advantage of the poor of the city.

Let us hope when we have a Ministry of Health all such work will be co-ordinated and subsidised by the State.

The Scottish Nurses' Club will be formally launched on Saturday, December 14th, when the opening ceremony will be performed by the Right · Honourable the Lord Provost of Glasgow, at three o'clock. The President and Trustees of the Club have issued invitations for this function, and we much regret that our engagements do not permit of our accepting that with which we have been honoured.

Miss H. Hawkins' letter in a recent issue, headed the " Deep Sighing of the Poor," in which she referred to the scandal that large numbers of dead in the East End of London were left unburied for an unseemly length of time, has aroused much indignation, as well it may.

Miss Mary L. Breay writes in this connection :—

" Miss Hawkins' letter about the dead lying unburied in the houses of the poor of London fills one with horror and indignation. May I suggest that if the Government and local bodies are so callous as to neglect this imperative duty of burying the dead, that a mortuary chapel should be built in every parish, and that the names of those who have laid down their lives for their country should be recorded in plain letters on the walls. Thus the chapel would be a memorial of the war and serve the dead and the living at the same time. And let the chapel be the most beautiful that can be built. Whoever has seen the lovely little chapel at Compton, near Guildford, designed by the late Mr. G. F. Watts, R.A., will know how beautiful it might be. The chapel outside is in the form of a cross inside a circle ; the latter represents eternity. I believe all the villagers made a stone and laid it in this building. Inside, the chapel is perfectly round and opposite the entrance door is the holy table with the symbol of our faith upon it. The walls are one mass of glowing colour, which entirely dissipates all thought of gloom and dreariness connected with death. Round the walls in artistic colouring are the words, " The souls of the righteous are in the hands of God." The centre of the chapel is empty, but there are benches of artistic design placed against the walls. The whole effect is beautiful and nothing can give one a better idea of the triumph of " life over death "—or rather the " continuity of life."

Royal British Nurses' Association.

(Incorporated by   Royal Charter.)

THIS SUPPLEMENT BEING THE OFFICIAL ORGAN OF THE CORPORATION.

OUR ROYAL CHARTER.

Numbers of the Members have requested, from time to time, that a photograph of Her Royal Highness the Princess Christian, President of the Royal British Nurses' Association, should be inserted in their official organ. We therefore asked for and obtained the gracious permission of Her Royal Highness to have it put into the Christmas issue. The Princess has ever had the interests of the nurses very close to her heart, and there are many movements connected with their profession which owe their success in large measure to the influence and support of Her Royal Highness. The Members of the Royal British Nurses' Association have, time and again, expressed with no uncertain voice their feelings of loyalty and devotion to their President for all her kindness to their Association, and for ever-ready sympathy and help in connection with any work which it finds good to undertake. But in the pages of Nursing History, both of the present time and time to come, her name will always be prominently associated with the grant of a Royal Charter to the nurses. For, in beautiful, old-time phraseology, the Preamble of the Charter commences, " VICTORIA, by the Grace of God of the United Kingdom of Great Britain and Ireland, Queen, Defender of the Faith, TO ALL TO WHOM THESE PRESENTS COME GREETING : WHEREAS, it has been repre-

HER ROYAL HIGHNESS PRINCESS CHRISTIAN PRINCESS OF GREAT BRITAIN AND IRELAND. PRESIDENT OF THE ROYAL BRITISH NURSES' ASSOCIATION.

sented to us by Our Most Dearly Beloved Daughter, Helena, Princess Christian," and there follow the representations made by Her Royal Highness as to why a Royal Charter should be granted to the Association, and later a list of Signatories to the Charter.

A Royal Charter is extremely difficult to acquire, particularly in modern times when the Companies' Act has come into force; almost any body can obtain incorporation under the Board of Trade, but the possession of a Royal Charter implies incorporation by the Crown. The most famous is, as most people know, the Magna Charta of King John, granted in 1215, and it was demanded in order to preserve the liberties of the English people. Ever since then Royal Charters have been associated with constitutional privileges, granted under the sign manual of a Sovereign of the Realm. The Royal Charter of the Royal British Nurses' Asociation offers to the nurses very far-reaching powers—powers which, if they would but combine and use them, would place their profession in the forefront of all women's professions and employments, and which could shelter and protect them individually. A close study of the Charter, too, shows the wisdom with which it was drafted, for, although it gives to the Corporation a status and a prestige which no other body of nurses in the Empire possesses, or is likely to possess, there is nothing in it to militate against the general good, or to favour any oppressive monopoly. It is, therefore, a great power in the hands of the nurses, and they owe to Her Royal Highness, the President of the Royal British Nurses' Association, a deeper debt than they realise that this priceless and historical document belongs to the Members of the Royal Corporation.

A CHARTER TEA.

The Executive Committee invite members of the Corporation, Members of the Societies affiliated to it and other Trained Nurses to tea at 10, Orchard Street on Tuesday, December 17th, from 3.30 to 6.30 p.m.

Instructions have been given that the Royal Charter shall be brought from the strong room at the Bank so that nurses who would like to see this document, which is of such paramount importance in the present struggle to safeguard their liberties and privileges, may have opportunity for doing so. All trained nurses will be cordially welcomed.

AMERICA AND THE NEW WORLD ORDER.

Mr. Price Bell, Editor of the *Chicago Daily News,* delivered an eloquent lecture on December 5th, under the auspices of the Corporation, at 11, Chandos Street, Cavendish Square, W. Mr. Herbert Paterson occupied the Chair and introduced the distinguished American journalist to the meeting. In commencing, Mr. Price Bell said that, as he was to speak to the members of a large and highly skilled profession, he would make no apology for devoting his remarks, not to anything pertaining to their life work, but to matters political. All who belonged to democratic countries, men and women alike, were politicians now, even the children breathed an air charged with political aspiration and political thought. Democracy had been reborn, and in its veins flowed a new and abounding life. Everyone in these days felt an enormously heightened responsibility for what goes on politically, and democracy was thoroughly out of conceit with secretive leadership and was minded more and more to project its will into the domain of political control.

The lecturer referred to the traditional devotion of America to principles of political and social liberty. She had, as a nation, always been a protagonist of freedom; all her wars had been fought for freedom; and all her threats of war had been in the interests of freedom.

American Democracy, Mr. Bell continued, was enthusiastically for a League of Nations. Cynics had called the proposed League of Nations " a Rainbow." Such persons held that our civilization is to be maintained, if at all, by *steel,* but the " rainbow " exercised a sure and universal mastery over steel. What was it which won the war against the Hun? Was it steel? Was it the big gun? Was it the aeroplane? Was it any material thing at all? It was the great and beautiful " rain-

bow " of free civilization's invincible ideal. Material weapons were wholly useless, unless behind them, supporting them, wielding them, was that most marvellous of all things—the righteously inspired human soul. " So," said Mr. Bell, " let us not dismiss the League of Nations idea because it is a dream. Personally, I thank God for the women and men of our world who dream dreams; but for them—but for the cooling springs of their prophecy and faith—we should parch and faint in a spiritual Sahara."

Mr. Bell next brought forward contentions based on the history of the great war, to support his belief in a League of Nations. He was aware that statesmen talked a great deal about the difficulties in the way of this great world political conception. He himself wished that they would talk less of those and display more confidence in one another and themselves; that they would be less fearful of the unknown; and remember the dramatic achievements which had come from marching boldly against the unknown. A League of Nations, as defined by Mr. Bell, was a league of law abiders, of respecters of sound morality, and a league of the defenders of the fruits of human progress. We talk much of national honour, but what reason and right ask is simply that we shall be honourable and do what in imperfect human nature lies to realise the supreme doctrine of humanity, " Thou shalt love thy neighbour as thyself." It was further explained that the proposed League of Nations would not bind any nations except by its treaties. In no way would such a league interfere with the domestic affairs of any single nation by, for instance, dictating as regards its fiscal or defensive policy. Neither would there be any system of subordination, but only one of co-ordination.

Speaking of Bolshevism, Mr. Bell said, " It is a horrible thing; it is civilization on the rack; it is the ghastly negation of everything for which humanity has hoped and prayed and toiled and bled. It is a mirror in which the misguided, callous, avaricious, criminal man may look upon himself. A thousand things, abhorrent to Christianity and to justice—these are the ugly and mis-shapen forebears of Bolshevism."

In Mr. Bell's opinion, British-American solidarity was the corner-stone of free civilization in the world. In closing, he advised his audience to neglect no opportunity by word or act to further such a re-union of our race as shall make it proof against any strain. More certainly than in any other way, this great object can be obtained by mutual tolerance of superficial differences, by mutual words and acts of friendship, by mutual sympathy and respect. All at their various posts of duty, in the Empire and elsewhere, could bear with them a mighty wave of influence for British-American harmony and happiness, and so for the well-being of the world.

The Chairman expressed the appreciation of those present of a brilliant lecture.

(Signed) ISABEL MACDONALD,
Secretary to the Corporation.

OUR VICTORY THANKOFFERING FOR STATE REGISTRATION.

The President of the Society for the State Registration of Trained Nurses begs to thank many friends of the cause for their generous contributions to the State Registration Campaign. The "Insignificant Minority" are well to the fore this week, and every shilling that can be spared will be welcomed in support of just legislation—and in opposition to plutocratic and charitable control of our profession. See page x.

See page x.

APPOINTMENTS.

MATRON.

Evelina Hospital for Children, Southwark, S.E. —Miss Judith E. Hancock has been appointed Matron. She received her Children's Training at the Sheffield Children's Hospital, and for the past year has been Assistant Matron at the East London Hospital for Children, Shadwell. Miss Hancock had her General Training at the Dreadnought (Seamen's) Hospital, Greenwich, and at the Samaritan Free Hospital for Women (four years' joint certificate); since then she has held the posts of Surgical Ward and Theatre Sister at Shadwell Children's Hospital and the Belgrave Hospital for Children, also of Night Sister at the Samaritan Free Hospital. Before returning to Shadwell as Assistant Matron, Miss Hancock was for more than three years a Sister in the Royal Naval Nursing Service Reserve.

London County Mental Hospital, Claybury, Woodford, Essex.—Miss Helen Lamb has been appointed Matron. She was trained at St. George's Hospital, Bombay, and has been Matron at Craig House, Morningside, Edinburgh.

Isolation Hospital, Pengam.—Miss Jessie A. Brown has been appointed Matron. She was trained at Belvidere Fever Hospital, Glasgow, and the Glasgow Royal Infirmary, and has been sister and assistant matron at Heathfield Hospital, Ayr; matron, Invalid Girls' Home, Bridge of Weir; sister at Muswell Hill Isolation Hospital, and has undertaken matron's duties and had experience of private nursing.

ASSISTANT MATRON.

Evelina Hospital for Children, Southwark, S.E. —Miss M. Irene Lindars has been appointed Assistant Matron. She was trained in Children's work for nearly four years at the Evelina Hospital; she then went to Westminster Hospital for General Training (four years' certificate), afterwards returning to the Evelina as Night Sister. From that post she was transferred to day duty as Surgical Sister; from the latter post she has now been promoted.

The King and Queen of the Belgians have been to the shooting range ground where are buried the bodies of persons shot during the German occupation. The Queen laid a wreath on the grave of Miss Cavell.

EXAMINATION OF NURSES IN SCOTLAND.

On November 12th and subsequent days the Local Government Board for Scotland held an examination for the certification of trained sick nurses and of trained fever nurses. The examination was held at Glasgow, Edinburgh, Dundee, and Aberdeen. The examiners were Professor Glaister, The University, Glasgow; Dr. Chalmers, Medical Officer of Health, Glasgow; Dr. Gordon, Aberdeen; and Dr. Ker, City Hospital, Edinburgh, who were assisted in the practical part of the examination by Miss Merchant, Matron of the Eastern District Hospital, Glasgow, and by Miss Lindsay, Matron of Belvidere Hospital, Glasgow.

The subjects of examination were Elementary Anatomy and Physiology; Hygiene and Dietetics; Medical and Surgical Nursing; Midwifery (for Poor Law and General-trained nurses); and Infectious Diseases (for Fever-trained nurses only). In all 214 candidates presented themselves for examination. Of these, 94 were examined in Anatomy and Physiology; 69 in Hygiene and Dietetics; 27 in Medical and Surgical Nursing (for Poor Law and General-trained nurses); 51 in Medical and Surgical Nursing (for fever-trained nurses); 23 in Midwifery; and 56 in Infectious Diseases.

The following candidates have now completed the examination and subject to the completion of three years' training in hospital to the satisfaction of the Local Government Board, are entitled to the certificate of efficiency granted by the Board :—

I. CERTIFICATE IN GENERAL TRAINING.

Eastern District Hospital, Glasgow.—Elizabeth M. Carson, Mary Frame, Medling MacIver, Margaret F. Pace, Marion W. Proctor, Isabella E. Somerville, Jane Wintour, Nellie Davidson.

Govan Poorhouse Hospital, Glasgow.—Jeannie Hannan, Georgina Mills, Isabella McGilp, Sophia S. Osman, Violet Sillars, Catherine B. Wilson.

Barnhill Poorhouse Hospital, Glasgow.—Mary H. McConnachie, Margaret McLellan, Mary W. Macpherson.

Paisley Poorhouse Hospital.—Eliza S. R. Stevenson, Agnes W. Taylor.

Craiglockhart Poorhouse Hospital, Edinburgh.—Nellie Aitken, Ann Iredale, Helen T. Pairman.

Aberdeen Poorhouse Hospital.—Helen Gill.

II. CERTIFICATE IN FEVER TRAINING.

Belvidere Hospital, Glasgow.—Margaret Reid.

Ruchill Hospital, Glasgow.—Annie S. Allan, Catherine H. Barlas, Agnes W. C. Brand, Janet M. Brown, Helen S. Cruickshank, Mary Flatley, Ella M. Forsyth, Edith Heughan, Caroline K. McBain, Euphemia W. F. Simpson, Margaret E. K. Smith.

County Hospital, Motherwell—Mary K. Lindsay, Elsie B. McEwan, Maud S. Wright.

Gateside Hospital, Greenock.—Margaret H. Gordon, Mary Howatson, Jeanie A. Matthews, Ella McGill, Margarita A. T. Shewan, Williamina S. Wilson.

Blawarthill Hospital, Yoker.—Mary A. Bowie, Rhoda M. Keillar, Jean A. McClure.

Duntocher Joint Hospital.—Christina J. M. Lindsay.

Combination Hospital, Johnstone.—Lily McQuillan.

Infectious Diseases Hospital, Paisley.—Isabella J. Gemmell.

Fever Hospital, Dunfermline.—Catherine V. Christie.

City Hospital, Edinburgh.—Gertrude Browne, Elizabeth Christie, Effie D. Clark, Jessie B. Cowie, Innes H. Craigen, Nancy M. Grieve, Isabella S. Henderson, Jean S. Jack, Marjory I. Myles, Margaret W. W. McArthur, Flora McLeod, Isabella S. Rennie, Joan F. H. Rigg, Margaret S. Scott.

King's Cross Hospital, Dundee.—Helen M. Garden.

City Hospital, Aberdeen.—Annie C. Cameron, Beatrice R. Davidson, Dorcas Fraser, Charlotte J. Grant, Annie S. Leith, Helen Mearns, Jessie A. Murdoch, Marion A. McAlpine, Georgina B. Riddell, Nellie L. Weir.

The Papers set at the examination were eminently practical and we congratulate those who passed on gaining their certificates.

PRIZES FOR NURSES.

The nurses' annual prize-giving was held at the Bristol General Hospital, where there was a large gathering of nurses and representatives of the various committees of the institution. Mr. G. A. Wills presided, and several of the speakers referred to the valuable work of the Matron, Miss Densham, and Dr. Albert Sim ; and thanks were conveyed to the nursing staff.

The prizes were awarded as follows :—Gold medal, Nurse Ethel Clark ; silver medal, Nurse Eleanor Keene. Certificates of efficiency : Nurse Dorothy Morris, Nurse Beatrice Godfrey, Nurse Ethel Panes. The Lottie Culverwell Memorial Prize, given by Mrs. Samuel Hosegood to the best nurse of her year : Nurse Ethel Clark. First prize on an examination on medical nursing : Nurse Clarie Wood ; second prize, Nurse Ethel Panes. First prize, surgical nursing, Nurse Ethel Panes ; second prize, Nurse Irene North. First prize, physiology, Nurse Eleanor Keene ; second prizes, Nurse Winifred Long and Nurse Dorothy Crocker. First prize, anatomy, Nurse Kate Wells ; second prize, Nurse Nellie Moody. First prize, practical nursing, Nurse Jessie Franklin ; second prize, Nurse Eva Heard.

QUEEN VICTORIA'S JUBILEE INSTITUTE FOR NURSES.

A meeting of the Council of Queen Victoria's Jubilee Institute for Nurses was held at 58, Victoria Street, S.W. 1, last Wednesday Captain Sir Harold Boulton, Bt., C.V.O., C.B.E., being in the chair.

The estimates for the expenditure during the coming year received very careful consideration, as it was realised that the expansion and many developments in connection with health work would involve an increased expenditure, but the Council felt that any retrenchment would be disastrous to the work which the Institute is carrying on for the benefit of the nation.

Most satisfactory progress was reported, more especially when the very great shortage of nurses, caused by the absence of some 600 of the Queen's nurses on war service, is taken into consideration. New districts are being formed in readiness for the hoped-for release of these nurses in the near future.

Special attention was called to the self-sacrificing and devoted work of the Inspectors, Superintendents and nurses during the prevalence of the influenza epidemic, and a resolution was passed expressing the Council's high appreciation for what they had done. The Council heard with the deepest regret of the death of nine of the Queen's nurses as the result of contracting the disease in the discharge of their duties

TRANSFERS AND APPOINTMENTS.

Miss Hannah F. Hobbs is appointed to Kingswood as Superintendent ; Miss Ida L. Benson to Watford as General Training Sister ; Miss Annie M. Stringer to Kilburn.

AN UNPARDONABLE ATTACK.

Sir Henry Burdett, the anti-registration protagonist for a quarter-of-a-century, and now the ardent supporter of the Employers' Registration Bill, drafted by the College of Nursing, Ltd., in opposition to the organized Nurses' Bill, lost his temper badly in his paper, *The Hospital*, last week ; and the scurrilous attack made upon Miss Isabel Macdonald, the very popular and greatly respected Secretary of the Royal British Nurses' Association is going too far, even for the employers' Press. Sir Henry and his anonymous correspondents must be made to realise, either in or outside the Law Courts, that virulent abuse of every trained nurse who dares to hold and express professional opinions distasteful to those advocated in the quack commercial nursing Press, must now stop. Thirty years of such methods would have taught anyone less pachydermatous than Sir Henry Burdett that the more he bullies the less effect results. That is a psychological fact so far as the convinced reformer is concerned. Tyranny, intimidation, insult, persecution—history proves to us that against conviction, courage and truth they are absolutely non-effective.

But we have also learned from the present war the inevitable doom of tyrants.

Sir Henry Burdett, in his thirty years' useless campaign in *The Hospital* and *Nursing Mirror* against the professional co-operation and organization of trained nurses has had scope enough. We advise him, during his declining years to modify the vitriolic ardour of his futile pen. We are tired of his twaddle.

THE BATTERSEA POLYTECHNIC.

SUPPLEMENTARY COURSES FOR TRAINED HOSPITAL NURSES AND CERTIFIED MIDWIVES.

The Hygiene and Physiology Department of the Battersea Polytechnic, Battersea Park Road, S.W. 11, the Head of which is Miss Hilda Bideleux, is arranging supplementary Courses of Training to meet the demand.

These courses are intended for (*a*) Fully trained Hospital Nurses, (*b*) Certified Midwives who have practised for at least two years, (*c*) Trained Matrons of Day Nurseries who are desirous of entering the Public Health Service as Health Visitors and Infant Welfare Workers, or Superintendents of Infant Welfare Centres.

The aim of the course will be to supplement previous training and experience by giving a more specialised training in (*a*) Public Health and Hygiene, (*b*) Maternity and Infant Welfare Care, (*c*) Food and Dietetics, including Practical Cookery. The length of the Course, which will begin on January 14th and April 29th respectively, will be 12 weeks, and the fee £6. Hours of attendance, 9.30–12.30 and 2–5 each day, except Saturday. At the end of the Course an examination will be held by Professor Henry Kenwood-Chadwick, Professor of Hygiene, University of London. Further information may be obtained from Miss Bideleux.

SARAH GAMP IN KHAKI.

The ways of the War Office have caused something of amusement as well as indignation during the war. An expert middle-aged gardener was enlisted in the summer and posted as an orderly to nurse sick Huns, whilst the fruits of the earth were left to rot until the services of a " land girl " could be procured. This is his ditty :—

They've put me in the Army (?)
  With non-commissioned rank,
And duties that debar me
  From corps, and 'plane and tank,
From battery and camp fire
  Route march and sentry go,
Tho' paid to serve the Empire
  With all the zeal I know.
Likewise from light to dark I
  Don't even *hear* a gun,
I'm Sarah Gamp in khaki,
  And nurse the pleasing Hun.

     (He might be less enchanting—
      It's said the case might be
     If I a limb were wanting
      And *he* were nursing me !)

Before I joined the Forces
  I led a busy life,
Whose coldest steel, of course, is
  The hefty pruning knife.
I planted, sowed and nourished
  Outside and indoor crops,
And proved, while all things flourished,
  The sturdiest of props,
Success repaid my labours
  In all the ends I sought.
I helped to feed my neighbours,
  And cost my country nought !

     Oh : what a transformation
      At this quaint time occurs,
     Eve's got my occupation,
      And I have one of hers !   C. B. M.

CHRISTMAS GIFTS.

With the lightening of the war cloud most people are looking forward to a Christmas which shall reflect in some measure our thankfulness that the Christ Child will this year find not a sword but peace upon the earth ; and one of our first instincts is to make the season a happy one for the children across whose lives the shadow of war has, in many instances, fallen with unavoidable heaviness.

CHRISTMAS BAZAARS.

At Messrs. Garrould's.

The Christmas Bazaar of Messrs. Garrould, 150-162, Edgware Road, is always a feature of this establishment and even in these days, though shorn of some of its pre-war glories, its attractions are varied enough to satisfy the most exacting. To begin with, there are dolls, dressed and undressed, English and French, beautifully modelled, one priced as low as 2s. 6d., and of English make, being a really beautiful model ; others priced from 5s. 11d. to £2 12s. 6d., would appeal to the heart of any child.

Then there are stockings of all sizes, stuffed with small toys and surprise packets ; moderate-priced games ; Noah's Arks, from a few shillings in price up to 2 guineas. There are dollies' cots, bears, cats, rabbits and elephants in plush ; Chinese lanterns, Japanese umbrellas, and a large collection of children's picture books and story books.

For grown-ups we noticed in a department just outside the Christmas bazaar some " cosy under-blouses," in a number of shades, which well deserve their name, and are just the thing to wear under a coat instead of the chilly muslin blouse at this season, when a woollen garment is always so comfortable. Their price (6s. 11d.) brings them within reach of most purses.

At Messrs. Gayler & Pope's.

Messrs. Gayler & Pope's establishment in High Street, Marylebone, W., is one which is in the centre of the nursing home district and near many hospitals, and is used by many nurses as their shopping place. At the present time its Christmas bazaar is being widely patronized, and Matrons, Sisters and Nurses are finding it most useful in meeting their needs for the toys and small presents, which go to make so much happiness in hospital wards at this season.

A visit of inspection will show the bazaar as a storehouse of desirable gifts—calendars and cards, drums, trumpets, crackers, stockings filled with trifles beloved of children, decorations for Christmas trees, dolls of all sorts, sizes and prices untearable picture books, and much besides.

Does anyone want to present a colleague with a gift sure to be appreciated, there are tea-sets for six persons from 13s. 11d ; and if nursing homes need extra plenishings, white-and-gold tea-pots, hot-water jugs and soup-bowls are to be found at most reasonable prices.

We also noticed at the head of the stairs leading to this department a " Teach-to-Walk Infant Balance," which would be a boon to mothers and nurses. By means of a strap round the waist attached to a handle bar, the child can be held in the upright position, while having perfect freedom of action.

At Messrs. T. Wallis & Co.'s.

Buy ! Buy ! Buy !

Everyone is in a spending mood this Christmas, whether they have money to spare or no.

Messrs. Wallis & Co., Holborn Circus, will help you to spend what you have, and purchasers will find there gifts to suit all tastes and all purses.

There are charming toys for the children of all descriptions, and actually dolls which are not prohibitive in price.

One fascinating person in yellow knitted cap and jersey was especially attractive.

The Christmas stockings (all sizes kept) just showed their varied contents through the transparent material. An ambulance set of cunning little khaki men, all complete with a stretcher, is, we hear, a very popular toy

The brass smoker's set will be an ideal present for our men home from the Front ; and in these days of expensive food, nothing can be more handy than the neat little luncheon cases. No one need be with unadorned tables this Christmas, in spite of the profiteering in fresh flowers, for Messrs. Wallis are selling lovely sprays of clematis, poppies and autumn leaves that almost defy detection.

Only would-be buyers must not delay, for this popular emporium is besieged.

Hot Water Bottles.

Hot water bottles are sure to give satisfaction as Christmas gifts, provided that the quality and workmanship are sound. This is assured in the Perfected Hot Water Bottle supplied by the Hospitals and General Contracts Co., Ltd., 19-35, Mortimer Street, W.I, with the one-piece stopper and neck, providing security against leakage, in three standard sizes.

Messrs. A. E. Braid & Co., Ltd., 30, Gower Place, W.C. 1, also supply hot water bottles of guaranteed quality at moderate prices ; and the Medical Supply Association, 167–185, Gray's Inn Road, W.C. 1, also offer a varied selection at reasonable terms.

For the Store Cupboard.

Do not forget in ordering in stores for Christmas to include some bottles of Bovril (be sure to return the bottles when empty), some cartons of Cook's Dried Farm Eggs, and some packets of Vi-Cocoa. You will feel the more secure when shops are shut and provisions difficult to obtain, and all are useful stand-bys to keep in the store cupboard.

A SPORTING OFFER.

Owing to the need for fuel economies and the conservation of coal supplies, the tendency in some quarters to push the use of electricity for cooking in National Cooking in the place of gas demands investigation, with a comparison of the costs (*a*) to the consumer in money, and (*b*) to the nation in coal. The British and Commercial Gas Company recently challenged an enthusiast as to the merits of electricity to a test before an independent umpire from the staff of the National Training School of Cookery. The result was a triumph for gas.

The electrician claimed that in cooking 15 million pounds of meat by electricity a saving would be effected of (*a*) 3,150 tons of coal, (*b*) of £2,500, (*c*) of 1,500,000 lb. of meat. The tests proved that there would be a *loss* (*a*) of 3,500 tons of coal, (*b*) of £10,000, and (*c*) there would be no saving in meat if it were properly cooked in both cases.

The umpire's report also revealed other disadvantages attending cooking by electricity.

CHRISTMAS SHOPPING.

At Messrs. Boots, Ltd.

Just now the show of seasonable gifts at the establishments of Messrs. Boots' Pure Drug Co., Ltd., is specially desirable. Attractiveness, combined with sound quality, are the distinguishing features of the tempting selection of gifts for Christmas offered by this firm.

Invalid Chairs.

No more acceptable gift could be made to an invalid than a wheel chair, and of such chairs the Surgical Manufacturing Co., 85 & 86, Mortimer Street, W. 1, have a wide selection. Moreover, there is the advantage that they are supplied on hire, so that, if a chair does not suit a customer after he has tried it, it can be exchanged for a different pattern, or it may be purchased at the listed price during the first month.

The Treasure Cot.

The Treasure Cot is, as its name implies, a valuable possession in any household where King Baby reigns. It is supplied in various designs by the Treasure Cot Co., Ltd., 124, Victoria Street, W. 1, near Victoria Station, where it is on view.

Hats.

If you want a hat don't forget to pay a visit to Madame Mills, 296, Regent Street, W.1. She will find something to suit you.

Useful and Dainty Footwear.

Dainty foot wear is always an acceptable gift, for the wise woman appreciates that she cannot be really well dressed unless she is well shod. At the many establishments of Maxfield & Sons there is a profusion of boots and shoes, for adults and children, dainty and charming, useful and enduring.

FOODS AND COMFORTS FOR INVALIDS MOTHERS AND INFANTS.

BYNOGEN.

Amongst the nerve foods frequently prescribed in illness and convalescence is Bynogen—a preparation of the well-known firm, MESSRS. ALLEN & HANBURYS', LTD., of Lombard Street, E.C. It is a combination of pure Milk Protein and the Glycerophosphates of Soda and Lime and Magnesia combined with the skill and knowledge for which this firm is famous.

SANATOGEN.

Sanatogen, as most of our readers know, is a product of GENATOSAN, LTD. (the British Purchasers of the Sanatogen Co., 12, Chenies Street, London, W.C. 1, of which Viscountess Rhondda is Chairman), and is owned and manufactured solely by the Company, which, with commendable promptitude, have displaced the German Sanatogen which was being largely used in this country at the outbreak of war, by a more perfect standardised form of the original preparation

BENGER'S FOOD.

This preparation, supplied by BENGER'S FOOD, LTD., Otter Works, Manchester, is frequently ordered in cases of enfeebled digestion. It is a farinaceous food containing the natural digestive principles of Trypsin and Amytopsin, with the result that it is very suited to persons of enfeebled digestion.

ROBINSON'S BARLEY

Robinson's "Patent" Barley, prepared by MESSRS. KEEN, ROBINSON & CO., LTD., London, E. 1, is invaluable in the preparation of barley water and for the dilution of milk, for the feeding of infants brought up by hand, it is an extremely satisfactory preparation, as is testified by its widespread use in hospitals, especially maternity hospitals, and by private nurses. In many households it has become a stand-by.

NESTLÉ'S MILK.

Nestlé's Milk, which is supplied, both in the sweetened and unsweetened form, by NESTLÉ'S, 6–8, Eastcheap, E.C. 3, and is on sale throughout the kingdom, is of proved value where it is necessary to resort to artificial feeding for infants. The records published in the Nestlé's Baby Books which have appeared annually since 1911, offer convincing proof of this.

VIROL.

Nor must we forget the usefulness of Virol in the feeding of delicate infants. The fact that it is used in more than 2,000 Hospitals and Infant Clinics is testimony to this fact. It is British made and British owned by VIROL, LTD., 145–166, Old Street, E.C.

INGRAM'S " AGRIPPA " BAND TEAT AND VALVE.

A Teat which will not slip off is of the highest importance for an infant's feeding bottle, and this is secured by using the " Agrippa " Band Teat supplied by MESSRS. J. G. INGRAM & SONS, LTD., Hackney Wick, E. 9, and obtainable through all chemists.

OUTSIDE THE GATES.
A HISTORIC MEETING.

At the meeting held at the Queen's Hall, on Monday, December 9th, an enfranchised sex came to meet the Prime Minister, who, in the words of Mrs. Henry Fawcett, chairman, had carried the greatest Reform Bill ever passed in this country, and had removed the stigma of disability from an entire sex.

Representative members of various Women's Leagues, Organisations and Societies were on the platform, including Lady Aberconway, the Lady Ampthill, Miss Barker, Lady Barrett, M.D., the Countess of Dudley, Miss Durham, Mrs. Bedford Fenwick, Mrs. Ogilvie Gordon, Muriel Lady Helmsley, Miss Amy Hughes, Hon. Emily Kinnaird, Dr. Janet Lane-Claypon, Mrs. Burleigh Leach, the Marchioness of Londonderry, and Mrs. Prothero. It was a special pleasure to us as representing the organised societies of nurses, to be on the platform when the Prime Minister, whose name will go down to posterity as having enfranchised women, came to greet women and to impress upon them, with eloquent earnestness, the importance of discharging their obligations as citizens of the State. We are not quite sure that the women present realised as a whole the extent of their indebtedness to Mr. Lloyd George, if they had, the quality of their welcome would have been more in keeping with the occasion, and they would have refrained from the heckling interruptions which, considering that the Prime Minister had spared precious time during an election campaign to address them, appeared out of place and undignified.

To a student of psychology it was interesting to observe in this representative meeting the temper of women generally, both from the applause and the silences. They desire to Punish the Kaiser, Expel the Huns, and make the Germans pay. None of the remarks which fell so tersely and crisply from the Prime Minister were more applauded than the following :—

" Those responsible for the atrocity of this war must be made responsible. The higher, the more exalted they are, the more necessary that they should be brought to justice."

" As to whether the Germans are going to be turned out of this country, I have repeatedly said that in my judgment these people, having abused our hospitality, must not get another opportunity to do so."

In regard to the third point women see no justice in this generation, and generations to come, being compelled to bear a staggering load of taxation to pay for the infamy of Germany.

The meeting ended with hearty votes of thanks both to Mr. Lloyd George and Mrs. Fawcett, and trained nurses in the audience observed with a smile that Mrs. Bedford Fenwick detained the Prime Minister in passing and had a word in his ear.

The women who were crowded out of the meeting called for Mr. Lloyd George, and he addressed them for a few minutes from the balcony of the Hall;

BOOK OF THE WEEK.

" YELLOW ENGLISH."*

At this moment, when the test question for our politicians is the alien menace in this country, the novel under our notice should be read with interest, for it is written in order to bring into prominence the spy system which was so active in this country prior to and during the war.

The successful banker, Otto Friedrich Shultz, early in his career had realised the need of a knowledge of women as well as men in order to succeed. He used that wisdom when by sheer force of will, the Marchioness was led to the altar a second time, and at the time the story begins she had fulfilled the desire of his heart by presenting him with a son. An English son, born of an English mother, just as he had planned ten years ago, when he had first seen Lady Mary Cranleigh, daughter of the impecunious Duke of Shadford. She had floated haughtily by him, leaning on the arm of her father, and then and there the rising young clerk, Shultz, had vowed in his mind that this aristocratic woman must become the mother of the son he saw he would need for his life's work.

He received a bad blow when he heard of her marriage, but he bided his time and married her some years later.

His life work was needless to say, the interest of the Fatherland at the expense of England, or, to speak more correctly, the Fatherland made it very much to his interest to play the part of spy.

Freddie, his little son, grew up a horrid little boy under the careful tutelage of his father. Everything, down to the smallest detail of the child's life, was carefully planned, so that in time he could fulfil his unworthy destiny. As soon as the child was born a German cousin was instructed to perfect herself in the English language in order that she might prove an able instructress in more subjects than one to Master Freddie Shultz.

At six years he was to be taught the importance of trifles, and also to keep his own counsel.

Lady Mary, although she had no inkling of the truth, was puzzled and disgusted at the crooked ways of her little son, and she conceived an instinctive dislike to the child she had borne, which she vainly tried to overcome.

She pours herself out to Major Couter, who had always loved her. She tells him that Shultz is no more her husband than Freddie is her son. " I go cold sometimes with horror when I watch that hard, perpetually-working machine in human form plotting, working, planning."

" For what ? "

" That is what I ask myself. Worldly ambition I could understand, riches, title, honour. No, it is something more. I know no more than you do, any more than I can explain why he has Freddie taken to his study every evening to teach him to watch, listen, report, and God knows what beside."

*By Dorota Flatau. London : Hutchinson & Co.

This outburst was on the occasion of her own daughter, Marigold, announcing her desire to finish her education in Germany, which desire had, of course, been planted in her breast by Father Frederick, as she was wont to call him.

It was not until the artless Freddie was grown into a man that the truth burst upon Lady Mary that both her husband and son were German spies.

In the meantime Freddie had married charming Joan, who, strange though it may seem, really loved her contemptible young husband, but then she, too, had married him in ignorance of the real state of affairs.

When Lady Mary's eyes were opened she denounces her husband.

" I have watched you for years," she was saying, " ever since the first year of our married life. Your mean household spying, contemptible though it was, I might have disregarded as serious, only that I found you carried these methods into every phase of life."

In return for her accusations the wily banker caused a rumour to be circulated that Lady Mary was mentally unbalanced, and he finally divorced her on some unfounded accusation.

But Lord Wellrock, as he was now known, was not to escape his just punishment, and the book closes on the scene of his trial. His miserable son met the fate he richly deserved, by being thrown over the cliff by the women relatives of the men who had perished at sea as the result of his treachery.

The author ends with an impassioned appeal " to tear out this canker that we have weakly fostered."

We mourn our valorous dead ; but can we mourn them honourably if we hold the hands, kiss the lips, nurture in our bosoms, the vipers that have caused their deaths ?

" Tear out this canker. Tear it out. Tear it out."

H. H.

COMING EVENTS.

December 14*th.*— League of St. Bartholomew's Hospital Nurses. Winter General Meeting, Clinical Theatre, St. Bartholomew's Hospital. 2.30 p.m. Social gathering, Nurses Sitting Room. Tea, music.

December 17*th.*—Royal British Nurses' Association. Charter Tea. (Royal Charter on view.) 10, Orchard Street, Portman Square, W. 3.30 p.m. to 6.30 p.m.

December 19*th.*—Royal British Nurses' Association. Lecture : " Bokhara and Samarkand " (fully illustrated by lantern slides) by Miss Annette Meakin, F.R.G.S. Chair : Miss Mildred Heather - Bigg, R.R.C., Vice - Chairman. The Rooms of the Medical Society of London, 11, Chandos Street, Cavendish Square, W. 2.45 p.m.

December 19*th.*—Central Midwives' Board. Penal Cases and Monthly Meeting.

December 19*th.*—Babies of the Empire Society. Conference. Mansion House, E.C. 3 p.m.

December 25*th.*—Christmas Day. A Happy Time in the Hospitals.

LETTERS TO THE EDITOR.

Whilst cordially inviting communications upon all subjects for these columns, we wish it to be distinctly understood that we do not IN ANY WAY hold ourselves responsible for the opinions expressed by our correspondents.

CONGRATULATIONS FROM HOLLAND.

To the Editor of THE BRITISH JOURNAL OF NURSING.

DEAR EDITOR,—It was with great pleasure that we noted from THE BRITISH JOURNAL OF NURSING your twenty-five years' feat as Editor.

We are utterly sorry that our congratulations will not reach you, together with those of other Corporations.

The reason for this delay is due to the decease of our beloved Miss v. Lanschot Hubrecht, which fact was the cause that the time of our members of the board was so taken up by the many necessary arrangements, that the reading of the foreign periodicals had to be postponed.

We trust, however, that you will still accept our most hearty congratulations, which before all, mean to express the hope, that we will still see you a long time as the leader of the BRITISH JOURNAL OF NURSING.

With our best wishes, we are,

Faithfully yours,

THE MEMBERS OF THE BOARD OF NOSOKOMOS.
Amsterdam.

CHILD WELFARE.

To the Editor of THE BRITISH JOURNAL OF NURSING.

DEAR MADAM,—I should like at once to disclaim the idea that anyone becomes " highly trained " by one course of lectures. But many of our voluntary visitors, have worked twelve years at a centre and have many courses of lectures and numberless consultations to their credit, and may thus have become experts in child-welfare. Rather than repeat my paper, may I refer all interested in finding out what I really said, to the report in the JOURNAL of November 23rd.

I advocate highly-trained specialists to supervise and co-operate with the service of local residents, which has its recognised place in all social effort, and while we wait for far-reaching national schemes to house and secure a clean, abundant milk supply for our teeming populations, some of us feel it well to tackle the wet feet of the children—a more manageable proposition after all.

Boot-repairing classes at our schools for mothers release pennies which can be spent on milk, and both have their place in the prevention of illness. We all know that every centre depends on its " personnel," and it is on this account that the League for Maternity and Child-Welfare provides these helpful lecture courses, so that we may approximate in all our centres to uniformity of teaching. Such conferences as suggested are often held by our Workers' Section of the above Association, and we are always glad of suggestions and welcome new members. Miss Wise, 22,

Canonbury Park, N. 1, is our Hon. Secretary, and will be pleased to give details. There are, at least, two organisations discussing vital points affecting health workers. They are : The Council of Professional Women, 92, Victoria Street, S.W. 1 ; and the Organisation of Social Workers, 5, Adelphi Street, Strand, W.C. 2. In addition, the Babies of the Empire Society is holding an important conference at the Mansion House on December 19th, at 3 p.m., at which all the points mentioned will be ventilated.

I am, yours faithfully,

KATE C. ATHERTON.

Kingsgate House,
107, Kingsgate Road,
Kilburn, N.W. 6.

THE DEEP SIGHING OF THE POOR.

To the Editor of THE BRITISH JOURNAL OF NURSING.

MADAM,—With regard to my letter in your issue of November 30th regarding the unburied dead in the poorer parts of London, I have been asked if the bodies referred to were not all lying in the public mortuaries. Certainly this was not the case. They were in the crowded homes where they had died. I know of one instance where the body of a man who had died of cancer of the throat in the Infirmary was brought to his home ten days after death, and it remained there for another thirty-six hours before the burial took place. His family only occupied two rooms in all.

Yours faithfully,

HENRIETTA HAWKINS.

AN URGENT NEED.

To the Editor of THE BRITISH JOURNAL OF NURSING.

DEAR EDITOR,—In the hot weather I had three months' holiday. I was very tired, but I thought to travel in a new part of India and see new faces and hear new voices would interest me and rest me, so I went to Sikkim, a small independent State between Napal and Bhulair, and truly I was well rewarded. I enjoyed my trip very much, but in all that State there is not a trained nurse and only an assistant surgeon, acting as civil surgeon with Indian assistants. I saw a nun (Tibetian) with her radius bone broken at the wrist, and they had put lotion on it for a sprain. She was twenty-one days in this condition ; and women who have illegitimate children have to go into the forest and there stay until it is all over. My heart ached much for those poor women.

Yours in work,

A. R. CREIGHTON.

OUR PRIZE COMPETITION.
QUESTIONS.

December 21st.—What diseases may be caused by faulty dieting ? Mention some of the effects which may follow the consumption of putrid or diseased meat.

December 28th.—Describe the signs and symptoms of acute bronchitis in an adult. Give an account of (*a*) the nursing and (*b*) the diet required in a case during (1) the acute stage and (2) the convalescent stage. What complications may occur ?

The Midwife.

JOY BELLS.

Come, rock the cradle for Him,
　Come, in the crib adore Him,
Dull care, I pray you, bury,
And in the Lord make merry,
　Sweet little Jesu, sweet little Jesu.

One of the joys of this Christmas will be that, for the first time in the lives of many little children, they can make merry without the sinister shadow of war being flung across the Christmas festival, and the grown-ups can enter unfeignedly into their merriment, without anxiety gnawing at a place in which children—all children, not the favoured few—shall be well born and have space, light, air, food sufficient for their needs, and that through their young lives the joy bells shall ring—those bells whose sound is so often stilled by the harshness and the injustices and the cruelties of humankind. Let us cherish the joy-bells, and do everything in our power to make melody for all with whom we come in contact, and especially for the little children.

　　"It is a comely fashion to be glad,
　　　Joy is the grace we say to God."

MOTHERHOOD—A CHRISTMAS GIFT.

their hearts and without listening for the dreaded knock accompanied by

　　"Just a little scrap of paper
　　　In a yellow envelope,
　　And the whole world is a ruin,
　　　Even Hope."

As the joy-bells fling their message over the countryside this Christmas—the bells which have been silent for four years on Christmas night—and as we kneel in adoration at the crib of the Christ Child—"Sweet little Jesu, sweet little Jesu"—we shall surely record a vow each one of us that so far as in us lies we will help to make the world

THE DEVELOPMENT OF SPEECH.

Dr. W. E. Robinson, in his book on "Baby Welfare," published by Mr. T. Fisher Unwin, says that "Speech develops slowly. At quite an early age—four months about—the infant crones to itself. A little later it begins to imitate sounds of words, and at about nine months it learns to respond with such words as 'ta,' 'dada' and 'mama.' In many babies, and especially when there are other children in the nursery, stringing together of words begins at about thirteen months. Where there is but one child, however, this stringing together of words is postponed to sixteen or eighteen months, or even later."

PRIVATE BROWN'S CHRISTMAS BOX.

"This 'ere is orl right for Christmas," says Bil' huskily to himself, as he tramps backwards and forwards in the cold, dirty, slushy streets. " Jist abart to get to bed I was, my first night back, too, when my gal said she felt queer and I best go for the nuss. So off I starts and when I gets to 'er 'ouse blest if I could wake 'er. Howsomever, I manages to at last and she pops 'er 'ead art of the winder. " Oo is it ? " she says and when she ketches sight of me khaki she ses, " If I didn't think it would be Mr. Brarn. I 'eerd you was 'ome. Jess you wait a minute," she says, and in a few twinks she opens the door and puts some mince pies and 'ot coffee into my 'ands. " To keep you art o' mischief whiles I finishes dressin'," she says. A fair sport I calls 'er, though I'd sooner 'ad a drop of Scotch. She arstes me a few questions as we goes along, and I felt a fair fool, it being the first occasion, yer see.

When we gets back poor old Nell warnt 'alf bad· and nuss she says, " Na, Mr. Brarn," she says, " I must trouble you to make yourself scarce," she says, " whiles I sees to yer wife." All right that fer a man whats fought for 'is country, ain't it only to 'ave one room wot 'e can call 'is own, and 'ave to walk the streets Christmas night when 'is missis is in 'er trouble ?

" You'll 'ave to alter this, Mr. Lloyd George, you and your Coalition. Strikes me that's abart all the coal we shall git, if the prices don't come down soon. 'Ark at me grousin' wen I might be art in the bloomin' trenches wif somefin' to grouse for. Last Christmas I were art in 'em, and Fritz 'e wern't 'alf lettin' loose, and me athinkin' abart my gal and wondering if I should ever bealive to go 'ome to marry 'er when my leaf come due.

Wonder 'ow she's gettin' on. I daresn't go in· I'm skeered o' that nuss. She's a starchy piece for all 'er mince pies, and corfee. Poor ole Nell ! She was fair knocked when I walked in to-day. She *said* it gave her a turn. It seems a long time. I 'opes she ain't wus nor she ought to be. " Orl right, nuss, 'ere I am. 'Ow's the missis ? Is it over ? Which is it, boy or gel ? Both ? Get out ! Yer kiddin'. No ? Stright ? Well I'm blowed ! Never mind, Nell, old dear, you'll get the extry allowance and there's that ere subsidy comin' for kids, as they say the women *means* to 'ave.

Good night, Sister, and thank yer. The same to you. I shall be merry to-night, I don't fink ! Give us a kiss, Nell. You done your bit, the same as I done mine. Thank God I'm 'ome with yer to-night. I used sometimes to think when I was in the trenches—but, there, you'd best get to sleep, old dear. *Four* of us. It don't 'alf seem rum. But I wishes us all four a 'appy Christmas, and I mean to see as we gets it for the future.

H. H.

MARGARET PATTESON.

AN APPRECIATION.

Dr. Annie McCall writes :—" Margaret Patteson, who passed away on November 21st, 1918, became known to me in October, 1899, when she first entered my house to train for the L.O.S. Already a fully-trained nurse, she had held several good appointments and had won golden opinions from all those with whom she worked.

In 1900 she became Matron of Rudgwick Sanatorium, Sussex, and only left that post towards the end of 1901 to take up the greater responsibility of the Matronship of Clapham Maternity Hospital. This she held until late in 1906, when her health made it imperative to take on less·work, and she took a trip to the Canary Islands for some months. Later again in 1910 she helped us as Honorary Tuberculosis Nurse at St. John's House, Battersea, for three years, until war broke out, when she felt it incumbent upon her to nurse in a Military Hospital first, and then for a year was Night Superintendent at Queen Mary Hospital, Roehampton (for armless and legless soldiers). Then she became Army Nurse in charge of ambulance trains, but her health again broke down, and after recovering she took the post of Home Sister to the London Homœopathic Hospital.

She was absolutely an ideal nurse, fulfilling all the best traditions of the nursing profession. A strong supporter of the Registration of Nurses, she kept herself up in all directions by reading and study. As a personal friend, I can hardly yet realise what I have lost. Unvarying in her kindness and consideration for the feelings of other people, she was an example in her devoted unselfishness, which characteristic is what made her the best· of friends. As a valued worker on the Committee of our hospital for the last twelve years she is truly mourned, and the Committee hope to start a small scholarship in her name.

CHRISTMAS.

Come sail with me
O'er the golden sea
To the land where the rainbow ends ;
Where the rainbow ends,
And the great earth bends
To the weight of the starry sky ;
Where tempests die
With a last fierce cry,
And never a wind is wild—
There's a Mother mild,
With a little child
Like a star set on her knee.
Then bow you down,
Give Him the crown,
'Tis the Lord of the world you see.

—From " Rough Rhymes of a Padre,"
By G. A. STUDDERT KENNEDY, M.C. C.F.

THE
BRITISH JOURNAL OF NURSING
WITH WHICH IS INCORPORATED
THE NURSING RECORD
EDITED BY MRS BEDFORD FENWICK

No. 1,603.   SATURDAY, DECEMBER 21, 1918.   Vol. LXI.

EDITORIAL.

A MINISTRY OF HEALTH.

Long delayed, long expected, and definitely promised we may hope that a Bill to establish a Ministry of Health will be part of the declared Government programme when the new Parliament assembles at Westminster next month.

The Bill introduced by Dr. Addison last Session, which will doubtless serve as a model for legislation with the same object in the future — placed upon the Minister of Health to be appointed under the Act the duty of taking " all such steps as may be desirable to secure the effective carrying out and co-ordination of measures conducive to the health of the people, including measures for the prevention and cure of diseases, the treatment of physical and mental defects, the collection and preparation of information and statistics relating thereto, and the training of persons engaged in health services."

The Bill further transferred to the Minister of Health " (a) all the powers and duties of the Local Government Board ; (b) all the powers and duties of the Insurance Commissioners and the Welsh Insurance Commissioners ; (c) all the powers of the Board of Education with respect to attending to the health of expectant mothers and nursing mothers and of children who have not attained the age of five years, and are not in attendance at schools recognised by the Board of Education ; (d) all the powers of the Privy Council and of the Lord President of the Council under the Midwives Act, 1902 ; (e) such powers of supervising the administration of Part I of the Children Act 1908 (which relates to infant life protection) as have heretofore been exercised by the Secretary of State."

Points of special interest to nurses in the proposed legislation are the transference to the jurisdiction of the Minister of Health of the powers and duties of the Local Government Board, which at present employs thousands of nurses. This is also important because it dissociates the infirmaries controlled by this authority from any connection with the hated " poor law " to which many of the poor will only apply for relief as a last resource. This point is of both economic and individual importance, because the expense is far less and the result more satisfactory if a case is taken in hand and treated at an early stage, than if it is allowed to develop ; and, further, because the wage earner is out of employment for a far shorter period.

The prevention of disease is a very important duty placed upon the Minister of Health. Consider, for instance, mental disease. With a delicate organ such as the brain any symptom of disease should be attacked in its incipient stage when the chance of effecting a cure is most hopeful. But, under the provision at present made for the treatment of cases of mental disease, a patient must be certified as insane before admission to an asylum (more properly a mental hospital) is possible. By that time the disease is in an advanced stage, and the prospect of a cure much more remote.

Another point of considerable interest to nurses in the Bill is that the Minister of Health is charged with the duty of securing the effective carrying out and co-ordination of measures for " the training of persons engaged in health services." Hitherto while many nurses have been trained in infirmaries under the Local Government Board, the training given has been limited to the needs of the institutions, and in no sense been arranged with regard to turning out the most efficient nurse. The Bill under consideration appears to place upon the Minister, responsibility for the quality of the training given to persons engaged in health services under his control.

OUR PRIZE COMPETITION.

DESCRIBE THE NURSING CARE OF A CASE OF DOUBLE PNEUMONIA.

We have pleasure in awarding the prize this week to Miss Maude Cullen, Queen Mary's Hospital, Stratford, E. 15.

PRIZE PAPER.

In a case of double pneumonia the nursing is of the highest importance. There is no means known of arresting the disease, which runs a definite course.

The patient must be kept absolutely at rest in bed. The room or ward well ventilated, and kept at an even temperature from 63° to 65° Fahr.; in some cases it may be necessary to raise this. Abundance of fresh air is required; the lungs being unable to work properly, the air admitted must be as pure as possible.

The patient will choose his own position. A pneumonia jacket, or gamgee, must be worn next the skin, and cover the back and chest. A flannel nightgown on top, which should be open down the back and fastened with tapes; this will allow changing, when necessary, with the minimum of disturbance to the patient.

The temperature, pulse, and respiration should be taken every four hours, and if the temperature is very high, as 105° or 106° Fahr., steps must be taken to reduce it; if continued it seriously affects the heart. Tepid or cold sponging may be resorted to in some cases, or the cold, or ice-pack, but it is necessary to closely observe the pulse all the time, if giving the cold treatment, and, if the pulse becomes weak, to immediately discontinue it.

For relieving the pain in the chest cold applications may be ordered, in the form of an ice-bag, cold compresses, &c. This treatment is of more use in the early stages, and for those only whose constitution can stand it.

Hot applications are preferred by many medical men, such as mustard or linseed poultices; these, if applied hot and made properly, should retain the heat for two to three hours. Poultices may often be discontinued after a few days.

Cough is a troublesome symptom, and may be relieved by a "linctus," containing ipecacuanha, squills, or some other expectorant. Linctus heroin (dose ʒi) is sometimes prescribed; as this contains some morphia it is valuable, as it acts as a mild narcotic.

The bowels must be kept freely open. Mist. alba, or salts, are often ordered to be given in the early morning. Calomel is useful, but should not be given unless specially ordered.

In cases of sleeplessness it may be necessary to give drugs, although simpler measures, such as tepid sponging, keeping the room quiet and dark, and giving a hot drink of milk, may be enough to induce sleep; but if not, the doctor may order a hypodermic injection of morphia to be given, as it is most essential for the patient to have mental or well as physical rest.

The most serious complication of pneumonia is heart failure. Should the heart show signs of weakening, strychnine may be ordered, or alcohol (brandy). The pulse rate will go up perhaps as high as 120 or more, and become irregular. The finger nails will be seen to become blue, also the lips. As much as ʒvi of brandy may be given in the 24 hours, but usually ʒiii is sufficient. Close watch must be kept on the pulse. When it goes up, the doctor usually orders brandy.

Delirium is another troublesome complication. It may be only slight, or, on the other hand, most marked; especially is this the case when the patient is an alcoholic subject.

A nurse should do all in her power to combat this distressing symptom. Often tepid sponging, a warm drink of milk, to which brandy is added, may induce sleep, if the delirium is slight.

One should never deal forcibly with a delirious patient, but as gently as possible; it is the best and really only way to try and coax, instead of using force with him. Usually, if the delirium becomes violent, the doctor orders morphia hypodermically.

The diet should consist of liquids only, in the early stages of the disease. Milk being the chief article of diet, it should be given regularly, at intervals of two to four hours. Egg (beaten up), beef-tea, chicken-broth are all nourishing. The strength of the patient must be maintained throughout the whole illness, because it is due to the proper feeding that his recovery to a certain extent depends.

If there is any sputum, the amount and character must be noted. In double pneumonia the "dyspnœa" may become troublesome. Oxygen gives relief in many cases, but it is not wise to continue its use too long.

A mixture of "ammonia c. ether" is often given in treating this troublesome complaint.

The back and mouth of a patient suffering from pneumonia both require special attention, as the neglect of such denotes bad nursing.

The crisis as a rule takes place from the seventh to tenth day; after that, the chief point to bear in mind is to guard the patient from taking a chill or having a relapse.

Brandy is sometimes ordered at this stage, as there may be a certain amount of prostration, and may be continued for some time after.

Convalescence is usually rapid. Tonics may be given, diet increased, and as soon as possible the patient should have a change of air.

There is hardly any other illness which calls for more careful nursing than pneumonia.

HONOURABLE MENTION.

The following competitors receive honourable mention :—Mrs. E. J. Gotlob, Miss J. Evans, Miss P. James, Miss N. Adams. We regret that an excellent paper from Miss Winifred Appleton only arrived on Wednesday morning.

QUESTION FOR NEXT WEEK.

What diseases may be caused by faulty dieting? Mention some of the effects which may follow the consumption of putrid or diseased meat.

DOPING.

It may be cold comfort to self-respecting members of the Nursing Profession in connection with being exploited by the *Daily Sketch*, in support of the sinking fund of the College of Nursing, Ltd., through the now very notorious Victory Ball at the Albert Hall, that the terrible vice of Doping has been dragged into the light of day at the inquest on the young actress Billie Carleton, found dead in bed after attending the Ball, and to which we allude in another column. Great public interest has been aroused in this sad case, and the prevalence of drug taking by the most vicious coterie of society and its hangers-on (a fact well known to trained nurses) has come as a rude shock, and, let us hope, as a salutary warning to the community in general. One good result of the exposure in the Westminster Coroner's Court is the wide publicity given in the daily press to the demoralization of persons addicted to " doping," as the more the terrible results of this vice are known, the greater the hope that the traffickers in murderous drugs will be brought to justice, and ignorant people saved from their cruel lust of filthy lucre. We would advise trained nurses to be keenly on the watch for sufferers from the " drug fiend," and to use their utmost endeavour to counteract the evil machinations of drug " profiteers " in our midst. It would appear that the police might be more alert in this connection !

Or do they not know there is a wide illicit traffic in the following dangerous drugs, which chemists may not sell without the presentation of a doctor's prescription, and that all such sales must be reported in the chemist's register?

WHAT THE DRUGS ARE.

The following is a list of the drugs in which there is an illicit traffic :—

Cocaine.—A white powder made from coca, a plant extensively cultivated in South America. By the medical profession it is largely used as a local anæsthetic. In normal times it is cheap. A small quantity worth a few pence is now illicitly sold in the West End for four or five pounds.

Heroin.—Another form of morphine.

Both cocaine and heroin are taken as snuff.

Opium.—For smoking a special preparation is used known as " chandoo." Opium-smoking carried to excess is utterly demoralising.

Haschisch.—The top leaves and tender parts of Indian hemp, dried for smoking and chewing and used as a narcotic in the East.

Morphine.—The chief alkaloid of opium. Once the use of morphine becomes a habit it is very dangerous, and brings about rapid moral degeneration.

THE ROYAL RED CROSS.

The King conferred the decoration of the Royal Red Cross upon the following ladies at Buckingham Palace on Friday, December 13th :—

FIRST CLASS.

Assistant Matron Margaret Weir, Territorial Force Nursing Service ; and Matron Emily Power, British Red Cross Society.

SECOND CLASS.

Queen Alexandra's Imperial Military Nursing Service.—Sister Annie Buyers and Sister Beatrice Thomas.

Queen Alexandra's Imperial Military Nursing Service Reserve.—Sister Mary Collier, Sister Anna Stuart, and Staff Nurse Matilda Tate.

Civil Nursing Service.—Matron Elizabeth Price and Matron Evelyn Pugh.

Voluntary Aid Detachment.—Mrs. Minnie Scott.

American Nursing Service.—Assistant Matron Alvira Stevens and Sister Letitia Kelly.

The King also conferred the following honours :—

THE MILITARY MEDAL.

Miss Mary Campbell, Voluntary Aid Detachment ; Miss Gertrude Johnston, Voluntary Aid Detachment ; and Sister Meta Hodge, Canadian Army Nursing Service.

Queen Alexandra received at Marlborough House the Members of the Military and Civil Nursing Services subsequent to their Investiture by the King with Decorations at Buckingham Palace.

QUEEN ALEXANDRA'S HOSPITAL FOR OFFICERS.

Her Majesty afterwards received Mr. Herbert J. Paterson, F.R.C.S. (Honorary Surgeon in Charge), and Miss Mary C. Sinzininex (Matron), of Queen Alexandra's Hospital for Officers, Millfield Lane, Highgate, and several Members of the Staff to whom she presented the Badge of the hospital.

NURSING AND THE WAR.

It is proposed that an Empire War Memorial Shrine and Cloisters, in the form of a Greek Cross, shall be erected in Old Palace Yard. We hope one of the 78 recesses to be used as small memorial chapels will commemorate trained nurses.

The Brussels correspondent of the *Times* writes from that city, on December 10th :—" The site of Nurse Cavell's grave in the Tir National seems, now to be established with sufficient certainty judging by the German plan of the cemetery shown to me there by the Belgian authorities.

" The first occasion was taken this afternoon by the British community to hold a commemoration service at the grave, conducted by the Rev. H. S. T. Gahan and attended by the British Minister, Sir F. H. Villiers, who laid a wreath from King George and Queen Mary, inscribed in memory of ' A brave and splendid Englishwoman.' Sir F. H. Villiers also deposited a wreath, likewise bound with the British colours, in the name of the British Legation and colony, to which the American Minister, Mr. Brand Whitlock, who was present, added a tribute of his own. In spite of a steady downpour, a large company did not shrink from the slippery, muddy walk across the wind-swept butts to the graveside. In addition to Lady Villiers and the members of the Legation staff and their ladies, those present included the Earl of Athlone, the Spanish Minister, and the Belgian Foreign Minister and Mme. Hymans.

" Among King Albert's first acts after his re-entry into Brussels was to visit, in company with his Queen, the Martyrs' Cemetery, where the latter laid a wreath, ' To Edith Cavell.'— *Elisabeth.*"

A general evacuation of British sick and wounded from Belgium and France, has been ordered, and is going on now. Of course, some cases cannot be moved, but most of the hospital staffs and women in the nursing services will come home. The demobilisation of nurses and V.A.D.s at home is also beginning to make the former consider their future. The past four years have been very strenuous, and the majority of war nurses mean to have " a nice long rest." This is wise ; they will thus begin a new " administration " refreshed and fit.

It must not be forgotten, however, that during the past four years, the training schools have certificated hundreds of young, up-to-date nurses, and many a post resigned is not now vacant. There is plenty of good work waiting to be done in private nursing, which, we fear, " war " nurses will not find to their taste after all the change and excitement. We believe the Overseas Nursing Association has vacancies abroad in our Crown Colonies for well-trained general nurses holding also the C.M.B. certificate, and information as to future spheres of work can be obtained at the office of the National Union of Trained Nurses'

Employment Bureau, at 46, Marsham Street, Westminster. There will also be every effort made to help nurses in every particular at the new Scottish Nurses' Club, 205, Bath Street, Glasgow. In Dublin, the nurses have their professional centre at 34, St. Stephen's Green, Dublin.

Last week's *Truth* asks :—
" Why should the Matron-in-Chief of Queen Alexandra's Nursing Service be allowed to hold her appointment for an indefinite period when the Pay Warrant limits the tenure of her office to a maximum of five years ? My War Office friends will, of course, tell me that the lady in question is highly qualified for her position, and from what I hear outside the War Office this is undoubtedly the case. None the less rules are made for observance, and, as the Matron-in-Chief has had an eight years' innings, I think the time has come for her to give a step of promotion to the Matrons and Sisters below her. General Goodwin is naturally anxious to have an efficient Matron-in-Chief at the head of the Nursing Service, but there are as good fish in the sea as come out of it.

" Apropos of this matter, I am by no means satisfied with the system, or rather with the want of system, of promotion in the Nursing Service. There is neither a time, nor any other, scale of promotion for the staff nurses and Sisters, who are absolutely at the mercy, tender or otherwise, of the Matron-in-Chief. Male autocrats are bad enough, but when autocratic power is given to female officials, especially when they are strong enough to hold their own, it is hopeless to look for impartiality of judgment. Women are not made that way. I think a Promotion Board should be set up for the Nursing Service, and I am disposed to think that the Director-General or his deputy, should be president of it."

We wonder if *Truth* has seen the offensive " Serf Clause," set up during the war, and without subscribing to which Sisters and nurses of the Military Nursing Service Reserve are not eligible for the £20 rise in salary. It is easy to exercise " autocratic power " with such a provision, and we demand once more that our Military Nursing Services shall be freed from the taint of tyranny and the Clause abrogated.

The members of the Nursing Board, as well as the Matron-in-Chief, are to blame for thrusting this ignoble system upon Sisters and nurses, during a war, when they must submit to it or fail to care for our devoted troops in their urgent need. To bleat about fighting for freedom and liberty and the " rights of man," and to permit this despotic system to continue at the War Office gives cause for the accusation of our enemies that we are a nation of hypocrites.

We hope *Truth* will look into this matter and help to have this injustice rectified.

TRUE TALES WITH A MORAL. 1930.

Another little Grand-daughter : What did you do in the Great War, Grannie ?

Grannie (bridling) : I appeared constantly in the pictorial Press in Nurses' uniform. Sweet studies."

EDITH CAVELL HOME OF REST,

WEDDING BELLS.

On December 17th, at St. Bartholomew's Church, Haslemere, by the Rev. W. Wragge, the marriage was solemnised between Miss Mary Gwladys John, Hon. Serving Sister, Order of St. John of Jerusalem, and Capt. Robert Nixon Armstrong Bailey, H.L.I. The hymns selected for the occasion were, " The Voice that Breathed o'er Eden," and " Now Thank We All Our God " (the latter being very appropriate, as Serving-Sister John was on duty at Etaples when the hospital was bombed and destroyed, and Capt. Bailey has also passed through many dangers). The happy pair left the church to the strains of the Wedding March.

the civilian dresses of the numerous well-wishers present.

The bride and bridegroom left Haslemere at five o'clock for Bournemouth, where the first part of their honeymoon will be spent. The bride's travelling dress was a saxe-blue costume with hat to match.

After the ceremony the ladies of the Coombe Head Committee, assisted by the Matron, Miss Hurlston, held a reception at Coombe Head, where the bride and bridegroom received the hearty congratulations of the many friends of the Home.

After the departure of Capt. and Mrs. Bailey, the visitors had an opportunity of seeing over the Home, and remarks of admiration were expressed on the excellent taste and the comfort displayed in all the arrangements. The bedrooms

EDITH CAVELL HOME, COOMBE HEAD, HASLEMERE.

The bride—who was married from the Home and given away by Mr F Rosher Vice-Chairman, in the unavoidable absence of Lt.-Col. Sir Richard Temple, Bart., C.B., C.I.E., Chairman of the Edith Cavell Homes—wore her mess uniform. She was attended by the Misses Payne and Pooley, nurse probationers, who were staying at Coombe Head ; they wore their indoor uniform. Lieut. P. C. Randall undertook the duties of best man.

The Nursing Sisters staying at the Home, with Miss Coventry's detachment of Girl Guides, formed a guard of honour. Among the congregation were a number of soldiers from the Australian Military Hospital's, their honourable " blues " giving a picturesque touch of colour to

—ten in number—are named after flowers, each guest having a separate room. " Jessamine " being occupied by Sister John, that flower was chosen for the table decorations with a centre vase of fine chrysanthemums. The large drawing-room looked very inviting, with its plentiful supply of easy chairs, sofas, and a handsome piano ; in fact, everything has been thought of to encourage the nurses to " rest " thoroughly. This room was decorated with pink and white flowers.

The nurses express warm appreciation of all the thoughtful kindness bestowed on them ; this, combined with the good air and beautiful walks, is an excellent tonic for them after their strenuous work of the past four years. They were very gratified when they heard the committee had invited Sister John to be married from Coombe Head ; it proved to them that these kind friends were anxious to have the guests use it as a real Home in every way, in the spirit in which Edith Cavell would approve.

THE ROYAL CHARTER TEA.

It was a happy thought that the Royal Charter—the precious document which is the unique possession of the Royal British Nurses' Association—should be brought from the safe at the bank where it has reposed for the last quarter-of-a-century, and shown to the members, whose priceless property it is.

The members evidently were in the same mind as their officers, and a steady stream on Tuesday afternoon last came to 10, Orchard Street, Portman Square, W., where a warm greeting from Miss Macdonald, and one of the real Scotch teas—for which she is famous—awaited them. In the place of honour they found the Royal Charter, engrossed on parchment, given by warrant under Queen Victoria's sign-manual, and sealed with the Great Seal, which was examined with the deepest interest.

Amongst those present were Mrs. Bedford Fenwick and Miss M. Breay named in the Incorporation Clause of the Charter, Mr. Herbert J. Paterson and Mrs. Campbell Thomson, the popular Hon. Secretaries, Mrs. Broadfoot, Lady Consul for India, and her daughter, Miss Saunders, and Miss Nicholls, both of whom attended the meeting at St. George's Hall in February, 1888, at which the Association was publicly launched ; Miss O'Brien, of the American Navy Nursing Service, Miss Alice Cattell, and many others interested in the organisation of nurses and the welfare of trained nursing.

The party was so enjoyable that at half-past six, instead of adieux being said, fresh tea was being brewed and fresh relays of cakes making their appearance—and disappearance. The general verdict of the members was that such social gatherings should be of frequent occurrence, and thus opportunity provided for friendly intercourse between the members of the Royal Chartered Corporation.

GIFTS.

The gift that makes the Dreamers into Doers :
The gift, through Joy or Sorrow, Light or Murk,
To play with all your soul and heart a Christ-like
    part ;
The gift of Discontent, to keep you driving
Forward and up, forever striving
For something better in the days hereafter ;
The gift of Kindness and the gift of Laughter
And all the gifts of Love and Faith and Friends
    and Purity and Truth,
And in your heart, until life's journey ends,
The priceless gift of Youth :
Hope that inspires and Courage that endures—
May all these gifts be yours.
                    From *The Canadian Nurse.*

THE SCOTTISH NURSES' CLUB.

On Saturday, December 14th, the Scottish Nurses' Club, 205, Bath Street, Glasgow, was opened by the Lord Provost (Mr. J. W. Stewart), the Marchioness of Ailsa, President, presiding at the successful opening ceremony, at which the large reception room was crowded. The Club, located in one of the most beautiful houses in Bath Street, is largely the outcome of the work for the nursing profession of Mrs. Strong, late Matron of the Royal Infirmary, Glasgow, and President of the Scottish Nurses' Association, a pioneer worker for the nursing profession who is still in the van of progress; and Dr. McGregor Robertson, who has proved such a true friend to nurses who are endeavouring to organize their profession on sound economic lines. Perhaps no body of workers need a professional Club, or appreciate it more, than trained nurses, who, whether they live in hospitals or are engaged in private nursing, or in branches of social service, long for a home of their own, for the best women are by instinct home-makers, and one of the trials of a nurse's life is that she so seldom has the opportunity of exercising that instinct.

The Club is appointed with great taste and is most comfortably, and, indeed, luxuriously furnished. To spend their off-duty-time in harmonious surroundings is to many nurses a greater rest than is often understood, for beautiful form and perfectly blended colours are not only an enjoyment but a real rest to nerves which are constantly at tension during duty hours.

The Scottish Nurses' Association, which formed the nucleus of the present Club, is one of a number of societies of nurses affiliated to the Royal British Nurses' Association, and the following telegram of congratulation was read at the opening of the Club, from Her Royal Highness Princess Christian, President of the Association :—

Please convey the congratulations of Her Royal Highness the President, the Hon. Officers, and the Executive Committee of the Royal British Nurses' Association, to the President, Trustees, and Members of the Scottish Nurses' Club, and their hope that the future may hold for it great success.

HERBERT J. PATERSON   *Hon.*
EMILY CAMPBELL THOMSON   *Secretaries.*

Lady Ailsa, in welcoming the Lord Provost, gave a brief account of the origin of the scheme, and referred to the office and recreation rooms of the Scottish Nurses' Association at 103, Bath Street, which had quickly enrolled 400 members. From that sprang the idea of forming a Club which might, in time, come to be recognized as the headquarters of the nursing profession in Scotland, and, thanks to the interest taken in the proposal by Sir Thomas Dunlop, when Lord Provost of Glasgow, and to the present Lord Provost, the scheme had materialised. She said that the Scottish Nurses' Association had realised the impossibility of running a Club of that kind under any one body, and emphasised the fact that the Club would be managed by nurses themselves for the whole body of nurses, as a house of their own, where they would have opportunities of comradeship.

The Lord Provost, in formally declaring the Club open, spoke in high terms of the willing and valuable service rendered by the profession of nursing to the community. He wished the Club every success, and hoped that the nurses would avail themselves fully of the advantages which it offered as a place of rest and refreshment in the midst of their arduous duties.

On behalf of the nurses, Mrs. Strong, who was warmly received, thanked the Lord Provost and Trustees for their interest, and gave the nurses a short address which was greatly appreciated. The vote of thanks was appropriately seconded by Miss Finn, Matron of the Abbey Hospital, Paisley, the nurses of which raised the money which was the means of originating the Club.

The Rev. M. McGibbon, of Glasgow Cathedral, was then called upon to dedicate the Club and bless its members, after which there was music, and visitors were served with tea.

We congratulate the Scottish nurses on their beautiful Club, and hope that with Miss M. R. Stewart as Secretary, and with a strong committee of management, formed of the nurses themselves, it will develop into headquarters to which Scottish nurses will naturally turn for rest, refreshment and professional help.

OVERSEAS NURSES' CLUB, EDINBURGH.

For some time past the Overseas Nurses' Club has been in use and greatly appreciated in Rutland Square, Edinburgh, and on Friday, the 13th inst., it was formally opened under the title of King George and Queen Mary Club, at 27, Drumsheugh Gardens, to meet the need of increased accommodation. The Marchioness of Linlithgow, President of the Edinburgh Branch of the Victoria League, which promoted the Club, occupied the Chair, and many influential people supported her on the platform, including Lady Jersey, Mrs. David Wallace (Hon. Sec.) and Miss Hay (Hon. Superintendent).

Lady Linlithgow said that nurses had come from all over the world to give their services, and, if necessary, to risk their lives, to succour the sick and wounded, and in that Club they would have a well-earned rest. No words could adequately express their feelings of gratitude to the nurses for their magnificent courage and endurance during the last four years.

Lady Jersey declared the Club open, and conveyed the grateful thanks of the Victoria League in London to the Edinburgh Branch for the work they had done. Nearly everybody who came from overseas wanted to visit Scotland. One reason of that was that wherever they went they would find Scotsmen doing good, gallant and faithful work. They heard a great deal about a League of Nations, and hoped and trusted it would come into existence.

But there was already a brotherhood of nations. Canada, South Africa, Australia, New Zealand, Newfoundland, India, Egypt, and all the Crown Colonies joined with the United Kingdom in a brotherhood that would stand together in peace and war.

Surgeon-General Wilson, in the course of a short address, paid tribute to the work of the nurses, and referred particularly to their heroism on the occasion of the bombing of a casualty clearing station at Bailleul and of the base hospitals at Etaples.

A vote of thanks to Lady Jersey, Lady Linlithgow, the Hon. Officers, and other workers, proposed by Dr. M'Kenzie Johnston, President of the Royal College of Surgeons, concluded the proceedings.

THE IRISH NURSES' ASSOCIATION.

A meeting of the Irish Nurses' Association was held at the Club Rooms, 34, Stephen's Green, Dublin, on Saturday, 7th inst.

The President, Miss Carson Rae, was in the chair. The usual routine business was transacted, and a letter was read from the secretary of the Scottish Nurses' Club, Glasgow, saying that members of the Irish Nurses' Association may have the use of the Club when visiting or passing through Glasgow, without the payment of fee or annual subscription, a courtesy warmly appreciated by all present. New members were elected.

M. L. O'KEEFFE,
Secretary.

TAINTED MONEY.

" Rather than touch a penny of that tainted money resulting from the College of Nursing Victory Ball I'd starve ! " writes an indignant Sister ; and she adds, "Now that the Billie Carleton inquest has exposed the source of some of the £16,000 profit, many other nurses feel with me."

Anyway, the professional Editor of this JOURNAL sympathises warmly with this expression of opinion.

Miss Billie Carleton was a beautiful young actress who attended the Ball, and who, at about 4 a.m., left in the company of a cinema actor— Lionel Herbert Belcher—Miss Olive Richardson, a Dr. Stewart, Miss Fay Compton, and Lieutenant Barraud. On the journey home to Savoy Court Mansions, Dr. Stewart was dropped near Knightsbridge, and Miss Fay Compton and Lieutenant Barraud were dropped together at her residence in Hereford Square, Belcher and Richardson returned with Billie Carleton, where they breakfasted in her bedroom, leaving the young actress in bed, where she was found sleeping heavily, and later dead, by her maid in the afternoon of the same day.

The inquest on this young girl has been widely reported, and stands adjourned until January 2nd, but the disclosures during the two enquiries at the Westminster Coroner's Court revealed widespread demoralisation amongst a group of people addicted to "doping" with opium. cocaine, heroin, and other deadly drugs, who, even down to the servant employed by a man dressmaker (de Veulle), to procure opium from a Chinese at Limehouse, attended the Victory Ball at the Albert Hall and paid cash in support of the "Nation's Fund for Nurses," run by Lady Cowdray and a Committee of actresses, in support of the College of Nursing, Ltd. The strong opposition of the organised Nurses' Societies, has been explained to this Committee of persons—who have no right whatever to interfere with the nurses' professional affairs—to having their profession based on vicarious charity, and their protest appeared in the press, before the Ball, at this method of obtaining money in their name.

Since the *exposé* at the aforesaid inquest, we have been asked if the late Miss Billie Carleton was a member of Lady Cowdray's Committee. She was not, but Miss Fay Compton is a member, and has publicly begged for the Nurses!

We need say no more than to advise the Members of our profession who resent association with the promoters of the Nation's Fund, to carefully read the scandalous revelations at the inquest, which appeared in the daily press on December 13th, and when the whole case is before the public (with reservations for the highly-placed, no doubt), that they will bring it to the notice of their new Member of Parliament, to prove how dangerous it is for professional women workers to be associated in any way, or controlled by, either financially or otherwise, the type of persons who are content to promote such a function as the Victory Ball in their name.

We spurn the "tainted money" acquired by such means.

IN A NUTSHELL.

Last week's *John Bull* puts the Nation's Fund for Nurses, in so far as the College of Nursing is concerned, in a nutshell in the following paragraph:

MISSING THE FUND.

Before we give our contribution to the Nation's Fund for Nurses, we should like to know where the money's going. The purport of the Fund is to benefit a limited company, "The College of Nursing, Ltd." What is the object of this concern? Has it anything to do with the passing of the Nurses' Registration Bill, which will shortly deprive the employers of nurses of their reservoir of cheap labour? The Fund must be already enormous. For instance, £16,000 was netted at the Albert Hall Ball, and £6,000 at a Tombola in Manchester. Who's going to administer it? And why are Lady Cowdray, Sir Arthur Stanley, and the other organisers calling this sinking fund for a company "The Nation's Fund for Nurses"?

With the Editor of *John Bull*, many trained nurses demand an answer to these questions. The

"Nation" has been entirely deluded by the misnaming of this appeal by Lady Cowdray, and it is high time the London County Council put a stop to the methods by which the Nursing Profession as a whole is being exploited through the War Charities Act, to finance the College of Nursing Company, and thus to thrust upon nurses the autocratic constitution of the College, of which intelligent nurses realise the danger to personal and professional freedom.

We are not surprised to learn, from an authoritative source that the subsidised daily press has been requested to leave out all reference to the College of Nursing, Ltd., and the so-called Nation's Fund for Nurses in reporting the "Doping" scandal in connection with the Victory Ball, by which they netted £16,000!

PLEASE NOTE.

Miss OLIVE RICHARDSON, of 2, Windsor Mansions, 296, Streatham High Road, daughter of the late Professor J. J. Richardson, and teacher of dancing, elocution and dramatic art, wishes to inform the public that she is in no way connected with the Olive Richardson who drove away from the Victory Ball in company with an officer and the late Miss Billie Carleton.

AMERICAN NURSES AND THE "SOUND" CONSTITUTION OF THE COLLEGE OF NURSING, LTD.

Miss A. Lloyd-Still, Matron of St. Thomas' Hospital, London, states in the *American Journal of Nursing* that the College Council knows nothing of invitations to American nurses to join it, but "I have been informed, however, by a member of the Council that a certain number of American nurses, who were impressed with the sound constitution of the College and its splendid aims, asked if they might not become members, or, at least associates."

If American nurses have had the opportunity of studying the constitution of the College, it is more than British nurses have; and it would be interesting to know what type of American nurse is prepared to sign an agreement to have her name removed by he Council from the College register *without power of appeal*, and considers such a constitution, which enforces this type of control, "sound." Our advice to such nurses is immediately, upon their return to their own free country, to cast an eye over that priceless document, the Declaration of Independence. Also why not send a copy of this "sound" Declaration to the Council of the College of Nursing, Ltd.? Too late this year, we fear, as a Christmas greeting.

APPOINTMENTS.

MATRON.

Isolation Hospital, Malvern.—Miss J. E. Gilbert has been appointed Matron. She was trained at the City Hospital, Edinburgh, and the Royal Berkshire Hospital, Reading, and has been Ward Sister and Deputy Matron of the Infectious Diseases Hospital, Huddersfield, Sister-in-Charge of the Sanatorium, Warrington, and Superintendent of Nurses at the Blackburn Fever Hospital.

Bideford and District Hospital, Bideford, North Devon.—Miss Jennie Jones has been appointed Matron. She was trained at Llanelly General and Eye Hospital, and has held positions of responsibility at the Infirmary, Aberystwyth, the General Hospital, Cardigan, and elsewhere.

Royal Victoria Eye and Ear Hospital, Dublin.—Miss E. M. Power has been appointed Matron. She was trained at the Adelaide Hospital, Dublin, and has held the post of Sister in the Royal Victoria Hospital for the last nine years.

SUPERINTENDENT NURSE.

Union Infirmary, Blackburn.—Miss Mary Alice Wood has been appointed Superintendent Nurse. She was trained at the Prescot Poor-Law Infirmary and has been Home Sister and Deputy Superintendent Nurse and Night Superintendent at Beverley Road Infirmary, Hull; Sister-in-Charge at Bradford Children's Hospital; and is at present Superintendent Nurse at the Lincoln Union Infirmary. She is a certified midwife.

NATIONAL UNION OF TRAINED NURSES.

NURSES' EMPLOYMENT CENTRE.

RECENT APPOINTMENTS.

Matrons.—Auxiliary Military Hospital, Glendarroch, N.B, Miss M. O. Wilson; War Hospital, Clopton, Miss A. Purchas.

Night Sisters.—Roehampton House, Miss D. M. Argent; St. Peter's Hospital, Covent Garden, Miss Keene.

Ward Sisters.—War Hospitals, Exeter, Misses L. A. Boniface, A. E. Ellis, E. Bleazby, L. Humphreys.

Nurse.—Paddington District Nursing Association, Miss A. M. Harding.

Nurse and Midwife.—English Hospital, Cairo, Miss Lake.

MEDALS FOR NURSES.

At a recent meeting of the Board of Management of the King Edward VII Hospital at Cardiff, the Sir William James Thomas medals for the three probationer nurses who had attained the greatest proficiency at the institution were awarded to the following:—Gold medal, Nurse Marie Goldsworthy; silver medal, Nurse Jane Nixon; bronze medal, Nurse Alice M. Thomas. Each of the recipients was congratulated in warm terms by the chairman, as was also the Matron (Miss Montgomery Wilson).

NURSING ECHOES.

Now that women have a voice in the making of our laws we hope that those relating to the law of libel in regard to venereal disease will receive attention.

The following instance of the way in which the disease is spread was given by Mr. E. B. Turner, F.R.C.S., at the third annual general meeting of the National Council for Combating Venereal Diseases, and is published in its third annual Report :—

"With regard to this disease, the law of libel affects both the layman and the doctor, and in different ways. The layman may become cognisant that a person is liable to spread this infection in the most ghastly and horrible way. I will give you one instance, and could easily multiply examples. Some time ago a girl went into a lock hospital; she was dissatisfied with her treatment there and took her discharge— as she had every right to do under our present system—being in a virulently infectious stage of the disease. She went away; in two or three weeks' time she came back to take tea with the Sister garbed as a nurse; she was nursing at the time, and was continuing to do so. Can you imagine anything more horrible than that a poor, unfortunate sick person should be attended by someone liable to give him or her a loathsome disease? The Sisters in that ward, the visitors to that hospital, could take no action whatever, because it is a distinct libel to say that any person is suffering from this disease; and had they said so, they would have been liable to any action which might have been brought against them. And, although a competent judge and jury might have found that there was no malice, and have, therefore, decided in favour of the defendant, still, an action brought by a person might easily result in the defendant being cast in damages, and in any case becoming liable for costs and thus fined for her altruistic exertions. That is how that law at present stands with regard to lay people."

Presumably trained nurses, having no legal status, rank as "lay people" in the eyes of the law.

Had we been a Sister in that hospital we would have risked the action for libel and the damages.

Bush nursing in Australia is work of real and wonderful national importance. A friend sends us the following little report :—

"Sister Greer told a wonderful story of heroic endurance last night before the National Council of Women. With the aid of many fine lantern slides, she described the work performed by the Bush nurses in the outlying districts from 10 to 80 miles away from railways.

The settlers and their wives and families find the Bush nurse the one person to whom they can look in dire emergencies, such as the accident occurring when a giant tree falls the wrong way, ptomaine poisoning, childbirth, &c. Where children are reared on a diet of white bread and corned beef, in parts where milk is unobtainable, the nurses find themselves with plenty to do; but every isolated settlement has its own peculiar difficulties. The ominous word 'drought' is again being whispered, and if it comes the central council of the Bush Nursing Association may find it necessary to do what it has never done before—appeal for financial help from Melbourne people.

Sister Greer told stories that sounded like fairy tales of magic growth of produce. She showed a slide where four children were rowing in the midst of the Snowy River, and their boat consisted of one-half a pumpkin! The women of Buchan use these pumpkins for all sorts of purposes, such as washtubs, washing-up dishes, and even cradles. There is an hotel of thirteen rooms at Gunyah Gunyah all built from one tree. From 12,000 to 14,000 palings are split from one tree, and these giants are valued at £50 each in the rough. Yet they are destroyed by fire in countless thousands merely to get rid of them."

It is proposed that the memorial to the late Miss Sowerbutts, Queen's Nurse at Hayward's Heath, shall take the form (1) of a tablet in St. Richard's Church, and (2) of a fund to be called the Nurse Sowerbutts' Memorial Fund for helping the work of the Association in Hayward's Heath. Amongst the suggestions as to the disposal of this Fund the following proposals were made at a well-attended meeting convened by the Hayward's Heath and District Nursing Association :—(1) The establishment of a Maternity Home, with two beds for abnormal cases, under the Government scheme of maternity and infant welfare; (2) the establishment of a Nursing Home, where two or three nurses could live together and form a local centre for nurses; (3) the provision of an additional nurse for Hayward's Heath; (4) the establishment of a nurses' pension scheme. It was resolved, on the motion of Mrs. Talbot Baines, seconded by Mrs. Parez, that primary consideration be given to a Maternity Home, and it was arranged to appoint a Sub-Committee to arrange for the raising of funds and report to the General Committee, who would submit their recommendations to a further public meeting.

EXAMINATIONS.

At the examination for nurses held in the fever hospitals of the Metropolitan Asylums Board, 58 nurses and probationers entered, and 53 passed the examiners.

The gold medal was won by Probationer E. E. Thwaites (South-Western Hospital), with 550 marks (91.6 per cent); the silver medal by Probationer A. J. Le G. Smith (North-Western Hospital), with 545 marks (90.8 per cent.), and the bronze medal by Probationer T. Austin (South Western Hospital), with 523 marks (87.2 per cent.)

THE WELLCOME PHOTOGRAPHIC EXPOSURE RECORD AND DIARY, 1919.

The publication of the Wellcome Photographic Exposure Record and Diary is always eagerly looked forward to by the many nurses who make a hobby of photography—a large and increasing number.

The present edition tells us that "however experienced a photographer may be, he will always find something to learn in this fascinating pursuit, but, the more experienced he is, the more will he recognize that there are certain necessities which are vital to success." These are: How to give a reasonably correct exposure, how to develop a plate correctly, and how to make a good print. There are many refinements and many up-to-date methods; but the foregoing points are fundamental. For the latest information on photography, consult the Wellcome Photographic Exposure Record and Diary, for, in the words of a distinguished member of the Royal Photographic Society, "the book improves every year, and whoever originally invented the Exposure Calculator deserves the combined thanks of the photographic world." It is published by Messrs. Burroughs, Wellcome & Co., Snow Hill Buildings, E.C.

AN ACCEPTABLE CHRISTMAS GIFT.

We have received from Messrs. Cadbury Bros., Ltd., Bournville, Birmingham, a parcel of the various preparations of cocoa for which the firm has a world-wide reputation. Their Cocoa and Milk Powder is a preparation which has only to be known to be appreciated; and no doubt when war restrictions are relaxed will be even more largely used in hospitals and nursing homes and by district nurses than at the present time. The great advantage of this preparation is that both milk and sugar are incorporated in it, so that it only needs the addition of boiling water.

The Cocoa Essence and Bournville Cocoa are also favourite preparations, and considerable attention has been given by the firm to their production just now, in view of the fact that the use of cocoa is specially urged by the Food Controller.

OUTSIDE THE GATES.

WOMEN CITIZENS

Polling Day, December 14th, passed without undue excitement, and we must preserve our souls in patience until the 28th inst. before knowing the result. Women were well to the fore with their votes, and their influence will have decided the fate of many candidates. Sixteen women candidates sought election, and it is computed that three or four may win success and proudly write M.P. after their names. Miss Christabel Pankhurst was given every chance—recommended by the Premier and well pushed by the Coalition Press — and Major Thompson, the favourite local candidate, retired most chivalrously in her favour—the type of man we women should help to support at some future day.

One of the few candidates to rouse enthusiasm was Mr. Bottomley in South Hackney. The women recognised he has stood by "Tommy and Jack" all through the war, and one flung her arm round his neck and said : "I've put a kiss to your name on the voting paper, now I give you another for yourself for what you have done for our boys in France." To which "Horatio" replied with his usual "vim" : "It's a good job for me the boys are still there !"

Everywhere women showed, by voting in large numbers, their appreciation of the responsibility of citizenship.

THE NURSES' VOTE.

We learn that 260 nurses from the London Hospital went in batches to record their votes. This is very good news as it establishes a precedent for trained nurses in similar institutions, where they have been denied this right. At Bristol, a group of nurses who had received literature from the Labour candidate presented themselves in the Central Division, and it was with the greatest difficulty that the officials convinced them they were not entitled to vote.

But why this discrepancy ? This matter must be at once taken in hand, and equality for all hospital nurses defined. Rouse up, nurses, and see to it yourselves and don't be put off by registration officials.

Our illustration is of exceptional interest and depicts nurses recording their votes on the historic 14th of December, 1918.

The Children's Jewel Fund aims at promoting the cause of child welfare throughout the kingdom ; fifty-five infant welfare centres have received grants as the result of the first appeal for jewels (the sale of which at Christie's in June alone reached over £26,000) but 5,000 centres are needed. The Doll Show, held from December 10th to 20th at Sunderland House, Mayfair, is one of the many schemes by which it is hoped that a sufficient sum of money will be raised to enable this object to be achieved. We own to a weakness for dolls, and this exhibit was something quite supreme.

A scheme for providing schools for the education of 2,000 tuberculous children, has been approved by the L.C.C. Education Committee.

NURSES RECORDING THEIR VOTES AT POLLING STATION.

A FOURTEENTH CENTURY CAROL.

Jesu, sweetë sorë, dear !
On poor-full bed liest thou here,
    And that me grieveth sore ;
For thy cradle is as a bier,
Ox and assë be thy fere,
    Weep I may therefor.

Jesu, sweetë, be not wroth,
Though I have no clout nor cloth
    Thee on for to fold,
Thee on to fold, nor to wrap,
For I have neither clout nor lappe,
But lay thou thy feet to my pappe,
    And wite thee from the cold.

LETTERS TO THE EDITOR.

Whilst cordially inviting communications upon all subjects for these columns, we wish it to be distinctly understood that we do not IN ANY WAY hold ourselves responsible for the opinions expressed by our correspondents.

"PUBLIC HEALTH NURSES MUST ORGANISE."

To the Editor of THE BRITISH JOURNAL OF NURSING.

MADAM,—Permit me to reply to your correspondent in t e issue of THE BRITISH JOURNAL OF NURSING of No em' er 30th.

I will take the side issues first. The teaching of boot-mending in Welfare Centres, to which such scornful allusion is made, is just one of the small matters which will help the mother in her " real duty towards her home." Those who have much experience in Infant Welfare work know how fatally boring it is to the mother if the one string of the proper feeding of infants is harped upon to the exclusion of all other subjects. The atrophied capacity for assimilating knowledge of the mother has to be coaxed and interested and invigorated if she is to profit by her attendance at the Welfare Centre.

Such classes as boot-mending, patching, cooking are useful in interesting the mother in various ways of managing and contriving, not only for the baby, but for the other children, too. It is a fairly general rule that " father " keeps the boots in condition, but with father away at the war, and the high price of boots (12s. 6d. for a pair for a boy of eleven, and then they are " through " in a fortnight !), added to the great difficulty in getting repairs done, surely it is better for mother to seize the chance of keeping the school children dry shod than that she should sit still and wait while politicians and philanthropists discuss plans for smoothing the many creases out of her very crumpled lot.

The suggestion that nurses engaged in Public Health work should hold conferences was forestalled some eighteen months ago, when the workers' section of the Association of Infant Welfare and Maternity Centres was formed. Only those who are actively engaged in Infant Welfare work are admitted to membership. Periodical Conferences are held, at which various aspects of the work are discussed ; and recently the meetings have been arranged at different centres, so that those attending may be able to study methods adopted in other localities than their own.

We are naturally anxious for the co-operation of all nurses engaged in this branch of social work, and would welcome any help in extending the scope of usefulness of the organisation.

F. E. WISE,
Hon. Sec. Workers' Section A.I.W.M.C.

22, Canonbury Park North, N.1.

STUDY AND READ.

To the Editor of THE BRITISH JOURNAL OF NURSING.

DEAR EDITOR,—I acknowledge with many thanks the 5s. prize which I was fortunate enough to win for the competition.

It is with great pleasure and interest I do the competitions. After one has finished training I think it so necessary to study and read up, as one is so apt to get slack. I have taken the BRITISH JOURNAL OF NURSING for a few years now, and wish it most heartily every success. I only hope we shall before long have State Registration, as I fear the war has not in any way helped to raise the standard of nursing in our training schools, but rather the reverse. One must hope for the best and look forward to better days in the near future.

Yours truly,
M. CULLEN.
Queen Mary's Hospital for the East End.

THE DEEP SIGHING OF THE POOR.

To the Editor of THE BRITISH JOURNAL OF NURSING.

DEAR MADAM,—It is reported in the press that the Southwark Board of Guardians recently complained to the Local Government Board of the long delays in the burial of the poor, who, through lack of hearses, had to be conveyed to the houses of their relatives in a fish cart.

A reply has just been received that the Local Government Board had been in communication with the Ministry of Labour with reference to skilled undertakers, and they understood the Ministry would consider the question of release from military service of men whose names were put before them by the Undertakers' Association. They asked that all names should be sent to Alderman J. R. Hurry, the Hon. Secretary of the association.

Yours truly,
POOR LAW SISTER.

[An appetising arrangement for those buying fish in the district !—ED.]

KERNELS FROM CORRESPONDENCE.

Country Matron writes.—" I note Sir Arthur Stanley calls the women who have worked and paid for State Registration, the ' Insignificant Minority.' I prefer the title of ' Old Contemptible.' What say you ? "

[We agree, but it does not matter a jot what w are called so long as we stick to our principles; and that we intend to do.—ED.]

We regret to hold over many letters and " Kernels."

OUR PRIZE COMPETITION.
QUESTIONS.

December 28th.—Describe the signs and symptoms of acute bronchitis in an adult. Give an account of (a) the nursing and (b) the diet required in a case during (1) the acute stage and (2) the convalescent stage. What complications may occur ?

The Midwife.

THE NAMING OF INFANTS' COTS AT QUEEN CHARLOTTE'S HOSPITAL.

The Committee of Queen Charlotte's Hospital are appealing for contributions for the naming of infants' cots in the hospital, and the appeal has already met with some success. For a gift of £105, the donor may have the right to name a cot, and donations for five cots have so far been received. In some cases they have been given as thank-offerings for the safety of a son during the war.

While during the war the general hospitals have been treating our wounded soldiers and sailors, Queen Charlotte's Hospital has been admitting the wives of our soldiers and sailors, of whom over 5,000 have been received into the wards or attended in their own homes, and many letters have been received from men at the front, expressing their appreciation of what has been done for their wives in their absence.

THE IDEAL HEALTH VISITOR.

By kind permission of the Jewish District Nursing and Sick-Room Help Association, a meeting of the Workers' Section of the Association of Infant Welfare and Maternity Centres, was held on December 4th at 24, Underwood Street, E., the subject under consideration being "The Ideal Health Visitor for Infant Welfare Work, and the Qualifications Necessary." Miss Isabel Macdonald, Secretary of the Royal British Nurses Association, was in the chair.

Miss French, Superintendent of the Loughborough Junction Maternity and Child Welfare Centre, suggested a two years' training which should include six months in a children's hospital, midwifery, six months' social training, and some experience in a welfare centre.

Miss Brownsdon, Matron of the American Welfare Wards, North Islington, advocated the three or four years' hospital training as the basis of qualifications, and said that experience as a school nurse is very valuable.

Miss Elliott, of St. George's House, Cable Street, considered three years' training, plus district midwifery experience, essential.

In the discussion which followed it was generally agreed that nothing but the best is good enough ; one speaker said if adequate salaries are paid the best will be forthcoming.

In summing up, Miss Macdonald thanked the speakers and emphasised the view that three years' training in the wards of a hospital should be an essential qualification for anyone holding a responsible position in infant welfare work.

HUNGERING FOR A CHILD.

Interviewed upon the leaving of foundling babies in Hampstead, the clerk to the guardians said that apart from the trouble it gives, it had brought to light the fact that there are an enormous number of women in England who are absolutely hungering for a child. " It is extraordinary the number who applied to adopt the children," he added.

CENTRAL MIDWIVES BOARD FOR SCOTLAND.

At the meeting of the Central Midwives Board for Scotland, held in the offices, 50, George Square, Edinburgh, Sir Halliday Croom in the chair, intimation was made of the appointment of Sir John Lorne MacLeod, as representative of the Convention of Royal Burghs in place of the late Sir Robert Kirk Inches.

PENAL BOARD.

The following are the decisions in the cases of midwives heard before the Penal Board :—

No. 1240. For failing to send the proper form for medical assistance in a case of still-birth, &c.

The midwife was cautioned strictly to observe the rules of the Board, and the local supervising authority was instructed to report to the Board at the end of one month upon her conduct as a midwife, and as to her fitness to take pulse and temperatures.

No. 179. For failing to advise medical assistance in the case of a child suffering from serious skin eruptions and for other breaches of the rules.

The midwife was suspended from practice for one month and the local supervising authority was instructed to report on her ability to take pulse and temperatures before she resumed practice.

No. 1724. For failing to send for medical assistance in a case of ophthalmia neonatorum and for other breaches of the rules.

The Secretary was instructed to remove the name from the Roll of Midwives and to cancel the certificate.

THE MENE ACCOUCHEMENT SETS.

Private nurses and midwives will be glad to have their attention directed to the Mene Accouchement Sets, which are procurable from drapers, ladies outfitters and chemists throughout the country. They are supplied both at 40s. and 20s., and contain mackintosh sheets, accouchement sheets, the dressings and supplies necessary to furnish both mother and infant's basket, and a supply of Mene towels, which are antiseptic, absorbent, and economical, and have the advantage that they can be destroyed by burning.

The Mene Accouchement Sets and Mene Towels are the specialities of Messrs. Robinson & Sons, Ltd., Chesterfield, and 168, Old Street, E.C.1.

THE
BRITISH JOURNAL OF NURSING
WITH WHICH IS INCORPORATED
THE NURSING RECORD
EDITED BY MRS BEDFORD FENWICK

No. 1,604.   SATURDAY, DECEMBER 28, 1918.   Vol. LXI.

PRINCIPAL EVENTS IN THE NURSING WORLD IN 1918.

The year now closing is one which will always stand out as a red-letter year, for two principal reasons—the cessation of hostilities and bloodshed in a war of unparalleled magnitude, and, after a struggle of sixty years' demand for the suffrage, for the granting of the Parliamentary Franchise to women in the United Kingdom.

" The old order changeth, yielding place to new," and the measure of power thus put into the hands of women workers is only yet dimly realized. If, then, we are sometimes tempted to exclaim—

" What is that which I should turn to, lighting upon days like these ?
Every door is barr'd with gold, and opens but to golden keys."

Let us take heart of grace and trust the prevision of the poet—

"Men, my brothers, men the workers, ever reaping something new :
That which they have done but earnest of the things that they shall do ;

For I dipt into the future, far as human eye could see,
Saw the vision of the world, and all the wonder that would be.

* * * * *

Heard the heavens fill with shouting and there rained a ghastly dew
From the nations' airy navies grappling in the central blue.

Far along the world-wide whisper of the south wind rushing warm,
With the standards of the peoples plunging through the thunder-storm :

Till the war-drum throbb'd no longer, and the battle flags were furl'd
In the Parliament of men, the Federation of the world.

There the common sense of most shall hold a fretful realm in awe,
And the kindly earth shall slumber, lapt in universal law."

THE HEALTH OF THE PEOPLE.

One thing that the war has taught the community is the supreme importance of the health of the people and of its conservation. The Bill brought in last Session by Dr. Addison, Minister of Reconstruction, to secure the effective carrying out and co-ordination of measures conducive to the health of the people, is an earnest of the Government programme for social reform and reconstruction in the new Parliament. Nurses and midwives who, coming into close touch with the people, have long been deeply conscious of conditions inimical to health, and who have been handicapped in their own work for physical and social betterment, by conditions which could and should be altered, await with impatience the opportunity of helping to influence legislation for the raising of the standard of national health. The war drum throbs no longer, thank God, on the battle fields of the world, but the trained nurse still marches breast forward against her immemorial enemies, and on the banner which she follows are inscribed the words, " War on disease and the conditions which produce it," " War on slums and the evils which they breed," " War on sweated labour and the misery it causes "; and on the companion banner gleam the words, " Prevention is better than cure," " Healthy homes breed healthy people," " A living wage for all." May the present generation see her demands fulfilled.

ROYAL BRITISH NURSES' ASSOCIATION.

An event of outstanding importance in the nursing world during the past year has been the affiliation of a number of important societies of nurses to the Royal British Nurses' Association, as the result of a conference, to which invitations were issued by Her Royal Highness Princess Christian, President of the Corporation. The Societies so affiliated are the Matrons' Council of Great Britain and Ireland, the Society for the State Registration of Trained Nurses, the National Union of Trained Nurses, the Fever Nurses' Association, the Scottish Nurses' Association, and the Irish

Nurses' Association. Such affiliation is not only an advantage to the Corporation, whose sphere of influence is thus enlarged, but to the affiliated societies, which, while retaining their own autonomy, benefit by the strength derived from union, and from the prestige and power which association under the Royal Charter confers. It is a unique and most powerful combine. A Consultative Committee, representative of the Affiliated Associations, has been formed, which, it is hoped, will keep them in touch with the Association and with one another.

Another important step taken by the Royal British Nurses' Association has been the adoption, by arrangement with the Editor, of THE BRITISH JOURNAL OF NURSING as the official organ of the Association. The JOURNAL now includes a Royal British Nurses' Association Supplement every other week, and the publication of the monthly organ of the Association has been discontinued. By this means forces are consolidated and the members of the R.B.N.A. get their Association news more frequently.

THE CENTRAL COMMITTEE AND THE COLLEGE OF NURSING, LTD.

The Nurses' Registration Bill of the Central Committee for the State Registration of Nurses —the parent Bill, which has behind it the considered opinion of the British Medical Association and the organized societies of nurses—has been revised and reprinted. A seventh draft of the Bill of the College of Nursing, Ltd., has also been published, and bears the impress of the patient negotiations of the Central Committee, inasmuch as it provides guarantees that the qualification for admission to the General Register, after the period of grace, shall be not less than three years' training and the passing of a central examination, and that a certain number of seats shall be secured on the Permanent Council, which is to administer the Act to registered nurses.

Nominally, also, the principle that the organized nurses' societies shall be represented on the first Council, has been conceded, but this concession, valuable as it appears on the surface, has been rendered valueless by the fact that the only duty which this Provisional Council can perform is to prepare and present to the Privy Council the rules required to be made under the Act for setting up the first General Nursing Council, on which the nurses' societies are not to be represented.

This is a dangerously subtle provision, as, superficially, it appears to concede to the organized societies the right which the College has persistently denied.

The Bill of the College of Nursing, Ltd., also incorporates the College, with its autocratic Memorandum and Articles of Association in the Bill, and virtually seeks to secure an unfair preference; indeed practically to obtain a monopoly for the College Register.

It must be remembered in this connection that the Memorandum of the College gives the Council the right to remove a nurse's name from its Register without power of appeal, and that right of appeal was only inserted in the Nurses' Registration Bill drafted by the College after strenuous representations on behalf of the Central Committee.

A new and most dangerous Clause of the Bill is that which empowers the Council to form as many Supplementary Registers as it pleases, thus undercutting the value of a three years' standardized certificate and dealing most unfairly with nurses by the registration of specialists, who will find themselves unqualified for the best positions in the hospital world and the most remunerative work outside.

The Central Committee, after carefully considering both Bills and adopting certain minor details in the College of Nursing Bill, expressed the unanimous opinion that the present Bill of the Central Committee is a better Bill than that drafted by the College of Nursing and should be adhered to.

It further resolved—

" That it is the considered opinion of the Committee that the Bill drafted by the Central Committee for the State Registration of Nurses should be presented to Parliament, and that the College of Nursing, Ltd., be formally invited to agree to this Bill, and join in getting it passed."

This invitation has been refused by the Council of the College of Nursing, Ltd., without consulting its members, and the responsibility therefore rests upon that Council of once again sowing dissension, where the various interests concerned in nurses' registration had been carefully co-ordinated, and three Bills amalgamated in one agreed Bill.

The radical difference between the two Bills and the reason for the impossibility of co-ordinating them is that the Bill of the College, however camouflaged, is framed in the interests of the employers, whereas that of the Central Committee safeguards those of the workers.

It is now proposed to introduce both Bills into the House of Commons, and it remains for Parliament to frame a just Bill, protecting this great body of professional women from interested control, and almost universal exploitation, by hospital committees and poor law guardians.

THE SOCIETY FOR THE STATE REGISTRATION OF TRAINED NURSES.

This Society has been actively on the alert, and has, from time to time, undertaken work at short notice in the interests of the State Registration movement, when quick decisions and action have been necessary.

In the past, before the formation of the Central Committee in 1909, this Society acted as the promoter of legislation for nurses, and most carefully guarded their interests, and defeated repeated attempts made by the nursing schools to assume absolute power over their economic condition; and at this crisis in the nursing profession, when, through the constitution of the College of Nursing, this policy is most active, the Society is appealing for financial support to save alive the soul of the profession of nursing.

Should the employers' Bill be forced, by social influence, through the House of Commons, nothing will then remain to the workers but to realize that they must take part in the drastic programme for the emancipation of the people already under consideration by the proletariat.

The members of this Society have conducted their political campaign with the utmost circumspection and with due regard to constitutional procedure, but the experienced leaders of the State Registration movement in this country have never lacked courage, and they do not intend to see the nursing profession enslaved, without recourse to methods against which no form of tyranny will be able to stand in the free England of the future.

THE ROYAL AIR FORCE NURSING SERVICE.

During the year the Royal Air Force Nursing Service has been organized, with a Matron-in-Chief as chief executive officer. The members have honorary rank as officers, the Matron-in-Chief ranking a major. Neither rank nor pay, however, compares favourably with that of the members of the Women's Royal Air Force, for which the training is three weeks, while that of the nurses is three years.

THE SPIRIT OF VOCATION.

It is with thankfulness and pride that, with peace within sight, we salute the trained nurses, who have foregathered from all parts of the British Empire, and have rallied round the flag wherever its red, white, and blue floated over the sick and wounded, whether behind the lines in comparative safety, or " standing to " under shell fire, efficient, disciplined, steadfast, putting the safety of their patients, and of fighting men, before their own, as did those also who went down into deep waters, done to death by a treacherous foe, untouched by humane feeling and regardless of the recognized rules of civilized warfare.

It is the tradition of the Navy to meet death with a cheer, and it is the tradition of the trained nurse to meet it with a smile.

A certain section of society claims to have discovered the nurse during the war, and it is the fashion to gush over her devotion to duty. But that devotion did not, as some would have us believe, awake with the roll of the war drum. It was nourished in stillness in childhood and cherished in girlhood; it surmounted difficulties in early womanhood till it gained the right to take its place by the bedside of sick and dying in hospital wards, that it might learn the best methods of caring for them, and it inspired the certificated nurse as, without ostentation, she took her place wherever her services were needed, by man, woman, or little child, bringing in her wake the skill and consolation inspired by the Spirit of Vocation.

It is that spirit which must be cherished in our hospitals if British nursing is to maintain the position it has established, and we should view somewhat with distrust the vocation which develops with the outbreak of war, and is limited in its interest to the needs of one sex.

" THE BRITISH JOURNAL OF NURSING."

This JOURNAL continues to be the only weekly organ which is professionally edited, and controlled, by nurses in the interest of the profession. It has over and over again provided practical proof of the indispensability to nurses of a voice in the press, for, without its fighting force, the profession would have been completely submerged.

The JOURNAL has always claimed a high educational standard for nurses, and the organization of the profession of nursing on a stable, self-supporting, economic foundation, in which policy it voices the views of the group of organized societies of nurses associated in the Central Committee.

The College of Nursing, Ltd., on the other hand, is endeavouring through the so-called Nation's Fund for Nurses to build up the profession on a charitable basis, raised by methods which rouse the indignation of every nurse who rightly esteems the honour of her profession.

We shall continue to claim for nurses the right of self-determination, self-support, and self-expression.

OUR PRIZE COMPETITION.

WHAT DISEASES MAY BE CAUSED BY FAULTY DIETING? MENTION SOME OF THE EFFECTS WHICH MAY FOLLOW THE CONSUMPTION OF PUTRID OR DISEASED MEAT?

We have pleasure in awarding the prize this week to Miss J. G. Gilchrist, Gillespie Crescent, Edinburgh.

PRIZE PAPER.

The diseases which are commonly met with in one's practical experience and may be termed constitutional are : *Rickets,* a disease of infancy most evident about the first and second years of life and characterized by impairment of general nutrition and by alterations in the growing bones. The essential cause is faulty dieting, the chief factors being the use of poor condensed milk, many proprietary foods (which nearly all contain starch), and too much starchy food generally, with a deficiency in animal fat, proteids and lime salts. Contributory factors are lack of sunshine, pure air and exercise. It is especially common in large cities amongst the poor, ill-clad and ill-housed. If the digestive disturbances can be remedied by early treatment, enabling good nourishment to be taken, deformities in the bones may be prevented and the child regain tone generally.

Late Rickets.—Recurrence of early rickets may be seen in rapidly growing girls, from nine to fifteen years, due to faulty dieting and strain put upon young children in poor districts where mothers are in the habit of going out to work all day, leaving the children to manage as best they can on " pieces," tea, &c., with a properly cooked meal occasionally. The disease may manifest itself in flat-foot, knock-knee and lateral curvature of the spine. Remedies are good feeding, regular meals, porridge, pure milk, eggs, fatty tonics—such as malt and cod liver oil, and Virol.

Scurvy may be seen in infants as well as adults, in rich as well as the poor. It is due to a limited diet—mainly the consumption of preserved, salted or artificial foods, and a lack of tonic properties such as are obtained in fresh fruit and green vegetables. In the child the exclusive use of sterilized milk may bring about the condition. The characteristics of this disease are usually seen in the swelling of the salivary glands, sponginess of the gums, unhealthy mouth generally, and pallor. Raw meat juice, fresh foods, whole milk, fruits—lemons and oranges especially—counteract the tendencies of the disease.

Anæmia.—The ordinary chlorosis is common in young girls, from fourteen to seventeen, who are underfed and overworked, especially if living or working in close, unventilated workshops and unhygienic homes. The appetite becomes capricious, and they usually come to prefer acids and highly spiced foods, which exaggerates the lack of hæmoglobin—the protein and iron contents of the blood—and cause further dyspepsia and constipation. Green vegetables, especially cabbage, which contains iron, and wholesome, easily digested foods, simply and well cooked, should be given.

Diseases due to over-indulgence or excess in foods which are richly prepared, fatty and sweet articles, alcoholic liquors and wine (such as champagne), are unnatural *obesity* and *gout.* Abstinence, plain food, exercise in open air are indicated.

Gastritis, inflammation of the stomach, may be caused by irritating, highly seasoned foods, frequent drinking of boiled tea with excess of tannic acid. Other organs, such as the liver and kidneys, may be affected in their functions by faulty dieting.

Eating fish out of season, or tainted or decomposed food stuffs of any kind, leads to poisoning of the digestive tract and interference of function.

Meat may be dangerous, through the development of putrefaction ; disease of a more or less virulent character may follow the presence of parasites which may not be killed in cooking.

In this country tuberculous or diseased meat rarely comes into the market, and the meat is usually sufficiently cooked to destroy the parasites, which may be worms of two kinds, the cestoda or flat worms—the nematoda or round worms. Should those parasites gain an entrance into the body, they usually adhere tenaciously to the intestinal mucous membrane, causing local irritation of more or less severity.

Bad meat has a very irritating effect on the alimentary tract as the result of the action of the bacteria, which produce an accumulation of poisons or ptomaines. Tinned meat is often subject to excessive decomposition, if at all moist or the tins imperfectly made, or air not wholly excluded.

The symptoms of ptomaine poisoning may be very severe—vomiting, purging, or diarrhœa, intestinal pain, collapse or shock ; mental prostration may be severe and the heart affected and beats slow. Prompt skilled treatment is necessary to get rid of the irritant and soothe the digestive canal.

HONOURABLE MENTION.

The following competitors receive honourable mention :—Miss A. E. Noblett, Miss Susan Grey, Miss May Farmer, and Miss Alice M. Burns.

THE JOINT WOMEN'S V.A.D. DEPARTMENT.

SCHOLARSHIP SCHEME.

The problem of what is to become after the war of the unit, who, by a misapplication of the English language, is called a " V.A.D." (Voluntary Aid Detachment), is one which is engaging the attention of a sub-committee of the Joint Women's V.A.D. Department at Devonshire House, and it is announced that the Joint Committee of the British Red Cross Society, and the Order of St. John of Jerusalem " have decided to give a sum of money for scholarships and for training, as a tribute to the magnificent work so generously given by V.A.D. members during the war." Only those members who served prior to January, 1917, will be included in the scheme.

The widespread lack of preparation of girls for the duties of life, whether in the home or the world, is one of the facts emphasised by the war, and we are glad that the lesson that serious training is a necessary preparation for a definite career has been taken to heart.

In August, 1914, there was a large reservoir of willing service to draw upon, but a great proportion of it was neither skilled nor competent. We have, therefore, only commendation for the effort to impress upon young women the need of honourably qualifying for any work undertaken, more especially when that work is concerned with so delicately balanced an organism as the human body.

It is, however, a debatable question whether the Joint Committee should spend money subscribed in the name of " the sick and wounded " to relieve parents of the obligation of maintaining superfluous daughters, by paying for their professional training. If the Department decides to help to place t e V.A.D.'s in suitable positions for training, and assist them, if they or their parents are unable to find the necessary fees, wherever possible such payments should, in our view, be regarded as loans, and the money subscribed to the societies associated under the Joint War Committee—at the cost of much self-denial, in many instances, on the part of the general public—conserved for future use. We wonder how parents, impoverished by the war and handicapped by the fees they are paying for the education of their daughters and for placing them out in the world, will appreciate paying for the education of the daughters of other people, in many instances better off than themselves !

The Committee has drawn up a list of professions and occupations towards which scholarships covering the cost of training or grants-in-aid will be given, under the headings " Type of Work," " General Conditions," " Qualifications," and " Approximate Length of Training," and a comparison of these is very instructive. First, the salaries to be earned when trained, are in some instances below the margin which will permit the worker to be self supporting ; and we hope the committee, if it spends public money on training, will also endeavour to obtain a rise

in the standard of pay for the trained worker, so that a living wage may be secured.

A point to be noted is the anomaly of remuneration in relation to the length of training. We give a few instances.

School Nursing. — Qualifications : Hospital training, special experience in children's diseases an advantage. Remuneration when trained, £60 to £120. Non-resident.

Welfare Supervisors.—Training : Six months to a year ; special courses for welfare workers, social study, diploma of recognized university and university degree an advantage ; experience in social work very helpful. Salary £120–£400. non-resident.

Hospital Almoners. — Training : Eighteen months, university degree an advantage. Salary £120–£400.

X-Ray Assistants.—Training : Six months. Salary in hospitals, about £60, resident ; £80 to £150, non-resident Private work (non-resident) may rise to £4 per week.

We wonder how many V.A.D.s, weighing the relative advantages of the different occupations and professions, will select nursing for which the length of training is four years, though " the course may be slightly reduced for members with long service." The pay is not given, but nurses know well that the salaries they can command (for most responsible work) make nursing the Cinderella amongst the professions. Who can wonder, therefore, if the V.A.D. rejects nursing as a career as too arduous and too unproductive, if she must serve an apprenticeship of at least three or four years to obtain a post as a school nurse at a salary of from £60 to £120 a year, when, after only six months' training, she can secure from £120 to £400 as a welfare supervisor ?

(There are also inequalities of rank which may here be noted, thus, while the Commandant-in-Chief of the Women's Royal Air Force holds the dazzling position of a brigadier-general, the Matron-in-Chief of the Royal Air Force Nursing Service is accorded the relatively humble rank of major.)

Such anomalies must be rectified, lest, with the way made easy for women to enter professions and occupations at once more attractive and remunerative than nursing, the stream of desirable candidates is diverted from this essential occupation.

Lastly, we note that the occupations and professions tabulated by the Committee are mainly those for workers who have a capacity as drudges. But the talents of a certain proportion at least of the V.A.D.s must lie in the direction of the arts and sciences which make the joy of life. If the greater proportion are content to be " hewers of wood and drawers of water," we should like to see opportunity offered to talent whatever direction it may take.

TRUE TALES WITH A MORAL.

Irate War Widow : " If I don't get my pension soon, I shall have to go on the streets and take to immortality."

Royal British Nurses' Association.

(Incorporated by   Royal Charter.)

THIS SUPPLEMENT BEING THE OFFICIAL ORGAN OF THE CORPORATION.

HER ROYAL HIGHNESS THE PRINCESS ARTHUR OF CONNAUGHT AND THE MARQUIS OF MACDUFF.

We have pleasure in reproducing this week a photograph of Her Royal Highness the Princess Arthur of Connaught and Lord Macduff. Her Royal Highness is a Vice-President of the Royal British Nurses' Association, and, as is well known, she takes a very enthusiastic and practical interest in all branches of nursing. For over three years and a half she worked at St. Mary's Hospital, Paddington; and for some time also in the wards of Queen Charlotte's Hospital. The Princess is in no sense one of those who can be accused of having merely "played at nursing," for she has shirked none of the difficult or trying duties in the daily round of the hospital wards, and has taken every opportunity which offered of acquiring a sound knowledge of nursing.

The Princess, who is Duchess of Fife in her own right, is the eldest daughter of the Princess Royal of England and the late Duke of Fife. Macduff was the patronymic of the first or Celtic Earls of Fife; and Dufagan Comes, who lived in the reign of Alexander the First is the first recorded Earl of Fife and was descended from the kingly stock of Moray. In the early days of Scottish history, Fife held a very high position as an earldom, probably because in former times it was the demesne of the Pictish Kings. In olden times the privileges of the Clan Macduff were three : first, that they should sit on the right of the Royal Chair on Coronation Day ; second, that they should lead the vanguard in every Royal battle ; and third, a remission for homicide on a fixed payment, and sanctuary at Cross Macduff.

LECTURE.

BOKHARA AND SAMARKAND.

We have seldom listened to a more fascinating lecture than that given by Miss Meakin, F.R.G.S., under the auspices of the Corporation on December 19th. In commencing Miss Meakin said that she would conduct her audience across the sandy desert of the wild Turkomans (the Parthia of the Ancients) to the Gates of Bokhara the Noble. The attitude of Russia in connection with Bokhara, for a considerable number of years, was explained and also why the present condition of affairs in Russia had opened up the Moslem States of Central Asia to the civilised world. She referred to the influence of the Bolsheviks in connection with Bokhara, and the dangers which might arise were they to possess themselves of the Moslem States on the Indian frontier.

Miss Meakin said that Bokhara's civilisation is a thousand years behind our own, her people are the strictest and most fanatical Mohammedans in the world. They are like grown up children so far as the outer world is concerned and have to learn before they can stand alone. " From what great Power or Powers are they to learn ? That is one of the nuts that the Peace Conference has to crack." Bokhara is not far from the frontiers of India and if the Indian Government does the duty that lies near it, said Miss Meakin, she will lend a helping hand to Bokhara. The lecturer strongly emphasised the importance of help for Russia. " The old Russia lies in ruins. Russia's noblest sons are fighting for the unity of Russia, just as America's sons fought in their civil war for the unity of America. Just as naturalised Germans penetrated England before the war and sapped her commercial wealth, so the Germans, who were naturalised Russians sucked the wealth of Russia, and if we do not help Russia they will do it again. Now is the day for English and Russian merchants to join hands and cope with the clever German, now is the time for Russo-British enterprise to develop the natural wealth of Bokhara."

The women of Bokhara are the most secluded in all the world, and the Russian residents were struck dumb with astonishment some years ago when the Amir of Bokhara suddenly announced that he was going to give a ball. " Would the ladies of Bokhara throw aside their great black horsehair veils for once ? " No such thing ; the real ladies of Bokhara could not be expected to leave the seclusion in which their lives were spent, even for a short time, and, if they could, they would not have been able to waltz ! This is how the Amir got over his difficulty—he sent invitations to all the Russians in or near his territory. Every man, every woman, no matter their degree or station were invited to the Amir's ball. And they all came, too, from the dignified Political Agent swollen with his own importance, to the boy who washed the bottles in the apothecary's shop. And the Amir peeped down on them from behind a curtain on a balcony above, and thought it a very fine sight indeed. It was quite right and proper in his eyes that the Russians should provide him with such an excellent show. It is the contemplation of other people's exertions that gives pleasure in the East. But more amusing reminiscences followed of the Amir's ball which, unfortunately, we have not the space to record.

The pictures which were put upon the screen were perfectly unique, and some were most wonderfully beautiful, and, as Miss Heather Bigg, who occupied the chair, remarked, it was very difficult indeed to say whether the lecture or the views had afforded the greater pleasure although personally she thought she had most enjoyed the lecture.

At the close of the lecture Miss Meakin said that she had ordered four of her books to be brought to the hall and they would be sold for the benefit of the Trained Nurses' Annuity Fund. To the great disappointment of some of the nurses they were all gone before they could walk across the hall, but we have looked at one of the copies and can inform them that the cost of the book is 3s. 6d. and it can be obtained through any bookseller on mentioning the name of its publishers, Messrs. Allen & Unwin. We have dipped into its pages and find it very fascinating indeed, in fact, some members went a second journey to far Bokhara, by way of its pages, on the evening of the lecture.

HER ROYAL HIGHNESS THE PRINCESS ARTHUR OF CONNAUGHT AND THE MARQUIS OF MACDUFF.

INVITATION TO SECOND CHARTER TEA.

Several members have explained that they were unable to accept the invitation of the Executive Committee to the "Charter Tea" at 10, Orchard Street on the 17th inst. owing to their being free,

in the daytime, only on a Saturday afternoon. It has therefore been arranged that there shall be a second "Charter Tea" on Saturday, January 4th from 3.30 p.m. to 6 p.m., to which trained nurses are very cordially invited.

QUALIFIED WOMEN FOR PUBLIC HEALTH WORK.

Some members of the Corporation ask us to announce that they have arranged that a Conference shall take place in their Clubroom at 10, Orchard Street, Portman Square, W. 1, on Saturday, January 11th, at 3 p.m. Miss Wise and Miss Alderman will read papers dealing with the urgent need for properly-qualified women for posts in all branches of Public Health Work. Miss Atherton will take the Chair, and an informal discussion will follow the papers. Tea will be served after the meeting. Conferences on such a subject are of the utmost importance at the present time, and the nurses, who have arranged that for 11th prox., sent up a request to the Executive Committee that a larger Conference should take place on the same subject under the auspices of their Association early in the new year. The Committee hope to hold this in February. Only fully-trained nurses may attend on January 11th.

APPOINTMENT.

Miss Ethel Wallis has been appointed Matron of Sherburn Hospital, near Durham. She was trained at the Royal Infirmary, Sunderland, and joined the Association during the current year.

OBITUARY.

It is with deep regret that we have to report the death of Dr. Percy Lush, who became a member of the Corporation in 1900. He always took a great interest in its work and has recently served on the General Council.

(Signed) ISABEL MACDONALD,
Secretary to the Corporation.

10, Orchard Street, London, W.

NURSING ECHOES.

For all the kind wishes received from friends far and near we return heartfelt thanks. A Happy New Year to all.

Once more Christmas has come and gone. We hear that a real " Victory " tone pervaded the hospitals and the festivities for the troops, and that a spirit of thankfulness inspired one and all—the glorious dead were not forgotten by the comrades who loved them.

One young soldier said to us :—" Just to be alive, how glorious ! But I took the risk. Yet when I think of the dead and broken—somehow I do not feel I ought to be so glad. I just lie awake nights springing with joy."

" Got a mother?" we asked.

" Yes—better than anybody's mother."

" Got a sweetheart?"

" You bet."

" That accounts for it. These two dear ones are just doing a bit of wireless—Honour the dead, help the broken, deserve happiness."

" Right you are."

A very enjoyable " At Home " was held recently at the County Hospital, York, in the Nurses' Home, where the Hon. Sec. of the York County Hospital Linen Guild and the Nurses' Needlework Guild held the annual show of garments sent by the members of the Nurses' Needlework Guild. 288 garments were shown, all most useful and pretty things for the Children's and Adult Wards. The Hon. Sec., Miss Ethel Crombie, who is an invalid and indefatigable in her good works for the hospital, personally manages both guilds. The members of the Linen Guild sent 627 articles of linen this year, making a total of 915 for both guilds. Several friends of the hospital were also present.

APPOINTMENTS.

MATRON.

Infectious Diseases Hospital, Kelso, N.B.— Miss J. M. Findlater has been re-elected Matron. She has been engaged in a Military Hospital during the war.

SISTER.

City of Westminster Union Infirmary, Fulham Road, London. – Miss Emma Marsh has been appointed Sister. She was trained at Marylebone Infirmary, where she was Staff Nurse and Sister, and has seen military service as staff nurse in the Reserve of Q.A.I.M.N.S. at the Lord Derby War Hospital, Warrington.

CROIX DE GUERRE FOR BRITISH WOMEN.

At the Scottish Women's Hospital, known as the Hôpital des Armées No. 30, installed in the Abbaye de Royaumont, not far from Villers-Cotterets, General Nourisson recently presented thirty Croix de Guerre to members of the staff. The hospital was in May subjected to heavy bombardment.

With Miss Ivens, the head physician, the list of women decorated includes : Miss Nicholson, Mrs. Berry, Miss Courtauld, Miss Maitland, and Miss Henry, the five surgeons ; Mme. Manuel, bacteriologist, Miss Storey, radiologist, Miss Collum, assistant radiologist, who was badly injured when the *Sussex* was torpedoed ; Miss Ramsay Smith, treasurer ; Miss O'Rorke, and Miss Lindsay, Matrons ; Miss Goodwin, Miss Anderson, Miss Inglis, Miss Chapman, Miss Rolt, Miss Smieton, Miss Armstrong and Miss Daunt, Nurses ; Miss Murray, Miss Fulton, and Miss Smeale, chauffeurs.

RECONSTRUCTION IN FRANCE.

Many of the splendid hospitals organised in the finest hotels in Paris have closed their doors, and the war nurses have gone home, or have flitted to pastures new. The Astoria is now given up to clerical workers for the British Peace Conference section, and Miss du Sautoy, the Matron, and Lady Hermione Blackwood have been entrusted with some very important reconstruction work at Pierrefonds by the British Committee of the French Red Cross, which, when they get the staff together, promises to be of deep interest and extremely useful, as every sort of organisation to help the people in the devastated areas is required to set civilised life running again. The British Committee is spending part of the grand sum of £360,000, subscribed to its funds this year, in tackling the immense question of the tuberculous soldier, and providing food, clothes, and crêches in France, where every penny can be well spent.

Miss du Sautoy is a practical organiser to her finger tips, and is just the woman to meet and overcome the tremendous difficulties to be faced in this work of healing social conditions. We wish her and her staff all success.

THE "NATION'S NOBLEST."

The reply sent to the press in answer to the letter of the Hon. Sir Arthur Stanley by the nurses who objected to the exploitation of their profession by such a function as the widely-advertised *Daily Sketch* Victory Ball, was apparently placed on the *Index Expurgatorius* of the lavishly subsidised Capitalist newspapers. It did not appear in one of them.

Manchester and Dublin are to repeat this type of function; let us hope not in its entirety, as the more details we hear, the more inexcusable were its methods. We presume neither Manchester nor Dublin wishes to tap ill-gotten gains for the " Nation's Noblest."

THE "GAZETTE" OF THE 3RD LONDON GENERAL HOSPITAL, WANDSWORTH.

The Christmas Number of *The Gazette*, the most witty of war hospital magazines is up to its usual first-rate form for 1918, and one regrets to realise that it may be the last. Fortunate those who have kept and bound their copies from its inception they are wise, as it ranks as the "Punch" of military hospital journals and as a mirror of the war,

"YOU DEAR, BRAVE FELLOW! MAY I KISS YOU?"
"LOR LUV YER, MISS, DON'T YOU THINK I HAVE
SUFFERED ENOUGH?"

The frontispiece by Mr. Noel Irving, the Editor, presents "The Empty Stocking," and little Fritz and Gretchen, plastered with the spread eagles, are shown howling copiously before a strip of land, shaped like a stocking, from Zeebrugge to St. Mihiel, now rescued from the rapacious clutches of the Hun.

Lance-Corporal J. H. Dowd, in presenting The Historic Day (11th ultimo) gives one a lively idea of the joy and pranks of the "bedridden" after the maroons went off. Splint cases hopping out of bed, flags waving, hands clasping, all to the mad sounds of revelry extracted from a distracted piano; empty beds, and men on crutches and supported by sticks, out of bed and out of doors " for the first time without permission!" The scrub ladies dancing the Highland fling in the corridors; and Sister discovering "another cork" the "morning after" to the amusement of "Donovan," the hero of so many pleasantries in the *Gazette*.

Private H. M. Hemsley presents the agony of a "brave fellow" when approached by a "Liza" with mistletoe. Behold them (by the kind consent of the Editor) on this page.

"Christmas, 1918," by Helen M. Nightingale, in touching verse gives thanks to God—

That those we loved the best,
Some living yet—some entered into
is rest—
In that dread hour made with unfaltering voice,
Whether for Life or Death, the hero's choice.

    *   *   *   *   *

Thanks be to God for those who come again,
Preserved by Him by air and land and main,
Thanks, too for those whose sacred memory
Makes real the dream of Immortality.

    *   *   *   *   *

Thanks be to God that now the Child is given
As very Prince of Peace from Highest Heaven,
That with the joy, which greets Emanuel's birth,
Mingles once more the joy of Peace on Earth !

"OUR DAY."

The response to the "Our Day" appeal of the British Red Cross Society and the Order of St. John amounted to a total of £1,146,395, a magnificent record of generosity from subscribers at home and overseas.

The Fund for Sick and Wounded to date amounts to £12,962,872 7s. 2½d.

THE PASSING BELL.

We regret to record the death in a nursing home in Hampstead on December 10th, of Miss Mildred Isabel Reid, a V.A.D. who, since the early days of the war, has worked steadily and devotedly. She died of acute septicæmia, due to an infection in her face, contracted while at work in a war hospital at Exeter.

A Sister who had her loyal co-operation for nine months, writes : "I thank God for her."

THE ROYAL RED CROSS.

At the Investiture held by the King on Thursday. December 19th, His Majesty decorated the following ladies with the Royal Red Cross :—

FIRST CLASS.

Sister Ethel Harwood, Q.A.I.M.N.S.R.; and Sister Mary Thomson, Q.A.I.M.N.S.R..

SECOND CLASS.

Queen Alexandra's Imperial Military Nursing Service Reserve.—Sisters Fanny Boulton, Mabel Campbell, Frances Hobbs, Sidney Rea, Janet Rodger, Priscilla Walker, and Staff Nurse Kate Rossi. *Territorial Force Nursing Service.*—Sister Esther Ashby. *Civil Nursing Service.*—Sister Mary Lintall. *Voluntary Aid Detachment.*—Miss Victoria Dunn and Miss Helena Nisbett.

The King held an Investiture at Buckingham Palace on December 21st, when he decorated the following ladies with the Royal Red Cross and one with the Military Medal :—

FIRST CLASS.

Matron Katherine Hagar, American Nursing Service (Harvard Unit).

SECOND CLASS.

Queen Alexandra's Imperial Military Nursing Service.—Matron Florence Tosh and Assistant Matron Rose Rooke.

Queen Alexandra's Imperial Military Nursing Service Reserve.—Sister Isabel Anderson, Sister Jeanie Cameron, and Sister Mary Dunbar.

Territorial Force Nursing Service.—Sister Alice Lowe and Sister Maud Taylor.

Civil Nursing Service.—Matron Emily Porter.

Voluntary Aid Detachment.—Miss Ruth Lindsay, Miss Annie Philip, and The Lady Tollemache.

American Nursing Service.—Sister Helen Hinckley.

THE MILITARY MEDAL.

Sister Linda Bowles, Queen Alexandra's Imperial Military Nursing Service Reserve.

Queen Alexandra received at Marlborough House the members of the Military Nursing Services who have been awarded the Royal Red Cross and the Military Medal, subsequent to the Investiture at Buckingham Palace.

Among the honours and awards for War Services announced in a Special Supplement to the *London Gazette* the following ladies are awarded the Royal Red Cross :—

FIRST CLASS.

Miss J. Durie, Matron, S.A. Med. Corps; Miss R. N. Fogarty, Matron, S.A. Med. Corps.

SECOND CLASS.

Miss E. Covey, Matron, S.A. Med. Corps; Miss A. O'Brien, Sister, S.A. Med. Corps.

NURSING AND THE WAR.

NURSES' UNIFORM GRANTS.

An Army Council instruction which has just been issued gives the following new rates of uniform allowance :—

Q.A.I.M.N.S., Q.A.I.M.N.S.(R.) and T.F.N.S.—£10 on enrolment, to cover the cost of a winter outfit; further instructions will be issued in due course as to the issue of any grant that may be approved for those who are required to provide themselves with a summer outfit *V.A.D. (Nursing Members), and Special Military Probationers.*—£4 each six months, payable in advance; in the event of their ceasing to serve within three months of becoming eligible for such a grant (otherwise than through illness or unavoidable accident) a refund of £2 will be required. V.A.D. (Nursing Members) and Special Military Probationers appointed prior to this date will receive the new rate of grant sanctioned above when the next six-monthly payment falls due. To prevent misunderstanding it is notified that the above increases are temporary, and will only continue while the present exceptional conditions subsist.

SISTERLY RECIPROCITY.

The Committee of the Scottish Nurses' Club, 105, Bath Street, Glasgow, has extended an invitation to members of the National Union of Trained Nurses, to make full use of the Club when in Glasgow. This courtesy has been acknowledged with much gratitude by the Executive Committee of the N.U.T.N.

Let us hope that before long English nurses in London will be in a position to offer reciprocity to their Scottish and Irish sisters in the use of a Club centre. Little birds are busy twittering!

TIME!

Bermondsey Board of Guardians have been informed by Dr. Bell, medical superintendent at their infirmary, that the probationer nurses, with few exceptions, refused to go on duty unless the whole day weekly leave was immediately restored. This had been stopped temporarily, and a half day substituted on account of the sick staff and the number of unfilled vacancies. On the promise that the whole day would be resumed they returned to duty. Dr. Bell added that the staff were in a state of unrest owing to the fact that they had not been granted any war bonus, whilst other boards had granted a bonus. The guardians decided to consider the grievances.

We do not approve of strikes where the sick are concerned. But we hope that Boards of Guardians will realise that drastic reorganisation in their Nursing Departments are necessary. The twelve-hour day or night must go. The strain on the nerves is too great.

COMING EVENTS.

January 1st, 1919.—New Year's Day.

ROYAL BRITISH NURSES' ASSOCIATION.

January 4th.—Charter Tea at 10, Orchard Street, W. 3.30 to 6 p.m.

LETTERS TO THE EDITOR.

Whilst cordially inviting communications upon all subjects for these columns, we wish it to be distinctly understood that we do not IN ANY WAY hold ourselves responsible for the opinions expressed by our correspondents.

FOR A JUST BILL.

To the Editor of THE BRITISH JOURNAL OF NURSING.

DEAR EDITOR,—Miss Sanderson and I are so glad that you have been asked to stand for Parliament, and deeply regret that you cannot enter for the present election, but it is good to know you will when opportunity offers, although I should have liked you to be one of the first elected. Maybe you will.

We are sending you a combined cheque for £5, for the Victory Thank Offering for State Registration; also that you have been given health and strength to work for the nurses' cause for so many years, and may you be spared to see the fruit of your labours in a just Act for the registration of nurses. The gambols of the Fund for Nurses (as it is *not* national it has no right to be called the Nation's Fund) make me furious; such things make for Bolshevism. I sometimes wonder when they will start a rummage sale, but as that would mean work and not fun and frolic I suppose we shall be spared that indignity.

I cannot tell you how much I should like to be able to share in all the work, but I hope you understand me well enough to know all that.

With every good wish for the success of your work, believe us, your sincere good wishers,

MARY BURR.

Les Capucines, Clarens Vaud,
Switzerland.

[A shop where "gifts" are sold in support of the Nation's Nurses has been opened by the Committee of this Fund in North Audley Street, London, so that we are not even spared this form of pauperisation. The plutocrat produces the Bolshevik.—ED.]

THE WOMEN SANITARY INSPECTORS AND HEALTH VISITORS' ASSOCIATION.

To the Editor of THE BRITISH JOURNAL OF NURSING.

MADAM,—In your issue of November 30th, you publish a letter from a correspondent, in which she urges the need for "a really good public health section."

I wonder if she knows that such a section already exists—"The Women Sanitary Inspectors' and Health Visitors' Association"?

The Association is not *exclusively* for trained nurses, but many fully-trained women are members, and as you will see by the rules (a copy of which I enclose), all the workers are trained, most of them very highly.

The Association, too, shares your correspondent's disapproval of the untrained voluntary worker, and is doing its best to ensure that Infant Welfare Workers shall, in future, be compelled to undergo an adequate training and pass a statutory examination before securing an appointment.

Yours truly,
M. BLANCHARD,
Trained Nurse and Infant Welfare Worker.
29, Broadwater Road,
Tottenham, N. 17.

[The handbook of the Association can be obtained by writing to the Hon. Secretary, Miss Sayle, 12, Buckingham Street, Strand, London, W.C. 2.]

A FACT OR A FARCE.

To the Editor of THE BRITISH JOURNAL OF NURSING.

DEAR EDITOR,—Being desirous to know the truth respecting Women's Franchise, may I ask whether it is a "fact" or a "farce"?

I am a "Queen's Nurse" living in apartments (I possess a key). In the district, as you know, we all live under similar conditions, or in District Homes. Last week I was informed I would have no vote.

I shall be indebted to you if you will kindly state through your invaluable organ, THE BRITISH JOURNAL OF NURSING (the only paper for trained nurses) if this is correct? Thanking you in anticipation.

I am, faithfully yours,
STATE REGISTRATIONIST.
Life Member National Union of Trained
Nurses, and Affiliated to R.B.N.A.

[A district nurse living in rooms with latchkey is certainly qualified for the Parliamentary franchise, but her name must be on the register in the district in which she has resided for six months. Each nurse should call at the Registration Office, obtain the prescribed form, fill it in, and then *see for herself* that her name is on the Register. It is no use waiting for any official to do his duty. This question of votes for Nurses must now be submitted to Counsel for a legal opinion, as many nurses' names were on the Register living in hospitals, and they voted, whilst others under identical conditions were refused registration.—ED.]

OUR PRIZE COMPETITION.

QUESTIONS.

December 28th.—Describe the signs and symptoms of acute bronchitis in an adult. Give an account of (a) the nursing and (b) the diet required in a case during (1) the acute stage and (2) the convalescent stage. What complications may occur?

January 4th.—State what you know about the result of taking the following drugs: Cocaine and morphine; and how the patients should be nursed.

LAST WORDS FOR 1918.

Yet do thy work; it shall succeed
In thine or in another's day;
And, if denied the victor's meed,
Thou shalt not lack the toiler's pay.

The Midwife.

CENTRAL MIDWIVES' BOARD.

ENGLAND.

In England the most important event in the midwifery world has been the passing of the Midwives Act, 1918 (which comes into force on January 1st next). The President of the Local Government Board announced, in the debate on the Committee Stage in the House of Commons, that " it is the intention of the Privy Council to give direct representation to midwives on the Board." The hopes of the midwives were raised high by this statement, but unfortunately the term "direct representation " was afterwards interpreted by Mr. Hayes Fisher (now Lord Downham) to mean the appointment of midwives to seats on the Board, under powers conferred on the Central Midwives Board by the Act. This, although a step forward, is not *direct* representation.

The Act, which received the Royal Assent on November 26th, repeals the Clause (Clause 9) in the principal Act giving County Councils the right to delegate their powers to District Councils, and makes provision for reciprocal treatment of midwives certified in other parts of His Majesty's Dominions.

SCOTLAND.

In Scotland we have to record with regret the death of Sir Robert Kirk Inches, representative on the Central Midwives' Board of the Convention of Royal Burghs. Sir John Lorne MacLeod has been appointed to succeed him.

The Scottish Midwives' Association, which has as its President the Duchess of Montrose, has held several meetings during the year. In our view the President of an Association of professional workers should always be a member of the profession concerned, and elected by her fellow members.

IRELAND.

The Bill " to ensure the better training of midwives in Ireland, and to regulate their practice " has become law during the year. The Bill was blocked in 1917 because the Irish Nurses' Association, which represents the interests of the midwives in Ireland, was not satisfied with the representation provided for midwives on the Board under Mr. Duke's Bill, namely, one midwife, out of a Board of thirteen persons, to be appointed by the Privy Council. The Irish Nurses' Association obtained the support of the Royal College of Physicians in Ireland, and, so effectively voiced its demand for representation of the midwives, that, when the Bill received the Royal Assent on February 6th, four out of eleven seats were secured on the Irish Midwives Board to certified midwives. These midwives are referred to in the Act as " midwives representatives," and are appointed by the Local Government Board, three out of the

four being appointed after consultation with recognised nursing associations in Ireland. The laurels are with the Irish Nurses' Association, which exercised such an effective influence on legislation in spite of vested interests and the unwillingness of the Government Department responsible for drafting the Bill.

The Midwives appointed on the Board are : Miss J. H. Kelly, Matron Maternity Hospital, Belfast ; Mrs. M Blunden, late Matron Lying-in Hospital, Cork ; Miss A. Michie, Superintendent for Ireland Q.V.J.I. ; and Miss G. O'Carroll, Matron Combe Lying-in Hospital, Dublin.

The resignation by Miss L. Ramsden of the position of Lady Superintendent at the Rotunda Hospital, Dublin, which she has held with distinction, has caused widespread regret.

MIDWIVES AND RAIDS.

It is to the credit of the midwives in London and elsewhere that, in spite of air-raids, their service of the poor in their own homes suffered no interruption, although in the East End of London, at least, the position was so menacing that the police obliged the midwives to wear shrapnel helmets and other protections in case of raids, when going to cases in the night. Their posts were posts of danger and honour, quite as much as those of nurses overseas, though no decorations reward services gallantly performed.

A STATE-AIDED MIDWIFERY SERVICE.

The proposals for a State-aided Midwifery Service made by the Association for Promoting the Training of Midwives, to which we referred last December, have since been revised and embodied in a memorandum as a basis for legislation. It is proposed that by means of an exchequer grant, a fee of 25s. per case, including ante-natal care, shall be ensured to midwives.

The Women's Co-operative Guild published an opportune pamphlet giving the views of the working women themselves in regard to a Midwifery Service. They consider that there should be a Public Health Service, free to all who desire to avail themselves of it.

NATIONAL BABY WEEK.

National Baby Week has now established itself as an annual function, with a permanent council, and at its Conference held in conjunction with an exhibition, in the first week of July, at the Central Hall, Westminster, and elsewhere, much useful propaganda work was done.

THE MATERNITY AND CHILD WELFARE BILL.

The Maternity and Child Welfare Bill became law in July. Discussion settled around the points as to whether the powers given under the Act should be entrusted to both large and small authorities. Eventually it was decided that the County Councils in England and Wales, exercising powers under the Act, should establish maternity and child welfare committees, and might delegate their powers to such committees with the exception of raising a rate or borrowing money.

BABIES OF THE EMPIRE.

The foundation of a Babies of the Empire Society, which has its headquarters in the General Building, Aldwych, of which Lord Plunket is chairman, has for its first object " To uphold the sacredness of the body and the duty of health." It has established a Mothercraft Training Centre at 29 and 31, Trebovir Road, Earl's Court, S.W.

The number of schemes on foot at the present time for the benefit of infants, prove that the nation is of opinion that all is not well with its babies. The rearing of healthy infants is one of the first essentials for putting mothercraft on a sure foundation.

CIVIC RESPONSIBILITIES WITH REGARD TO CHILD WELFARE.

Amongst the excellent pamphlets published by the National Baby Week Council, 27, Cavendish Square, London, W. 1, is one by Dr. Harold Scurfield, D.P.H., Medical Officer of Health for Sheffield, the motto of which is " Every child a chance, and every family a home." It deals with the subject under the headings : Healthy parents, efficient mothers, reasonable income, efficient medical service, and, on the last point, says :—

" EFFICIENT MEDICAL SERVICE.

" The mother has not yet got an efficient medical service at her disposal for herself and her children, and the provision of this is one of the after-war problems which the citizens have to settle.

" We need a system by which there will be secured a family doctor for each family. The relations of the family doctor to the special institutions such as School Clinics, Tuberculosis Dispensaries, Maternity and Child Welfare Centres and Venereal Disease Clinics will have to be determined. The family doctor must be linked up with the consulting surgeons and physicians, and the hospitals, convalescent homes, midwives, district nurses and mothers' helps, so that his patients may have the benefits of these services in time of need. More lying-in hospitals, more children's hospitals and open-air schools are required. Especially do we need more hospitals for crippled children on the lines of Lord Mayor Treloar's Hospital at Alton.

" Besides this, arrangements must be made for dentists to look after the teeth of the children. This has been done to some extent with regard to the children of school age by School Clinics and the system will have to be extended.

" The Poor Law medical service will obviously become involved in the changes which take place.

" Another matter urgently requiring attention is the reform of out-patient departments. These are at present swamped by cases which ought never to be sent there. Mothers who take their children to out-patient departments are frequently required to spend the whole day in the waiting-room, to the great detriment of their homes. Out-patient departments ought to be restricted to accidents, cases requiring special treatment, and those cases which are sent by a general practitioner for a consultant's opinion.

" The Maternity and Child Welfare Centre is the institution which chiefly affects babies and young children, and it will be right to say a few words on this matter. County Councils and Sanitary Authorities are now required to establish Maternity and Child Welfare Centres, and the representatives of the citizens must see that these are as efficient as possible. There should be provided advice and hospital treatment if required for expectant mothers ; medical attendance under certain circumstances and hospital treatment, if required, during confinement ; and advice and hospital treatment, if required, for both mother and baby after confinement, the advice to be continued, in case of the baby, up to the school entrance age. As regards hospital treatment, I believe the usual way is for the Sanitary Authority which establishes the Centre to make arrangements with the existing hospitals, but some sanitary authorities may find it advisable to establish lying-in hospitals and infant hospitals.

" At present we have medical supervision of children from birth up to the age at which they leave school, but no provision has been made for the gap between leaving school and the age of sixteen, when those who go to work come under the scheme of the Insurance Act.

" In many districts there are voluntary societies working in the interests of mothers and children, and it is very necessary that these voluntary workers should be linked up with the work of the Maternity and Child Welfare Centre. Cordial co-operation is needed, also a spirit of tolerance. Voluntary workers sometimes seem to think that an official paid by the Sanitary Authority must be soulless and void of sympathy. It is, of course, absurd to suppose that a hospital nurse when paid her salary by a voluntary hospital or the Queen Victoria District Nursing Association is sympathetic, and that the same woman, when her salary is paid by a County Council or a Sanitary Authority, must necessarily become hard of heart and lose her sympathy with the people amongst whom she works.

" Another danger is that the voluntary worker will not appreciate the difficulty in giving sound advice to mothers with regard to their infants. Each infant is a study in itself and until recently even the medical profession has not appreciated what a large amount there is to be learned about babies. Care is therefore needed lest the voluntary worker should develop into a quack doctor."

Lightning Source UK Ltd.
Milton Keynes UK
UKHW030658140922
408851UK00008B/688